T0330040

Second Edition

International Sport Management

Eric W. MacIntosh, PhD

University of Ottawa

Gonzalo A. Bravo, PhD

West Virginia University

Ming Li, EdD

Western Michigan University

Editors

HUMAN KINETICS

Library of Congress Cataloging-in-Publication Data

Names: MacIntosh, Eric W., 1977- editor. | Bravo, Gonzalo A., 1959- editor. |
Li, Ming, 1959- editor.
Title: International sport management / Eric MacIntosh, Gonzalo Bravo, Ming
Li, editors.
Description: Second Edition. | Champaign, Illinois : Human Kinetics, [2020] |
Previous edition: 2012. | Includes bibliographical references and index. |
Identifiers: LCCN 2018029543 (print) | LCCN 2018030727 (ebook) | ISBN
9781492556794 (e-book) | ISBN 9781492556787 (print)
Subjects: LCSH: Sports administration--Cross-cultural studies.
Classification: LCC GV713 (ebook) | LCC GV713 .I585 2020 (print) | DDC
796.06/9--dc23
LC record available at https://lccn.loc.gov/2018029543

ISBN: 978-1-4925-5678-7 (print)

Copyright © 2020 by Eric W. MacIntosh, Gonzalo A. Bravo, and Ming Li

Copyright © 2012 by Ming Li, Eric W. MacIntosh, and Gonzalo A. Bravo

All rights reserved. Except for use in a review, the reproduction or utilization of this work in any form or by any electronic, mechanical, or other means, now known or hereafter invented, including xerography, photocopying, and recording, and in any information storage and retrieval system, is forbidden without the written permission of the publisher.

The web addresses cited in this text were current as of November 2018, unless otherwise noted.

Acquisitions Editor: Diana Vincer; **Developmental Editor:** Melissa J. Zavala; **Copyeditor:** Bob Replinger; **Proofreader:** Leigh Keylock; **Indexer:** Beth Nauman-Montana; **Permissions Manager:** Dalene Reeder; **Graphic Designer:** Whitney Milburn; **Cover Designer:** Keri Evans; **Cover Design Associate:** Susan Allen; **Photograph (cover):** © Martin Rickett/PA Images via Getty Images; **Photographs (interior):** ©Human Kinetics, unless otherwise noted; **Photo Asset Manager:** Laura Fitch; **Photo Production Manager:** Jason Allen; **Senior Art Manager:** Kelly Hendren; **Printer:** Sheridan Books

Printed in the United States of America   10   9   8   7   6   5   4   3   2

The paper in this book is certified under a sustainable forestry program.

Human Kinetics
P.O. Box 5076
Champaign, IL 61825-5076
Website: www.HumanKinetics.com

In the United States, email info@hkusa.com or call 800-747-4457.
In Canada, email info@hkcanada.com.
In the United Kingdom/Europe, email hk@hkeurope.com.

For information about Human Kinetics' coverage in other areas of the world,
please visit our website: **www.HumanKinetics.com**

E7119

Tell us what you think!
Human Kinetics would love to hear what we
can do to improve the customer experience.
Use this QR code to take our brief survey.

We dedicate the second edition to the memory of Dr. Earle Zeigler, a pioneer, leader, and instrumental figure in sport management who helped pave the way for many scholars in the field.

Contents

Part IV Management Essentials in International Sport

Part V International Sport Business Strategies

Foreword

As one who has been associated with the field since its beginnings, I have the great pleasure to be writing the foreword to this book, which signifies the ever-expanding domain of sport management around the world. That this book is the second edition is a testament to its quality as well as its utility as a textbook. I would also like to point out that the most esteemed Dr. Zeigler wrote the foreword for the first edition. Because he is indisposed, I have been asked to write the foreword. I am thankful for the opportunity. It is indeed an honor to follow Dr. Zeigler and take his place in the book. He is my mentor and benefactor.

Sport management as a specialized field of study and practice has grown considerably since it was initiated in 1985. Although North America was the birthplace of the field under the leadership of the venerable Dr. Zeigler, the growth of the field is exemplified by the existence of a sport management association to represent every continent. More significantly, the North American Society for Sport Management reports that more than 95 journals deal directly with sport management, its subfields such as sport marketing, and allied fields.

Although sport management has at its core the management of sport as it is practiced and purveyed, it is also shaped by the political, legal, technological, competitive, and cultural factors that shape the organizations worldwide. Thus, these nuances need to be understood and managed appropriately for the benefit of clients and customers. Those who want to promote and manage sport around the world will find this book helpful because it outlines the rudiments of sport on the world scene. More important, the book serves to educate students and managers on the intricacies of managing sport organizations in different cultural and political contexts.

Eminent authors have contributed to this book by writing chapters covering sport management as it is practiced in all continents, including the Arab world. The chapters span the spectrum of Olympic sport, Paralympic sport, youth sport, professional sport, and so on. In addition, some of the chapters deal with the international sport federations that manage the variety of sport offerings. Note as well that some of the chapters cover critical negative influences in sport, such as doping, which is discussed regarding the role of the World Anti-Doping Agency and its management. I am sure that the book will serve as a comprehensive introduction to sport management as it is practiced across the globe. Students are exposed to key management theories and practical examples from around the world.

The editors, Eric MacIntosh, Gonzalo Bravo, and Ming Li, renowned scholars in their own right, should be congratulated on assembling an outstanding cast of authors to write chapters on carefully selected contexts and contents. Note that two of the editors hail from continents other than North America—Gonzalo Bravo from Chile in South America and Ming Li from China. All three editors have traveled widely around the world, and those experiences have served them well in distilling the content and context to be covered, and in selecting the authors to write the various chapters. The chapters stand as testament to the scholarship of the authors who wrote them.

This book fills a void in texts dealing with sport management as practiced around the world. Although students and their teachers are the prime beneficiaries of this edition, scholars will also find the book enticing because the book as a whole and the chapters within will stimulate critical thinking on additional conceptualizations and research in international sport management.

Packianathan Chelladurai, PhD, LLD, FNAK
Distinguished Professor
Troy University
Troy, Alabama, United States
Professor Emeritus—University of Western Ontario, Canada
Professor Emeritus—Ohio State University, United States

Preface

Published in 2012, the first edition of *International Sport Management* was the first book to deal specifically with the topic of international sport in a systematic way. To our delight, the first edition was well received. Adopters of the textbook spanned the globe. Since then, interest in the topic of international sport management has grown. A quick scan of sport management programs around the world reveals that the topic is taught in many undergraduate and graduate programs in Europe, North America, South America, Oceania, Africa, and Asia—a testament to just how international the topic of sport truly has become.

A consequence of this growth was a need to revise the first edition to provide what we hope is another quality product from leading sport management scholars around the world. In this, the second edition, we have revised the book to address some of the suggested changes to help truly internationalize this contribution. This volume has 55 authors who are native of or currently work at universities in Europe (Germany, England, other), Australia, Chile, Canada, Asia, Norway, the United States, and Africa.

Although we do not attempt to define the consistently debated geographical boundaries of a region, we have made every effort possible to put together a textbook that speaks to the vastness of sport overall in a region such as Europe by retaining authors who have centralized experience as researchers and sport management teachers for that region. In the revised edition, we have included further details on the development of sport management internationally and additional material on the academic societies currently in practice.

As editors to this volume, we bring with us life experiences in various regions of the world, scholarly work in those regions and others, and different cultural perspectives generally as researchers and practitioners. We believe that these varied experiences help with the content of the book and challenge us in our own ways to come up with a product we believe is much more international in scope.

Revisions in this book include new chapters on a history of international sport, world anti-doping and ethics for clean sport, youth sport events and festivals, digital media and fantasy sport, corruption in sport, and a challenge presented by international scholars on the way forward in sport management research. We have also expanded part II, Field of Play in International Sport, to include new chapters on North America, Latin America and the Caribbean, Western Europe, Eastern Europe, Africa, the Arab world, Oceania, North Asia, and South and Southeast Asia. We believe that these additions complement the existing roster from the first edition of chapters, all of which have undergone updates and revisions to reflect the various continental shifts in sport management.

The world of sport management continues its growth with the sharing of information at the disposal of researchers around the globe. The unprecedented availability of knowledge and the cross-pollination of disciplines of research continue to challenge sport management research and practice. Consequently, this new edition is in response to those challenges and the suggestions of the first adopters of the text who provided insightful feedback and commentary to ensure that this revised edition meets the needs of the modern classroom. Similar to the first edition, this edition introduces the principles and practices of the business and management of international sport and discusses sport governance, business activities, and the cross-cultural context of sport. We have included several new illustrations and cases embedded in the chapters to reflect the current situation in sport. Each of the 25 chapters has several case studies and learning activities that illustrate a multitude of real-world examples in international sport. The case studies, drawn from primary industry sources, newspapers, and journals, are intended to provide the student with the opportunity to apply concepts outlined in the chapters to real-world situations.

In addition, we have included a new instructor guide that will help the teacher use the course content and develop a curriculum for students.

The instructor resources available at www. HumanKinetics.com/InternationalSportManagement include a sample syllabus and a section on how to integrate case studies from *Case Studies in Sport Management* into teaching a course. Each chapter in the instructor guide includes ideas for class activities, essays, suggested readings or resources, and tips for teaching specific topics. The test package offers over 200 questions in multiple choice, fill-in-the-blank, true–false, and short-answer or essay formats. Each question is identified by topic. Instructors may use each chapter's bank of test questions as is or create customized tests. The presentation package contains PowerPoint slides of the main ideas of each chapter. These slides may be used as is or incorporated into customized classroom lectures.

A goal of this revised edition of the book is to combine relevant theoretical and practical insights from scholars that demonstrate the importance of international sport management. This text strives to incorporate the relevant theoretical advances in international business and organizational management literature and pedagogy in a manner that either undergraduate or graduate students in sport management can easily comprehend. To meet this goal, each chapter is organized to assist the student through the inclusion and highlighting of chapter objectives, key terms, learning activities, and review and discussion questions. The text includes extensive bibliographies and reference sections to help support the work of researchers and practitioners in the field. This text is intentionally written for use by students in sport management programs throughout the world and is not limited to a North American perspective. As editors, we hope that this orientation provides a solid account of international sport management in a way that is easily digestible and interesting for students around the globe and that will help advance the field in general.

Part I

Issues in International Sport Management

WORLD BASEBALL CLASSIC 2017 WorldBaseballClassic.com WORLD BASEBALL CLASSIC 2017

Alex Trautwig/WBCI/MLB Photos via Getty Images

The Dominican Republic baseball team during the 2017 World Baseball Classic (WBC), the premier international baseball tournament that gathers the best 16 national teams and professional players in the world. The WBC takes place every four years and has been in existence since 2006. In 2017, more than 1 million fans attended the 40 games that were played in six venues across the globe, including Seoul, Tokyo, Miami, Zapopan (Mexico), San Diego, and Los Angeles. Broadcasts of the 2017 WBC reached 415 million viewers in 182 countries.

Development of Globally Competent Sport Managers
Key Concepts and Emerging Trends in International Sport

Michael Pfahl, PhD
Bangkok University

Ming Li, EdD
Western Michigan University

Eric W. MacIntosh, PhD
University of Ottawa

Chapter Objectives

After studying this chapter, you will be able do the following:

- Understand the importance of globalization and its effect on the sport industry.
- Be familiar with the terminology and key concepts related to the globalization of sport.
- Appreciate and understand emerging global sports and markets.
- Understand the basic competencies and skills required to manage a sport organization in an international environment.

Key Terms	
globalization	localization
glocalization	regionalism
internationalization	nationalism
commodification	

The international nature of modern sport requires sport organization personnel to modify their personal and management practices to remain effective and competitive. Although modern sport has always had an international element to it in events like the World Cup and Olympic Games, numerous forces have given rise to a greater diversity in sport coverage, events, and participants. Technological changes and advancement have transformed broadcasting revenues, creating more sport entertainment options for fans and more revenue streams for organizations than ever before. Capital investment has moved with great speed, creating new stadia, teams, and merchandising opportunities. Athletes are perceived (and oftentimes act) like entertainment celebrities, moving from place to place employing their skills and aptitudes for the masses. This introductory chapter to *International Sport Management* is intended to help sport managers develop an understanding of some key concepts and critical issues of managing sport business around the world.

Key Concepts

In this section, key concepts are defined to aid in understanding the terminology used in the international sport world. These terms include globalization, internationalization, regionalism, nationalism, glocalization, and localization.

Globalization

"**Globalization** is a process of political, economic, and cultural penetrations among nations. In the context of sport, globalization refers to the increased interactions and integration among sport organizations and enterprises around the world" (Eschenfelder & Li, 2006, p. 211).

Globalization in sport has been described as being driven by economic considerations more often than not, although cultural elements play a role. The balance between the two is difficult to find. A search for such a balance can be seen in the emphasis that the International Olympic Committee (IOC) places on culture as part of its governing ideology. The demonstration of cultural uniqueness through hosting the Olympic Games (i.e., Opening and Closing Ceremonies) and through the local efforts for disseminating broader Olympic values through Olympic Day all speak to cultural elements within the globalization of sport (*Olympic Day*, 2010). Rather than allowing money to be the sole driving force behind the Olympic Movement, the IOC and related national Olympic committees strive to use educational, cultural, and athletic experiences to facilitate social development and change.

Yet the economic incentives of hosting an Olympic Games are touted as a primary reason to bid for them. Although the economic and cultural elements are often seen as being in conflict with each other, the IOC strives to show how they can be combined for the betterment of all the world's peoples.

Despite the importance of culture in globalization debates and in sport, economic considerations do play a significant role because of the need to expand markets and drive profits by international companies using sport as a sponsorship platform (Coakley & Donnelly, 1999, in Horne, 2006). The economic impact of sport can be felt in the areas of media, the aforementioned corporate sponsorship and influence, branding and celebrity culture, and the general sense of commercialization of sport (Horne, 2006).

When sport managers are driven by the search for diversification in assets, capital flows, and new markets to enter with existing products or product associations, changes to sport occur. For example, corporate sponsorship and influence have moved beyond supporting sport, and corporate entities can now be found in the offices of current sport ownership where interest in controlling sport organizations is increasingly falling to those who have amassed the largest fortunes. To illustrate, AC Milan (Italian Serie A), one of the largest and most popular football clubs in the world, is owned by Yonghong Li, a Chinese business tycoon; Chelsea (English Premier League) is owned by Russian-Israeli billionaire Roman Abramovich; Manchester United (English Premier League), another successful and globally popular football team, is owned by American Malcolm Glaser, who also owns the Tampa Bay Buccaneers (National Football League); Aston Villa (English Premier League) is owned by Chinese billionaire Tony Jiantong, who is the owner of Recon Group; and Manchester City (English Premier League) is owned by Sheikh Mansour, a member of Abu Dhabi's ruling Ali-Nahyan family. The result is the need to recoup the initial investment through actions to accumulate profit (in the interest of the owners), perhaps at the risk of fielding competitive teams or pursuing championships (in the interest of the fans).

Sport ownership also can contribute to a company's global expansion. Recently, Lizhang Jiang, a Chinese real estate investor and general manager of Shanghai Double-Edged Sports, became a minority owner of both the Minnesota Timberwolves and the Minnesota Lynx. The involvement of a Chinese owner would help open the Chinese market to these two sports franchises, along with various merchandising, broadcast, marketing, and sponsorship opportunities. This move solidifies the NBA's quiet work for "an international group to become involved in ownership on a minority level" (Withers, 2009, p. 7), part of its decades-long move toward creating a global market for its products. For more than 20 years, the NBA has been slowly making inroads with its brand around the world. The NBA has hosted international tournaments, played exhibition games outside America, and welcomed numerous international players to its teams. Although other professional leagues have engaged in international markets, the NBA has arguably been the most successful to date.

Internationalization

Internationalization is a term used to describe the worldwide dissemination of sport, driven, in part, by the development of the 20th-century consumer culture. In addition, the term refers to the movement of athletes around the world in the pursuit of work (Magnússon, 2001). This trend occurred despite "sport not being controlled or produced in a single country" (Keys, 2006, p. 187). Sport, as an element in the internationalization of cultures, could be claimed by nations (both politicians and citizens) as "an expression of intrinsically national characteristics" (Keys, 2006, p. 188). Coakley (2003) identified three main areas that paved the way for the internationalization of sport: market economies, changing demographics including increased disposable income and greater leisure time, and large-scale capital investment by public and private sources. Although these elements could not, and cannot, be found in every country in the world, they do indicate the driving forces behind the last 100 years or so of growth in the popularity of sport, participation in sport (and athletics and

CASE STUDY

Development of Formula One's Global Reach

Formula One is the world motorsport championship that began in 1950. Steve Matchett, former Benetton Formula One team mechanic and current color commentator for the Formula One broadcasts on Fox's Speed Channel in the United States, said that the sport "has grown to become one of the leading sport businesses in the world, a colossal multi-billion-dollar industry" (Matchett, 2005, p. 22). With even the smallest components costing substantial sums and the race prize amounts kept relatively secret, Formula One is built on mystery, excess, politics, and glamour (Pfahl & Bates, 2008). Formula One cars are arguably the world's most exotic automotive machines. In years past, the championship was run primarily on European race circuits, although a handful of races were run in countries such as Australia, Brazil, South Africa, and the United States (depending on the year). The teams operated from bases in England, Germany, and France, although the drivers were from all over the world.

By the 1990s the sport had grown in popularity, and the governing body, the Fédération Internationale de l'Automobile (FIA), and the marketing entity for the sport, Formula One Management (FOM), began to set eyes on emerging global markets. The driver of this expansion was the broadcast rights sold by FOM across the world and the increasing sponsorship money that followed the massive international broadcasting and fan base of the sport. FOM pushed for new tracks to be built in rising economies such as those of Malaysia, Turkey, and China. By 2009 the championship boasted a 17-race schedule that ran from March to November and raced in 19 countries (including, for example, Italy, Bahrain, Hungary, and Brazil). Although some have questioned the viability of the FIA and FOM's strategy, Formula One remains the top motorsport competition in the world.

exercise in general), and importantly, the **commodification** of sport and athletes. In this case, commodification refers to the influence of economic forces on the structure and practice of sport. Today, with the available technology, commodification of sport is at an all-time high.

As many sport leagues, teams, athletes, and companies become more internationalized, various cultural elements taken from the home country or local region emanate across the world by television, radio, and computers. For example, the English Premier League is the most popular football league (domestically, regionally, and internationally) not only because of the quality of play in the league but also because of the associated English cultural elements broadcast around the globe with each match (e.g., language, fan culture). These elements are evident in the United States where, for example, the official supporter organization of the Columbus Crew (Major League Soccer) has adopted the chanting and singing of songs during match play, an international occurrence, but one with special connections to British football. British hooliganism (see Giulianotti, Bonney, & Hepworth, 1994) has even found its way to Columbus, Ohio, as 100 Crew supporters, ironically named the Hudson Street Hooligans, clashed with 30 or so supporters from the English Premier League side West Ham United during a friendly match (Leonard, 2008). Although this image is not the one that English football would prefer to present to the world, it does show that the cultural characteristics of the British version of the sport find their ways to other communities through the internationalization of sport.

The internationalization of sport has increased opportunities for fan involvement and enjoyment and has provided exposure to cultures from around the world, because of developments in television, satellite, computer, and computer-mediated technologies. For example, American fans of the Italian Serie A football league can watch league matches from the comfort of their homes on the Fox Soccer Channel, Thai fans can wake up early in the morning to watch live broadcasts of the American National Football League games by satellite television, and soccer enthusiasts all over the world watched the 2018 FIFA World Cup games being played in Russia live by online streaming. Many major sport teams around the world have multiple-language websites (e.g., NBA in Chinese) that offer unique content for fans in different countries to maximize sponsorship and marketing opportunities, especially merchandise sales. Overall, many professional sport leagues and teams engage in internationalization strategies.

Regionalization

Within the framework of internationalization lies regionalization. Blocs of countries or market areas within a specific geographical, cultural, or economic condition have developed in the modern era. Although groups of nations have come together for various purposes throughout history, in the era of globalization formal entities such as the European Union, the Association of South East Asian Nations, and the Non-Aligned Nations (Baghdadi, 2009) have developed in response to various forces of globalization and internationalization. In the world of sport, regionalization has also taken hold as governing bodies for various sports have created confederations and regional tournaments in addition to the larger, global ones run by international federations such as Fédération Internationale de Basketball (FIBA).

For example, the Union of European Football Associations (UEFA) is the powerful European football confederation that runs the UEFA Champions League and other competitions that are broadcast worldwide. These events receive almost as much attention as the World Cup itself. Although the competitions draw from European domestic leagues (e.g., England, Italy), the tournaments themselves are broadcast around the world. Fans are able to cheer their teams at an entirely different level of competition than in the domestic leagues. For the sponsors, the championships are an important advertising platform, although not quite at the cost level of the Olympics or World Cup. Although other regional confederations host similar tournaments (e.g., African Nations Cup, Asian Champions League), none generate the excitement that surrounds the European championships.

Regionalism, based on a geographical area (e.g., Southeast Asia) made up of a set of countries with similar characteristics, plays an important part in international culture, specifically in sport. Regional competitions and teams maintain an international presence at a lower cost of operation than large, international competitions. Thus, they can be run more frequently and have the benefit of generating neighborhood rivalries among countries or communities. Examples of regional sport include the Southeast Asian Games and the Pan American Games. But anytime that international cultural flows (of any kind) move through countries or regions, the possibility exists that not everyone will understand and accept the inherent diversity of ideas or practices. Despite the global nature of modern sport, at its heart, sport remains locally centered.

Nationalism

As the various forces of globalization developed, expanded, and exerted their influences over local cultures, a countermovement developed with the intention of retaining or promoting a national identity (nationalism). **Nationalism**, or a shared sense of what a country stands for or is composed of, is a socially constructed concept with ever-changing rituals, practices, and historical foundations (Horne, 2006). It is closely linked with individual and community perceptions of national identities, although nationalism takes many forms (e.g., civic, ethnic) (Bairner, 2001). The most common form of nationalism is promoting the characteristics of the nation-state itself. For example, although what it means to be an American varies by person, there is a mainstream, some might say hegemonic, version of being an American, which includes loyalty to family, country, and religious or traditional values. Additionally, a common expression of nationalism includes language that refers to *we* or *us* used in relation to another, a *them*.

Naisbitt (1994) characterized the tension between local and global as a paradox in which "the more universal we become, the more tribal [local] we act" (p. 131). By tribal, Naisbitt is referring to the local cultures of communities, which includes the nation (Maffesoli, 1996). Arguably, the increased globalization occurring in the 21st century has put nationalism into question in terms of whether or not globalization has led to the increase or decrease in nationalism. Bairner (2001) viewed globalization and nationalism as opposite sides of the same coin whereby increased knowledge of other cultures helps to raise awareness and understanding of local cultural elements.

Sport is arguably the most popular form of nationalist behavior given the masses of people that become emotionally charge in support of their Olympic team. Perhaps, the most visible of the connection between national team and nationalism is associated with the men's World Cup football tournament. Countries with long, sometimes violent, histories with each other—for example, Japan and Korea, and Germany and Poland—tend to see a rise in nationalism ahead of an actual match as media references to the history and other memories are dredged up (Maguire, Poulton, & Possamai, 1999; McCormack, 2002).

The pressures of globalized cultures can weigh heavily on local cultural elements. Individuals must negotiate the tensions inherent within a web of local, national, and international connections. Local cultural traditions and the need to retain cultural identity can clash with increasing capitalist ideals (wealth, status, stardom) (Friedman, 1990). Sometimes, the outside cultural forces are rejected, sometimes they are embraced, and other times hybrids of both are accepted. Hybrid forms are known as **glocalization** (Giulianotti & Robertson, 2009), or "the combining of global and local themes" (Horne, 2006, p. 133), which creates a new entity out of one or more cultural elements. In New Zealand, for example, the 20th century saw the rapid development, spread, and popularity of rugby after its introduction to the country in the 19th century. The country used the national team as a springboard to encourage social integration, culminating in the All Blacks rugby team, through which "distinctions between social classes, between town and country, between regions, between colonisers and colonised, were both dramatized and bridged" (Perry, 2005, p. 159).

Localization

Closely related to glocalization is localization. **Localization** is the adaptation of nonlocal elements to the local context (e.g., language, rules). Local culture should be seen in terms of the global cultural flows of which it is a part (Appadurai, 1990; Wakeford, 2003), meaning that the interconnectedness of global and local communities influence each other and require knowledge of both to understand each. Most major sporting teams and leagues have links on their main websites to specific language websites (e.g., Chinese, Japanese, Spanish). Slowly, these entities are also producing exclusive content for these local sites rather than merely translating what was presented on the main English (or Italian or Korean) page. Mobile telephones, computer-mediated communication, and wireless devices have redefined *local* to mean a focus on individual preferences of content, and platforms such as Twitter and YouTube allow users to generate their own content such as current news and reports. Although developments such as YouTube might be driven by profit motives and used to attract additional sponsorship monies, they also speak to the tightening of global ties that are a part of internationalization and globalization discussions with local situations.

In sum, within the duality of global and local, sport managers must make strategic decisions to establish a brand presence in local markets while identifying ways in which to establish or increase an international presence. Differences in global, national, regional, and local communities make this task a challenging one. Sport managers responsible for making the strategic, cultural, political, and economic decisions for sport teams or organizations must be prepared for the challenges of the new sport landscape. They must be equipped with skills, abilities, and worldviews that are inclusive yet can differentiate cultural elements.

Emerging Sports

Although established leagues and their teams in professional sport (e.g., EPL, La Liga, NBA, and so on) and mega and major sport events (e.g., Olympics, FIFA, PGA tour events, Wimbledon, and so on) are now mainstays of international sport, several sport entities are increasing in size and prominence. For example, stand-up paddling, adventure racing, ultradistance competitions, and bouldering (now on the Olympic program) are emerging sports that highlight physical and athletic prominence. Emerging sports lack the mass exposure (for the moment at least) and monetization of major sports leagues or events (Socolow, 2016). One such sport entity, e-sport, is emerging at so rapid a rate that the IOC is grappling with the decision of whether or not to include it within the Olympic program. Some professional sport leagues (e.g., NBA) have already started to venture into partnerships and business opportunities with this technology sector.

Another example of an emerging sport that showcases technological advancements is drone racing. Like e-sport, drone racing can be played in sport stadia or arenas, creating additional entertainment and revenue streams within sport facilities. Owners

of these facilities now can use it to attract new fans and demographics that may be less enthusiastic about traditional sports playing within those same facilities.

Newzoo (2018) defined e-sport as "competitive gaming at a professional level and in an organized format (a tournament or league) with a specific goal (i.e., winning a champion title or prize money) and a clear distinction between players and teams that are competing against each other" (p. 7). The British Esports Association sees it as "competitive video gaming, where people [amateurs or professionals] play against each other online and also at spectator events in indoor arenas, usually for a cash prize" (British Esports Association, 2017, p. 3). There is little question that e-sport is emerging at breakneck speed. "[It] is on course to become established as one of the leading global sports" (Nielson, 2017, p. 6). Performance Communications (n.d.) concurs with such claim with a number of statistics:

> In 2013, people spent 1.5 billion hours watching Activision games being played, compared to the NFL's seven billion. Sky Sports has already broadcast the FIFA Interactive World Cup, Amazon paid $1 billion for games streaming site Twitch. . . . If we accept that participation is an important driver of fandom—an estimated 260 million people play football, while 1.2 billion play computer games—some futurists believe eSports could become the world's most popular pastime. (p. 26)

It was estimated that in 2018 e-sport enthusiasts worldwide will number 165 million and the e-sport audience will be around 380 million. In the same year, the global e-sport industry will realize $906 million in revenues, 77 percent of which will come from investments of other industries (Newzoo, 2018, p. 7).

The viewership or spectatorship for e-sport tournaments continues to grow. For example, the Season 4 Finals of League of Legends was held in the Seoul World Cup Stadium, Asia's largest soccer stadium with a seating capacity of 40,000 in 2016. All seats were taken. According to Newzoo (2018), 588 major e-sport tournaments were held worldwide in 2017, and ticket revenues collectively reached $59 million. The prize money for those tournaments was about $112 million.

The emergence of e-sport, where video and real-life play converge, challenges the traditional definition of sport (Delaware North, 2015) and provides tremendous opportunities for brands to tap into some key demographics. In 2014 Amazon acquired the e-sport streaming network Twitch for $970 million in part because the network attracts over 100 million viewers a month, allowing Amazon to grow their brand. Many professional sport teams and leagues see e-sport as an excellent opportunity to cultivate their fan base. "The top-tier soccer league in the Netherlands was among the first national sports leagues to launch a full FIFA league season with esports teams branded by the soccer clubs" (Newzoo, 2018, p. 10).

Finally, e-sport will feature at the 2022 Asian Games as a medal event, raising this question: Will the Olympics be next to feature e-sport?

Emerging Markets

Developing nations with high economic growth rates and potential are commonly referred to as emerging markets (Khanna & Palepu, 2010). With this criterion in mind, Brazil, China, India, and Russia, commonly known as BRIC nations, along with a number of other countries, are often cited as emerging markets. The economic growth in these emerging markets offers tremendous opportunities for sport organizations to expand into these nations (PWC, 2011). More and more international sports events are being held in emerging markets. "Emerging markets are increasingly engaging with and investing in top-level sport: the next three Olympic Games will be staged in Asia" (Nielson, 2017, p. 2). Major sport event properties have chosen these emerging markets to host their events including, for example, Russia's hosting of the 2018 FIFA World Cup and the 2014 Winter Olympic Games, China's hosting of the 2008 Summer Olympics and the 2022 Winter Olympic Games, and Brazil's hosting of the 2014 FIFA World Cup and the 2016 Summer Olympic Games. The sport market in the aforementioned four BRIC countries outpaced the overall global sport markets between 2006 and 2010 with a compound annual growth rate of 7.7 percent (PWC, 2011, p. 13).

American professional sport leagues have been capitalizing on the large populations and the growing middle-class base of these emerging markets for more than two decades (Bode, 2014). For example, for growth of its brand the NBA has strategically targeted China, one of the top emerging markets in the world. As such, the NBA has sent players to conduct clinics and participate in public appearances. The increased fan base and viewership will likely lead to greater consumption of NBA products. Besides the NBA, the NHL, NFL, and MLB have also been establishing and maintaining their physical presence in China and many European countries for some time, again highlighting the internationalization of sport.

Nielsen Sports, an international sport marketing company, in its annual report released in 2017 titled *Commercial Trends in Sports*, gives three pieces of advice about the emerging international sport markets:

1. The sporting landscape is changing, opening up major opportunities in new markets.
2. A deep understanding of how emerging markets are approaching sport is required—right up to state level.
3. Knowledge transfer from mature to emerging markets will be an increasingly valuable asset (Nielson, 2017, p. 3).

Development of International Competencies for Sport Managers

The modern sport world requires sport managers to be knowledgeable and aware of the importance of their own and other's cultural preferences. Hanvey (1976, p. 2) identified five main areas that influence international sport understanding:

1. Perspective consciousness (understanding differences)
2. State-of-planet awareness (understanding global issues)
3. Cross-cultural awareness (understanding cultural diversity and similarity)
4. Systematic awareness (operations of international organizations)
5. Options for participation (conducting sport business)

Sport managers need to have competence in these skill sets if they wish to work within the modern sporting landscape. For emerging sport managers, these experiences will teach them as much as discussions regarding theoretical skill sets will. The skill sets include personal reflexivity, sensitivity to cultural differences, and flexible expertise.

Personal Reflexivity

First, sport managers need to be reflexive about themselves, their actions, and their worldviews. Reflexivity describes the state of being self-critical or analytical. It encompasses personal reflection on attitudes or actions to understand why they came about and what outcomes they produced. Why should a person examine the self when the goal is to understand others? Primarily, a person needs to be able gauge where he or she stands on issues and what knowledge is known versus inferred. As social beings, humans are a balance of self and other, (co)constructing life each day. In other words, we are individuals within communities of other individuals who interact and share ideas to create understandings of the world around us. As George Mead (1934), the father of modern sociology, noted,

> No individual has a mind which operates simply in itself, in isolation from the social life process in which it has arisen or out of which it has emerged and in which the pattern of organized social behavior has consequently been basically impressed upon it. (p. 222)

Further, nothing in this world is absolute, isolated, or permanent because we are all linked together in some way, especially with our natural environment (Pfahl, 2002; Plamintr, 1994).

When we take the time to learn more about ourselves, we can learn about our relations to and with others and even about other people in deeper and meaningful ways. In terms of sport, you might be a person who cheers for the underdog at a sporting event and considers such an action a part of who you are or something you value. But this behavior is associated with cultural values from the community in which you were raised. Learning this lesson about yourself helps you gather information from others (e.g., dialogue, observation) and begin to understand how they view the world or, in this case, a sport league, team, or event. Of course, new experiences and lessons mean that changes can occur to existing beliefs or value structures, but this change is only natural (and probably useful

for sport managers working within international sport). The self is social and socially constructed, yet a person takes her or his own journey, one on one with the environment. Thus, to understand others, we must begin by understanding the self because understanding ourselves provides ways of understanding others.

Sensitivity to Cultural Differences

Second, sport managers need to be receptive and sensitive to cultural differences (Harris & Moran, 1991). Most people are aware of the legislation against discriminatory hiring or promotion practices as well as the more severe laws against racially or ethnically motivated hate crimes. Sport managers face a more subtle challenge in relation to cultural sensitivity, one that usually places one set of cultural values at odds with another. For example, an NBA team's use of Spanish language on jerseys can be seen as a sincere outreach gesture to an excited but underserved fan community. But the action might be insulting to others, who view it as using culture to sell tickets without a sincere interest in Hispanic culture.

Another example comes from the 2010 World Cup and the infamous vuvuzela horn. The vuvuzela is a descendant of a traditional cultural musical instrument found across Africa. Many observers in the media and football fans called for the horns to be banned, mostly because of the high levels of noise that they produce, which could endanger a person's hearing with prolonged exposure and interfere with broadcast commentary. Former FIFA president Sepp Blatter squashed all notions of banning the instrument, saying,

> I have always said that Africa has a different rhythm, a different sound. . . . I don't see banning the music traditions of fans in their own country. Would you want to see a ban on the fan traditions in your country? (Baxter, 2010, p. 2)

Blatter's decision lay at the intersection of cultural traditions in one community and standards of behavior in another (most negative complaints and comments came from Western or Caucasian corners). If Blatter banned the horns, he risked having the move being viewed as racially motivated or, at the very least, culturally insensitive, especially because the event was the first World Cup held in Africa (and one that he championed). Yet his comments, however positive, can be interpreted in another way because he praises the difference of Africa, a continent with numerous cultures. This account illustrates the complexity of culture in international sport. Hence, culture has been broadly used in this chapter. It might mean traditional conceptualizations of cultures (e.g., nations, regions), it might be used to explain what it is like to work within an organization (i.e., organizational culture), or it might mean cultures within cultures (e.g., surf culture). In any case, sport managers must balance the notions of difference and similarity; homogeneity and heterogeneity; and local, regional, national, and international aspects. Sport managers need to appreciate that culture has a strong influence on how a person perceives the world, and acts and reacts when dealing with others.

In a vast world of numerous cultures, how can this be done effectively? Newspapers, magazines, journals, mediated programming, and other sources provide constant access to international issues in sport and beyond. In terms of direct industry practice, sport managers can examine the methods that sporting events and teams around the world use to engage fans, to market themselves, and to exist within different cultural realms. Such an investigation will provide a solid base from which to reexamine practices in a person's own organization or industry and adapt them to international contexts in a culturally sensitive way.

Flexible Expertise

Third, a sport manager requires a flexible expertise. Understanding oneself and others and then communicating with them involves a fundamental worldview that values flexibility and adaptation. Opening up oneself to other cultures, influences, and knowledge requires a person to challenge personal (and perhaps deeply held) beliefs or practices, find information that runs counter to belief systems, or learn something not previously known. Sport managers who maintain flexible and adaptable behaviors and practices will be better placed to seize opportunities, create them where they have not been capitalized on, and manage challenges to operations.

Sport managers, then, must develop operational expertise, communication expertise, and systems and critical analysis expertise that are grounded in technical, human relations, and conceptual skills and the principles of learning organizations (Katz & Kahn, 1978; Senge, 1994), although they differ slightly in size and scope. Operational expertise involves knowledge of marketing, sales, finance, accounting, economics, and personnel management—the foundations of business practices. The combination of the foundations with integrated strategic thinking (i.e., systems and critical analysis expertise) is the ultimate expression of operational expertise. Remember, however, that these skills are gained through both education *and* experience. Effective sport managers must have communication expertise to be able to communicate thoughts, ideas, and concepts from around the world or from their own backyard. Finally, international sport managers need well-developed systems and critical analysis expertise to see the interrelationships among various organizational and market variables as well as the ability to balance macro and micro perspectives within a given issue.

The first component to flexible expertise is operational expertise. To some extent in a market system, operational expertise is understandable and translatable across cultures. But some nuances must be addressed. Examples include accounting and financial regulation that differ across countries or regions (e.g., European Union), approaches to sales and marketing that vary along a continuum of relationship, and perhaps most difficult, the challenges of working for or managing people from other countries or cultures where different regulations or laws govern work.

A second expertise is communication. Communication involves the knowledge of oneself and how to communicate various messages because the world is (co)constructed among individuals within communities (Baxter & Montgomery, 1996). Communication expertise can be thought of as communication competence, or the ability to "effectively exchange meaning through a common system of symbols, signs, or behaviors" (Bourhis, Adams, Titsworth, & Harter, 2004, p. 28). Communication competence is difficult to achieve because others have different perspectives, sense-making processes, and goals. Understanding and developing strong communication skills allow sport managers to interact with others to make sense of the world and communicate with others in their organization to achieve goals and effect change. Cultural and international differences such as distance, language differences, and cultural practices (e.g., silence, relationship development) create *noise*, which affects the ability to communicate with others. A sport manager can develop communication skills to deal with these issues by using a systems approach—one that simultaneously understands person, culture, and context (Hersey, 1984). For example, the National Football League (NFL) has several international websites (Canada, China, Japan, Mexico, United Kingdom, and NFL-Latino.com). To overcome distance issues (time, too, because NFL games are shown in the middle of the night or early in the morning in some of these countries), each site is complete with videos, broadcast schedules, local news and information, and community content (e.g., user-generated content) to keep the game alive within each community. The Chinese and Japanese websites are created using a template that accounts for stylistic needs for the characters in each language. Creating websites in this manner shows that the personnel at the NFL understand the importance of integrating cultural practices into their marketing and information efforts. Although they cannot overcome all barriers, cultural and otherwise (e.g., time), this example demonstrates the importance of cultural sensitivity in sport business practices.

In conclusion, developing all three expertise areas is a never-ending process. The journey is the key to the development of a sport manager. Throughout this journey, sport managers have numerous opportunities to use these expertise areas in relation to the issues explored in this chapter and throughout the book.

Summary

The concepts and current issues within the world of international sport discussed in this chapter and the competencies necessary to work within and among them are of supreme importance to sport managers. Sport managers who are able to understand and work with the numerous social forces affecting sport will be able to play important roles in creating the future of international sport.

Issues such as globalization, regionalism, and localization place a responsibility on sport managers to reach across country and cultural borders and learn about other people and communities. Enabling and constraining these efforts are complex issues including politics, economics, laws, and cultural beliefs and practices. Communication, then, becomes a significant key to success. Time, patience, open mindedness, and a willingness to learn and develop personal skill sets will all serve a sport manager well in the international sport world. The remainder of this book is dedicated to building on the issues discussed in this chapter. By the end of the book, the reader should have a better understanding of the complexities inherent in the modern sport landscape and a deeper knowledge of his or her place within the international sport world.

Learning Activity

The chapter discussed the importance of communication and communication competence. Reflect on recent interpersonal or group interactions that you have had yourself or witnessed with others in terms of interactions with people from another country. Are you able to identify interactions that were not effective? Why? Can you identify ones that were effective? Why?

Review Questions

1. How does globalization influence sport today?
2. Describe the tension that exists between homogeneity and heterogeneity in terms of sport and culture.
3. What are the differences between global, international, and regional sport? Provide examples of sport in each.
4. Discuss the global trends in emerging sports and markets.
5. What are three competencies needed by international sport managers? Provide examples of each.

The Globalized Sport Industry:
Historical Perspectives

James J. Zhang, PhD
University of Georgia

Demetrius W. Pearson, EdD
University of Houston

Tyreal Y. Qian, MS
University of Georgia

Euisoo Kim, MBA
University of Georgia

Chapter Objectives

After studying this chapter, you will be able to do the following:

- Define the concept of globalization and recognize its impact on the sport industry as a whole.
- Recognize that certain aspects of contemporary global sports have emerged from the past and are connected with many different sport forms today.
- Understand the historical evolvement of modern sports from indigenous, local, or regional games to become global competitions.
- Identify major forces and critical junctures that have contributed to the intensification of sport globalization.
- Comprehend the sport industry as a growing global business and understand issues and challenges surrounding the demand and supply of sport in a globalized marketplace.

Key Terms

Industrial Revolution	labor movement
modern sport	sport globalization
sport business	

Globalization, assimilation, and acculturation are elements that have given rise to
how people within their respective societies internalize aspects of life through myriad
ideologies, including politics, religion, governance,
economics, child rearing, education, and social
etiquette. Coakley (2017) operationally defines
globalization as

> a process through which financial capital,
> products, knowledge, worldviews, and cultural
> practices flow through political borders and
> influence people's lives. Globalization often
> involves exchanges of resources and elements
> of culture—but those exchanges are seldom
> equal, because some nations have more power
> to export and infuse their money and ways of
> life into other societies. (p. 429)

In fact, globalization is not a new concept.
According to Eitzen (2012), a globalizing economy
has been in existence and evolving for over 500
years. This international exchange of life experiences, inventions, and ideologies grew exponentially during the late 19th and 20th centuries in
part because of major advancements in transportation (air, land, and sea), communication (tele-
phone, telegraph, television, film, etc.), and technology (satellites, microcomputers, Internet, etc.).
Consistent with the interchange of consumable
products and services are the migratory patterns
of people and customs that are both accepted and
rejected (Banjeree & Linstead, 2001; Rowe, 2003).
This chapter explores the many aspects of globalization evolvement and the interconnectedness
that currently exists through international sport
involvement. In this chapter, we first examine the
growth of sport during the **Industrial Revolution**
and the spread of American sporting values. Then,
we trace the development of international athletic
arms race and militarism throughout the 20th
century and major surge of **sport globalization**
in the late 20th century. Finally, we close out the
chapter by discussing contemporary development
trends in globalization of the sporting goods industry, international migration and sport, sport **labor
movement**, and benefits of international athletes
in sport teams and leagues.

Growth of Sport During the Industrial Revolution

Physical activity contests of many sporting natures
and their ancillary components (e.g., equipment,
facilities, rules, and training regimens) have been
exchanged, emulated, and inculcated for centuries.
However, never has globalization or internationalization of sport been as pervasive and widespread
as it is today. Nations around the world are now
participating in various aspects of the sport marketplace.

"Quasi-sports" (i.e., early activities reminiscent
of institutionalized sport forms), games, and related
physical contests can be traced to antiquity in many
countries around the world. According to Sage
and Eitzen (2013), these activities had a narrow
geographical base historically and were traditionally local and endemic to a particular region. Many
of them originated within the indigenous culture,
were delivered by nomadic tribesman and traders, or were inculcated by proselytizing explorers
and conquerors. According to Howell and Howell
(1988), the first real evidence of sport and games
was found in the Early Dynastic period of the Sume-
rian civilization circa 3000 to 1500 BC.

Various archeological artifacts depicting early
forms of boxing and wrestling were unearthed. But
Howell and Howell note that some of the archeological finds depicting such competitive challenges
may not have been what sport historians would
commonly perceive as sport and games. The aforementioned physical contests were engaged in, but
many were never recorded, particularly those of the
lower class (Howell & Howell, 1988). Therefore,
many sport historians tend to focus attention on
the Greek National Festivals (aka "crown games"),
and specifically the Olympic Games (Coakley, 2017;
Howell & Howell, 1988; Swanson & Spears, 1995;
Woods, 2016). These games are noteworthy because
they incorporated a modicum of organization and
structure. In addition, evidence of their contests
abounds through etchings, pottery, sculptures, and
literature.

Arguably, the most notable acculturation of
indigenous games and quasi-sport forms were

the bastardized contests of the Romans usurped from the Greeks. Their belligerent ethos was considerably different from that of their vanquished counterparts, whose sport orientation reflected an aesthetic appreciation for contests of an athletic nature that included the love of rhythm, beauty, and music. The Romans were more pragmatic and brutal in their employment of physical contests and games. Coakley (2017) noted that these spectacles created opportunities to hone the skills of the military, entertain a disillusioned citizenry, and rid the empire of social undesirables (e.g., criminals, heretics, POWs, Christians, and disobedient slaves). In addition, man versus animal and animal versus animal contests, as well as bear baiting and bull baiting were staged. Thus, the term *quasi-sport* appears to be an appropriate designation for such activities. The orientation of the Greeks and Romans toward competitive athletic contests was considerably different.

As noted earlier, globalization of sport forms is not of recent origin (Maguire, 2004), nor is it limited to North America. Nonetheless, this section of the chapter will use the onset of sport globalization primarily during the Industrial Revolution in Europe (1780s) and North America (1820s) that subsequently led to the Gilded Age and the exponential growth of sport in the United States (Barney, 1988; Coakley, 2017). This era is often referred to as the age of progress (Glassford & Redmond, 1988, p. 140). This quintessential period in the development of contemporary sport (Coakley, 2017) enabled it to become a major global commodity.

Born during the Industrial Revolution, **modern sport** developed extensively during the 19th and 20th centuries (Glassford & Redmond, 1988). Technological advances in various areas spurred the development and expansion of diverse sport forms. This seminal period (1875-1925) is noteworthy as a starting point because it reflects and encompasses the organization and institutionalization of the many tenets endemic to organized sport. Among them were standardized rules and guidelines, documentation of results and statistics, codes of conduct for participants and spectators, sanctioned facilities and equipment, appropriate attire, and eligibility requirements. These milestone changes occurred during the Industrial Revolution period to the mid-20th century and helped lay a strong foundation for today's sophisticated sport marketplace, which is currently reflective of international athletic contests and federations as well as their ancillary trappings.

Maguire et al. (2002) contend that a long-term historical and comparative approach can help explain how certain aspects of contemporary global sport have emerged from the past and are connected with many different sport forms today. This analysis of the development and expansion of sport during the Industrial Revolution must include a discussion of the salient contributions of Great Britain and its cultural imperialism. As the most powerful country in Europe during the 19th century, its culture and recreational pastimes were instilled within its distant global colonies. At one point, "the countries of the Empire accounted for a quarter of the world's population" (Woods, 2016, p. 215), including colonies in Africa, India, Singapore, Hong Kong, Australia, New Zealand, the West Indies, Canada, and America. Great Britain's sporting values and influences were so pervasive that it was dubbed "The Mother of Sport" (Glassford & Redmond, 1988, p. 134) even though its many contributions were more in the areas of structure, formalization, and standardization. Suffice it to say that most major sports of the 19th century were organized and exported from Great Britain. Other countries noteworthy for their influence on early sport forms included Germany, Sweden, Denmark, and Norway. They resented British culture and rejected the concomitant sporting customs in favor of their own national sport systems that embraced gymnastics and sundry winter sports (e.g., skiing, figure skating, curling, etc.).

Great Britain's contribution to international sports can also be attributed to its spread of soccer, currently the most popular sport in the world ("The History of Soccer," n.d.) although the origin of soccer is in question because various forms of the game were played centuries ago in China, Japan, Greece, Rome, and the British Isles. But the contemporary form of soccer is believed to have begun in England in 1863 (FIFA, 2017). Because of Great Britain's immense influence internationally around the turn of the 19th century, the game spread rapidly around the world. Football (soccer) associations were formed in such countries as the Netherlands and Denmark (1889), New Zealand (1891), Argentina (1893), Chile (1895), Switzerland and Belgium (1895), Italy (1898), Germany and Uruguay (1900), Hungary (1901), and France (1907). Currently, people in over 210 countries play soccer and vie for the coveted World Cup every four years.

The popularity and pervasiveness of British games and the English sport system purported to inculcate certain revered values such as honesty, fair play, sportsmanship, initiative, courage, patriotism, and loyalty (Glassford & Redmond, 1988). These attributes were perceived to be outcomes of sport participation and elements that would produce leaders in business and government. In essence, sport arguably became Great Britain's most important cultural export during the late 19th century. Its world prominence was so profound that it became the impetus for the structural underpinnings of the modern Olympic Games. Baron Pierre de Coubertin, the French aristocrat and architect of the reconstituted Olympic Games in 1896, was instrumental in the early international sport movement (Gems, Borish, & Pfister, 2017; Maguire, 2004). Impressed with what he saw and learned during his visit to England and its public school sport system, de Coubertin sought to emulate this pedagogical concept. In so doing, he linked the British system of sport and games with the early Olympic credo to create the modern Olympic movement (Howell & Howell, 1988; Woods, 2016). The implications of this unprecedented amalgamated concept are without question one of the most galvanizing and polarizing aspects in sport history.

Originally staged in Athens, Greece, with 14 participating nations, the Olympics remain as the most celebrated multisporting event worldwide, with over 200 nations competing (Woods, 2016). This international sporting event, predicated on de Coubertin's Olympic creed, has embodied the geopolitical and sociocultural issues endemic to all countries at one time or another. Although plagued by boycotts, bombings, hypernationalism, terrorism, and global warfare that led to the cancellation of three Olympic Games, they have withstood these global challenges and continue to rein as the most prominent purveyor of sport, in spite of the multitude of international sporting events that have emulated its concept.

Spread of American Sporting Values

The American influence on sport globalization primarily occurred concurrently with the Olympic movement. After Canadian-born physical educator James Naismith invented basketball, his Young Men's Christian Association (YMCA) disciples exported it, as well as baseball and track and field, to China and its provinces in the mid-1890s (Cui, 2015; Ling, 2008). The proselytizing missionary work and sport promotion of David Willard Lyon and later Robert Gailey in 1898 at Chinese colleges laid the foundation for national athletic championships. The most noteworthy was the 1915 Far East Games, a regional variation of the Olympic Games (Gems et al., 2017). The Japanese were also early converts and consumers of American sport. American-educated Japanese students learned the game at U.S. colleges and in the 1890s brought it back to their country, where it became the sport of choice.

YMCA-endorsed sports were often incorporated into the U.S. War Department's agenda as a conduit to channel and rebuff hostile insurgent threats to colonial rule and American acculturation. Akin to the Roman Empire's employment of quasi-sport contests to entertain and distract a disgruntled populace, the U.S. War Department incorporated YMCA-sanctioned sports and religious tenets as diversions. This military ploy helped spread American sports and its sporting values after their conquest of Spain during the Spanish-American War in 1898. As a result, American sports were spread to the newly acquired Spanish colonies: Cuba, Puerto Rico, Guam, and the Philippine Islands. Filipinos were most receptive to baseball, basketball, and boxing. Manila, where the Manila Carnival was held, invited other Asian nations to participate in what would be known as the Far Eastern Olympics. Basketball became the national sport, and boxing produced numerous world champions over the years (Gems et al., 2017). The U.S. military's sport influence was so pervasive in the Philippines that some military leaders arrogantly contended, "Baseball had done more to 'civilize' Filipinos than anything else" (Seymore, 1990, pp. 324-325).

The U.S. Army was also instrumental in the exportation of American sport forms to Europe during their deployment in World War I. Pope

CASE STUDY

The NBA's Road to Globalization

The NBA is seemingly the most rapidly growing sport league in the United States and perhaps across the globe. The influx of international basketball players into the NBA did not occur until April 8, 1989, when the Fédération Internationale de Basketball (FIBA) modified the policy that forbade professional basketball players from participating in FIBA competitions and allowed those foreign professionals to play in the NBA without being disqualified from representing their countries in the Olympics. The NBA 2016-2017 season witnessed a record-breaking international presence marked by the participation of 113 foreign players from 41 countries and territories (NBA, 2016). The internationalization of the NBA has greatly enhanced the image of the league as a pioneer in terms of promoting diversity and the multicultural profile of the teams.

Internationalization is a slow process, and developing a fan base loyal to a sport culture that is not endemic can be difficult, if not impossible. In 1992 the NBA connected to non-American markets by forming the Dream Team, including Michael Jordan and Earvin "Magic" Johnson. Major efforts like these use cultural heritage, governmental relations, facility infrastructure, and human resources in local communities. In the past 25 years, this strategy has helped the league achieve phenomenal success. The NBA now broadcasts its games in 215 countries and territories, has established 13 international offices, and has actively engaged with 320 million fans across the globe (NBA, 2012). The NBA Global Games, also known as the preseason tours or exhibition games, are a series of games featuring NBA teams that are played outside the United States and Canada. Since its outset, the Global Games have been a powerful tool to reach out to the passionate and growing fan base overseas. Along with offering fans a unique immersive experience, the Global Games provide a great opportunity for teams and players to experience different cultures and bond with one another through community service, fan events, and social activities.

In addition to mounting an all-out effort to explore foreign markets, teams in the NBA have also been revolutionizing the way that sport is marketed and consumed by attracting a more diverse and engaged fan base in the international marketplace to increase viewership and broaden sponsorship appeal. Over 287 million people in China watched newly signed Yao Ming play his first game in the 2002-2003 season. Even after Yao Ming retired, the Rockets are considered China's NBA team (Blinebury, 2016). The benefits of maintaining a close tie with the Chinese fan base is demonstrated by the Rockets' six major partnerships with companies based in China, including Peak, Scisky, and ZTE, some of which have moved on to be major NBA sponsors (Feigen, 2016).

(1997) maintained that the military personnel deployed were more than soldiers. They were athletes as well. *Scientific American* noted this point: "Uncle Sam has created not only an army of soldiers . . . but an army of athletes" (Pope, 2010, p. 199). This sentiment was mirrored by Naismith (1941, p. 140): "The development of the game by military forces has been in some measure responsible for the spread of basketball into the foreign countries." The vision linking sport and the military was not necessarily a new strategy. Sport emerged as a part of the American spirit and traveled wherever the U.S. military was deployed. After WWI, all West Point cadets were required to engage in major sports and learn how to teach them. The aggressive dis-semination of American sport forms throughout Europe culminated in the Inter-Allied Games of 1919, in which 29 nations participated. According to Pope (2010, p. 200), "Never before had so much information about a sports event reached so many publications in so many countries." Newspapers around the world covered the Inter-Allied Games. The YMCA also facilitated the expansion of American sporting values by radioing the results of the World Series to military personnel stationed in war zones from 1917 through 1919. In addition, the military also procured large amounts of athletic equipment; prepared rulebooks and training manuals; secured specialists, venues, and prizes; and constructed contest brackets and schedules.

In essence, the military became international missionaries of American sporting life.

International Athletic Arms Race and Militarism

Throughout the early decades of the 20th century, sport became more prominent, political, and pervasive worldwide in spite of the Great Depression and a propagandized Berlin Olympic Games in 1936. Infamous for its anti-Semitic stance and racist ideology, the 1936 Olympic Games contributed to the expansion of sport through early television broadcasts and Leni Riefenstahl's film coverage. Her state-of-the art slow-motion and underwater photography in *Olympia* proved to be a major breakthrough for coaches and athletes seeking to improve athletic performance (Gems et al., 2017). Telecast of baseball and football in America in 1939 also helped spread those sport forms nationally and internationally. For example, Negro League baseball teams traveled to Japan, Hong Kong, Hawaii, and the Philippines in the 1920s and 1930s; during the 1940s, touring Black all-star teams played throughout Latin America and in winter baseball in the Mexican Leagues (Heaphy, 2003).

Sports and political ideology gained greater significance during the 1930s and 1940s in fascist regimes in Europe and Asia, notably in Italy, Germany, Spain, and Japan. Even during the buildup and onset of World War II, sports were expanding globally. American professional baseball clubs were playing teams north and south of its borders, as were Canadian hockey teams. Both leagues (MLB and NHL) received government approval to continue playing during the war years to maintain public morale. Although the Olympic Games were canceled in 1940 and 1944, they resumed in the country that contributed most to its revitalization: Great Britain. Politics were a salient factor in determining which nations participated, and this factor would be a cornerstone of future Olympic Games.

The postwar years ushered in a more modern world as major advancements in technology occurred (e.g., nuclear armament). Growing political tensions, international territorial disputes, and the space race brought about a Cold War between former WWII allies: the United States and the Soviet Union. This rivalry ultimately led to an unprecedented military buildup in both countries and an ensuing athletics arms race (Gems et al., 2017). The United States, the Soviet Union, and allies of both countries employed sport, somewhat as Germany had done several decades earlier, to promote their sociopolitical agenda. Globalization occurred not only in sport forms and their structural aspects but also with athletes, equipment, apparel, coaching techniques, and performance enhancers.

Globalization of Sport in the Late 20th Century

Since the late 1980s the world economy as a whole has become significantly more international; exports and imports have grown over one and a half times faster than GDP (Kobrin, 2015). Besides the escalation and dissemination of globalization in areas such as transportation, communication, technology, and international migration of labor and residents, the world economy is becoming more closely integrated at a faster pace than ever before. Economic globalization and integration are influenced by such components as international trade of goods and services, capital and financial investment, multinational corporations, and labor migration. Internationalization of sport has been significantly strengthened in the last decades as manifested in the prosperity of the sporting goods industry and the sport labor market, the popularity of professional sport teams and leagues, and the increasing prominence of international sporting events. Simultaneously, ethical concerns and controversial issues associated with this growing trend have arisen (Zhang, Pitts, & Kim, 2017).

Sport is widely considered a universal language that transcends national boundaries. At its best, sport brings people together, teaching teamwork and tolerance regardless of participants' origin, background, religious beliefs, or economic status (Dyreson, 2003). The age of mass communication and interplanetary technology since the 1960s has contributed immeasurably to the ever-expanding sport industry. The rapid advancement of new information, communication, and transportation technology, which eliminates the formidable obstacles for sport exchange created by time, space, language, and ideology, and an interconnected global market that enables free mobility of capital, knowledge, labor, and culture, have greatly enhanced the **sport business** opportunities at the individual, organizational, and national levels (Andreff & Szymanski, 2006; Zhang et al., 2017).

Internationalization is a nonnegligible phenomenon in recent decades as sport-related businesses have mushroomed worldwide with the involvement of governments, ventures, companies, and organizations. Many governments look for opportunities to host international sport events, hoping to boost economic development and secure up-to-date facilities and infrastructure. For instance, the host country of the 2018 Winter Olympic Games, South Korea, was one of the bidding countries for the 2010 and 2014 Winter Olympics. After South Korea was selected as the host country, extra highways and high-speed trains to Pyeongchang, the host city, were constructed and some sport facilities such as a bobsleigh track were built for the first time in the nation's history. Sporting goods enterprises operate affiliate companies internationally, aiming to secure competitive advantages in such areas as low operating and labor cost. One of the most famous sporting goods companies, Adidas, is known to operate 145 subsidiaries throughout the globe, including the continents of Europe, Asia, and North and South Americas as of 2015 (Adidas Group, 2016). International sport organizations such as FIFA and IOC have tremendous influence on some of the sport policies that sport organizations in individual countries must follow. For instance, FIFA banned countries such as Indonesia, Kuwait, and Benin from participating in international soccer matches because they broke the FIFA rule that a government cannot interfere with its football association (BBC, 2016).

Over the last few decades, three salient themes appear to have emerged in the process of internationalization:

1. Geographical shifting of the production and consumption of sport goods and services
2. Promotion of diversity and inclusiveness, as well as compliance with international production and consumption standards, to remain competitive in the global marketplace
3. Rapidly growing influence of the emerging economic powers, notably the BRICS countries (Brazil, Russia, India, China, and South Africa), which have extensively shaped the contours of the global economy, challenged the existing

Learning Activity

Students form groups. As a group, identify one sport and discuss the historical evolution of the sport. Use index cards or computer graphing to build key time blocks to illustrate how the sport evolved from an indigenous, local, or regional game to a global competition. Identify the major forces that contributed to the sport's globalization.

order, and raised both challenges and opportunities (Armijo, 2007; Jain, 2006)

The internationalization of sport has also increased the exposure and extended the outreach of professional sport teams whose marketing strategies can consider both the international and home markets. The rising spending power of middle-class households in the developing economies (along with their large populations) has enticed major professional sport franchises to those countries. Examples of professional teams' and leagues' marketing efforts to broaden the base of fans and supporters internationally include globally renowned soccer clubs such as FC Barcelona and Manchester United hosting preseason tours abroad and providing youth and club training that focused on the Asian continent, MLB scheduling its season-opening games abroad, and the NBA playing regular-season games in some of the emerging economies (Zhang et al., 2017).

Globalization of the Sporting Goods Industry

With today's globalized economy, geographical and cultural boundaries are continuously transcended. Many nations and regions have strategically developed and adopted a comprehensive plan to use sport events and sport participation as catalytic agents to transform communities, revitalize urban environments, improve public infrastructure, promote project destination images for tourism and business, enrich residential quality of life, nurture an active lifestyle, enhance societal harmony and solidarity, and promote interorganizational collaborations and work efficiency (Zhang, Huang, & Wang, 2017).

Internationalization of sports has also played a key role in enhancing the global awareness of a city or country, and building a harmonious sense of community within the region (García, 2004). Sport tourism, for example, has redefined the extrinsic value of sport, suggesting that hosting international sport events or tournaments could stimulate economic growth, enhance destination image and branding, generate positive publicity, and showcase the development of local society (e.g., Hallmann, Kaplanidou, & Breuer, 2010; Huang, Mao, Wang, & Zhang, 2015; Richard & Jones, 2008). Mega sport events such as the World Cup and the Olympic Games command considerable international attention and accommodate the growing interest in sport tourism (Green & Chalip, 1998). Similarly, Preuss and Alfs (2011) analyzed how China used the 2008 Olympics and worldwide media coverage to convey messages related to promoting better business relations, attracting more foreign investment and potential future tourists, and accumulating symbolic capital. To some extent, hosting mega sport events can help the host send tailored information to focal external audiences and improve the image and the perception of certain aspects of the host city or nation.

Because sport contests and athletes are promoted and covered extensively through global media lenses, what athletes wear, endorse, and use as equipment are of paramount concern. All these items have become internationalized commodities in the landscape of sport. The global sporting goods industry, which consists of sporting equipment, apparel, and athletic footwear, is one of the most conspicuous facets of the internationalization of sport because it is a highly structured, differentiated, and labor-sensitive segment. Because people around the world enjoy playing, following, and participating in sport, sport leagues and some sport-related organizations are among the top 150 global licensors. Examples of these licensors include the PGA Tour, Major League Baseball (MLB), National Basketball Association (NBA), English Premier League (EPL), German Football Association (DFB), The Enthusiast Network (sport media platform), and Kawasaki (motorsports bikes and goods) (License Global, 2017). Yet in some parts of the world where trademark protection and royalty payments are not effectively regulated and monitored by the law, piracy and trademark infringements are prevalent, causing serious reputational and financial damage to brands and licensors (Baker, Liu, Brison, & Pifer, 2017). Issues surrounding trademarks, copyrights, and licensing rights lead to interesting research streams with empirical significance for sporting goods companies and law firms. Moreover, the recent clashes between large sport organizations and student-athletes in terms of the use of personal image and likeness illustrate the controversies and complexities behind the sizable financial gains generated by the sport-related companies, raising questions about whether student-athletes are appropriately compensated for their contribution to the sport enterprise as sport revenues and coaches' salaries have soared in the past decades.

Few people foresaw the exponential growth of the sporting goods industry. In the early 1980s, only brand names like Wilson, Spaulding, Rawlings, and Titleist enjoyed public recognition (Lipsey, 2006). By 2017 the sporting goods industry was ranked as one of the top revenue producers; over 20 companies had sales surpassing US$1 billion (Lipsey, 2006). As the scale and scope of sporting goods businesses have grown exponentially, the industry has become more sophisticated, extending into goods and services above and beyond the traditional jersey, T-shirt, and collectible items. The early sport equipment and apparel manufacturers like Adidas, Spaulding, Penn, Everlast, Wilson, Hillerich & Bradsby, and others, whose products were sold around the globe before the mid-20th century, gave rise to a sport marketplace that is more competitive and pervasive than ever. The global sporting goods industry has grown steadily over the past decades. European and North American brands, including Adidas, Nike, Puma, Reebok, and Under Armour, to name a few, dominate the industry. Although some Asian brands such as Mizuno and Li-Ning, are growing in popularity, they are comparatively focused on domestic or regional markets. The international nature of modern sport brought about a volatile mix of opportunities and challenges to the extremely competitive sporting goods industry and its relevant businesses (Nadvi, Lund-Thomsen, Xue, & Khara, 2011). On one hand, the booming sponsorship market provides unprecedented venues for major sporting goods brands to promote and associate their products with professional sport clubs, leading sport tournaments and events, and superstar players through various types of sponsorship deals. On the other hand, the

Learning Activity

Pick any sporting goods company. Conduct a comprehensive review of literature through print and online resources. Outline the trajectory of the migration of this company in terms of its manufacturers. Present your findings to the class.

popularity of the brands and subsequent increased demand for their products also give rise to ethical and legal concerns pertaining to the supply chain. Poor working conditions, unfair labor standards, and questionable regulatory practices have caused international outcry and protests in the past (Van Tulder & Kolk, 2001).

International Migration and Sport

Without a doubt, technological advances in broadcasting and communication have helped transcend national and regional boundaries and made it easy to deliver sport products and services, yet it is today's convenience of on-site presence of human resources that has ultimately pushed the sport industry to new heights. Essentially, human knowledge, skills, capabilities, and talents are key driving forces for continued internationalization of sport. On the positive side, international migration, a global phenomenon that is increasing in scope and impact, profoundly facilitates sport inclusion, interaction, and integration. It also tends to remove the borders and isolation within sports played worldwide. For example, Laotian immigrants enjoyed playing sepak takraw and introduced the sport in Canada in the 1970s. The sport gained popularity as a school activity, and the increased interest in the sport from the public led to the establishment of the Sepak Takraw Association of Canada (STAC) in 1998 (STAC, 2017). In addition, many Latino and Hispanic immigrants from Latin America enjoy playing soccer as a leisure activity in the United States. Targeting these populations around the metro Atlanta area, Atlanta United Football Club joined Major League Soccer (MLS) and began playing in 2017 as a member of the Eastern Conference (Henry, 2015). The emergence and growing popularity of diverse sport forms offer additional opportunities for sport and nonsport organizations and businesses domestically and internationally to penetrate new markets and demographic segments. In the meantime, migration has also resulted in slave-like conditions, drained talent from their homes to richer countries, and produced inequality. The negative perspectives of talent migration are included in further discussions in this chapter.

Sport Labor Movement

Historically, noticeable transcontinental patterns in the recruitment and subsequent retention of sport talents were initially identified in the late 1980s and early 1990s when a sport labor movement occurred between North America and Europe in professional football, basketball, and ice hockey (Butler & Dzikus, 2015; Maguire, 1996, 2008). For instance, Maguire (1996) found that Canadian migrants who had experience with Canadian ice hockey leagues contributed significantly to the development of British ice hockey leagues in the 1990s, which had a low standard in play and marginal status as a sport. Ever since, the global movement of athletes has become a prominent feature of the internationalization of sport in a variety of contexts around the globe. Notable examples are Ichiro Suzuki, a Japanese professional baseball outfielder who played for the Seattle Mariners, New York Yankees, and Miami Marlins of MLB; Kristaps Porzingis, a Latvian professional basketball player for the New York Knicks of the NBA; Diana Lorena Taurasi, an American professional basketball player for the Phoenix Mercury of the Women's National Basketball Association and UMMC Ekaterinburg of Russia; and Lionel Andrés "Leo" Messi, an Argentine professional footballer who plays for Spanish club Barcelona (Zhang et al., 2017). By 2017 over 600 former or current NHL players from many countries were employed in 36 different hockey leagues located in Asia and Europe (Fisher, 2017).

Impact on the Competitive Landscape

Athletes not only go abroad to play for sport teams and leagues but also may become citizens of a foreign country to compete in international sporting events. For example, Korean-born short-track speed skater Hyun-soo Ahn, also known as Viktor Ahn, became a Russian citizen in 2011 after he failed to make the Korean national team for the 2010 Winter Olympics. He also had conflicts with the Korean Skate Union. As a member of the Russian national team, he won three gold medals during the 2014 Winter Olympics. A growing number of countries grant citizenship to talented athletes in an effort to build their competitiveness internationally. Therefore, migration has significantly influenced the landscape of the sport industry (Schwartz, Jamieson, & Pitts, 2015). Talented international athletes and coaches provide teams with better performances, higher quality of games, and hefty financial returns. In this respect, professional sport teams in both developed and emerging economies naturally search for the best athletes around the globe within the budget allowance.

Some football clubs within the EPL have experienced the effect of talented international players and coaches on team performance and beyond. After Sheikh Mansour bin Zayed al-Nahyan took over Manchester City Football Club in 2008, the club signed high-profile players and coaches with the capital investment from the new owner. Since then, Manchester City enhanced its competitiveness and won the EPL championship during the 2011-2012 season after 44 years of waiting and again during the 2013-2014 and 2017-2018 seasons. The club was financially successful as well. Manchester City announced a record high profit of £20.5 million (about US$30 million) in the 2015-2016 season, with its fourth place finish in the EPL and qualification into the semifinals of the Champions League for the first time in its history (Conn, 2016). The Chelsea Football Club followed a similar path as Manchester City within the EPL. As a consequence, the competitive landscape within the EPL changed greatly. Newly rising teams placed within the top four and pushed traditionally well-performing teams like Liverpool Football Club out of the top four for an extended period. Likewise, Chinese professional soccer clubs spent huge amounts of money and made headlines with astonishing transfer fees and weekly salaries. World-class players who have moved to the Chinese Super League (CSL) include Jackson Martínez (Atlético Madrid to Guangzhou Evergrande for £32 million [about US$43 million]), Ramires Santos do Nascimento (Chelsea to Jiangsu Suning for £20 million [about US$27 million]), Oscar dos Santos Emboaba Júnior (Chelsea to

Shanghai SIPG for £52 million [about US$70 million]), and Carlos Tevez (Boca Juniors to Shanghai Shenhua for £71 million [about US$96 million]) (O'Rourke, 2016; Price, 2017; Telegraph, 2016). In fact, the signing of some of the best international players brought enough experience and strength to the top Chinese clubs that they could compete against their counterparts from other Asian countries in the AFC Champions League; eventually some Chinese clubs were able to win championships (Duerden, 2015).

Athletes as Commodities

With respect to athletes, significant numbers of them move between cities, countries, and continents for better career opportunities. Contemporary sport settings are as diverse and distinct as professional soccer in Europe and South America, collegiate sport, professional baseball, and basketball in North America, as well as professional soccer and basketball in Asia where more opportunities for international athletes are available. The liquidity of sport labor has been one of the most symbolic characteristics of the internationalization of sport as the flows of global sport labor have become increasingly multidirectional. According to research published by the International Center for Sports Studies (CIES), an independent study center based in Switzerland, in 2013 in the major soccer leagues in Europe, ranging from the "big five" leagues of the EPL, Germany's Bundesliga, Spain's La Liga, Italy's Serie A, France's Ligue 1, to other top divisions from Austria to Ukraine, the number of nonresident alien players reached record levels; 36.1 percent of all players were internationals in the leagues in which they played (Harris, 2013). In 2017, as suggested by the follow-up study, at least one national representative from each of the 174 countries surveyed in the research was playing overseas (Poli, Ravenel, & Besson, 2017). Brazil is the top exporter of soccer talent in the world (1,202), 65 percent of whom play in UEFA leagues. France (781) and Argentina (753) secure second and third place in terms of the number of players representing clubs abroad, followed by Serbia (460), England (451), and Spain (362) (Poli et al., 2017). Table 2.1 lists the country of origin of NBA international players during the 2016-2017 season, which depicts a record of 113 international players from 41 countries or territories. These numbers indicate that the globalization

Table 2.1 Country of Origin of 2016-2017 NBA International Players

Country of player origin	Number of players
Argentina	4
Australia	8
Austria	1
Bahamas	1
Bosnia and Herzegovina	3
Brazil	9
Cameroon	3
Canada	11
Cape Verde	1
Congo	1
Croatia	5
Czech Republic	1
Democratic Republic of the Congo	2
Dominican Republic	1
France	10
Georgia	1
Germany	3
Greece	2
Haiti	1
Israel	1
Italy	2
Latvia	2
Lithuania	3
Mali	1
Montenegro	3
New Zealand	1
Nigeria	1
Poland	1
Puerto Rico	1
Russia	1
Senegal	2
Serbia	3
Slovenia	3
South Sudan	2
Spain	8
Sweden	1
Switzerland	2
Tunisia	1
Turkey	3
Ukraine	2
Venezuela	1
41 countries	**113 players**

Data from NBA (2016).

in sport has contributed to the active cross-border and cross-continent movement of sport labor in the most recent decade, which was not feasible or even imaginable a few decades ago when the industry was less integrated.

Nonetheless, the domination of Western nations in the capitalist system also renders the international sport migration detrimental in a sense that European clubs appropriate soccer talents from Africa. Obviously, as opposed to their African counterparts, European clubs are more powerful financially and capable of manipulating the terms and contracts on which an African soccer player is traded. Because the majority of talent-exporting countries in Africa still struggle against poverty, most clubs there are trade dependent, resulting in the deskilling and underdevelopment of African soccer. In other words, a vicious circle is formed on terms and conditions established by European interests (Darby, Akindes, & Kirwin, 2007). Arguably, European professional soccer benefits from the unequal trades; they achieve their development and prosperity at the expense of those on the periphery of the global economy.

Labor movement in North American sport displays a similar pattern. For instance, MLB has witnessed a substantial rise in international players over the past two decades. Although only about 10 percent of MLB players were born outside the United States in 1985 (Tainsky & Winfree, 2010), over 25 percent of MLB players are now foreign born. During the 2016 MLB season, international players from 18 countries and territories outside the United States accounted for 27.5 percent of the entire player pool. The Dominican Republic led the way with 82 players. Venezuela ranked second with 63. Cuba was third with 23. The 15 other countries or territories that sent players to the MLB teams were Puerto Rico (17), Mexico (12), Japan (8), South Korea (8), Canada (6), Panama (4), Colombia and Curaçao (3 each), Brazil and Taiwan (2 each), and Aruba, Australia, the Netherlands, Nicaragua, and the U.S. Virgin Islands (1 each) (Thornburg, 2016).

A similar pattern can be observed in North American collegiate sport. In the 1999-2000 academic year, 5,858 student-athletes participated and competed in the NCAA Division I, Division II, and Division III, as nonresident aliens (NCAA, 2000). This number jumped to 18,366 during the 2015-2016 academic year (table 2.2) as an increasing number of international athletes chose to sign with the NCAA (NCAA, 2016). A diverse and inclusive environment attracts an influx of talented international athletes who have become invaluable assets for programs in their quest for championships. Likewise, the NCAA also provides competitive scholarships, top-level educational institutions, state-of-the-art facilities, professional coaches, and fierce competition for international student-athletes to improve both their quality of play and their lives (Love & Kim, 2011). Besides bringing international sport talent to the United States, the NCAA has also been active in reaching out to international audiences beyond the United States. Through the partnership between the Pacific-12 Conference (Pac-12) and Alibaba Group Holding Limited, the world's largest online and mobile commerce company, at least one regular-season collegiate men's basketball game will be played annually in Shanghai and streamed online across the country (Soper, 2015). Besides playing games in China, the Pac-12 Men's Basketball All-Stars paid a visit to Australia and played against the Australian Olympic team (Pac12, 2016a). With a growing global impact, the exhibition game has turned into an important marquee event of Pac-12 Global, "an initiative that promotes goodwill and showcases the Conference and its member institutions in China and around the world through student-athlete exchanges and sport" (Pac12, 2016b).

In an effort to promote sport participation, organize sport competitions, enhance cultural and academic exchanges among college students in the world, and ultimately elevate harmony and cooperation among future leaders of the world, the Fédération Internationale du Sport Universitaire (FISU) (International University Sports Federation) was established in 1949. FISU's main responsi-

Learning Activity

As a class, discuss four recent examples of international sport labor movements that have been in the news. Describe how each of the examples affects the stakeholders involved.

Table 2.2   2015-2016 NCAA Student-Athletes Considered Nonresident Alien

Sport	Nonresident Alien	
	Men	Women
Baseball	269	0
Basketball	735	465
Beach volleyball	0	69
Bowling	0	9
Cross country	422	423
Equestrian	0	14
Fencing	40	39
Field hockey	0	249
Football	273	0
Golf	763	608
Gymnastics	2	39
Ice hockey	642	344
Lacrosse	250	99
Rifle	3	7
Rowing	131	265
Rugby	5	13
Sailing	6	0
Skiing	56	57
Soccer	2,641	923
Softball	0	130
Squash	84	54
Swimming	552	566
Synchronized swimming	0	3
Tennis	1,687	1,589
Track, indoor	735	772
Track, outdoor	902	808
Triathlon	0	1
Volleyball	66	398
Water polo	62	66
Wrestling	30	0
Total	**10,356**	**8,010**

Data from NCAA (2016).

bility is the supervision of both of the Summer and Winter Universiades (i.e., World University Games), as well as the World University Championships. The General Assembly representing its 170 national university sports federations is FISU's main governing body. FISU is funded through subscription, organizing and entry fees, television incomes, and marketing activities. The Universiade is the second largest participant sport event in the world, smaller only than the Olympic Games. As many as 12,000 athletes and delegation members from 170 countries compete for more than 300 sets of medals. Each Universiade can attract over 100,000 tourists and spectators from all over the world to the hosting city (International University Sports Federation, 2017). Influenced by FISU's vision and ideals, increasingly greater numbers of university students seek athletic participation and competition opportunities in cross-border or overseas countries. International higher education has developed rapidly in the past two decades. Besides benefiting from the surge of globalization, the rapid increase of international higher education has been facilitated and governed by the General Agreement on Trade in Service (GATS) among the World Trade Organization (WTO) members. According to the Organization for Economic Co-Operation and Development (OECD), in 2003 more than 2.1 million international students were in the OECD areas and in other nations that provided data. As noted in the OECD's statistics, about 4.0 million students studied outside their home countries in 2015 (OECD, 2017). This number has doubled since 2000 at an average annual rate of about 7.0 percent. It has been suggested that 7.0 million students will be studying abroad by 2025 (Baker et al., 2016). International movement of student-athletes is consistent with this trend. For instance, over 17,000 international student-athletes were studying and competing at NCAA member institutions in the United States during the 2016-2017 academic year (NCAA, 2017). These international athletes usually represent a high level of competition that has raised the level of play and significantly shaped the contour of collegiate sport. As a result, colleges and universities are increasingly expanding their recruiting efforts beyond their national boundaries. Given the

upward trend in the number of international student-athletes participating in a variety of men's and women's sports at all divisional levels, international student-athletes have become a common presence in intercollegiate athletics (Ridinger & Pastore, 2000). Meanwhile, according to the Association of International Educators (NAFSA), slightly over 1.5 percent of all U.S. students studied abroad for credit during the 2014-2015 academic year (NAFSA, 2017). The small percentage represents a lack of international experience for U.S. college students. Even so, an increasing number of young athletes in the United States are seeking opportunities to play sports internationally. This trend has created a new niche market for sport organizations such as Sport Changes Life, TeamGLEAS, and Global Players, which provide programs, services, and scholarships that enable student-athletes to train, compete outside the United States, and develop communication and leadership skills in a foreign environment (Lipshez, 2017; Sport Changes Life, 2017; Thompson, 2013). The increasing globalization of sport and sport businesses has brought about a need for a new emphasis within the sport business management education community and has set new demands for professional preparations (Zhang, Chen, & Kim, 2014).

Benefits of International Athletes in Sport Teams and Leagues

The incessant flow of talented players has not only shaped international cultural exchange but also expedited global programming of media coverage of sport and a gradual narrowing of gaps in athlete income levels (Maguire, 1996). Early research studies on team nationality composition have demonstrated that the country of origin is an important factor for sport consumers in evaluating the quality of products (Han, 1989; Hoang & Rascher, 1999). Further empirical inquiries into the influence of the presence of international players reveal that sport leagues and teams benefit from increased attendance, higher TV ratings, and consequently elevated revenue by having more foreign players (Oates & Polumbaum, 2004; Pedace, 2008;

Learning Activity:

Conduct a literature review on the effect of international athletes on team performance and revenue generation. Using the methods outlined by Tainsky and Winfree (2010), develop regression equations and calculate stadium, broadcasting, licensed product, or social media revenues generated by adding an international player to a team's roster.

Tainsky & Winfree, 2010). A study by Tainsky and Winfree (2010) revealed that every additional international player added to an MLB roster could increase stadium revenue by US$595,632 annually. Such internationalization of sport labor is an important component of creating more inclusive and integrated sport marketing efforts, providing incentives for sport organizations to become more international by signing foreign athletes or scheduling more games outside the home country.

Summary

With the constant progression and interdependence of people and communities around the globe, the discussions on internationalization have been not only a subject at the economic foreground but also a hot topic in the world of sport. The universal appeal of sport contributes to the lucrativeness of the sport industry and the enormous business opportunities for all parties involved. Internationalization and commercialization have drastically changed the landscape of modern sports, converting them from mere recreational or leisure activities that showcase physical athleticism and dexterity into a highly remunerative global enterprise. Moreover, the sport industry is becoming increasingly professionalized.

It has grown to be an important economic sector on a global scale, and its products and services are significant contributors to employment generation, wealth creation, and value reorientation.

Today, the world of sport has become a dynamic landscape in which the trend of internationalization is an unstoppable force. This chapter sheds light on a plethora of topics surrounding the growth of the sport industry in an increasingly interconnected world. The authors have argued that in today's society, sport serves as an essential source of social and cultural exchange, political influence and might, as well as economic development. With this in mind, the challenge for policy makers, practitioners, and scholars is to recognize, identify, and adapt to the ever-changing international sport environment. The content of this chapter is intended to provide cases that occurred not only in North America, Europe, and Oceania but also in the often-overlooked developing economies. Essentially, the ability of people around the world to participate in and watch sport is fundamentally swayed by the socioeconomic conditions and political structures within their respective countries. In the past, most international marketing and academic efforts have focused on the sport industry in developed countries. But economic progress and the rise of developing countries have demonstrated the necessity to commit more attention, resources, and scholarship to recreational, amateur, and professional sport development in this emerging marketplace. The authors have made a concerted effort to present an etiological perspective of sport internationalization, as well as an overview of challenges and opportunities in contemporary sport management in a somewhat borderless international sport marketplace. We advocate a more systematic approach to advance the sport industry worldwide, calling for future endeavors to promote the exchange of ideas, to encourage sharing of best practices, and to support further cutting-edge research in global sport management studies.

? Review Questions

1. What are the implications of the NBA's marketing strategies for other major sport organizations if they look for opportunities in the global market?

2. What have been key stages in the historical evolution of modern sport from indigenous, local, or regional games to global competitions?

3. What major forces and critical junctures have contributed to the intensification of sport globalization?

4. What are the impacts of international migration and athlete movements on the globalization of sport?

5. Using the NBA as an example, discuss how a professional sport league can effectively penetrate the international market.

Part II

Field of Play in International Sport

China versus Thailand during the 2018 Asian Football Confederation (AFC) Women's Asian Cup that took place in Amman, Jordan. China defeated Thailand 3-1 for third place. Japan won the gold after defeating Australia 1-0. The top five teams qualified for the 2019 FIFA World Cup. The AFC Women's Asian Cup is a biannual championship for national teams' members of the AFC. The event has been in existence since 1975, with China winning the highest number of titles.

Francois Nel/Getty Images

Sport in North America

Michael Odio, PhD
University of Cincinnati

Shannon Kerwin, PhD
Brock University

Chapter Objectives

After studying this chapter, you will be able to do the following:

- From a historical perspective, discuss the important trends in the evolution of sport leagues structure over the past one and one-half century.
- Recognize the economic and cultural importance of sport in North America.
- Identify differences as well as similarities between sport organizational structures in the United States and Canada versus those in other countries.
- Describe the role the government has in delivering and influencing sport in Canada compared with the United States.
- Evaluate the role of commercial or professional sport within the American and Canadian sport delivery systems.
- Explain differences and similarities among sport leagues within the United States and Canada.
- Discuss the major differences in the approaches to intercollegiate athletics in the United States and Canada.

Key Terms

Sport Canada	Amateur Sports Act (United States)
Canadian Sport Policy	Fitness and Amateur Sport Act (Canada)
NCAA	
U Sports	YMCA
Title IX	United States Olympic Committee

Key Events

NFL Super Bowl. One of the most viewed sporting events in the United States, as well as Canada. The 2018 Super Bowl (LII) was held in Minneapolis, Minnesota, on February 4, 2018. Despite the historical popularity of this event, only 104 million people watched the 2018 Super Bowl, the smallest television audience since 2009 (CBS News, 2018).

Major League Baseball World Series. Contested since 1903, this annual fall event consists of a best-of-seven series of games in which the winner takes home the title of World Champion of baseball.

Pan American and Parapan American Games 2015. Forty-one member nations participate in this event, held every four years in the year before the Summer Olympic and Paralympic Games. The event is the world's third largest multisport games (Toronto2015, 2015).

U.S. Open Women's Tennis Championship. Since 1987 the U.S. Open has been the fourth and final major tennis event (internationally) of the Grand Slam each calendar year. In 2017 the women's championship gained record-breaking television ratings, increasing by 36 percent (Haring, 2017).

Daytona 500. The pinnacle of auto-racing championships in the United States, for six decades this auto-racing event has presented top-notch races to sold-out crowds. The Daytona International Speedway seats 101,000 people and is home to several national race car events.

Canadian Women's Open (Golf). This golf championship is an official event of the Ladies Professional Golf Association Tour and is sponsored by Canadian Pacific Railway. The Women's Open professional golf championship is managed by Golf Canada and is hosted across Canada annually.

Key People

Christine Sinclair, captain of the Canadian national soccer team, scored the second-most goals in international competition

LeBron James, NBA player and activist

Scott Blackbum, CEO of the United States Olympic Committee

Kirsty Duncan, minister of Sport and Persons With Disabilities, oversees Sport Canada

Graham Brown, CEO of U Sports, Canada

Carlos Cordeiro, president of the United States Soccer Federation

Serena Williams, tennis player, 23 Grand Slam singles titles

Kevin Plank, CEO of Under Armour

The main purpose of this chapter is to contribute to the general body of knowledge concerning how sport is organized in North America compared with other parts of the world. The distinctive sport organizational characteristics of the United States and Canada are discussed in the context of their historical development through the evolutionary process and up to current practices. This chapter also seeks to facilitate an enhanced understanding of the ways in which environmental influences in terms of management proficiency, government, public, legal, economics, culture, and competition have influenced North America's sport structural development. This topic is relevant to today's sport managers who are striving to establish structural frameworks that meet the needs of their constituents and achieve the basic purpose and goals of their organizations.

The United States and Canada are major players in international sport and have unique and complex domestic sport systems. At the elite levels, both countries are among the top of the medal count for every Olympic and Paralympic Games, and they boast some of the most popular sport leagues that attract top talent from around the world. Sport is also a major part of the cultural identity for both countries, stemming from modern sports invented in the region, indigenous games of the region's native populations, and the growth of sports brought by immigrants. This chapter explores some of the historical context for the growth of sport in the United States and

Canada as well as the current landscape, including the role of government, the way in which sport is legislated, professional sport leagues, college sport, and more.

Geographical Description and Demographics

The United States and Canada are part of the North American continent. Canada and the United States comprise a wide range of geographic regions and climates, which includes the humid subtropical climate of Florida, the frigid winters of Winnipeg, large mountain ranges along the western side of both countries, and the Great Plains, which stretch from the arctic region of Canada to the southern United States. The countries have a combined coastline of over 215,000 miles (350,000 km).

Sport in the United States and Canada is usually closely associated thanks to the countries' many cultural similarities, common language, and their long border, the longest international border in the world. Although many sports are popular across both countries, the diverse geographic and demographic characteristics of each country have led to many local differences. The two countries differ greatly in terms of population; the population of the United States is well over 300 million, almost 10 times larger than Canada's population of 36 million. Both countries are highly urbanized; about 80 percent of the population lives in cities. Both have large immigrant populations; about 13 percent of the U.S. population and 22 percent of the Canadian population are foreign born.

Background and Role of Sport

Exploring the history of North American sport greatly helps in understanding how a handful of unique sports developed and were later exported to the rest of the world. We begin with a brief explanation of how certain sports began and evolved. We then identify significant sport milestones that brought major changes, and finally we provide some insight into the cultural and social significance of sport in North America.

United States

The most prominent sports in the United States are baseball, basketball, and American football. All these sports were developed in the latter half of the 19th century, beginning as amateur pursuits that became professional over time and spread in different ways. Baseball, the oldest of the major U.S.-born sports, likely evolved from a combination of European ball and bat games such as cricket and rounders (Springfield College, 2015). Originally popular in the New York region, the sport spread across the country through its popularity among soldiers in the Civil War who returned home, continued playing, and eventually formed leagues (Schaefer-Jacobs, 2012). American football followed a similar evolution from rugby and association football around the same time, but it was spread through college campuses rather than independently owned teams (PFRA Research, n.d.). Unlike baseball and American football, basketball is not a direct descendant from another sport. Instead, it was invented by Dr. James Naismith as a suitable indoor physical activity for a physical education class at the Young Men's Christian Association (Springfield College, 2015). The sport spread through other **YMCAs** in the northeastern United States and southern Canada before being picked up by other organizations and eventually forming into professional teams and leagues. The forming of multiple leagues in baseball, the involvement of college administration in football, and the grassroots origins of basketball all influence how these sports were governed, then and now.

Although sport in the United States in its early history was more of a pastime and diversion for soldiers, college students, and others, sport quickly became an important social, cultural, and political component of the nation. For example, Jackie Robinson's breaking the color barrier in professional baseball mirrored the country's struggle with race relations throughout the 20th century (Hill, 2007). Likewise, the intense rivalry between the United States and the Soviet Union in the Olympics embodied the ongoing Cold War between the two world superpowers (Guttmann, 1988). Today, the role of sport in American society continues because professional athletes are seen as important public, social, and political voices (Vasilogambros, 2016).

Canada

Sport has a long and rich tradition in Canada. Many of the most popular sports in North America were first played in Canada and by Canadians. The games of the native peoples, such as lacrosse, had been played long before Canada was established as a nation, and they continue to be played and celebrated in communities across the country.

Many sport clubs were established in the second half of the 19th century, and Montréal served as the hotbed for organized sport in Canada. Although early Canadian sport had been mostly an experience for the upper classes, the growing industrialization and urbanization of Canada led to increased free time for the working classes (Metcalfe, 1987). Sport served as a popular diversion for many men, and eventually for women as well. The YMCA played an important part in the dissemination of new games and in the provision of the space and facilities needed for many of the most popular sports (Johnson, 1979).

Up until the mid-20th century, sport had been mostly a recreational activity pursued by interested participants, wealthy benefactors, and, at the higher levels of competition, by those able to afford the costs associated with many sporting pursuits. In 1961 the federal government of Canada passed Bill C-131, the **Fitness and Amateur Sport Act**. This formal piece of legislation identified sport as being a legitimate concern of the federal government. This legislation and the programs and policies that followed rapidly transformed the Canadian sport

CASE STUDY

Carla Qualtrough

Carla Qualtrough is a successful lawyer, dedicated volunteer, and Paralympic swimmer. Carla has been visually impaired since birth. Through her position within the Canadian ministry, Carla is dedicated to diminishing inequality and championing diversity initiatives across Canada. Qualtrough has degrees in political science from the University of Ottawa and law from the University of Victoria. Carla practiced human rights law in Delta, British Columbia, Canada, for several years, and through her work with the Canadian Human Rights Commission, she has been named one of Canada's Most Influential Women in Sport six times. She received a Queen Elizabeth II Diamond Jubilee Medal in 2012.

Through her commitment to human rights issues, Carla chaired the Minister's Council on Employment and Accessibility in British Columbia and was an adjudicator with the Workers' Compensation Appeals Tribunal. Passionate about the power of sport and physical activity to change lives, Carla has volunteered locally, nationally, and internationally, including with the International Paralympic Committee and for the Toronto 2015 Pan and Parapan American Games. She has been president of the Canadian Paralympic Committee and chair of the Sport Dispute Resolution Centre of Canada. Carla was on the Board of the Canadian Centre for Ethics in Sport, and was vice-chair of the Delta (British Columbia) Gymnastics Society. As an athlete, Carla won three Paralympic and four World Championship medals. On November 4, 2015, Qualtrough was named the minister of Sport and Persons With Disability in the 29th Canadian Ministry.

system into a state-financed and state-controlled organism (Macintosh, Bedecki, & Franks, 1987).

Governance of Sport

The governance of sport in North America varies between Canada and the United States. Specifically, unlike in most other large and developed countries, the United States' government plays a small role in the management and direction of the nation's sport system (Sparvero, Chalip, & Green, 2012). This more free-market approach has allowed a diverse mix of public- and private-sector organizations operating at different levels across a variety of sports to emerge as major components of the sport system. Within the Canadian sport context (Thibault, 2017), the free-market system is far less prominent than in the United States counterpart. Within Canada, professional sport is governed in the free-market system, but amateur sport (the predominant form of sport delivery in the country) is governed by **Sport Canada**, a branch of the national government system housed within the Department of Canadian Heritage.

Learning Activity

Compare and contrast the governance of sport in the United States and Canada. What elements of the free-market system are similar in both countries and what elements are unique?

Finally, community sport is the most diverse level, consisting of recreational leagues and other forms of participation for people of all ages. Because of the continually rising obesity rates, one of the most concerning issues has become youth sport participation. Although participation rates are rising, the cost of playing sports has limited opportunities for many (Rosenwald, 2016). In all, the governance of the sport delivery system in North America is complex and decentralized, consisting of a diverse set of organizations. Although many great athletes are produced by the system, it has many weaknesses and imperfections. The following section explores the system further and discusses the role of the government in delivering sport within the United States and Canada.

United States Sport Delivery System

Although the federal government of the United States lacks an explicit and coherent national sport policy, it is still influential in the overall governance of sport. Public-sector organizations operate at different levels of sport and coexist with a number of nongovernmental organizations that have also emerged as leaders at each level of sport. This section outlines the most notable and influential ways that the U.S. government has been involved in sport.

The federal government of the United States has been directly involved in sport through legislation, court cases, and through some programming and policy efforts. In 1978 the **Amateur Sports Act** was passed, taking away the Amateur Athletic Union's (AAU) power to govern the country's participation in international competition. The act empowered the **United States Olympic Committee**, a private nonprofit organization, to govern the nation's sport development including governing bodies for specific sports (Sparvero et al., 2012). Another federal law that directly affected the governance of sport was Title IX of the Education Amendments of 1972. **Title IX**, as it is more commonly known, prohibits sex discrimination in educational institutions receiving public funding, which affects most high school and college athletics. Despite applying only to educational settings, the law is credited with creating a major resurgence in the participation of and the support for women's athletics overall.

Other influences of the federal government include major court cases, such as those deciding the legality of players' unions for professional athletes, and Major League Baseball's ongoing exemption from antitrust laws (Hylton, 1999). The United States Congress has held special investigations into the performance-enhancing drug policies of professional sport leagues, and hearings on the governance policies of the National Collegiate Athletics Association have altered policy within those organizations. The final way that the federal government directly influences sport is through the President's Council on Fitness, Sports, and Nutrition. Originally established in 1956 through an executive order concerning youth fitness, the coun-

cil has been expanded to address the physical health of all Americans through education, programs, and initiatives involving partnerships between public, private, and nonprofit entities (U.S. Department of Health and Human Services, n.d.).

State and local governments play a role in sport through other means. Because public education is mostly governed at the state and local level, the funding decisions for sport at public schools and universities are made at this level of government, affecting both varsity sports and physical education for students. Likewise, decisions about facilities, programming, and access for sport in the community are made through state and municipal parks and recreation departments. This financing function plays a role for professional and private sport enterprises as well. However, the practice of local governments funding the building or renovation of stadia and arenas for professional sport franchises has become widely criticized (Kennedy & Rosentraub, 2000).

A number of organizations have emerged at different levels of sport because of the government's hands-off approach. Among them are professional sport leagues, governing bodies for college sport, travel and club teams for youth sport, and a variety of gyms, health clubs, and other organizations that focus on different ages and functions.

At the community and recreational level, over 36,000 health clubs and gyms offer opportunities for fitness and athletic participation (International Health, Racquet, and Sportsclubs Association, 2017). Private clubs like Planet Fitness and Cross-Fit, which primarily target adults, are among the most financially successful across the United States (Wang, 2016). Other organizations like the YMCA and Boys and Girls Clubs of America serve several functions for people of different ages and abilities, but they also play an important grassroots role in the development of youth athletes (Green, 2005).

Canada's Sport Delivery System

Unlike the free-market-driven sport system in the United States, the Canadian system is largely driven by government policy. Specifically, Sport Canada is the federal government organization that oversees most of the funding, programs, and policies relating to sport in Canada. Thus, when considering the constituent parts of the Canadian sport system, understanding the basic tenets of Canadian federalism is useful. In a general sense, the provincial governments are responsible for recreation, education, and health care, sectors that are typically responsible for sport and physical activity (Simeon, Robinson, & Wallner, 2014).

The Canadian sport system, like the systems in most countries, is influenced greatly by the international sport community. The Canadian national sport organizations (NSOs) oversee most aspects of their individual sports, but much of what they do is dictated by the standards established by international federations and organizations who act as governing bodies for major games and other international competitions. Although control over the rules governing sport in Canada is mostly determined by international interests, the majority of the funding and support for the individual NSOs comes from the public sector (Thibault, 2017).

Specifically, within the federal government there is a sport branch within the International and Intergovernmental Affairs Sector of the Department of Canadian Heritage. Each of the positions in this department (e.g., director general of Sport Canada) is occupied by a member of the civil service. The current government of Canada has an elected member of parliament (MP) serving as minister of Sport and Persons With Disabilities.

Like the sport systems throughout Europe, the provincial governments have given municipalities (or regional governments) responsibility, for the most part, for the service delivery for education, through local school boards, and for recreation, through municipal parks and recreation departments. With that being said, the federal government also plays an important role in ensuring basic service delivery across the country and transferring funds to the provincial governments to support these services (Houlihan, 1997).

Perhaps the most significant recent development in the Canadian sport system is the update of the **Canadian Sport Policy** (CSP). In 2012 Sport Canada reconvened to expand the CSP from the originally drafted 2002 policy. The original CSP, released in 2002, identified a vision of "a dynamic and leading-edge sport environment that enables all Canadians to experience and enjoy involvement in sport to the extent of their abilities and interests and, for increasing numbers, to perform consistently and successfully at the highest competitive levels" by the year 2012 (Canadian Heritage, 2002, p. 4).

Learning Activity

Compare the importance of provincial and territorial governments in Canada with the importance of governments at a corresponding level in the United States and other countries in terms of delivering and influencing sport.

By 2012 Sport Canada revisited their mandate and established their vision to be

> the notion that Canada is a leading sport nation where all Canadians can pursue sport to the extent of their abilities and interests, including performing at the highest competitive levels; and where sport delivers benefits, for increasing numbers, to individual health and well-being, and contributes to socioeconomic outcomes. (Canadian Heritage, 2012a, p. 1)

A desired outcome of the CSP 2012 is to increase the number and diversity of Canadians who participate in sport in the 10-year period from 2012 to 2022. This goal recognizes the importance of managing how people are introduced to sport, how they engage in recreational sport, and how they engage in competitive sport.

Currently a great deal of discussion is occurring about the Canadian sport system. Without a doubt, the most pressing issue is the question of funding. Recently, certain stakeholders, led by the Canadian Olympic Committee, have become much more organized in their efforts at lobbying the government for increased funding. But with the dramatic cost overruns associated with funding high-performance sport and the myriad other issues (e.g., public health, culture, and heritage) that fall under the federal government mandate, the private and public sectors will again evaluate the significance of funding high-performance sport. Furthermore, the discussion of the government's role in funding high-performance sport is becoming increasingly relevant, because the rising rate of obesity in Canadians is a disturbing reality. Specifically, it has been noted that spectatorship in sport was assessed at 40 percent of the population who were 15 years and older in 2010, whereas only 26 percent reported participation in sport (Canadian

CASE STUDY

Sport in Canada

The Canadian Sport Policy (2012) is a federal government policy with a vision for "a dynamic and innovative culture that promotes and celebrates participation and excellence in sport" (Canadian Heritage, 2012a). The policy provides direction and focus for all governments, institutions, and organizations that are committed to realizing the positive effects of sport on individuals, communities, and society. These entities include but are not limited to national, provincial, and territorial sport organizations; sport clubs; ministries; municipalities; and event rights holders within the country. Furthermore, the policy encourages new partnership formations between local and national entities, domestic and international sport associations, and sport and nonsport bodies.

As discussed in the chapter, much of the Canadian sport delivery system relies on federal government support, and the survival of most sport organizations depends on the funding programs administered by the Department of Canadian Heritage. Traditionally, the federal government has been primarily interested in supporting sports that appear in the Olympic Games, giving special attention to those sports in which Canadians have the highest likelihood of winning medals. Although this type of treatment of high-performance international sport fits with the political goals of the federal government, some debate has begun around the appropriateness of public financing of an elite sport system that supports a small number of Canadian athletes. Critics of the current funding formula include those who believe that sport should not be a sector that government regulates and funds, as well as those who believe that the rising rates of inactivity and obesity in Canadians, particularly in the youth population, are deserving of greater attention. These critics believe any investment government makes in sport should be at a grassroots level that promotes physical activity for all Canadians.

As the new Canadian Sport Policy is envisioned and drafts are developed for 2022, the government must critically review (1) organizations and institutions where partnerships will be most effective in the delivery of sport to diverse populations across the country and (2) the appropriateness of funding allocations at the grassroots or high-performance levels of sport in the country. As sport policy coordinator, you must move the policy draft forward. Review the relevant sections of this chapter. Based on this material, develop a memo to your government cabinet ministers that argues for enhanced federal government support of sport at either the grassroots (local) level or high-performance (international and national) level. Support your choice with material from the chapter.

Heritage, 2012b). This relatively low participation rate is further complicated when looking at the low participation of minority groups such as women and indigenous people (Canadian Heritage, 2012a).

Management of Sport

Throughout North America, the management of sport varies depending on the country and financial structure of the sporting system (Hums & MacLean, 2017). Specifically, in the United States the prominence of professional and collegiate sport (and the profitable nature of those sport sectors) influences how these sport sectors are managed. For example, many of these organizations are managed by paid staff who are directed toward profit or revenue maximization. In Canada the prominence of the community sport sector influences the management of sport; many sport organizations are managed by a small paid staff or a relatively large group of volunteers. The following sections outline the management of sport in professional sport, collegiate sport, and community sport within North America.

Professional Sport

Professional sport leagues and competitions are the most visible and highly publicized component of sport in the United States and Canada. Some of the leagues (e.g., the NFL and NBA) and tournaments (e.g., Masters Golf Tournament) garner widespread national and international attention and feature domestic as well as international athletes. Although many of these competitions closely resemble their counterparts in other countries, North American sport has a few distinguishing features.

The most prominent professional sport leagues are centered on the sports developed and grown in North America: American football, basketball, and baseball. The National Basketball Association (NBA) and Major League Baseball (MLB) have teams in both the United States and Canada. On the other hand, each country has its own professional football league, the National Football League (NFL) in the United States and the Canadian Football League (CFL) in Canada. The two leagues have several different rules, vary in league size (the NFL is much larger in number of teams and in terms of commercialization and media dollars), and are played on different-sized fields. The next most popular sport leagues are the National Hockey League (NHL) and Major League Soccer (MLS), which also operate with teams in both countries. Among the other notable leagues are the Women's National Basketball Association, the National Women's Soccer League, and the National Lacrosse League.

Unlike most comparable leagues in Europe and other parts of the world that have open systems of team promotion and relegation, the North American sport leagues have a closed system in which current team owners in the league make decisions on approving the addition of teams to the league as well as their sale or transfer. This style of operation for the league has been likened to a cartel (Fort & Quirk, 1995) and is accompanied by other practices such as revenue sharing and strict rules about player movement meant to maintain a competitive balance and parity between all teams. For example, each of the top North American sport leagues holds an annual draft to determine what teams new players are allowed to sign with.

Another notable practice in North American sport is the trend of using public money from local government to fund the building of sport facilities for professional teams (Povich, 2016). Although not unique to North America, this issue intersects with the team's relationship with local government, particularly in the United States, thus playing a role in the practice of franchise relocation. Further, the Canadian public has usually been quite reticent, if not strongly opposed, to the idea of using public money to support professional sport. Some

Learning Activity

Do a search of the open-league system of European sport leagues. What would be the effect on professional sport in North American if the leagues shifted to an open-league system like those of Europe?

provincial governments have used lottery revenue to support their professional sport teams, but the federal government was strongly rebuked in their one attempt to offer funding support to professional sport franchise operations. Public opinion in Canada is that public money should be spent on grassroots sport development rather than on billionaire sport owners and millionaire athletes (Sam, 2011).

The United States and Canada also host many high-profile individual sport competitions and tournaments such as NASCAR, the Professional Golf Association (PGA) and Ladies Professional Golf Association (LPGA), and several men's and women's tennis tournaments including the U.S. Open. Mixed Martial Arts (MMA), particularly under the Ultimate Fighting Championship (UFC), has also grown a large fan base, drawing in massive audiences for their televised events. Although team sports collectively garner most of the media attention, the professional sport landscape in North America is large and diverse.

College Athletics

The role of intercollegiate athletics in the United States is a unique facet of the country's sport system. Particularly for basketball and American football, which have minimum age limits for entry at the professional level, many prospective athletes first spend time playing their sport in college before advancing. College sport is considered a high level of competition that attracts elite athletes, including many current and future Olympians, in a wide range of sports.

College sport competition began in the northeastern United States with rowing, American football, and baseball in the mid to late 19th century. In 1906, to protect players from the increasing injury and death rate of college football, President

Funding Stadia in North America

Although public financing of stadia and arenas is somewhat common in the United States, large-scale public financing of professional sport facilities in Canada has rarely occurred (Church, 2008). As discussed by Buist and Mason (2010), the media in the United States typically frame financing of sport facilities as a positive contribution to civic pride and community engagement. In Canada, however, both the media and the public largely view the funding of new sport facilities as an economic drain that provides no financial gain to a community or region (Ligaya, 2013).

Background

As the commissioner of the National Women's Soccer League, you have decided that you will go through a league expansion and add one new team to the league. Your director of communications has done some research and has determined that expanding to the Canadian market (i.e., Vancouver, British Columbia) may provide enhanced revenue streams because of the popularity of soccer in the country, as well as the

lack of rival professional women's soccer organizations and leagues. With the potential of this type of expansion, you realize that a new stadium build may be inevitable in a bid proposal from a Canadian city. Your board of directors assigns you to do some searches through media documents and scholarly articles, and complete the following tasks:

♦ Define three pros and three cons of publicly funding a new stadium in Canada.

♦ Define three pros and three cons of privately funding (corporate sponsorship) a new stadium in Canada.

♦ Construct a memo to your board of directors that outlines (*a*) the pros and cons from tasks 1 and 2 and (*b*) provides a recommendation (with explanation) regarding which funding structure (public or private funding) would be best suited for a stadium build in an expansion city such as Vancouver, British Columbia, Canada.

Theodore Roosevelt called for better organization and governance of college sport (NCAA, 2010). As a result the Intercollegiate Athletic Association of the United States (IAAUS) was formed. It later changed its name to the National Collegiate Athletic Association (NCAA). The **NCAA** is currently the largest governing body in American college sport. It has over 1,100 member institutions, including public and private colleges and universities, and it administers championships in 90 men's, women's, and coed sports.

The NCAA is divided into three divisions that each have their own legislative abilities and pass rules that distinguish them from the others (NCAA, n.d.). Division I, the most visible, contains the largest universities in the country and has a more spectator-driven format, along with the highest levels of revenues and expenditures compared with the other levels. At each level, member institutions are organized into conferences that organize the schedules and can engage in other activities such

as hosting conference championships and sharing revenue.

Other notable governing bodies in college sport are the National Association of Intercollegiate Athletics (NAIA), the National Junior College Athletic Association (NJCAA), and the National Christian College Athletic Association (NCCAA). Colleges and universities individually negotiate entry into the various governing bodies based on their preferences for the organization's rules, emphasis, and requirements.

The most salient and controversial issue involving the higher levels of college sport is the principle of amateurism maintained by the NCAA. Amateurism has been a core principle for the NCAA since its inception, but despite many changes to the rules over the years, there is widespread criticism of a system that allows the NCAA and its member institutions to use the likeness of their athletes in promotional materials for revenue generation while preventing the athletes from doing the same (Huma

& Staurowsky, 2012; Southall & Staurowsky, 2013). As the Olympics has moved away from amateurism and the Amateur Sports Act has removed the United States' emphasis on amateurism for international competition, the NCAA remains the last major sport organization in the United States that maintains these ideals.

In Canada, interuniversity competition also exists, where university competition is overseen by **U Sports** (formerly Canadian Interuniversity Sport [CIS]), and competition between colleges is governed by the Canadian Colleges Athletic Association (CCAA).

In the beginning, university sport competition was governed by the Canadian Interuniversity Athletic Union (CIAU), which was reconstituted in 1961 and was represented by the various universities from across Canada (U Sports, 2017). With this reconstitution came financial assistance from the federal government, and universities thus began to commit themselves to excellence in their sport programs. In the 1970s the financial commitment was expanded to the CIAU to include funds for travel equalization, increases for national championship travel, and involvement in international competition (e.g., World University Games).

As financial commitment increased from the federal government, the CIAU recognized their mandate was to serve national priorities:

1. Coordination, promotion, and development of high-performance sport
2. Provision of administration and technical leadership, policy direction, consultative services, and financial resources to function effectively as the primary agent for excellence in sport policy (U Sports, 2017)

In 2001 the CIAU was renamed to Canadian Interuniversity Sport (CIS). A global rebranding of the CIS was announced in 2016. The goal of the rebranding strategy was to give Canadian student-athletes and national championships the visibility, appreciation, and reward they deserve through the new name—U Sports (U Sports, 2017). As noted on the U Sports website,

> The U Sports brand aims to create a massive change in the way Canadians see university sports in the digital era. Our commitment is to revitalize our place in the national sport con-

versation by using every technology possible to highlight, celebrate, and present the accomplishments of these remarkable young individuals who pursue the toughest double major of all; full-time scholar and full-time athlete. (n.p.)

Currently, U Sports represents 56 member universities, 12,000 student-athletes, and 7,700 games and events per year (U Sports, 2017). The organizational structure of U Sports, presented in figure 3.1, demonstrates the commitment to communication and social media within the U Sports brand.

In addition to U Sports in Canada, the Canadian Collegiate Athletic Association (CCAA) has been involved in the governance and delivery of high-level competitive opportunities in intercollegiate sport since 1974 (Canadian Collegiate Athletic Association, 2017). Before the formation of the CCAA in 1974, national-level collegiate competition was initiated in British Columbia, Alberta, Saskatchewan, and Manitoba when the 4-West Championships were formed, in seven sports, in 1971. Following these competitions, Ontario and Quebec initiated similar competitions in 1972. The success of these championships resulted in the formation of the CCAA.

Today, CCAA student-athletes compete in seven sports at 10 CCAA national championships, each hosted by a CCAA member college (Canadian College Athletic Association, 2017). The 94 member institutions of the CCAA include colleges, universities, and technical institutes located in eight provinces and regionally governed by five member conferences.

Community Sport

The most popular sports and physical activities in the United States are fitness sports (e.g., walking, high-impact intensity training, jogging, and weightlifting), outdoor sports (e.g., camping, fishing, and trail running), and individual sports (e.g., triathlon, martial arts, golf, and bowling). The settings for these activities range from private homes to parks, schools, and health clubs. Local governments strive to provide opportunities for sport through schools for children and through parks and recreation departments for people of all ages.

According to a report from the Physical Activity Council, 27.5 percent of Americans did not participate in sport or physical activity in 2016 (Physical

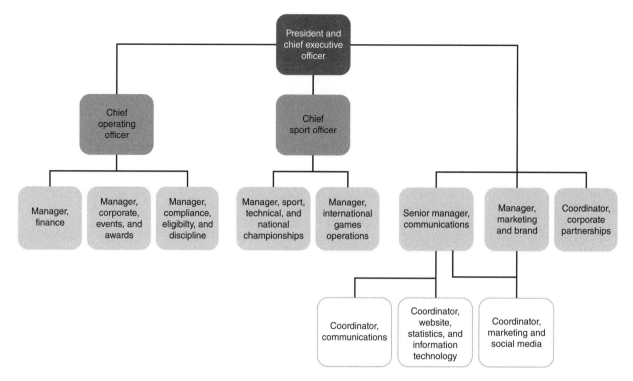

Figure 3.1 Organizational structure of U Sports.
U SPORTS

Activity Council, 2017). The report points to specific trends in physical activity based on income levels; the lowest income households have the highest rates of inactivity. As previously mentioned, the rising cost of sport participation, especially for youth team sports, creates a barrier for many, even with the services offered by local governments.

As described earlier, sport and recreation in Canada are primarily a municipal concern, because the education system and municipally operated recreation departments are the primary providers of sport and recreation opportunities. Unlike the European sport system, which includes much more active involvement by local sporting clubs in providing opportunities and school systems that place less emphasis on competitive sport, the Canadian sport and recreation system depends heavily on public financing and support (Macintosh & Whitson, 1990). Therefore, community sport is often thought of as local not-for-profit sport leagues that provide opportunities for children and municipally operated recreation programs. Although private sport clubs

are present in Canada, high membership fees usually limit access for the public.

Major Sport Events

Within North America, states, provinces, and territories host many annual or quadrennial sporting events. These national and international events typically have large international viewership. Regarding professional sport in North America, the World Series (Major League Baseball), Super Bowl (National Football League), Grey Cup (Canadian Football League), and Stanley Cup (National Hockey League) are all examples of professional sporting events that rotate annually to host cities within their respective leagues. In addition, both the United States and Canada host amateur sporting events on a quadrennial basis. For example, the Pan American and Parapan American Games are held the year before the Summer Olympic and Paralympic Games and have been hosted by Toronto, Ontario (Canada); Winnipeg, Manitoba (Canada); and Indianapolis,

Indiana (United States). These events draw large numbers of athletes and spectators from across the globe and have television audiences in the millions.

Summary

This chapter discussed sport systems within North America, specifically addressing the distinctive and common features of the sport frameworks of the United States and Canada in the context of the historical development of those countries, sport delivery systems, governmental involvement in sport, diverse professional and collegiate institutions, and sport practices. Moreover, differences between sport in North American and the rest of the world were explained through the various roles played by the government, public, economy, competition, and federal and local laws.

Review Questions

1. Evaluate the role of the federal government in the Canadian and American sport delivery systems.
2. Evaluate the role of the state, provincial, or territorial and local government in the Canadian and American sport delivery systems.
3. Discuss the cultural significance of sport in North America.
4. Discuss the importance of sport clubs like the YMCA in sport delivery and growth in North America.
5. What has been the most impactful federal action (e.g., legislation, court ruling) on the sport delivery system in the United States?

Sport in Latin America and the Caribbean

Gonzalo A. Bravo, PhD
West Virginia University

Charles Parrish, PhD
Western Carolina University

Chapter Objectives

After studying this chapter, you will be able to do the following:

- Explain why governments in the region become involved with the sport industry.
- Explain the differences between governance and government involvement in sport.
- Discuss the role that sport plays in the development of social identities across Latin American and Caribbean communities.
- Discuss the impact that sport has on the economies in the Caribbean and Latin America.
- Explain the role of sport as both a unification and economic tool in the Caribbean.
- Identify major games and sport events held in Latin America and the Caribbean.

Key Terms

cultural proximity	Caribbean Free Trade Association (CARIFTA)
regional and national identity	Caribbean Community (CARICOM)
baseball academies	public limited sport company (PLSC)
club model	

Key Events

Pan American Games. Hosted every four years since 1951, it is a multisport festival for members of the Pan American Sport Organization (ODEPA).

Central America and Caribbean Games. Hosted since 1926, it involves members of the Central American and Caribbean Sports Organization (ODECABE).

Caribbean Baseball Series. Hosted since 1949, it is a major baseball tournament for club champion members of the Baseball Caribbean Confederation.

Caribbean Premier League. Established in 2013 by the West Indies Cricket Board, it is an annual Twenty-20 cricket tournament featuring six of the region's top professional teams.

Copa América. This event is the main football tournament for national teams affiliated with the South American Football Confederation (CONMEBOL).

Copa Libertadores de América. This event is the prime club championship cup for football club members of the South American Football Confederation (CONMEBOL).

Key People

Edson Arantes do Nascimento (Pelé), Brazil. The most influential football player of the 20th century (1956-1977). Appointed as the first sports minister in Brazil (1995-1998). Author of *Pelé Law*, which reformed professional football in Brazil.

Whycliffe "Dave" Cameron, Jamaica. President of the West Indies Cricket Board (WICB) since 2013 and former executive with the Jamaican Cricket Association.

Marta Vieira da Silva, Brazil. Considered one of the best female footballers of all time. The top scorer in Women's World Cup history through 2018. Named FIFA World Player of the Year five times (2006-2010).

Flor Isava-Fonseca, Venezuela. First woman to be appointed as a member of the International Olympic Committee. Currently an honorary member of the IOC.

Willi Kaltschmitt Luján, Guatemala. Member of the IOC Executive Board (elected in 2012). Also member of the executive board of the World Baseball Softball Confederation. President of the Central American Sports Organization (1982-1990).

Sir Frank Worrell, Barbados and Jamaica. Legendary cricketer for the West Indies in the 1940s through 1960s. Perhaps best known for becoming the first black West Indian to captain the West Indies cricket team in an international test series.

This chapter examines how sport is currently organized in Latin America and the Caribbean. Specifically, it looks at the role of government and other nongovernmental organizations in shaping a country's sport structure and system. Although important differences exist among the sport systems across Latin America and the Caribbean, many similarities are present as well.

Geographical Description and Background

Geographically, Latin America and the Caribbean encompasses a vast area within the Americas that extends for more than 8 million square miles (21 million sq km) from the Rio Grande, the border between the United States and Mexico, all the way to the southern point in Patagonia. This area represents almost two-thirds of the Americas or one-fifth of the world's total land area (Wiarda & Kline, 2007).

The idea of Latin America as a region is not strictly geographic; instead it is a concept that better relates with the notion of **cultural proximity** between nations (Ksiazek & Webster, 2008). Latin America is commonly referred to as the area that is culturally bound by a common language with a strong Hispanic and Portuguese influence, where most countries share similar cultural and historical roots (Eakin, 2004). Most notable is Spanish as a common language (Brazil being the exception) and Catholicism as the primary religion. In addition, many countries share a common base in law,

history, and colonial experience. Despite these similarities, Latin America is also diverse and heterogeneous. In terms of ethnicity, no single group is predominant. Williamson (1997) identified four ethnic groups in Latin America: the mestizo (a term that describes someone whose background is European and Native American Indian); people of European descent; Native Indians; and people of African descent. The predominant group or groups vary by country.

The Caribbean is also a unique geographical region rich in cultural diversity. The Caribbean region encompasses the chain of islands situated south of North America, east of Central America, and north of South America inclusive of the Lucayan Archipelago, Greater Antilles, and Lesser Antilles. Because of cultural similarities, Guyana, Suriname, and French Guiana on the South American continent are also considered part of the Caribbean region. The legacy associated with pre-Columbian peoples combined with European colonization and North American influences have had a profound and lasting political, economic, and cultural impact on the region. For example, McCree (2016) notes that the region can be subdivided into four major linguistic zones, including Spanish (Cuba, Dominican Republic, Puerto Rico), French (French Guiana, Guadeloupe, Haiti, Martinique), Dutch (Aruba, Bonaire, Curacao, Suriname), and English (17 countries and territories).

For the purpose of identifying the nations and territories of Latin America and the Caribbean, we use the list of member states that are part of the United Nations Economic Commission for Latin America and the Caribbean (ECLAC), which includes 20 countries in Latin America and 13 in the Caribbean. In Latin America the countries included are Argentina, Bolivia, Brazil, Chile, Colombia, Ecuador, Paraguay, Peru, Uruguay, Venezuela, Costa Rica, Cuba, Dominican Republic, El Salvador, Guatemala, Haiti, Honduras, Mexico, Nicaragua, and Panama. In the Caribbean, the counties are Antigua and Barbuda, Bahamas, Barbados, Belize, Dominica, Grenada, Guyana, Jamaica, Saint Kitts and Nevis, Saint Lucia, Saint Vincent and the Grenadines, Suriname, Trinidad and Tobago, and Puerto Rico. Although included in this list, Puerto Rico, an unincorporated territory of the United States, is only an associate member of the ECLAC. In 2016 the estimated overall population of Latin America and the Caribbean surpassed 600 million people (ECLAC, 2015).

Role of Sport

Although several native and pre-Columbian ritual games like the Mesoamerican ball games in Mexico and the ball game of *batey* played by the Taíno peoples of the Greater Antilles and Lucayan Archipelago (Bahamas and Turks and Caicos islands) existed at the time of the Spanish conquest, none of these activities played a significant role in shaping today's Latin American sporting scene because they were practiced mostly for survival or for celebratory or religious rituals. Modern sports, as we know them today, arrived in Latin America and the Caribbean during the postcolonial or modern era, from the late 19th century through the first half of the 20th century, particularly with the influx of Anglo-Saxon immigrants (Arbena & LaFrance, 2002). British and American merchants, militaries, sailors, missionaries, and educators who traveled to the major cities in Latin America and the Caribbean created a turning point in defining the cultural basis of what would be the preferred sports in the region. These people, along with their religious missions, educational objectives, military operations, and commercial ventures, brought their favorite pastimes and sports (Arbena, 2002). Thus, football, rugby, cricket, and tennis became the primary sports practiced in areas where British immigrants lived, and baseball became the preferred pastime for those who lived

in cities where American businesspersons relocated or military bases were established.

In the Caribbean the situation was not very different. As Cobley (2010) notes, cricket "was the quintessentially English game that took root throughout the British West Indies during the nineteenth century . . . football was established in all four of the European colonial zones" (p. 377). Over time these sports evolved from their association with the colonial ruling elite to expressions of popular culture and postcolonial regional identity. After World War II, many Caribbean societies established themselves as independent countries. During this postcolonial era, sports such as cricket, football, and athletics (track and field) continued to gain popular appeal. Of course, other sports, such as netball, basketball, water sports, tennis, and golf among others, are common features of the sport and leisure landscape as well.

Besides the American and British presence in Latin America, immigrants from Germany, Switzerland, Italy, Spain, and France also exerted a great deal of influence in the diffusion of European sports. The creation of social and sporting clubs throughout the region contributed not only to preserving the cultural identity of their members but also to introducing new sport practices to Latin Americans (van Bottenburg, 2001). But despite the influence of the 19th century Anglo-Saxon and other European immigrants, over the last four decades a number of other global and domestic forces have contributed to encouraging people to consume new sports. An overall increase in the standard of living, technological advances in communications, more government involvement, and the expansion of global corporatism have all boosted the popularity of sport across the region. Hence, basketball, volleyball, motor sports, golf, and a wide array of nature-based and adventure sports have become extremely popular in many Latin American countries. Today, football is indisputably the most popular sport in most countries, but baseball is also highly popular in a number of countries, particularly in the Dominican Republic, Cuba, Venezuela, Nicaragua, and Panama.

The role that modern sport plays in Latin America and the Caribbean today is not much different from that in other regions of the world. Beyond the common attributed values related to health, well-being, community development and social inclusion, economic benefits, and national pride (Chalip, 2015), sport in Latin America and the Caribbean also plays a powerful role in reinforcing social identity for the many different ethnic groups and communities. Whether by strengthening individuals' identification with their neighborhood, town, region, country, social class, or gender, sport in general, and football in particular, helps Latin Americans answer the question "Who are we?" (Capretti, 2010, p. 246). From the social amateur club to the most acclaimed professional teams, people across the region highly identify with the teams or clubs that they have some affiliation with. In many instances, a person's affiliation to a club serves as a proxy to unravel the social group or neighborhood or even political affiliation where this person belongs (Elsey, 2009). In Latin America, football clubs are often associated with both ends of the social spectrum; some attract the wealthy and educated, and others have a fan base mostly made up of the working class. Typical examples of teams associated with the more affluent are Club Deportivo Universitario de Lima (Peru), Fluminense in Rio de Janeiro (Brazil), River Plate in Buenos Aires (Argentina), and Club Deportivo Universidad Católica in Santiago (Chile). Although mostly associated with the working classes, the following popular and successful teams attract fans from every corner of society: Alianza de Lima (Peru), Flamengo in Rio de Janeiro (Brazil), Boca Juniors in Buenos Aires (Argentina), and Colo-Colo in Santiago (Chile). Although this spontaneous association of football teams and social class might be true, the recent corporatization of professional sport across the region has helped to mitigate this occurrence. Today, teams like Colo-Colo in Chile and Boca Juniors in Argentina attract supporters from across the social spectrum.

Sport in Latin America and the Caribbean also plays a ubiquitous role as a part of most governments' broader public policies. Cuba (1976), Nicaragua (1986), Brazil (1988), Colombia (1991), and Venezuela (1999) have all recognized the right of sport for their citizens in their respective constitutions. In those countries sport is much more than leisure or fun. Instead, sport is a right that is viewed as being at the same level of importance as educa-

tion, health, or housing. Many other countries have also recognized the value of sport in their constitutions, although they have not elevated sport as a constitutional right. Thus, Mexico (1917), Panama (1972), Honduras (1982), Guatemala (1985), Paraguay (1992), Peru (1993), and Ecuador (1998) have all explicitly indicated in their constitutions the importance of sport for the life and well-being of their citizens (Bermejo Vera, Gamero Casado, & Palomar Olmedo, 2003).

In the Caribbean, sport also serves multiple roles throughout many functions, including education, health, social and economic development, and diplomacy. Perhaps the most conspicuous role of sport in the region may be **regional and national identity**. Houlihan and Zheng (2015) suggest that sport provides an opportunity for small states to assert national sovereignty, cultural distinctiveness, and achieve differentiation from their former colonial power. In the West Indies, much has been written about the Windies cricket team and its function as a pillar and symbol of postcolonial regional sovereignty. As Griggs (2006) highlights, the profound success of the West Indies from the 1970s and into the early 1990s (including a 15-year unbeaten streak in test matches) is a remarkable achievement. But perhaps more important than the team's run of dominance was its ability to serve as a structured institution that managed to unite the insular West Indies region. When political institutions failed to establish a unified and sustainable nation state (i.e., the West Indies Federation), the West Indies cricket team succeeded in becoming a unifying force for the demonstration of a diverse yet progressive and distinct Caribbean regional identity. But the team's recent decline in test cricket during the 21st century alongside the failure of basketball as a tool for regional integration suggests that sport is limited in its ability to bind culturally diverse and independent nation states in an era when digital media have exacerbated the effects of globalization (Mandle & Mandle, 2002).

The success of individual athletes and national teams at major international sporting competitions is a point of national pride and symbolizes the successes attributed to the independence movement of the second half of the 20th century. Contemporary sporting icons, such as sprinters Usain Bolt and

Learning Activity

Choose any three countries from Latin America or the Caribbean and find one sport hero (athlete) for each country. Prepare a brief report on these sport heroes and reply to the following questions: What sport did these athletes excel in? What did they do to now be recognized as heroes? Are these athletes' fame recognized beyond their own countries? To what extent do these athletes contribute to raising awareness of their countries around the world? What happened to these athletes after they retired from sport? Do they play any other significant roles in their home countries beside sport?

Elaine Thompson (among many others), are hailed as national heroes for their global achievements and simultaneously serve as objects of and cause for the celebration of Jamaican nationalism. Likewise, past successes of Trinidad and Tobago's Soca Warriors national football team served as a vehicle for the expression of national pride. Specifically, the team's historic qualification for the 2006 FIFA World Cup in Germany was accompanied by droves of flag-waving supporters from Port of Spain to Scarborough and beyond.

Governance of Sport

The sport system across Latin American countries has two distinguishing characteristics. First, it is made of clubs, associations, and federations or national governing bodies; second, it is supported and funded by a government structure. In many countries, government also provides the legal framework in which the sport system operates. Although governments across the region exert a good amount of influence in the way that sport is governed, the governance of sport is for the most part autonomous from the government, because it falls under the jurisdiction of the Olympic Movement. This is true for those organizations that are part of the national Olympic committee in each country. Therefore, the governance of sport is organized in a pyramidal system that runs from "the global to continental, national, and local levels" (Geeraert, 2016, p. 6). On the other hand, for the hundreds of grassroots, voluntary, and even commercial organizations that do not fall under the umbrella of the Olympic Movement, governance of sport occurs in multiple forms, such as laws for civil associations, regulations that control the standards of business practices, and consumer protection laws. The differences between government and governance in sport is that government is mostly concerned with the development of policies and laws related to sport (e.g., laws to prevent violence and hooliganism in sport events, laws that provide tax incentives to companies, laws that assign a certain percentage of the national budget to the funding of sport events, and so on). In contrast, governance is about the mechanism by which sport organizations are steered, managed, ruled, or controlled (O'Boyle & Bradbury, 2013). In Latin America and the Caribbean, where government has a strong presence and involvement in sport, these two functions are closely intertwined.

The club system, or **club model**, reflects the region's early European influence on sport. The club model, as it occurs in other parts of the world, is mostly organized around private single-sport or multiple-sport organizations. For the most part, the club model represents the foundation of the Olympic Movement, which in addition to the hundreds of clubs is also made up of associations (local level) and federations (national level), or, as they are commonly known, national governing bodies (NGBs). Accordingly, although the entire club model and its Olympic structure occur outside the government's jurisdiction, these structures are heavily influenced by government actions and policies.

Although government involvement in sport has increased over time in a number of countries in Latin America (see Bravo et al., 2018; Lopez de D'Amico, 2012), sport is not supported exclusively by public funds. The club system, fundamentally a private structure, has also provided longstanding financial support for the sporting system in many countries. In many Latin American countries the foundation of the sport system resides outside the school system, a trend that resembles what occurs in European countries and in direct opposition to what occurs in the United States. Currently, sport clubs are perhaps the most common way in which sport is organized in Latin America. Clubs may be single-sport clubs or multiple-sport clubs. Some

Club Deportivo Universidad Católica: The Largest Multisport Club in Chile

In April 2017 Club Deportivo Universidad Católica (CDUC) reached its 80th anniversary. The club is among the most important multisport clubs in Chile. Over the years, the club has gained an international reputation not only within South America but around the world. Historically, athletes from CDUC competed internationally in a number of disciplines including track and field, boxing, basketball, alpine skiing, field hockey, rugby, equestrian, tennis, and synchronized swimming. In many instances, these athletes also represented Team Chile in major international sport events such as the South American Games, Pan American Games, and the Summer and Winter Olympic Games. In football many of Católica's professional players have also represented Chile's national team. The Chilean squad that participated in the 2010 FIFA World Cup in South Africa included six players from CDUC, two current and four former. All these players were developed in the club's academy system and then went on to play professionally in leagues all over the world including Argentina, Italy, Mexico, and Russia. During the 2014 World Cup in Brazil, CDUC was represented by seven players, one player currently playing in CDUC and six others who at that time were under contract for clubs in Italy, England, Spain, and the Netherlands.

CDUC was launched in Santiago, Chile, under the auspices of Pontificia Universidad Católica de Chile, which was ranked as the number one university in Chile and among the top three in Latin America. Back in the 1930s CDUC served as the athletic department of the university. Its purpose was to administer and promote the participation of students in competitions with other universities, particularly with its archrival Universidad de Chile. The professional football team of CDUC made its debut in 1937 in the second division of the Chilean league. In the 1980s CDUC became administratively independent from the university. During that time, the club created its own legal and financial structure that provided the institution with a firm and lasting financial structure.

Traditionally, members of Club Deportivo Universidad Católica have been associated with the more affluent and educated segments of the Chilean society. "La Católica" or "la UC," as the team is commonly referred to by their supporters, has won 13 national titles in the first division and 2 in the second division, and it reached three semifinals (1960, 1966, 1969) in Copa Libertadores de América (South American Cup). In addition, in 1994 La Católica obtained a first place in Copa Interamericana, a cup played between the champions of the Copa Libertadores de América and the winner of CONCACAF's Champions Cup (North America, Central America and the Caribbean). In 2009 the football division was separated administratively from CDUC to become a **public limited sport company (PLSC)**, which is a for-profit organization formed by stockholders who provide the funds to operate the team. Similar to many other teams in Europe, La Católica has shares that are publicly traded on the stock exchange.

Unlike other multisport clubs that host professional football in Chile, CDUC became an exemplary model for Chilean sport organizations as well as others clubs across South America. The club directed its efforts to develop not only a world-class football team but also a world-class infrastructure for the practice of Olympic sports.

---

clubs emphasize social benefits through the practice of sport, and others focus more on the development of high-performance athletes. Also, some clubs support professional sport. The entire club model and its Olympic structure of clubs, associations, federations, and confederations are, in fact, a fundamental part of the sport system in any country. But despite the fact that many sport clubs in Latin America operate outside the educational system, many successful football clubs started as a part of a major university, such as Club Universidad de Chile and Club Deportivo Universidad Católica in Chile, Club Universitario de Deportes de Lima in Peru, Liga Deportiva Universitaria de Quito in Ecuador, and the team Tigres from Universidad Autónoma de Nuevo León in Mexico. Many of these clubs have kept their names and identities linked to their alma mater but have replaced their collegiate adminis-

Learning Activity

Conduct a brief search on the web and identify three successful sport clubs in South America. Describe the characteristics of each of these clubs. Are these single-sport clubs? Multisport clubs? Private? Public? What types of sports do these clubs offer their members and supporters? What are the main sources of funding?

trative and financial dependence in their business structure with a more professionalized approach.

The structure and governance of sport in the Caribbean share several key features with those in Latin America because of similarities with past European influences and later integration within the global sport industry. For example, a key defining characteristic of the governance of sport in the region is the role of sport clubs and their relationship with local, national, and international sport federations. As Cobley (2010) states, West Indian press coverage of organized cricket matches can be traced back to Barbados in the early 1800s. Although the sport had been around before then, St. Ann's Garrison Cricket Club was representative of a broader movement that saw the development of many other exclusive British sport and social clubs during the mid to late 19th century. Today, cricket clubs are accessible to a wider segment of the population and, for the most part, are less exclusive in purpose and practice because they serve as coordinating institutions for both elite-level and recreational play. Likewise, football clubs, aquatic clubs, as well as sport clubs in general offer participation opportunities for youth and adults of various ages and skill levels. Some clubs support elite-level professional teams that participate in national leagues, yet the revenue generated by most clubs in the region is not sufficient to provide lucrative wages that would prevent the movement of the most talented domestic players to leagues abroad. In fact, some leagues, such as the Women's Premier (football) League in Trinidad and Tobago, fail to generate sufficient revenue beyond government subsidies to fund critical league operations (Cabralis, 2016).

The administration of sport clubs is typically bound by a set of internal bylaws designed to promote good governance with oversight from a board of directors or similar committee. Common features of club governance also include audited financial statements for fiscal transparency, the identification of club officials and their formal role within the structure of the club, and a declaration to abide by rules of domestic, regional, and global regulatory bodies. For example, a football club competing in the national league in Jamaica would be required to abide not only by its own bylaws but also by the regulations and guidelines imposed by the Jamaican National Premier League (national governance), CONCACAF (regional governance), and FIFA (global governance). Likewise, a track club in the Bahamas would need to ensure that its operations are compliant with the constitutions set forth by the Bahamas Association of Athletics Associations (BAAA); the North American, Central American, and Caribbean Athletics Association (NACAC); and the International Association of Athletics Federations (IAAF). Unfortunately, several examples exist to highlight the limitations of governance in preventing unethical behavior. Perhaps none are more noteworthy than the recent FIFA corruption scandal involving numerous Caribbean sport officials. In the wake of the scandal, a renewed and spirited commitment to good sport governance has been at the forefront of sport managers in the region, spanning the upper ranks of regional governance officials, including the Caribbean Association of National Olympic Committees, and trickling down to member national associations and member sport clubs.

Another characteristic related to the governance of sport in the Caribbean that is consistent with Latin American countries (and beyond) is government involvement and influence. The role and influence of the Brazilian government, highlighted by the power afforded to the Ministry of Sport, is well documented (Bravo, 2013; Rocha, 2016). Many Caribbean countries also feature a ministry of sport (or a similar agency that encompasses sport) as a branch of the national government, with both a supportive and regulatory function. For example, in 2018 Olivia Grange, Jamaica's minister of Culture, Gender, Entertainment, and Sport, promoted a wide variety of initiatives in an effort to enhance women's sports, continue the development of the country's Special Olympics program, and develop an official policy for the safeguarding of children in sport, among many other activities. Beyond the development of sport policy, which as Darko and Mackintosh (2015) emphasize is challenging on many levels for small Caribbean nations, governments across the region also invest in sporting infrastructure in support of grassroots and elite-level sport. In addition, governments have enacted targeted policies and continue to invest funds in support of hosting mega sporting events. As Keech (2016) emphasized, the government of Grenada demonstrated a unique international collaborative approach to finance the reconstruction of the National Cricket Stadium in 2007. The government later invested US$500,000 to acquire the rights to host a 2015 cricket test match between the West Indies and England. These investments were part of a broader tourism policy designed to foster economic development in Grenada. With respect to the stadium project, the Chinese government's monetary investment is one of many examples of BRICS countries' strategic engagement with **CARICOM** member nations (Montoute & Abdenur, 2018). In terms of interregional cooperation, Caribbean nation states have demonstrated a willingness to develop and enact complex collaborative initiatives in support of economic development, particularly in the sport tourism sector. For example, the 2007 ICC Cricket World Cup was staged across eight Caribbean nations. As Rampersad (2011) pointed out, the logistical challenges were immense, but from a profits and tourism perspective, the event generated more revenue than any other previous world cup, despite poor local spectatorship.

Economics of Sport

Although many Latin American countries experience similar challenges in their attempts to develop their sport systems, several important differences across the region add to the complexity of the task for some countries. Larger and more productive economies, like those of Brazil and Mexico, have developed a more advanced and multifaceted sport system because of their greater wealth. In contrast, smaller economies have not achieved the same level of progress in their sporting systems because their

social, economic, and even political systems are not as stable and developed. All of this means that sport, as an economic activity, has not been able to develop at the same pace across the region.

Across Central America and the Caribbean, where the economic potential of the sport industry is often underappreciated, the contribution of baseball to the overall economy of the Dominican Republic is an interesting case to examine. Historically, the Dominican Republic has been a consistent source of talent for Major League Baseball (MLB) in the United States. In 2013, out of 856 players signed in MLB, 241 of them (28 percent) were from outside the United States. Of the 241 foreign-born players, 207 (or 85.9 percent) were from Latin America and the Caribbean. The largest single nationality from this group came from the Dominican Republic, which was represented by 89 players (Berry, 2013). Over the years, the 10 to 12 percent proportion of Dominicans playing in MLB has been constant. In 2016, 83 players in MLB were from the Dominican Republic (Lagesse, 2016). The presence of Latin American players is even more evident in Minor League Baseball (MiLB). It is estimated that of the more than 7,000 players who play in MiLB, about 25 percent come from the Dominican Republic, making Dominicans the largest group of foreign players in both major and minor league baseball (Gregory, 2010).

The economic impact of MLB on the island today is significant. According to baseball scholar Robert Ruck, the baseball industry brings in a half billion dollars to the island. Each MLB baseball academy on the island spends roughly "US$125 million a year . . . that's after paying perhaps an additional $200 million in signing bonuses to young Dominican players, plus whatever comes home from the estimated $400 million paid to Dominican major leaguers" (Ruck, cited in Lagesse, 2016, pp. 10 and 11). **Baseball academies** are full-time facilities operated by MLB franchises in the Dominican Republic that develop baseball talent. Because of the large supply of talented baseball players available at relatively low cost, MLB teams began establishing baseball academies in the late 1980s to recruit and prepare young players for a future life in the United States. The academies operate similarly to subsidiaries of a foreign company (Klein, 1991), and some critics argue that the economic impact is short lived

Learning Activity

Go to the MLB of DR (Dominican Republic) website and research how many and what MLB teams have academies in the Dominican Republic. Select two teams that currently have academies in this country and investigate how these academies are run and funded. In addition, find out what role these academies play in the big picture of the business of Major League Baseball.

because it does not provide the needed elements to ignite a significant change in an impoverished economy (Spagnuolo, 2003).

As in the Dominican Republic, the sport economy in other Caribbean countries is underdeveloped. Rampersad (2011) framed sport as a secondary social institution in Trinidad and Tobago and noted that the sport industry is "at the nascent stage of development" (p. 99). Consequently, he argues, the industry is not a primary source of employment and may be characterized by amateurish structures and organization, poor management practices, and general reliance on external support (i.e. government and corporations). Toomer's (2015) description of the sport industry in Jamaica also indicated an overreliance on government subsidies and grants and framed the commercial sport industry as "semiprofessional in nature because most sporting competitions are heavily reliant on amateur athletes. . . . Only the sport of horse racing can be classified as a local commercial sporting industry" (p. 468). This general description of the economics of sport (i.e., amateurism, reliance on external support) could apply not only across countries in the Caribbean but also across Latin America. This circumstance is largely due to comparatively smaller economies that are not developed to a level capable of sustaining professional sport as a commodity.

Despite the challenges associated with developing economies, significant financial investments and an emphasis on economic development policies grounded in sport continue to be formalized across the region. For example, the Jamaican government has identified sport as a critical component to the nation's national development plan and has committed to developing its sport industry further for the purposes of contributing to the nation's gross domestic product (GDP) (Toomer, 2015). A key component of sport as an economic driver in Jamaica and other Caribbean nations centers on the ability of sport events (large and small) to contribute to tourism in the region. According to the **Caribbean Community (CARICOM)**, a consortium of 20 Caribbean countries, tourism has become the most significant productive sector with respect to contributions to GDP. The tourism and travel industry has been identified by leaders of CARICOM member countries as a high-priority segment of the economy because of its potential to drive growth in other economic sectors, such as construction. Specifically, sport tourism possesses social and economic value. Local athletic championships and other sporting events, such as regional and international tournaments, work to stabilize arrivals to member countries and account for a notable percentage of the overall tourism and travel industry (CARICOM, n.d.).

Although the size of the sport industry across the region represents only a fraction of the total industry on a global scale (PWC, 2011), in larger economies like Mexico and Brazil the sport industry has played an important part in the economy for years. For example, in 2012 the total size of the sport industry in Brazil was estimated at R\$31 billion, equivalent to US\$6.3 billion, or 0.6 percent of the GDP (Menin, 2013). Moreover, between 1996 and 2000, the economic growth rate for the sport industry in Brazil grew at faster pace than the nation's GDP (Graça & Kasznar, 2002). Although sport in Brazil represents a fast-growing market, it is surprising that few national governing bodies (NGBs) can support their operations through private sponsorships. Similar to what occurs in other countries across the region, many Brazilian NGBs still rely on public funding to support their day-to-day operations alongside sponsorship dollars from public companies.

Management of Sport

Anecdotal evidence suggests that in Latin America, managers and employees working in both the public and private sport sectors do not have much expertise or sufficient professional background to operate these organizations effectively. Consequently, poor managerial practices are common

Learning Activity

Identify the two most popular sports in Mexico and Brazil. Also, provide a brief description of two professional leagues in these countries. Are the most popular sports in each country the same? In terms of the organization of the professional leagues, can you discern any similarity or major differences in the way that these leagues are organized and funded in each country? Can you identify which league in each country is the most successful?

in amateur and community sport organizations as well as among professional sport organizations. For the most part, these poor practices are characterized by loose approaches to bookkeeping and financial management and minimal transparency in documentation of operations. A lack of professionalization of the people who work in the sport sector can partially explain the problems described earlier. An additional explanation can be found in the lax hiring practices that some governments use when appointing civil employees in the sport sector. Studies show that public-sector employment in Latin America is still characterized by the practice of patronage, a discretionary allocation of jobs to reward followers and fortify political status and personal relationships (Grindle, 2010). The employment of well-trained employees and managers in an organization is important because mismanagement and abuse of power often lead to the corruption of an organization (Doig, 1995).

Although monitoring malpractice and corruption in sport is not solely the responsibility of governments, a recent report of Transparency International states, "Part of the work on sport and corruption must focus on how governments behave" ("Corruption and Sport," 2009, p. 6). The intersection between career professionalization and the remodeling of public service administration has been acknowledged as exerting a significant influence within the process of modernization of governmental structures (Nef, 2007). This breakthrough suggests that governments in Latin America must focus not only on improving their

own public administrative civil services but also on understanding how and where the education and training of sport sector personnel takes place.

The FIFA scandal on world football that was unveiled in 2015 resulted in 14 people being arrested on the charge of corruption, specifically taking bribes and kickbacks from sport marketing companies that bid on television and marketing rights. The investigation revolved around collusion between official members of CONMEBOL and CONCACAF regarding media and marketing rights. Thirteen of the 14 individuals arrested were from Latin America, including many presidents of football governing bodies (Perez & Forero, 2015). Similarly, the former president of the Rio 2016 Organizing Committee and member of the IOC Carlos Nuzman was arrested in September 2017. Nuzman was accused of paying bribes in exchange for votes to secure Rio de Janeiro as the host city of the 2016 Olympic Games (Hyde, 2017). Unfortunately, these two cases are not isolated because corruption in sport today is much more common than it might appear to be (Masters, 2015).

From a different perspective, and despite the many cases that taint sport in the region, signs of maturity and development are apparent. One sign of maturity is the professionalization of football in Brazil, at least for the teams that historically have a large base of supporters. Thus, the total value of the 40 largest and most successful teams in 2017 reached R$10.26 billion (about US$3.1 billion), compared with R$6.29 billion in 2013 (BDO, 2017). Almost 90 percent of the value increment achieved in the last five years (2013 to 2017) was due to the economic performance of the best and better-positioned 10 teams in Brazil including Flamengo, Palmeiras, Corinthias, Grêmio, Atlético MG, Cruzeiro, Internacional, Fluminense, São Paulo, and Botafogo (BDO, 2017).

Despite the significant incremental growth in the value of Brazilian football, critics argue that more money does not always result in better management. This conclusion also applies to the Chilean football league. Despite an increase in revenue stemming from the Television Football Network, which guarantees an incremental payment to all clubs in the first and second division of the Chilean football league, the improvement and capitalization of clubs has not occurred because management practices

CASE STUDY

Evolution of the Brazilian National Football Championship

The Brazilian National Football Championship, also known as Brasileirão or Série A, is the main professional football competition among clubs in Brazil. It is through this tournament, along with the champion of the Brazilian Cup, that Brazilian teams are selected for the Copa Libertadores de America, the most important competition among South American football clubs. The format and management of Série A has evolved alongside changes to Brazilian football throughout history.

Until 1971, unlike other South American countries, Brazil did not have a national competition to determine its champion. The major obstacle to organizing a national competition was the travel of teams in a country with continental dimensions. The distances between cities made a national competition logistically challenging. In addition, the difficulty in finding common schedules to satisfy the multiple constituencies was a problem because state championships and overseas exhibition games filled the calendars of all Brazilian clubs. In response to these challenges, in 1971 the Brazilian Sports Confederation (CBD), which was responsible for Brazilian football at the time, launched the Brazilian National Football Championship, which over the years became the most important competition for football clubs in Brazil. During the 1970s the national championship served widely as a platform for propaganda serving the interests of the military government that ruled Brazil from 1964 to 1985.

In its earlier years, a main problem with the national championship was frequent changes to the rules governing the tournament. Among the various formats adopted were the knockout system (1959-1968) and the mixed groups and playoffs system (1967-2002). At the end of 1979 the CBD was dissolved and the Brazilian Football Confederation (CBF) was born, which started to organize the new national championship. In 2003 the Brazilian National Football Championship adopted the regular-season system in which all the teams faced each other at home and away to differentiate the competition from the Brazilian Cup (also organized by the CBF), which was played in a knockout system by 91 clubs representing all Brazilian states.

Currently, the main challenge faced by the Brazilian National Football Championship is overcoming the imbalance that exists between Brazil's different regions. Of the 20 participants in 2018, 4 (20 percent) are from the north and northeast, the economically poorest regions in the country. The other 16 (80 percent) clubs are from the south and southeastern part of Brazil, which includes the most developed states in the country. An additional problem of the Brazilian National Football Championship is its schedule of competition, which runs from April to December. This schedule conflicts with the European season and causes Brazilian clubs to lose their main players in the middle of the competition because they are often transferred to European clubs during this time frame. The main problem that clubs still face, however, is the neglect of the CBF with respect to the national tournament. The main product managed by the CBF is the Brazilian national team. As a result, the Brazilian National Football Championship, and its participating clubs, is a secondary priority. Therefore, in the future the clubs will have to run their own league that will organize the competition according to their own interests.

Ary José Rocco Júnior, PhD
University of Sao Paulo, Brazil

have not changed much (Soria & Maldonado, 2016). Therefore, attendance is still low, violence in the stands has not been eradicated, minimal investment in infrastructure has occurred, and teams' executives continue spending much more than their budgets allow. Unfortunately, and despite the success of Latin American players in the best leagues in the world, management of local leagues has not evolved at the same pace as their production of high-caliber players. According to the International Center for Sport Studies (CIES), in May of 2018 more than 3,000 Latin American professional football players were playing overseas (Poli, Besson, & Ravenel, 2018). A high dependence on transfer fees has been recognized as one of the problems affecting the management of football clubs in the

Learning Activity

Investigate the issue of violence and hooliganism in professional football in Latin America. Which leagues in which countries present the most problems? What have governments of these countries done to curb these problems?

Learning Activity

Choose any of the football championships described in this section and prepare a brief report on the historical and cultural significance of these championships.

region (Miller, 2012). Many clubs invest most of the resources that come from the transfer of talented players to acquire new players, leaving minimal or no resources to reinvest back into their own clubs.

Major Sport Events

Over the past 90 years, Latin American and Caribbean countries have hosted major world sporting events like the FIFA World Cup, Summer Olympic Games, and the ICC Cricket World Cup. The men's FIFA World Cup has been hosted seven times in Latin America, including the first version in Uruguay in 1930. The other countries that have hosted the FIFA World Cup have been Brazil in 1950 and 2014, Chile in 1962, Mexico in 1970 and 1986, and Argentina in 1978. The Summer Olympic Games have been held twice in Latin America, in Mexico City in 1968 and in Rio de Janeiro in 2016. In 2007 eight Caribbean countries jointly hosted the ICC Cricket World Cup. The Caribbean also hosted the ICC T20 Cricket World Cup in 2010 as well as the ICC Women's T20 World Cup in 2010 and 2018. In addition, several regional multisport events of medium to large size such as the Pan American Games, Central American and Caribbean Games, and South American Games are also organized in the region. The main football championships are Copa América, the South American Championships of Nations (organized every four years since 1916); Copa Libertadores de América, the South American Club Championship (organized every year since 1960); and the Central American Football Union Nation Cup (organized every two years since 1991). Copa América and the Nation Cup in Central America are men's only competitions; the Copa Libertadores started a female version in 2009.

Other single-sport tournaments organized in the Caribbean are the Caribbean Baseball Series, the Caribbean Premier League in cricket, and the CARIFTA Games in track and field. The Caribbean Baseball Series, or Series del Caribe in Spanish, is an annual baseball tournament played since 1949 by the national champion teams of Puerto Rico, Venezuela, Cuba, the Dominican Republic, and Mexico. From 1949 to 1960 the Caribbean Baseball Series included four countries: Puerto Rico, Cuba, Panama, and Venezuela. Because Fidel Castro banned professional baseball in Cuba in 1961, Cuba self-excluded from the Series del Caribe until 2014. From 1970 until today, participants included the champion teams of the Dominican Republic, Puerto Rico, Venezuela, Mexico (since 1971), and Cuba (Latino Baseball, 2015).

The Caribbean Premier League was established in 2013 by the West Indies Cricket Board. The annual Twenty-20 cricket tournament features six of the region's top professional teams. The CPL T20 event is unique because the competing teams are often from different island nations, which requires strategic logistical planning.

Following the dissolution of the West Indies Federation (1958-1962), the **Caribbean Free Trade Association (CARIFTA)** was organized to foster economic and political integration among English-speaking countries in the region. In 1972 the organization launched the CARIFTA Games, a junior-level track and field event, in support of this goal. A year later the Caribbean Community (CARICOM) replaced CARIFTA as the unifying institution for member countries, but the event continued and retains its original name to this day. This tournament showcases some of the top-level amateur talent in a region known for its development of some of the best track and field athletes in the world. Olympic gold medalists such as Usain Bolt, Yohan Blake, and Shaunae Miller Uibo are among the list of former champions. Over its history, the CARIFTA Games have rotated among 13 countries in the region, each seeking to capitalize on the economic impact associated with the influx of visitors that accompanies the event and to enhance its national profile.

Summary

Most sports that are popular in Latin America and the Caribbean arrived in the region more than a hundred years ago. Essentially, sports were cultural imports that were brought from Europe at the end of the 19th century or at the turn of the 20th century. Two distinguished features characterize the way that sport is organized in Latin America and the Caribbean. First is the role played by clubs, associations, and national governing bodies, and second is the supporting role played by governments. Clubs represent the actual place where the sport activity takes place. Clubs can be of multiple forms, from single to multiple sports, from public to private, and from recreational to professional sport. On the other hand, government involvement in sport in Latin America and the Caribbean occurs in a way that is not much different from how it occurs in other regions of the world. Governments' presence exists at multiple levels, from municipal and provincial to the national level. Although the extent of this involvement varies from country to country, governments' main role is to provide the necessary funding to the sport system in each country. Because governments' influence is strong, many countries have raised the status of sport to a constitutional level. Many governments rationalize their involvement and subsidization of sport because they think that sport can serve as a vehicle to achieve a number of higher social ends. From helping to develop healthy habits in the population to developing national pride, sport is seen as a powerful vehicle that helps reinforce social, regional, and national identity. Despite this perceived importance, the sport industry in many Latin American and Caribbean countries still lags behind when compared with other regions of the world. Although the overall social value of sport is high, the economic value of many sport enterprises is still not significant in terms of the impact to national economies. In addition, managerial practices in many private and public sport organizations are still substandard, or at best are a work in progress. Nonetheless, many governments see the potential to develop an industry that can significantly contribute to the country's economic development. Recent sport mega events hosted, or soon to be hosted, in the region, such as the 2014 FIFA World Cup in Brazil, the 2016 Summer Olympics in Rio, the 2019 and 2023 Pan American Games in Lima and Santiago de Chile, and the 2018 Youth Olympic Games in Buenos Aires, show that many countries are still committed to raising the standard of the sport industry in this part of the world.

? Review Questions

1. How does sport contribute to reinforcing the notion of social and national identity in Latin America and the Caribbean?

2. How did colonization influence the structure of sport in the Caribbean?

3. What are the differences between government involvement in sport and governance of sport?

4. Discuss the role played by clubs in the entire sport system of countries across Latin America and the Caribbean. How many types of clubs can you find in these countries?

5. What is a public limited sport company?

6. Explain why various governments in the Caribbean region are involved in the sport industry and describe two specific roles they play in the administration of sport.

7. In consideration of the 2007 Cricket World Cup, describe why hosting this sporting event was a complex undertaking. Do you foresee more international megaevents being hosted in a similar manner in the future? Why or why not?

8. Explain the main challenges faced by the Brazilian National Football Championship.

9. Explain the relationships among sport events, sport tourism, and economic growth.

Sport in Western Europe

Brice Lefèvre, PhD

University Lyon, University Claude Bernard Lyon

Guillaume Routier, PhD

University Lyon, University Claude Bernard Lyon

Guillaume Bodet, PhD

University Lyon, University Claude Bernard Lyon

Chapter Objectives

After studying this chapter, you will be able to do the following:

- Define Europe and Western Europe geopolitically and culturally in relation to sport management.
- Outline the region's common approaches to the philosophy, organization, and financing of sport.
- Identify the main trends in terms of viewership of live sport events and participation in sport or physical activity.
- Identify the main national similarities and differences in terms of sport participation patterns in Western Europe.
- Discuss the methodological challenges of national sport comparisons in Western Europe.

Key Terms

sport	EU definition of sport
sport participation	categories of sport goods and services expenditure
European Union (EU)	
work plan for sport	traditional pillars of sport participation in Western Europe
traditional sport system	
economics of sport	omnivorism

1. Switzerland
2. Greece
3. Luxembourg

Key Events

1924 Chamonix Olympic Games. Organized by the French Olympic Committee, the event was designated by the International Olympic Committee as the first Olympic Winter Games. They were organized in the French city of Chamonix, in the Alps. The Games gathered 16 nations and 258 athletes.

European Sport for All Charter, 1975. Adopted by the sport ministers of European member states, it had the goal of making sport accessible to all people and supporting high ethical values in sport.

Fall of the Berlin Wall, 1989. Event that paved the way for German reunification and a wave of anti-Communist revolutions across Eastern Europe, which had a significant effect on the landscape of European sport and on understanding sport-doping issues.

Bosman ruling, 1993. European Union legal ruling that allowed freer movement of athletes between teams.

Creation of the English Premier League of football, 1992. One of the most watched sport leagues in the world, its creation represents a turning point for European professional football and sport, generating high revenues, notably through high broadcasting rights and sponsorship deals.

1992 Barcelona Summer Olympics. The Olympics was organized in Spain for the first time. These Games saw the first official participation of professional athletes. They are often cited as an example of a positive impact and legacy of hosting the Olympics on the regeneration of a city.

Key People

Lord Sebastian Coe, former Olympic athlete, political figure, and chief executive of the London 2012 Olympic bid team.

Tony Blair, formerly prime minister of Great Britain, played a role in the London 2012 Olympics bid and

personally intervened on behalf of Formula One to allow an exception to a ban on tobacco advertising in sport.

Andy Burnham, former sport minister for England.

Pierre de Coubertin (1863-1937), French historian and educator, played a central role in the revival of the modern Olympic Games and was a founding father of the International Olympic Committee.

Alice Milliat (1884-1957) was a sportswoman who strongly contributed to the development and inclusion of women in the Olympics, notably through the creation of an international federation and the Women's Olympics.

Juan Antonio Samaranch (1920-2010) was a Spanish sports administrator and minister of sport under Franco regime and served as IOC president between 1980 and 2001. During his presidency the Olympic

Games became the megaevent that it is, through sponsorship, broadcasting, and commercialization.

Sepp Blatter (1936-), a Swiss football administrator, is the former president of the Fédération Internationale de Football Association (FIFA) between 1998 and 2015. He strongly contributed to the development of football, the FIFA organization, and the FIFA World Cup, but his tenure was tarnished by numerous controversies and corruption allegations. He has been banned for six years from FIFA activities.

The overall aim of this chapter is to draw the picture of sport consumption in Western Europe. In this sense, **sport** is considered in both its social and economic dimensions. Indeed, Andreff (1999, p. 135) observed that **sport participation** was "an act of consumption" that engages sport specific expenditures such as clothes, sport products and material, tickets and fees for using sport equipment, traveling, and tourism. According to this view, sport participation and, more broadly, sporting and leisure activities create various primary and secondary sport markets (Andreff, Bourg, Halba, & Nys, 1994). Sport can then be analyzed though the lens of both its economic and social aspects.

To appreciate the various challenges in relation to the sport sector in Western Europe, this chapter discusses the political and governance dimension of sport, demographic considerations in sport consumption, and participation in sport and physical activity sectors.

Geographic Description, Demographics, and Background

On March 25, 1957, Germany, Belgium, France, Italy, Luxembourg, and the Netherlands signed the two treaties of Rome, creating the European Economic Community (CEE) and the European Community of Atomic Energy, which are usually considered the first two foundational pillars of the birth of a political Europe. Later, on February 7, the CEE entity became the **European Union (EU)**, with

the signature of the Maastricht treaty. Sixty years later and after several additions, the EU comprises 28 member states: Austria, Belgium, Bulgaria, Cyprus, Croatia, Czech Republic, Denmark, Estonia, Finland, France, Germany, Greece, Hungary, Ireland, Italy, Latvia, Lithuania, Luxembourg, Malta, the Netherlands, Poland, Portugal, Romania, Slovakia, Slovenia, Spain, Sweden, and the United Kingdom. But Europe remains a continent that is difficult to define because it is simultaneously one and several, which is well illustrated in the EU motto "United in diversity."

Because defining Europe is not an easy exercise, defining Western Europe is similarly difficult. Traditionally, **Western Europe** is defined geographically but also politically. According to the United Nations (i.e., Western Standard Countries Codes for Statistical Use), Western Europe comprises 9 countries: Austria, Belgium, France, Germany, Liechtenstein, Luxembourg, Monaco, (the) Netherlands, and Switzerland. But for other standards, notably UNESCO's, Western Europe comprises 23 countries: Andorra, Austria, Belgium, Denmark, Finland, France, Germany, Greece, Ireland, Iceland, Italy, Liechtenstein, Luxembourg, Malta, Norway, the Netherlands, Portugal, San Marino, Spain, Switzerland, Sweden, the United Kingdom, and Vatican. From a geopolitical point of view, the West–East division also refers to the Cold War, which goes beyond geographical boundaries. During the Cold War (1945-1991), Western Europe comprised the countries situated west of the Iron Curtain, which were the European countries belonging to NATO with the exception of Turkey, plus the neutral ones.

Learning Activity

Compare the composition of the European Union, the Euro Zone, and the border-free area called Schengen. Using a web search, distinguish the countries that belong to all three of these areas from those that do not.

These countries were allied with the United States of America (USA) and formed what was commonly called the Western bloc or capitalist bloc. This definition will be used in this chapter mainly because the political systems in Europe strongly influence sport and its development as a cultural, social, and economic phenomenon, and because it excludes the very small nation-states that are not representative of Europe because of their small population (e.g. Monaco, San Marino, Vatican, and so forth).

Consequently, we define Western Europe as made up of Belgium, Denmark, Germany, Ireland, Greece, Spain, France, Italy, Luxembourg, the Netherlands, Austria, Portugal, Finland, Sweden, the United Kingdom, Iceland, Norway, and Switzerland.

From a geographic and climatic viewpoint, Western Europe is extremely diverse, which has a significant influence on sport consumption and participation. Europe is often described as a peninsula of peninsulas, a peninsula being a piece of land surrounded by water on three sides. Western Europe has the Arctic Ocean on the north, the Atlantic Ocean on the west, and the Mediterranean Sea on the south. The European continent is generally divided into seven geographic regions, four of which are included in Western Europe as we defined it: Scandinavia (Iceland, Norway, Sweden, Finland, and Denmark), the British Isles (the United Kingdom and Ireland), West Europe (France, Belgium, the Netherlands, and Luxembourg), and South Europe (Portugal, Spain, Italy, and few small states). The fifth and sixth areas, Central and Southeast Europe, integrate several Western European countries according to our definition: Germany, Switzerland, Austria, and Greece. The last area is East Europe. Climate varies from polar climate in the far north, Atlantic climate for the countries facing the Atlantic ocean, mountain climate in the Alpine region, continental climate in northern countries (e.g., Sweden, Finland), and a dry and warm Mediterranean climate in the south. These differences particularly influence the development of outdoor versus indoor sports, and summer versus winter sports. The performance of Norway at the Winter Olympics is illustrative of these differences and specificities. In terms of demography, Western Europe comprises the most populated European countries: Germany (about 82 million inhabitants in 2018), the United Kingdom (about 66 million), and France (65 million), as well as sparsely populated countries like Iceland (about 330,000) and Luxembourg (590,000).

Overall, according to our definition Western Europe gathers about 420 million inhabitants. In terms of economies, Germany, the United Kingdom, France, and Italy are among the top 10 largest economies in the world in terms of gross domestic product (GDP), and Luxembourg, Ireland, Norway, and Switzerland are among the top 10 economies in terms of GDP per capita. Consequently, we can consider Western Europe a wealthy area.

Role of Sport

Because of its important social and economic impact, sport has taken a growing place in European development programs and more generally in EU strategy. Consequently, the EU designed in 2017 a dedicated **work plan for sport** that comprises three key challenges: integrity of sport, economic dimension of sport, and sport and society. Essentially, EU's aim is to (1) ensure integrity for those under 18 years old and fight against corruption and doping though the good governance of sport; (2) stimulate economic activity, especially in terms of jobs, through support of innovation and the construction of a specific sport market; and (3) fight against exclusion, preserve and improve individuals' health, and protect the environment through the promotion of sport and physical activity for European citizens. In that sense, sport is used as a platform to address numerous social, economic, and political challenges.

> Sport plays a positive role in the cross-sectoral cooperation at EU level and thereby helps to ensure sustainable development and to adequately tackle the overarching socio-economic and security related challenges facing the EU, including migration, social exclusion, radicalization that may lead to violent extremism, unemployment, as well as unhealthy lifestyles and obesity. (Council of European Union, 2017, p. 3)

Learning Activity

Although the Council of European Union sees sport almost exclusively as producing positive outcomes for populations, reflect on the potential mixed and negative consequences of sport participation, attendance, and viewership.

Regarding sport participation, nonparticipation rates in Europe remain as high as the differences between countries, confirming the need for public intervention for the promotion of sport and physical activity (Downward & Rasciute, 2011). This has been the case since the ratification of the European Sport for All Charter that addresses the importance of participation for all, a confirmation of the importance of sport participation irrespective of geographical, social, education, and gender aspects. Sport has to be accessible to everyone to fit with the European idea of sport for all. But because of the strong differences between national and regional contexts, designing global sport policies based on few general indicators such as participation rates and frequencies appears difficult, as well as inefficient.

Governance of Sport

In 2007 the European Council adopted a resolution institutionalizing new trans-Europe cooperation about sport named Enlarged Partial Agreement on Sport (EPAS). This platform of cooperation between governments aimed to foster a dialog between EU member states, public authorities, sport federations, and nongovernmental organizations (NGOs) to contribute to better governance of sport. In that sense, EPAS constitutes a tool that should help Europe tackle current sport threats and challenges. The Erasmus+ program also supports, notably financially, development, exchange and transfer, and the realization of innovative ideas and actions through Europe. This cooperation between various stakeholders also contributes to the development of the European dimension of sport. In the same vein, the European week of sport aims to raise awareness of the benefits of regular sport and physical activity among European citizens, irrespective of their age and level of fitness. In emphasizing local initiatives, it aims to encourage people to #BeActive on a regular basis.

The **traditional sport system** in Western European countries is based on a system of interdepen-

CASE STUDY

Sport in France

In France, public authorities are strongly and directly linked to sport federations that are delegated to organize the sport and its development within the national territory, although each of numerous actors has a specific role. For instance, within the sporting movement, national federations are given by the state a direction to organize the sport, its rules, and its competitions; to deliver local and national titles; and to select athletes to represent the country. This mandate is renewed every four years. The French National Olympic Committee (FNOC) is the representative of the Olympic Movement and deals with public authorities about common-interest issues such as the preservation of the Olympic spirit. It collaborates with both sport federations and public authorities to prepare and select

elite athletes for Olympic Games. Last, it gives its opinion on the delegation of public service to national federations. The state, through the ministry of sports and its decentralized directorates, is centered on the functions of coordination and regulation. Specifically, it deals with safety issues in controlling sport equipment and formations (i.e., role of administrative police). As for the elite level, the state is the administrative tutor of federations in the sense that it establishes, in coordination with them and the FNOC, the lists of elite athletes and conducts the fight against doping. Last, it warrants the development of sport for all by conducting actions such as the Sports Day, supporting small rural clubs, and ensuring equal access to sport equipment within the territory.

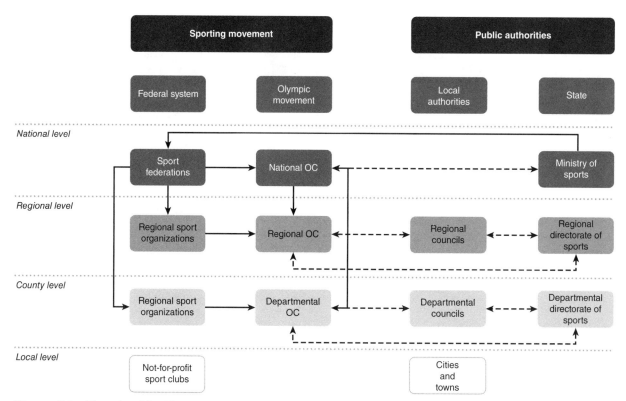

Figure 5.1   The simplified French sport organization system.

Based on information from Ministère Des Sports. Available: http://www.sports.gouv.fr/IMG/pdf/orgasportfrancais_sigles5.pdf

dences between various sport institutions that can be actors, producers, organizers, managers, and administrators. This system is generally organized as a pyramid. Elite sport is on top, organized by international and national institutions (i.e., governing bodies and federations), and grassroots sport is at the bottom, organized by not-for-profit organizations and clubs. Excluding professional sport, the historic actors of the organization of sport in Europe are the ones from the "sporting movement" comprising the federal system, the Olympic movement, and public institutions made up of states and local authorities. Each of these actors is active at the regional and local levels to implement national sport policies, and interactions occur at each level. Figure 5.1 proposes a simplified structure of the French sport organization system.

Economics of Sport

The analysis of the **economics of sport** and its challenges in Europe is not an easy task partly because of the growing importance of economic and monetary

factors influencing sports and sporting activities. It consists, according to Andreff et al. (1994), of looking at both sides of a coin by focusing on the origins of sport funding, the recipients of these expenses, and the activities that they generate. To shed light on these two aspects, surveys and studies are regularly conducted to produce relevant data and knowledge that, in turn, should influence policies.

First, to identify the main European sport funders and the amounts invested, we can rely on a study conducted by the consultancy firm Groupe AMNYOS (2008). Second, we focus on sport-related employment in Western Europe using the Labor Force Survey from Eurostat, the statistical office of the EU. Third, we focus on trade in sporting goods. Fourth, we look at households' sport-related consumptions and expenses in Western Europe using Eurostat's data.

To understand the meaning of the data, the **EU definition of sport** is important to keep in mind because it comprises three levels: a statistical, a narrow, and an extended definition. The statistical definition comprises all sporting activities that have their own statistical category in the Statistical Classification of Economic Activities in the European Community classification (NACE, 2002, 2008). Within this category, we can find, for instance, professional athletes, sport coaches, and instructors. The narrow definition gathers all activities considered as sport inputs, that is, all goods and services necessary to participate in sport, to which we add the elements from the statistical definition. Finally, the extended definition gathers all activities in which sport is an input, that is, all goods and services related to sport but that are not necessary to participate, to which elements from the narrow definition are added.

Structure of Sport Funding

According to a study commissioned by EU Directorate-General Education and Culture (SportsEconAustria et al., 2012) including the 27 countries, sport represented about 1.13 percent of the European GDP when using the narrow definition and 1.76 percent when using the extended definition. When considering the more restrictive definition, the statistical definition, which concerns the organized sport sector, it represents less than 0.3 percent of the EU GDP. Furthermore, we can observe that the sport sector when direct and indirect impacts are concerned was evaluated at 2.98 percent of the EU GDP and corresponded to 2.12 percent of overall employment. According to the study from Groupe AMNYOS (2008), Eastern European countries allocate a smaller share of their GDP to sport, for instance, 0.21 percent for Bulgaria, 0.38 percent for

Lithuania, and 1.13 percent for Estonia, in comparison with Western European countries, which invest more in that sector, for instance, 1.76 percent for France, 1.67 percent for the United Kingdom, and 1.42 percent for Germany.

When looking at the funding of sport, the picture is clear: Private funding (households and firms) represents the most significant share in comparison with public funding (state and local authorities). Sport is on average funded at 63.8 percent from private funding, and more precisely at 49.7 percent from households. On average, public funding in Europe was about 36.2 percent in 2008, with 24.3 percent funded by local authorities. This structure has been quite stable since 1990.

The case of France is interesting. Until 2011 household expenditure was on average greater than public administrations' expenditure (national and local, 47 percent and 44 percent, respectively), while firms' funding remained relatively low (less than 10 percent). From 2012 the hierarchy was changed mainly because of the economic consequences of the 2007 financial crisis. Although household expenditure still increased (an increase of 7 percent between 2007 and 2013), this growth was lower than public administrations' expenditure (an increase of 26 percent between 2007 and 2013). Therefore, the share of public funding in France went from 42.5 percent in 2005 to 47.8 percent in 2013, while the share from household expenditure decreased from 47.4 to 43.6 percent (see table 5.1).

The sport sector is therefore an important sector with significant potential. Moreover, the European

Table 5.1 Structure of Sport Expenditures in France (2005-2013)

	2005	2006	2007	2008	2009	2010	2011	2012	2013
Households	47.4%	47.0%	46.8%	46.4%	45.4%	46.6%	45.8%	44.7%	43.6%
Public administrations	42.5%	42.9%	43.5%	44.1%	44.8%	44.0%	45.0%	46.0%	47.8%
Firms	10.1%	10.0%	9.7%	9.8%	9.8%	9.6%	9.2%	9.0%	8.7%
TOTAL	30.6	31.9	33.1	33.8	33.7	34.3	36.0	36.5	38.1
GDP	1,772.0	1,853.3	1,945.7	1,995.8	1,939.0	1,998.5	2,059.9	2,086.9	2,116.6
% of GDP	1.73	1.72	1.70	1.70	1.74	1.72	1.75	1.75	1.80

Data from Bergonzoni (2016).

sport sector showed strong resilience after the 2007 financial crisis in comparison with other economic sectors, possibly because of the maintenance of effort and expenditure from public actors, especially local ones. In France sport expenditure growth was greater than GDP growth: Between 2007 and 2013, sport expenditure increased by 15 percent whereas GDP increased by only 9 percent.

The European sport model (elite and professional sports at the top and grassroots and mass participation at the bottom) generally uses "trickle-down effects" to justify funding elite sport, presuming that success at the elite level will increase mass participation (Bosscher, Sotiriadou, & Bottenburg, 2013). But this model shows some fragility; expenditures become increasingly specialized and contribute more to the top of the pyramid than the bottom (Groupe AMNYOS, 2008). Private expenditures (households and firms) mainly go to elite and professional sports (mostly through broadcasting and TV rights), and public expenditures, especially those from the states, tend to follow the same orientation.

In the meantime, funding for mass participation becomes increasingly complex. Because of the progressive disengagement of public actors, not-for-profit organizations, which are the basis of the system, have to develop new strategies and competencies, especially from a financial perspective.

Those sport organizations are extremely dependent on volunteers, and without this "invisible labor," not-for-profit organizations could not operate as they do now (Chantelat, 2010). As an example, in France in 2005, the financial value of volunteers' time and skills in not-for-profit sport organizations was evaluated at €5.6 billion (US$6.9 billion) when both direct and indirect (i.e., construction, maintenance, and access to sport facilities) funding from public administrations was considered (Chantelat, 2010). Figure 5.2 illustrates the current streams of funding for various types of sport (i.e., elite sport, competitive recreational sport, health and recreational sport), demonstrating the plurality of funding origins and the complexity of the sport system.

Employment in Sport

When specifically focusing on employment within the sport sector, the Labor Force Survey conducted by the EU provides relevant information regarding the status of workers and their sociodemographic characteristics such as age, gender, and education levels (using the ISED classification). The definition used by Eurostat refers to the statistical definition that gathers sport activity economic sectors from the NACE classification, but it brings another dimension through related occupations according to the ISCO classification by integrating sport and fitness workers outside the sport sector. The figures

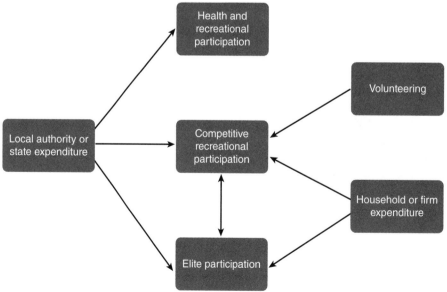

Figure 5.2 The simplified European sport funding system.
Based on Groupe AMNYOS Consultants (2008).

presented consider the number of workers irrespective of their amount of work; no distinction is made between full-time and part-time jobs (i.e., they are not full-time equivalent values).

At first, we can observe that in 2016, 86 percent of jobs from the sport sector were located within Western European countries. This portion had remained relatively stable despite a slight decrease observed starting in 2013 (see table 5.2).

Within Western European countries, gender balance in terms of workers within the sport sector is relatively even, even if the portion of males remains slightly larger (54.9 percent) than that of females. But the gap is being progressively reduced; between 2011 and 2016, the number of male workers increased by 6.1 percent and the number of female workers increased by 18.6 percent.

Regarding age, most sport workers in Western European countries are between 30 and 64 years of age, representing about 58.5 percent of workers in 2016. The most rapidly growing age group is the 65 and older age group, which increased 107.6 percent. The 15 to 29 years old age group increased by 12.1 percent, and the 30 to 64 years old age group increased by 10.6 percent.

Last, we observe that the majority of jobs within the sport sector in 2016 required moderate qualifications; 48 percent of them were upper-secondary and postsecondary nontertiary education jobs, jobs of levels 3 and 4 from the 2011 ISCED classification. In comparison, jobs from levels 5 to 8 represented only 35 percent of jobs. But the global trend has been toward an upgrade in terms of qualification since 2011. Specifically, while the number of workers from levels 0 to 2 decreased by 5.4 percent between 2011 and 2016, the number of workers with qualifications from levels 5 to 8 increased by 37.2 percent (table 5.3).

Trade in Sporting Goods

Using the COMEXT data published by Eurostat, it is possible to assess the value of the sporting goods trade in Europe (imports and exports) within and outside the EU. Within this database, sporting goods are identified according to the Harmonized System classification and then gathered according to sport disciplines. The following categories can be found: skis and associated materials; skates; boats and nautical sport materials; golf materials; racquet sport materials; balls; gymnastics, athletics,

Table 5.2   Part of Western Europe in European Employment in Sport

	2011	2012	2013	2014	2015	2016
Part of Western Europe (%)	88	88	87	86	86	86

Based on data from Eurostat (2017).

Table 5.3   Employment in Western Europe (2015)

Sociodemographic characteristics		Number of persons employed in sport (thousands)	Distribution of persons employed (%)	Evolution 2011-2016 (%)
Gender	Women	730.5	45.9	18.6
	Men	860.8	54.1	6.1
Age group	15-29	611.1	38.5	12.1
	30-64	928.7	58.5	10.6
	65+	48.3	3.0	107.3
Education level (ISCED)	0-2	269.7	17.0	–5.4
	3-4	760.6	48.0	6.1
	5-8	554.8	35.0	37.2

Based on data from Eurostat (2017).

and swimming materials; fishing materials; bikes; parachutes; sport clothes; sport shoes; and sport and hunting guns.

In 2017, 87.2 percent of European imports and 87 percent of exports were produced by Western European countries. Imports from these countries increased by 18.3 percent between 2006 and 2015, while exports increased by 29.2 percent over the same period. These trends strongly contributed to the reduction of the trade balance deficit, which fell by 70 percent between 2006 and 2017. But all countries from Western Europe (see figure 5.3) do not present the same situation of deficit; Italy, the Netherlands, Belgium, Portugal, and Finland present trade surpluses.

Three countries can be considered the biggest contributors in terms of imports: Germany, the United Kingdom, and France. In 2016 they represented 20 percent, 14.8 percent, and 13.6 percent of sport goods, respectively. This result is not surprising because these are the richest countries in Europe, having the largest GDPs in 2016 (OECD, 2016). As for exports, Germany remains the strongest European contributor, followed this time by Italy and the Netherlands. In 2015 they represented 18 percent, 17.5 percent, and 15.8 percent of exports, respectively, from Western Europe.

Private Expenditure on Sporting Goods and Services

To get an idea of household sport consumption in Western Europe, the Eurostat data, particularly the 2010 Household Budget Survey, focusing on household expenditures on sport goods and services, can be used. This study includes the 28 EU countries and provides information regarding five **categories of sport goods and services expenditure**: (1) recreational and sporting services; (2) major durables for outdoor recreation; (3) equipment for sport, camping, and open-air recreation; (4) maintenance and repair of other major durables for recreation and culture; and (5) major durables for indoor recreation.

The overall value of household expenditures is estimated at €52,078,000 (about US$70,000,000) (Purchasing Power Standard), representing 1.2 percent of their overall expenditures. This value also constitutes 75 percent of the overall expenditures in the sport sector in Europe, and it represents 61 percent of overall expenditures. In that sense, in Western Europe the consumption of sporting goods and services takes a bigger place in household budgets and expenses in comparison with countries from Eastern Europe (i.e., 0.6 percent of their overall expenditures) (see figure 5.4).

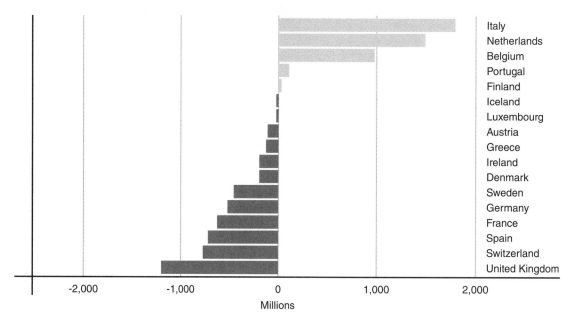

Figure 5.3 Trade balance of Western European countries.
Based on data from Eurostat (2017).

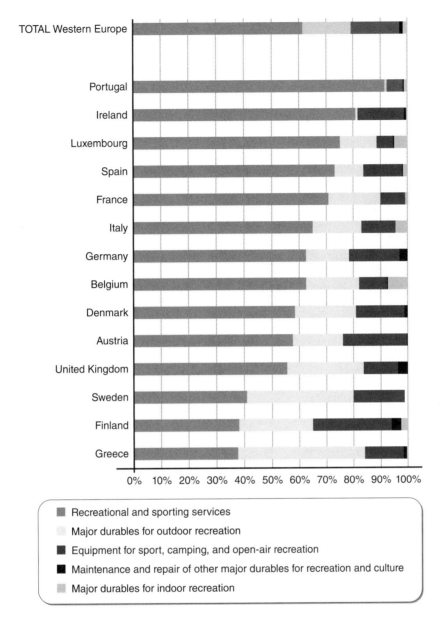

Figure 5.4 Distribution of household sport expenditure in Western Europe by country and category.
Based on data from Eurostat (2017).

Management of Sport

As indicated in the previous section, Governance of Sport, the state and public authorities have a significant role in the traditional sport system in Western Europe through the funding and management of elite sport and the funding of recreational participation.

Keep in mind, however, that the direct management of sport is related to where and when participation is executed within a sport structure, as well as the nature of the structure. Most sport participation is individual and self-organized. The management role here of the state and the public authorities mainly deals with offering public spaces, sport venues, and facilities to the public.

For those who participate within a sport organization, about 25 percent go to commercial places and about 15 percent join not-for-profit clubs. Commercial organizations (e.g., health and fitness clubs, golf clubs, five-a-side football organizations, indoor climbing structures, and so on) are privately owned and structured (e.g., independent or franchised). The following sections provide further information about the places of participation and memberships.

Places of Sport and Physical Activity Participation

Among sport participants in Western Europe, the favored places (see table 5.4) tend to be parks or outdoors and the home, although fitness centers and sport clubs are also preferred places for participation.

This table shows some notable differences for participation preferences between the countries of Western Europe and those of the EU. Participants in Western Europe favor parks and outdoors (+11 points), not-for-profit sport clubs (+8 points), and health and fitness centers (+8 points). For the other

EU countries, the privileged place of participation is at home (+13 points of difference). The other places do not present remarkable differences.

Beyond the classic north–south division observed earlier, there are important differences and specificities, and the at-home category is the most discriminant. In Germany (+13 points gap) and in Sweden (+13 points), at home is the privileged place of participation for almost half the population (46 percent). In contrast, at-home participation concerns a little more than 1 person out of 10 in Italy (13 percent, –20 points), in Spain (14 percent, –19 points), and in Portugal (14 percent, –19 points). Part of this difference can be explained by geography and, consequently, climate characteristics, the latter countries being sunnier and warmer overall. Health and fitness centers are used by numerous Swedish participants (40 percent, +23 points), whereas they are not much attended by French participants (5 percent, –12 points). One possible

Table 5.4 Places of Sport and Physical Activity Participation in Western Europe (row percentages, n = 12,283)

	At home	Parks or outdoors	On the way	Fitness center	Sport club	At work	Sport center	School or university	Elsewhere	DK
Sweden	46	55	38	40	12	16	6	6	3	1
Germany	46	42	27	16	21	15	5	4	2	2
Finland	43	72	47	27	7	15	12	5	5	1
Austria	43	54	30	19	12	10	5	5	9	1
United Kingdom	40	38	22	21	11	18	9	4	6	4
Denmark	39	50	29	26	22	18	7	7	3	3
Belgium	38	32	29	11	17	13	9	6	5	4
Netherlands	35	37	29	18	23	13	10	6	5	2
Luxembourg	35	36	11	14	16	11	9	7	4	3
Greece	31	33	41	20	8	10	5	3	4	0
France	27	42	16	5	17	16	7	5	5	4
Ireland	27	44	14	16	18	7	7	5	6	2
Portugal	14	44	25	17	7	5	3	4	5	2
Spain	14	51	31	19	9	6	11	2	4	1
Italy	13	36	23	15	7	4	19	4	5	2
Western Europe (15 countries)	33	42	25	17	14	13	9	4	4	3
Others (13 countries)	46	31	26	9	6	11	5	6	3	7

Based on data from European Commission (2014).

explanation is that the French sporting culture is strongly associated with not-for-profit clubs and public funding, and they are more reluctant to join commercial organizations. On-the-way is the participation place for more than 2 people out of 5 in Finland (47 percent, +22 points) and Greece (41 percent, +16 points), although on-the-way participation concerns only 1 person out of 10 in Luxembourg (11 percent, –14 points). Last, it can be observed that about three-quarters of Finnish participants (72 percent, +30 points) take part in sport and physical activities in parks and outdoors, indicating a strong cultural orientation toward natural environments.

Membership

In Western Europe, affiliation with a club (see table 5.5) concerns about 30 percent of the population. Sport clubs (14 percent) and health and fitness clubs (12 percent) recruit the most. Sociocultural clubs (3 percent) and other types of clubs (1 percent) represent marginal shares of participants.

The Western Europe population is significantly more involved (+15 point gap) in sport club and health and fitness center participation compared with other EU countries, made up of a +9 point difference for sport clubs and a +6 point difference for health and fitness centers. Important differences are also evident among Western European countries. Northern European countries demonstrate the highest rates of club affiliations, and Southern European countries show less developed not-for-profit club networks.

With a ratio of four individuals out of five who are not members of a sport organization, we find without surprise the countries of Portugal (88 percent, +18 point gap) and Greece (83 percent, +13 point gap). In the northern part of Western Europe, less than half of the population from Sweden (47 percent, –24 points) and Denmark (47 percent, –23 points), a little more than half of the population in the Netherlands (54 percent, –17 points), and three out of five persons in Germany (60 percent,

Table 5.5 Rates of Membership in Sport Organizations in Western Europe (row percentages, n = 15,689)

	Not a member	Health or fitness center	Sport club	Sociocultural club	Other	DK	Total
Portugal	88	6	4	2	0	0	100
Greece	83	11	5	1	1	0	100
Italy	80	6	7	3	2	2	100
Spain	79	10	7	3	1	1	100
France	74	4	16	4	1	2	100
Finland	70	13	12	7	1	0	100
Austria	70	16	13	3	2	0	100
United Kingdom	69	18	11	2	2	2	100
Belgium	68	11	16	5	2	2	100
Ireland	65	15	19	4	2	0	100
Luxembourg	65	13	21	5	2	0	100
Germany	60	14	24	4	0	1	100
Netherlands	54	19	27	3	3	0	100
Denmark	47	25	25	9	1	1	100
Sweden	47	33	22	8	2	0	100
Western Europe (15 countries)	70	12	14	3	1	2	100
Others (13 countries)	85	6	5	2	1	2	100

Based on data from Eurostat (2017).

–13 points) participate outside sport organizations. When looking at the extremes, the proportion of people participating in sport organizations is 4.3 times higher in Sweden than in Portugal.

Other national differences can also be observed. For instance, note a stronger role of health and fitness centers in Sweden (33 percent, +21 point gap) and Denmark (25 percent, +13 points). In the same vein, the Netherlands (27 percent, +13 points) and Germany (24 percent, +12 points) demonstrate a stronger role of not-for-profit clubs in comparison with other countries of Western Europe. Overall, sport participation and place clearly differ among the countries of Western Europe.

Major Sport Events

In terms of regular events, men's football results from England, Spain, Italy, Germany, and France are regularly broadcast and dominate media discourse. Annual regular tennis tournaments such as Roland Garros, Wimbledon, Rolex-Monte Carlo Masters, and Mutua Madrid Open have national and international coverage. Further, cycling races such as the Tour de France, the Tours of Italy and Spain, and the most prestigious one-day races, called *classiques*, organized in France, Italy, Belgium, and the Netherlands (e.g., Milan–San Remo; the Tour of Flanders, Paris–Roubaix, Liege–Bastogne–Liege, and the Tour of Lombardy) are followed in many countries.

Some of the most prestigious and attractive events in this region include the Champions League and the Europa League in football, the EuroLeague of basketball, the EHF Champions League in handball, and the European Rugby Champions Cup. The following category deals with regular but infrequent European competitions that are generally organized every two or four years depending on the sport (e.g., every four years in football, every two years for the European Athletics Championships) and hosted in various European countries following a bid process similar to the Olympics. An exception is the Six Nations Championship, the top European national competition in rugby, which happens every year. The final type is international events such as world cups, championships, and the Olympic Games, which are organized in Western European countries on an irregular basis.

Considering the diversity of sport interests within Western Europe (see later sections), the countries' wealth, the quantity and quality of sport infrastructures (e.g., stadia, indoor arenas, swimming pools, and so on), and the proximity between locations and sites, these events are quite regularly hosted in Western Europe, even if they have different audiences and impacts. For instance, the World Men's Handball Championship in France, World Women's Handball Championship in Germany, IAAF World Championships in London, UCI Road World Championships (road cycling) in Bergen (Norway), IIHF World Championships (ice hockey) in both Koln (Germany) and Paris, and World Figure Skating Championships in Helsinki (Finland) were hosted in 2017.

The analysis of participation in live sport events has multiple dimensions. One approach consists of looking at live attendance, whereas another consists of looking at mediated attendance, particularly through television (TV) broadcasting. The distinction is important to have in mind because the significance of sports and sporting events may vary according to the approach used. Several types of data can be used to identify the most popular sports and events to attend and watch. Eurostat data are useful in that regard, especially because they allow analyzing these figures according to gender, age, and education level.

Overall, we observe that viewership of live sport events concerns a large part of the population of Western Europe. Despite the lack of data, we can say that in 2011 about 44 percent of Western Europe inhabitants had taken part in a live sport event at least once during the previous year and about 15 percent attended more than six sport events over the same period. Behind these global figures, however, huge differences are evident among countries. Data from figure 5.5 show that inhabitants from Southern European countries participate less often in live sport events. At the extremes, we find that 72 percent of the population of Greece never attended sport events, compared with a rate of 46 percent for Luxembourg.

The popularity of sport can also be evaluated through media diffusion and television broadcasting in particular. Because no comparative data are available, identifying the sports most broadcast in

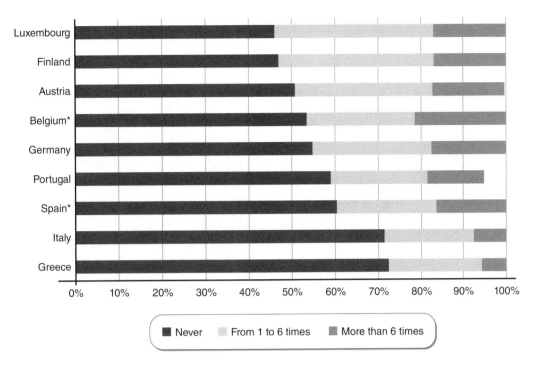

Figure 5.5 Live sport events attendance (over a 12-month period) in Western Europe per countries and per frequency (2011, persons aged 25 to 64).

Based on data from Eurostat (2017).

Western Europe is difficult. Nevertheless, a focus on the case of France is interesting.

First, the evolution of TV broadcast in Europe in general and in France in particular has significantly influenced the diffusion and consequently the watching of live sport events. In 1995 the French Audio-Visual Superior Council (CSA) counted 7 channels broadcasting sport (3 with pay per view). In 2016 the number was 35, with 22 pay-per-view channels, which belonged to 16 media groups. Between 2000 and 2016 the volume of TV sport programs increased by a multiple of four, rising from 50,846 to 211,677 hours. This rise is essentially due to the increase of media groups and channels, especially the number of pay-per-view channels (95 percent of broadcast hours), in response to increasing demand from spectators.

In France the six sports that are most often broadcast on free-to-air channels are football, cycling, tennis, rugby, basketball, and motorsports. These sports represent more than half of TV sport event programs, and 10 sports represent about 85 percent of the sport event programs, indicating a strong concentration of the market around a small number of sports. If the popularity of football, tennis, and motorsports remains high, their relative share tends to decrease on free-to-air channels, whereas rugby and cycling have increased their share since 2012, and basketball has increased its share since 2010. But this structure change in sport event TV programs has to be linked with the increasing number of sports broadcast, and after a reduction between 1994 and 2010, the offers have been strongly diversified since 2010 as demonstrated in figure 5.6.

Between 2012 and 2014 in France, the number of sports (excluding the Olympics) broadcast on free-to-air channels increased by 58 percent, from 24 to 38 sports. This significant increase is notably due to the arrival of a new channel (L'Equipe 21) that broadcast 15 sports that were not offered on

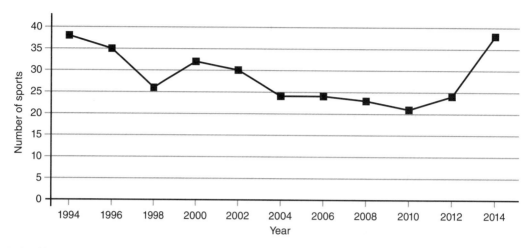

Figure 5.6   Number of sports broadcast on free-to-air channels in France.

other free-to-air channels. Besides the analysis of volumes and number of sports, audience scores and rankings are interesting. First, note that since 1995, all TV programs that gathered more than 11 million spectators in France are sport programs. Second, although women's sports broadcasting is significantly lower that men's, major women's sport events are receiving more and more interest and consequently bigger audiences. A prime example is the Women's Football World Cup; the France–Germany game gathered 4.1 million spectators in France. The France–South Korea (2.8 million), France–USA (2.3 million), and Mexico–France (2.2 million) games from the same competition gathered several million spectators each, which are noticeable figures for a country of 66 million inhabitants and are among the top 10 audiences of free-to-air channels, when the traditional five channels are excluded. Even minor sports that are rarely broadcast can attract huge audiences during major sport events, and we may wonder whether there is a causal link between the two (i.e., scarcity creating interest when finally broadcast) or whether TV channels are missing huge opportunities when they broadcast only major events.

Sport Participation

The 2013 Eurobarometer (*Eurobaromètre 412*) (European Commission, 2014) provides important information about sport and physical activity participation. It is produced by Eurostat, EU's statistical service, and it follows previous editions from 2002

Learning Activity

In your own country, identify the top five sport activities that have the highest participation rates, that broadcast events the most often (total hours per year), and that attract the biggest audiences. Explain these results and compare them with the case of France.

and 2009. The existence of such a tool and the regularity of its use demonstrate how the sport sector in general and sport participation in particular are of importance for the EU. This Eurobarometer relies on a standardized questionnaire translated into the various languages of EU country members and a sample of 1,000 respondents in each country. The population at stake comprises individuals aged 15 years old and above from the 28 member states. The overall sample comprises 27,919 respondents.

According to our definition, Western Europe comprises northern and southern countries: Finland, Sweden, Denmark, the Netherlands, Germany, the United Kingdom, Ireland, Belgium, Luxembourg, Austria, France, Italy, Spain, Portugal, and Greece. With the exception of very small countries in terms of population such as Malta and Cyprus, the remaining 13 countries (out of 28) correspond to countries from the former Eastern bloc: Estonia, Latvia, Lithuania, Poland, Czech Republic, Slovakia, Hungary, Romania, Slovenia, Croatia, and Bulgaria.

Sport and Physical Activities: Five Pillars and National Specificities

Table 5.6 presents the 10 sports with the highest participation rates in France (Lefèvre & Thiéry, 2010), Spain (Estadística, 2015), Switzerland (Lamprecht, Fischer, & Stamm, 2014), and England (Department for Culture, Media and Sport, 2011). Although informative, these results should be taken with caution because some sports have different names and are not grouped in the same ways. But the results are quite stable. For instance, the rankings remained the same in Switzerland between 2008 and 2014 and in France between 2000 and 2010.

Walking, swimming, cycling, keeping fit, and running represent the five **traditional pillars of sport participation in Western Europe**. Geography and natural resources, equipment, and cultural aspects explain some of the variance in sport participation among countries in Western Europe.

Sporting activities are defined here according to four dimensions: frequency of participation, place of participation, membership in a sport club, and the motives behind sport participation. In the following analyses, estimates for each country are produced using the country-specific weighting proposed by Eurostat. These estimates of the differences between each country and the overall Western Europe population require using a weighting for this population that respects the demographic share of each country. This calculation is needed because, for example, the over-15-years-old population in Germany is 148 times bigger than the one from Luxembourg. Only the biggest differences are interpreted in the following sections.

Frequency of Participation

The sport and physical activity definition used in the Eurobarometer questionnaires is quite restrictive (oriented toward sport, without a broad temporal reference, and subjective), but its advantage is that it strongly differentiates individuals. To ease

Table 5.6   Top 10 Activities With the Highest Participation Rates (Over a 12-Month Period) for France, Spain, Switzerland, and England

Rank	France (2010)	Spain (2014)	Switzerland (2014)	England (2010-2011)
1	Walking	Cycling	Hiking	Walking
2	Swimming (leisure)	Swimming	Cycling	Swimming or diving (indoors)
3	Cycling (leisure)	Walking, hiking	Swimming	Health, fitness, gym, or conditioning activities
4	Gym and well-being activities	Running	Skiing	Cycling (health, recreation, training, competition)
5	Running	Gym and well-being activities	Running	Swimming or diving (outdoors)
6	Winter sports	Football	Fitness, aerobic	Snooker, pool, billiards (excluding bar billiards)
7	Hiking, mountaineering	Body toning, bodybuilding	Gymnastics	Tenpin bowling
8	Bowls	Padel	Football	Football
9	Football	Tennis	Dancing (with jazz dance)	Jogging, cross-country, road running
10	Body toning, bodybuilding	Basketball	Walking, Nordic walking	Keepfit, aerobics, dance exercise (including exercise bike)

Samples: Residents 15 years old and older except for Switzerland (15-74 years old) and England (16 years old and older)

Reading: In Spain the fourth activity in terms of participant numbers for the last 12 months is running.

the interpretations, frequencies are gathered for four categories: DK (don't know), never, sometimes (less than once a week), and regularly (at least once a week).

In Western Europe (see table 5.7), nonparticipation concerns two persons out of five (39 percent), occasional participation is evaluated at 16 percent, and regular participation concerns more than two persons out of five (44 percent at least once a week). People from Western Europe participate more than people from Eastern Europe do. Nonparticipation rates differ by 12 points, and the gap for weekly participation is larger at 15 points.

Beyond the overall figures, important differences can be observed between countries from Western Europe. Specifically, populations from northern Western Europe participate the most, whereas in certain southern Western European countries, more than half of the population does not participate in sport and physical activity. These differences in terms of participation are the consequence of numerous factors such as cultural differences,

> ## Learning Activity
>
> Conduct a web search and compare the rates of sport participation in your country with those in Western Europe.

general and sport-specific cultures, political history (for instance, social democratic or conservative political regimes), and democratic systems, in terms of economy and religion (for instance, Protestant versus Catholic countries).

Countries in general, and European countries in particular, are rarely culturally uniform and homogenous, and this characteristic has a strong influence on sport participation and consumption. The complexity is also present at the level of participants who increasingly participate in multiple sports and activities (Bodet, 2009). This multiple practice pattern is called **omnivorism** (Lefèvre & Ohl, 2012). In this case, sport participations

Table 5.7   Frequency of Sport Participation in Western European Countries (row percentages, n = 15,689 for Western European countries)

	DK	Never	Sometimes	Regularly	Total
Sweden	0	9	21	69	100
Denmark	0	14	18	68	100
Finland	1	15	19	66	100
Netherlands	0	29	13	58	100
Luxembourg	0	29	17	54	100
Ireland	0	34	14	52	100
Germany	0	29	23	48	100
Belgium	0	31	21	47	100
United Kingdom	0	35	19	46	100
Spain	0	44	10	46	100
Austria	0	27	28	45	100
France	0	42	15	43	100
Greece	0	59	10	31	100
Italy	0	59	10	30	100
Portugal	0	64	8	29	100
West (15 countries)	0	39	16	44	100
Others (13 countries)	1	51	20	29	100

Reading: 69 percent of Swedish people claim to participate regularly in sport (at least once a week).

Based on data from Eurostat (2017).

Learning Activity

In your own country, what are the regional differences in terms of types and rates of physical activity and sport participation? Which factors and variables can explain these differences? What is their nature (e.g., geographical, historical, cultural, economic, and so on)?

should not be considered independently, but combined, which is the case of the portfolio approach that focuses on the number of sports and physical activities performed (Sullivan & Katz-Gerro, 2007) and their types (Lefèvre & Ohl, 2012). Last, sport participation and consumption are also strongly influenced by individual and sociological characteristics such as age, gender, social position, and place of residence. These variables should also be considered when comparing countries and cultural groups such as Scheerder & Vos (2011) did for Belgium and Llopis-Goig et al. (2017) did for France and Spain.

Summary

One definition of Western Europe is the region that corresponds to the Cold War's Western bloc, most of which are part of the European Union.

Sport is a focus of European Union's policies. Nevertheless, although these countries belong to the same political entity, and common European Union tools have been developed, comparing countries in relation to the diverse issues of sport consumption is a difficult exercise because of the lack of uniformity in the objectives and methods used. In addition, despite communalities in terms of sport funding structure, employment rates in sport, and economic importance, national differences are significant in terms of viewership of live sport events and participation in sport and physical activity. For instance, walking, swimming, cycling, keeping fit, and running represent the five traditional pillars of sport participation in Western Europe, but the popularity of certain sports is observed only in certain countries. In the same vein, sport participation frequencies vary strongly according to country, and the Northern European ones show higher rates than their Southern European counterparts. This north–south division is observed in relation to many sport issues and sport structures in this area. Consequently, if Western Europe is compared with other regions of the world in regard to sport issues, the reader should keep in mind the heterogeneity of these countries and their cultures, which have significant influence on the way that sport is defined and consumed.

? Review Questions

1. Why does sport represent a key component of European Union policy?
2. What are the definitions of sport, and what are the implications for sport policy and governance?
3. Who are the main funders of sport in Western Europe?
4. What are the most popular sports in Western Europe? Are there differences between viewership of live sport events and participation in sport and physical activity?
5. For Europe in general and Western Europe in particular, what are the limitations in analyzing sport at the country level?

Sport in Eastern Europe

Peter Smolianov, PhD
Salem State University

Chapter Objectives

After studying this chapter, you will be able to do the following:

- Define Eastern Europe geographically and demographically in relation to sport management.
- Outline the regions' common approaches to the role of sport in society and to sport governance, management, and economics.
- Describe scientific methods in developing and supporting participants and coaches in Eastern Europe.
- Depict the structures of sport clubs and societies, and sport schools and universities.
- Discuss the challenges of developing and enforcing policies particularly aimed at fighting corruption and doping in Eastern Europe.

Key Terms	
GTO	long-term athlete development (LTAD)
sport societies	sport schools
Spartakiads	sport universities

1. Slovenia
2. Czech Republic
3. Moldova
4. Bosnia and Herzegovina
5. Montenegro
6. Albania
7. Croatia
8. Macedonia

Key Events

1947—beginning of the Cold War. An ideological, economic, and sports battle over what system was better: USA-style capitalism or USSR-style socialism. Participating in the Olympic Games from 1952 to 1992, the USSR, or later the Unified Team, was the most successful country during the Cold War, leading other Eastern European nations.

1980—Summer Olympic Games, Moscow, USSR. The first Olympics staged in Eastern Europe, boycotted by the United States and its political allies to protest the Soviet invasion of Afghanistan, prompting the Soviet-led boycott of the 1984 Summer Olympics in Los Angeles.

1984—Winter Olympic Games, Sarajevo, Yugoslavia. The first Winter Olympics staged in Eastern Europe during the sport development peak in the country, where factories were owned by workers, living standards were high, and citizens were free to travel and work abroad, followed in the 1990s by increased freedom, breakup of the country, violent nationalism, and war.

1986—USSR leader Mikhail Gorbachev. Launched a policy of glasnost (openness) and perestroika (economic restructuring), and urged increased political and economic freedoms across Eastern Europe, leading to the breakup of the USSR in 1991 and other Eastern European countries, the deterioration of living and sport conditions for most citizens, and the departure of many athletes and sport specialists for better conditions in the West in the 1990s.

2000—Russia elected President Vladimir Putin. Curtailed democracy and revived the country as economic, political, military, and sport power, threatening the United States' global domination, particularly through growing cooperation with China in key industries including sport.

2014—Winter Olympic Games, Sochi, Russia. The most expensive Olympics in history, which converted the region into a year-round sea and alpine resort with new venues, roads, railroads, airports, power plants, and other infrastructure utilizing technologies for environment protection.

Key People

Lev Matveev, Soviet and Russian sport scientist, who developed the theory of periodization used as a foundation of sport training across the world.

Tudor Bompa, Romanian sport scientist who advanced and popularized the theory of training periodization in the English-speaking world.

Vladimir Platonov, Soviet and Ukrainian sport scientist who integrated multiple sciences into a system of preparation to competitions used internationally.

Ivan Abadjiev, Bulgarian national weightlifting coach who used the USSR training principles to develop a training system used across the globe.

Roman Abramovich, Russian businessman and the first oligarch in English football who bought the poorly performing Chelsea FC on the brink of financial collapse and made it a dominant team in European football and a global brand, setting a best-practice standard for club owners around the world.

Mikhail Prokhorov, Russian businessman who bought the Moscow CSKA basketball team and turned it into one of the best in Europe and bought the NBA New Jersey, later Brooklyn, Nets, being the first person from overseas to acquire such a deep stake in a major American sport team.

This chapter examines the evolution and contemporary state of sport systems in Eastern Europe, focusing on the valuable practices as well as on problematic issues of sport in Eastern Europe, particularly corruption and doping. Eastern bloc countries pioneered sophisticated fitness and sport concepts used around the world, such as multisport national clubs and healthy mass festivals from Czech lands; low-cost recreational facilities for maximum social inclusion and efficient elite athlete development in East Germany; training and periodization methods developed in Bulgaria, Romania, and Russia; and healthy long-term athlete development from Hungary. Russia has been the epicenter of both great and ugly phenomena of Eastern European sport development before, during, and after the USSR—from the world's most advanced guidelines for lifelong fitness of all citizens and individualized parametric training for high performers to artificial performance enhancement schemes and devices, resulting in dramatic scandals and disqualifications. Indicative cases are used in this chapter to exemplify positive and negative sides of sport in Eastern Europe.

Geographical Description, Demographics, and Background

Eastern and Western Europe can be separated in many ways geographically, culturally, and politically, and Eastern Europe can likewise be defined in many ways. Because rapid sport development in the second part of the 20th century was closely connected with the Cold War, for the purpose of historical analysis we separate Europe into former Western and Eastern political blocs based on the capitalist NATO and socialist Warsaw Pact alliances, which had significant influence on the ways in which countries' sport systems have grown. The term *Eastern bloc* is used here to refer to the former states in Central and Eastern Europe that were under the direct influence of the former Union of Soviet Socialist Republics (USSR). Being close neighbors, many of these nations shared Slavic language and cultural traditions and were connected through knowledge of Russian language, which was taught at schools of Warsaw Pact countries and in other states that used to be satellites of the USSR.

The Warsaw Pact countries included Albania, Bulgaria, the former Czechoslovakia (current Czech Republic and Slovakia), the former German Democratic Republic (East Germany), Hungary, Poland, Romania, and the former USSR itself. This bloc also initially included the former Yugoslavia (current Bosnia-Herzegovina, Croatia, Kosovo [partially recognized], Macedonia, Montenegro, Serbia, and Slovenia), which should also be considered part of Eastern Europe. Besides the geographic and Slavic connections, Yugoslavia's socialist orientation and close political ties with the USSR and Eastern bloc for most of the Cold War period allowed its sport system to borrow many fundamental Eastern European practices and structures, just as other former USSR friends did, including China and Cuba.

The 15 republics that were part of the USSR and now are independent countries include, in Eastern Europe, Belarus, Estonia, Latvia, Lithuania, Moldova, and Ukraine; in Central Asia, Armenia, Azerbaijan, Georgia, Kazakhstan, Kyrgyzstan, Tajikistan, Turkmenistan, and Uzbekistan; and Russia, the largest country in the world by area, stretching from the Atlantic Ocean to the Pacific Ocean and occupying a substantial part of continental Europe and the entire northern portion of Asia.

Despite the disintegration of the USSR and the transformation of Eastern bloc socialist countries during the 1990s into independent states and their assimilation into global free-market capitalism, these nations retained many distinct elements of their former elaborate Soviet-style sport systems. These systems were designed to provide high-performance sport with sufficient public resources for stress-free progression of predisposed participants to any desired level of competition and with support from mass fitness and recreation programs at childcare, schools, colleges, universities, and places of work, all of which contributed to international success as well as national health, productivity, and military readiness. The sport systems were also designed to build partnerships between multisport clubs and medical and academic education programs that provided conditions for well-rounded long-term athlete development; to nurture athletes into competent coaches, physical educators, and other sport specialists who progressed through specialized sport schools and universities; and to coordinate teams of medical, pedagogical, and exercise scientists who provided training and fitness methodologies for all with a dual goal of national wellness and performance.

Role of Sport

The philosophical and organizational principles inherited by present-day Eastern Europe from the former monarchies of the region and the Eastern bloc led by the Soviet Union continue to guide comprehensive governmental leadership of scientific, educational, and medical support aimed at maximizing mass fitness and elite sport performance. The mechanisms provide lifelong paths in sport from grassroots to professional careers and ensure expertise of all involved with sport, including uniform education; ranks and rewards for participants, coaches, and referees; a pyramidal structure of sport clubs, schools, and universities; and unified plans of amateur and professional competitions. Sport governing organizations in this centralized, integrated, and increasingly democratic system carry difficult responsibilities for equitable spending of state money, ethical achievement of ambitious goals, and enforcement of rules and control over doping and corruption.

Coaches run this sport system because they are employed by the state and rewarded according to achievements of participants. According to the East European notion of sport as preventative medicine, the coaches assume the roles of holistic physicians as well as spiritual leaders, being well educated in biomedical and pedagogical sciences. Coaches receive help from medical doctors and scientists to nurture participants through long-term development process, directing each participant to the sport appropriate for individual health conditions.

Mass fitness, health, fun, and artistic expression had been priorities of sport traditions in Eastern Europe. Competitive festive sport participation by one-third of the USSR population contributed to peaceful socioeconomic progress by means of balancing the stress from work with rich sport, arts, and cultural recreation. In an attempt to introduce more democracy, the government liberated the country's political and economic systems by setting the republics free in 1991 and privatizing public assets, which, regretfully, resulted in the shift of wealth to the elite, a decline in life standards for the majority, and wars among the disintegrated republics, which claimed over 100,000 dead and

wounded and over 3 million displaced from their homes.

Preoccupied with a market economy in 1991 through 1999, the government was largely concerned with making sport profitable. As a result Russian sport lost much of its public funding, which caused deterioration in mass participation and in the number of qualified coaches, managers, and scientists. Russian youth were found to be 20 percent less fit in the 1990s than they were in the 1970s, and the country's elite sport performance deteriorated. The capitalist reforms of the 1990s brought a long period of stress and reduced affordable sport and recreation services, which led to an increase in the number of cases of depression, smoking, alcoholism, drug addiction, suicide, antisocial behavior, and crime (Igoshev & Apletin, 2014).

Reforming their economies and political structures, dealing with border issues, and fighting wars, many of the former Soviet republics and Eastern bloc member countries initially reduced their emphasis on sport. In the two decades after 1990, the interaction of sport and society changed dramatically in Eastern Europe as the Soviet bloc dissolved and public resources devoted to mass sport decreased. Following the 1989-1990 political and economic transition, Hungarian sport, like other Eastern European sport systems, had to adapt to new economic and legal circumstances of capitalism, particularly in how sport was financed (Gál, 2012). Bulgaria also found that the transition from a planned to a free-market economy led to a withdrawal of many subsidies and services to sport. At a time when their real incomes were dropping, people could ill afford to pay for sport participation. "Sport for all" changed from a way of life to a matter of choice (Girginov & Bankov, 2002). Similarly, in Romania, after decades of nearly free sport and recreation services and increasing choices of facilities and programs accompanied by noisy propaganda and aggressive ways to encourage sport participation, people found it difficult to devote time and money to sporting recreation, which is now far from a way of life (Suciu et al., 2002). These post-1990 changes had a somewhat negative effect on mass participation and elite sport performance in the former socialist countries.

In the 21st century, the Russian government started to restore political and economic stability, and the quality of life increased because of higher investments in education, health care, and sport. Russia was second in the medal tallies at the 2010 Youth Olympic Games and at the 2011 World Summer Universiade. The Russian Paralympic team moved from 11th place in 2004 to 8th in the 2008 Summer Games, and in the Winter Paralympics the Russian athletes moved from the 5th in 1994 and 1998, to 4th in 2002, and to 1st in 2006 and 2010. Under President Putin's leadership, the mass fitness and international sport programs started to regain their importance after the year 2000. Sport development has been particularly emphasized since 2007 when the Russian city of Sochi won the bid to host the 2014 Winter Olympics. In 2008 the Russian Sport Ministry was reestablished with a higher status and broader responsibilities, employing 220 administrative staff in the head office and 310,974 coaches and other sport specialists across the country. Physical education was increased from two to three times a week with a revitalized **GTO** (Ready for Labor and Defense) fitness program in all Russian schools. The Sport Ministry has committed to reach the following goals by 2020:

- Have 40 percent of the overall population, 20 percent of disabled individuals, and 80 percent of students participating in sport.
- Attract everyone to exercise three to four times or 6 to 12 hours a week.
- Ensure that 45 percent of all organizations have sport clubs.
- Employ 360,000 qualified public coaches and other sport professionals.
- Place within the top three in all future Olympics and Paralympics by total medal count.

The goals of winning in the 2014 Sochi Olympic Games and increasing the number of regular sport participants in Russia from 25 million in 2011 to 43 million in 2015 were achieved, and a long-term goal was set to increase sport participation to 70 percent, or 100 million (Sport Ministry, 2012, 2017). The increased investment in sport showed its first positive effects on national health; in 2009 through 2011, for the first time since the capitalist reforms started, the number of Russians diagnosed with alcoholism and drug addiction decreased (Inchenko, 2014).

Learning Activity

Discuss the cultural and political issues that a Western sport manager should keep in mind when working with Eastern European counterparts. Consider the achievements as well as socioeconomic problems experienced in the region.

Governance of Sport

From 2007, all sport-related organizations and activities in Russia have been guided by the federal law on physical culture and sport, which is based on the following principles:

- Free access to sport for physical, intellectual, and moral development of everyone, and consecutive connection in physical education across ages
- Unified nationwide legislation, combining top-down state or public and bottom-up organizational regulations in compliance with international agreements
- State or government guarantees of sport-related rights to citizens, prohibition of discrimination and violence, assistance to persons with disabilities and other groups requiring special social protection, and provision for safety of participants and spectators
- Interaction between federal or national and local governments in the field of sport and between sport authorities and federations, and development of all types and components of sport as a social and educational voluntary activity

Similar laws are being enacted across countries of Eastern Europe, reflecting the region's sport traditions of mass lifelong fun participation for health and communal harmony.

Eastern European sport scientists have been developing policies for guiding and regulating lifelong participation of all in fitness and sport. Everyone is encouraged to pass the GTO fitness tests from 1931 in Russia. Compared with fitness programs across the world, the unique options of GTO include minimal cost to participants, a fitness knowledge test, recommendations for all ages, and a variety of sports to be tested on (Keating, Smolianov, Liu, Castro-Piñero, & Smith, 2018). The GTO webpage offers high-quality videos with audio and text instructions supported by interactive instant messaging or texting and voice assistance by trained operators.

GTO test scores are used as a criterion for high school, college, and university graduation. In addition, GTO tests are part of fun festivals and competitions for everyone. In Moscow, for example, between 2011 and 2015 over 1.5 million residents attempted to pass GTO requirements, the number of people who regularly exercise increased to over 3 million, and 450,000 people were taking part in multisport community competitions for all ages and families every year (Vinogradov, 2016). The GTO Without Borders festival for people with a disability connected rehabilitation and Paralympic sport using resources of governments, nonprofit foundations, educational organizations, and medical organizations. GTO tests were adapted for Paralympic participant categories and integrated with wheelchair fencing, basketball, rugby, and Nordic walking as well as parapowerlifting and paraworkout.

Although GTO has been increasingly popular, commercial companies promote their expensive tests. The Cooper Institute for Aerobics Research (2013), based in the United States, signed an agreement with the Hungarian School Sport Federation to test all school-aged children in Hungary using FitnessGram, which is used in over 65,000 schools across the United States and in 20 international locations. FitnessGram requires a budget for equipment and for assessment software costing US$599 for the first year and US$149 for renewal (Keating et al., 2018).

After passing the GTO tests, participants are to progress through three junior, three senior, and four master ranks in 143 sports. Each rank requires specific results against such criteria as seconds or meters as well as victories in competitions at a certain level. This ranking system is designed to guide healthy **long-term athlete development (LTAD)**, to monitor performance, and to ensure a proper distribution of public resources. In the 21st century, LTAD guidelines focused on age-appropriate training have been implemented by national gov-

Learning Activity

Many Eastern European-style sport schools have been developed in Australia and Canada. Research one of these schools and discuss special accommodations and services provided to athletes.

erning bodies of most sports in Canada and other English-speaking countries such as Australia, New Zealand, the United Kingdom, and South Africa, and they started to be used in the United States in 2009 (USA Hockey, 2018). These guidelines, authored by Balyi (2001) from Hungary, stem from the USSR and Eastern European sport development approaches outlined by Riordan (1980) and Shneidman (1978). Modern theories of training, particularly periodization, pioneered by Matveev (1964, 2008) from Russia, were further developed and applied by Bompa (1983, 2009) from Romania, Platonov (1988, 2005) from Ukraine, and other sport scientists and coaches. But the integration of LTAD with mass fitness testing, emphasized by Matveev (2008), has not yet been fully applied in any country.

To support LTAD in Eastern Europe, governmental sport officials provide recommendations on most aspects of athlete development based on scientists' advice. The guidelines for coaches include such criteria as the minimum starting age for each sport and uniform training and educational curricula. Coaches regularly visit schools and invite sport-predisposed children to sport clubs. Another distinct sport management feature of Eastern Europe is that since the early 1970s, groups of scientists in pedagogy, medicine, psychology, physiology, biomechanics, biochemistry, and engineering have been consulting the national teams for improved athlete performance and health. In 2012 the Russian Sport Ministry supported the summer Olympic sports with 41 scientific groups, the winter sports with 15 groups, and Paralympic and other special-needs sport activities with 26 groups. In addition, it coordinated 98 sport conferences in 2011. In 2014 Moscow's Russian State University of Physical Education, Sport, Youth, and Tourism attracted over 900 participants from 17 countries to a congress, Nation's Health: A System of Lifelong PE as a Foundation of Public Health, which published two 600-page volumes of 370 presented research papers to advance systems of lifelong fitness, particularly GTO.

The public **sport schools** connecting mass and elite sport and supporting LTAD developed in 1950 through the 1970s across the USSR were emulated in Eastern Europe, China, and Cuba in the 20th century (Riordan, 1980; Smolianov & Zakus, 2008) and in the 21st century are spreading across the world to countries such as Australia, Belgium, Canada, Finland, Germany, Italy, the Netherlands, Singapore, Sweden, and the United Kingdom (BBC, 2004a, 2004b; Davies, 2008; Way, Repp, & Brennan, 2010; Wynhausen, 2007).

To ensure a continuation of athletes' careers, the national governments in Eastern Europe support and direct the education, certification, and rewards of sport personnel. Coaches enter special **sport universities** and progress after graduation through five certification stages. Many successful sport countries, particularly those from the former Eastern bloc, adopted Soviet-style sport education that included a government-funded network of sport universities. In Poland the University of PE in Warsaw enrolled 6,500 students in 2014 and employed 400 academic staff in 2013 to educate PE teachers, coaches, and specialists in physiotherapy, recreation, and tourism, and to serve as a center of sport science and training. Similar universities exist in the Polish cities of Cracow, Gdańsk, Katowice, Poznań, and Wrocław. Sport universities are also important for successful sport systems in most of Eastern Europe. The greatest variety of degrees, numbering 55, including sport management, are available at Russian State University of Physical

CASE STUDY

Corruption in Polish Football

Poland's former minister for sport was arrested in 2007 under suspicion of corruption, having allegedly accepted bribes when awarding building contracts for public sporting facilities to construction companies (Cafebabel, 2008). The corruption in Polish football has been exposed since 2001, when dealings between referees became publically known. The Polish Football Association was blamed for ignoring the problem, and some board members were themselves under suspicion. Twenty-nine clubs were caught up in the scandal, and 116 people were implicated (Cafebabel, 2008).

In 2008 Polish soccer was shaken to its core when it came to light that match results were being manipulated and licenses were being distributed in crooked ways (Stasik, 2012). The former president of the Upper Silesian club GKS Katowice informed the police that matches between Polar Wroclaw and Zaglebie Lubin had been fixed. In 2008 a prominent Polish player admitted that he and his club bought the match for €25,000 (about US$35,000). The corrupted player was sentenced to a year in prison on probation and had to pay a €37,000 (about US$52,000) fine, but he was allowed to continue playing soccer, including for the Polish national team. That incident was not an isolated one in Polish soccer. The public prosecutor had ongoing investigations in 2012 against 17 clubs. In the Polish Extra League, the highest class in the country, 6 clubs were cleared of corruption charges in 2012. The clubs were demoted, but they subsequently received amnesty and were punished only with point deductions and fines (Stasik, 2012). Although it is debatable that Poland's lack of victories can be blamed on the recurrent scandals and corruption, the fact is that Poland lacks a tried and tested successful national soccer team. Most of the many talented Polish players play abroad; 18 of the 26 players who were on the national team in 2012 played outside Poland. As the economic and social consequences of corruption become more pronounced, a failure to address corruption in sport may lead to public desensitization (Chien, Kelly, & Weeks, 2016) of corrupt practices and growing cynicism about the place of sport in society (Kihl et al., 2017).

Education, Sport, Youth, and Tourism in Moscow, Russia.

Economics of Sport

Sport systems are subsidized and coordinated by national governments to attract regional and local resources to both mass and elite sport in Eastern Europe, although private and commercial income sources, common in the West, are becoming increasingly important, particularly for professional sport sold as entertainment. Leading the world by making sport facilities, programs, and professional instruction available to all at no or minimal cost, the USSR government had been allocating increasing amounts of money that reached US$2.2 billion annually in the 1970s. In comparison, the Russian federal sport budget was only US$680 million in 2009, although it increased to US$1.8 billion in 2011, US$1.7 billion in 2012, US$1.6 billion in 2013, and US$1.3 billion in 2014 on the run-up to the 2014 Winter Olympics and Paralympics in Russia. The national **sport societies**, or networks of community and organizational clubs, have provided affordable conditions for all from first steps to high performance in most Olympic sports across Eastern Europe, financed and managed by the army (e.g., Russian SKA and Serbian Red Star), police, and security forces (e.g., Russian and German Dynamo), as well as trade unions of key industries, from agriculture and manufacturing to transportation and education. Citizens have been involved as participants and in the governance and management of sport through these multisport societies at places of study, work, and service. These sport societies lost their strong governmental support in Eastern Europe, so they have privatized some of their assets and operations since the 1990s. But a new 21st century step in the promotion of the multisport approach was the foundation of the European Multisport Club Association, which brought together 17 **multisport clubs** in a network dedicated to both professional and grassroots sport, sharing best club practices of Eastern and Western Europe.

To share resources fairly, amateur and professional competitions in each sport have been managed in integration and governed by one national federation in most of Eastern Europe, particularly in Russia. But attempts to create independent profitable leagues and teams are increasing (Pochinkin,

2006). Together with political and economic pluralism, ownership types in sport organizations, particularly professional sport teams, have become diverse in Eastern Europe since 1990, from private and publically traded companies to state or government owned and organization owned. As many as 25 percent of Russian premier league football clubs in 2004 combined ownership of municipal or regional governments and oligarchs (Pochinkin, 2006), and at least half of German clubs must be owned by members or fans. The rule was introduced in 1998 to help prevent debt of both East and West German clubs, but exemptions were granted to clubs such as Bayer Leverkusen and VfL Wolfsburg, owned by Bayer and Volkswagen (Bundesliga, 2017). The balance between investments into mass and elite sport is becoming harder to maintain in capitalist Eastern Europe. To support healthy physical activities for all, the Russian president asked to redirect public funds toward mass sport from professional teams subsidized through public companies. For example, Russian Railways sponsors Lokomotiv Moscow soccer, Yaroslavl hockey, and Novosibirsk volleyball clubs; VTB Bank sponsors soccer and hockey Dynamo Moscow clubs; and Gazprom sponsors soccer clubs Zenit and Volgar and volleyball club Zenit Kazan (lenta.ru, 2016).

An important task for the Russian Olympic committees is the search for new financial sources in increasingly capitalist economic conditions. The Russian winners of the 2012 Olympic Games were estimated to receive between US$500,000 and US$1 million from the federations alone, before any endorsement money. The Russian Olympic Committee counted on the rich to reward winners. The head of the Summer Sports Association has US$30 billion, so if he gives every winner $1 million, it is not very much for him (Johnson, 2012). In preparation for the 2008 Olympics, the government helped to deploy billionaires to participate in the effort; the country's 10 richest businessmen, in addition to aiding other sport projects, donated US$12 million to the Fund for the Support of Olympians (Schwartz, 2008). Russian corporations increasingly finance sport, devoting over $1 billion to the 2014 Sochi Olympics. The Russian gas and oil company Gazprom reportedly chose not to sign sponsorship contracts but instead simply to donate US$130 million to the country's Olympic teams to help them prepare for the 2012 London and 2014 Sochi Games (RT, 2010).

Management of Sport

The way that sport has been managed and developed in Eastern Europe, particularly Russia, was influenced by frequent wars, making preparation for military fitness permanent. Professional sport had started and was developed largely within the armies of Eastern Europe, including commercial and relatively independent soccer, ice hockey, and basketball as well as all other Olympic sports. Centralization, rational organization, competent personnel, and effective system of training, education, and competitions as well as creative application of best global practices spread from the army to the entire Russian sport system (Pochinkin, 2006).

Mass fitness and participation in over 100 sports is integrated today with preparation of athletes for international competitions led by the Russian governmental sport authorities. Coaches, employed by the state and rewarded according to achievements of participants, run this sport system. According to the East European notion of sport as preventative medicine, coaches assume the roles of holistic physicians as well as spiritual leaders, being well educated in biomedical and pedagogical sciences. Coaches receive help from medical doctors and scientists to nurture participants through a long-term development process, directing each participant to the sport appropriate for individual health conditions and opening more opportunities for talented athletes to progress.

In the 1920s the Soviet government established the National Physical Culture Department with regional and local branches, and scientists and coaches were commissioned to construct uniform mechanisms for all to participate in recreation and sport. This structure, from the 1920s in the USSR and from the 1950s in the rest of Eastern Europe, created a comprehensive sport system seen neither before nor after the existence of the socialist Eastern bloc. In 1990s this system lost much of its public funding and resources together with mechanisms of comprehensive monitoring and science-based management. As a result, all types of instruction and control weakened, leading to increased corruption and careless treatment of athletes.

Corruption has become a significant issue for sport across the world. Commercial growth has raised concern about the unsatisfactory way in which administrators handle sport (Kihl, Skinner, & Engelberg, 2017). Corruption and doping are critical issues for current sport in Eastern Europe and beyond, because Eastern Europeans are buying and selling Western clubs including American New Jersey, later Brooklyn, Nets, English Chelsea, Scottish Hearts, and Dutch Vitesse Arnhem. The oligarchs who took control of the professional teams previously owned by state industries now use these clubs to gain political power, money, and fame. Evidence from the analysis by Salzman (2015) shows that the transition from public socialist to private capitalist ownership in the Eastern European soccer has created less fair league conditions and introduced more corruption, crime, and violence. For example, in 2004 police raided FC Zakarpattya, a club of the Ukrainian Premier League, and 36 armed men were arrested. The club president was charged with robbery, kidnapping, and terrorism. Another example of the violence brought by gangs was with the club FC Tavriya (Salzman, 2015). Wracked by corruption and mismanagement, Romanian football is also in crisis. Because 75 percent of football players in Romania said they were paid late, the second highest percentage of 31 European countries, players may be tempted to take money for unscrupulous reasons and for fixing matches (Giulianelli & Malyon, 2017). The decades following the dissolution of the USSR in 1991 brought new freedoms, accompanied by commercialization and criminalization of sport. In 1996 a law was introduced that imposed severe punishment for bribery among participants, coaches, referees, managers, and organizers of sporting events. Offenses such as influencing a game outcome led to a fine of 500 times the minimum salary and up to six months in prison (Pochinkin, 2006). In 2010-2011 fines for giving or taking bribes were raised to 100 times the amount of the bribe.

As with the fight against corruption, anti-doping policies have yet to produce results in Eastern Europe. One or two decades might not be enough to build new legal, financial, and cultural control mechanisms that would be effective in the new capitalist conditions.

The Russian performance at the 2010 Winter Games was influenced by drug scandals. Subsequently, Russia adopted stricter penalties for doping violations, cooperated more closely with event organizers and regional sport authorities, became actively involved with such international organizations as the 16-country Anti-Doping Working Group within the European Council, and introduced new courses aimed at prevention of doping at schools and universities, as well as anti-doping television programs.

After Russia won the 2010 and 2014 Winter Paralympic and 2014 Winter Olympic Games, finished fourth at the 2012 Olympics, and finished second at the 2012 Paralympics, the country's doping schemes were featured in competing nations' media reports and documentaries and were investigated by the World Anti-Doping Agency (WADA) (see also chapter 14). The IOC decided against a ban of Russian athletes at 2016 Rio Games, instead reversing the presumption of innocence for Russian athletes and deferring to the sport federations to reinstate individual athletes (Ruizjan, 2017). But the Russian Paralympic team was banned from 2016 Rio Games, including athletes who never used doping (see the case study Russian Roulette in chapter 14). In 2017 a report commissioned by WADA indicated that Russian officials orchestrated a doping program at the Olympics and other competitions that involved or benefited 1,000 athletes in 30 sports. The country's team was banned from the 2018 Winter Olympics, including 28 athletes cleared by the Court of Arbitration for Sport, but the International Olympic Committee (IOC) allowed many athletes from Russia to compete without displaying their country's symbols. President Putin claimed that the IOC was manipulated by U.S. interests who wanted to use doping scandals to embarrass his government ahead of the 2018 presidential elections in Russia (Duerden, 2017).

New stricter Russian laws remove coaches and officials who violate anti-doping rules and punish them with fines and imprisonment for coercing young athletes into doping (CBC, 2016; Giles, 2017). These efforts will return better results when sporting communities in Eastern Europe and across the world focus more on the health of participants than on underdeveloped doping tests and the protection of administrators from responsibility for drug abuse. The practice that should be used to minimize corruption and doping is equal and fair support of athletes and coaches in all Olympic and nationally

Learning Activity

Compare media coverage of drug abuses by Western and Eastern European athletes. Who suffered and who benefitted from these scandals?

popular sports. Instructors and competitors in a spectrum of disciplines could be paid as much as doctors, lawyers, engineers, and scientists.

Major Sport Events

Olympic-style mass sport festivals were a key vehicle for the integration of mass and elite sport across time. Such festivals originated in Czech and German lands in the 1860s, mainly through workers' and union movements. The Czech Sokol movement was founded in 1862 as a youth sport and gymnastics organization inspired by the German Gymnastic Movement and provided physical, moral, and intellectual training for the nation through fitness programs and massive gymnastics festivals. This training spread across all regions populated by Slavic cultures. Besides offering physical training and athletic contests, the Polish Falcons from 1867 also included national dances and songs. Continuing its festivals, the Sokol movement celebrated 150 years in 2012.

Following the Czech, German, and ancient Greek traditions, the Soviet sport authorities had been developing the **Spartakiads**, which is a mass multisport festival that includes more sport disciplines than the Olympic Games. In the Soviet Union the Spartakiads began in 1928. By 1975 one-third of the USSR population participated in Spartakiads. Post-Soviet Russia revitalized the Spartakiads in 2002, making them annual events integrated with school competitions. The 2011 Youth Spartakiad had four tiers of competition: first at individual educational institutions, then at the municipal and regional levels, and finally in the national finals.

Recent growth of the region's global importance is indicated in the successful Russian bid for hosting the 2014 Winter Olympic Games, the 2013 Summer Universiade, the 2017 FIFA Confederations Cup, the 2018 FIFA World Cup, the 2013 World Championships in Athletics, the 2015 World Aquatics Championships, the Russian Grand Prix from 2014, and the 2016 World Ice Hockey Championships. Reflecting the Eastern European notion of sport as serious fun, Putin and other top Russian officials and business people together with former international hockey stars play for the Night Hockey League (NHL), one of many amateur leagues, with 200 teams across Russia. Eastern Europe connects East and West through the Kontinental Hockey League (KHL) and its junior divisions, which started in 2008, growing out of the Russian Superleague. The KHL includes European teams from such countries as Finland, Latvia, and Slovakia as well as teams from such Asian nations as China and Kazakhstan. The KHL is a premier professional ice hockey league, second in the world after the North American NHL by level of play. Twenty-nine teams and over 400 players competed in 2016-2017. With the growth of the league and local talent, the number of Canadian players in the KHL decreased from 69 in 2014 to 41 in 2016; even so, more than 60 North American players competed in the 2016 KHL. In addition to the sporting events outlined in the beginning of the chapter and in this section, the following events demonstrate the important role of Eastern Europe in both professional and amateur sport:

- The 2012 UEFA European Championship in Poland and Ukraine, the highest level of football competition for Europe's national teams, was held in Eastern Europe for the first time. Sixteen national teams played 31 matches in eight stadia in eight cities for a prize fund of US$241 million.
- The Russian Grand Prix is an auto race held annually in Sochi since 2014 as part of the Formula One World Championship with a seasonal prize fund of US$700 million.
- The Kremlin Cup, Moscow, Russia, tennis tournament has been held annually since 1990 as part of the ATP World Tour and Premier Tournament on the WTA Tour. The prize fund was US$790,208 in 2017.
- The Gagarin Cup, Russia, is awarded annually to the champion of the Kontinental Hockey League (KHL), a premier international professional ice hockey league with the highest total attendance in Europe.

Learning Activity

Select one professional entertainment sport event and one mass-participation event in Eastern Europe and research different aspects of the events' socio-economic impact. How have the events benefited the local community and its quality of life?

- The 2018 FIFA Football World Cup in Russia was the most watched sport event in the world. Thirty-two national teams played 64 matches in 12 stadia in 11 cities for a prize fund of US$400 million.

Eastern Europe continues to lead the world in integration of recreational and elite sport events. A tournament for fans held in 2018 FIFA World Cup Russia brought together 200 football supporters from 16 countries who played and lived together. This unique Fan World Cup with a draw, group stage, and elimination round united rivals and encouraged healthy mass football participation (Smirnova, 2018).

Summary

The management of sport in Eastern Europe is based on the philosophy of a harmonious science-guided development of each individual and on a highly integrated system of physical culture and sport led by federal authorities as part of national education and health policies. Sport was delivered with passion, original inquiry, dedication, and rigor in the USSR and Eastern bloc. Present-day Eastern Europe has inherited the following practices that appear to be useful for successful sport management across the world:

- Coaches qualified to prevent mass illnesses and achieve high performance.
- Uniform guidelines for integrated mass and elite participation, regulation, and long-term athlete development; education and certification of athletes, coaches, and referees; sport schools and universities; and integrated plans of competitions.

? Review Questions

1. How would you define Eastern Europe in relation to sport management?

2. What are some Eastern European approaches to the role of sport in society and to sport governance, management, and economics?

3. Which Eastern European methods are useful for using science in sport development, management, and governance?

4. How have Eastern European structures of sport clubs and societies, sport schools, and universities benefited the world?

5. Which healthy sport practices has present-day Eastern Europe inherited from the former USSR?

6. Which mechanisms ensure lifelong participation and career progression in sport systems of Eastern Europe?

7. How could corruption and drug abuse be reduced based on the approaches of Eastern Europe?

Sport in Africa

Jepkorir Rose Chepyator-Thomson, PhD
University of Georgia

Samuel M. Adodo, PhD
University of Benin, Nigeria

Emma Ariyo, MS
University of Georgia

Chapter Objectives

After studying this chapter, you will be able to do the following:

- Understand the role of sport in African societies.
- Comprehend the role of women's sport in society.
- Explain how African countries use sport as soft power.
- Understand issues facing the sport of boxing in Uganda.
- Identify and explain the role of sport federations and associations in Africa.
- Gain information about issues in management and governance of sport in a variety of environments.
- Understand the structure, administration, and management of football in Nigeria.
- Describe professionalization and commercialization of premier leagues in Africa.
- Understand the role of sponsorship in African sport.

Key Terms

Confederation of African Rugby (RA)
African Cricket Association (ACA)
Confederation of African Athletics (CAA)
Confederation of African Volleyball (CAV)
Confederation of African Football
Netball Association of Africa Region (NAAR)

1. Congo
2. Central African Republic
3. Equatorial Guinea
4. Benin
5. Togo
6. Lebanon
7. Jordan
8. Kuwait
9. Qatar
10. Eritrea
11. Uganda
12. Rwanda
13. Burundi
14. Malawi
15. Swaziland
16. Lesotho

Key Events

All-Africa Games. A continental-based multisport event for athletes from all countries of Africa, the All-Africa Games provides opportunities for athletes to display their skilled performance while representing their home countries.

African Union Sports Council. Organ of development for sport in Africa that works with international sport organizations in professional development of sport managers and administrators, promotes sport for development in established zones across the continent, and organizes the All-Africa Games.

Association of National Olympic Committees of Africa (ANOCA). Instrument of unification for African national Olympic committees and helps in promotion of the Olympic ethos and in a variety of sporting activities in the continent while working cooperatively with government and nongovernment organizations.

Association of African Sport Confederations (AASC). Promotes unification of African sport organizations while making sure that their administration and functionality is sound and without discriminatory practices; occurs through the General Assembly and Executive Bureau.

Key People

Lydia Nsekera, Burundi, chair of the IOC Women in Sport Commission, committee member for Olympic football tournaments, women's football, the FIFA Women's World Cup, and the FIFA council, and served as member of the Organizing Committee of FIFA at the 2013 FIFA's 62nd Congress.

Issa Hayatou, Cameroon, a key historical figure in African football as head of the Confederation of African football for 29 years, contributed significantly to the growth of African football in the era of globalization as the number of African teams that qualified for the FIFA World Cup increased from 2 to 5 and the African Cup of Nations expanded by 50 percent (from 8 to 16).

Fatma Samba Diouf Samoura, Senegal, is FIFA secretary general, a top-ranking official in FIFA, and a symbol for women birthing a new era for women sport administrators across Africa and around the world.

Lamine Diack, Senegal, past president of IAAF (1999-2015) and the Africa Amateur Athletics Confederation, and a member of the IOC and the National Olympic and Sport Committee of Senegal and the Executive Committee of the Supreme Council for Sport in Africa (SCSA) from 1973 to 2008. He transformed athletics, bringing unity to the diverse African populace and cultivating the sport within and outside Africa during his reign.

Sam Ramsamy, South Africa, member of International Olympic Committee, vice-president of FINA (International Swimming Federation), president of South African Swimming, and chairman of the Commonwealth Games Association. He was the key person to use sport to fight for the removal of apartheid, spearheading the development of sport along nonracial lines and leading the South Africa sport industry to be managed and administered along nonracial lines.

Didier Yves Tébily Drogba, Ivory Coast, the all-time top scorer for his country with 65 goals from 104 appearances, was named African Footballer of the year in 2006 and 2009 and is known for his humanitarian work and his role in bringing peace to his country with a plea for a cease-fire after five years of civil war.

Hezekiah Kipchoge Keino, Kenya, is a running legend, an inductee of the World Sports Humanitarian Hall of Fame in 1996, and founder of the Kip Keino Foundation, whose purpose is to improve the quality of life and provide education to underprivileged children in Kenya.

The sport industry started from small beginnings along the coastal regions of Africa. Sport for the masses was introduced through the school system, where the European sports—cricket, football, rugby, netball, and athletics—were taught to youth and children and elite sport was taught and promoted through high-class school systems and private sport clubs that dot the continent. The purpose of this chapter is to discuss the role and governance of play in African sport, explicate management and economics of the sport industry, describe major events that characterize the sport industry, and provide information about key sport leaders who make the sport industry known nationally and globally. The chapter begins with continental geography, demographics, and background characteristics. It then describes the role of sport in African societies, sport governance and management, structure of sport, and major events. Case studies provide details on two important aspects of sport in Africa.

Geographical Description, Demographics, and Background

The African continent, the oldest of the seven continents and second only to Asia in size, is replete with all forms of geographic diversity. The most distinguishing geographic features include the Sahara Desert in northern Africa, the Kalahari Desert in southwest Africa, and the Great Rift Valley that stretches from the Dead Sea in Israel to Lake Tanganyika, the second deepest lake in the world after Lake Baikal in Eastern Asia, and contains on its valley floor several freshwater lakes. On the north–south extremes of Africa are the Atlas and Drakensburg Mountains, respectively. The tallest mountain, Kilimanjaro (19,340 feet [5,894 m] above sea level), and second tallest, Kenya (17,000 feet [5,182 m] above sea level), occupy middle-eastern Africa, in the countries of Tanzania and Kenya, respectively.

Learning Activity

Discuss the significance of the Nile River and explain human diversity along its route from its source to its mouth at the Mediterranean Sea. Discover by Internet search the types of sporting activities popular along the river, past and present.

The prominent rivers that score the continent include the Nile River, stretching from Uganda to Egypt and emptying into the Mediterranean Sea; the Congo river, the second longest in Africa, flowing through the country of the Democratic Republic of Congo; the Niger River, the third longest river in Africa, flowing across the western African countries of Guinea, Mali, Niger, and Nigeria; and the Zambezi River, the fourth longest, which touches the countries of Angola, Zambia, Zimbabwe, and Mozambique before it empties into the Indian Ocean at the Mozambique Channel. The continent has the world's second largest (by area) freshwater lake, Lake Victoria, which stretches across three countries: Kenya, Uganda, and Tanzania.

The indigenous peoples of Africa have occupied the continent since its discovery as the oldest of the seven continents. The African continent has a "multi-faceted history and culture [that] reach back through empires of early antiquity to the first known site for human life" (Seidman & Anang, 1992, p. 1), and it currently houses diverse ethnic groups—Bantu, Nilotic, and Nilo-Hamitic people—and recent immigrants from Europe and Asia. The most populated country, Nigeria, has over 250 ethnic groups, including three major ethnicities: Yoruba, Igbo, and Hausa-Fulani (Rotberg & Obadina, 2007). Asians, primarily from India and the Middle East, arrived in Africa in the late 19th century (Oonk, 2004) and occupy the coastal regions of eastern Africa. Among them are Arabs.

The sport industry is at its infancy in the continent. The development of the industry through various sports started with the advent of European tutelage in Africa during the colonial period, when the introduced sporting activities took precedence over indigenous games and sports (Chepyator-Thomson, 2014). The introduction and spread of

European sports to African people took place in cities in the form of club competitions. During colonial times, sport clubs were introduced to both the coastal regions and the interior areas of Africa.

Role of Sport

Sport serves as an engine of economic revitalization and sociocultural integration in communities and nations across the continent. Sport promotes formation of comradeship among friends, bonds families together, generates revenues, and encourages community engagement in business enterprises. It serves as a unifying tool because it brings together people of different multicultural upbringing (Vidacs, 2011). In Kenya, sport reigns supreme and is thus included in national development plans, serving as a means to meet national policy objectives. In South Africa, the African National Congress used the party's Reconstruction Development Programme to improve the socioeconomic conditions of underprivileged communities following the 1995 Rugby World Cup (Boshoff, 1997). In Saayman, Saayman, and du Plessies's (2005) perspective, sport brings economic impact to communities and allows people to network and conjure business activities.

The sport industry in Africa is dominated by businesses and the formation of cross-cultural relationships that involve European-introduced sports—soccer, rugby, cricket, and netball. Cricket is popular across English-speaking Africa and is central to the lives of elite city dwellers and visitors at rural tourist resorts. In Tanzania, for instance, according to Ndee (2010), tennis courts are located close to five-star hotels where tourists play the game during leisure hours. The female-only sport netball, common originally in British English-speaking Afri-

Learning Activity

Select three major sports in Africa and explain their influence in local and global contexts. Discuss the extent to which Uganda can benefit from inclusion of newcomers to the sport, women boxers. Discuss as well the types of sponsors that can be used to elevate the sport in Uganda.

CASE STUDY

Boxing in Uganda

Boxing plays a significant role in situating Uganda on the world map and has become the country's leading sporting export. The rise and dominance of boxing in Uganda is partly attributed to former president Idi Amin, who symbolized the greatness (and importance) of the sport while he served in the King's African Rifles during the British colonial period in Uganda, long before he became Uganda's president (Mazrui, 1986). Amin believed that the government had the duty to support all sporting activities in Uganda and thus funded the Uganda national boxing team, the Bombers.

In recent times, the Uganda Boxing Amateur Federation (UBAF), one of the biggest and most successful sport federations in the country, has faced a management crisis (Isabirye, 2017, p. 1). The International Boxing Association (AIBA) suspended the UBAF for seven years because of inconsistent leadership, corruption, and heavy meddling in administration by the central government. The administration squabbles paralyzed the struggling structure of the Uganda boxing fraternity, leaving coaches, referees, judges, and trainers with no access to equipment, materials, and information from the international body that would help promote the game. Because of the administration wrangles, companies and private sponsors were afraid to invest in the sport because of the failed leadership structure and organization. Brewer and Pedersen (2010) posit that commercialization of sport through sponsorship of competitions, teams, and athletes plays an important role in the development and sustainability of the sport as well as promotes the image of the sponsor. Sponsorship plays a significant role in the development and promotion of a sport, because corporations not only get to promote their products and brands through investing in sport but also give leverage to the sporting entity and hence develop a strong emotional connection with the people it serves and the various communities around the country.

The increasing importance of sport as a cultural force enhances the unity and prestige of a nation and has guided governments to employ massive intervention in sport activities (Houlihan, 2005). Therefore, the government of Uganda, through the Ministry of Education and Sport and the National Council of Sport, is currently involved in rebuilding the sport by stabilizing the management as well as providing equipment, money, manpower, and advisory services to jump-start the sport (Isabirye, 2017), after many years of inactivity within the boxing community. Uganda cannot compete with other countries and athletes or have a competitive advantage because of the lack of exposure to modern equipment and structure of competition. The country and the boxing federation do not have a national training gym to nurture and prime boxers to participate in regional and international boxing events. There is urgent need for education about sport policies and implementation. The government needs to provide directives about physical education and sport and how local clubs and the federation can work together to improve the welfare and performance of the athletes. The future of the sport lies in attracting newcomers and making an international impact.

---

can countries and popular in contemporary Africa (Chappel, 2005), provides women with excellent economic opportunities for social mobility.

Sport as a soft power puts African countries on the world map—Kenya through track and field, Cameroon through soccer, and South Africa through rugby—and permits globalization of human resources and sport sponsorships, given that many African athletes have taken residences abroad by participating in European football leagues or taking part in global sport competitions representing their adopted countries. Soft power is defined as a nation seeking "to achieve [its] goals in the international arena through attraction rather than coercion" (Delgado, 2016, p. 1). For example, note the spectacular performances of a nation's athletes at mega sport events like the Olympics, where athletes take home medals. Athletes of international standing have become instruments of change, transforming their nation's communities and reverberating abroad with the likes of Africa's track and field heroes Kipchoge Keino of Kenya, Nawal El Maoutawakel of Morocco, Maria Mutola of Mozambique, and John Akii-Bua of Uganda;

soccer players Didier Drogba of Ivory Coast and Roger Miller of Cameroon; and basketball great Dikembe Mutombo of the Democratic Republic of Congo. These athletes not only put Africa on the world map but also transformed the continent economically through development of various business enterprises and promoted unity among the diverse ethnic groups that live within their nations' borders. The sport of boxing played a dominant role in putting Uganda on the world map and unifying the nation ethnically and socially. In staging mega sport events, countries like India (Commonwealth Games) and Brazil (FIFA World Cup 2014 and Olympic Games in 2016), two rapidly expanding economies, announced through these events that "they had finally arrived on the international stage" (Grix & Houlihan, 2014, p. 577).

Governance of Sport

Governance is critical to effective functioning of sports organizations. According to Hill, Kerr, and Kobayashi (2016), "effective governance is necessary for any group to function, whether one is a public entity, not-for-profit organization, school, sport club or corporate business" (p. 211). In Africa, sports are governed through confederations and associations. Governance cities are largely located in northern and western-African countries, with only one sport—netball—being female specific. These federations and associations organize and manage sport competitions and work together with major international sport bodies to hold mega sport events in the continent like the 2010 FIFA World Cup, Rugby World Cup, and Cricket World Cup, all held in South Africa.

The **Confederation of African Rugby** is the governing body and organizes continental competitions. The body oversees the organizing and running of rugby for R15s and 7s and women's rugby. The southern African region dominates rugby competition, although recently the eastern African countries of Kenya and Uganda have offered a serious challenge. The South Africa Rugby team occupies a superior position by winning the Rugby World Cup in 1995 and appearing in the film *Invictus*. The **African Cricket Association** manages cricket tournaments, and the sport is most prevalent in the southern region of Africa, particularly South Africa, Zimbabwe, Namibia, and Zambia,

Learning Activity

Select two sport confederations and discuss similarities and differences in governance structures. If you were to start a new sport, what critical elements would you include and why?

as well as in the eastern Africa countries of Kenya, Uganda, and Tanzania. The **Netball Association of Africa Region** governs and oversees all netball sport competitions. This female-only sport is played predominantly in the southern region of Africa. The Malawi Queens, the national team for Malawi, rule the continent and currently rank fifth in the world. The **Confederation of African Athletics** oversees all aspects of athletic competition, including the major athletic event in the continent, the African Championships. The **Confederation of African Volleyball** governs the sport and administers all women and men's volleyball championships. The **Confederation of African Football** is the organ of governance and administration of African football, representing all football federations in the continent.

Sport confederations and associations legitimized the development of sport structures and competitions, instigated the creation of jobs and generation of revenues in countries where sport competitions are held, and promoted unity and solidarity among players and spectators. Competitions held annually, every two years, or every four years affect local communities economically, create revenues that promote national economies and ethnic integration, and promote international notoriety and engagement with foreign sport enterprises.

Economics of Sport

Football is by far the most prominent sport in the continent. The strong presence of professional and the commercialization of the sport started with the development and promotion of premier leagues. Football premier leagues are part and parcel of Africa's economy and are a mainstay of societies in terms of social and economic development. The premier leagues are a subset of football associations under the sport governing bodies. The development of a premier league system in Africa significantly altered the way that sport business is developed and promoted within each African country and across the continent. For instance, in South Africa, the "inception of the premiere soccer league laid the foundations for the million Rand business and heavily commercialized entity that professional soccer in South Africa is today" (Darby & Solberg, 2010, p. 119). According to Darby and Solberg (2010), commercialization and corporatization is increasingly "fueled by sponsorship from large commercial entities such as South African Breweries, South African Airways, TV broadcasting companies and Vodacom" (p. 119). The revenue generated has transformed underserved communities, making the league "the most economically viable and well-organized league in sub-Saharan Africa (Darby & Solberg, 2010, p. 119). The South African Premier Soccer League is a franchise system in which rich entrepreneurs have ownership, with the "most powerful entrepreneurs helping transform and steer South African football into its current profitable state" (Darby & Solberg, 2010, p. 120). According to Darby and Solberg (2010), "South Africa's status as the economic powerhouse on the continent alongside the hosting of the 2010 World Cup seems set to herald a prosperous future for the Premier Soccer League, one that will allow it to continue to retain local labor and attract talent from elsewhere in Africa" (p. 127). In Kenya, the premier leagues entertain people with weekend games that generate lots of revenue.

In many African countries, most of these premier leagues exist with the support of the government or private sponsorships. In South Africa, the Premier Soccer League relies on corporate sponsorships and is considered one of wealthiest in Africa. In Ghana, the Ghana Football Association (GFA) and the national team benefit from corporate investments, although the extent to which it benefits youth leagues is unclear (Darby & Solberg, 2010). The two premier league teams in Ghana, the Accra Hearts of Oak and Asante Kotoko, are considered financially stable because they "pay higher wages, signing bonuses and win bonuses to players" (Darby & Solberg, 2010, p. 122). Unfortunately, the GFA faces challenges stemming from a poor administration and governance structure, affecting the premier league because it is not independent from the association, contrary to the situation in South Africa, where in a two-tier structure the Premier Soccer League is autonomous from the South Africa Football Association (Darby & Solberg, 2010, p.

122). Eighteen teams form the premier league in Kenya (also known as SportPesa Premier League), and sponsorship comes from a variety of sources, primarily from international sponsors such as Puma and SuperSport. Local sponsors include sugar companies, banks (Kenya Commercial Bank), the government of Kenya, Kenya Defense Forces, Kenya Power, and Kenya Ports Authority, who support the league and the Kenya Football Federation (Kenyan Premier League Limited, 2018). The league generates a total income of 270.9 million shillings which benefits many communities and cities and goes to pay for marketing, advertising, and staff payroll (Kenyan Premier League Limited, 2018; AllAfrica. com, 2018).

In contemporary times, the major sports, rugby and cricket, bring lots of business and revenues to communities and nations. South Africa has been the main beneficiary. The 1995 Rugby World Cup, the 2003 Cricket World Cup, and the 2010 FIFA World Cup brought a tourist boom to South Africa; about 309,554 foreign tourists spent about R3.64 billion during the event (FIFA, 2018). FIFA, which took the lion's share of benefits from the World Cup in South Africa, is considered the "sport's Wall Street and Pentagon combined [as] it was set to earn about 2.25 billion pounds from TV rights, exceeding its income from the two most recent World Cups combined" (Pilger, 2010, p. 21). Economic gains in South Africa from sport—football, rugby, and cricket—represent significant investment in the sport industry in the country (Stander & van Zyl, 2016). The FIFA World Cup can be said not only to have put South Africa on the world map but also to have shown the world that the country can be considered a possible destination for various types of investment. South Africa spent millions of dollars to attract sport tourists, done largely to "raise external revenues" expected to happen through "increased tourism and heightened awareness of South Africa as a destination for tourists and international capital" (Giampiccoli, Lee, & Nauright, 2013, p. 229).

The South Africa Rugby Union created an enterprise to commercialize its heritage, the Springbok Experience Museum. This commercial rugby museum sells sport memorabilia and artifacts (Grundlingh, 2015). The professionalization of rugby helps "solidify the Springbok brand through its heritage." The South Africa Rugby Union markets its heritage as a "commodity that showcases the Springbok brand on a very competitive sports market" (Grundlingh, 2015, p. 107-108). The development of this heritage venture is significant because tourists come to witness "South Africa's unique social and political heritage," which constitutes an experience-based economy (Grundlingh, 2015, p.108). In South Africa today, rugby is a "professional, multinational, highly commercialized business machine" (Parker, 2013, p. 102) and "offers unique experiences and business opportunities" (Gedye, 2017) through utilization of "new private equity investment" and global private investors, with solicited interest coming from U.S. companies and a Hong Kong-based company, Carinat Sports Marketing (Gedye, 2017, p. 1). South Africa gained "an inflow of R4 billion and generated gate revenues of R80 billion" (Versi & Nevin, 2003, p. 1) from holding the Cricket World Cup and had, according to the Global Cricket Corporation, "up to 300 million households [that watched] the 54 games spread over 43 days."

Wrestling is another important sport in the continent. The West Africa countries take the lead, especially Senegal. The sport generates revenues for economic development in various cities and communities and has allowed social mobility among sport players in countries wherever the sport is played. Wrestling has "become a million dollar spectacle, mostly because of big telecom sponsors, TV stations, and new media channels [and] this has led to the most successful wrestlers becoming media-stars and billionaires, giving young men in this African country a very different perspective" (Bobst, p. 1). Senegalese youth have a passion for the country's ancient sport, and on a good day, fans fill a 60,000-seat stadium in the capital, Dakar (Heuler, 2006).

Another sport practiced in Africa is the East Africa Safari Rally, the most popular international event in the World Rally Championship (WRC) outside Europe (Kamweru, 2008). The event is often considered the biggest international sporting occasion in East Africa. The East Africa Safari Rally is a platform for car manufacturers to showcase their latest models. With the influx of car manufacturers into East Africa, the regional economy was boosted, especially in the hospitality industry because of the large number of crews that took part in the event. The event is a generator of national and local economic and social development (Horne & Man-

Learning Activity

Beyond the content provided in this section, critically examine how these sports influence communities and nations, considering where they are most prominent in the continent, using an Internet search and your own experiences.

zenreiter, 2006). The East Africa Safari Rally was a catalyst for social change because of the investment in infrastructure, technology, and the livelihood of the people within and around the hosting cities, promoting sport tourism, regional economies, sociocultural cohesion, and the car-racing industry in the region.

In summary, numerous competitive sport events are held throughout the continent on annual basis or every two or four years. The premier leagues are the mainstay for diverse groups of people who depend on them for economic revitalization of communities and cities, for player social mobility, for general welfare of people who attend weekend competitive matches, and for involvement in corporate social responsibility activities that target youth in both rural and urban locations. The prominent sport country is South Africa because it has hosted the three mega sport events—in soccer, cricket, and rugby—successfully in the past. The future of professional sport in the continent rests on growing these sports. South Africa is becoming a powerhouse in the three major sports in the continent, but other countries are coming up to challenge that country's superiority in the not-too-distant future.

Management of Sport

Proper management is critical to the development of sport. With globalization, many skilled athletes and players take up residences abroad to be part of renowned European soccer clubs or sport franchises that give them a return on their investment, making management of sport essential to development. The demand for competent managers in clubs and federations is paramount given the enormous public interest and growth of sport in the continent (Eksteen, Malan, & Lotriet, 2013). The authors argue that club managers need to possess competencies centered on "budgeting, managing personnel and facilities, controlling and directing [as well as] communicating management [in form of] writing, media relations and advertising and fundraising" (Eksteen, Malan, & Lotriet, 2013, p. 934). The administration process, according to Abdl-Galil Muhammad and Abdallah (2016), includes "planning, organizing, directing, and follow-time management" (p. 93). Proper management engenders excellent documentation of sport activities and achievements and good record keeping, which are critical in football administration. Sound record keeping, organization, and execution of plans are essential to all sports, particularly football, given its important position in the continent. In West Africa, the Ghana Football Association, along with its Premier League Board, are tainted with corruption "because they fail to provide proper records of their activities" (Yeboah, Adams, & Akotia, 2017), a problem that FIFA has been implicated with in recent times. In Egypt, Hamza and Abdelmonem's (2018) research

CASE STUDY

Football in Nigeria

The administrative structure of sport in Nigeria starts with the Federal Ministry of Youth and Sports Development (2017). The minister serves as the chief executive and the accounting officer. The ministry has oversight functions for youth matters and sport development at all levels (national, state, local government, and institutions). The structure of sport is such that government totally controls sport development through the Ministry of Youth and Sports Development, which in turn regulates the activities of all the sport associations and football clubs in the country.

An example of club structure is found in Nigerian football, which starts with the state-owned clubs, constituting 90 percent of clubs in the Nigerian Premier League, private clubs owned by individuals or corporate shareholders, and finally community clubs. The club structure shows the prevalence of state-owned clubs because the state government uses football to show that they care for the welfare of the citizens. The state-owned clubs are financially supported mostly from the state treasury. A specific department or agency is set up by the state government to manage the club, and the office of the state governor or state ministry of sports manages the clubs.

The Nigeria Football Federation (NFF), which is affiliated with FIFA, organizes football among clubs, states, and national levels, by statutorily regulating the sport. A president leads the NFF with a board made up of football administrators across the country. The board constitutes the law-making body of the NFF. The president administers football through a general assembly made up of the various football associations' chairmen and chairpersons from the 36 states of Nigeria including the Federal Capital Territory (FCT). The National Football Association Act of 1990 gives the sole power to organize football in Nigeria to the NFF, which in turn issues a license to the League Management Company (LMC) (2017) to manage the Nigeria Premier League on behalf of the NFF. In contrast, the State Football Association is responsible for the organization and administration of football at the grassroots level. At the club level, the NFF administers a three-tier league system for men and a two-tier league system for women. Men have the Nigeria Premier League (NPL) with 20 teams, the Nigeria National League with two groups of 16 teams, and the Nigeria Nationwide League Division One (4 groups of 10 teams) and Division Two (52 teams). Women have the National League and the Nationwide League.

The Nigeria Football Association Act (Decree No. 10) and the Nigeria Professional Football League Decree (Decree No. 11) were promulgated in 1990 and merged in 1992 as Decree No. 101, constituting the laws required for football administration. Decree No. 101 was a product of a near FIFA ban of the country for frequent interference, particularly as it relates to the dissolution of the Board of Football Association in Nigeria. Decree No. 101, however, created more problems than it set out to solve. The decree gave the government absolute power to control the NFA, which stunted the growth and development of football because of unnecessary government bureaucracy, inefficiency, and corruption.

Learning Activity

Discuss issues and perspectives on corruption and scandals in African sport in comparison with major international sporting governance bodies and consider solutions to the problems of corruption and sport inefficiency.

Learning Activity

Conduct an Internet search on athletics in Africa and discuss how the new IAAF eligibility regulations for female classification will affect women athletes who wish to participate in international sporting competitions, as compared with women in Western countries.

documented that sport federations are critical to the achievement of goals and objectives of sports clubs. The research findings point to the significant impact of experience and possession of skills on quality of strategic decision-making made in sports federations, with "transformational leadership being of one of the most appropriate management methods for leading change process in [sport] organizations" (Hamza and Abdelmonem, 2018, p. 122). Despite issues facing management of sport, it must be recognized that sport management is in its infancy in Africa, and only a handful of programs are present. Even in South Africa, only certain universities have sport management as a degree option (Steyn, Hollander, & Roux, 2014).

Major Sport Events

Prominent sport events occur on an annual basis or every two or four years in Africa. Among them are marathons, the All-Africa Games, and the African Cup of Nations. Marathons are held annually and occur on scenic routes (South Africa), bring profound changes to the lives of vulnerable youth (Sierra Leone), and fund wildlife activities that safeguard the country's wild animals from extinction (Kenya). The All-Africa Games, a multisport event, is held every four years. The African Cup of Nations competition is held biennially in odd-numbered years so as not to conflict with the World Cup, and the Confederation of African Football (CAF)

is in charge of the competition. Other major sports include the Rugby World Cup (1995), Cricket World Cup (2003), and FIFA World Cup (2010). All these sporting events were held in South Africa.

Summary

Sport in Africa is a massive undertaking, particularly given its infancy status. But sport has served Africa well. It is an instrument of integration, economic development, and progress. Sport internationalizes the continent, putting it almost on par with other continents in sports like track and field. Through major sport events, the production of skilled labor for football leagues on other continents, and the medals that African athletes receive at the Olympics Games, Africa has effectively used sport as soft power on the global stage. Sound governance and policy are critical to the effective administration and management of sport, although corruption has slowed progress. Sport has elevated business activities through the presence of premier leagues and major sport events. Despite predicaments associated with colonialism and independence, sport in Africa is predicted to rival sport of other continents in the future, led by leaders, women in particular, who have taken key positions in managing and leading sport federations and Olympic committees.

? Review Questions

1. Discuss the sports' importance to the sport industry in Africa.
2. Review government involvement in football administration and management in Nigeria.
3. Discuss the functions and roles of sport federations and associations in the continent.
4. The premier league system is entrenched in the economies of the communities in which teams reside. Explain.
5. What sport leaders demonstrate Africa's influence on the world of sport?
6. Identify and explain the major sport events that make up the sport industry in Africa.

Sport in the Arab World

Mahfoud Amara, PhD
Qatar University

Chapter Objectives

After studying this chapter, you will be able to do the following:

- Explain the differences and similarities in the sport systems of Arab countries.
- Discuss the foundations of how the sport industry developed in the Arab world.
- Identify the most popular sports practiced and followed in the Arab world.
- Identify some of the key characteristics of national sport systems in the Arab world.

Key Terms	
Arab Games	Ministry of Youth and Sport
Asian Games	Gulf Cooperation Council
Pan African Games	FIFA 2022 World Cup in Qatar

1. Congo
2. Central African Republic
3. Equatorial Guinea
4. Benin
5. Togo
6. Lebanon
7. Jordan
8. Kuwait
9. Qatar
10. Eritrea
11. Uganda
12. Rwanda
13. Burundi
14. Malawi
15. Swaziland
16. Lesotho

Key Events

Pan African Games. The Pan African Games, also known as the All-Africa Games or the African Games, is a continental multisport event held every four years and organized by the African Union (AU) with the Association of National Olympic Committees of Africa (ANOCA) and the Association of African Sports Confederations (AASC). The first Games were held in Brazzaville, Congo, in 1965. The Games seek to promote African unity and the shared history of colonialism, decolonization, and African solidarity.

Asian Games. The Asian Games, or Asiad, held every four years, is the largest multisport event (42 sports) after the Summer Olympics. The first edition took place in New Delhi, India, in 1951. The Games are organized by the Olympic Council of Asia. In addition to Olympic sports, the Games include other traditional sports practiced by millions in the continent, such as wushu, pencak silat, sepak takraw, and kabaddi.

Mediterranean Games. This multisport event comprises countries from the Mediterranean Sea region. The Games are held every four years. The Arab region con-

tributed to the development of the Games. The idea was proposed at the 1948 Summer Olympics by Muhammed Taher Pasha, chairman of the Egyptian Olympic Committee and vice-president of the International Olympic Committee (IOC). The first edition of the Games was held in Egypt in 1951.

Pan Arab Games. These Games are organized by the Arab League in partnership with Arab national Olympic committees and sport federations. The Games, held every four years, aim to raise interest in sport as an educational tool and strategy that seeks to prepare strong youth who believe in their Arab identity. In addition, the Games provide a competitive environment for Arab youth to enhance their sporting skills, helping them to represent their nations better in international sporting festivals. The first Games were organized in Egypt (Alexandria) in 1953.

Islamic Games. The Islamic Games, known also as the Islamic Solidarity Games, are equivalent to the Olympics for Muslim countries that are members of the Islamic Council. The Games are organized by the Islamic Solidarity Sports Federation (ISSF). The first Games were held in Saudi Arabia in 2005. The second Games were organized in Indonesia in 2013, and the third edition was held in Azerbaijan in 2017. The first Games were open for males only. The following editions were open for female athletes as well. The Games are also open to non-Muslim athletes who are citizens of Muslim countries that are members of the Islamic Council.

Gulf Cooperation Council (GCC) Games. This quadrennial multisport event was established and first held in 2011. The event brings together monarchy states in the Arabian Gulf, which are members of the Gulf Cooperation Council.

Key People

Muhammed Taher Pasha, from Egypt, is the founder of the Mediterranean Games. He was the chairman of the Egyptian Olympic Committee and a member of the executive commission of the International Olympic Committee from 1952 to 1957.

Nawel El Moutawakel, a 400-meter hurdler, was the first woman from an Islamic nation to win an Olympic medal and the first Moroccan athlete of either sex to win a gold medal. In 1998 El Moutawakel was chosen to be a member of the International Olympic Committee. She was chairwoman of the evaluation commission for the selection of the host city for the 2012 and 2016 Summer Olympic Games. She was IOC vice-president from 2012 to 2016.

Gabriel Jemayel, from a prominent Lebanese Maronite family, was influential in political affairs in Lebanon and established *Comité internationale des Jeux méditerranéens* in 1961.

Princess Haya of Jordan is the daughter of King Hussein of Jordan and the wife of the ruler of Dubai, **Sheikh Mohammed bin Rashid al-Maktoum**. She was president of the International Equestrian Federation (FEI) from 2006 to 2010.

Sheikh Ahmed Al-Fahad Al-Ahmed Al-Sabah is a Kuwaiti and current president of Olympic Council of Asia. He is also a member of the International Olympic Committee.

Nasser al-Khelaifi, from Qatar, has been the chairman and chief executive of Paris Saint-Germain since October 2011. He is also chairman and chief executive officer of beIN Media Group, chairman of Qatar Sports Investments, president of the Qatar Tennis Federation (QTF), and vice-president of the Asian Tennis Federation for West Asia (ATF).

The chapter examines how sport has evolved in the region and explains how the political, cultural, and economic contexts have shaped the meaning of sport. The region is divided geographically between Asia and Africa. Although Arabic culture and civilization is influential, the region is home to many ethnic groups and religious communities. The chapter begins with background on how the sport industry has developed in the Arab world. It then identifies the most popular sports practiced and followed in the Arab world. A discussion about the role of government in the development of sport in Arab countries follows. The chapter ends by identifying some of the sport governing bodies that rule the sporting scene in the Arab world. Considering the space constraints of the chapter, this information cannot be comprehensive or present an exhaustive analysis of the sport industry in the Arab world, but it will introduce the reader to the major features of sport in the region.

Geographical Description, Demographics, and Background

For some authors the Arab world, framed also as the Middle East and North Africa, is at the crossroads of the three monotheist religions. It is also the birthplace of several civilizations: Mesopotamian, Egyptian, Greco-Roman, and Arab. One of the legacies of colonization is the famous French and British Sykes–Picot Agreement, which designated the borders of the region, the consequences of which are seen in the current ethno-religious conflicts. Decolonization has shaped the region along various politico-ideological lines. One consequence is the divide between the North Africa (the *Maghreb*) region and the Middle East (the *Masherq*) region, which have come to be represented as different, culturally, economically, and politically. Being situated between the two regions, Egypt wants to be seen as the leader of the Arab world. The region has also been a location for internal conflicts and proxy wars in Lebanon, Sudan, Algeria, Egypt, Iraq, and more recently in Libya, Syria, and Yemen. Hence, the focus on the region today in international news tends to be centered on questions of the trinity of energy, security, and immigration, considering that Arab countries are big producers of oil and gas and that the region is a border to sub-Saharan Africa and a transit to Europe (9 miles [15 km] by sea from Tangier, Morocco). Other aspects tend to be neglected in comparison with current news of turmoil in the region.

With a combined population of around 422 million inhabitants, the Arab region includes 22 countries: Algeria, Morocco, Tunisia, Mauritania, Libya, Egypt, Sudan, Somalia, Djibouti, Jordan, Saudi Arabia, UAE, Qatar, Bahrain, Oman, Yemen, Kuwait, Iraq, Palestine, Syria, Lebanon, and Comoros. Spread around North Africa, the horn of Africa, and the Middle East (including the Arabian Peninsula), these countries define themselves as Arab and are members of the Arab League, which is the regional institution that has the ambition to promote and protect Arab agendas within the international community. The Arab League is vividly criticized by intellectuals and the general population alike for not being able to resolve internal conflicts that the region has been facing for the last 50 years or so and for not having the power to prevent direct or indirect foreign military interventions in the region. One of the biggest challenges for the Arab League is the ongoing Arab–Israeli conflict over the question of the Palestinian occupied territory. Although Arab culture and heritage is dominant, other ethnic groups live in the region, including Kurds scattered through Iraq and Syria, Turkmen mainly in northern Iraq, and Berbers in North Africa. Sometimes the question of ethnicity is intermingled with the question of race and religion. Not all Arabs are Muslims, and not all Muslims are Arabs, which is not always clear cut in international public opinion and mind-set, influenced by cliches about the region in the media as well as in other cultural production about the region.

Role of Sport

The main sporting event under the Arab League umbrella in partnership with national Olympic committees and national federations is the **Arab Games**, a sporting festival held every two or four years to promote sport culture and sport competition in the region. Those Games are not recognized officially by the International Olympic Committee, but they are good opportunities for young elite athletes in the region to compete and prepare for other continental and international competitions. As in any other region, there are rivalries in sport. The most heated rivalry is between Egypt and other North African countries such as Algeria, Tunisia, and Morocco. Rivalries are also found between countries in the Gulf region, particularly in the competition for the Gulf Football Cup, the most important sport tournament in the GCC, the **Gulf Cooperation Council**.

The process of the diffusion of Western sport into the region has taken different means and routes. One major influence was the presence of colonialism in its various forms, namely direct colonialism or protectorates. Sport was part of the strategy, or the "civilizing mission," of most colonial administrations. Conversely, nationalist movements used it as a tool of resistance against colonialism in the struggle for independence. Case in point is the struggle of the Palestinian Authority to be recognized by the international sport system and the Olympic Movement. Palestine had to wait until 1995 to be recognized as a nation in the Olympic Movement, and it is waiting to be recognized as a state by the United Nations. The appropriation of the dominant model of sport, despite its colonial origin, was seen as a necessity by newly independent countries in the Arab region. For independent nations seeking to gain full recognition, the integration into international federations and the International Olympic Committee became highly symbolic. Although some nations do not have a chance of winning a single medal in the Olympics, having the flag of the nation raised during the Opening and Closing Ceremonies is important to consolidating national unity. As in other regions of the world, sport has been shaped by nation-state construction and the political ideology of the leaders of the nation, party, and monarchy states. The Arab world in the 1960s and 1970s was divided between the Eastern and Western blocs. This division affected some of the decisions about participating in or boycotting international events. Not all Arab nations boycotted the 1980 Olympic Games. The same was true for the 1984 Olympic Games, which witnessed the historic victory of the Moroccan **Nawel El Moutawakel** in the 400-meter hurdles, the first gold medal for Morocco in the Olympics and the first by an Arab woman.

Sport even before the independence of Arab countries has been central in Arab culture and identity, including both modern sport as a product of globalization and traditional sport practice. A number of traditional games are still being practiced and celebrated in the region despite modernization, including horse riding, camel racing, falconry, traditional wrestling, and martial arts. Some of these sports are being transformed by technology. Now falconry and hunting are practiced with the assistance of GPS and 4-by-4 Jeeps, and for camel racing jockeys are now replaced by robots. Modern sport is now part of the fabric of Arab societies, although it occurs at different intensities depending on variables such as demography, GDP, urbanization, level of literacy, and government budgets for sport and recreation.

Sport has played some role in nation-state building in Arab countries. Sport was integrated by newly independent countries, particularly from the late 1950s to the early 1970s in nation-state formation and engagement with the international community. Sport has been used for the mobilization of the populace around Arab regimes' political ideologies (see Fatès, 1994). Starting from the early years of independence, the staging of regional games such as the **Pan African Games** (1978 in Algiers) and Mediterranean Games (1959 in Beirut, 1967 in Tunis, 1975 in Algiers) was important in showcasing the path toward development and nation-state building. Of course, the staging of the 2022 FIFA World Cup in Qatar will be a milestone for the region. Qatar has presented the event as an opportunity to bridge the gap between the Arab region and the rest of the world.

Football is not only a sport but also a lifestyle and religion-like institution that mobilizes millions. For Palestine refugees in Jordan, Al-Wihdat Football Club is more than a football club. It symbolizes the history of the Palestinian struggle and recognition as a nation. The same is true inside Palestine and the Gaza Strip where, as suggested by von der Lippe (2014), "the idea of Gaza football as an act of a masculinity of resistance through their continuing involvement in the everyday activities marks out an ordinary place that is not controlled by the [Israeli] military" (p. 1803). In most Arab countries, as argued by Tuastad (2013),

> with a suppressed or largely absent civil society, football has remained one of the few if not the only arena open for exposure of social and political identities, and the football arenas are where political messages are first communicated and struggle with authorities initiated. (p. 1)

The rival football clubs Al-Zamalek and Al-Ahly in Egypt are case in point. The two institutions are in parallel to other governmental and nongovernmental organizations in the country. Both clubs have more group members than may be in the party in power and even the Egyptian army, the biggest in the Arab world. Matches involving these two teams are occasions for power demonstrations. The football stands on those occasions become symbolically liberated territories from security control and from the control of regime doctrine that couples religious authority with nationalist sentiments. Amara (2012) argued that

> as an alternative to the official and rigid discourse of nationalism, football chanting is an opportunity for youths to take control of their identities. More importantly, it is a mode by which they may recover their right to speak about themselves, in their own language and codes; to interrogate history, faith, culture and politics; and to assert the right to speak directly to decision makers without an intermediary, on behalf of what they refer to in their songs, the "silenced" people. (p. 55)

One of the questions that has been central to sport, at least when the Arab region is mentioned or

Learning Activity

Qatar and other countries in the GCC (Bahrain, the UAE, and Oman) are facing a number of challenges in their strategy for elite sport development to improve sport performance, particularly in Asia and internationally. They are competing with nations such as China, Japan, Azerbaijan, South Korea, and Uzbekistan. They have a smaller population from which to develop a sustainable base of elite athletes. In groups, discuss how these countries are overcoming these challenges. What measures are needed to develop a viable elite sport system? Which sport should they focus on in their strategy?

represented in sport, is that of gender and women in sport. One could argue that the Arab world's readiness to integrate values of (Western) modernity has been judged in relation to the development and visibility of women in sport, particularly sport that represents the public space and a woman's body that symbolizes privacy (and *awra*, or private parts of the body, in Islamic). Women's bodies in sport have been at the center of the struggle between so-called secular and conservative wings of Arab societies. For some, revealing women's bodies in sport symbolizes liberalization from tradition, and for others, it symbolizes a form of submission to Western culture. PE lessons in schools, access to sport stadia, and participation in sport are being shaped by the debate in society (including in the media and political spheres) on gender questions and separation or not between genders. The 2012 London Olympics are considered a highlight when it comes to representation of Arab women in the Games. All Arab countries sent female athletes to the Games, including Saudi Arabia, which is branded as ultraconservative (although currently undergoing radical change in its political system). This development has been facilitated by the change of policy and rules of international sport federations with regard to the hijab (the veil) in sport. International sport federations banned headgear, including the hijab and turbans, in competition, officially on the basis of safety. This policy affected the participation of veiled women in competitive sport. The Fédération Internationale de Basketball (FIBA) was the last international federation to lift the ban after two years of trial.

In terms of sport practice, football, of course, is the most popular, followed by other team sports such as handball, volleyball, and basketball. This ranking goes back to the history of these sports and their significance in nation-state building. Although in other Arab countries, football is dominant, in Lebanon, because of the socio-religious fabric of a nation made of 18 religious groups and the influence of the Lebanese diaspora, basketball is the most popular sport among fans and sponsors. Thanks also to the nexus between business, politics, and sectarian identity, derbies between basketball teams attract more interest than derbies in football, although the latter have gained momentum in recent years. With the influence of globalization (or Americanization), urban sports such as the following are emerging:

- Parkour in the Gaza Strip is becoming a lifestyle for youth Gazaoui in the absence of spaces for leisure (Al Jazeera, 2017; Thorpe, 2014)
- 3v3 basketball in the streets of Algiers, Casablanca, and Tunis, mixed with rap and urban basketball clothing
- Surfing and scuba diving on beaches such as Sham al-Cheikh in Egypt and Salala in Oman, the new destination for tourism in the region

In terms of sport performance, Arab countries seem to perform better in football because of investment from governments and sponsors. Arab countries managed to qualify for the FIFA World Cup, as shown in table 8.1, and a few (Morocco, Tunisia, and Algeria) managed to reach the second round of the competition.

In terms of international sport performance, athletes from the Arab world are doing better in other sports, even though they are neglected, than they are in football. Football, despite its popularity and the resources it mobilizes, has not had any medals won so far by Arab nations in the Olympics. Track and field, thanks to athletes such as Said Aouita (Morocco), Hicham Al-Guerrouj (Morocco), Naoual Moutawakil (Morocco), Hassiba Boulmarka (Algeria), Noureddine Morcelli (Algeria), Taoufik

Makhloufi (Algeria), Nouria Merah-Benida (Algeria), and Mutaz Essa Barshim (Qatar), to name a few, produced the majority of medals for Arab nations in the Olympics. Other chances of winning medals occur in sports such as weightlifting, taekwondo, boxing, and wrestling. Some countries in the region, because of demographic constraints, are implementing a naturalization policy for foreign athletes to improve the country's performance on

Table 8.1 Arab Countries in the FIFA World Cup

Country	Year
Algeria	1982, 1986, 2010, 2014
Morocco	1970, 1986, 1994, 1998, 2018
Tunisia	1978, 1998, 2002, 2006, 2018
Saudi Arabia	1994, 1998, 2002, 2006, 2018
Egypt	1934, 1990, 2018
Kuwait	1982
Iraq	1986
UAE	1990

the international stage. Bahrain won two medals at the Rio 2016 Olympic Games thanks to naturalized athletes from Kenya; Ruth Jebet won a gold medal in the women's 3,000-meter steeplechase, and Eunice Kirwa won a silver medal in the women's marathon. These results cannot be seen as a direct product of grassroots sport in Bahrain, but even top nations in the Olympics maintain their world ranking by pursuing a similar policy of attracting outstanding foreign athletes and benefiting from the relaxed regulations of some international federations on nationality and citizenship. Arab nations do better in Paralympics than they do in the Summer Olympics, but as in other nations, the Paralympics is still considered a minor event.

Economics of Sport

Because of the oil boom in the Gulf region in recent years, a new trend of public and private investments in European football began. The aim is to brand the region as a new destination for tourism and business, and to link sport to other new sectors

CASE STUDY

Aspire Zone Foundation

Aspire Zone, at the heart of the city of Doha, Qatar, is a hub for sport science, research, education, and sport community provision. Key organizations include Aspire Academy, Aspetar for sport science and medicine, and Aspire Park. Aspire Zone is one of the legacies of the Doha 2006 **Asian Games** and a venue for a number of multisport facilities, including an indoor sport facility for women only. Families use the large park for walking, running, and picnicking. Aspire Academy has the ambition to be the center of sport excellence not only in Qatar but in the entire Arab region. Established in 2004, the academy is mandated to provide sport training and high school education to local and foreign students (around 6,000) with sporting potential. It has an ambitious talent identification program that has assessed in excess of 38,000 talented young people from the Qatar primary school system as well as people nominated by the various Qatar sport federations. In 2007 Aspire Academy opened its satellite branch in Senegal to oversee its sport for develop-

ment program, Aspire Football Dreams. According to the official webpage of the academy, "more than 3.5 million kids have been screened in 17 countries with 18 to 20 scholarships awarded each year." Questions have been raised in the Western media about the real agenda of this program, which is perceived as a way for Qatar, which has a small population, to import young, talented athletes from Africa. To be fair, European football clubs have been opening academies in Africa to bring young talents to play in European professional leagues for more than two decades now. To sustain its elite sport development system and to give graduates from Aspire Academy international experience and the opportunity to play in professional leagues abroad, Aspire Academy has teamed up with KAS Eupen, a Belgian professional football club that currently plays in the Jupiler Pro League (First Division). The Belgian club was taken over by Aspire Zone Foundation in 2012 while it was still playing in Second Division.

such as tourism and hospitality. This goal explains the presence and visibility of airline companies as sponsors of European clubs as well as major sport events around the world, such as Emirates' naming of Arsenal stadium, Qatar Airways' sponsorship of FC Barcelona, and Etihad's renaming of Manchester City FC's stadium. One of the strategies behind this direct or indirect investment in sport is to diversify the economy and manage the transition to the post-oil era. Some argue that the return on investment is minimal and that the main rationale is place branding and developing "soft power" by using sport arenas to network with international business and politics.

Milestones:

- Across Europe, US$1.5 billion has been spent by Middle Eastern investors and groups on team ownership.
- Abu Dhabi Holdings spent US$330 million for a 90 percent share in Manchester City FC in 2008.
- Qatar Sports Investments spent US$130 million for a 100 percent stake in Paris St. Germain in 2011.
- During the 2009-2010 season, jersey sponsorship by Middle Eastern companies was worth about US$24.6 million.

One success story in the Arab region when it comes to the economics of sport and sport investment in general is beIN Sports, the biggest sport TV network in the region. When launched in November 2003, it was branded Al Jazeera Sport, part of Al Jazeera Network. Ahead of the 2014 World Cup in Brazil, it was rebranded as beIN Sports and moved under different management to beIN Media Group. It broadcasts today in 43 countries across the globe—in the Middle East and North Africa (MENA), France, Spain, Turkey, the United States, Canada, Australia, Indonesia, Hong Kong, and the Philippines. Covering more than 20 sports internationally, the group claims to have more than 50 million subscribers around the world and 30 million social media fans. The chairman and chief executive officer of the group, Nasser Al-Khelaifi, is also the chairman of Paris Saint-Germain (PSG) Football Club in France. beIN Sports Arabia, in

particular, offers a number of programs for various sports as well as commentators from across the Arab region with different styles. Viewers can switch between different dialects—Egyptian, Algerian, Tunisian, Moroccan, and Khalidji (accent from the Gulf region). The beIN Sports TV network offers top-of-the-range studios with high-quality equipment for match analysis accompanied by former football stars and coaches from Europe and Brazil. beIN Sports, although Qatari owned, presents itself as a network that raises the flag of all Arabs in the global sport arena. The beIN Sports TV network has recently signed a partnership with the International Olympic Committee to start a new channel devoted to Olympic Sports in preparation for the 2018 and 2024 Olympic Games.

Governance of Sport

In most Arab countries, sport depends heavily on governmental funding, particularly where sport programs are supervised by the government under the **ministry of youth and sport** or under the umbrella of national Olympic committees. Most of the budget for sport would go to football because of its popularity and political dimension. Funding of sport is defined by the central government in general, from the ministry to departments, municipalities, and districts. The exception is the UAE, which is formed by federal states and where the sport system is organized under three sport councils—Dubai Sport Council, Abu Dhabi Sport Council, and Sharjah Sport Council. An interesting example is Lebanon, where a quota system among the different religious groups that make up the country (officially 18) shapes representation with sport governing bodies and clubs (Reiche, 2011). According to Nassif and Amara (2015, p. 1),

> Although there is no official distribution of power according to religious affiliations inside the national sport system, compromises are, however, informally in place to promote an internal "peaceful climate" within various sport institutions. These informal arrangements and tacit agreement between different protagonists, allow every community to have influence in the national sport system, although very often this led to situations of mismanagement and division, which in turn have strongly affected the implementation of sport policies in the country.

Although the norms of good governance are not in favor of government intervention in running sport and in electing heads of sport governing bodies, political leaders, military personnel, and members of royal families have a long history of being involved in sport. In a study of the sport and development agenda in the Arabian Peninsula, Amara and Theodoraki (2010) concluded that sport, as product of the dynamics between business, politics, and sport, serves the following purposes:

◆ The profusion of risky and bold mega sport projects linked to major urban developments

◆ The extensive use of the intangible values and images (goodwill, fair play, and well-being) of sport, which people generally hold, to increase brand awareness and sales

◆ The "glocalization" of the activity of the various agents (and their business interests) who engage with sport, moving between global trends and local context (Giulianotti & Robertson, 2004)

◆ The central role of the royal families, as both political and business elites, in facilitating the networking between international sport organizations and global and local business interests

Dependency of sport on governing bodies and the scarcity of sponsorship money coming to elite sport, with the exception of football and other high-profile events hosted in the region, make sport vulnerable to manipulation for political interests and intervention (Chen & Henry, 2012). Sport governing bodies in the region have been suspended by FIFA and the IOC in recent years. In 2009 FIFA suspended the Iraqi Football Association (IFA). The Iraqi Olympic Committee disbanded the IFA, and security forces seized control of its headquarters. Following the disruption of the Lebanese national championship because of political and judicial interference, FIBA suspended the Lebanese Basketball Federation (LBF) on July 11, 2013, for four years. In 2015 the International Olympic Committee suspended Kuwait for the second time in five years over government interference in the country's Olympic movement, thus obliging Kuwaiti athletes to compete as independent Olympic athletes under the Olympic flag at the Rio 2016 Olympics.

Kuwaiti athletes received two medals, one gold, but they were not counted for Kuwait because of the suspension.

Major Sport Events

Today, sport is becoming instrumental in the transformation of the region, particularly in the Arabian Peninsula (also known as the Gulf region). Significant investment is injected into the staging and sponsorship of leading global sport events and professional clubs, and the building of sporting infrastructure (see table 8.2). As an indication, around 60 international major events are hosted in Qatar annually. The aim is to open the Arabian Peninsula to the world of business and finance through branding the region as a hub for international sporting events. The organization of the **2022 World Cup in Qatar**, the first megaevent organized by an Arab country, despite the numerous bid attempts by Egypt and Morocco, will be a milestone for the region. The event, meant to be

Learning Activity

Qatar's successful bid to host the 2022 FIFA World Cup caught everybody by surprise. Qatar was competing with nations such as the United Kingdom and the United States. The World Cup will be the first mega sport event to be hosted by an Arab nation. Qatar's population is about 2 million, and the majority of them are non-Qataris. Qatar is ranked among the top countries in the region for business and competitive economy. Sport is becoming a key component of Qatar's development and international relation strategies. A number of issues have been raised about Qatar's bid and its preparation to host the FIFA World Cup. The event has been promoted by Qatar as the World Cup for the entire Arab region. Describe the economic, commercial, and geopolitical domains surrounding the 2022 FIFA World Cup in particular and the international football system in general.

Table 8.2 Major Single and Multisport Events Hosted in the Arabian Peninsula

Country	Important events	Major and single multisport events
Qatar	IAAF Diamond League ATP and WTA tour events FINA Swimming World Cup FIBA 3v3 All Stars Modern Pentathlon Champion of Champions	Asian Games 2006 2015 AIBA World Boxing Championships 2015 IPC Athletics World Championships 9th FIG Artistic Gymnastics World Challenge Cup, 2016 Fédération Internationale de Gymnastique Artistic World Gymnastics Championship 2018 Athletics World Championships in 2019 FIFA World Cup 2022
Bahrain	Bahrain FIA Grand Prix	Bahrain FIA Grand Prix
UAE	McLaren Cup Polo Omega Dubai Desert Classic (Golf) Dubai Duty-Free Tennis ITU World Triathlon Abu Dhabi Emirates Airline Dubai Rugby Sevens DP World Tour Championships (Golf) Abu Dhabi Grand Prix	2019 AFC Asian Cup

an event for the entire Arab world, has been at the center of political friction between Qatar and other countries of the Gulf Cooperation Council, namely the Kingdom of Saudi Arabia (KSA), Bahrain, and the United Arab Emirates (UAE). Morocco submitted yet again another bid to host the 2026 World Cup after unsuccessful bids in 1994, 1998, 2006, and 2010, competing this time against a joint bid by Mexico, Canada, and the United States. Despite the modernization projects underway and a growing market in the region, the challenge to overcome in hosting international sport events remains economic and mainly political. A number of countries in the region have been going through political turmoil and instability for the last 50 years, so the priority is to rebuild their countries and satisfy the needs of a growing educated youth population seeking decent jobs and better living standards. Qatar could be the exception as a one-country host of the FIFA World Cup. A more viable model, which seems to be encouraged by international sport federations to reduce financial risk and improve management before and after the event, is to opt for joint bids. We may see in the future a joint bid between two or three countries from North Africa or the Middle East for mega sport events.

Management of Sport

Management of sport in the Arab world depends on the political system and other political factors, such as questions of identity. The other dimension is that of economy. The one-party and military systems in the Arab region, such as in Syria, Iraq, Algeria, and Egypt, were highly involved in the affairs of national Olympic committees and national federations. For those countries, sport was (and still is) a means to mobilize youth around their political ideologies (Baath party in Syria and Iraq, National Liberation Front in Algeria, and Dostour party in Tunisia, to name a few). Sport has been mobilized for national prestige by the building of sport facilities symbolizing the modernization of the country under the guidance of the nation's leader. To reduce the influence of regional identities, Algeria, which pursued socialist ideology after its independence, replaced in the 1970s the names of football clubs by those of national corporations. In Lebanon, religious-political groups play a direct role in the management of sport clubs and federations. Hezbollah, in addition of having its own army, also has its own TV channel, newspapers, and, of course, affiliated sport clubs (e.g., Al-Ahd Club) and sport centers.

The same is true for other political movements with different religious obedience: Christian Maronite (Sagesse Club), Druze (Al-Safa), and Sunni (Ansar Club). In the Arabian Peninsula, *Choyoukh*, or noble families and princes, play an important role in the management and finance of sport federations and clubs. The divide between private and public sectors is not always clear cut.

Having said this, the private sector is present in the growing sport industry of event management, sponsorship, and fitness clubs, particularly in the emerging business centers from Ramallah in Palestine to Tangier in Morocco. According to a recent report by the Josoor Institute (2017) based on research undertaken in 17 countries in the MENA region (including Turkey), the value of the MENA sport and event industries stands at US$15.8 billion and US$8.7 billion, respectively. Most of the time national corporations intervene in the finance of sport clubs to overcome deficits resulting from the high salaries of professional players and coaches or budget cuts, particularly for nations depending on oil revenues.

The military and police forces are also involved in the management of sport centers and sport clubs (e.g., Royal Army FC in Morocco, Military Club in Egypt, Syrian Army FC in Syria, Union of Police in Egypt, Air Forces FC and Police FC in Iraq) and own parallel sport competition system. The final of the national cup between army regiments may be staged before the national cup of civil clubs and broadcast live on national TV. To rationalize funding and maximize the use of the state-of-the-art Duhail stadium, in 2017 the Qatari Ministry of Culture and Sport in collaboration with military and police institutions merged the two clubs Lakhwiya (police) and Al Jaish to form Duhail Club, which would dominate the Qatar professional league.

Summary

The Arab World with its 22 countries and different histories, geography, and ethnic and religious makeup offers an interesting context for the study of politics and the business nexus of sport. Sport is shaped by the nature of the political system and by business, economy, and demography. Egypt, the most populated Arab country, offers a range of examples of sporting practice and amateur and professional sport, including a parallel system of sport in the police and the military. Egypt has been dominating sports such as handball, squash, and football. But considering its long history in comparison with other countries in the region, Egypt has so far performed poorly in international elite sport, particularly in the Olympics, possibly because of the disparity in sport finance between football and other sports. For countries with a small population, such as Bahrain, that have to compete in Asia with top sporting nations, naturalization of African athletes is seen as a strategic component in a national sport strategy to have a presence in international sport. Wealthy oil countries such as Qatar and the UAE have used sport to aid urban development and place branding (Doha and Dubai as sport capitals in the region) using airlines, tourism, and the retail industry. Hosting major sport events and sponsoring top European clubs are part of the strategy to develop alliances through sport with international business. Qatar will host the first mega sport event in the region, the FIFA 2022 World Cup. This event is the pinnacle in the region with regard to sport development (or sport and development). The Arab world is undergoing a number of transitions in economic, political, social, and cultural domains. Global sport, particularly Internet and satellite sport TV broadcasting, is shaping different forms of sport consumption and access to major sport brands and professional sport leagues—the Premier League in football, the NBA in basketball, Rolland Garros in tennis, and Formula One for car racing, to name a few. The derby between FC Barcelona and Real Madrid mobilizes millions of viewers in the Arab region. Nowadays, fan loyalty in the Arab region is divided between local and international clubs.

? Review Questions

1. In which sports are Arab countries performing well in the Olympics?
2. What is the controversy about women's bodies in sport in Arab Muslim contexts?
3. How is sport being implemented in the transformation of the Arabian Peninsula?
4. Name examples of key sport events organized by the UAE.
5. What is the business value of the MENA sport and event industries?
6. How does religious identity influence the national sport system in Lebanon?
7. What are the reasons behind the dominance of beIN Sport over sport TV broadcasting in the region?
8. How was modern sport diffused in the Arab world?
9. Explain the strategy of Aspire Academy for elite sport development.

Sport in Oceania

Trish Bradbury, PhD
Massey University, New Zealand

Popi Sotiriadou, PhD
Griffith University, Australia

Chapter Objectives

After studying this chapter, you will be able to do the following:

- Understand sport in the Oceania region.
- Identify the geographic region, cultural background, popularity of sport, and the economic impact of sport in Oceania.
- Understand the key structures involved in managing sport in Oceania.
- Understand professional sport in Oceania.
- Understand the variety of major events held in Oceania.

Key Terms

Australian Institute of Sport (AIS)
Australian Olympic Committee (AOC)
Australian Paralympic Committee (APC)
Australian Sports Commission (ASC)
Australian University Sport (AUS)
High Performance Sport New Zealand (HPSNZ)

New Zealand Olympic Committee (NZOC)
Paralympics New Zealand (PNZ)
Sport New Zealand (Sport NZ)
University and Tertiary Sport New Zealand (UTSNZ)

Key Events

The **Sport Management Association of Australia and New Zealand (SMAANZ)** was established in 1995. SMAANZ encourages scholarly inquiry into sport management research and provides opportunities to present results at annual conferences and seminars.

The **Rugby World Cup** is a men's rugby union tournament contested every four years between the top international teams. The tournament was held for the first time in 1987, when the tournament was cohosted by New Zealand and Australia. Since then, Australia hosted the tournament in 2003 and New Zealand in 2011.

The **Pacific Games** is a multisport event, with participation exclusively from countries around the South Pacific Ocean. The event, held every four years, began in 1963. It was hosted by Suva, Fiji, and Papua New Guinea (PNG) in 2015.

The **Commonwealth Games** is an international multisport event involving athletes from the Commonwealth of Nations (also known as the Commonwealth), an intergovernmental organization of 52 member states that are mostly former territories of the British Empire. The Games were first held Canada in 1930. New Zealand hosted the Commonwealth Games in 1950, 1974, and 1990, and Australia hosted in 1938, 1962, 1982, and 2006. Australia's Gold Coast City is hosting the event in 2018.

The **World Masters Games** is an international multisport event held every four years and open to people of all abilities and most ages. Depending on the sport, the minimum age criterion ranges from 25 to 35 years. Toronto staged the first World Masters Games in 1985. Australia hosted the event in 1994, 2002, and 2009, and New Zealand hosted in 2017.

Key People

Sir Peter Blake, a New Zealand yachtsman and leader who led New Zealand to many victories in such events as the Whitbread Round the World Race, the Jules Verne Trophy, and the America's Cup. He was appointed a knight commander of the Order of the British Empire in 1995 for his services to yachting and youth development.

Sir Edmund Hillary, a New Zealand mountaineer, explorer, and philanthropist, who was the first confirmed climber to summit Mount Everest. The Hillary Commission for Sport, Fitness, and Leisure was named in his honor. Hillary is recognized as one of the 100 most influential people of the 20th century.

Dame Valerie Adams, a New Zealand shot-putter and four-time world, three-time world indoor, two-time Olympic, and three-time Commonwealth champion. She holds the New Zealand, Oceanian, Commonwealth, and equal world championship records. She is the first woman to win four consecutive individual titles at the World Track and Field Championships and is one of only nine athletes to win world championships at the youth, junior, and senior level of an athletic event.

Dawn Fraser is an Australian freestyle champion swimmer. She was named the Australian of the Year in 1964 and was inducted into the International Swimming Hall of Fame in 1965. Dawn was made a member of the Order of the British Empire in 1967. In 1998 she was appointed an officer of the Order of Australia and was voted Australia's greatest female athlete in history.

In 1999 the International Olympic Committee named her the World's Greatest Living Female Water Sports Champion.

Sir Donald Bradman was an Australian cricketer, widely acknowledged as the greatest batsman of all time. Bradman's career test batting average of 99.94 is often cited as the greatest achievement by any sportsman in any major sport.

Catherine Freeman was inducted into the Sport Australia Hall of Fame in 2005 as an athlete member for her contribution to the sport of athletics. She lit the cauldron in the Olympic Stadium at the 2000 Sydney Olympic Games, and after her gold-medal performance in the 400-meter race, she danced through a victory lap carrying Australian and Aboriginal flags, becoming a great ambassador of sport for indigenous Australians.

Although all the countries in Oceania have a strong sport culture and various successes to showcase their passion for sport, the focus of this chapter is on New Zealand and Australia. These two countries have developed strong sport structures and policies, and have systems in place that allow sport organizations to deliver sport at the professional, amateur, and community levels. This chapter offers an understanding of the role that sport plays in Oceania, specifically in New Zealand and Australia, and discusses sport and its development from a cultural basis, recognizing the key organizational structures and specific sport organizations involved in administering sport.

Geographical Description, Demographics, and Background

New Zealand and Australia are part of the wider region of more than 10,000 islands known as Oceania. Oceania stretches out over the Pacific and part of Southeast Asia, covering Australasia, Melanesia, Micronesia, and Polynesia. This region comprises a mixture of well-developed countries (e.g., New Zealand and Australia) as well as less- and least-developed countries (e.g., Cook Islands, Papua New Guinea, Samoa, Fiji, Vanuatu, and Tonga) (Sak & Karymshakov, 2012).

In mid-2017 New Zealand's population was estimated at 4,793,700 (Statistics NZ, 2017) and Australia's at 24,644,437 (Australian Bureau of Statistics, 2017). In New Zealand approximately 51 percent of the adult (16 years and over) population is physically active five days a week for a minimum of 30 minutes (Ministry of Health, 2017). Of the 17,000 5- to 18-year-old school-age youth surveyed, the majority take part in three or more hours of sport and recreation per week. Swimming is the most popular activity (Sport New Zealand, 2012).

Over time, the Oceanian culture has seen an increasing influence from Western culture. As the British Empire expanded so did the popularity of sport in Australia and New Zealand (Collins & Jackson, 2007). Therefore, sport in New Zealand and Australia largely reflects their British colonial heritage; some of the most popular sports are rugby union, cricket, soccer, and netball (Cashman, 1995). Rugby, for instance, was introduced in the mid-1800s in both countries, and cricket in 1825 in New Zealand (Ministerial Taskforce on Sport, Fitness and Leisure, 2001) and in the early 19th century in Australia.

Role of Sport

Most countries in Oceania appear to have an international sporting presence and a strong sport culture. For instance, some of the main sports played in Samoa are rugby union, rugby league, and Samoan cricket called kilikiti (Khoo, Schulenkorf, & Adair,

CASE STUDY

Kilikiti, the Samoan Cricket!

Kilikiti evolved from the game of cricket that the English missionaries brought to Samoa in the early 19th century. The Samoans adopted the game and renamed it kirikiti. Eventually, the game became the national sport of Samoa, and it spread throughout Polynesia to countries like Fiji, Tokelau, Tuvalu, and Tonga. It is played in most Pacific countries, including by Samoans in New Zealand and Australia. The change of name happened almost naturally because Samoans had difficulty pronouncing the English word *cricket* properly, so they called it kirikiti. Later on the pronunciation of the letter *r* changed to *l* in the Samoan language, so the name then changed to kilikiti.

Among the key differences between cricket and kilikiti are the bats, which are triangular and crafted from hibiscus or breadfruit tree! The ball is smaller and the wickets are taller than in traditional cricket. During the game, we see a bowler and a wicket keeper at each end, and when the ball is hit over the boundary on the full, the batsman scores two runs. But the most critical point of differentiation would have to be the fact that there is no limit to team size when playing kilikiti. Most players are all-rounders, and a kilikiti game is a multiday community event full of singing, dancing, and feasting. Entire villages compete, and everyone is involved, whether as player, cook, or spectator. Kilikiti sounds like backyard cricket, doesn't it?

2014). At the 2016 Olympic Games in Rio, Fiji won the men's rugby sevens gold medal in a thrilling match against Great Britain ("Olympic Results, Gold Medalists and Official Records," 2017). In addition, PNG topped the medal tally at the 2015 Pacific Games hosted in Port Moresby (Sotiriadou & De Bosscher, 2017). Women's cricket in PNG is also successful, winning the International Cricket Council East Asia Pacific Women's Trophy in Samoa in 2017 without losing a single match and qualifying for the Women's World Cup in Sri Lanka.

Although most countries in Oceania are culturally similar, some differences in popular sport and sporting preferences are evident, and the most popular sports in Oceania vary from country to country. For instance, one of the most popular sports in Australia is cricket, and the most popular sport among Australian women is netball. Australian rules football is the most popular sport in terms of spectatorship and television ratings.

As in Australia, netball is the dominant sport for females in New Zealand. Soccer has the highest sport registration base (New Zealand Football, 2016), but rugby union is the most popular sport, as it is in Papua New Guinea (Boyd, 1996). Rugby in New Zealand, according to Fougere (1989), cited in Owen and Weatherston (2002), "is more than

just the national sport; . . . it borders on the status of a *de facto* religion and is an important part of the nation's sense of identity" (p. 1). New Zealand's national rugby union team, the All Blacks, are the most successful rugby team of all time, compiling a 77 percent winning record over approximately 550 tests in their playing period of 1903 to 2016 (All Blacks, 2017). Based on World Rugby's ranking system, the All Blacks have been in the number one spot since 2009 and have been named World Rugby's Team of the Year consecutively from 2010 through 2016 (All Blacks, 2017).

Other sports popular in New Zealand and Australia at the participation and elite levels are swimming, cycling (road, track, and mountain biking), and surfing, in which both countries have excelled by winning medals in Olympic and world championship events.

Governance of Sport

The central government provides most of the funding for sport delivery at the national, amateur, and community levels in New Zealand and Australia, but local governments, charities, and private funding also contribute to the pool of money. Private investment is the foremost provider of funds at the professional sport level.

Sport in New Zealand and Australia

In New Zealand, the Sport, Fitness and Leisure Act established the Hillary Commission for Sport, Fitness and Leisure in 1987 as the organization responsible for developing and encouraging sport, fitness, and leisure participation (NZ Institute of Economic Research, 2000). Then in 2000 a ministerial taskforce, Getting Set for an Active Nation, commonly known as the Graham Report, named after the author of the report, was undertaken (Ministerial Taskforce on Sport, Fitness and Leisure, 2001). This report assisted the government in defining and developing a clear policy framework and vision for sport, fitness, and leisure over the next 25 years (Ministerial Taskforce on Sport, Fitness and Leisure, 2001). Thus, in 2001 the Sport and Recreation Agency Bill was introduced to Parliament to create a new organization titled Sport and Recreation New Zealand (SPARC) (Sport and Recreation New Zealand, 2002). SPARC was officially launched in June 2002 with the intention to promote, encourage, and support the taskforce's vision for a healthier, more physically active nation. It replaced the Hillary Commission, the NZ Sports Foundation, and the policy arm of the Office of Tourism and Sport to form a more dedicated and focused sport body. In 2011 **High Performance Sport New Zealand (HPSNZ)** was established as a subsidiary of SPARC, which was rebranded to **Sport New Zealand (Sport NZ)** in 2012. The New Zealand government provides funding for sport through the Sport NZ group, a public-sector entity comprising Sport NZ and HPSNZ (Sport New Zealand, 2015).

Similar developments took place in Australia during the early 1980s with the establishment of the **Australian Institute of Sport (AIS)**, Australia's strategic high-performance sport agency located in Canberra. Soon after this initiative, in 1985 the **Australian Sports Commission (ASC)** was established (Sotiriadou, 2009). The ASC, Australia's primary national sport administration and advisory agency, operates under the Australian Sports Commission Act 1989. Its four key goals are to

1. increase participation in sport,
2. increase international success,
3. provide sustainable sport, and
4. enhance ASC capability to lead, partner with, and support Australian sport efforts.

In August 1987 the government formalized their decision to rationalize federal assistance to Australian sport, and the AIS merged with the ASC as the agency responsible for general sport participation as well as high-performance sport (Sotiriadou, Quick, & Shilbury, 2006).

Sport New Zealand and the Australian Sports Commission

The Sport New Zealand Group is a wholly owned crown agency charged with supporting young people and adults' sport participation and elite athletes' sport performance (Sport New Zealand, 2015). Their vision is "For New Zealand to be the world's most successful sporting nation" (Sport NZ, 2015, p. 1) with a focus on "getting more Kiwis, especially kids, into sport, and producing more winners on the world stage" (Sport NZ, 2015, p. 1). These aims are intended to be achieved by being participant focused, system led, and performance driven, focusing on young people, local delivery, competitive sport, and high-performance activities (Sport NZ, 2015).

In Australia, the Australian Sports Commission, the statutory authority responsible for government sport policy, works with national sport organizations (NSOs) through the Australian Institute of Sport and the Sport Performance and Development Group to promote the sport philosophy of the Australian government. This philosophy is reflected through the ASC's two-fold aim to

1. increase community participation in sport through programs for various groups of people including juniors, women, people with disability, indigenous people, and the elderly, and
2. achieve international elite-athlete success through sport excellence and high-performance programs (Australian Sports Commission, 2011).

Success in achieving results in community participation is measured by the proportion of the Australian population participating regularly in sport and of specific underrepresented groups participating regularly in sport. The Australian sport system offers the Australian population various opportunities to engage in sport activities through sport clubs. As such, local clubs and sport managers offer facilities, programs, and competitions that allow various segments of the population like young participants, females, indigenous people, people with disabilities, and people from all ethnic backgrounds and genders, to play, coach, or volunteer. This process is called the attraction, retention, transition, and nurturing of sport development, and sport clubs are an essential part of that process (Sotiriadou, Shilbury, & Quick, 2008).

High Performance Sport New Zealand and the Australian Institute of Sport

Operating as a subsidiary of Sport NZ, HPSNZ's purpose is to get more winners on the world stage. HPSNZ is a one-stop shop for New Zealand's elite athletes, enabling them to concentrate solely on training and performance (Sport New Zealand, 2015) using a strategy and investment approach designed to build "a performance-driven, athlete-focused and coach-led system" (High Performance Sport New Zealand, 2015a, p. 3). HPSNZ's vision is "More New Zealanders winning on the world stage at Olympic/Paralympic Games and World Championships in targeted sports," and its mission is "Creating a world-leading, sustainable high performance sport system" (High Performance Sport New Zealand, 2015, p. 4).

In Australia, for elite athletes to achieve and sustain international success, the government established the Australian Institute of Sport as Australia's strategic high-performance sport agency. The AIS is responsible for leading the delivery of Australia's international sporting success. This success is measured by medals at Olympic, Paralympic, and Commonwealth Games, world rankings, and results at benchmark events, including world championships and world cups, and the number of athletes and teams of world and international class (Commonwealth of Australia, 2011).

Three Principles of Managing Elite Sport in Oceania

Sotiriadou and De Bosscher (2017) suggested that managing high-performance (HP) sport is a function of three principles:

1. developing athletes and creating pathways to success,

2. examining the environment within which athletes can develop, and

3. using that information to shape, implement, and evaluate HP strategies, policies, and plans.

In Oceania, particularly in countries such as New Zealand and Australia, these three principles are evidenced in various ways.

First Principle   Sport organizations, especially local sporting clubs in Oceania, help identify athlete development pathways within their sport. Athlete development programs and strategies encourage participation and promote excellence. But creating successful athlete attraction, retention, transition, and nurturing processes through developmental pathways represents a sport development challenge to sport organizations that cannot identify or fill in gaps in developmental pathways. Some sports get the balance of athlete continuation and progression right, whereas others struggle. An example in the Australian context is represented in two football codes, the Australian Football League (AFL) and soccer (A-League). Both codes are popular at the grassroots level of participation. But the pathways to the top tier of the AFL game are clearly structured, and the sport experiences better talent retention and transition to the elite level compared with soccer and the A-League.

Learning Activity

In groups, discuss the key reasons that would help explain why some sports fail to design and deliver successful athlete development pathways. In your discussion, consider the nature of the selected sport (e.g., popular sport, Olympic sports, early specialization sports, nonorganized sports, professional sport) and the ways that can influence athlete development, the income sources of the sport, its infrastructure, the competitions structure, the pool of talented athletes, and the people and organizations involved. Also, consider the barriers that people or children are faced with that influence their decision or capacity to progress to higher levels of participation.

Second Principle   The environment of high-performance sport in Oceania is shaped at the macro, meso, and micro levels. Specifically, the commercial, political, social, and cultural environment in which people live, including the economy, demography, geography and climate, urbanization, politics, and national culture, affect the operation of sport organizations. Therefore, managers need to formulate the strategies that best fit the historical, cultural, and political context of the sport system. At the meso level, countries in Oceania offer financial support to sports, and a well-established sport structure and governance is necessary for the development of sport, both at grassroots and elite levels. Coaches, national and international competitions, and scientific research and innovation are also essential for the development of elite athletes. Yet the success of individual athletes can also be attributed to micro-level factors such as genetics as well as more controlled factors like coaching or training.

Third Principle   Most nations in Oceania are strategic in the way they produce elite athletes. Consequently, national sport systems have moved beyond the application of sport sciences and coaching as a sole base for elite-athlete success. High-performance strategy formulation involves the development of the organization's (or team's or athlete's) mission—what the organization or team does and what it aims to achieve. Then, sport organizations at the national level (like Tennis New Zealand or Swimming Australia) are ready to develop their HP strategies. After sports have completed their HP strategy formulation, HP managers need to facilitate strategy implementation, the process of putting the formulated strategies into action. Managers are required to communicate the strategies to coaches, athletes, and sport scientists to execute HP activities that will yield the best results. Strategy evaluation is the process of measuring performances, analyzing variance between set and achieved goals, and taking corrective action if goals have not been achieved (Sotiriadou & De Bosscher, 2017).

New Zealand and Australian Olympic and Paralympic Committees

The **New Zealand Olympic Committee (NZOC)** represents both the Olympic and Commonwealth Games movements in New Zealand and is recognized as the national Olympic committee (NOC) for New Zealand. Their vision is "to inspire excellence and pride in New Zealanders and enable New Zealand's elite athletes to achieve on the world's stage" (NZOC, 2017a). Their mission is to use their "unique mandate as a member of the International Olympic Movement to maximise benefits for New Zealand and New Zealand sports and athletes" (NZOC, 2017b, p. 2).

Parallel to the NZOC is **Paralympics New Zealand (PNZ)**, the body responsible for Paralympic sport and athletes with a disability, which is recognized by the International Paralympic Committee (IPC) as the national Paralympic committee (NPC) in New Zealand. Their vision is "excellence and equity through sport" and their mission is to lead, excel, champion, and advocate for athletes with a disability on the national and international stage (PNZ, 2017).

The **Australian Olympic Committee's (AOC)** responsibility, like the NZOC's, is to select, send, and fund teams to partake in the Olympic Summer and Winter Games. Similarly, the **Australian Paralympic Committee (APC)**, like the PNZ, is responsible for preparing Paralympians for the Paralympic Summer and Winter Games. The AOC is a nonprofit organization, independent of government, and funding is derived from income distributions from the Australian Olympic Foundation, grants from the International Olympic Committee (IOC), licensing, sponsorship, and fund-raising activities of the AOC, and state Olympic councils and their corporate appeal committees. In recent times, however, the ASC and the AOC decided to collaborate to progress the idea of a new national sport lottery and other prospective new revenue sources (Australian Olympic Committee, 2017). The urgency of the matter was prompted not only by government pressures for sport organizations to become more financially

Learning Activity

In your groups, discuss how the geographical location of countries in Oceania and other environmental factors influence the types of sports played as well as opportunities for athlete travel and international competitions.

viable but also by the consistent drop in elite-athlete performances, in particular since the 2000 Sydney Olympics (Sotiriadou & Brouwers, 2012).

National, Regional, and Supporting Sport Organizations

A national sport organization, like New Zealand Football (NZF), is the national governing body of a particular sport, a keeper of the code, you might say. Their role is to promote and control the activity of a particular sport for the majority of people participating in that code, from community to elite or international levels, and to foster, develop, and promote sport by providing training, enjoyment, recreation, and competition (Chelladurai, Radzi, & Daud, 2017). At the grassroots level, NSOs, NZF for example, provide financial and sport-specific resources supporting their affiliated regional sport organizations (RSOs) like the Northern or Central Football Federations. At the elite level, they are responsible for selecting national teams or individuals to represent their sport at international

CASE STUDY

New Zealand Football and the 2015 Pacific Games

New Zealand Football's (NZF's) under 23 men's team, the Oly-Whites, participated in the 2015 Pacific Games, hosted by Papua New Guinea (PNG). New Zealand would not normally compete in these Games, but the Oceania Football Confederation (OFC) and the Fédération Internationale de Football Association (FIFA) jointly decided that the Pacific Games would be a qualifier for the 2016 Olympics. The Oly-Whites travelled to PNG with confidence and high hopes. They won the semifinal 2-0 against Vanuatu, sending them to the Games and Olympic qualifier final. The Vanuatu Football Federation (VFF) then submitted a protest under FIFA's Statutes, Article 7, claiming that New Zealand fielded an alleged ineligible player. The OFC disciplinary committee upheld the protest, reversing the score 3-0 and disqualifying New Zealand. NZF contested and appealed to the OFC without success.

According to Article 7, to be eligible a player had either to be born in New Zealand, have Kiwi ancestry, or have lived continuously in New Zealand for five years after the age of 18 (FIFA Statutes, 2015). In this case, the alleged ineligible player was born overseas, had no New Zealand relatives, and was only 20 years of age. Some commentators suggested that Vanuatu's protest was encouraged by the Pacific Games Council, the local community, and the OFC, all of whom allegedly disliked NZF and New Zealand in general. A key question was this: How did Vanuatu know there might be a problem with a New Zealand player's eligibility? The individual had already played in FIFA-sanctioned tournaments and World Cups, so his ineligibility was not obvious. Had Vanuatu been briefed, and had they prepared the protest before the game? If not, how did they prepare the protest in the two-hour time limit allowed following the game? Had evidence been prepared by the OFC to be used when an opportune time arose? Or did the problem arise because NZF backed the "wrong person" in the 2015 FIFA presidential election? NZF originally agreed to vote for this person but because of allegations of corruption and other unethical behavior, they changed their mind. (We now know that this longstanding president was charged with criminal mismanagement.) This issue created a divide among the OFC and its members because NZF was the only member nation to vote against the OFC-preferred candidate. Some believe that NZF and the Oly-Whites' coach must have known that the player was ineligible. Commentators questioned whether New Zealand was trying to pull a fast one by sneaking a player into the squad, assuming that no one would check. In addition, New Zealand's coach openly criticized the local organizing committee for arranging substandard accommodation, inferior playing conditions, and a demanding playing schedule. These criticisms were widely publicized both within PNG and overseas. These comments put the New Zealand team offside with the Games hosts and made a volatile local community even more hostile. These Games were designed to create "bonds of kindred, friendship, and brotherhood . . . without any distinctions as to race, gender, religion or politics" (Pacific Games Council Charter, 2010, p. 4), which was not the New Zealand experience.

Learning Activity

A number of rumors and opinions circulated. Many questions were posed and considered: Did NZF go through the appropriate processes to ensure that all players were eligible to compete in the Pacific Games and Olympic qualification tournament? Was an outright gamble taken with the player's eligibility status, or was it a calculated decision? Who in NZF was responsible for establishing player eligibility? Was NZF trying to protect this person? Was it administrative incompetence or misinterpretation of the statutes? Consider the answers to these questions using evidence offered in the case study and by visiting online sources to verify your opinion.

competitions and for developing and financing a high-performance program for pre-elite and elite athletes.

A regional sport organization has responsibilities at the regional or state grassroots level and the elite level. At the grassroots level, they develop and promote their sport within their region through schools and clubs. At the elite level, their role is to select and resource regional teams or individuals to represent the region at national competitions, manage competitions, and provide appropriate services to regional or state athletes (e.g., travel, sponsorship, coaches, and equipment). Other examples of RSOs include Judo Victoria and Surfing NSW in Australia and the Auckland Touch Association and Volleyball Bay of Plenty in New Zealand. In summary, NSOs support RSOs and are affiliated with a regional world body and an international federation (IF). For example, NZF is affiliated with the Oceania Football Confederation, and both are affiliated with the Fédération Internationale de Football Association (FIFA). Swimming New Zealand is affiliated with the Oceania Swimming Association and the Fédération Internationale de Natation (FINA), and Cycling Australia is affiliated with the the Oceania Cycling Confederation and the Union Cycliste Internationale (UCI).

University Sport in New Zealand and Australia

University sport has held a significant place in New Zealand's and Australia's heritage of sporting success. The first interuniversity sport competition in New Zealand was held in 1902. The New Zealand University Sports' Union (NZUSU) was created in 1957 with the purpose of coordinating interuniversity sporting activities domestically and internationally. The NZUSU serviced tertiary students until 2012, when student Union membership became voluntary, thus reducing funds available to the Union and contributing to the decline of the national University Games competition and associated events, and ultimately, the Union itself. In 2015 **University and Tertiary Sport New Zealand (UTSNZ)**, a new collectively funded organization, was established. Its first executive director was appointed in 2016. UTSNZ's goals include reviving competitive intertertiary sporting competitions, lifting the standard of those competitions, and developing pathways to international opportunities (UTSNZ, 2017). In Australia, similarly, **Australian University Sport (AUS)** facilitates opportunities for students to participate in competitive sport at a regional, national, and international level. A key event that AUS organizes on an annual basis is the Australian University Games, a national event open to all universities in Australia.

Economics of Sport

Sport in Oceania offers opportunities for people to engage in exercise and play sport in their spare time, volunteer and work in the sport industry in various capacities, spectate at games and competitions at large stadia or enjoy local competitions at community venues, and watch elite players and athletes compete on the international stage. This ever-increasing activity, as well as overall household expenditures on sporting goods and services, offers a significant multilayered economic contribution to the sport industry across Australia and New Zealand.

In Australia, for instance, the sport sector employs over 75,000 Australians, and every year Australian households spend more than A$8.4 billion on sporting services and products (ABS, 2011). Supported by lucrative television broadcasting rights agreements, corporate sponsorships, and spectator interest, the sport sector in Australia is growing by 3.5 percent per year, achieving a total turnover of A$6.2 billion (McMillan, 2011).

In New Zealand, the sport sector employs approximately 55,000 people and contributes 2.3 percent to the GDP, which equates to NZ$5 billion per annum covering sport and recreation industries, physical and human infrastructure, and volunteer contributions (AERU, 2015). Volunteers make a significant contribution to the sport and recreation sector. Close to 1 million adults volunteer 68 million volunteer hours over a 12-month period. In dollar terms, this effort equates to an estimated NZ$1,031 million (Sport NZ, 2017). Overall, approximately NZ$987 million is spent on sport and active leisure activities, equipment, and services.

New Zealand exports and imports sport and recreation commodities such as horses, leisure wear, ski equipment, swimwear, sporting footwear, bikes, yachts and other crafts, and outdoor recreation equipment, to name a few. Imports of these commodities increased from NZ$451.8 million to NZ$521.5 million during the 2010 to 2014 period, but exports decreased from NZ$455 million to NZ$312.8 million (AERU, 2015).

Management of Sport

Through the 1990s professional sport in New Zealand and Australia experienced significant developments. Rugby union became professional in 1995 because World Rugby (called the International Rugby Board [IRB] at the time), repealed all amateurism regulations, meaning that players could be paid (Owen & Weatherston, 2002). Because international rugby became professional, rugby in New Zealand and Australia had no choice but to become professional to keep in step with the international scene (SANZAAR, 2017). For the first time, New Zealand Rugby had to negotiate with and contract professional rugby players. In 1996 SANZAR (South Africa, New Zealand, Australia Rugby) was formed, and a professional, well-paid competition, the Super 12, began with five New Zealand teams, three Australian teams, and four South African teams competing for the title. In 2017 this competition was called Super Rugby. The organization grew to 18 teams and was renamed to SANZAAR to include Argentine rugby. The competition evolved from 12

teams in 1996 to 14 in 2006, 15 in 2011, and 18 in 2016, now including teams from Argentina and Japan as well as New Zealand, Australia, and South Africa, but it will be reduced in 2018, eliminating South African and Australian franchises.

Also in 1995 the Vodafone Warriors rugby league team joined the Australian Rugby League (ARL) competition. This was the start of New Zealand teams playing in various Australian professional sporting competitions, known as Trans-Tasman leagues. Other sports to follow suit included football with the Football Kingz joining the Australian National Soccer League (NSL) in 1999, which was renamed the A-League in 2004. The New Zealand Breakers joined the Australian National Basketball League (ANBL) in 2003, and from 2007 through 2016, five New Zealand netball teams participated in the ANZ Trans-Tasman Championship. As of 2017 both New Zealand and Australia are running standalone domestic competitions. The New Zealand competition is called the ANZ Premiership Netball League with six teams, and the Australian competition is called the Suncorp Super Netball with eight teams. Most of these professional sports are privately owned but are governed by nonprofit sport organizations. New Zealand, as a country, does not own or operate any professional leagues.

Both countries have successful elite-athlete development systems that provide talent for domestic and overseas professional sport competitions as diverse as English Premier League Football, Rugby League, Rugby Union, and County Cricket in the United Kingdom and the National Football League, Major League Baseball, the National Basketball Association, the Womens' National Basketball Association, and the National Hockey League in North America (Hoye, 2015).

Major Sport Events

States in both New Zealand and Australia host a series of annual or biannual professional and amateur sporting events that highlight their passion for sport and strong cultural ties with sporting events. Victoria, Australia, for instance, is home to the Formula 1 Australian Grand Prix, Rip Curl Pro Bells Beach, Australian Open Tennis, and Boxing Day Cricket Test. Queensland hosts the Australian PGA Championship, the Australian Surf Life Saving Titles, the Gold Coast Airport Marathon, the Magic

Millions Racing Carnival, and the Pan Pacific Swimming Championships. New Zealand plays host to events such as the ASB Men's and Women's Tennis Classic, NZ Golf Men's (PGA) and Women's (LPGA) Opens, Crankworx Festival and Enduro (Mountain Biking) World Series, and the World Rally Championships. Many other events are hosted on a one-off basis like the World Masters Games, Rugby Union and Rugby League World Cups, numerous yachting events like the Youth Sailing World Championships, and the International Ski Federation's (FIS's) World Cup events in freestyle skiing, snowboarding, and freeski halfpipe.

Summary

This chapter has provided a brief overview of sport in the Oceania region with a focus on New Zealand and Australia. Sport in these countries has a long history; British immigration and sporting preferences affect the types of sports played even today. Both countries are sport mad. Sport at the community through to the international or elite and professional levels are played, spectated, coached, refereed, and even debated.

Learning Activity

Select an international mega sport event held in North America or Europe and compare it with a mega sport event in Oceania. Pick a few aspects to research for comparison. Some examples to consider are finances, sponsorship, marketing, and revenues. Which aspects are similar? Which are dissimilar? Why do you think this is the case?

The two countries have a similar structure of organizations that support sport from the community to international or elite echelons and receive government funds to support sport operations like Sport NZ and the ASC with a national reign.

Lastly, professional sport and the hosting of domestic and international sport events were presented. Australia provides professional sport competitions, but New Zealand does not and thus plays in these Trans-Tasman leagues. Examples of the vast number of events hosted in both countries were also provided.

? Review Questions

1. What are the lead organizations of sport in New Zealand and Australia?
2. What are the key roles of these organizations?
3. How have the cultural and historical backgrounds of sport in Oceania influenced sport today?
4. List the similarities and differences between sport in New Zealand and Australia.
5. Explain what a Trans-Tasman league entails in regard to professional sport.

Sport in South Asia and Southeast Asia

Megat A. Kamaluddin Megat Daud, PhD
University of Malaya, Kuala Lumpur

Wirdati M. Radzi, PhD
University of Malaya, Kuala Lumpur

Govindasamy Balasekaran, PhD
Nanyang Technological University, Singapore

Chapter Objectives

After studying this chapter, you will be able to do the following:

- Appreciate the heterogeneous characteristics of the region that influence regional sports governance.
- Identify key economic, political, and social considerations that shaped the management of sports in the region.
- Recognize the role of the public sector in governing regional sports structures.
- Understand the role of sport in the region.
- Identify the influence of religion, tradition, and culture in sport activities in the region.
- Recognize the types of national and popular sports being played at the grassroots and competitive levels.

Key Terms

purchasing power parity (PPP)
South Asian Association for Regional Cooperation (SAARC)

Association of the Southeast Asian Nations (ASEAN)
South Asian Games (SAG)
Southeast Asian (SEA) Games

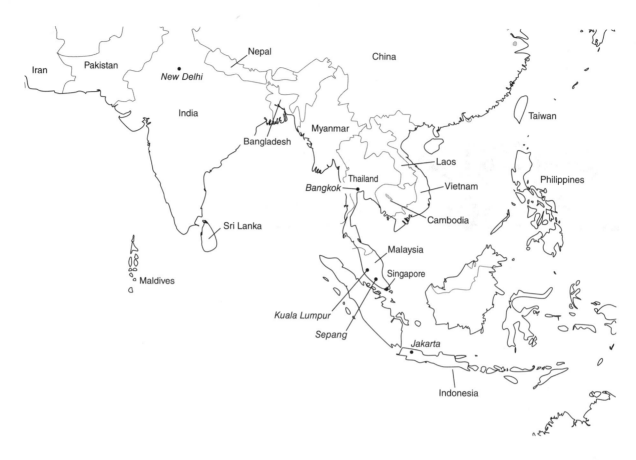

Key Events

Establishment of Asian Association for Sport Management (AASM) in 2002. A scholarly and professional organization for the study of sports management in Asia.

2010 Commonwealth Games in New Delhi, India. This quadrennial multisport event is a solidarity game that brought together the former colonies of the British Empire. It is the second biggest multisport event in the world after the Olympics with 53 nations competing.

2010 Hockey World Cup in New Delhi, India. Officially known as the Hero Honda FIH World Cup Delhi 2010.

The event was held from February 28 to March 13, 2010. The Hockey World Cup is a quadrennial event, comparable to the FIFA World Cup series.

2018 Asian Games in Jakarta and Palembang, Indonesia. The third largest multisport event after the Olympic Games and the Commonwealth Games with 46 nations competing, officially named the 18th Asian Games for 2018. The Asian Games is a quadrennial event. It was founded in New Delhi, India, in 1949. The 2018 event was the first with two host cities.

Key People

Sheikh Salman bin Ibrahim Al-Khalifa, president of the Asian Football Confederation AFC (based in Kuala Lumpur, Malaysia).

HRH Sultan Ahmad Shah, president of the ASEAN Football Federation AFF (based in Kuala Lumpur Malaysia).

Poul-Erik Høyer Larsen, president of the Badminton World Federation BWF (based in Kuala Lumpur).

Sachin Tendulkar, former Indian cricketer regarded as one of the best batsmen of all time.

Nicol David, longest reigning world number 1 in women's squash (108 weeks), currently ranked seventh in the world.

This chapter examines sport in two regions, South Asia and Southeast Asia. In terms of development, countries are classified as developed, developing, less developed, and least developed (Nielsen, 2011), which is a unique feature of the region. For instance, based on Nielsen (2011), the South Asian region is made up almost entirely of countries categorized as developing (e.g., India, Pakistan), less developed (e.g., Bangladesh), and least developed (e.g., the Maldives). The Southeast Asian region consists of a developed country (e.g., Singapore) and developing countries (e.g., Thailand and Malaysia). Developed countries have advanced industrial economies, high incomes, and democratic governments. The gross domestic product (GDP) of these countries is in excess of US$10,000 per capita. Developing countries are the bottom group of the International Monetary Fund's (IMF) hierarchy of advanced economies. Less-developed countries have low levels of output, low living standards, and limited technology. They have a GDP per capita of US$5,000 or less. The least developed country includes countries with no significant economic growth, low literacy rates, and per capita GDP of US$1,000 or less (World Bank, 2016).

This divergent socioeconomic, political, cultural, and religious background of the region is the starting point of our discussion on managing sport in the region. This chapter seeks to understand the role that sport plays in South Asia and Southeast Asia. It outlines some of the sport management structures and issues within the region, complexities that are present, and the results of social dynamics that were put in place to manage sport in the region.

Geographical Description, Demographics, and Background

To promote clarity, the geographical description and demographic makeup of South Asia and Southeast Asia are discussed here. This background is important to frame the discussion of sport in the region.

South Asia

South Asia is geographically defined as the region located at the southern end of the Asian continent, also sometimes known as the Indian subcontinent. South Asia is made up of India, Pakistan, Nepal, Bhutan, Sri Lanka, Bangladesh, and the Maldives. It is one of the world's most densely inhabited regions, having a population of more than 1.5 billion people. The region has a rich combination of ethnic backgrounds and religious affiliations: Buddhists, Hindus, Muslims, and Christians. The region also boasts an illustrious political history whereby archaeological evidence of past ancient civilization points to the region's ancient political and economic prosperity. The population of India is made up of two major ethnic groups: the Indo-Aryan and the Dravidian. These groups share more than 1,000 languages, 18 of which are recognized as India's official languages (Chelladurai et al., 2002). The European intrusion in the region started in the 15th century when Portuguese merchant vessels sailed into the nearby waters. Colonization ended in the late 1940s when many nations in the region gained independence from their colonial masters.

At present, South Asia is an emerging economic force. India is the world's third largest economy after China and United States (Chelladurai, et al., 2013). According to the World Bank Group report (2016), South Asia continues to be the world's fastest-growing region economically. Leading the pack is India, a large emerging market economy in the region. India is ranked number 3 in the world in GDP (gross domestic product) based on **purchasing power parity (PPP)** (World Bank, 2018). PPP is a method of understanding the long-term exchange rates of money based on relative price levels in two countries. PPP is also used to compare the income of people by adjusting for differences in prices in various countries.

The nations of South Asia have formed the **South Asian Association for Regional Cooperation (SAARC)** to enhance regional cooperation and development. Established on December 8, 1985, SAARC has a specific aim to promote economic, social, and cultural cooperation among member states. The member states comprise (in alphabetical order) Afghanistan, Bangladesh, Bhutan, India, the Maldives, Nepal, Pakistan, and Sri Lanka. Other members of the SAARC with observer status are Australia, Burma, China, the European Union, Iran, Japan, South Korea, Mauritius, and the United States (Central Intelligence Agency, 2017). An observer country has direct or indirect interests or stakes in any of the SAARC member countries.

Southeast Asia

Southeast Asia covers a vast area that borders the Indian subcontinent in the west, China in the north, and Australia in the south. Measuring 1,746,000 square miles (4,523,000 sq km), the region is divided into two smaller regions: the mainland nations of Southeast Asia (Cambodia, Laos, Myanmar, Thailand, and Vietnam) and the maritime nations of Southeast Asia (Indonesia, Malaysia, the Philippines, Singapore, and Brunei). The regional diversity consists of "over five hundred million population, one thousand languages, and a religious smorgasbord of Animism, Buddhism, Taoism, Hinduism, Islam and Christianity. This sheer diversity of Southeast Asia defies simple categorization" (Chong, 2005).

The geographical composition of the region also plays an important role, especially in shaping the historical, political, and past and current conditions. Originally, Indian and Chinese traders came to Southeast Asia in search of spices and other products to be exchanged in the barter trade system at various ports. Eventually, the merchants began to settle down and influence local ways of living. Ancient mega structures such as the Angkor Wat in Cambodia and the Borobudur in Indonesia are temples dedicated to Buddhist and Hindu deities. These magnificent testaments of the architectural genius and engineering technology possessed by the people of Southeast Asia were influenced by the Indian voyagers (Abdul Wahid, 1970). In terms of political history, with the exception of Thailand, most countries in Southeast Asia were colonized by the West from the 16th to the 18th centuries. Colonialism replaced the native economic, legal, and education systems and altered the geopolitical boundaries of the region (Hashim, 1992).

The 19th and 20th centuries saw the gradual withdrawal of the Western powers and the beginning of newly independent modern nation states. Southeast Asia maintained its regional cooperation through the formation of the **Association of the Southeast Asian Nations (ASEAN)** in August 1967. ASEAN preserves its main purpose, which is to accelerate economic growth, social progress, and cultural development of the region, as well as to promote regional peace and stability (ASEAN, 2018). ASEAN membership consists of 10 states (listed in alphabetical order): Brunei, Cambodia,

Indonesia, Laos, Malaysia, Myanmar, Philippines, Singapore, Thailand, and Vietnam. The association has 11 dialogue partners: Australia, Canada, China, the European Union, India, Japan, South Korea, New Zealand, Russia, the United States, and the United Nations (Central Intelligence Agency, 2017). ASEAN also promotes cooperation with Pakistan in areas of mutual interests, and Papua New Guinea is a state member with observer status.

Southeast Asia is an emerging economic power, emulating the economic success of South Asia, specifically India. The region has a GDP of approximately US$37 billion and purchasing power parity (PPP) of current international dollar 10.69 units (International Monetary Fund, 2016). A country like Singapore has already attained developed status through significant economic development, whereas countries like Laos and Vietnam are experiencing a slower economic growth rate. The United States, Japan, China, and Korea are major trade partners with the region.

Role of Sport

Sport, especially in South Asia and Southeast Asia, has always been viewed as an important tool in social integration (Megat Daud, 2000), as well as an avenue to develop national identities. People generally identify with their national team during international sport competitions. Outstanding performances by a national team lead to an increase in the nation's international eminence, such as the internationally successful Indian national cricket team that is revered among the Indian populace (Nalapat & Parker, 2005). South Asia and Southeast Asia are part of the largest continent in the world and are exceptionally diverse in experiences—ethnically, culturally, religiously, sociologically, economically, and politically (Mangan, 2003).

Learning Activity

Read the sidebar Sepak Takraw: From Peasant Game to International Sport and search the Internet for a video of sepak takraw being played. Construct your own ball out of crumpled paper and play a game of circular sepak takraw with a few of your friends or classmates.

Traditional Sport

In multicultural, multiethnic, and multireligious South Asian and Southeast Asian communities, the interest in sport transcends the differences and shared objectives. Sports introduced in the region by the colonizers are still popular today. Before the introduction of the Western concept of team sports in the region in the 20th century, the natives indulged in activities that are physical and sport-like in nature (Brownfoot, 2003).

Similar conditions were observable in other parts of the region. Traditionally, the majority of Thais were involved with agriculture, so folk and craft games were more popular (Sriboon, 2007). One such game that gained reputation in the region is sepak takraw. Originally thought to be a game introduced by Chinese traders to Southeast Asia, sepak takraw is considered by many countries in the region as their own traditional game. Sepak takraw was already popular in Malaysia and Thailand by the early 1400s ("Sepak Takraw," n.d.). The term itself depicts the presumed two nations that originated the game: *Sepak* is a Malay word meaning "kick," and the word *takraw* is Thai for "rattan," because the ball is made of rattan. The game was known in Thailand as takraw. Sepak takraw is the formal name of the game, a name that paid homage to the two Southeast Asian countries that claimed to have created the modern and structured version of the game. Not surprisingly, Malaysia and Thailand were considered traditional rivals at this game, and the rivalry is a much awaited feature at any sepak takraw event. Today, sepak takraw is played

Sepak Takraw: From Peasant Game to International Sport

Sepak takraw is a game of speed, agility, and dexterity. The origin is said to be Chinese. In Thailand at Wat Phra Kaew, murals of the game being played by the monkey god, Hanuman, can be found. Sepak takraw was also mentioned in the Malay Annals, an epic that chronicled the life of the Malaccan sultans that was said to have been written in the 14th century. In 1829 the Siam Sports Association drafted the first rules for sepak takraw competition, retaining its original circular form of play. In 1833 the badminton-styled netting was introduced. Today, sepak takraw requires an area measuring 44 by 20 feet (13.4 by 6.1 m) with a center line dividing the court. The ball is spherical and can be made of either rattan or synthetic fiber. The three-person team in sepak takraw is called a *regu*, and two *regus* play against each other. The formation of the players' position is quite similar to that of volleyball. Two players flank the net placed in the middle of the court at either side. The server, or *tekong*, is at the center of the court. The top of the net measures about 5 feet (1.5 m). The tekong serves the ball, which has a circumference of 1 foot, 4-1/2 inches (42 cm) and weighs 6 ounces (170 g), to the other court using the feet. The ball is pitched to him or her by one of the players at his or her side who flanks the net. The regu on the other side then attempts to receive the ball using either the feet or the head. The objective of the game is to maintain the ball airborne as long as possible.

The team that allows the ball to drop or fall outside the court lines loses a point. The game is played in two sets, separated by a two-minute rest. The scoring system is similar to other net games such as badminton and volleyball. When either the serving side or the receiving side commits a fault, a point is awarded to the opponent's side, including the next service. The winning point total for a set is 21 points, unless the set is tied at 20 to 20. In that case, the set shall be decided on a difference of 2 points, up to a ceiling of 25 points (International Sepak Takraw Federation, 2016).

Sepak takraw has evolved into a full-fledged, international sport having its own international sport governing body, the International Sepak Takraw Federation (ISTAF). Currently, ISTAF includes 21 member countries: Thailand, Indonesia, Singapore, Brunei, Malaysia, Korea, Laos, China, Myanmar, Philippines, Japan, Sri Lanka, India, Pakistan, Bangladesh, Vietnam, United States, Canada, Puerto Rico, Iran, and Brazil. The federation also lists 8 playing countries that have been granted observer status: Germany, Switzerland, Sudan, Nepal, Denmark, Colombia, Mongolia, and Hong Kong. The current headquarters of ISTAF is in Singapore. Sepak takraw is included in international multisport events such as the SEA Games, the Asian Games, the World Games, as well as having its own regional and international single-sport events.

Learning Activity

Identify one folk or traditional sport or sport-related activity that you know of. Would you define it as a sport in modern context? In what way does traditional sport influence or shape our understanding of sport?

competitively at the biannual regional games and the **Southeast Asian (SEA) Games**, which will be explained in detail later in the chapter.

Other traditional games reflect the societal life of the region and often involve everyday activities such as plowing the fields. At the end of the harvest season, farmers organize a celebration as a symbol of seasonal change and an opportunity to enjoy recreation. Folk and traditional games are still very much alive in many parts of South Asia and Southeast Asia, such as traditional kite-flying games that are played on the east coast of Malaysia. These activities provide farmers respite from the hard work of toiling in the fields. The simple games evolved to community events where people gather to celebrate the end of the harvest.

Modern Sport

As mentioned earlier, the South Asia and Southeast Asia regions were formerly colonized by the West, notably the British, Dutch, Portuguese, and Spanish. Along with the Western law and other systems, the British also introduced Western sports to the whole empire (Brownfoot, 2003). Currently, football is unrivalled as the favorite pastime in many Southeast Asian countries such as Indonesia, Malaysia, Vietnam, and Thailand. In the Indian subcontinent, cricket, another modern Western-styled sport, is considered the national sport. Cricket players are revered by the populace. Legendary names such as Imran Khan of Pakistan and Sachin Tendulkar of India reverberate along the corridors of cricketing fame.

Badminton is also popular among the locals in countries like Indonesia, Malaysia, and India. Lim Swee King, Misbun Sidek, and Prakash Padukone and current stars like Taufek Hidayat and Lee Chong Wei are iconic badminton players from the region that will forever inspire millions of young sport people in South Asia and Southeast Asia.

In terms of elite sport participation, football is popular in South Asia and Southeast Asia. In India, cricket and hockey (also known as field hockey in contrast with North American ice hockey) are the most popular sports. Badminton and squash are examples of sports that are dominated by athletes from South Asian and Southeast Asian countries, which have produced world champions such as Pakistani squash champions Jansher and Jahangir Khans, Indonesian badminton champion Taufek Hidayat, and Malaysia's longest reigning world number 1 squash queen, Nicol David, and badminton ace Lee Chong Wei. These sport stars benefit from the sport development policies and programs of their countries, and they now become the source of inspiration for sports development at the grassroots level.

Governance of Sport

Throughout South Asia and Southeast Asia, the role of the government appears to be important in the development of mass sport as well as sport at the elite level. Regardless of the economic status of the nations in the regions, the role of the public sector in sport is instrumental within local sport development structures. The active involvement of the public sector in local sport points to the emphasis given to sport by governments as part of the nation-building agenda. Nations are reconstructing their own image and identity as independent nations, and sport has always been regarded as contributing to the participation of the masses in rebuilding the national identity.

In India, the National Sports Policy was proclaimed in 1984 but was later replaced in 2001 on claims that it was not implemented properly and that its goals were not realized (Chelladurai et al., 2002). The objectives of the 2001 National Sport Policy are twofold: to promote sport at a broad level and to achieve excellence at the elite international level. The policy also stated the responsibility of state governments to push for the development of mass sport. In Malaysia, sport is also regarded as an important component in the nation-building process and as a significant contributor to Malaysian society (*National Sport Policy*, 1989).

Similarly, in Singapore, although the initial emphasis of the government was to promote the policy of sport for all among Singaporeans, the pursuit of excellence in sport became the focal point of the government with the initiation of Sports Excellence 2000 (SPEX 2000) in 1993 (Horton, 2002). A further policy on sport participation was announced by the Singaporean government in May 2008 through the Singapore Sport Council with the Let's Play Campaign. Singapore aspires to be the leading city for sport in Asia, heralding the evolution of Singapore sport from the grassroots level to international sport participation. Table 10.1 presents some of the regional competitions and the frequency of such events.

A review of some of the national sport policies in the region reveals the increasing effort made by governments to regulate local sport. Governments in the region are beginning to invest more in the development of sport and using it as part of national developmental programs. The government of Singapore has considered sport policy a "particularly malleable and high profile policy instrument" (Green, 2007).

The commercialization and globalization of sport have prompted many regional governments to consider including elite sport programs in their sport policy. The emphasis is no longer just about promoting sport at the broader base; achieving excellence in sport along the way is crucial. National sport policies in countries such as Singapore, India, and Malaysia would have repercussions in terms of financial allocations to either category of sport participation. Tensions may arise, especially when a small number of elite athletes compete for funds with a community sport program for the elderly that is aimed at a larger segment of the population. Countries in the region face this continuing dilemma, and absolute solutions are absent. Sport managers would have to manage and improve the mechanisms in place and balance priorities when deciding between the needs of the population and the aspirations of the country.

Economics of Sport

According to Manzenreiter (2007), although sport has been associated with the business sector for a long time, a straightforward equation of sport with profit making and commercialization is a recent phenomenon. This view is exemplified by the complexity of estimating the global market size of sport-related goods and services. The market value of the global sport industry was roughly made up of gate revenues for live sport events, television broadcasting rights fees, merchandising, sport sponsorships, and other related business activities. Although data on sport GDP in South Asia and Southeast Asia have not been comprehensively compiled to date (largely because sport is not considered or categorized as a revenue-generating sector in many developing countries), the annual budgetary allocations for sport from governments remain high or are on the increase. One country that has compiled data is Singapore, which recently announced that its sport GDP has crossed the S$1 billion mark.

Asia as a whole is now riding on the prospect of China's burgeoning economy. Megaevents such as the Formula One Grand Prix are good revenue generators for local regional economies. For example, following the success of the Malaysian Grand Prix in Sepang, Singapore wanted a piece of the action in hosting the event. Table 10.2 presents the number of attendees at the Grand Prix in Sepang and Singapore.

Table 10.1 Frequency of Regional Competitions

Competition	Frequency
SEA Games	Biennial
Asia Games	Every four years
AFC Football Championship	Biennial
South Asia Games	Biennial
Commonwealth Games	Every four years
SEA Universities Games	Biennial
Pacific Games	Every four years

Table 10.2 Formula One Grand Prix Attendance in Sepang, Malaysia, and Singapore

Year	Sepang, Malaysia	Singapore
2013	120,000	87,509
2014	87,228	85,704
2015	80,604	86,970
2016	83,828	73,000

CASE STUDY

Singapore Sport Industry

Since gaining independence from Britain in the mid-1960s, Singapore has grown exponentially to become the financial and commercial hotspot of its region. Many of the world's leading corporations have regional headquarters in Singapore. They have been attracted by its stability, the quality of the communications infrastructure and the built environment, and its proximity to the tremendously exciting growth markets of China and India.

Although Singapore does not possess world-renowned athletes and record holders, it aspires to capitalize on the sport services sector as a major income generator for its economy and as an international operational hub for international sport organizations (ISOs). Singapore has been actively promoting and positioning itself to attract multinational sport companies to locate their business in the country. The investment paid off when major international and regional sport events were held in Singapore over the last two years. Some of the world-class events are the Youth Olympics, Asian Youth Games, and the Men's Hockey Junior World Cup. With the Singapore government committed to growing its sports industry, Sports Singapore (SportsSG) believes that more companies will realize its untapped potential (Roberts, 2005; "Sports Investment," 2009).

Management of Sport

The field of sport management in Asia is gradually changing in line with the rest of the world. South Asian and Southeast Asian countries are slowly making their presence felt. The progress that they are making now mirrors that of their Western counterparts. The new markets appear to be tempting for marketers, especially when the product is in demand in the South Asia and Southeast Asia market.

Cultural Implications for Sport Managers

Managing sport in a multiethnic, multicultural, and multireligious society, especially in Asia, requires special knowledge and skill. At the outset, it would be unwise to disregard the cultural differences that exist and the deeply embedded ways of life of the various societies (Abraham, 1988). Abraham argued further that, although cultural differences must be taken into account when making management decisions, they are not the main impediment that necessarily affects the institutional structure of work in a systematic and consistent way over a prolonged period (Abraham, 1988). Abraham suggested that the management perspective (including sport) must be directed toward creating an economic climate that enhances local initiative and entrepreneurship. Mendoza (1992) further advised that local managers need to look objectively at their own cultural values, use them to filter practices that were based on Western or foreign values, and critically select practices from local or foreign values that support positive management practices.

According to Chatterjee and Pearson (2003), as Asian management emerges as an area of intellectual and practical attention, no other managerial concern attains more significance than the ethical dimension in ethically divergent contexts. This issue is particularly relevant because the challenges they present are rooted in the cultural, social, religious, political, and managerial traditions of Asian countries. Western approaches are based on individual freedom, democratic nuances, universalism of rules, and a focus on strategy. In contrast, attachment to extended family, deference to social interest, thrift, respect for authority, and fulfilling traditional obligations are key Asian characteristics. Universalistic principles and practices of the mainstream management ideas need to be explicitly accommodative and responsive to Asian context-relevant imperatives.

Sport managers must be sensitive to these values when making decisions. For instance, religious holidays must be observed, and locals must be consulted on the relevant aspects. For example, planning a water-based sport event during the fasting month of Ramadan in Indonesia would be insensitive to the locals. Indonesia is the largest Muslim-majority country in the region. In observance of Ramadan, Muslims fast from dusk to dawn for a whole month and usually refrain from rigorous physical activity to conserve energy. Although Muslim athletes are known to compete in sporting activities while continuing to fast, water-based activities are considered problematic because of the chance of swallowing some of the water while participating, which would render the fast to be broken. In addition, Muslims use the lunar (not Gregorian) calendar to determine when Ramadan begins and ends; therefore, sport managers are advised to determine the matter before making any decision.

Training Sport Managers

Operating and managing today's sport industry efficiently requires extensive knowledge and skill. Sport needs qualified, competent managers to manage it (DeSensi et al., 1988). Career paths associated with sport management are not as well defined as they are in other vocational areas (Parks & Quarterman, 2003). Initially, sport managers are usually hired from visible groups such as professional sport or college athletics. Especially in Asia, this situation is typically exemplified by hiring a former professional footballer or a physical education (PE) teacher to become a sport director for a university's sport program. The objective of PE academic programs is to train PE teachers to be proficient in sport science knowledge such as human anatomy, sport physiology, biomechanics, and so on; the PE curriculum was never designed to train

Learning Activity

Think about any sport-related policy in your institution. Who created it? What is it about? Who will be affected by it? Discuss with your classmates the extent of influence that a sport policy wields over a certain group, community, or country. Think also about the policy systems, processes, and pathways in the discussion.

sport managers (Lizandra, 1993). The academic preparatory programs are of paramount importance as the demand for skilled and competent managers in sport rises alongside the phenomenal growth of the industry. The University of Malaya, the first university in Malaysia, started the initial baccalaureate program in sport science in 1995, becoming one of the earliest in the region to do so, more than two decades after Ohio University started its sport administration programs (Radzi, 2000).

Major Sport Events

The regions have hosted many international sport megaevents including the Commonwealth Games (Kuala Lumpur 1998, Delhi 2010), the Youth Olympic Games (Singapore 2010), the Asian Games (India, Thailand, and Indonesia), as well as regional multisport events (such as the South Asian Games and the SEA Games) and single-sport events, such as the Formula One Grand Prix, the Hockey World Cup, and the BWF World Championships. The Formula One race was the first ever night race in Asia, a unique feature that also doubled as an effective marketing tool (Cheng & Jarvis, 2010). This further promoted the region in organizing mega sport events.

Regional sports play an important part in fostering stronger cooperation among the nations in the region. Regional sports have deeply embedded historical backgrounds that are often a result of the sociopolitical and economic dynamics among regional nation-states. As mentioned earlier in the chapter, all the regions organized themselves into regional cooperation entities such as the SAARC and ASEAN. Later, interest developed to strengthen multilateral ties through sport and other social initiatives. For example, the first **South Asian Games (SAG)** was held in Kathmandu, Nepal, in 1984. The motivation for the event was to strengthen cooperation and relationships among South Asian countries through sport. Note that although Afghanistan is a member of the regional economic cooperative, the nation was barred from participating in the event because of allegations of human rights violations. The event was initially held annually, but from 1985 onward it was held every other year.

The Southeast Asian Games (SEA Games) were initially styled as the Southeast Asian Peninsular Games (SEAP). The first SEAP Games were held

Learning Activity

Select an international sport megaevent in North America and compare it with a sport megaevent in South Asia and Southeast Asia. Pick a few aspects to research for the comparison; some examples are financial, sponsorship, marketing, and revenue. Which aspects are similar? Which are dissimilar? Why do you think this is the case?

in Bangkok in 1959, and it too had an objective of promoting regional cooperation through sport. The 9th SEAP Games held in Kuala Lumpur saw the unveiling of a new name for the event—the SEA Games. The SEA Games are a biennial event. The 2009 Games were hosted by Laos, and the 2011 Games were hosted by Indonesia. The 2017 Games were hosted in Kuala Lumpur.

Sport marketers must understand the various political, philosophical, cultural, and religious norms that affect the value system of the country in question. Sport marketers in northern Thailand may be able to list an alcoholic beverage manufacturer as a major event sponsor, but having the same event sponsorship in southern Thailand would draw protests from the district's majority Muslim population.

Summary

The evolution of sport in South Asia and Southeast Asia saw the development of individual life skills and talents, the assimilation of Western-based sport, and participation at the international level in a number of Western sports. Another important point is that hitherto, sport has always been a public concern. The involvement of the private sector, especially in terms of funding and sponsorship, is not as prevalent then as it is now because of the social context of sport participation. Lately, sport in South Asia and Southeast Asia has developed into a commercial endeavor. Multinational corporations have invested millions of dollars in sport programs. The local sport management circumstances were largely influenced by the development of this field in other developed countries in North America, Europe, and Asia. Issues that plagued regional sports, especially in South Asia and Southeast Asia, have also affected the management of modern sport, such as overreliance on government funding, sport governance, modernization needs, moral and ethical issues in sport, and the dilemma between the priorities for mass sport participation and the aspiration for sporting excellence.

From observation, the management of sport and sport organizations in South Asia and Southeast Asia is in need of development and modernization. Various factors may affect development, but one thing remains for certain—sport has continuously been receiving support, particularly from governments and sponsors.

Clearly, the role of the government is central to the development of sport in South Asia and Southeast Asia. This relationship is evident mainly through the financial allocations and expenditures on sport made by governments as well as the promulgation of sport-related legislation that some may see as controlling mechanisms. Some factions deem this control appropriate on the premise that governments are merely accounting for public expenditures in sport as opposed to dictating the direction of local sports. A possible dilemma is that future expenditures and development of public sport programs will target only a few selected elitist sports. For example, funding may be concentrated on sport events that have the potential to bring fame and fortune to the country, and spending may be limited for grassroots mass sport.

As with any discipline, sport management should go through the professionalization process (Koehler & Lupcho, 1990). Essentially, this process covers three phases (Parks & Quarterman, 1998):

Phase 1—Building of theoretical foundations and a body of knowledge

Phase 2—Creation of a distinctive subculture

Phase 3—Sanction and acceptance by the community

This region appears to have gone through the first phase and is well into the second phase. Local scholars in Asian sport management are being trained locally and abroad for that same purpose. The establishment of the Asian Association for Sport Management (AASM) in 2002 signified the start of the second phase, which could speed up the process leading into the final phase, when the community would be aware of the need to have professionals managing sport in South Asia and Southeast Asia.

❓ Review Questions

1. What traditional sports are the most popular in countries in this region?

2. Discuss how colonial rule influenced and shaped sport development in the region.

3. How has the global sport industry affected sport in this region?

4. What is your opinion about the effect of globalization of sport in the two regions?

5. Discuss the differences between managing sports in the West, in South Asia, and in Southeast Asia.

6. Discuss the economic trends important to sport in the region and the opportunities that these developments might bring for sport organizations, sponsors, and other businesses.

Sport in Northeast Asia

Yong Jae Ko, PhD
University of Florida

Di Xie, PhD
Active Sport International Co., Ltd., China

Kazuhiko Kimura, MS
Waseda University, Japan

Chapter Objectives

After studying this chapter, you will be able to do the following:

- Define Northeast Asia as an economic and geophysical continent.
- Be familiar with the sport governance systems in China, Japan, and South Korea.
- Compare and contrast the approaches taken by China, Japan, and South Korea in governing their respective sport systems.
- Identify the major legislations enacted by nations, particularly China, Japan, and South Korea, for sport development.
- Understand the arms race among China, Japan, and South Korea in Olympic sports.
- Identify major international and continental sport events held in Northeast Asia.

Key Terms

All-China Sports Federation (ACSF)
Asian Games
centralized sport governance system
Chinese National Games (CNGs)
East Asian Games
Japanese Ministry of Education, Culture, Sports, Science and Technology (MEXT)
Japan Sports Agency (JSA)

Japanese Sport Association (JASA)
Ministry of Culture, Sport and Tourism in South Korea
Korean Olympic Committee
mixed sport governance system
National Council of Sport for All (NCSA)
sport governance system
State General Administration of Sports (SGAS)

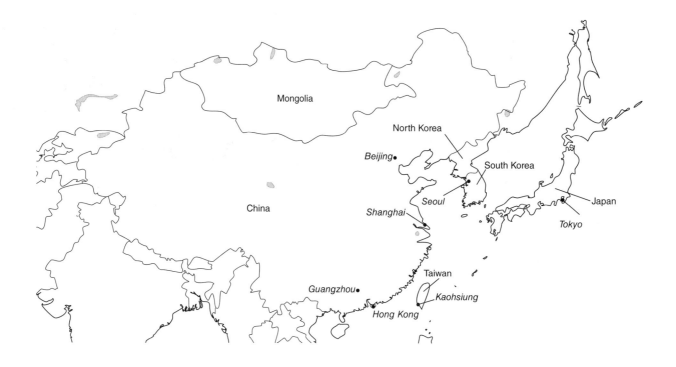

Key Events

FIFA 2002 World Cup in Korea and Japan, first FIFA World Cup event held in Asia.

1988 Olympic Games in Seoul.

2008 Olympic Games in Beijing.

2009 East Asian Games in Hong Kong, the fifth East Asian Games, hosted more than 2,300 athletes who competed in 22 sports.

2010 Asian Games in Guangzhou, China, hosted athletes from countries throughout East Asia, Southeast Asia, and the Middle East who competed in 42 sports.

2014 Asian Games in Incheon, South Korea.

2017 Asian Winter Games in Sapporo, Japan, hosted about 2,000 athletes and officials from 32 countries and regions.

2018 Winter Olympics in Pyeongchang, South Korea.

Key People

Zaiqing Yu, vice president of the 2022 Beijing Winter Olympic Games, vice president of the International Olympic Committee from 2008 till now.

Chiharu Igaya, president of the Japan Triathlon Union (JTU) and Japan Olympic Academy, joined the International Olympic Committee in 1982.

Daichi Suzuki, first commissioner of the Japan Sports Agency (JSA), won the gold medal for 100-meter backstroke at the 1988 Seoul Olympics.

Kun-Hee Lee, honorary president of the Korean Olympic Committee since 1996 and a member of the International Olympic Committee since 1996.

Zhongwen Gou, director of the State General Administration of Sport in China and president of the Chinese Olympic Committee.

Un Yong Kim, vice president of the International Olympic Committee for many years and president of the World Taekwondo Federation until mid-2000, a major figure in the sport industry of Korea and the Olympic Movement.

A powerful sport boom has been under way in Asia, particularly in Northeast Asia, over the last four decades, evidenced by the successful staging of the Seoul Summer Olympic Games in 1988, the Nagano Winter Olympic Games in 1998, the 2002 World Cup cohosted by Japan and South Korea, the 2008 Beijing Olympics, and the 2018 Pyeongchang Winter Olympics. The boom is also evidenced by the success of athletes from nations in Northeast Asia in various international competitions. This chapter introduces the sport industry in various nations in Northeast Asia, specifically examining the structure of the sport industry and the policies and issues concerning its development in three core nations—China, Japan, and South Korea. In addition, the influence of geopolitical and cultural factors on sport governance in these three countries will be reviewed.

Geographical Description, Demographics, and Background

There is no commonly accepted version of the geographical makeup of Northeast Asia (NEA). According to Kim (2004), NEA is a region that encompasses Greater China (including Hong Kong, Macau, and Taiwan), Japan, Mongolia, North Korea, South Korea, and the Russian Far East. The United Nations Environment Programme (2004) defines NEA as a subregion of Asia comprising five countries: China (including Hong Kong, Macau, and Taiwan), Japan, Mongolia, North Korea, and South Korea. This area "has the highest population of all the subregions with a total of 1.48 billion people (United Nations Environment Programme, 2004, p. 9). While discussing sport in this region, this chapter focuses on the three biggest sport nations in the region in Asia—China, Japan, and South Korea.

The countries in this region are rising in economic power in the world. China (including Hong Kong, Macau, and Taiwan), Japan, and South Korea collectively accounted for about one-fourth of world GDP in 2000 (Kim, 2004). As of September 2002,

NEA was home to the world's five largest holders of foreign-exchange reserves: Japan (US$443.1 billion, or 19.3 percent of the global total), China (US$259.4 billion, or 11.3 percent of the global total), Taiwan (US$156.1 billion, or 6.8 percent of the global total), South Korea (US$117.1 billion, or 5.1 percent of the global total), and Hong Kong (US$108.2 billion, or 4.8 percent of the global total) (Kim, 2004, p. 8).

Besides those amazing economic strengths, NEA consists of people of racial, linguistic, and cultural complexity. Although NEA nations have their own distinct linguistic forms of expression, many have their roots in the Chinese language. The cultures of the NEA countries can be labeled as neo-Confucian because the ideology of Confucianism is their shared common cultural root (Hu, 2006). As a set of ethical and philosophical beliefs, Confucianism developed from the teachings of an ancient Chinese scholar called Confucius, who lived in the 6th century BC (Yao, 2000).

China, the world's largest country by population, is home to more than 1.38 billion people (Central Intelligence Agency, 2017). The world's population is now nearly 7.4 billion, so about one in every five people on earth is Chinese. Physically, China is the third largest country in the world after Russia and Canada, and the largest nation in Asia, encompassing an area of 3,705,000 square miles (9,597,000 sq km) (Central Intelligence Agency, 2017). China has 34 province-level administrative units, including 4 municipalities, 23 provinces (including Taiwan), 5 autonomous regions, and 2 special districts. China's economy has experienced a more than 10-fold increase in GDP since 1978 after changing from a centrally planned system to a market-oriented economy. Reforms by China's Communist government started in the late 1970s with the phasing out of collectivized agriculture. Restructuring expanded to include the gradual liberalization of prices, fiscal decentralization, increased autonomy for state enterprises, the foundation of a diversified banking system, the development of stock markets, the rapid growth of the nonstate sector, and the opening to foreign trade and investment (Central Intelligence Agency, 2017). Measured on a purchasing power parity basis that adjusts for price differences, China in 2008 stood as the second largest economy in the world after the United States, although its large population means that per-capita income is still in the lower-middle range (Central Intelligence Agency, 2017). Today, China plays an important role in the global economy.

The development of the sport industry in China has gone through four stages: the formation stage (1985-1990), the market-oriented development stage (1991-2001), the sport industry revitalization stage (2002-2008), and the post–Beijing Olympic stage (2008-present). The mid- and late 1980s was an important period in the development of the sport industry in China. Before 1990 China never had the opportunity to host a high-profile international sporting event. With steady economic growth, Beijing hosted the country's first large-scale international sport event, the 11th Asian Games, in 1990. China invested ¥2.5 billion (US$525 million) to build or renovate facilities to stage the event. The Beijing Asian Games served as a precursor to China's sport facilities construction boom, because the country went on to bid for the 2000 Summer Olympics.

After the successful hosting of the Beijing Asian Games in 1990, China became an attractive place for a variety of international events because of its rapid economic growth. A professional football league was formed in 1994, and a professional basketball league followed in 1995. During this period, sport media became a strong player in the promotion of the sport industry in the country. In 1993 China hosted its first Sporting Goods Fair. More than 200 manufacturers displayed their products. During the sport industry revitalization stage, the entire nation had one focus: to make the 2008 Olympics the most successful ever in the history of the Olympic Movement. Marketing through sport for nonsport products and marketing of sport products became the main themes of this stage. How to use and maintain the sport facilities built and used in the Olympic Games, how to maintain the level of sport consumption, and how to strengthen the sporting goods market and develop the sport service industry are some of the main issues of the post–Beijing Olympic stage.

Japan has the 10th largest population in the world with about 126.5 million people (Central Intelligence Agency, 2017). Its gross national income is the highest in the subregion (United Nations Environment Programme, 2004). Administratively, Japan is subdivided into 47 prefectures (or subnational jurisdictions). After experiencing tremendous growth in the years from 1960 to 1990, the Japanese economy suffered a severe recession in the early 1990s. Slow recovery has occurred since the economic downturn. Japan's GDP in 2008 was US$4.844 trillion.

According to Cheng (2009), the development of the sport industry in Japan can be divided into six eras. The six eras include the beginning era (1880-1940), the expanding era (1950-1960), the highly developing era (1960-1970), the maturing era (1970-1980), the transiting era (1980-1990), and the second growing era (1990-2000). During the beginning era, modern sport was introduced to Japan from the West. The Mizuno Corporation, the world's oldest sporting goods company, was established in the early 20th century during this era (Harada, 2010).

Many sport facilities were built in the expanding era. Leisure sport took shape during the highly developing era. The period from 1980 to 1990 saw the booming of health clubs as Japanese participation in various recreational or health-related sports such as golf increased tremendously. The government recognized the sport sector as an industry during this era (Harada, 2010). Professionalism and commercialization in sport were the two key traits of the second growth era in the sport industry in Japan. For example, the Japanese Soccer League, or J League, was formed in 1991. The sport industry in Japan has experienced another growth period in the first decade of the 21st century.

Compared with China and Japan, South Korea has a relatively small population (51,181,299 people in 2017) (Central Intelligence Agency, 2017). Geographically, its land area covers 38,023 square miles (98,480 sq km). Because of the rapid growth of its economy, South Korea was labeled one of the four dragons in Asia (alongside Hong Kong, Singapore, and Taiwan) in the 1980s. It has since become one of the most economically dominant nations of Asia. In 2008 its GDP was US$1.278 trillion.

The sport industry experienced a great leap in the 1980s after the nation successfully hosted the Seoul Asian Games in 1986 and the Seoul Olympic

Learning Activity

Research and write a brief report to describe the implications of Northeast Asia's strategic significance in the world economy for sport industry managers.

Games in 1988. The Japan–Korea World Cup in 2002 was another stimulus to the sport industry in Korea. Professional sport, amateur sport, and sport events play an important role in the 21st century in Korea. Collectively, they were valued at approximately $348 million (Cheng, 2006). Specifically, the professional sport market alone is about US$246 million. According to Kim (2004), the total number of spectators for professional sport games was more than 20 million in 2001.

Role of Sport

To depict the status and development of the sport industry in NEA, conducting a detailed appraisal of the major sport nations in the region—China, Japan, and South Korea—is useful because they have become dominant among Asian nations on the world's sport stage. Figure 11.1 is an illustration of the total medal count of China, Japan, and South Korea in each of the Summer Olympic Games from 1976 through 2016. The combined medal count of these three countries as a percentage of the overall medals won by all Asian nations in the past 10 Olympic Games, including the 2016 Rio Olympic Games, is revealed in figure 11.2. As figure 11.2 shows, the medals won by athletes from China, Japan, and South Korea collectively made up a large percentage of all Olympic medals won by Asian competitors. In the Beijing 2008 Olympic Games,

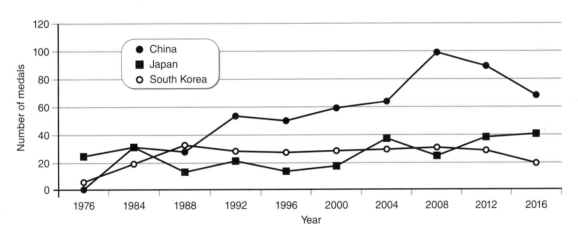

Figure 11.1 Total medal count of China, Japan, and South Korea in the Summer Olympic Games from 1976 through 2016.

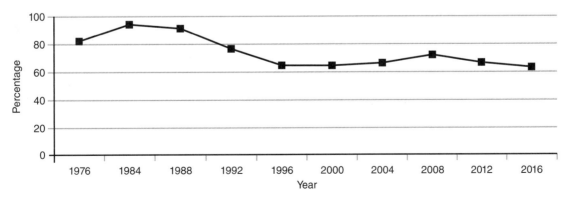

Figure 11.2 The combined medal count of China, Japan, and South Korea as a percentage of the medal count of all Asian nations in the Summer Olympics from 1976 through 2016.

Arms Race in Olympic Competition Among Nations in Northeast Asia

Japan and South Korea collectively received 31 medals, accounting for 82 percent of all medals awarded to Asian nations in the 1976 Montreal Olympic Games. The return of China to Olympic competition in 1984 not only drastically increased the number of medals won by the Asian nations but also started an arms race among these three Northeast Asian countries. At the Los Angeles Olympic Games, Chinese and Japanese athletes won the same number of medals (32) for their respective countries, and South Korean Olympians won 19 medals. The combined medal count of these three countries accounted for 92 percent of the overall number of medals conferred to Asian Olympic competitors. At the Athens Olympic Games, Asian Olympians took home 181 medals, of which 130 were contributed by China, Japan, and South Korea combined, accounting for 66 percent of the total medals won by Asian countries. Among the 220 medals awarded to Beijing Olympic participants from various Asian nations, 156, or 71 percent, were won by these three nations (100 by China, 25 by Japan, and 31 by South Korea). The medal-winning trends over the years have several interesting characteristics.

◆ Since the 1988 Seoul Olympic Games, South Korea has become a noteworthy Olympic medal producer, outmatching Japan in the next three Olympic Games. Its medal count has been consistent between 27 and 33.

◆ Japan dropped out of the second-place position as an Olympic medal-producing powerhouse in Asia after the 1984 Los Angeles Olympic Games. Its Olympic medal count decreased substantially from 32 at the Los Angeles Games to 14 at the 1988 Seoul Games, 22 at the 1992 Barcelona Games, 14 at the 1996 Atlanta Games, and 18 at the 2000 Sydney Games. In the 2004 Athens Games, however, Japan regained second-place

position over South Korea, surpassing the nation's previous best performance in history at the 1984 Los Angeles Games, reaching 37. In the recently finished Beijing and London Olympic Games, its medal count was 25 and 38, respectively.

◆ The domination by China, Japan, and South Korea in Asia is gradually slipping. The medals won by these three nations together accounted for 92 percent of the total medals awarded to Asian Olympians at the Los Angeles Olympic Games. But the percentage was down to around 66 percent at the 2004 Athens Olympic Games. It went up slightly to 71 percent at the 2008 Beijing Olympic Games (because of the unprecedented performance of the Chinese athletes). This trend implies that a greater number of Asian nations are becoming stronger Olympic medal contestants. In 1984 the national anthems of only 6 Asian nations were sung at that Olympic Games. Two decades later, athletes from 16 Asian nations had the opportunity to stand on the medal award podiums at the 2004 Athens Olympic Games. Seventeen Asian Countries were represented in the medal chart of the 2008 Beijing Olympic Games.

◆ The return of China to Olympic competition in 1984 brought a new sense of competition among nations in Asia.

Besides the just mentioned characteristics, the medal-winning trends are a microcosm of the political and economic competition among these three nations. Historically, animosity existed for a long time between Japan and its two close neighbors. Japan invaded China and Korea multiple times over the last two centuries. This animosity has found its way into various geopolitical and economic competitions and rivalries among the three nations.

Learning Activity

Look up the medal count, by sport, for China, Japan, and South Korea in the 2016 Summer Olympic Games. Identify the strengths and weaknesses of the elite sport development strategies of each of these nations. Justify your answers.

the three nations collectively fetched nearly one-fourth of the gold medals.

The following section provides an overview of sport development in Northeast Asia. Also included is an examination of the issues related to sport governance, such as government agencies, sport-related government legislation and policies, and nongovernmental agencies and organizations in sport in Northeast Asia, particularly in each of China, Japan, and South Korea. The last part of the section examines the organized sport system in each of the nations.

Sport in China

Although China is known for its martial arts and table tennis, badminton, basketball, and running are gaining popularity, especially running. "Running has now become the most important sport for Chinese recreational athletes. 44 percent of sports-playing Chinese count running among their main activities" (Klingelhöfer, 2017, n.p.). According to Sohu.com (2017), the portion of the Chinese population that participated in sport in 2017 was about 34 percent, or 434 million people. The sport population in China was defined as those who take part in sport activities two or three times a week, for more than a half hour each time, and at proper exercise intensity. In large metropolitan areas, the number may be higher. For example, about 50 percent of the Beijing population reported that they participated in exercise at least once a week (The Economist Corporate Network, 2016). According to Statista (2018), approximately 67 percent of the population of China is sports consumers who watch live or highlights sports coverage or read about sports frequently or talk about sports frequently.

One of the premier journals of its kind in the world maintains that "one-third of Chinese people frequently exercise" (The Economist Corporate Network, 2016, p. 3).

The size of the Chinese sport industry was about US$217 billion in 2015 (The Economist Corporate Network, 2016). The figure accounts for approximately 1.9 percent of China's GDP. It is predicted that the sports-to-GDP ratio may reach 3 percent by the year 2025 (The Economist Corporate Network, 2016).

In a blog regarding the status of the Chinese sporting goods industry, Daxue Consulting (2018) estimated that the consumption of sporting goods and equipment accounted for about 66 percent of the Chinese sports market. The remaining 34 percent came from sports services, entertainment, and other. Among all the sporting goods categories, the top three are sports equipment and accessories (28.45 percent), followed by training and fitness equipment (24.9 percent) and sports protection equipment (10.65 percent). While the domestic demand for sports goods and equipment are increased, Chinese sporting goods industry is highly influenced by the demand of the global market (Daxue Consulting, 2018).

According to IBISWorld (2017), there were 1,484 sporting goods and equipment manufacturers in China. This particular sector demonstrated an average annual growth rate of 9.8 percent from 2012 to 2017 and had $30.6 billion in sales in 2017. The sales were attributed to the increase in consumer interest because multiple world-class sports events were held in China during this period. The sporting goods wholesaling sector in China demonstrated similar impressive performance in the same period. Its sales, estimated at around $43.5 billion in 2017, were growing at an annualized rate of 6.9 percent. There were 8,296 sporting goods wholesalers in China in 2016 (IBISWorld, 2017).

With the growth of the sport industry in China, many foreign sport agencies have started operations in China. IMG, Octagon, Infront, Frontier, and Detsu are a few names on the list. The NFL, NBA, and MLB all have branch offices in China. Take IMG as an example. Asia has been a huge part of IMG's international expansion. IMG China was founded in 1979. Since then, IMG China has been responsible for founding and shaping many of the professional leagues in China, including those for badminton, football, and basketball. After William Morris Endeavor Entertainment (WME) purchased IMG in 2013, IMG China hosted Color Run and Tough Mudder events in China, and coordinated some local entertainment events as well, such as Shenzhen Fashion Week and Ultimate Fighting Championship.

Sport in Japan

Before the introduction of Western sports, Japan had made progress in traditional sports called budo, which were born in the 12th century and flourished mainly among the warrior class. They include kendo (Japanese stick fencing), jujutsu (known today as judo), kyudo (Japanese archery), and others (Web Japan, 2017, p. 1). After the Meiji Restoration (1868), various kinds of Western sports were introduced into Japan. Baseball arrived in 1872, thanks to an American. During the 1870s, track and field events and soccer were introduced, followed by ice skating and rugby during the 1890s. In 1911 an Austrian gave skiing instruction to the Japanese army. In those days, Western sports were played by few people, but through the educational system, they spread throughout the country. Western sports were also stressed as a form of mental discipline at first, but now Japanese have come to enjoy them as recreational activities (Web Japan, 2017, p. 2).

Baseball is one of the most popular spectator sports in Japan. During the season, night games of professional baseball are broadcast almost daily and gain high audience ratings. Since Nomo Hideo became a player for the Los Angeles Dodgers in the United States, many people have become interested in Major League Baseball. Millions watch the All-Japan High School Baseball Championship Tournament held each summer. With the establishment of the J League in 1993, soccer became more popular. Soccer has now become the second most widely practiced sport among boys in elementary school, after swimming. J League games are well attended (Web Japan, 2017, p. 2).

The Japan Amateur Sports Association (JASA) organized the first National Sports Festival in 1946 for the purpose of reviving sport and raising the morale of Japanese citizens. These summer and autumn meets became annual events. In 1948 the first Winter National Sports Festival was held, and this too became an annual event (Web Japan, 2017, p. 2).

The Emperor's Trophy is awarded to the prefecture that earns the most points in the competition. The Japanese government has designated the second Monday of October as Sports Day, declaring it a national holiday to promote the importance of sport and commemorate the Tokyo Olympics.

Tokyo hosted the 3rd Asian Games in 1958, and in 1994 the city of Hiroshima hosted the 12th Asian Games. The 1st Winter Asian Games were held in Sapporo in 1986 and the 2nd in 1990. The Summer Olympics will again be held in Tokyo in 2020 (Web Japan, 2017, p. 3).

According to the results of a national survey conducted by the Sasakawa Sports Foundation (2014), the most popular physical activities in Japan were leisurely walking (22.0 percent), fitness walking (18.1 percent), calisthenics and light exercises (12.8 percent), weight training (8.4 percent), jogging and running (5.3 percent), cycling (3.1 percent), yoga (2.3 percent), golf at a driving range (1.9 percent), catch ball (1.6 percent), and swimming (1.3 percent). "The number of sports enthusiasts who exercise regularly more than once a week was estimated to be 76.51 million or 73.7 percent of the people ages 20 and older in Japan" (p. 66). Although baseball is the most popular nontraditional spectator sport in Japan, it ranked only 12th in terms of the participation rate of Japanese male adults and 18th in terms of the participation rate of Japanese adults (Sport Life Data, 2014, Sasakawa Sports Foundation).

According to the research of Ministry of Economy, Trade and Industry of Japan (2013), the total market of the sport industry in Japan was US$10.4 billion (1US$ = JP¥79.79). It included sporting goods (US$2.1 billion), sport facilities (US$2.4 billion), sport services and information (US$2.4 billion), education and public sector (US$2.4 billion), and other sports (e.g., sport gambling) (US$1.4 billion). On the other hand, the total market of the sport industry in the United States was US$47 billion, four and a half times that of the Japanese sport industry. The biggest sector of the sport industry

Structure of the Sport Industry in Japan

As in other nations in Northeast Asia, the sport industry in Japan has grown tremendously over the last decade. This case provides a brief illustration of the sport industry in Japan.

Harada (2010) maintained that the sport industry in Japan has three key sectors: the sporting goods industry, the sport facility industry, and the sport service and information industry. As shown in the model depicted in figure 11.3, interactions among these three sport industry sectors have created several composite sectors, such as the sport facility management industry, the sport-related distribution industry (i.e., the industry created to move products from manufacturers to retail stores to consumers), and the hybrid sport industry. The interactions of the sport industry with other industries have also created some other industry segments such as sports medicine, food sold in sport facilities and events, and sport facilities and events as tourism destinations. E-sport, a new phenomenon, is a joint product of the information technology industry and the sport industry.

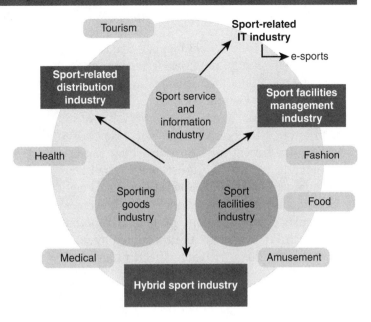

Figure 11.3 The interactions among the three main sport industry sectors in Japan have created additional sectors.

Adapted by permission from M. Harada, "Development of the sport industry: Japan's experience." Paper presented at the 2010 Annual Conference of the Asian Association for Sport Management (Kuala Lumpur, Malaysia, 2010).

in the United States was sporting goods (US$4.26 billion) (Plunket Research, 2013).

Sport in South Korea

As for traditional sports, Korea is known for taekwondo and ssireum. These sports existed long before the introduction of Western sports, such as baseball, basketball, and football. Taekwondo is Korea's national sport. Since 1973 when the World Taekwondo Federation (WTF) was formed as the legitimate governing body, the traditional martial art of taekwondo has spread to 191 countries and WTF has become one of the largest sport organizations. Taekwondo became an official event at the 2000 Sydney Olympics (WTF, 2010).

The modern history of sport in Korea began in the late 19th and early 20th centuries when Western countries, notably England and the United States,

introduced their modern sports such as football (1882), baseball (1905), basketball (1903), and volleyball (1917) to Korea through missionary work and business (Ok, 2007). Today, sport is closely linked with Korean national identity. Sport plays a role in continuing to change Korean society with emphasis on cultural diffusion and national assimilation (Ok, 2007). Historically, sport has been used as a venue for political, ideological, and symbolic competition between nations (Chehabi, 2001). International sporting events such as the Olympic Games have been used as a political tool to generate national identity and prestige (Stevenson & Nixon, 1987). Athletic success in megaevents (the Olympic Games and FIFA World Cup) is considered an achievement that represents the power of a country. This is the case in South Korea, where the increased patriotism inspired by international sport has been used as political means of creating national identity and assimilating various groups.

The international sporting community recognized the Korean success over the last two decades in hosting the 1988 Seoul Olympics and the 2002 Korea–Japan World Cup. Considering the size and population of Korea, its success in the international sport arena has been impressive. Golf, marathon, taekwondo, judo, wrestling, archery, shooting, badminton, field hockey, and short-track speed skating are among the sports in which Koreans have excelled. The Korean national football team has qualified for the FIFA World Cup finals eight times, continuously since 1986, an achievement unparalleled in Asia. Many professional football and baseball players have been recruited by major professional clubs in Japan, the United States, and Europe. Since the mid-1990s, Korean golfers have won LPGA and PGA tournaments, which has facilitated phenomenal growth of the sport in Korea (Korean Overseas Information Service, 2008).

This fast-growing sport industry needs highly talented and educated professionals to manage organizations and people. Currently, sport management and marketing is the most popular area of study within the field of sport and physical education. Interest in and awareness of this field continue to increase.

Sport as an industry segment in South Korea was born with production of sport apparel and shoes to export in the 1970s (Ministry of Culture, Sport and Tourism, 2006). Today, the sport industry has become one of the fastest growing industries. Measured by annual revenue generated by sport organizations and consumer expenditure, the sport industry increased in size from US$22.4 billion in 2006 to US$36.5 billion in 2011 ($1 = ₩1,000). The industry makes up 2.44 percent of GDP in 2006 and 2.95 percent in 2011, larger than the proportion in the United States (1.71 percent) or Japan (2.02 percent). The Korean sport industry has been classified into three general segments: (1) facility and management, (2) sport products and merchandising, and (3) sport services (sport events, marketing, information, and other sport services) (Ministry of Culture, Sport and Tourism, 2012).

The most popular sports and physical activities in South Korea are football, jogging and walking, mountain climbing, bodybuilding, soccer, cycling, and swimming. South Koreans hope to participate in swimming (12.7 percent), yoga (7.9 percent), golf (6.8 percent), mountain climbing (6.6 percent), bodybuilding (4.2), cycling (3.8 percent), dancesport (3.5 percent), tennis (3.1 percent), badminton (3.0 percent), and mountain biking (2.8 percent). Mountain climbing is popular because about 70 percent of the country is mountainous. The common reasons not to participate in exercise are lack of time (44 percent), lack of interest (13.6 percent), body weakness (10 percent), lack of money (7.9 percent), laziness (6 percent), lack of physical skill (3.9 percent), lack of facilities (3.6 percent), and others (9.8 percent) (Ministry of Culture, Sport and Tourism, 2015). Understanding such constraints will help managers and marketers develop successful segmentation and targeting strategies.

Governance of Sport

Most nations in Northeast Asia have an administrative unit in the central government that oversees sport-related affairs and operation. The State General Administration of Sport, or SGAS, in China (formerly, the State Sports Commission); the Ministry of Education, Culture, Sports, Science and Technology in Japan; and the Ministry of Culture, Sports and Tourism in South Korea are the administrative units in the national governments responsible for sport development in the three major countries. Nevertheless, the **sport governance system** used in China differs substantially from those adopted by other nations in the region. The term **centralized sport governance system** can be used to label the sport governance system in China.

A centralized sport governance system refers to "the sport managing system in a nation in which a specific government unit at every level of government is responsible for overseeing sport-related affairs and operations" (Eschenfelder & Li, 2006, p. 208) and for the promotion and development of sport. On the other hand, the sport governance system adopted by other Northeast Asian countries approximates the one referred to by sport economists as a **mixed sport governance system**. The governments in nations that adopt the mixed sport governance system have a great deal of involvement in developing sport policies for the public sector, but they exercise limited supervision over the sport operations controlled by the private sector.

Role of Government in Sport in China

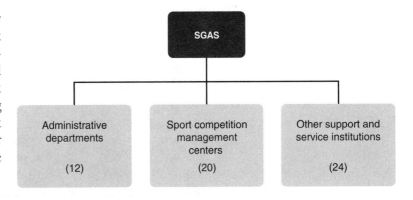

Figure 11.4 Administrative structure of the SGAS.

Before the 1980s the Chinese sport governance system was a huge state-run enterprise. The Chinese government was responsible for funding and overseeing sport-related affairs and operations under a centrally planned, hierarchical economic system (Jones, 1999). The country's adoption of the open-door policy in the 1980s led to the transformation of the sport system in China. The sport governance system then gradually evolved under the free-market system to become more self-sufficient (Hong, 2003). The State Sports Commission was restructured to become the State General Administration of Sport in 1998. Although the sport governance system has been reformed considerably in the last two decades, the government at all levels still has extensive control of sport operations in China.

The **State General Administration of Sports (SGAS)** is an administrative unit under the State Department. As shown in figure 11.4, SGAS has 12 administrative departments, 20 sports competition management centers (e.g., the water sports management center and the winter sports management), and 24 other support and services institutions, such as the National Olympic Center, the Institute of Sports Scientific Research, and the Beijing Sport University. The SGAS is closely tied to the All-China Sports Federation and the Chinese Olympic Committee. Besides forming strategies for sport development, overseeing their implementation, and developing mid- and long-range sport development plans, the SGAS has the following major responsibilities (The State Council, 2015):

◆ To research, develop, implement, and supervise the policy and regulations of sports

◆ To guide and promote the reform of the sports industry, plan the long and medium term development strategy for national sports, and coordinate the development of regional sports

◆ To implement and guide the national exercise project and national physical exercise standard, and monitor the health of all athletes

◆ To plan the development of China's athletic sports, coordination of national sports events and games

◆ To fight against performance-enhancing drug use and other unfair competition acts

◆ To manage foreign affairs related to the sports industry, enhance cooperation with other countries and regions, especially with Hong Kong, Taiwan, and Macao

◆ To organize and participate in major international sports events, and assist the hosting of such events in China

◆ To support research and development of sports technologies

◆ To implement policies governing the sports industry, develop the sports market, and formulate criteria for sports businesses

◆ To examine the eligibility of national sports associations

◆ To undertake other projects assigned by the State Council

To fulfill the nation's Olympic strategies and ambition, the SGAS and sport authorities at the provincial level have played a key role in promoting sport development in China. One of the strategies is sponsorship of the **Chinese National Games (CNGs)**. Modeled after the modern Olympic Games, the CNGs are the largest and most important sport extravaganza in China. Each province-level administrative unit sends a team to compete in the CNGs. The preparation for and competition at the CNGs allow the government to cultivate elite Chinese athletes for major world competitions.

The essence of Chinese Olympic strategies and ambition is a unique system of selecting and training elite athletes (figure 11.5). China is one of the few countries in the world that dedicate and use spare-time sport schools extensively to train and prepare future elite athletes. A spare-time sport school is a boarding school specializing in sport and established to train Olympic hopefuls. Students are selected for their athletic talent. They take academic classes in the morning and engage in rigorous sport training sessions in the afternoon. These sport schools serve as a reserve pool for elite sport teams at the provincial and national levels. Many issues are associated with this centralized athlete development system, including early entry (e.g., diving starts at age four or five), arbitrary selection methods, poor training facilities and conditions, inhumane training methods, inadequate education, and cost inefficiency. On the other hand, this system provides China with an advantageous position for winning medals in the Olympic Games and other world sport competitions, leading to tremendous national pride among its citizens.

The Sports Law of the People's Republic of China became effective on October 1, 1995, becoming the first fundamental legal document for sport since the current regime was established in 1949. The Sports Law establishes the main tasks and key principles in managing the sport industry, confirms the importance of mass sport, and identifies the duties and responsibilities of sport-related organizations. Essentially, the law sets the framework for the development of sport in China (Jones, 1999). The enactment of the law signified that the sport industry in China had entered a new era under the protection of the country's legal system. Based on the Sports Law, local governments at provincial and city levels have the right and authority to make their own rules for managing sport within their jurisdictions. The Sports Law was modified twice, in 2008 and 2016.

The Plan for Olympic Glories was released by the SGAS in 1995. The plan outlined three goals: (a) restructuring the system in elite sport training and management, (b) enhancing the elite athlete delivery pipeline and system (including sport schools), and (c) maintaining the nation's leading position in world sport competition, particularly the Summer Olympic Games (Chinese Olympic Committee, 2009). In 2001 SGAS developed the 2001-2010 Plan for Olympic Glories as a guiding document for it to prepare for the 2008 Beijing Olympic Games. China's success in the Games signified that the mission outlined by this plan was accomplished. SGAS again drafted a new document, the 2011-2020 Plan for Olympic Glories, in 2011 (State General Administration of Sport, 2011). China's Olympic strategy paid off because it placed second in the total medal count in both the 2012 and 2016 Summer Olympic Games (The Economist Corporate Network, 2016).

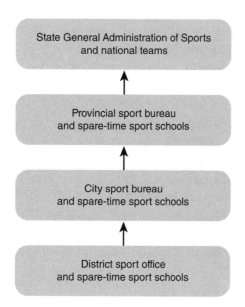

Figure 11.5 Chinese elite athlete preparation and delivery pipeline.

In 1995 the State Council promulgated the guidelines for a National Fitness Program. The guidelines were drafted with the aim of improving the health and the overall physical condition of the general population. The guidelines encouraged everyone, especially children and adolescents, to engage in at least one sporting activity every day, learn at least two ways of keeping fit, and have a health examination every year. The hope was that by 2010 about 40 percent of China's population would be regularly participating in physical activity and that clear improvement would take place in the physical fitness level of Chinese citizens (Chinese Olympic Committee, 2009). In 2016 the State Council released Healthy China 2030, a new plan for improving national nutrition and health (The State Council, 2017).

The Chinese government released a high-profile policy in 2014, Opinions on Accelerating the Development of the Sport Industry and Promoting Sport Consumption, aimed specifically at facilitating the growth of the nation's sport industry. It called for the government to take full advantage of the critical role that the sport market plays in resource allocation and formation of an effective competitive structure within the market, ultimately advancing the sports for all movement, developing elite sports, and building a strong sporting nation (The State Council, 2014). For the first time the Chinese central government recognized sport as an economic development tool (Liu, 2017).

Role of Government in Sport in Japan

Japan has significantly changed its sport governmental system. The **Japanese Ministry of Education, Culture, Sports, Science and Technology (MEXT)** established the **Japan Sports Agency (JSA)** as an extraministerial committee in October 2015 to promote and develop sport for the success of 2020 Tokyo Olympic and Paralympic Games. JSA has seven divisions.

Two major governmental policies and laws serve as basic blueprints for sport development in Japan: the Sports Promotion Law and the Basic Plan for the Promotion of Sports. The Sports Promotion Law, enacted in 1961, was intended to encourage and increase sport participation. This law not only provides a legal basis for promoting sport in the country but also clearly outlines the duty of both national and local governments in the promotion and development of sport. In addition, this law has facilitated the promotion of sport by creating a system for maintaining and improving sport facilities, establishing the position of physical education advisor at municipal boards of education, and providing guidelines for organizing and funding the National Sport Festival (MEXT, 1991).

The Basic Plan for the Promotion of Sports is another important legislation. The Japanese government, particularly the MEXT, launched the Basic Plan for the Promotion of Sports in 2000. Under the same premises outlined in the Sports Promotion Law of 1961, this policy serves as a comprehensive guideline for governments at various levels to promote sport development and achieve a number of long-term goals, such as (1) improving regional sport environments with a view to achieving lifelong participation in sport, (2) improving Japan's international competitiveness, and (3) enhancing the link between lifelong and competitive sport and school education and school sport (MEXT, 2000).

MEXT is striving to promote sport through increasing sport opportunities for children, promoting sport activities in line with the life stages, improving community sport environments, and enhancing international competitiveness of athletes. In March 2012 the MEXT formulated the Sport Basic Plan pursuant to the Basic Act on Sport enacted in June 2011 (MEXT, "Law and Plan," n.d.).

Japan's first Sport Basic Plan was established in March 2012, pursuant to the Basic Act on Sport. Within the new plan, in the interest of realizing the basic ideas set forth in the Basic Act on Sport, mention is made of the key principles of sport promotion for the 10-year period from fiscal year 2012, as well as the comprehensive and systematic measures to be advanced over the next five years. JSA developed the second Sport Basic Plan in March 2017.

Sport Governance in South Korea

The **Ministry of Culture, Sport, and Tourism in South Korea** is the administrative unit in the national government responsible for developing and implementing policies to promote culture, arts, sport, and religion in the country. The Sports Bureau is one of the offices in the ministry. A number of sport-related government legislations in South Korea have profoundly affected the development of sport in the nation.

The National Sport Promotion Act was government legislation enacted in 1962 (and revised in 1982) to increase people's physical fitness and mental health by promoting sport participation. This legislation influenced all aspects of the sport industry in South Korea, including intercollegiate athletics, amateur and professional sport, and leisure sport activities in schools, job settings, and local communities. The SaengHwalCheYuk movement (sport for all) began with the Hodori plan in 1989. The sport for all movement in Korea grew rapidly because of increased health awareness accompanied by economic growth and proactive implementation of welfare policies by the government after the 1988 Olympic Games in Seoul (Korean Overseas Information Service, 2007). To generate revenues and support the various segments of the sport industry, the Seoul Olympic Sports Promotion Foundation (SOSFO) was established in 1989 after the 1988 Seoul Olympics (Ministry of Culture, Sport and Tourism, 2006).

A few years later, the Korean government developed its first Five-Year National Sports Promotion Plan (1993-1997) to increase sport participation and leadership in the world sport business. The plan focused on five major tasks: (*a*) to improve the quality of life of citizens through sport, (*b*) to provide continued support for elite sport, (*c*) to increase international corporative efforts, (*d*) to advance sport science and its application, and (*e*) to solidify the sport administration system. The plan was quite successful because public interest in sport grew after the 1988 Seoul Olympics (Ministry of Culture, Sport and Tourism, 2006). A major sport facility construction boom occurred during this period, during which 49 stadiums, 74 arenas, 17 swimming pools, and 1,728 neighborhood sport facilities were built (Korean Overseas Information Service, 2007).

The second Five-Year National Sports Promotion Plan (1998 to 2002) modified and incorporated several major tasks (e.g., to make the 2002 Korea–Japan World Cup successful and to improve the efficiency of sport administration). In particular, the government developed a strategic plan to foster the sport industry in Korea during this time by (*a*) supporting development of high-quality sport products and branding efforts, (*b*) improving sport facility management, (*c*) fostering the sport service sector (sport information systems and highly qualified sport marketers), and (*d*) creating a long-term sport development plan (Ministry of Culture, Sport and Tourism, 2006).

The third Five-Year National Sports Promotion Plan (2003-2008) focused on (*a*) a drastic increase in sport participation, (*b*) improvement of elite sport to be among the top 10 in the world, (*c*) national and balanced development of regions through the growth of the sport industry, (*d*) improvement of the national image through increased international sport relationships, and (*e*) development of a positive political and cultural environment between North and South Korea by promoting sport exchanges (Ministry of Culture, Sport and Tourism, 2015).

In 2008 Cultural Vision 2008-2012 was proposed and implemented to increase sport participation further and to enhance competitiveness in the sport industry and the quality of the sport system. In 2013 Sport Vision 2018 was proposed, focusing on social change, enhancement of national image, and economic development through sport. As a result of the systematic planning and implementation of sport policies, sport participation (at least once a month) among Koreans increased from 48.3 percent in 1989 to 62.2 percent in 1997 and 65.6 percent in 2015 (Ministry of Culture, Sport and Tourism, 2015).

Table 11.1 shows government expenditures on sport in South Korea in the period from 2000 through 2006, which shows government financial investments correlated with the increased number of sport participants during the same period.

Noting the increased public interest and greater participation in sport, the Korean government considered sport a major industry segment. The Sports Industry Promotion Act was enacted by the Ministry of Culture and Tourism in October 2007 to provide systematic support for further development of the sport industry in Korea. Specific tasks were to (1) establish a basic developmental plan for the sport industry, (2) train market-oriented industry professionals, (3) provide sport facilities and funds, (4) establish business organization in the sport industry, (5) appoint the sport industry support centers, (6) strengthen the competitiveness of the national sport industry, including improvement of sport product quality and marketability, and (7) promote professional sport. The Taekwondo Promotion Act was passed in July 2005 to improve and develop the global position of taekwondo by building and managing a taekwondo park and promoting taekwondo to contribute to national development.

Nongovernmental Sport Agencies

The nongovernmental sport agencies in Northeast Asian countries have played a critical role in promoting sport development in the region. The All-China Sports Federation (ACSF), the Japanese Sport Association (JASA), and the Korea Sports Council are examples of such nongovernmental sport agencies.

Learning Activity

Discuss the advantages and disadvantages of the sport governance systems adopted by China, Japan, and South Korea. Which system is the best for achieving success in the Olympics and other international sport competitions? Which system best promotes public interest and participation in sport?

Nongovernmental Sport Agencies in China

The Chinese Olympic Committee (COC) is a nongovernmental, nonprofit national sport organization whose major objective is to develop sport and promote the Olympic Movement in China. The COC represents China in handling international affairs related to the Olympic Movement. The **All-China Sports Federation (ACSF)** is also a national nongovernmental, nonprofit sport organization that oversees an array of sport associations in China. The ACSF is an important linkage between the government and those involved in sport. The aim of the ACSF is to (a) strengthen ties between athletes and others who engage in sport to promote the development of elite sporting excellence, (b) increase public participation in sport activities and improve health

Table 11.1 Annual Budget for Sport Segments in South Korea

Segments	2000	2001	2002	2003	2004	2005	2006
Elite sport	47.1	51.2	54.1	53.1	68.4	79.6	98.3
Sport for all	9.0	21.0	29.7	32.7	31.1	23.5	25.8
International sport participation and relations	123.0	90.0	73.7	54.2	7.3	8.0	13.9
Other sport industry	0.3	0.8	1.4	2.6	2.5	2.7	11.0
Total	180	164	159	143	109	114	149
(percent of government budget)	(.19%)	(.16%)	(.15%)	(.13%)	(.09%)	(.08%)	(.10%)

Amounts are in millions of U.S. dollars. One dollar is roughly equivalent to 1,000 South Korean won.

Adapted from Ministry of Culture, Sport and Tourism (2006).

outcomes for all Chinese, and (c) improve sporting achievements in the world arena. Although both the COC and ACSF are supposed to be nongovernmental in nature, they are under the supervision and guidance of the SGAS. In fact, the current director of the SGAS, Mr. Gou Zhongwen, is also the current president of the COC. The profound involvement of government in sport is a characteristic of the sport governance system in China.

Nongovernmental Sport Agencies in Japan

The **Japanese Sport Association (JASA)** and the Japanese Olympic Council (JOC) are the two major nongovernmental agencies that provide leadership in sport development in Japan at the national level. Although the JASA is mainly responsible for promoting lifelong sport, or sport for all, in the country, the role of the JOC is to improve Japan's international sport competitiveness. Before the Seoul 1988 Olympic Games, the JASA was the sole entity and governing body in sport in Japan and had the dual responsibility of promoting competitive sport and sport for the public. The unsatisfactory performance of Japanese Olympic athletes in the Seoul 1988 Olympics led to the creation of a separate entity to oversee competitive sport and raise the level of Japan's competitiveness in the world of sport. The JOC was then created out of a former committee within the JASA as a single legal corporation in 1989 (Ministry of Education, Culture, Sports, Sciences and Technology, 1991). Figure 11.6 depicts the nongovernmental sport governance structure in Japan

As figure 11.6 shows, the JASA fulfills its duties in sport development in coordination and collaboration with other nongovernmental agencies, such as the Japan Sports Association for the Disabled, the Nippon Junior High School Physical Culture Association, some national sport federations, and the prefectural amateur sport associations or the local chapters of the JASA.

Nongovernmental Sport Agencies in South Korea

In South Korea, besides the leadership provided by the Ministry of Culture, Sport and Tourism, many nongovernmental sport organizations assume the responsibility to advance sport. One of those organizations is the **National Council of Sport for All (NCSA)**, authorized by the Ministry of Culture, Sport and Tourism in 1991. Three main objectives of NCSA are to (a) enhance people's health and fitness through promotion of sport for all, (b) lead people to effective sport and recreation systems, and (c) build a basis for unification of the Koreas (North and South Korea) by developing identity and patriotism among Koreans worldwide. The main business of the organization includes (a) promoting sport clubs and amateur sport participants by supporting federations and hosting various club leagues and festivals, (b) promoting sport for all by offering public sport services to citizen, extracurricular activities for youth, and exchange programs between Korea and other nations (e.g., China and Japan), and (c) developing sport-for-all welfare programs by supporting disabled amateur sport participants and hosting such events as Mother's Festival and Senior's Festival (NCSA, 2007, internal source). In 2016 NCSA was merged with Korean Olympic Committee (Ministry of Culture, Sport and Tourism, 2015).

The **Korea Sports Council (KSC)** was established in 1920 to train national athletes, help improve the physical fitness of all Koreans, and create a wholesome social atmosphere through the promotion of sport. The council also helps develop Korean culture and international friendship through participation in various international sport events and by hosting national and international sport events. The KSC has hosted numerous international sport events (e.g., the 1988 Seoul Olympics; 2018 Pyeongchang Winter Olympics; the 1986, 2002, and 2014 Asian Games; and major international conferences (e.g., the 6th Sports-for-All Congress in 1996 and the IOC Executive Board Meeting in 1998). The **Korean Olympic Committee (KOC)** was established in 1947. In 1968 the KSC adopted the Korean Olympic Committee as a suborganization. Currently, the KSC has 47 member associations (Ministry of Culture, Sport and Tourism, 2006, internal source).

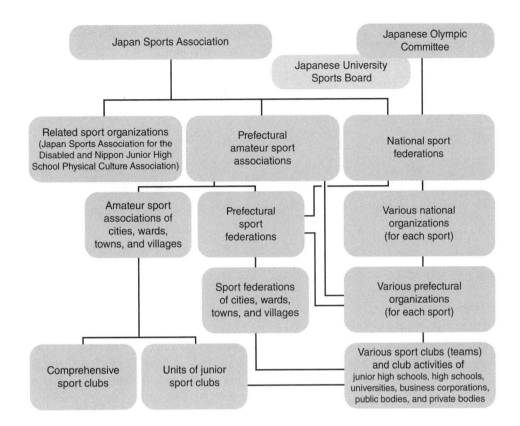

Figure 11.6 Nongovernmental sport governance structure in Japan.

The **Seoul Olympic Sports Promotion Foundation (SOSFO)** was established in 1989 as a public corporation to promote public interest in accordance with the National Sports Promotion Act. Its goal is to preserve and promote the outstanding achievements of the 1988 Seoul Olympic Games and to raise and manage the Sports Promotion Fund to support various sport agencies and organizations (Seoul Olympic Sports Promotion Foundation, 2007a, internal source). Specifically, the foundation focuses on the following specific objectives and business areas: (*a*) managing the Seoul Olympics commemorative businesses, (*b*) managing the Olympic facilities and construction of sport infrastructure, (*c*) providing various sport organizations (e.g., the Korean Olympic Committee, the National Council of Sport for All, the Korea Sports Association for the Disabled) with financial support through creative fund-raising efforts (e.g., cycle and motorboat racing, and Sports Toto), (*d*) supporting research in sport science, and (*e*) fostering the sport industry (Seoul Olympic Sports Promotion Foundation, 2007b).

For example, the SOSFO has been supporting the KOC and KSC (US$43.2 million) and Korea Sports Association for the Disabled (US$68 million) annually. In addition, the foundation has been supporting the Korea Institute of Sport Science (KISS), which has established and maintained an extensive sport-related information database. The KISS has published sport science journals including the *Korean Journal of Sports Science* and the *International Journal of Applied Sports Science* in English and has hosted international conferences such as the Asian Sports Science Conference. In addition, the SOSFO developed national sport centers (90 sites), grass and

Learning Activity

In a small group, compare and contrast the functions and roles of nongovernmental sport agencies in China, Japan, and Korea in promoting sport development.

urethane sport facilities (547 sites), football centers and parks (3 centers and 16 parks), and village sport facilities (3,186 sites), and it helped develop the stadia for the 2002 Korea–Japan FIFA World Cup (6 sites). In 2007 the SOSFO contributed US$230.1 million overall to the promotion of national sport. To raise funds for its sport promotion activities, the SOSFO runs several businesses such as cycle racing, motorboat racing, and a lottery called Sports Toto (Seoul Olympic Sports Promotion Foundation, 2007b). Recently, the name of the organization has been changed to Korea Sport Promotion Foundation (KSPO).

The Taekwondo Promotion Foundation was established in July 2005 to help develop and manage Taekwondo Park and to promote the sport. The goal of the foundation is to raise the status of taekwondo, a national sport in Korea, to a world martial art and a sport in the global community.

Professional Sport

Although sumo wrestling, the oldest professional sport in the region, if not the world, has been in existence in Japan for more than 1,000 years, professional sport as a whole in Northeast Asia is relatively a new phenomenon. The first professional baseball league was established in 1936 (Daly & Kawaguchi, 2003).

China had no professional sport league until 1994 when football became the first sport to take that road. Since then, professional competition has started in other sports, including basketball, volleyball, badminton, table tennis, and go (encirclement chess). China Basketball Association (CBA) events attract an average 80 percent box-office rating. Professional volleyball, table tennis, and badminton also have high fan appeal. The follow-ing details briefly describe some professional sport leagues in China:

◆ China Basketball Association (CBA)—established in 1995

◆ Chinese Football Association Super League (CSL) (formally the Football A League)—established in 2004

◆ China Table Tennis Super League (CTTSL)—established in 2003

◆ Chinese Volleyball Association (CVA)—established in 1996

◆ China Badminton Super League (CBSL)—established in 2009

Professional sport in China is still in the developmental stage. In 1998 the Football A League had an average of 21,300 on-site spectators per game and a total of 5,800,000 spectators over the year. Scandals and charges of match fixing and corruption hit the sport in the early years of the 2000s, causing a loss of spectators and sponsors. Most clubs are losing money and having a hard time surviving. For the 2005 season the league had no title sponsor. In March 2009 Italian tire manufacturer Pirelli signed a three-year, multimillion-euro agreement with the Chinese Football Association (CFA) to become the title sponsor of China's Super League. With new leaders named at the CFA in early 2009 and new sponsorship deals, the league was expected to improve over the following years.

Many Chinese athletes have joined professional leagues in other countries and are currently playing overseas. For instance, basketball stars Yao Ming and Yi Jianlian played in the National Basketball Association in the United States for a number of years. Zhu Ting, famous female volleyball player and the MVP for women's volleyball in the Rio Olympic Games, was recruited to play for a professional volleyball club in Turkey in 2016. Many football players have been enlisted to play in other countries. One of the latest examples was Li Weifeng of the Korean Football League. This go-global phenomenon has a number of significant implications to sport management education and the sport industry in China. First, to produce effective client representatives, the Chinese sport education system must be able to prepare sport agents who are not only proficient in English but also familiar with the operations of professional sport leagues in other parts of the world. Second, the phenomenon helps increase the public's interests in a particular sport, in both watching and participating. For example, many Chinese people love basketball because Yao Ming played in the NBA.

Many high-profile sporting events have been held or will be held in China, including the HSBC Championships in Shanghai (golf); the ATP World Tour Masters 1000 in Shanghai and the China Open in Beijing (tennis); the World Games of 2009 in Kaohsiung, Taiwan; the Formula One World Championship; the Chinese Grand Prix in Shanghai; the Fifth East Asian Games in Hong Kong; the 2011 Summer Universiade in Shenzhen; and 2014 Youth Summer Olympics, and 2022 Winter Olympic Games.

The major professional sports in Japan are baseball, football, and sumo wrestling. Professional athletes also participate in horseracing, bike racing, boat racing, golf, boxing, tennis, and many other sports. The Nippon Professional Baseball (NPB) was formed in 1950. The NPB has two divisions, the Central League and the Pacific League, each made up of 12 teams. All teams except one are named after their corporate owners or sponsors rather than the cities or regions in which they play. For example, the Tokyo Yakult Swallows are owned by Yakult Honsha Co., Ltd., a corporation that sells probiotic milk-like products.

J League became the first professional football league in Japan in 1993. From 10 clubs at its inception, the league has grown to 52 clubs in three divisions. In autumn 2016 B League started as an integrated professional basketball league of 36 clubs (two divisions). The following is a list of professional sport leagues in Japan.

◆ Nippon Professional Baseball (NPB)—established in 1950

◆ J League—established in 1991

◆ Japanese Professional Sumo League—established in the Edo period (1603-1867)

◆ B League—established in 2016

Professional sport in Korea was born with professional boxing and wrestling. But it was not until 1982 when the Korea Baseball Organization (KBO) was formed that professional sport became a significant industry segment in Korea (Ministry of Culture, Sport and Tourism White Book, 2006). Currently, Korea has 10 professional leagues in nine sports:

◆ Korea Baseball Organization (KBO)—established in 1982

◆ The Korean Professional Football League (KPFL or K-League)—1983

◆ Korean Basketball League (KBL)—1996

◆ Women's Korean Basketball League (WKBL)—1997

◆ Korea Volleyball Federation (KOVO)—2004

◆ Korea Professional Golfers' Association (KPGA)—1968

◆ Korea Ladies Professional Golf Association (KLPGA)—1978

◆ Korea Professional Bowling Association (KPBA)—1995

◆ Korea Boxing Commission (KBC)—1947

◆ Korea Ssireum Association (KSA)—1981

In 2014 baseball (6,754,619 attended baseball events) was the most popular spectator sport among Korean people, followed by soccer (1,858,333), basketball (1,500,449), and volleyball (446,402). Factors that negatively influenced spectatorship included lack of interest (33.2 percent), lack of time (27.7 percent), lack of event and facility available (13.8 percent), watching on TV (13.3 percent), and lack of money (5.2 percent) (Ministry of Culture, Sport and Tourism, 2006). Understanding such constraints will help sport managers and marketers develop successful segmentation and targeting strategies for professional sport organizations.

Learning Activity

Select one of the Korean sport leagues and research its structure and governance. See whether you can identify the sponsoring companies and their relationship with the organization. Present your findings in class.

Major Sport Events

Because the nations in Northeast Asia are becoming politically, economically, and culturally important to the world, many international sport organizations are bringing their events to countries in this region. The four Olympic Games held in Asia so far were all hosted by nations in Northeast Asia (Japan in 1964, South Korea in 1988, China in 2008, and South Korea in 2018). In addition, this region is the favorite option for many international sport federations to organize their competitions. For example, the World Championship of the International Table Tennis Federation (ITTF) took place in Korea. The **Asian Games**, held every four years, are a major international sporting event in the region. This competition includes athletes from the entire continent of Asia, except Russia, as well as athletes from island nations in Southeast Asia.

To strengthen the ties among nations in East Asia, the national Olympic committees in the region discussed the idea of having an East Asian Games and endorsed the plan in 1991. In the following year, the Coordination Committee of the East Asian National Olympic Committees (EANOC) was officially formed and its charter was passed. Shanghai, China, was selected to hold the inaugural **East Asian Games** in 1993. The EANOC was renamed the East Asian Games Association (EAGA) that year. The East Asian Games is a smaller multisport event held every four years. Only members of EAGA (China, including Hong Kong, Macau, and Taiwan; Japan, Mongolia; North Korea; and South Korea) take part in the Games.

Summary

This chapter provided a brief introduction to sport in Northeast Asia, a region encompassing a number of nations that are culturally, economically, and politically important to the world, such as China, Japan, and South Korea. This region has experienced tremendous growth and development in sport in the early 2000s. In addition, the region has also demonstrated its dominance on the world sport stage, which is reflected particularly in the success of the Northeast Asian nations in the Olympic Games. Among most Asian nations, an administrative unit is established in the central government to administer sport, but the systems that each country adopts in managing sport are different. In addition, the nongovernmental sport agencies also play a critical role in promoting sport development in the region.

? Review Questions

1. Can you justify why Northeast Asia is considered a strategic region in the world, both politically and economically?

2. What are the most popular professional sport leagues that exist in the NEA area?

3. What are the key laws or major legislations enacted by China, Japan, and South Korea for sport development?

4. What are the interesting characteristics of the arms race in Olympic sports among China, Japan, and South Korea?

5. What major international and continental sport events have been held in Northeast Asia?

Part III

Governance in International Sport

Canada defeated Brazil 82-49 during the group stage of women's wheelchair basketball at the 2016 Rio Paralympics Games. Brazil and Canada made it to the quarterfinals. The United States won the gold medal by defeating Germany 62-45. The 2016 Rio Paralympics were held in Rio de Janeiro, Brazil from September 7-18, 2016. It was the first time the Paralympic Games took place in Latin America.

Alexandre Flourier/Getty Images

Olympic and Paralympic Sport

David Legg, PhD
Mount Royal University, Canada

Laura Misener, PhD
Western University, Canada

Ted Fay, PhD
State University of New York at Cortland

Chapter Objectives

After studying this chapter, you will be able to do the following:

- Explain the historical development of the International Olympic Committee and the International Paralympic Committee.
- Describe the structure and governance of the Olympic and Paralympic Games.
- Identify the major issues at stake for a city hosting the Olympic and Paralympic Games.
- Discuss the primary challenges in the future for the Olympic and Paralympic Games as it relates to gender equality and testing.
- Explain the primary issues related to the inclusion of athletes with a disability into the Olympic Games.

Key Terms

International Olympic Committee (IOC)
Olympic Movement
International Paralympic Committee (IPC)

Olympic Charter
National Olympic Committee (NOC)

Arguably, the **International Olympic Committee** (IOC) has adroitly positioned itself, its Olympic Games, and its corresponding interlocking five-ring logo as one of the most recognizable and dominant international brands in the world. Founded in 1894, the IOC is undoubtedly a preeminent sport brand. The IOC, as a sport and cultural movement, has power and influence well beyond the normal reach of governments, beyond the scope and power of international trading unions, defense alliances, and international financial institutions (Burton & O'Reilly, 2010a). The **International Paralympic Committee (IPC)** is the corresponding governing body for athletes with an impairment. It has grown quickly from its first Games in Rome in 1960 where just over 400 athletes from 23 countries competed to the more recent Games in Rio de Janeiro where over 4,000 athletes competed in the same venues used two weeks earlier in the Olympic Games. Today, bid cities for the Olympic Games also must bid for the Paralympic Games, and this agreement has been extended until 2032. The two organizations are independent and different in their governance structures; the IOC has appointed members, and the IPC has an elected board from the membership consisting primarily of representatives of the national Paralympic committees.

This chapter provides a brief historical context of the International Olympic Committee (IOC) and International Paralympic Committee (IPC), along with an overview of their respective organizational structures. The focus, however, is primarily on the current and future organizational, sociocultural, financial, and legal issues facing the IOC, the IPC, the respective national Olympic and Paralympic committees (NOCs and NPCs), the designated organizing committees of the Olympic Games (OCOGs) and Paralympic Games, and the related international sport federations (IFs) responsible for conduct, including rules and officials, of each Olympic and Paralympic sport. Space limitations preclude us from going into depth about any of the domains of these key stakeholders of the Olympic and Paralympic Movements. Therefore, we will focus on the core issues that jointly challenge both the IOC and the IPC by intertwining their relationship from a leadership and management perspective.

Formation of the IOC and IPC

Based in Lausanne, Switzerland, the IOC has a charter, or constitution, a flag, an organizational anthem, and some of the other typical symbols of nations. As a comparison, the United Nations has 192 member nations, but the IOC recognizes 205 national Olympic committees (Burton & O'Reilly, 2010a). At the Sochi 2014 Winter Olympic Games, 2,873 athletes competed in 98 events from 15 winter sport disciplines representing 88 NOCs (IOC, 2015). In Rio de Janeiro in 2016, more than 11,000 athletes from 205 national Olympic committees participated including first-time entrants Kosovo, South Sudan, and the Refugee Olympic Team. In March 2016 IOC President Thomas Bach had declared that the IOC would choose 5 to 10 refugees to compete in the Games to recognize the global refugee crisis, which was being most prominently felt in Europe, where migrants from various African and Middle Eastern nations such as Syria were attempting to flee from civil strife.

The IPC, based in Bonn, Germany, was founded in 1989 and took over its first Games management with the 1992 Summer Paralympic Games in Barcelona. It has been somewhat dependent on the IOC for financial, logistical, and political support as far as the hosting of the Paralympic Games is concerned, but it is otherwise independent of the IOC. The Paralympic Games, which involve elite athletes with physical and sensory disabilities, are now one of the world's largest quadrennial mega sporting events. At the 2016 Summer Games 4,328 athletes from 159 national Paralympic committees (NPCs) competed in 22 sport disciplines (Paralympic Movement, 2017a). Meanwhile, in Sochi in 2014, 547 athletes from 45 NPCs competed in five sports in the Paralympic Winter Games (Paralympic Movement 2017b).

Since 1988 the Paralympic Winter and Summer Games have occurred approximately two weeks after the Olympic Games at the same location, in the same facilities, and under the same or a similar management structure of the host organizing committee for the Olympic Games. Today the organizing committees of the Olympic Games (OCOGs) are mandated by the IOC to organize and conduct the

Learning Activity

Many people have criticized cities that want to bid to be hosts of the Games, citing lack of legacies and unfair funding models. Often these groups are called "No Olympics," and their efforts, in part, have caused a number of cities to withdraw their interest in bidding. One example is Boston, which retracted its bid for the 2024 Games. Select at least one official Games bid site and one of the nonofficial ones that perhaps take a more critical and independent view of bidding. Write a one- or two-page paper that compares and contrasts the positions of these different perspectives and present your opinion on the issue.

Paralympic Games, and this agreement extends until 2032 (Paralympic Movement, 2016).

Olympic and Paralympic Organization Structure and Governance

Governing, policy, and decision-making structures differ substantially within the International Olympic and Paralympic Committees. Table 12.1 gives a brief overview of the governance of each organization. The IOC describes itself as the "supreme authority" of the **Olympic Movement**, which supports a philosophy of life, in which the blending of sport and culture with art and education aims to combine in a balanced way the human qualities of body, will, and mind. It currently consists of 115 individual members elected to eight-year terms and then an unlimited set of multiple terms thereafter. An executive committee consisting of 15 members, including a president, 4 vice presidents, and 10 members at large, is then elected and assumes overall responsibility for the administration, management, and overall policy decisions of the IOC. The president is elected to an initial eight-year term with an option for an additional four-year term if supported by the members (Hums & MacLean, 2009).

The IPC is composed of the IPC General Assembly (highest decision-making body), a governing board (executive body), a management team, and various standing committees and councils. The governing board is currently composed of 15 members, of which 12 are elected at the IPC General Assembly (president, vice president, and 10 members at large). The governing board, collectively, is the representative of the IPC General Assembly. The governing board is responsible for setting the policies and for ensuring that the directions set by the membership at the IPC General Assembly are implemented. The governing board is elected every

Table 12.1   2018 Snapshot of Olympic and Paralympic Governance

Quick facts	Olympic	Paralympic
Current headquarters	Lausanne, Switzerland	Bonn, Germany
Current website	www.olympic.org	www.paralympic.org
Founder	Baron Pierre de Coubertin	Sir Ludwig Guttman
First president	Demetrios Vikelas (1896)	Dr. Robert Steadward (1992-2001)
Current president	Thomas Bach	Andrew Parsons
Total number of presidents	9	3
Governance and voting members	119 individuals	176 nations
Year of founding Games	1896 Athens, Greece	1960 Rome, Italy
Year of founding Winter Games	1924 Chamonix, France	1976 Örnsköldsvik, Sweden
Number of NOCs and NPCs	206	176
Number of sports (IFs)	36	29

four years and members can serve a maximum of three terms (Paralympic Movement, 2017c).

The IOC is further organized, structured, and managed by its 27 IOC commissions (e.g. Athletes Commission, Evaluation Commission, Marketing Commission), its relations with all organizing committees of Olympic Games (OGOGs), 206 national Olympic committees (NOCs), and a number of other recognized and affiliated organizations representing a wide range of international sport-related entities.

The governance of each of the 36 Olympic sports is then controlled independently by international sport federations (IFs) and their related national sport governing federations or bodies (NSFs or NGBs). Thus, the IOC cooperates and collaborates directly and individually with each of these international federations as well as through the auspices of an umbrella coordinating organization, the Global Association of International Sport Federations (GAISF), formally known as SportAccord and before that the General Association of International Sport Federations.

The IPC operates, arguably, with more transparency and democracy through the aegis of its biennial general assembly, which includes representatives from all member groups. These include national Paralympic committees (NPCs), 4 international organizations for sport for the disabled (IOSDs), the representatives of Paralympic sports that include 10 IPC managed sports, 7 IOSD sports, 19 independent Paralympic sport federations (IPSFs), and 5 IPC regional organizations (Paralympic Movement, 2017d).

The **national Olympic committee** (NOC) and national Paralympic committee (NPC) are usually separate organizations in each nation; the committees have separate boards of directors, financing, and organizational structures. This arrangement, however, is changing. In the United States, for example, one organization, the USOC, is responsible for both Olympic and Paralympic sports.

Relationships With Outside Stakeholders

A number of new entities have become more directly involved in international sport governance as it relates to Olympic and Paralympic Games management. Several factors have contributed to

this development, including the relaxing of the eligibility rules and criteria to allow openly professional athletes to compete in the Olympic Games, the emergence of the Paralympic Games as a major multisport quadrennial world event, and the inclusion of new Olympic and Paralympic sports on the Games program. Additions to this interlinking international sport governance model relevant to the Olympic and Paralympic Games include

- professional sport organizations (PSOs) such as sport franchises, leagues, tours, and circuits beginning in 1992;
- professional athlete unions and professional athlete representatives (PPUs and PARs) beginning in 1992;
- the Court of Arbitration for Sport (CAS), created in 1993, to adjudicate international athlete eligibility issues, breaches of fair play issues, and so on;
- the World Anti-Doping Agency (WADA), created in 1999, which acts as an independent testing and research organization established to eliminate the use of banned performance-enhancing substances and techniques from international sport competition; and
- sport organization and event sponsors (SOs and ESs) that provide critical support and funding to athletes, organizations, and events.

Figure 12.1 demonstrates the plethora of organizations related to the Olympic and Paralympic Movements and attempts to show the direct interrelationships.

Learning Activity

Select a sport in which professional players compete in the Olympics. Discuss some of the pros and cons of Olympic competition for the professional tour or association (e.g., ATP or WTA for tennis, PGA for golf, FIS for ski racing) or for a professional league (e.g., NBA or WNBA for basketball, MLS or Premiership for soccer, NHL for hockey) as well as for the players, their agents, and unions.

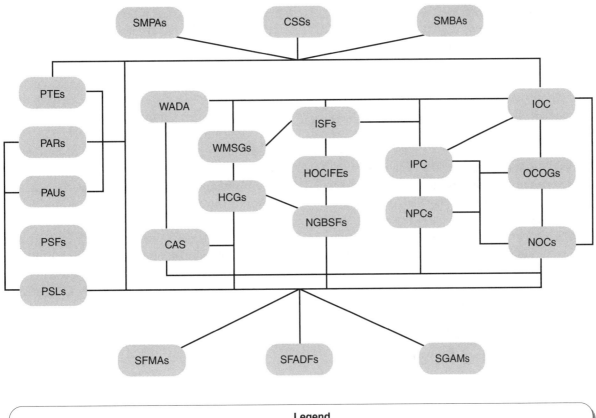

Figure 12.1 Universe of key international sport governance and industry relationships.

Reprinted by permission from T. Fay, L. Velez, and J.B. Parks, "A North American Perspective on International Sport, in *Contemporary Sport Management*, 4th ed., edited by P.M. Pedersen, J.B. Parks, J. Quarterman, and L. Thibault (Champaign, IL: Human Kinetics, 2011), 404. Created by Ted Fay, 2006.

A perfect example of why these additional groups are included can be drawn from the multiple stakeholders and governing bodies involved in negotiating the availability of professional ice hockey players for the Olympic men's ice hockey tournament. The National Hockey League and its club owners withdrew their support for suspending the regular season for two weeks in February for the 2018 Winter Olympic Games in Pyeongchang, Korea. This decision broke the pattern set in 1998 when the Nagano Olympic Games included NHL players for the first time. The Owners may have dropped their support for the Olympic hiatus because they are concerned about injuries and fatigue to players as well as the financial repercussions of extending the regular season and playoffs for an extra month. Despite the best-ever television ratings achieved at the 2010 Vancouver Games and the men's semifinal games in Sochi being the highest rated hockey games ever on NBC (TV by the Numbers, 2014) clear agreement on the value of Olympic ice hockey competition is lacking among its primary stakeholders, which include the International Olympic Committee (IOC), the International Ice Hockey Federation (IIHF), the National Hockey League (NHL), the National Hockey League Players Association (NHLPA), as well as other entities such as the Kontinental Hockey League (KHL), the new Russian professional hockey league (Burton & O'Reilly, 2010b). Although the NHL decided not to allow its hockey players to participate in the 2018 Olympic Games, some high-profile players such as Alex Ovechkin vowed to attend and play regardless (Sportsnet, 2017).

History and Commercial Development of the Olympic and Paralympic Games

The modern Olympic Games were not always the colossal mega sporting and cultural event that they have become since 1984. During the founding period of the modern Games from 1896 to 1928, the form and organization of the Games were not standardized or consistent. The events instead resembled a "culture or identity" Games for nations and amateur athletes who could afford it (Brittain, 2010). For example, athletes competed in events over a period of 79 days for the 1904 St. Louis Olympic Games, which were little more than a sideshow attached to the St. Louis World's Fair of 1904. With the exception of nominal participation in a few sports practiced only by the elite social classes of the times (e.g., golf and tennis in 1900 and 1904), women were excluded from the Games until 1924 (Johnson, 1993, 1996).

Other historical tidbits of the Olympic Games reveal that the evolution of games management occurred in fits and starts. For example, the awarding of gold, silver, and bronze medals for first, second, and third places started at the third Olympic Games in St. Louis in 1904. The Olympic Games in Antwerp, Belgium, in 1912 marked the first occasion when the Olympic flag was raised at the Opening Ceremony and the Olympic Oath was recited by and for competitors. The first Olympic village, first Closing Ceremony, and first official inclusion of women into the Olympic Games did not occur until Paris in 1924. Often, the host country included indigenous sports ranging from lacrosse to rugby as medal events.

Attendance by nations in the founding period often depended on the cost of travel, thus giving an advantage to the richer nations of Europe and North America. Participation by Asian, African, Caribbean, and South American nations remained low until the 1960s (*Olympics History*, n.d.; *NOCs & Athletes*, n.d.).

As decolonization was birthing new and independent nations around the world, the IOC stepped forward to assist those countries in creating sport programs. During the 1960s, the IOC created the precursor to the Olympic Solidarity program, which now funds NOCs to develop and manage these programs. As the money from television rights grew in 1984, so too did aid to NOCs. The IOC's 2015 Annual Report reported that just over US$45 million was spent on the world program and another US$47 on the continental program (Olympic Movement, 2017a).

Globally, many identify 1948, when Sir Ludwig Guttmann introduced the first Stoke Mandeville Games for World War II veterans with spinal-cord-related injuries, as the founding year of the Paralympic Movement. The first Paralympic Games, however, did not take place until 1960, when it was held in Rome two weeks following the Olympic Summer Games. This event came about because of Guttmann's proposal to then IOC president Avery Brundage that the Paralympic Games occur in parallel to the Olympic Games in the Olympic city (Brittain, 2010). Between 1964 and 1984, the Paralympic sport leaders attempted to conduct parallel Games in Olympic cities or, if not within the actual Olympic city, at an alternate site within the same country. During this time, the Paralympic Games became more diverse concerning an athlete's type of disability. The 1972, 1976, and 1980 Games saw the increasing inclusion of athletes with visual impairments, amputations, and cerebral palsy (Brittain, 2010).

The Olympic Movement in the 1970s and 80s was also dealing with tremendous change and crisis, including fallout from the massacre of Israeli athletes and coaches at the Olympic Games in

Munich in 1972; boycotts of the 1976 (Montréal), 1980 (Moscow), and 1984 (Los Angeles) Games from various nations; and the excessive public debt incurred by Montréal in 1976. Following the Summer Games in Moscow in 1980, the IOC, under the leadership of its new president, Juan Antonio Samaranch (1980-2001), began to institute dramatic changes to the IOC Charter that led to a revaluing of the Olympic Games as a global brand. Beginning with the launching of a new marketing and corporate sponsorship strategy built from the unexpected financial success of the Los Angeles Olympic Games in 1984, Samaranch was able to persuade IOC members to purge any reference in the **Olympic Charter** to the term *amateur*, thus redefining athlete eligibility and opening the door to participation of openly professional athletes into the Games after 1988 (Mickle, 2010a).

From a Paralympic perspective, the significant turning point was the 1988 Games in Seoul. The Paralympic Games were held for the first time in the same venues as the Olympic Games and incorporated other commonalities such as using the same athletes' village. For this reason, many consider the Seoul Games to be the start of the modern Paralympic era.

The IOC, which had begun to correspond more regularly with Paralympic leaders, requested that one umbrella organization be established with which to communicate. This request was, in part, the genesis of the International Paralympic Committee. Dr. Robert Steadward had met with IOC president Juan Antonio Samaranch in Calgary, Canada, during IOC meetings leading up to the 1988 Olympic Winter Games. Steadward stressed to Samaranch the importance of continued meetings between Paralympic leaders and the IOC leadership (Legg & Steadward, 2011). This ultimately led to the formal agreement between the IOC and IPC, which, as discussed earlier, means that bid cities bid for and host both Games.

Considerations for Staging the Games

The hosting of Olympic and Paralympic Games has many challenges and opportunities for the host city and nation. Among these are the costs in bidding; various challenges facing the host city; additional costs resulting from the expansion in the Olympic family; the continuous growth of media in size, price, and scope; and environmental impacts.

Bidding Costs

Despite IOC reform efforts, the costs of bidding for the privilege of hosting an Olympic and Paralympic Games continue to increase. Preuss (2008), in his work *Economics of Olympic Bidding*, provided a detailed history of the Olympic bidding process from Munich in 1972 through Beijing in 2008. Preuss, who has served as consultant to a number of Olympic candidate cities, illustrated the cost–benefit relationship of being part of the bidding process and theorized that a city and nation could maximize their cost–benefit ratio by being a finalist in the Olympic bidding process but not the ultimate winner.

As an example, the three finalists for the 2018 Winter Olympic and Paralympic Games (Pyeongchang, South Korea; Munich, Germany; and Annecy, France) spent approximately US$21 million to US$42.5 million during the bidding cycle by the time the winner was announced on July 6, 2011. And this sum did not take into account the total cost of bidding by Pyeongchang, because this bid was their third after narrowly missing being selected for the 2010 and 2014 Winter Games ("2018 Olympic Candidates," 2010). Tokyo also spent as much as $150 million on its failed 2016 bid, and about half that much for its successful 2020 bid, and Toronto decided it could not afford the $60 million necessary for a 2024 bid (Council on Foreign Relations, 2017).

Challenges for Host Cities

Whatever the actual costs of bidding, the cost of hosting can be much more challenging to pin down. In part, the difficulty lies in trying to forecast seven years in advance the state of the global, regional, and national economies to produce estimates of revenue from broadcast, sponsorship, and ticket sales and projections of the demand for public spending (Preuss, 2004). The volatility of global economic and security issues and the unpredictability of currency markets (e.g., U.S. dollar versus the euro versus the yen or yuan) can wreak havoc with the best-laid plans of any Olympic and Paralympic Games host organizing committee ("London 2010 Budget," 2010). National politics can also dramatically affect support for public spending, as occurred with the change in government that took place in the United

Kingdom just two years before the 2012 Olympic and Paralympic Games ("London 2010 Budget," 2010). Differences between initial budgets and final costs for hosting Games also range dramatically. In Sochi the initial budget was $10.3 billion, but the final cost was over $50 billion. Rio de Janeiro was budgeted at $14 billion, and the final cost was estimated to be over $20 billion. London 2012 went from $5 billion beforehand to $18 billion in total cost. Vancouver was projected to cost $2 billion, but the final estimates of costs ranged around $7.6 billion (Council on Foreign Relations, 2017).

Perhaps because of these financial issues, few cities are willing to bid for and host the Games. Only two cities officially bid to host the 2022 Winter Games. The Games were awarded to Beijing, the third Asian city in a row to host Olympic and Paralympic Games (Pyeongchang in 2018, Tokyo in 2020, and Beijing in 2022). The number of cities bidding for the 2024 Summer Games was also smaller than the number that bid previously; cities such as Hamburg, Rome, Budapest, and Boston all bowed out, and only Los Angeles and Paris remained. The IOC, perhaps recognizing that the number of cities might continue to decrease, took the unique step of awarding the Games for both 2024 and 2028 at the same time to the only two cities left bidding—Paris and Los Angeles (Panja, 2017; "Business Model," 2017).

The most recent Games being considered are the 2026 Winter Games. Cities such as Calgary and Sion are pondering whether they wish to bid (Klingbeil, 2017).

Additional Costs of Expansion

Although the number of cities bidding for Olympic Games is declining, the IOC has attempted to enable smaller centers to still be in the game as an Olympic summer candidate city by creating a new Olympic property—the Youth Olympic Games (YOG) for aspiring Olympic athletes between the ages of 14 and 18. These games debuted in Singapore in August 2010. The YOG unveiled the winter version in Innsbruck, Austria, in February 2012. In the first case, the Youth Olympic Games were hosted by a nation-state that likely would never be able to host an Olympic–Paralympic Games, and in the instance of Innsbruck, the IOC will return to a former Olympic (1964 and 1976) and Paralympic (1984 and 1988) city, thus allowing the IOC to extend itself to more cities itching to be directly connected to the Olympic brand (Mickle, 2010b). The Games were held in Nanjing in 2014 and in Lillehammer in 2016. Future Games will be held in Buenos Aires in 2018 and in Lausanne (home of the IOC headquarters) in 2020.

Billed as one of the key legacies of Jacques Rogge's tenure as IOC president (2001-2012), the YOG has generated skepticism about whether it is a strategic extension or a dilution of the Olympic brand. Some international federations and national Olympic committees have expressed concern over the new costs of YOG events and their interference with well-established existing competitions. Some skeptics believe that the Youth Olympic Games is a way for the IOC to maintain its brand presence in a battle for global sport brand supremacy with FIFA. The IOC hopes perhaps that the YOG will help it connect to a younger audience, foster youth participation in sport, and increase the interest of youth in the Olympic Games (Mickle, 2010b).

Observers speculate, however, that as with the Olympic and Paralympic Games, the cost burden to cities of hosting this event will steadily increase. Singapore, for example, reportedly spent nearly US$400 million to host nearly 3,600 athletes from 202 countries in 26 Olympic sports. This amount is more than 3 times the estimated original cost of nearly US$120 million and well over 10 times the US$30 million cost originally estimated by Rogge himself when the Games were approved in 2007 (Mickle, 2010b). Note that no parallel Youth Paralympic Games has yet to be created under the behest of the International Paralympic Committee.

Media Coverage

As the IOC makes a strategic effort to move into new regions of the world with new events such as the Youth Olympic Games and to build on its sizable reserves, estimated at nearly US$500 million, garnered through the sale of its international broadcast rights and corporate sponsorships, it is unclear how and to what extent it will be able to maximize and protect its digital rights in the universe of decentralized social media and social networking sites. Questions have arisen over who will control the rights of social media and networking sites used by Olympic and Paralympic athletes before, during, and after Olympic and Paralympic Games. These developments will likely create new complexities surrounding intellectual property rights that need to be negotiated by and between NOCs and NPCs with their respective athletes, coaches, and officials as well as with the IOC, IFs, and OCOGs. This situation is further complicated by the efforts of the IOC and IPC to capitalize on the popularity of their star athletes by building greater fan interest with the Olympic and Paralympic Games (Lombardo, 2010).

As Olympic-related media continue to increase in size, price, and scope, concern is also growing over controls and suppression of a free press that can effectively shut out solo journalists who are often openly critical of the IOC or a host city's conduct in organizing the Games. This action is similar to the leverage that the IOC has been able to impose on various host cities and host governments in its attempts to control ambush marketing efforts by companies, organizations, and corporations not officially related to NOCs or the IOC (Rosner & Shropshire, 2011). For example, the host city contract between the Vancouver 2010 Organizing Committee and the IOC stated that no propaganda or advertising material could be within view of spectators at the venues or television cameras covering the sports or "in the airspace over the city and other cities and venues hosting Olympic events during the period of the Games." In response, before the Games, Vancouver's city council passed an omnibus by-law amending dozens of existing laws, including the creation of so-called free-speech zones and blocks of the city where no political pamphlets, leaf-lets, graffiti, or "non-celebratory posters" would be allowed (Burton & O'Reilly, 2010b; Mickle, 2010a).

Environmental Impact and Games Legacies

Because of its efforts to institute reforms regarding the processes of bidding, awarding, and hosting of the Games (Olympic, Paralympic, and Youth), the International Olympic Committee has perhaps become increasingly concerned over the legacies of a given Games, including the lasting impacts on the local and regional environments of the physical infrastructure requirements for facilities, transportation, communication, public health, and security. Unique now among the factors considered by the IOC Review Commission in its progress reports on Olympic candidate cities is a new focus on universal design that would provide adequate and appropriate accessibility and accommodation for people with disabilities, including the ability to host the Paralympic Games. The results of these efforts also allowed greater accessibility for people with disabilities who attend either the Olympic or Paralympic Games as working professionals (e.g., members of the media, OCOG personnel) or as spectators. Given previous criticism over the cost and lack of use of Olympic venues after the Games had ended (known as white elephants), the IOC has also encouraged greater use of temporary structures for spectator seating, media and broadcast facilities, and the large structures necessary to accommodate a given Olympic and Paralympic village (Burton & O'Reilly, 2010b; Crary, 2010; Mickle, 2010a). Even so, Games' facilities in many instances have gone unused afterward, although the most recent Games in Rio are an exception.

As a result, regardless of the advances in environmental awareness and the practices by OCOGs, often working in cooperation with national, regional, and local governments, to use the requirements of hosting of an Olympic Games as a means to regenerate blighted sections of their cities, a healthy skepticism remains over whether these efforts really help the people targeted by displacement from their neighborhoods. Typically, displaced people lack the political and economic power to resist these changes. Such public debates over housing rights and neighborhood regeneration efforts have occurred consistently since Seoul in 1988, where

Learning Activity

Many critics have sounded the alarm over restrictions imposed by the International Olympic Committee's effort to protect its top sponsors from creative ambush marketing by its competitors. In doing so, the IOC has imposed new requirements, like those imposed at the Vancouver 2010 Games, on the host city and the regional and federal governments of a given Olympic Games related to free speech of citizens during a specified period before and during the Games. In small groups, discuss examples you have seen of ambush marketing and whether you think these restrictions are appropriate. Why or why not?

720,000 people were forcibly evicted (10 percent received replacement housing). In 1992 in Barcelona, 600 families were displaced and housing prices rose 240 percent between the time the city won the right to host the Games and their actual start, which led to secondary displacement (many of whom were Roma). The building of the Olympic Stadium (now Turner Field) in Atlanta for the 1996 Games coincided with the arrests of 9,000 homeless people between 1995 and 1996 and the evictions of tens of thousands of low-income residents. In 2000 in Sydney, the acceleration of gentrification in the city caused housing prices to double between 1996 and 2003. As had occurred in Barcelona, the Roma experienced a disproportionately negative effect from the Athens Games in 2004, but the Olympic Village provided 10,000 people with subsidized housing. Beijing in 2008 was an apparent disaster for housing; approximately 1.5 million people were evicted to make way for Games construction. In Vancouver a report by the United Nations Special Rapporteur on adequate housing found that Canada was not doing enough to protect people from Olympic construction (United Nations General Assembly, 2009). In particular, the construction of the Vancouver Olympic Village displaced over 3,000 homeless people. In London the redevelopment of a number East London neighborhoods notorious for poverty and crime forced 1,000 people from their homes (Center on Housing Rights and Evictions Report: Fair Play for Housing Rights, 2007). Most recently the Rio Games were plagued with accusations of evictions and the evaporation of other legacies from various perspectives (Kommenda, 2017; Geiling, 2016).

Social and Ethical Issues in Olympic and Paralympic Sport

Social and ethical issues in Olympic and Paralympic sport often emerge from the disparities between the stated mission and principles of the Olympic and Paralympic Movements and the actual realities of what happens at the Games. As one example, women do not share equally in the number of participants, sports, and power and voice in the decision making (Carr, 2009). The Institute for Diversity and Ethics in Sport provides an annual racial and

gender report card. The report on international sport concluded that "the leadership in international sport is an exclusive club of men." The desire for a greater equity paradigm also challenges the IOC and IPC with respect to transgendered and sexual ambiguous athletes (e.g., Semenya). Although it does not give justice to the importance of these topics, the following section explores some of the more pressing social and ethical issues found in both the Olympic and Paralympic Movements and presents them as introductions to the area.

Gender Equity

Despite the IOC's charter goal of promoting equal rights of men and women, when the Games first began women athletes were not even invited to compete. Pierre de Coubertin, the founder of the modern Olympic Games, thought that the inclusion of women would be "impractical, uninteresting, unaesthetic, and incorrect" (Johnson, 1996). He also believed that the Olympic Games should "be reserved for the solemn and periodic exaltation of male athleticism with internationalism as a base, loyalty as a means, arts for its setting, and female applause as its reward" (Johnson, 1996). At the 1900 Olympic Games, 23 women competed in six sports: tennis, sailing, croquet, golf, ballooning, and equestrian. Boxing, the only sport not available to women at the 2008 Olympic Games in Beijing, was actually held as a demonstration event for women at the 1904 Olympics in St. Louis. The local organizing committees of the host cities of the early Olympic Games were often responsible for organizing separate women's events until 1912, when the IOC took charge of setting the event schedule (Wamsley, 2008). Women were officially included in the Olympic Games starting with Paris in 1924. Not until Tokyo in 1964 was a women's team event, volleyball, added to the Olympic event schedule. Women's basketball and team handball followed in Montréal in 1976 (Johnson, 1996; Pfister, 2000).

Although women's participation increased over the next few decades, in 1954 the IOC voted to limit events for women to those "particularly appropriate to the female sex" (Olympic Women, 2008; British Columbia Supreme Court, 2009).

In 2009 a coalition of international female ski jumpers filed a lawsuit in Vancouver on the grounds that ski jumping was offered only for male competitors. The court in Vancouver ruled that the women were being discriminated against under the Canadian Charter of Human Rights and Freedoms but that they had brought the wrong violators into court (British Columbia Supreme Court, 2009). Despite finding that the Vancouver Organizing Committee for the 2010 Winter Olympics (VANOC) was discriminatory, an adverse decision was entered against the women because it was determined that VANOC had no power to set the Olympic program. The judge stated, "The IOC made a decision that discriminates against the plaintiffs. Only the IOC can alleviate that discrimination by including an Olympic ski jumping event for women in the 2010 Games" (British Columbia Supreme Court, 2009, p. 42). Although the criteria for adding new events to the Olympic program are not discriminatory against women per se, past discrimination seems to have played a factor. The judge in Canada further found that the IOC's actions stem from historical discrimination against women in ski jumping because in 1949 men's ski jumping was "grandfathered" into the Olympic Games "for the sake of the Olympic Tradition" (British Columbia Supreme Court, 2009, p. 29). More recently a similar issue emerged when the USA women's hockey team refused to play in the Ice Hockey Women's World Championships until male and female athletes were equally compensated (Clarke, 2017).

Although the issue of gender equality is far from over, there is hope that changes are occurring. Canada's *Globe and Mail* highlighted that many of Canada's leading sport administrators were women

Learning Activity

Break into small discussion groups and brainstorm all the different forms of prejudice and discrimination that might be experienced by members of different identity groups seeking to participate in the Olympic or Paralympic Games as participants or governance. What groups might feel marginalized, and why? If given the opportunity to provide suggestions to the IOC and IPC, what would you recommend? What are some of the complexities and challenges in achieving equity in sport, particularly at the international level?

(Maki, 2017). The IOC has also made efforts to be more gender balanced by increasing the number of women on their commissions, but the reality was that in 2016 only 24 of 106 IOC members were women (Olympic Movement, 2017b). Another article highlighted that globally speaking women were also missing in international sport leadership ("Women Are Missing," 2016). The IOC has addressed gender imbalance by promoting the first ever gender-equal Games when Argentina hosted the Youth Olympic Games in 2018 (Around the Rings, 2017).

Gender Testing

A second issue related to female participation is gender testing. When drug testing was introduced to the Olympics in 1968, so was gender verification testing. The first gender tests conducted at international track events were visual exams, but the IOC used chromosome testing (obtained from a mouth swab) at the 1968 Games in Mexico City. Testing was mandatory only for female athletes. If the test was negative, the female had to undergo further testing. Unlike drug testing, which focused on ensuring an equal playing field for all athletes, gender testing involved deeper concerns about the femininity, or lack thereof, of certain female athletes (Wamsley, 2008).

Inclusion of Athletes With Disabilities

Disability sport began with a desire to reintegrate persons with disabilities into mainstream society, which has been further described in an article published by Legg, Fay, Hums, and Wolff (2009). These authors noted that for over 60 years this issue has held a significant place within the growth and development of disability sport. Inclusion is a topic that inspires tremendous emotional undertones based on philosophical debate and practical issues related to autonomy, economies of scale, and equity. Not surprisingly, then, inclusion is one of the most "discussed, debated, and contentious issues facing disability sport and the Paralympic Movement" (Steadward, 1996, p. 26).

Beginning in the early 1990s, the IPC under the direction of its first president, Dr. Robert Steadward, created the Commission for the Inclusion of Athletes with a Disability (CIAD). CIAD played

CASE STUDY

Caster Semenya

One of the most sensational sport stories of 2009 and 2010 was the Caster Semenya case, which involved a 19-year-old female track and field athlete from South Africa who won the 800-meter event at the 2009 IAAF World Championship race in Berlin in a time more similar to a top men's result than a top women's result. Because of Semenya's muscular build, masculine appearance, and accelerated improvement, the IAAF suspended Semenya from further competition, pending the results of a series of gender verification tests. A year later on July 6, 2010, official results from the IAAF medical examiners cleared Semenya to resume international track competition as a woman, positioning her as the favorite for Olympic gold in London in 2012 (Goldman, 2010). The results of those tests were not made public.

Semenya issued a public statement in 2010 declaring that the circumstances before and after her win in Berlin in 2009 had violated her human rights, including her rights to privacy and dignity. Semenya was just 18 years old when she won the world title, and questions about her gender placed her into the international spotlight. "Since my victory in the female 800 m event at the Berlin world championships in August last year, I have been subjected to unwarranted and invasive scrutiny of the most intimate and private details of my being," said Semenya (Longman, 2010). Some of those details include Australian press reports stating that she did not have either a womb or ovaries and was going through hormone treatment similar to the type that other "gender ambiguous" athletes have received in the past (Goldman, 2010). Ironically, the introduction of hormone therapy in this case, which purportedly was intended to "womanize"

an athlete such as Semenya to help make her less dominant as an athlete, begins to blur the line with the antidoping efforts that focus on identifying those who seek to gain an advantage by increasing strength and speed through the use of anabolic steroids and human growth hormone (HGH).

Was Semenya cheating? Should she and other gender ambiguous athletes be banned from competition based on the traditions and norms of fair play? To understand the rationale in support of gender testing and the complexities of trying to develop a reliable and valid testing procedure, we need to look back at some of the more sensational stories about athletes who were suspected of or caught gender cheating in the Olympic Games.

Suspicion reigned in sports such as track and field between 1932 and 1968 over whether a given athlete was a male posing as a woman. Ironically, Ewa Klobubowski of Poland, who was a bronze medalist, became famous as the first female to fail a chromosome test in 1964, yet she gave birth to a son in 1965, bringing into question the reliability of the newly introduced chromosome test at that time. The Caster Semenya case is a perfect example of what initiated gender testing in the 1960s—"a culture of hyper competition and suspicion" (Olympic Women, 2008).

Semenya has since continued to compete and excel. In 2012 she was chosen to carry South Africa's flag during the opening ceremony in London and most recently won a gold medal at the Rio Olympic Games in the 800-meter event. In 2017 at the World Track and Field Championships, also in London, Semenya won the bronze medal in the 1,500 meter and gold in the 800 meter.

---

a central and successful strategic role in lobbying the 1994 Commonwealth Games held in Victoria, Canada, to grant events for athletes with a disability with full medal status (Christie, 1997). Athletes with disabilities were allowed to compete in what was previously an able-bodied competition, and their medals were as respected as any other and contributed to the overall medal tally. Four years later when the Commonwealth Games were held in

Malaysia, the inclusion of athletes with a disability was not followed, but inclusion returned in 2002 when the Games were held in Manchester, England. In 2006 the International Commonwealth Games Federation (ICGF) declared that all Games starting in 2006 must have full medal status events for athletes with a disability.

The hope was that this model would be followed in the Olympic context, but this was not to be the case. Dick Pound, a senior IOC member from Canada, noted that within the Olympic Games there were lots of choices and

> whenever there are choices to include or exclude [the idea that] you're talking about "discrimination" is a moot point, or a debatable point. Any exercise of distinctions requires discriminating. We [the Olympic Games] cannot be all things to all people. (Clark, 1992, p. 4)

Two wheelchair events had been included as demonstration status since the 1984 Games, and in 2004 in Athens athletes and administrators finally challenged the IOC's stance. Two athletes from the United States who were scheduled to compete in their respective events, Cheri Blauwet and Scot Hollenbeck, wrote to the United States Olympic Committee (USOC) requesting support to contest the IOC's decision. In addition, a personal letter dated July 20 to IOC president Jacques Rogge from the president of the Canadian Paralympic Committee (CPC), Patrick Jarvis, suggested that a terrible injustice was about to unfold at the birthplace of the modern Olympic Games (Legg, Fay, Hums, & Wolff, 2009).

> As it related to the situation in Athens where the athletes competing in the wheelchair demonstration events are being excluded from the Opening Ceremony and being denied privileges afforded to all others who are members of their country's contingents. It appears to be discriminatory and I appeal to the IOC that they act in accordance with the underlying values of the Olympic Movement such as the sense of fair play, respect and sport for all.... We are of the opinion that they should be treated the same as other athletes in Athens or not participate in any fashion: please do it the right way or don't do it at all. (Jarvis, 2004)

IOC officials responded by stating in a series of press releases and press interviews that the wheelchair athletes in Athens were being treated exactly the same way as any athlete who had ever competed within an Olympic demonstration event. The events remained as demonstration status, the practice was cancelled, and no events for athletes with disabilities occurred in Olympic Games thereafter.

What transpired instead was a discussion on whether the two Games should be merged. Given his past advocacy for inclusion into the Olympic Games, it was not surprising when Dr. Robert

Steadward suggested that putting the Olympic and Paralympic Games together would create efficiencies and allow the Paralympics to take advantage of the public support for the Olympic Games. Steadward suggested that the natural evolution of the Paralympic Movement would call for it to be included more in the Olympics. "I wouldn't mind seeing the 100-metre men's final, the 100-metre women's final, the 100-metre wheelchair final and the 100-metre final for blind runners," he said. Pointing to the intense national pride that emerged in Vancouver during the Olympics in 2010, he said that it was a shame for the Paralympics to have to "re-energize" the city 10 days later (Battistoni, 2010).

Phil Craven, president for the IPC from 2002 to 2017, rejected the idea of combining the Olympic and Paralympic Winter Games into one megaevent, saying that the Paralympic Movement was doing just fine on its own. Craven said that the Paralympics had become a force of their own over the last decade and would be diminished if they were melded into the Olympic Games:

> Any coming together would, I think, by its very nature, be restrictive from a logistics point of view. We have it as we like it at the moment, and we don't see any need to change. We believe by having the Paralympics and the Olympics separate, we're able to have our own identity while coming together in a festival of sport that gives a wonderful face to the world of what sport can do.

Gilbert Felli, then executive director of Olympic Games for the IOC, stated in 2010 that the two groups had worked out an agreement that allowed the IOC to assist the IPC but merging the two Games together would hamstring both, resulting in the participation of fewer Paralympic athletes. Craven also dismissed the idea of the Paralympics being held in advance of the Olympics to take advantage of the more than 10,000 media and broadcasters who typically descend on an Olympic host city. Historically, far fewer journalists stick around for the Paralympics, but Craven was adamant that the Paralympics wanted to stand on their own merit. "I believe the Paralympic Games have to attract the media in their own right," he said (Battistoni, 2010).

A final issue is the valuing and recognition of Paralympic versus Olympic athletes. A prime example of this was evident in Canada in 2004 after the Athens Olympic and Paralympic Games when

Chantal Petitclerc shared the honor of Athletics Canada's Female Athlete of the Year (Jack Davies Trophy) with Perdita Felicien, winner of the hurdles competition in the 2003 IAAF World Championships. Despite being the heavy favorite, Felicien did not finish in the finals of the 110-meter track event at the Olympics in Athens in 2004, tripping over a hurdle. Petitclerc, on the other hand, won the Olympic 800-meter wheelchair track exhibition event at the Olympic Games as well as four Paralympic gold medals at various distances. The question was whether the accomplishments of Petitclerc and Felicien should be valued equally. In a *Globe and Mail* article following the 2004 Games that profiled Petitclerc as one of Canada's Nation Builders, she noted her discomfort with the perception that it is easier to win a Paralympic medal than an Olympic one: "That may have been true 15 years ago. That's not the case now" (Wong, 2004, p. F1). Two weeks after Athletics Canada announced its Jack Davies Trophy cowinners, *Maclean's Magazine*, Canada's national weekly news magazine, named Petitclerc the 2004 Canadian of the Year (Gillis, 2004).

Even with outstanding performances by athletes such as Petitclerc and others, Paralympic sport is not always seen as elite. As noted by Bell (2002), "The issue is really quality of competition" based on an able-bodied standard. The reality according to Bell (2002) is that only a few events mirrored the competitiveness found in the Olympic Games. Bell (2002) determined that from 1960 until 2000 Olympic athletes had a 1 in 10 chance of receiving a medal, whereas Paralympic athletes had a 6 in 10 chance. Bell (2002) also clarified, however, that he was not suggesting that Paralympic performances equated to poor performances; instead, they were fraught with poor quality of competition that could not be considered equal to that found in Olympic competitions. He recognized that the men's 1,500-meter and women's 800-meter wheelchair races that had been showcased as Olympic exhibition events from 1984 through Athens in 2004 were exceptions.

A final issue is whether athletes with a disability should be encouraged and allowed to compete directly against able-bodied athletes. Brian McKeever, a Canadian athlete with a visual impairment qualified as a cross-country ski racer for both 2010 Olympic and Paralympic Games. Others such as Oscar Pistorius, Natalie du Toit, and Natalie Partyka have also competed in both Olympic and Paralympic Games, and athletes with a disability have competed in the Olympic Games going as far back as 1904 (Legg, Burchell, Jarvis, & Sainsbury, 2009).

Olympic and Paralympic Games of 2036—the Inclusive Games?

Considering all the issues and challenges presented relating to the Olympic and Paralympic Games, considering and envisioning a future Games may be worthwhile. Already the Summer Games for 2024 and 2028 have been awarded to Paris and Los Angeles, and a few cities have indicated an interest in bidding for and hosting the 2026 Winter Games. But what about the Games in the 2030s? How might they look? Already discussion has arisen about the inclusion of e-sports into the 2022 Asian Games and potentially the 2024 Olympic Games being held in Paris (Geekwire, 2017).

Another vision of a future Games might be one focusing on inclusion being staged for the first time in a primarily Islamic nation. To conclude this chapter, let us explore the following hypothetical ideas based, in part, on what has happened recently in the international sport arena.

After narrowly losing out to the winning bid of Delhi and Mumbai, India, for the 2032 Games, Turkey was finally rewarded by the IOC for its years of persistence and commitment to the Olympic ideals as evidenced by decades of unsuccessful bids to stage the Summer Olympic Games. The controversial selection of Istanbul to host the 140th anniversary Games was ironic given the centuries of war and animus between Greece, the ancient land of the Olympic Games, and neighboring Turkey, which were exacerbated by the centuries-long dispute over control of the island of Cyprus. Perceived as a statement of the power and ability of the Olympic Movement to bring peace to historically war-torn places, this achievement positioned the IOC and its new president, Dmitry Chernyshenko, president and CEO of the hugely successful 2014 Olympic and Paralympic Winter Games in Sochi, Russia, to be strongly considered for a 2036 Nobel Peace Prize.

Beginning with the 2008 Olympic and Paralympic Summer Games in Beijing, China, and followed by the successful staging of the 2014 Winter Games in Sochi, the 2016 Summer Games in Rio de Janeiro, the 2024 Summer Games in Paris, the 2028 Games in Los Angeles, and the 2032 Summer Games in India, the IOC successfully shifted the locus of its financial, marketing, and media strategies from its traditional European and North American base deep into the heart of the largest of the world's new economies (Rosner & Shropshire, 2011). Following the lead of several international federations involved in some of the larger Olympic sports (e.g., FIFA, FIS, and FIBA) and their bold strategies of placing their respective single-sport world championships in the new economies of Brazil, Russia, India, and China together with South Africa and Turkey (aka BRIC-SAT), the IOC was able to take a low-risk approach by piggybacking on the logistics and infrastructure already in place from past single-sport megaevents (e.g., track and field, basketball, and skiing) to ensure a successful multisport extravaganza that the Olympic (Paralympic) Games had become (*Brazil's Decade of Sport*, 2010).

The decision to invite wheelchair basketball, wheelchair rugby, and a select number of previously Paralympic-only track, swimming, and cycling events to become official Olympic sports in time for the 2024 Olympic Summer Games in Paris forced the IPC to reconsider its separate but equal position with respect to the IOC. Faced with losing its top athletes and most marketable sports to the Olympic Games, the IPC capitulated and agreed to be absorbed as a new division of the IOC in 2025 with full inclusion occurring for the first time at the 2022 Olympic Winter Games held in Beijing, China (*China Embraces*, 2009). This groundbreaking inclusive arrangement between the IOC and IPC was achieved as the result of years of international advocacy and pressure by the United Nations and the European Parliament along with individual governments, labor unions, corporations, and volunteer groups that have been working to remove barriers to full participation in many sectors of civilized society in partial fulfillment of the UN Millennium Goals (United Nations, 2006) and the Convention on the Rights of Persons with Disabilities (United Nations, 2007).

The acceptance by the IOC in 2020 that all Paralympians would henceforth be referred to as Olympians was a testament to the resolve, persistence, and dedication of a number of former Paralympic and Olympic athletes with a disability, beginning with the track and skiing athletes who competed in the first Olympic exhibition events in Sarajevo and Los Angeles in 1984 through to Athens in 2004 (Legg, Fay, Hums, & Wolff, 2009; Legg, Burchill, Jarvis, & Sainsbury, 2009). But it was Oscar Pistorius's highly publicized quest to qualify for the 2008 and 2012 Olympic Games, along with the bid of Canadian Paralympic champion Brian McKeever to become the first Paralympian to qualify as a Winter Olympian at the 2010 Vancouver Olympic Games, that provided the tipping point for sport governing bodies and sporting officials to begin to question the future of the Paralympic Games in relation to the Olympic Games (Legg, Burchill, Jarvis, & Sainsbury, 2009).

Some sport historians cited the debate that occurred after the 2010 Winter Paralympic Games in Vancouver between the first and second presidents of the IPC, Dr. Robert Steadward and Sir Philip Craven, over the purported right place for the Paralympic Games to be governed and staged by the IOC as a critical turning point in the eventual full integration of Paralympic athletes as Olympians beginning with the 2028 Olympic Winter Games in China (Battistoni, 2010). In addition, a separate agreement was negotiated in 2025 by the IOC with Special Olympics International (SOI) regarding its continued use of the term *Olympic* in its name and its ongoing oversight of the major international multisport Winter and Summer Games in odd-numbered years for athletes with an intellectual disability. A similar agreement was also reached between the IOC regarding the Deaflympics for athletes who are deaf or have a significant hearing impairment.

The 2036 Istanbul Summer Olympic (Paralympic) Games were also noteworthy regarding fair play and doping, as well as gender equity—all issues that had long plagued the Olympic Movement. A new, relatively simple genetic test developed by an international consortium of sport scientists virtually brought to an end over a half century of drug and blood doping. Critics hailed this achievement as the start of a new era of fair play. Arguments over whether athletes who underwent genetic regeneration, hormonal therapy, smart limb replacement, or augmentation therapies were now able to compete against athletes with more "normalized" bodies as decided by the Court of Arbitration for Sport (CAS), thus favoring a more inclusive, open, and transhumanist approach (Wolbring, 2008).

The 2036 Summer Olympic Games also followed the precedent-setting 2034 Winter Games, where for the first time in Olympic history more women than men competed. This feat was the result of an extensive audit by the IOC Olympic Program Commission, chaired by Angela Ruggiero, IOC vice president and four-time U.S. Olympic ice hockey medalist (1998-2010), that created a new set of equity principles forcing international federations of Olympic sports to balance their event schedules, funding, and leadership and coaching figures with respect to gender. The audit also resulted in the addition of women's ski jumping in the Winter Games and a return of softball for women in the Summer Games. Ruggiero's leadership, based on the principle of universal access and equity in sport for all, helped take the IOC to a position opposite its founding in 1896 as an exclusive bastion of white, male privilege to being a farsighted organization that truly lives its principle of valuing diversity, equity, and fair play. Many journalists speculate that Ruggiero will become the first female IOC president, succeeding Chernyshenko when his term of office ends in 2042.

Is this future a reasonable scenario of Olympic and Paralympic sport? We shall have to wait until 2034 to see how much of this becomes reality!

Summary

The Olympic and Paralympic Games have been linked and have had somewhat parallel histories. Each has had to deal with issues pertaining to governance, equity, management, and enabling fair competition at the highest levels. The future of the two Games is now more intertwined than ever before, and tracking how they have grown, evolved, and contributed to our sporting systems worldwide will be interesting.

You should now have an in-depth understanding of how the Olympic and Paralympic organizations evolved, how they are structured, and how their histories may continue to intertwine. Cities wanting to host the Games certainly face a number of significant issues, and you should have new insight into what those are and how the IOC, IPC, and host cities can address them to ensure a bright future for the Games. In particular, we highlighted issues related to gender equality and the inclusion of athletes with a disability. We concluded with presenting a hypothetical future of the Games based in part on our reading of current events and trends. We hope that these ideas provide a base for further examination of sport at the international level and the role that you as a future professional can play in its evolution.

? Review Questions

1. What are the differences in structure and governance between the International Olympic Committee and the International Paralympic Committee?

2. What are key issues affecting the Olympic and Paralympic Games?

3. How has the inclusion of athletes with a disability been managed in the Olympic Games?

4. What are the challenges of bidding for and hosting Olympic and Paralympic Games?

5. How has gender equality been pursued in the Olympic Movement, and what effects has gender testing had on this effort?

International Sport Federations

Li Chen, PhD
Delaware State University

Chia-Chen Yu, EdD
University of Wisconsin—La Crosse

Chapter Objectives

After studying this chapter, you will be able to do the following:

- Define international sport federations.
- Describe the major managerial functions of international sport federations.
- Outline the common organizational structure and governance model of international sport federations.
- Describe the relationship between international sport federations and other international sport governing bodies, such as the IOC.
- Explain how international sport federations are financed.
- Identify the stakeholders of international sport federations.
- Identify the key managerial issues facing international sport federations.

Key Terms

Association of International Olympic Winter Sports Federations (AIOWF)

Association of IOC Recognized International Sports Federations (ARISF)

Association of Summer Olympic International Federations (ASOIF)

confederations

international (sports) federation (IF)

International Olympic Committee (IOC)

national Olympic committee (NOC)

national sport federation (NF)

Olympic Movement

organizing committee of the Olympic Games (OCOG)

International sport federations, also simply referred to as IFs in the Olympic vocabulary, are governing bodies in various sports at the international level. They play a significant role in promotion of global sport development and the **Olympic Movement**, which supports a philosophy of life in which the blending of sport and culture with art and education aims to combine in a balanced whole the human qualities of body, will, and mind. Although the **International Olympic Committee (IOC)** is the highest governing body for the Olympic Movement, the IFs are mainly responsible for administering each of the sports at the international level. In this chapter, we discuss how the IFs, IOC, and other Olympic organizations cooperate with each other to set up rules and policies for Olympic competitions, and develop and promote international sport in the world. Also we describe the mission, purpose, and operations of a typical IF and its relationship with other Olympic sport organizations, ranging from the IOC to the **organizing committees of the Olympic Games (OCOG)**, which are authorized by the IOC to organize the Olympic Games, and the **national Olympic committee (NOC)**, which is the national sport governing body in each country. Furthermore, issues related to management of an IF are discussed.

What Are International Federations?

An **international sports federation** is a nongovernmental organization established to govern one or more sports at the international level. Although most IFs represent only one sport, a number of them oversee several sports, such as the Fédération Internationale de Natation (FINA), which sanctions swimming, diving, high diving, water polo, synchronized swimming, and open-water swimming.

Although each IF maintains independence and autonomy in governing its own sport or sports to be continuously recognized by the IOC, the IF must cooperate with the IOC to make sure that its statutes, practices, and activities conform to the Olympic Charter, which is a set of rules and guidelines established by the IOC to organize the Olympic Games and govern the Olympic Movement. According to the Olympic Charter (Olympic Charter, 2016a), the common missions and roles of the IFs within the Olympic Movement include the following:

a. to establish and enforce, in accordance with the Olympic spirit, the rules concerning the practice of their respective sports and to ensure their application;

b. to ensure the development of their sports throughout the world;

c. to contribute to the achievement of the goals set out in the Olympic Charter, in particular by way of the spread of Olympism and Olympic education;

d. to support the IOC in the review of candidatures for organizing the Olympic Games for their respective sports;

e. to assume the responsibility for the control and direction of their sports at the Olympic Games;

f. for other international multisport competitions held under the patronage of the IOC, IFs can assume or delegate responsibility for the control and direction of their sports;

g. to provide technical assistance in the practical implementation of the Olympic Solidarity programmes;

h. to encourage and support measures relating to the medical care and health of athletes (p. 58).

Besides its role in the Olympic Movement, an IF governs and promotes a particular sport or a set of sports internationally. As indicated by Theodoraki (2007) and the IOC (2017a), other purposes of IFs include (a) to administer and monitor operations and competitions of the sport worldwide, (b) to engage in the development and promotion of the sport and related regulations and policies, and (c) to organize international championships and other competitions. For example, the types of competitions and events organized by the International Biathlon Union (IBU) consist of the BMW IBU World Cup Biathlon, IBU Cup, Junior Cup, and IBU Open European Championships (IBU, 2017).

The major functions of the IFs are consistent with their common missions in promoting their sports, organizing competitions, encouraging participation, and developing new programs (FINA, 2017a; ITTF, 2017). The following are the major functions of an IF:

a. Cooperating with the IOC for recognitions and participation of the Olympic Games

b. Functioning as a legislative body of rules, regulation, and policies for its sport

c. Determining competition levels

d. Playing a role in defining eligibilities and statuses of competitions

e. Determining affiliations with business organizations

f. Developing rules, policies, and measures against illegal or unethical practice in the sport

g. Making a decision on the equipment and site requirements for competitions

h. Determining qualifications of judges or referees and appointing the officers

i. Collecting, analyzing, examining, and maintaining all data and records of the sport federation (FINA, 2017a; ITTF, 2017)

The IFs also collaborate with the OCOG for all the technical functions during the Olympic Games. Each IF is responsible for technical control and elements of the competitions of its sport, including the schedule, field of play, and training sites. All equipment must comply with the rules of the IF. According to the Olympic Charter (2016b), the major responsibilities of IFs concerning technical functions at the Olympic Games include the following:

a. Establishing the technical rules of their own sports, disciplines, and events

b. Establishing the results and ranking of Olympic competitions

c. Selecting judges, referees, and other technical officials from the host country or from abroad

d. Enforcing, under the authority of the IOC and the NOCs, the rules of the IOC concerning the eligibility of the participants before the Olympic Games (preliminaries) and during the Olympic Games

e. Establishing an appeal process for all technical matters concerning their sport and from which all rulings and decisions including any related sanctions or measures, are final and without appeal

f. Requiring technical provisions such as training facilities, technical equipment at the venues, technical installations, and so on (pp. 89-90)

CASE STUDY

Federation Taking Leadership in Determination of Playing Eligibility

At the Summer Olympic Games at Rio, Brazil, in 2016, the World Anti-Doping Agency (WADA) called on the International Olympic Committee (IOC) and International Paralympics Committee (IPC) to decline all athletes' entries from Russian teams because of suspected drug usage.

The International Olympic Committee left athletes' eligibility up to the respective sport federations. The Fédération International de Natation (FINA) took on the role of investigating and determining whether Russian athletes were eligible to participate in the Olympic competitions of swimming, diving, and water polo. Although FINA banned seven Russian swimmers from the Rio Olympics because of evidenced violations of doping, FINA determined that Russian athletes in synchronized swimming, diving, and women's water polo were in compliance with the eligibility requirements to participate because the ongoing doping testing did not affect those athletes.

Although the U.S. Anti-Doping Agency stated that the IOC passed the baton to the sport federation, which might have had insufficient expertise to address the situation, the IOC insisted that the federation was in the position of authority to identify such important issues for the integrity of international sport competition and that the federation, rather than the IOC, could take the decisive leadership on this matter. The IOC officer stated that the respective sport federation should be responsible for analyzing each athlete's record of auto-doping, determining the reliability of international testing, and making sure that the playing field was level. Russian Olympic minister Alexander Zhukov believed that this stance was a well-considered decision of FINA. Russian athletes were allowed to compete in the Olympics, and the pressure that had been on the athletes from Western media diminished.

International Federations and the Olympic Movement

Although all IFs are autonomous and independent, they can be classified into four categories based on whether their sports are part of the official programming of the Olympic Games and the degree to which they are recognized by the IOC. Each of these categories has an international federation associated with it. These associations may act as spokespersons to discuss common issues or interests of the members and decide on their calendars of competitions with the IOC. The IOC does not recognize all IFs. Those IFs recognized by the IOC become one of the four main constituents of the Olympic Movement. Only the IOC-recognized IFs are eligible to have their sports included in the Olympic Games, but many sports with IOC-recognized IFs do not compete in the Olympic Games (Fairley & Lizandra, 2011) because of the restrictive rules of the IOC and the scope of the Olympic Games.

The associations of IFs for sports included in the Summer and Winter Olympic Games are the Association of the Summer Olympic International Federations (ASOIF, 2017) and the Association of the International Olympic Winter Sports Federations (AIOWF). The associations of IFs recognized by the IOC but whose sports are not included in the Olympic Games are the Association of the IOC Recognized International Sports Federations (ARISF) and the General Association of International Sports Federations (GAISF) or SportAccord.

All these associations are formed to ensure that member IFs have a close relationship with the IOC but still maintain their authority, independence, and autonomy (IOC, 2017b). The following are the four categories and their federations recognized by the IOC. These categories indicate whether the sports could be included in Olympic competitions or compete internationally only outside the Olympic Games.

◆ **Association of Summer Olympic International Federations**. Currently 28 IFs are affiliated with the Association of Summer Olympic International Federations (ASOIF) (2 others have recently been added) and are recognized and permitted to participate in the Summer Olympic Games. ASOIF represents the common interests of all affiliated IFs in the Summer Olympic Games and governs all related professional issues of the Summer Olympic Games (IOC, 2017b).

◆ **Association of International Olympic Winter Sports Federations**. Similar to ASOIF, the Association of International Olympic Winter Sport Federations (AIOWF) is recognized by the IOC and is responsible for organizing the Winter Olympic Games. Sports of seven IFs are currently included in the competition programs of the Winter Olympic Games (see table 13.1).

◆ **Association of IOC Recognized International Sports Federations**. The Association of IOC Recognized International Sports Federations (ARISF) consists of 37 member IFs that compete internationally but not as part of the Olympic program (ARISF, 2017). Such IFs include cricket, bowling, and motorcycle sport.

◆ **SportAccord**. SportAccord is made up of 92 international sport federations (IFs) and 17 associated members (organizations of international games and sport-related international associations). The IFs in this category could be either members or nonmembers of the IOC. Examples of associated members are the Commonwealth Games, World Games, and school sport (SportAccord, 2017a). The mission of SportAccord is to "unite and support its members in the co-ordination and protection of their common aims and interests, while preserving and respecting their autonomy" (SportAccord, 2017b).

The primary mission of the IFs recognized by the IOC is to cooperate with the IOC and administer the designated sports at the global level. The IFs work closely not only with the IOC but also with the national governing bodies (NGBs) or national sport federations in each country. Each affiliated national sport federation must also be recognized by the national Olympic committee (NOC) in its country. At present, the number of member nations affiliated with an IF that is represented in the Summer Olympic Games ranges from 35 to 214. The International Association of Athletics Federations (IAAF) is the largest IF, involving 214 countries and territory affiliations (International Association of Athletics Federations [IAAF], 2017), whereas the Union Internationale de Pentathlon Moderne (UIPM) has only 35 member nations (IOC, 2017b).

Currently, 35 official sports with their respective IFs appear with the status of official sports on

Table 13.1 International Sport Federations Recognized by the IOC for the Summer and Winter Olympic Games

Sport	Name of federation	Founding year
Summer Olympic Games (28)		
Aquatics	(FINA) Fédération Internationale de Natation	1902
Archery	(WA) World Archery Federation	1931
Athletics	(IAAF) International Association of Athletics Federation	1912
Badminton	(BWF) Badminton World Federation	1934
Basketball	(FIBA) Fédération Internationale de Basketball	1932
Boxing	(AIBA) Association Internationale de Boxe	1946
Canoeing	(ICF) International Canoe Federation	1924
Cycling	(UCI) Union Cycliste Internationale	1900
Equestrian	(FEI) Fédération Equestre Internationale	1921
Fencing	(FIE) Fédération Internationale d'Escrime	1913
Football	(FIFA) Fédération Internationale de Football Association	1904
Gymnastics	(FIG) Fédération Internationale de Gymnastique	1881
Golf	(IGF) International Golf Federation	1958
Handball	(IHF) International Handball Federation	1946
Hockey	(FIH) Fédération Internationale de Hockey	1924
Judo	(IJF) International Judo Federation	1951
Pentathlon	(UIPM) Union Internationale de Pentathlon Moderne	1948
Rowing	(FISA) Fédération Internationale de Sociétés d'Aviron	1892
Rugby	(WR) World Rugby	1886
Sailing	(WS) World Sailing	1907
Shooting sport	(ISSF) International Shooting Sport Federation	1907
Table tennis	(ITTF) International Table Tennis Federation	1926
Taekwondo	(WTF) World Taekwondo Federation	1973
Tennis	(ITF) International Tennis Federation	1913
Triathlon	(ITU) International Triathlon Union	1989
Volleyball	(FIVB) Fédération Internationale de Volleyball	1947
Weightlifting	(IWF) International Weightlifting Federation	1905
Wrestling	(UWW) United World Wrestling	1912
Winter Olympic Games (7)		
Biathlon	(IBU) International Biathlon Union	1993
Bobsleigh and skeleton	(IBSF) International Bobsleigh and Tobogganing Federation	1923
Curling	(WCF) World Curling Federation	1965
Ice Hockey	(IIHF) International Ice Hockey Federation	1908
Luge	(FIL) International Luge Federation	1923
Skating	(ISU) International Skating Union	1892
Skiing	(FIS) International Ski Federation	1924

Data from websites of International Federations, the IOC (2017b), and ASOIF (2017).

CASE STUDY

Process for a Sport to Be Included in the Olympic Games

For inclusion in the Summer or Winter Olympic Games program, a sport and its IF must first be recognized by the IOC. The IF of an unrecognized sport can make a formal petition to the IOC, but it must ensure that all activities of the sport adhere to the fundamental principles and rules of the Olympic Movement and the by-laws adopted from the IOC. The IOC takes approximately two years to observe the federation and its sport to determine whether the sport should officially become a recognized sport (Fairley & Lizandra, 2011). After the IF has become recognized, it may then petition to add the sport to the Olympic program if the sport is perceived to be widely practiced and meets certain criteria. Nowadays, the IOC has approved 28 IFs as recognized sports for the Summer Olympic Games and 7 for the Winter Olympic Games. The list of sports recognized by the IOC is presented in table 13.1.

For the recognized sports that are not included in the Olympic program, the IFs of the recognized sports can present their proposals to the Olympic Programme Commission of the IOC to request consideration. Their requests may be approved if the sports are widely practiced around the world with restricted criteria. The sports for men need to be played in at least 75 countries across four continents, and the sports for women must be played in at least 40 countries across three continents to be qualified in the Summer Olympics program. The Winter Olympics program requires a sport to be practiced in at least 25 countries across three continents (Fairley & Lizandra, 2011). For the 2016 Summer Olympic Games, the IOC Executive Board added two sports, golf and rugby, to the Olympic Games. Baseball, softball, karate, surfing, sport climbing, and skateboarding, for example, have been approved by the members of the IOC to be part of the 2020 Olympic Games because of their international and local appeal for spectators and fans of the Olympics (Chavez, 2016, August 3).

After each of the Olympic Games, the Olympic Programme Commission reviews the composition of the sport program, including sports, disciplines, events, and the number of athletes in each sport for the Olympic Games. The commission ensures that the Olympic program continues to meet the expectations of future sporting generations. The Olympic Programme Commission developed 35 criteria in five categories to define the procedure of evaluating sports for the Olympic program. The five categories include (a) Olympic proposal (e.g., number and list of events), (b) value added to the Olympic Movement (e.g., legacy), (c) institutional matters (e.g., antidoping and compliance with WADA code), (d) popularity (e.g., ticket sales and attendance), and (e) business model (e.g., targeted additional revenues during the Olympic Games) (IOC, 2017c). For example, softball and baseball were dropped from the Olympic program after the 2008 Olympic Games but will be added to the 2020 Olympics.

Learning Activity

Identify a sport (either summer or winter sport) that has been added or dropped from the Olympic program in recent years. Discuss the reasons why it was included or excluded from the Olympic program. Do you agree or disagree with the rationale and decision to add or drop this particular sport? Why or why not?

the program of the Olympic Games. The program of the Olympic Games (hereafter, "the Olympic program") refers to all competitions of the Olympic Games established from each edition of the Olympic Games by the IOC. The Olympic program consists of the sports, disciplines, and events (Olympic Charter, 2016a) and encompasses core sports and additional sports for both the Summer and Winter Olympic Games. Currently, the Winter Olympic Games consist of 8 core sports.

The Summer Olympic Games, on the other hand, contain at least 28 core sports approved by the executive board of the IOC (2016, August 3), and more sports may be added to its programming. For the sports to remain in the Olympic program, the IFs of the sports must adopt and implement the World Anti-Doping Code.

International Federations and Other International Sports Governing Bodies

In terms of its relationship with the IOC, the IF is involved in the preparation for the Olympic Congresses and serves on various IOC commissions. In addition, the IF also provides suggestions and opinions to the IOC about candidate cities' technical capabilities to host and organize the Olympic Games in coming years.

Moreover, the IFs also maintain professional relationships with associated international federations or continental associations that help the IFs promote their sports at the international level. Such associated international federations include the Commonwealth Games Federation, International Paralympics Committee, International School Sport Federation, and International University Sports Federation. For example, the World Archery Federation (WA, 2017) formerly named the International Archery Federation (FITA), is the governing body of the sport of archery. It contains 156 members of national federations and other associations of archery recognized by the IOC. It has been supported by the archery federations at the continent level and the associated international federations mentioned earlier for achieving its missions internationally.

Learning Activity

Find examples from websites, newspapers, or magazines on changes of rules in your favorite sports in the past three years. Discuss the influences of such changes on the operation of those sports.

International Federations and National Federations

Besides maintaining a close relationship with other international sport governing bodies, an IF also cooperates with **national sport federations** (NFs). An NF is a sport governing body responsible for promoting the development of the sport in an individual country. For instance, the International Basketball Federation (FIBA) has built a stable relationship with the Chinese Basketball Association (CBA) and provides assistance for its daily operation and administration in the aspects of strategic plans, financial and event management, promotion of basketball, media relations and communications, sponsorship, and marketing. Another example is that the Fédération Internationale de Football Association (FIFA) keeps a close relationship with the Spain Soccer Association regarding rule changes and qualifications of players who participate in World Cup competition.

Although the national sport federation of a particular sport (i.e., the national governing body, or NGB) provides opportunities for people to participate in that sport, it also has to implement the rules and regulations set up by the IFs, which sometimes change to adapt to new issues surrounding the sport. For example, the Fédération Internationale de Natation (FINA) released decisions in July 2009 regarding the use of high-tech swimsuits in FINA-sanctioned competitions. Before 2009 FINA did not have specific rules prohibiting materials and design of swimwear that may aid swimmers' speed, flow, and endurance. When a swimwear manufacturer launched the high-tech LZR Racer swimsuits in early 2008, more than 130 world records were broken, including seven (in eight events) by Michael Phelps during the Beijing Olympics (Crouse, 2009). The high-tech materials assist swimmers by repelling water, aiding flow, and enhancing buoyancy, which are critical elements in competitive swimming (Fermoso, 2008; Roberts, Kamel, Hedrick, McLean, & Sharp, 2003). The major controversies and concerns came from whether the new world records were set as a result of the swimmers' performance or the new swimwear technology. Thus, FINA established new rules and regulations to respond to the concerns about the use of high-technology swimwear fabric during swimming competitions. The NGB affiliated with FINA for swimming in each country has to implement and comply with the new rules and regulations on swimwear. The new rules were enforced beginning on January 1, 2010. Some of FINA's major requirements for swimsuits are as follows (Fédération Internationale de Natation, [FINA], 2017b):

◆ Type of material: The material used for swimsuits can be only "textile fabric(s)" defined for the purpose of these rules as material consisting of natural or synthetic, individual, and nonconsolidated yarns used to constitute a fabric by weaving, knitting, or braiding. The definition of "textile" will be made by a group of scientific experts chosen by FINA.

◆ Surface covered: Men's swimsuits shall not extend above the navel nor below the knee, and for women, shall not cover the neck, extend past the shoulder, nor extend below the knee.

◆ Thickness: The material used shall have a maximum thickness of 0.8 millimeters (0.031 in.).

◆ Buoyancy: The swimsuit shall not have a buoyancy effect above 0.5 Newton measured after application of vacuum.

◆ Use: In the regulation approved by the congress, the swimmer can wear only one swimsuit and no taping is allowed.

◆ Construction: No zippers or other fastening system is allowed. Seams shall be limited to functional systems and shall not create outside shapes (FINA, 2017b).

As a result, in July 2010 FINA published a list of FINA-approved swimsuits for open-water competition (FINA, 2017b) that swimmers can choose from for approved competitions of FINA and national governing bodies. If competitors want to wear swimsuits with a new design, construction, or materials that are not on the FINA-approved swimsuits list, manufacturers of such swimwear need approval of FINA for swimwear to be worn in competition (FINA, 2017b). To implement FINA's new rules for swimsuits, national governing bodies thus enforce new regulations and require their swimmers to wear approved swimwear during competitions. For example, the United States Swimming Association amended that "only swimsuits complying with FINA Open Water swimsuit specifications may be worn in any USA Swimming sanctioned or approved open water competition" (USSA, 2010). Thus, swimmers competed in competitions sanctioned or approved by USA Swimming must wear suits approved by FINA.

Management of International Federations

As mentioned previously, each IF is responsible for only one sport or a group of similar sports. Management of the IFs is based on a set of comprehensive missions and an extensive system that permits them to function well at various competition levels, such as worldwide or continental competitions. The managerial authority of an IF is given by its general assembly, which is made up of the national sport federations or associations. As the governing body of the sport, the IFs are primarily independent governing bodies that manage the sport (International Basketball Federation [FIBA], 2017). Their officers are elected democratically and carry ambassador responsibility for the sport, but they must be recognized by the IOC (Hums & MacLean, 2004).

The sports of many federations are currently not included in the Olympic Games. The mission, structure, and routine operation of these federations are largely similar to those of the federations affiliated with the IOC. The following two federations demonstrate the similarities and differences:

◆ The World Baseball Softball Federation (WBSF, 2017) is a member of the Association of IOC Recognized International Sports Federations (ARISF) but was not in the Association of Summer Olympic International Federations (ASOIF) before June 2017. The 2020 Summer Olympics, however, will include baseball and softball, a decision approved by the IOC Executive Board in June 2017. The 2020 Olympic Games will have 33 sports containing 339 competitive events and 5 new sports that will be introduced in Tokyo. The WBSF serves as the worldwide governing body for the sport of baseball. It sanctions play between teams sponsored by the national baseball federations of member countries through tournaments such as the Baseball World Cup, the World Baseball Classic (in conjunction with Major League Baseball), and the Intercontinental Cup (WBSF, 2017). Its organizational mission includes promoting the sport of baseball, organizing world competitions, and ensuring the cooperation of national federations to improve the sport. Its organizational structure is similar to that of other federations in the Olympic program. WBSF is operated by an executive committee that includes a president, vice presidents, secretary general, treasurer, and members at large. All decisions of the federation are made by the committee and approved by the president (WBSF, 2017). WBSF, not the IOC, is the highest authority for organizing international competitions in baseball and softball.

◆ The International Life Saving Federation (ILS), a member of the General Association of International Sports Federations (GAISF), is an international not-for-profit, nongovernmental, and non-Olympic organization that is composed of national lifesaving organizations. The ILS works to support and coordinate lifesaving development activities of member federations and regions. Its general assembly has the highest authority for external audit and contains the Departments of Drowning Prevention, Lifesaving, and Sport, as well as board committees such as commissioners, equity and diversity, and finance. As with Olympic federations, these committees provide essential functions for the federation.

Confederations

Confederations are zoned or regional governing bodies of national sport federations for countries located in the same continent. They are the umbrella governing bodies of the IFs in each continent. For example, the Fédération Internationale de Football Association (FIFA) has six confederations:

◆ Asian Football Confederation (AFC) in Asia

◆ Confederation of Africa Football (CAF) in Africa

◆ Confederation of North, Central American and Caribbean Association Football (CONCACAF)

◆ South American Football Confederation (CONMEBOL) in South America

◆ Union of European Football Associations (UEFA) in Europe

◆ Oceania Football Confederation (OFC) in Oceania (Fédération Internationale de Football Association [FIFA], 2017)

Learning Activity

Visit the website of the Union of European Football Associations and describe the major functions of the confederation.

The missions of the continental sport confederations are consistent with their IFs. They should adhere to the rules and regulations of the IFs, cooperate with the IOC, and assist their member national sport federations. The continental sport confederations are responsible for organizing continental competitions and championships among member nations located in the continent. Examples of such continental competitions and championships are the Asian Games and the European Football Championship.

Membership

The national sport federations make up the primary membership of the IFs. Each IF has its established constitution that clearly states the membership eligibilities and qualifications. The general membership rules of the IFs maintain that the national sport federation should (*a*) be recognized by the IFs with eligibility and qualifications, (*b*) agree to pay subscriptions or dues, and adhere to the rules and eligibilities of the IFs, (*c*) be responsible for the sport in its country and organize teams to participate in international competitions, and (*d*) be subject to suspension and termination if a member association commits any violation (International Basketball Federation [FIBA], 2017; FIFA, 2017).

Although some IFs, such as the International Table Tennis Federation, allow personnel honorary membership (International Table Tennis Federation [ITTF], 2017), other IFs divide the membership into different categories. For instance, the International Tennis Federation (ITF) categorizes its member associations as Class A, B, or C memberships. Each membership category has a set of particular requirements and benefits (ITF, 2017). A national sport federation must be successful in the procedures of application, election, review, and approval by the executive board or board of directors of a particular IF before it would be granted membership in that IF. After a national sport federation is granted membership with an IF, it assumes all membership rights, obligations, and responsibilities (ITF, 2017).

190 Chen and Yu

Governance Models

The governance models used by the IFs are similar in terms of organizational authorities, functions, and relationships with other governing bodies. Figure 13.1 depicts a common governance model of the IFs and their relationships with confederations, national federations, the IOC, and the national Olympic committees.

Most of the IFs use a congress or assembly formed by member nations as a legislative body to develop rules and policies and to approve changes recommended by the executive committee. Consisting of the president, vice presidents, secretary, and other officers, the executive committee (or board of directors, bureau, or central board) has the responsibility of managing the IF. With a fixed term to assume the leadership roles in the organization, the president and executive committee are usually granted power to handle federation affairs. Numerous standing committees or commissions, ranging from 4 to more than 20, are functional groups responsible for a variety of tasks delegated by the executive committee or the president.

All decisions made by the standing committees must be ratified by the executive committee or the president according to the FIFA statutes or constitution. Figure 13.2 shows another example of the management structure of an IF, the Fédération

Learning Activity

Visit the websites of two IFs (e.g., FIBA, FIVB) and compare their governance models.

Internationale de Natation (FINA), the governing body in international aquatics (FINA, 2017a).

Finance

All IFs are primarily considered not-for-profit membership organizations based on their stated philosophies and missions. The revenue generated may be used mainly to support functions of the federations, the operations of the organizations, and further development of the sport (Chen, 2004). Although some IFs have experienced a shortage of funds in operations, many IFs have been successful in revenue generation through fund-raising, broadcast rights, naming rights, and sponsorships for worldwide sporting events.

Most IFs charge annual membership dues or subscriptions from their member nations. The amount of income from this source, however, is insufficient to offset the expenses incurred from operations. To cover the costs, many IFs actively pursue and develop partnerships, create sponsorship opportunities, and solicit donations. Other

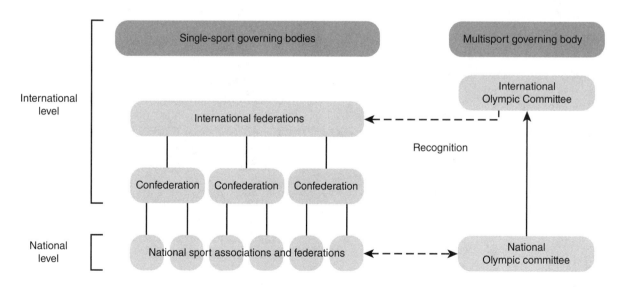

Figure 13.1 A common governance model of IFs and their relationship with the IOC.

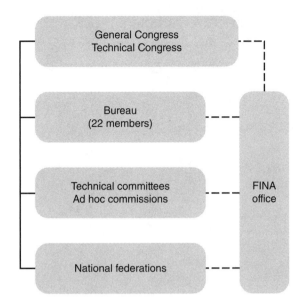

Figure 13.2 Organizational flow chart for the International Aquatics Association.

commercial activities often engaged in by IFs to generate necessary revenues include licensing, advertising, and selling broadcasting and naming rights (Chen, 2004; FINA, 2017b).

The revenue generated from these business activities improves the financial bottom line of the IFs and allows them to focus on their core activities, such as holding competitions and events, promoting global development of their sport, and providing monetary support to their member nations as needed (FINA, 2017b).

The revenues and expenses of the International Federation of Association Football (FIFA) for fiscal year 2015 provide us an opportunity to examine the financial operation of an IF. FIFA generated a total of US$1.152 million in 2015. Of the total revenue, 84 percent was from FIFA event-related revenue (e.g., the World Cup), including sales of television broadcasting rights (US$628,520), marketing rights (US$257,472), brand licensing (US$11,762) and FIFA hospitality rights (US$35,000), and financial income (US$98,371). The expenditures of FIFA in the same year included event-related expenses (US$781,646), development-related expenses (US$160,789), governance (US$17,252), personnel expenses (US$92,106), and other operating

expenses (US$79,288). The total revenue for FIFA in 2015 was US$1.152 million, which was lower than the total revenue generated in 2014 (US$2.096 million). Table 13.2 illustrates FIFA's Statement of Comprehensive Income for 2014 and 2015 (FIFA, 2016).

Table 13.3 is the consolidated balance sheet of FIFA for its fiscal year 2014 and 2015. As of December 31, 2015, it had total assets of US$2.993 million, including current assets of US$1.971 million and noncurrent assets of US$1.02 million against current liabilities of US$1.5 million and noncurrent liabilities of US$149,917. Compared with year 2014, FIFA had total assets of near US$3 million, including current assets of US$2.13 million and noncurrent assets of US$804,000, against current liabilities of around US$1.3 million and noncurrent liabilities of US$131,000, respectively. FIFA thus had total liability of US$1.652 million and reserves of US$1.34 million for a total of near US$3 million for year 2015, compared with total liability of US$1.4 million and reserves of US$1.522 million for a total of near US$3 million for year 2014, as shown in the balance sheet (FIFA, 2016).

The balance sheet of FIFA in 2015 also shows equity (reserves) of around US$1.34 million, which provides a strong financial foundation to support the functions of the federation and demonstrates the effectiveness of the financial management. Because IFs have no ownership, the revenue generated from the activities is used either to cover expenditures of the federation itself or to support the organization of international competitions. The more popular

Learning Activity

After studying the 2015 financial report for FIFA, what are your predictions for each category (increase or decrease) in the income statement for the year to come, given that the World Cup will be held in Russia in 2018? Do you expect revenue to be greater than expenses or vice versa? Conduct a search to estimate the results. How accurate are your predictions?

Table 13.2   FIFA 2014 and 2015 Statement of Comprehensive Income (in US$)

Revenue		
	Year 2015	**Year 2014**
Television broadcasting rights	628,520	742,638
Marketing rights	257,472	465,084
Licensing rights	11,762	54,230
Hospitality rights	35,000	110,637
Other event-related revenue	40,096	537,368
Other operation income	80,524	77,828
Financial income	98,371	108,244
Total revenue in events, operation, and finance	1,151,745	2,096,029
Expenses		
	Year 2015	**Year 2014**
FIFA World Cup	−547,196	−788,040
FIFA club protection progamme	−29,293	−34,024
Other FIFA event expenses	−178,157	−79,448
Operation expenses	−190,473	−189,277
Financial expenses	−30,284	−156,791
Total expenses in events, operation, and finance	−975,403	−869,026

Data from FIFA (2016).

Table 13.3   FIFA Consolidated Balance Sheet at December 31, 2014 and 2015 (in US$)

Assets			Liabilities and equity		
	Year 2015	**Year 2014**		**Year 2015**	**Year 2014**
Current assets	1,971,446	2,127,606	Payable	61,652	66,115
Cash and cash equivalents	801,624	1,083,069	Derivative financial liabilities	886	32,959
Receivables	239,532	181,098	Accrued expenses and deferred income	1,439,954	1,177,909
Derivative financial assets	25,765	6,654	Current liability	1,502,492	1,276,983
Prepaid expenses and accrued income	199,272	179,527			
Noncurrent assets	1,021,118	804,102	Noncurrent liabilities	149,917	131,827
Property and equipment	302,944	196,846			
Intangible assets	32,980	26,889	Total liability	1,652,409	1,408,810
Financial assets	685,194	580,367	Equity (reserves)	1,340,155	1,522,898
Total	2,992,564	2,931,708	Total liability and reserve	2,992,564	2,931,708

Data from FIFA (2016).

a sport is globally, the more effective the IF must be in obtaining the resources or developing sound programs to generate revenues. Financial management is always a challenge to IFs and other sport governing bodies. Sound leadership and an effective financial management system ensure the survivability of the federation and continuous promotion of the sport in the world.

Summary

International sport federations (IFs) are governing bodies in various sports at the international level. IFs are mainly responsible for administering particular sports internationally. They maintain their independence in governing a specific sport or set of sports. IFs work closely with the IOC and national governing bodies (NGBs) or national sport federations in each country. The major functions of IFs are consistent with their mission of promoting their sports, organizing competitions, and developing new programs. Confederations are regional governing bodies of national sport federations for the countries located in a same continent. They are the umbrella governing bodies of IFs in each continent.

After carefully studying this chapter, you should be able to define each type of international sport federation, describe the major organizational structure and governance system, understand the relationship between international sport federations and other international sport governing bodies, and comprehend the major financial resources that IFs use to support their operations and satisfy their stakeholders.

? Review Questions

1. Describe the basic relationship among international sport federations, the IOC, and national sport governing bodies.

2. What are the major purposes and missions of international sport federations?

3. If a sport is not currently part of the Olympic program, what is the process for the IF of that sport to petition for inclusion?

4. What are the major categories of criteria that the Olympic Programme Commission uses to evaluate sports for future Olympic programs?

5. What is the relationship between the international federation in a particular sport and the governing body of the sport in a nation?

6. What are the major financial resources supporting the operation of an international sport federation? You may list all possible categories.

The World Anti-Doping Agency and Ethics in Sport

Clayton Bolton, EdD
Texas A&M University—Commerce

Samantha Roberts, PhD
Texas A&M University—Commerce

Chapter Objectives

After studying this chapter, you will be able to do the following:

- Understand ethics and ethical behavior in sport.
- Discuss the use of performance-enhancing drugs (PEDs) as a form of unethical behavior in sport.
- Discuss doping as a major issue in international sport.
- Describe the history of doping in sport.
- Discuss the introduction of the World Anti-Doping Agency (WADA) and its role in the fight against doping in sport.
- Discuss the challenges faced by WADA and national anti-doping organizations (NADOs).

Key Terms

banned substance

ethical dilemma

ethics

gamesmanship

governance

moral values

national anti-doping organizations (NADOs)

performance-enhancing drugs (PEDs)

regional anti-doping organizations (RADOs)

sportsmanship

transparency

USADA

WADA

Maybe it is the flawed thinking and concept of peer accountability. Members of an organization (in our case professional sport, amateur athletics, intercollegiate athletics, and even youth sport) are intended to operate on the understanding that everyone is playing fairly and that each member, team, and individual is abiding by the same rules. We can learn from the lessons of countries failing to realize that their neighbors may not always act properly or tell the truth. For example, in 1938 British prime minister Neville Chamberlain once shouted, "Peace in our time," under the impression that an elected leader in Germany would somehow operate ethically and keep his word that Germany would not go to war with Great Britain. Soon after, the Luftwaffe, the German Air Force, bombed London and the rest of Great Britain on a routine basis. Additionally, months earlier, Hitler had told the world that Jews were not being mistreated and his administration, and indeed an entire country, hid the fact that the Holocaust had begun to ensure that the 1936 Olympic Games, held in the German capital, Berlin, would go ahead with a full international presence.

Scandal and questions regarding ethical decision-making processes in sport are not new. For many years, athletes have been using PEDs (or being fed them without their knowledge), coaches have been rewarding athletes for cheating, and those in positions of power in sporting organizations have been subject to allegations and investigations regarding decisions made and, in some cases, payments taken. Examples range from the awarding of the World Cup to the fall of the likes of Barry Bonds and Sammy Sosa, and from the worldwide disgrace of Lance Armstrong to the banning of an entire Russian Olympic team from competition.

It has been said that former Chicago Cubs first baseman Mark Grace was the first to utter the phrase "If you're not cheating, you're not trying hard enough" (Rankin, 2012, para. 1). Said another way, "If you're not first, you're last!" once uttered by fictional character Reese Bobby in a comedy movie about NASCAR, *Talladega Nights: The Ballad of Ricky Bobby* (Miller & McKay, 2006). Do we live in an era of "you do what must be done" to be a champion, to finish first, win a gold medal, be famous, be rich? Has the quest for greatness become an all-out assault on cutting corners, taking risks, operating outside the rules, and then lying to cover all tracks of your deception? The idea that fans of the Chicago White Sox baseball team would believe that an illiterate baseball giant from South Carolina would not dare to take money to throw the World Series in 1919, a scandal that ushered in the phrase "Say it ain't so, Joe" (referring to player Shoeless Joe Jackson) seems somewhat normal now. Did eight players on that team actually fix games, and did a rumored gambler from New York, Arnold Rothstein, get away with stealing the World Series in 1919? Yes . . . but does it matter?

"There is no honor among thieves" is an often-used phrase and the title of several novels, movies, and even songs. This concept is acted out in the opening scenes of the movie *The Dark Knight* (Thomas & Nolan, 2008), when many of the men working for the main villain (The Joker), one by one assassinate the others to gain more of the money, or loot, being stolen from a bank. The idea is that all are interested in simply gaining more for themselves, regardless of the costs or the way in which they get recognition, fame, or the possibility of the financial reward that these days always seems to come with being crowned champion. In contrast, the song "The Champ" (Haynes, Thielk, & Montilla, 2011) by Nelly talks about being a champion of the world based on blood, sweat, and grind as opposed to an unknown or at least unseen competitive advantage—or in so many cases today, an illegal or inappropriate advantage.

Some may ask whether we have reached a point in the world of sport where there is a standard lack of honor among thieves. The authors of this chapter truly hope not, because if we accept that concept, then we must believe that everyone cheats and that no honor remains in sport. Therefore, we must expect that everyone is cheating and the only hope is that we do not get caught.

Ethics and Ethical Behavior in Sport

Doing the right thing in the face of adversity or in a difficult situation is how many define ethics or ethical decision making. Expressed a slightly different way, when faced with a decision of right or wrong where there are consequences, we may confront an ethical dilemma. **Ethics** is defined by Merriam-Webster as "a theory or system of moral values, the discipline dealing with what is good and bad and with moral duty and obligation, as well as the principles of conduct governing an individual or a group." Academic literature is awash with articles and books about ethics and ethical theory, including discussions of deontology, teleology, and intuitionism (see table 14.1).

Depending on your view of the world, your ethical perspective or lens will shift according to your own beliefs, opinions, and **moral values**. In the sport arena, this perspective becomes even more important—some of the behaviors we see on or off a field of play often push this ethical boundary and, depending on the view of those in charge of sport or the media or you as a fan, the response to this behavior varies. These moral values and the way in which we arrive

at right or wrong can be as simple as most reasonable people agreeing that not telling the truth is not appropriate and is a lie. Moral values are the standards by which we define right and wrong and could include deciding to be honest or not, paying taxes owed or not, being paid for work you actually perform as opposed to accepting financial remuneration for not doing much, or making a promise and then keeping it. These decisions, to do what is perceived or considered to be right or wrong, are based on a set of traits each person has (see table 14.2) and dictate how we would respond to any given situation. Some

Table 14.1 Ethical Theories

Action ethics "Thinking about doing"		
Deontology	**Teleology**	**Consequentialism**
Actions are right in and of themselves.	Actions are right because they achieve the purpose of the agent.	Actions are right because of their consequences (i.e., the end justifies the means).
Kant (1724-1804)	Aristotle (384-322 BC)	Bentham (1748-1832) Mill (1806-1873) Singer (1946-)
Agent ethics "Thinking about being"		
Emotivism	**Intuitionism**	**Virtue**
Right living is an expression of the emotions, rather than of rationality.	Right living is instinctive (i.e., morality is universally accessible).	Right living is derived from the moral character of the agent.
Stevenson (1908-1979)	Ross (1877-1971)	Aristotle (384-322 BC) MacIntyre (1929-) Hauerwas (1940-)

Data from Barry (2012).

Table 14.2 Contrasting Ethical Traits

Traits that promote good ethics	Traits that promote bad ethics
Self-control, rationality, an ability to gain some distance from an emotional event or issues	Recklessness, emotionalism, a tendency to act with emotion and self-interest
Honesty and integrity, an interest in achieving something of value	Drive and desire, an interest in succeeding by whatever means
A sense of fair play	A win-at-all costs attitude
Patience, a willingness to wait for the opportunity	Opportunism, a tendency to jump at the first attractive offer one receives
Constancy, singleness of purpose, the development of a life and career guided by clear values	Adaptability, vacillation, a tendency to embrace values that work or that are currently popular
Courage, a willingness to stand by personal values in the face of difficulty	Strategic shrewdness, an unwillingness to let extraneous values stand in the way of success
Altruism, a tendency to look out for the rights and interests of others	Survivalism, a tendency to take care of oneself and let others take care of their own problems

Based on Kretchmar (1994).

Learning Activity

Think about people who have influenced, and continue to influence, you and your decision-making processes. Whom do you turn to when faced with an ethical decision? Why? Do you look to more than one other person to help you? What might the issue be if you turn to more than one person?

of these traits are innate to us as individuals; others can be influenced and molded by those around us, like family, the wider community, religion, government, or any other entity that affects the thoughts of the individual. In sport, these influencers would also include coaches, teammates, team owners, the media, and other external organizations that an athlete might work with.

Ethics in sport is based on four key virtues or pillars (Hanson & Savage, 2012)—fairness, respect, responsibility, and integrity—that together form the foundation of the key construct of **sportsmanship**. These pillars can be seen in figure 14.1. In this construct, the cultivation of virtue and character occurs through healthy competition, in which the goal is not just to win but to win fairly and knowing that everything has been left on the field of play, through maximum effort. It is argued that, in Ancient Greece, athletic competition was based on sportsmanship and "a personal sense of honor" (Shaven, 2016) but also "law, oaths, rules, vigilant officials, tradition, the fear of flogging, the religious setting of the games contributed to keep Greek athletic contests clean" (Shaven 2016, para. 2).

Many examples from across the sporting world demonstrate this ideal of sportsmanship. In golf, Bobby Jones, the legendary amateur golfer, called a penalty shot on himself in the 1925 U.S. Open

Fairness	Integrity	Responsibility	Respect
Established rules and guidelines are in place for all athletes and coaches to follow Seeking an unfair competitive advantage over an opponent to create an uneven playing field violates the integrity of sport No discrimination in sport based on race, gender, or sexual orientation Referees must apply the rules equally to both teams and cannot show bias or personal interest in the outcome	Any athlete who seeks unfair competitive advantage over his or her opponent demonstrates a lack of personal integrity and violates the integrity of the game (e.g., diving in soccer or flopping in basketball) Intentionally deceiving an official or referee into making a bad call, which only hurts the credibility of the officiating and ultimately undermines the integrity of the game	Players and coaches need to take responsibilty for their performance, as well as their actions on the field Athletes and coaches should not make excuses as to why they lost the game (e.g., blaming officiating) Focus on aspects of the game that can be controlled (i.e., What could you have done better?) Be up to date on rules and regulations governing their sport Conduct of players and coaches should be honorable off the field, as well as on it	All athletes should show respect for teammates, opponents, coaches, and officials All coaches should show respect for their players, opponents, and officials All fans, especially parents, should show respect for other fans, as well as both teams and officials

Figure 14.1 Key virtues of sportsmanship.
Data from Hanson and Savage (2012).

tournament in Worcester, Massachusetts, and lost in a playoff by one shot. Jones, when told that his honesty was to be commended, said that he didn't "know any other way to play the game." Eighty-five years later at the 2010 Heritage Classic on Hilton Head Island, Brian Davis, a British golfer on the PGA tour, called a penalty on himself while in a playoff. Although it could be argued that he made a proper ethical decision, it cost him his first PGA tour win and in excess of $1 million dollars in prize money.

West Ham United legend Paolo Di Canio earned international praise and FIFA's Fair Play Award in 2001 for his actions in a match against Everton FC when, with a clear scoring opportunity, he caught the ball to stop play as Everton's goalkeeper Paul Gerrard lay on the ground injured. At the 2016 Olympic Games in Rio, American Abbey D'Agostino and Nikki Hamblin of New Zealand tripped each other accidently and fell during a 5,000-meter race. Instead of arguing or racing each other to the finish, they opened their arms and helped each other for the remaining distance, completing the race.

The Olympic Games stand for this idealized notion of sportsmanship. Founder of the modern Olympic Games Pierre de Coubertin once said, "The most important thing in the Olympic Games is not winning but taking part; the essential thing in life is not conquering but fighting well" (BBC, 2014, para. 2). This idea became the foundation of the Olympic creed, established by the International Olympic Committee (IOC) as part of the Olympic triad, designed to inspire athletes from around the world to embrace the Olympic spirit, represent the values of the Games and perform to the very best of their ability. To this end, in 2000 at the Sydney Olympic Games, the issue of performance-enhancing drugs was added to the Olympic oath, a promise read by a nominated athlete from every competitor at the start of an Olympic Games. Australian women's hockey captain Rechelle Hawkes read the Olympic Oath at the Sydney Games in 2000, which states, "In the name of all competitors, I promise we shall take part in these Olympic Games, respecting and abiding by the rules which govern them, committing ourselves to a sport without doping and without

Learning Activity

What other examples of sportsmanship can you think of? How did they happen? Who was involved? Why do you think they are examples of sportsmanship?

drugs, in the spirit of true sportsmanship, for the glory of sport and the honor of our teams" (Clark, 2016, para. 1). Indeed, in 2015, David Howman, then WADA director general, said:

> The intrinsic values of sport, often referred to as "the spirit of sport," is the celebration of the human spirit, body and mind, and is characterized by values such as ethics, honesty, respect for rules, self-respect and respect for others, fair play and healthy competition. If sport is void of these values (and others) it might be argued it is no longer sport. (Howman, 2015, para. 3)

In spite of this idealized view of sport and the earlier examples, it could be argued that the notion of sportsmanship, although based in the idea of the spirit of fair play, is becoming somewhat of an antiquated concept (Beller & Stoll, 2013). Increasingly, we hear stories of athletes trying to gain any kind of advantage over their rivals, either fairly or unfairly. The idea that "Winning is everything . . . and the only thing" appears to be the pervading theme in many sporting competitions around the world. **Gamesmanship**, in which competitive advantage is sought by any means, has led athletes and coaches to seek any edge and, as a result, to pay less attention to the well-being of opponents. Ultimately, the argument that "if the referee or official doesn't catch it, it's not cheating" prevails. According to Hanson and Savage (2012), the following are examples of gamesmanship:

- Faking a foul or injury (e.g., diving in soccer, flopping in basketball)
- Attempting to get a head start in a race
- Tampering with equipment (e.g., corking a baseball bat to hit the ball farther)
- Committing covert personal fouls (e.g., grabbing a player underwater during a water polo match)

◆ Inflicting pain on an opponent with the intention of knocking him or her out of the game (e.g., the "Bountygate" scandal involving the New Orleans Saints)

◆ Using performance-enhancing drugs

◆ Taunting or intimidating an opponent

◆ Lying by a coach about an athlete's grades to keep him or her eligible to play

The Olympic motto *Citius, Altius, Fortius* means "faster, higher, stronger." In today's sporting world, the question becomes, how are athletes running faster, jumping higher, becoming stronger? Is sportsmanship still the foundation of sport, as Pierre de Coubertin once envisioned, or has gamesmanship won the day?

Volkwein (1995) suggests that the development of modern elite-level sport is the pinnacle of the performance demands of society. This development is primarily sociocultural in that winning at all costs is key, success is overemphasized, and the athlete is the main element of uncertainty. In addition, the commercialization and globalization of sport has led to significant financial and material considerations that must be addressed. These pressures lead to **ethical dilemmas** for athletes, coaches, and all those who have a stake in sport. How can I win? What do I need to do to be successful? Because athletes' livelihoods are tied to their performances on the track, on the pitch, on the field, or in the pool, this material can become paramount. British sprinter Dwain Chambers was

CASE STUDY

Bountygate

The NFL has long frowned upon bounties, calling them "non-contract bonuses," but an underground culture of the practice is said to exist, and team management allegedly turns a blind eye to the practice. League rules specifically forbid payment of bonuses based on performances against an individual player or team, as well as bonuses for on-field misconduct. The NFL's stance here is that such practices undermine the integrity of the game and would allow teams to use such payments to circumvent the salary cap, thus circumventing financial regulations. The collective bargaining agreement with the NFL Players Association also forbids this practice, as does the standard NFL player contract.

Despite this prohibition, an investigation that concluded in 2012 found that during the 2009 through 2011 seasons, 2009 being the year that the New Orleans Saints won the NFL's biggest prize, the Super Bowl, Saints' coaches and players were awarding cash payments to players who injured selected members of the opposing teams they played. An investigation discovered that between 22 and 27 players, as well as head coach Sean Payton, were involved in the bounty scheme. Among those rumored to be targeted were quarterbacks Brett Favre and Kurt Warner during the 2009 playoffs. It emerged that the Saints had also targeted Aaron Rodgers, Matt Hasselbeck,

and Cam Newton, again all quarterbacks, during the 2011 season.

Saints defensive coordinator Gregg Williams apparently developed the program, in which "'knockouts' were worth $1,500 and 'cart-offs' $1,000, with payments doubled or tripled for the playoffs" (ESPN, 2012, para. 1). At the time the scandal hit the headlines, four players who played for Williams with the Washington Redskins told authorities that he had operated the same kind of system there. Indeed, allegations were made against Williams reaching back to 1997!

Some of the players involved in Bountygate, as well as both Williams and Sean Payton, were banned by the NFL for their parts in the scandal. Payton was banned for the entire 2012 season, the first coach in modern NFL history to be banned for any reason.

Research by Hassett and Veuger (2012) found that the Saints didn't injure more players than other teams in the league did, despite the bounty payment system that appeared to be in place. In fact, they argued, "In each year of the bounty program, the Saints injured fewer players than the average for the league" (Hassett & Veuger, 2012, para. 10). They went on to say that this finding proves that the players were not following the coaches' direction. On the other hand, why would they be injuring more players than any other team if they were explicitly targeting certain people?

banned for two years after becoming embroiled in the BALCO scandal in 2003. He wrote candidly in his autobiography about what he did and that he made the wrong decisions, but he also noted that he knew that others on the start line were using PEDs and that he not only had a family to support but also had terms in a sponsorship agreement that required him to remain among the world's top three sprinters. He asks readers: What would you do?

Performance-Enhancing Drugs in Sport

"Usain Bolt! It's very, very tight but I think he has done it. . . . He's saved his title. . . . He has saved his reputation. . . . He may have even saved his sport."

Steve Cram, BBC commentary of the men's 100-meter final at the IAAF World Athletics Championships in Beijing, China, 2015

As Usain Bolt crossed the line in the final of the 100 meters at the IAAF World Athletics Championships in Beijing in 2015, the world of track and field appeared to sigh with relief. Bolt had beaten U.S. rival Justin Gatlin to win the gold medal. In the run-up to the final, the race and the rivalry was portrayed in the media as good versus evil, the savior against the destroyer. In a sport that has regularly been tarnished by the use of **performance-enhancing drugs (PEDs)**, Gatlin has served two doping bans—one for a year (reduced from two years on appeal) in 2001 and another in 2006, originally an eight-year ban reduced to four, again on appeal.

This type of story, however, is not an isolated incident. The history of sport is replete with stories of athletes using PEDs to gain an edge, and, as such, it continues to be an area of focus for those in the sport industry. It has been written that the ancient Greeks and Romans began using herbal types of drink and potions as well as eating the hearts and testicles of animals to produce greater stamina and strength in athletic competition. In the late 1800s athletes such as lacrosse players and cyclists used substances like wine and cocoa to try to improve performance. At the 1904 Olympics, British-born U.S. runner Thomas Hicks was given a near-lethal mix of brandy and strychnine by his trainers to pre-

vent him from stopping in the marathon. Likewise, athletes began experimenting with heroin, cocaine, and caffeine from the early 1900s. Nazi scientists and chemists created medical stimulants in the 1930s and early 1940s with the hopes of creating a master race, and results were evident in the success of the German Olympic team that hosted the 1936 Olympic Games in Berlin (Potter, 2012).

Regardless of where you place the origin, PEDs have been a subject of hot debate and public outcry for decades—from the testing of athletes at Olympic and international sporting events to intercollegiate testing in the United States, from the banning of substances by nearly every professional association worldwide to the increasing pace of substance development. Much like other forms of corruption in sport, the use of PEDs is as big as any topic in the world of sport and ethics discussions. As such, the word *doping* is often used to refer to any practice involving prohibited substances (PEDs) or other methods that give an athlete an unfair advantage over other competitors.

History of Doping

As previously stated, sport has a long history of drug use, as can be seen in table 14.3. It was in the 1960s, however, that authorities began to realize the extent of the issue and initiated testing procedures and policies. The Winter Olympic Games in Grenoble, France, and the Summer Olympic Games in Mexico City, both in 1968, introduced mandatory drug testing, marking the first real attempt of the International Olympic Committee (IOC) to come to grips with the use of PEDs. The Games in Mexico City saw the first athletes have to return medals for using illegal substances, including one Swedish athlete who drank two beers before an event. Four years later in Munich, testing was in place for narcotics and stimulants. Subsequently, anabolic steroids were added to the banned substance list of the IOC in 1975. The Games the following year in Montréal was the first time that steroids were tested for (Andren-Sandberg, 2016).

Many of the substances used in sport at the time were invented in the former Eastern Bloc, particularly in the aftermath of World War II when German scientists defected to the Soviet Union to help the Russians, who were seeking to be successful on the world stage. Indeed, the Soviet weightlifting team's success at the time was in part attributable to their use of performance-enhancing drugs, the formulas for which had been brought east from Germany. In the United States, a physician for the U.S. weightlifting team in the mid-20th century, John Ziegler, learned from his Russian counterparts that American athletes needed chemical assistance to remain competitive. Steroids found their way into professional football in the late 1960s, as teams began hiring strength and conditioning coaches, who were charged with the task of growing a new breed of bigger, bulkier players. Taking their cue from the weightlifting world, these coaches turned to steroids as the fastest way of accomplishing this goal (Andren-Sandberg, 2016).

During the 1970s PEDs were still light years ahead of the drug detection mechanisms in the scientific arena. At the Munich Games, East Germany fielded a team of female swimmers sporting man-sized muscles and deep voices. They won most of the medals, and although there was much talk about the likelihood that they were using **banned substances**, not one of those athletes tested positive. It later became clear that the athletes themselves were the victims of a mandatory doping program overseen by East German Olympic officials, who injected the swimmers with steroids without their informed consent. Several swimmers of that era have reported that they began receiving steroid injections at age 13 and have suffered serious long-term health consequences, ranging from liver damage to infertility, as a result of doping. The systematic doping began in 1974 when party lead-

Learning Activity

The Iron Curtain Project contains stories as well as videos and real-life accounts of the abuses of mainly female athletes in both East and West Germany in the 1970s. Research the Iron Curtain Project. Do you think this kind of systematic doping program could happen today? The answer here is yes. What do you think the implications of such a program are? How can sport deal with these types of cases? What responsibility does sport have to athletes who are given substances without their knowing?

Learning Activity

The list of events in doping history presented in table 14.3 is not exhaustive. See if you can fill in other key dates and cases related to doping in sport. Perhaps you can identify sports we have not included here, such as boxing, wrestling, cricket, and others.

ers met with the East German Sports Performance Committee to decide how best to guarantee gold medals and international glory. What they came up with was State Plan 14-25 (PBS, 2016).

Doping Explosion

Doping really became an issue of focus in sport in the 1980s. The surprise testing at the Pan Am Games in 1983 caused many athletes to withdraw before competition. At the 1988 Olympic Games in Seoul, the world's focus become trained on track and field when Canadian sprinter Ben Johnson was stripped of his gold medal in the 100 meters for testing positive for stanozolol. The race became known as the "dirtiest race in history" (Moore, 2012) when it emerged that six of the eight finalists faced accusations of using PEDs during or after their careers, failed drugs tests, or were banned from the sport for supplying illegal substances to other athletes. This story was one of the first of its kind to be front-page, worldwide news involving a high-profile international athlete and concerning steroid use (Mehaffey, 2012). Johnson was banned from the sport for life in 1993, after failing another test.

The 1990s saw the first ban of steroids in Major League Baseball when rumors about players, including Jose Canseco, started surfacing. Even though then commissioner Fay Vincent sent a memorandum to all major league clubs, no investigative or testing program with any teeth was in place in professional baseball at the time; it would be 2004 before the MLB would begin a testing and penalty program. In 1998 star slugger Mark McGwire admitted to using what became known as androstenedione, which is essentially a precursor to steroids but was not a banned substance at the time (Carroll & Carroll, 2005). McGwire once said, "I remember trying steroids very briefly in the 1989-1990 offseason, and then after I was injured in 1993,

Table 14.3 Landmark Events in Doping History

Year	Event
776 BC	Greek Olympians use substances from herbs and animals to increase stamina and performance.
Late 1800s	Bukowski becomes early pioneer for anti-doping research (horseracing).
1896	Welsh cyclist Arthur Linton dies after taking cocaine and heroin at the Tour de France.
1904	Thomas Hicks, a marathoner, nearly dies from a brandy and strychnine mixture.
1928	The International Association of Athletics Federations (IAAF) is formed and is the first body to prohibit the use of PEDs.
1930s-40s	Nazi scientists and chemists develop drugs designed to help create a master race of German athletes.
1960	Danish cyclist Knud Jensen dies, and drugs are discovered in his system during his autopsy, creating bans from the UCI.
1967	Tommy Simpson dies in the Tour de France, and the creation of the IOC Medical Commission quickly follows.
1968	The first testing of any kind occurs at the Winter Olympics in Grenoble and at the Summer Games in Mexico City.
1972	The first tests for stimulants are conducted at the Munich Olympics.
1976	The first true steroid testing occurs at Montréal Olympics, although few were caught (German female teams dominate again).
1988	Ben Johnson wins gold in the "dirtiest race in history."
1998	The Festina Affair occurs at the Tour de France.
1999	The World Anti-Doping Agency (WADA) is formed.
2001	Lahti doping scandal occurs.
2002-03	The BALCO scandal arises, involving Marion Jones, Tim Montgomery, Dwain Chambers, and Bill Romanowski.
2006	Operacion Puerto occurs in cycling.
2007	The Mitchell Report is released, detailing the extent of steroid use in Major League Baseball.
2012	The U.S. Postal investigation report is released by USADA, involving Lance Armstrong and teammates.
2013	Supplements scandal arises in Australian sport, involving Essendon (AFL) and Cronulla Sharks (NRL).
2016	Russian doping scandal occurs.

I used steroids again. . . . I used them on occasion throughout the '90s, during the 1998 season" (AP, 2010, para. 23). This event is significant, primarily because at the time baseball was recovering from a lockout season in 1994 and needed something to rekindle the public's interest in the sport. In 1998 McGwire of the St. Louis Cardinals and Sammy Sosa of the Chicago Cubs (big rivals at any time of the season) were battling for the single-season home run record held by baseball legend Roger Maris. Both ended up eclipsing Maris' mark, and baseball was growing in popularity again. Given,

however, that the record was achieved with the aid of substances and that McGwire later admitted that he had knowingly cheated and lied about it, we have to wonder whether it was worth the glory to live with the shame.

A scandal involving some of sport's biggest names erupted when the Bay Area Laboratory Co-Operative (BALCO) was raided by federal agencies in 2002. A new substance they had introduced, which had become known as "The Clear," was added to testing protocols. As a result, multiple gold medalists from the Olympic Games, including Marion Jones and Tim Montgomery, Olympic athletes like Dwain Chambers and Kelli White, and stars from other sports including Jason Giambi and Barry Bonds (baseball) and Bill Romanowski (NFL) were implicated. Many received drugs bans. The case of Marion Jones was particularly difficult for the sport to manage given that she had dominated the Olympic Games in Sydney two years previously, winning three gold medals and two bronzes at the event. Jones lost everything—her reputation, her endorsement deals, and her freedom, eventually serving a jail sentence in 2008 for her involvement in the scandal and for check fraud.

Hundreds of cases of drug use in sport could be used to provide examples in a chapter such as this, but we cannot ignore perhaps the biggest scandal of them all—the U.S. Postal investigation in cycling. Although cycling has a long history of PED use, from Tommy Simpson in the 1960s to Floyd Landis in 2006, from Festina to Operacion Puerto, the investigation that led to the demise of Lance Armstrong is perhaps the most important and tragic one. When the **United States Anti-Doping Agency (USADA)** reported about doping in the U.S. Postal cycling team, they described "the most sophisticated, professionalized and successful doping program that sport has ever seen" (USADA, 2012, para. 1). Armstrong, who had won seven consecutive Tour De France titles from 1999 through 2005, had often been accused of using PEDs but had never had a positive test result released and would often pursue legal avenues against those who had accused him. Then, because of the USADA investigation, Armstrong granted an interview with Oprah Winfrey during which he admitted to using banned substances, doping, and using human growth hormones. He acknowledged that he could not have won seven consecutive titles without the use of all of those banned and illegal techniques.

But Armstrong's legacy was based on more than just his Tour de France victories—he survived cancer, founded the nonprofit organization LiveStrong, which has raised millions of dollars to fund cancer research, and became a living legend in the eyes of many (Macur, 2014). After the testimony of former teammate Floyd Landis in 2006, who himself had served a doping ban, it became apparent that Armstrong may not have been the perfect model citizen everyone thought he was. Although he was not found guilty of any violations in early

2012, by fall of that same year the Union Cycliste Internationale (UCI) stripped him of all seven of his Tour de France titles. Other sanctions and the loss of his endorsers came shortly afterward. Like Marion Jones, Armstrong has lost many millions of dollars, but unlike Jones, he has continued to be involved in various legal battles over contracts, bonuses, and investments he made during his more than a decade of deception, with many still to be resolved.

Lance Armstrong became the face of the U.S. Postal scandal, but most of the riders who were part of that team also received doping bans for their part in the use of PEDs (a six-month ban for each member who testified against Armstrong). Although the Festina Affair and Operacion Puerto had previously put the sport of cycling in the headlines, the U.S. Postal scandal really lifted the lid on doping in the sport. Of the 33 Tour de France races held between 1980 and 2012, 17 were tainted by winners who had used PEDs. Granted, Armstrong won 7 of those races, but riders from other teams won the other 10. Although not condoning Armstrong's behavior during his time on the Tour, some believed that he became the scapegoat of a generation of cycling destroyed by the use of PEDs in the peloton. Clearly, as Macur (2014) suggests, the final chapter in the Lance Armstrong story is still being written.

World Anti-Doping Agency (WADA)

WADA's mission is to lead a collaborative world-wide movement for doping-free sport.
  (WADA, 2017, para. 1)

Central to any discussion about PED use and doping in sport is **WADA**, the World Anti-Doping Agency. The end of the 20th century saw a new beginning of an international effort to police as well as educate all those involved in sport on doping and the dangers involved. On November 10, 1999, WADA was established, based on a document produced at the World Conference on Doping in Sport held in Lausanne, which became known as the Lausanne Declaration, earlier that year. This document provided for the creation of an independent international anti-doping agency to be operational for the Olympic Games held in Sydney in 2000. The need for a global and coordinated fight against doping in sport, based on the core values of integrity,

Learning Activity

Compare the core values of WADA with the key virtues of sportsmanship in figure 14.1. Is there any commonality between the two? Is WADA based on this ideal of sportsmanship?

accountability, and excellence (WADA, 2017), was the foundation for the introduction of WADA, which was established under the initiative of the International Olympic Committee (IOC). The organization, based in Canada, is supported by intergovernmental organizations, governments, public authorities, and other public and private bodies that are involved in the fight against doping in sport and is made up of equal representatives from the Olympic Movement and public authorities. Funding for WADA comes from both the IOC and a group of national governments.

To promote a global approach to addressing the issue of PED use in sport, international standards were developed for laboratories, testing, an annual prohibited list, including updated banned substances, and for therapeutic use exemptions (TUE), which gives permission for athletes to use substances like salbutamol found in asthma inhalers that would otherwise be banned. The World Anti-Doping Code is the core document that harmonizes anti-doping policies, rules, and regulations within sport organizations and among public authorities around the world. This document works with the five aforementioned international standards to try to unify a previously disjointed and uncoordinated anti-doping effort. WADA has been able to secure a number of international declarations that have commended and ratified the policy code it has developed, and the policy has been approved by the United Nations Educational, Scientific and Cultural Organization (UNESCO) as an international convention, an organization that all major countries are members of.

One of the biggest challenges facing WADA as an international organization is its **governance**, in that "the governance mechanism (e.g., formal documents, organizational structure) specifies how rights, authority, and responsibility are distributed among the participants in order to monitor performance and achieve goals" (Sawyer et al., 2008, p.

11). Currently, WADA has a 38-member foundation board, made up of an equal number of representatives from the IOC and from national governments. Day-to-day operations are also handled by a 12-member executive committee, again made up of representatives from both the IOC and national governments, as well as a number of subcommittees with much narrower remits, responsible for areas such as finance and administration. WADA's overarching responsibilities can be seen in figure 14.2. The issue here is that, even with these international standards, not every country adopts and operates to these rules and regulations. A rigorous global anti-doping program needs everyone to be singing from the same proverbial hymn sheet; stakeholders need to accept that PED use is a problem in sport and they must be prepared to preserve the values of sport, which means being free from doping. More than 650 sport organizations have accepted the WADA Code, including the International Olympic Committee (IOC), the International Paralympic Committee (IPC), all international federations (IFs) and all IOC-recognized IFs, national Olympic and Paralympic committees, and national anti-doping organizations (NADOs). To be fully compliant with the code, sports are required to undertake three steps:

1. Acceptance—agrees to the principles of the code, to implement and comply with all rules and regulations within it

2. Implementation—the process that an anti-doping organization goes through to amend its rules and policies so that all mandatory articles and principles of the code are adhered to

3. Enforcement—enforces its amended rules and policies in accordance with the code

Until the introduction of WADA, there was a scarcity and splintering of resources required to conduct research and testing, a lack of knowledge about specific substances and procedures being used and to what degree, and an inconsistent approach to sanctions for those athletes found guilty of doping (WADA, 2017). Although some sports like athletics have sought to adopt a more consistent approach with sanctions given to athletes, this isn't always operationally true. In the last few years, sprinters Asafa Powell and Tyson Gay failed drug tests—the former was banned for 18 months, the latter for 12 months. The IAAF has recently intro-

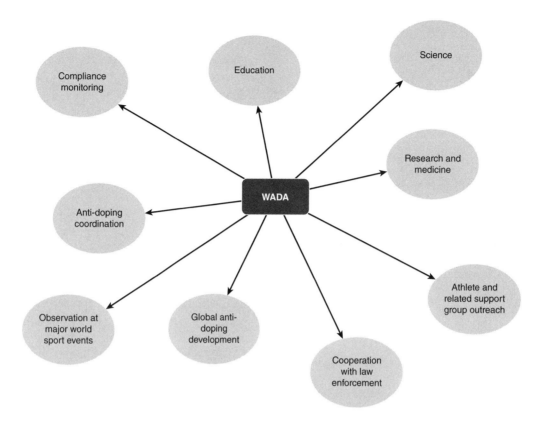

Figure 14.2   Responsibilities of WADA.

duced a four-year ban for a first failed test, which is far longer than in many other sports.

Transparency is an issue that WADA continues to wrestle with. The need to be transparent, so that everyone knows the rules and can abide by them, is important given the global nature of the fight against PEDs in sport. With what have been seen to be systematic doping practices in sports like cycling, but also in countries like East Germany and now in Russia (see the case study Russian Roulette), not all organizations and countries that have signed up to the WADA code are following the rules. This behavior reflects negatively on the sports involved and the wider anti-doping fight.

Regional Anti-Doping Organizations

To operate on a global scale, WADA established regional and national anti-doping organizations. The **regional anti-doping organizations (RADOs)** are in place to facilitate countries within those regions to come together to discuss the latest chal-

lenges, advances, and education and to ensure that countries are complying with the World Anti-Doping Code and that all athletes in all their respective countries and in all sports are being subject to the same anti-doping protocols and processes. RADOs have offices in Africa, the Americas, Asia, Europe, and Oceania.

National Anti-Doping Organizations

Each country within a region is responsible for testing national athletes in and out of competition, as well as other athletes from other countries competing within its borders at certain times, adjudicating anti-doping rules violations, and providing anti-doping education. In complying with World Anti-Doping Code, **national anti-doping organizations (NADOs)** must agree to the tenants of the code, must amend its own rules and policies to include the articles and principles of the WADA code, and must agree to enforce rules and policies in accordance with the WADA code. These NADOs have much more of a role in the day-to-day implementation of anti-doping rules and, therefore, their importance in the fight against PED use in sport cannot be understated. Three of the most prominent NADOs are the United States Anti-Doping Agency (USADA), United Kingdom Anti-Doping (UKAD), and the Russian Anti-Doping Agency (RUSADA).

USADA

In the fall of 2000 the United States Olympic Committee (USOC) decided to create its own independent organization designed to provide education, lead scientific initiatives, conduct testing, and oversee results management for the processes of all United State Olympic Committee endeavors including sport national governing bodies, their athletes, and events. USADA manages the anti-doping program from its office in Colorado Springs, Colorado, for the U.S. Olympic, Paralympic, Pan American, and Para Pan American sports. The agency is a signatory of the World Anti-Doping Code and fully complies with all aspect of WADA and the code.

UKAD

UK Anti-Doping was established in 2009 after it was suggested to the British government that an independent body be set up to tackle PED use in sport, with a particular focus on the Olympic and Paralympic Games to be held in London in 2012 (the United Kingdom had been awarded the Games in 2007). The Drug Free Sport Directorate at UK Sport handed over responsibility for testing and education to UKAD, and case management responsibilities previously carried out by national governing bodies of sports were given to the newly formed agency. According to UKAD, their responsibility is "the implementation and management of the UK's anti-doping policy and ensuring that sports bodies in the UK comply with the code" (UKAD, 2017). More than 40 Olympic, Paralympic, and professional

CASE STUDY

Russian Roulette

If you look back at the history of doping in sport, you will notice that many Russian athletes have been sanctioned for failing drugs tests. Indeed, Russia has had the most (37) Olympic medals stripped for doping violations—triple the number of the next country on the list.

In 2014 German television channel ARD reported on a state-sponsored doping program in Russia, comparing it with the East German programs in place in the 1970s and 1980s. As a result, WADA began investigating, which led to the IAAF's decision to suspend Russia from world track and field events indefinitely. Other NADOs tried to assist WADA in testing Russian athletes but found their paths blocked by armed federal security service agents. Allegations made about the 2014 Winter Olympics in Sochi, from a Russian former lab director, led to the commission by WADA of an independent investigation. The investigation, by prominent sports lawyer Richard McLaren, found that the Russian Ministry of Sport and the FBS had operated a "state-directed failsafe system" ensuring that positive test results were expunged from records, a "disappearing positive [test] methodology" (DPM) from "at least late 2011 to August 2015," a four-year state-sponsored doping program (McLaren Report, 2016).

In response to these findings, WADA announced that RUSADA should be regarded as noncompliant with respect to the World Anti-Doping Code and recommended that Russia be banned from competing at the 2016 Summer Olympics. The International Olympic Commission (IOC) rejected that recommendation, stating that the IOC and each sport's international federation would make decisions on each athlete on an individual basis. Of the entire Russian team sent to Rio de Janeiro for the Olympic Games, 270 athletes were cleared for competition and 167 were removed because of doping. The International Paralympic Committee, on the other hand, voted unanimously to ban the entire Russian team from the 2016 Summer Paralympics, having found evidence that the DPM was also in operation at the 2014 Winter Paralympics. The Olympic Athletes from Russia were of considerable focus during the 2018 Winter Olympics, given that Russia as a nation was banned from participating in Pyeongchang.

sports are subject to the robust testing programs in place. UKAD also undertakes scientific research to identify and detect new methods of enhancing performance.

RUSADA

Established in 2008, RUSADA is affiliated to WADA and operates all anti-doping programs for Russian Olympic and Paralympic sport. But significant issues with PED use have arisen in Russia, and at the time of writing, RUSADA has had its WADA accreditation suspended.

Challenges in the Fight Against PED Use in Sport

Although WADA is at the forefront of the pursuit for clean sport, the organization, and indeed the cause as a whole, faces significant challenges. Questions have been raised about just how independent WADA is from the IOC, especially given that a large proportion of funding comes from that organization. As previously discussed, the transparency of its practices has also been questioned. Four significant challenges in particular need to be highlighted: the role of the Court of Arbitration for Sport (CAS) in the anti-doping fight, issues around the uptake of policy regulations, the development of new substances, and the number of sports that have become signatories to the World Anti-Doping Code.

Role of CAS

The Court of Arbitration for Sport (CAS) is an independent institution that provides an environment to facilitate the settlement of sport-related disputes through arbitration or mediation. Many doping cases have ended up in arbitration. Athletes have sought to have a ban reduced, and WADA, or governing bodies, have wanted to have sanctions upheld or even extended. With this option available, and with many cases being overturned, a sport-wide standardized set of sanctions for PED use seems unlikely.

Policy Regulations

The Whereabouts Rule, which was introduced in 2004, has led to much divided opinion in the world of sport. According to the rule, athletes are required to select one hour per day, seven days a week, when they are to be available for random drug tests without receiving any notification beforehand. Athletes can be on holiday or moving house, but they need to let authorities know where they will be for an hour every day in case they are to be tested. UKAD has a system called ADAMS (Anti-Doping Administration and Management System) that allows an athlete to log in to the UKAD website and update any required information.

The rule was challenged in the European courts in 2009 by the Belgian sports union, Sporta, who argued that the system violated Article 8 of the European Convention on Human Rights, and by FIFPro, the international umbrella group of football players' unions, stating that the rule raised issues related to data protection and employment.

Not all IFs and NGBs agree with the whereabouts rule; both FIFA and UEFA have raised concerns about the rule, claiming that it violates an athlete's right to privacy, as has the BCCI (Board of Control for Cricket in India). On the other hand, a significant number of sport organizations, governments, athletes, and other individuals and organizations have expressed support for the whereabouts requirements, including the IAAF and UK Sport. Again, with such a disparate adoption of this type of rule, not everyone is trying to address PED use in sport in the same way.

New Substances

As technology and understanding of the human body continue to develop, so too do the substances available for athletes to use to cheat. Throughout history, substances have been introduced to the world of sport that testing mechanisms weren't ready for. Anabolic steroids, human growth hormone (hGh), erythropoietin (EPO), and meldonium have bypassed testing, meaning that athletes using these substances have been able to continue to compete without fear of sanction. Only when the scientists behind testing programs catch up will these athletes be caught. When tests were developed to detect EPO, a rash of cyclists ended up being banned by the UCI.

Signatories to the Code

Sport organizations that have signed up to the WADA code include, but are not limited to, the International Federation of American Football (IFAF), the World Baseball–Softball Confederation

CASE STUDY

Double Fault?

Although many say she is known more for her off-court looks, endorsement money, and model-like persona, Maria Sharapova would have gone down in sporting history as one of the great players in women's tennis. She moved to America as a young child, at around 9 years old, with her father from her native Russia, and she joined the Bollettieri Tennis Academy in Florida soon afterward. Her career took off with a win over Serena Williams at Wimbledon in the finals in 2004, and she followed that up with two French Open titles and multiple wins on the international circuit. She has been ranked as high as number 1 in the world on multiple occasions. She was the world's highest paid female athlete for several years, and *Forbes* estimated her earnings at $29.7 million in 2015, after she signed high-dollar endorsement deals with companies like Nike, Avon, Evian, TAG Heuer, Porsche, Tiffany & Co., and Head. But in the spring of 2016 her world changed dramatically. Sharapova announced that she had failed a drug test during the Australian Open earlier that year. She stated that she had been taking a drug known as mildronate, which contains meldonium, for about 10 years, mostly for issues related to shoulder

surgeries and comebacks from those injuries. The drug, meldonium, was added to the WADA prohibited list on January 1, 2016. Sharapova and her group of doctors, trainers, coaches, and managers claimed that they did not know the substance was banned until the positive test result in Australia.

In early June of 2016 the International Tennis Federation (ITF) handed down its punishment for the failed drug test. Sharapova received a two-year ban from competing in the sport. She and her advisers appealed that decision to the Court of Arbitration for Sport (CAS). In the fall of 2016 CAS reduced her punishment by 15 months and gave her an opportunity to return to tennis in the spring of the following year. Since that time, she has seen limited court action—indeed, some of the larger tour events and Grand Slams have refused to give her wild-card entry to competitions. She sustained an injury going into the summer of 2017 and is now uncertain about when she will return to competition.

Where her career goes from here remains to be seen. As with all cases of this kind, only time will tell.

(WBSC), and the International Ice Hockey Federation (IIHF). Although these IFs are included, WADA, at this point in time, does not have any influence on the anti-doping practices of the National Football League (NFL), Major League Baseball (MLB), the National Hockey League (NHL), and the National Basketball Association (NBA), primarily because of the process of collective bargaining in these sports. More testing isn't necessarily high on the agenda of these leagues, which have some of the most lenient doping bans in the world of sport. Would the NFL institute a four-year ban for failing a drug test? Probably not, but what message does that send out to the rest of the sporting world?

Summary

The governance and representatives of WADA, RADOs, NADOs, Olympic committees, and governing sport bodies; managers, trainers, and coaches;

and athletes all face challenges associated with the use of PEDs. The lengths to which elite athletes, teams, and even nations will go to cover up illegal and unethical acts should not surprise anyone in 2017. Because of pressure to win, to represent, to carry on traditions, and to gain almost God-like fame and fortune, governing bodies face a barrage of issues, such as corruption due to bribes and gambling, coercion, and nations wanting to show the world a good face and a strong standing on the athletic field of play. People holding key positions need to uphold the highest degree of integrity and be above the almighty power of winning at whatever cost.

We as sports fans, as academics, and as the next generation of sport managers need to ask ourselves the following questions:

◆ Does sport have a moral obligation to uphold an ideal of sportsmanship?

◆ At what point will stakeholders say, "Enough is enough," and really start dealing with PED use in sport?

◆ How do we teach the next generation of athletes about the key virtues of sportsmanship?

◆ Does culture influence those virtues? How do we address those differences?

◆ Can we mitigate the pressure to win?

◆ Should doping be legal?

Chances are that we will never come up with the answers to all these questions, because as we can see, some are always going to push the proverbial envelope, to try to gain even the smallest advantage over their rivals. How we manage that, how we mitigate the effect of that behavior become of critical importance as we move forward in sport.

? Review Questions

1. What forms the foundation of the key construct of sportsmanship?
2. Where did the use of performance-enhancing substances originate?
3. When did the "Doping Explosion" occur?
4. When, where, and how was the World Anti-Doping Agency introduced?
5. What steps are sports required to undertake in order to be compliant with the WADA Code?

Professional Sport Leagues and Tours

James Skinner, PhD
Loughborough University London

Jacqueline Mueller, MSc
Loughborough University London

Steve Swanson, PhD
Loughborough University London

Chapter Objectives

After studying this chapter, you will be able to do the following:

- Explain the structure and common features that underpin the governance of international professional sport leagues.
- Describe specific professional sport leagues in North America, Australia, Europe, and Asia.
- Explain the economic nature of professional sport leagues including the differences between the operation of leagues in North America, Australia, Europe, and Asia.
- Identify how professional tours have established themselves in the international sport management landscape.

Key Terms

competitive balance

league governance

commercialization

cartel

equalization policy

monopoly power

salary cap

draft

players associations

At one level, professional sport leagues and organizations are no different from any other type of business organization. First, they have investors, mainly the franchise owners, who desire an adequate return on their investments. Second, they use suppliers of sport equipment, food and league merchandise, and subcontractors, such as security firms, merchants, facility cleaners, and so on that provide vital services directly to the franchises. Third, the franchises have employees (namely, the players but also backroom staff, administration, maintenance workers, and so on) who seek financial remuneration, job security, good working conditions, and an opportunity to grow. Finally, franchises have customers, the spectators who demand to see their team win championships (Oebbecke, 1998). Beneath the surface, however, we begin to see that although the professional sport industry has an economic rationale anchored in the principle of profit maximization, its business practices are unique and distinctive. This chapter explores these unique differences by examining the nature of professional sport leagues and tours and the models that shape their governance structures and operational practices.

Structure and Governance

This section outlines the structure and common features of international professional sport leagues in team sports throughout the world. The governance of sport leagues operates at different levels, depending on the league. Leagues may be governed at the international, regional, national, or local level, as highlighted in figure 15.1.

Although sport may be governed globally, regionally, or only nationally, professional sport leagues tend to follow one of a few models of ownership and management. Not all professional sport leagues operate at an international level, but those that do are generally governed by regulatory bodies that monitor and control all aspects of international competition by establishing game rules and codes of conduct that must be enforced at regional, national, and local levels.

The International Cricket Council (ICC) is an example of a league that operates at an international level. This type of organization is unique because it governs across national borders and has policy integrated within national leagues and

Figure 15.1 Governance of sport at different levels.

governing bodies. The ICC's governance structure is clearly defined on its website (International Cricket Council, n.d.). The council operates on behalf of 105 member countries in two levels of membership, full and associate. A former third category, affiliate membership, was removed at the ICC Annual Conference in London in 2017, when all former affiliate members were moved to the associate category, which now has 92 members. With the acceptance of Afghanistan and Ireland into the full membership category and the expulsion of the United States, the ICC now has 12 full members; most are represented at the international level. Voting rights of each membership type reflects its importance within the organization (Hoye & Cuskelly, 2007). Nine committees fulfill specific governance functions, as depicted in table 15.1.

Table 15.1 ICC Subcommittee Structure and Membership

ICC subcommittee	Membership	Main responsibilities
ICC Annual Conference	Delegates from all full and associate member governing bodies	Ratifies major decisions, considers applications from potential new member countries, appoints the ICC president
ICC Executive Board and IDI Board of Directors	Presidents or chairmen of the 12 full-member countries and 3 representatives of the associate members	The key policy body for international cricket, responsible for major financial and commercial policies
ICC Chief Executives' Committee	CEOs of the 12 full members, an appointed secretary and chairman, and the executive officio composed of the chairman of the Cricket Committee and the chair of the Women's Committee	Key forum for making recommendations on the business of cricket; refers policy to the ICC Executive Board for approval
ICC Cricket Committee	An appointed chairman, two past players, two representatives of current players, a team coach representative from a full member, an umpires' representative, a referees' representative, a Marylebone Cricket Club representative, an associate representative, a media representative, a women's representative, and the executive officio composed of the president and CEO of the ICC	Makes recommendations to the CEC on matters of the game of cricket
ICC Audit Committee	Representatives from four full members, an independent appointment and an independent chairman, and the president and CEO of the ICC	Reviews the ICC's financial reporting process, internal controls, risk management, audit process, and compliance issues
ICC Code of Conduct Commission	Twelve nominated representatives from each of the full-member countries and four nominated representatives from associate countries (Hong Kong, Scotland, Papua New Guinea, United Arab Emirates)	Oversees formal enquiries into conduct which may be prejudicial to the interests of the game and makes recommendations to the ICC Executive Board
ICC Development Committee	Two associate member directors, three associate representatives from the Central European Committee, a global affiliates representative, three full-member representatives, and the executive officio	Reviews and monitors all policy matters relating to the structure and delivery of the ICC Global Development Program
ICC Finance and Commercial Affairs Committee	Five appointed members and the executive officio (ICC president and CEO)	
ICC Nomination Committee	Five appointed members	
Dispute Resolution Committee	Two code of commission representatives, two CEC representatives, and an ethics officer	
Membership Committee	Five permanent members, the chair of the associate members, an independent chair of audit, the Cricket Committee chair, the ICC chairman, and the ICC CEO	

Data from International Cricket Council (2017).

Like cricket, other sports have governing bodies that operate as leagues at the international level. The Fédération Internationale de Football Association (FIFA), one of the largest international sport governing bodies, has overseen the phenomenal growth of world football and the increasing profile of the World Cup. Tomlinson (2005) describes how the world governing body of the game has established partnerships that have changed the financial base of the game and established the FIFA World Cup as a "major global spectacle and . . . a marketing opportunity for the world's most powerful corporate investors" (p. 39). FIFA is one of the world's oldest and largest nongovernmental organizations. Founded in 1904, it has since expanded to include 211 member associations (FIFA, 2017). Tennis is another sport that has its governance at an international level. Starting out as an amateur sport, tennis became professional many years ago, much to the advantage of players. Women players compete in the WTA Tour, and men on the ATP Tour, which is now divided into ATP Tour events and Grand Slam events. In golf, the PGA Tour is a primary organizer of top professional competitions, and consists of six different tours across multiple continents; three operating in the United States, and three other development tours in Canada, China, and Latin America collectively (PGA Tour, 2018).

Regional sport leagues operate across international boundaries but tend to be isolated to a particular geographical regional location. For example, UEFA is the administrative and controlling body for European football. SANZAR (South Africa, New Zealand, and Australian Rugby Unions) emerged because of occurrences in rugby union in Australia, South Africa, and New Zealand. In early 1995 Rupert Murdoch's News Limited introduced its Super League competition in Australia as an attempt to control the administration of rugby league worldwide and, in turn, provide product for cable and pay television (Fitzsimons, 1996). In Australia, a bitter struggle ensued between Super League and the Australian Rugby League (ARL), the traditional governing authority of the code. The ugly struggle created ongoing hostility between both clubs and players (Masters, 1997). One of the most significant outcomes was a massive increase in player salaries, which resulted from the restricted market of player talent, the potential presence of two elite competitions, and the financial support

provided to Super League by News Corporation and to the ARL by the Optus telecommunication company. With salaries of rugby league players seemingly out of control, rugby union officials in Australia, New Zealand, and South Africa became concerned that they were going to lose most of their leading players to rugby league. This unease led to the formation of the Southern Hemisphere Consortium, collectively known as SANZAR. The consortium announced on June 23, 1995, before the commencement of the Rugby World Cup, that it had signed a 10-year joint-venture agreement with Rupert Murdoch's News Corporation worth US$550 million over 10 years, with a 5-year option (Skinner et al., 2003). In return for News Limited's heavy investment in rugby union, the Southern Hemisphere Consortium was required to provide two products. The first was a Super 12 competition of 5 regional teams from New Zealand, 4 from South Africa, and 3 from Australia, which in 2006 transformed into the Super 14 as an additional Australian team and a South African team entered the competition. The entry of another Australian team resulted in an additional name change to Super Rugby in 2011. In 2016, 3 more teams were added to Super Rugby, which resulted in the current total of 18 franchises—6 South African, 5 Australian, 5 New Zealand, 1 Japanese, and 1 Argentinian team. But because of reduced spectator numbers and intense travel, SANZAR announced in April 2017 that the league would be reduced to 15 teams for the 2017-2018 season (SANZAR, 2018). Two South African teams, Kings and Central Cheetahs, will from this point onward compete in the Europe Pro 12 (which will be renamed into Europe 14 after they join). The third team to leave Super Rugby is the Australian team Western Force, which has not been granted a license to compete. The second product offered by the Southern Hemisphere Consortium was a Tri-Nations series among the three countries.

At the national level the structure and features of professional sport leagues vary depending on the sport. Some leagues modify their "rules of play, eligibility, and behaviour of governing bodies" (Noll, 2003, p. 542). The National Basketball Association (NBA) in North America, for example, has rules that are slightly different from those of the International Federation of Basketball Associations (FIBA), which NBA players must abide by during international competition (Noll, 2003). By contrast, FIFA exerts much greater control over national leagues. FIFA has established a pyramid of authorities to control the increasing international complexity of football (Giulianotti, 1999). As a result, "FIFA has invested its 204 member associations [211 members as of 2017] authority at national level" supported by "the formation of continental football confederations as middle tiers of control between the national and the international levels" (Giulianotti, 1999, p. 27). Each national league, however, can have its own structural variations. For example, the emergence of the Premier League in England in 1992 resulted in premiership clubs becoming independent members of a consortium whose control extends to the marketing of the league independent of the lower leagues. The national governing body (NGB), the Football Association (FA), has responsibility for overseeing the running of the England teams (Morgan, 2002).

At the lower levels, clubs, players, and coaches abide by the rules and regulations established by the international governing body (IGB) when competing in international competitions, but they may play under different rules and regulations when participating in regional or national leagues. Clubs competing in national league competitions are affiliated with the NGB, which in turn is affiliated with the IGB. Players are registered with their NGB, and to play in international events they need to be registered with their IGB. In some leagues, coaches are required not only to be properly licensed, as in Japan, but also to hold appropriate coaching qualifications as stipulated by the relevant governing body.

Economic Nature

Professional sport is a business operation capable of generating billions of dollars in revenue every year, but how does an organization make a business out of sport? In a business the aim is to destroy the opposition, but in sport a team needs to have someone to battle against or there is no point. Sport is an industry in which teams need competitors to make a product. Sport leagues use rules and regulations to encourage **competitive balance** to maintain fan enthusiasm by keeping them in suspense. Competitive balance is a concept often used by governing bodies to justify exemptions and interventions made to ensure that the outcome of competitions remains uncertain. Smith and Stewart (2010) drew on the work of Morgan (2002) when they suggested that

there are "four major trans-national models for the **league governance** of sport at the highest level" (p.10). League governance refers to the system by which professional sport leagues and organizations are directed and controlled. The following sections discuss these models.

Pyramidical Hierarchical Model

The first model that Morgan (2002) identified was the traditional pyramidal hierarchical model that can be seen in "traditional European sports such as swimming and badminton and collegiate sport in the United States" (Smith and Stewart, 2010, p. 10). Morgan suggested that in such a model the national governing body (NGB) is the key decision maker of the "structure, conduct and marketing of the sport" (p. 49). The NGB has control of "the key assets such as the national team brand and the ability to reward members through the distribution of revenue" (p. 49). He went on to suggest that when the sport has significant commercial value at the highest international level, the model would succeed. Before rugby union became a professional sport in 1995, it operated under this model. To some extent Morgan suggested that this model can still be seen in the SANZAR rugby union discussed earlier. This Southern Hemisphere consortium of national rugby unions maintains "a hierarchical governance system within their respective countries" (p. 50).

In general, this model is becoming obsolete with the continued **commercialization** of professional sport. Commercialization refers to the application of business principles to professional sport to run it as a business, generally to profit from it. Amara et al. (2005), however, argued that the control of international football (soccer) can be conceptualized as a hierarchical model. In this model, "FIFA was the ultimate authority in world soccer with responsibility for the premier competition, the World Cup, and with UEFA and national FAs occupying lower tiers in the authority structure" (p. 191). Although this description is simplified, "in this model of power, clubs and then players lay at the bottom of the decision-making hierarchy" (p. 190). In the contemporary setting, Amara et al. (2005) suggested that it has become "impossible to think in terms of a national or international governing body as being the sole author of its own sport's destiny" (p. 191). They suggested that many new factors within the contemporary sport environment indicate that the

Learning Activity

Investigate the clubs that make up the G14 group of teams in Europe between 2011 and 2017. How do these teams exert influence on the governance of football in Europe?

traditional hierarchical model is no longer relevant. These new elements include the rise of the G14 clubs (the 14 most powerful and influential clubs in European football), the strategic ownership alliances established between satellite broadcasters and powerful clubs that have provided enhanced broadcasting opportunities for both parties, and the pressure that can be applied by other groups such as **players associations**, which are a collective and representative voice of professional players involved in a particular sport and established to safeguard the interests of their members, player agents, and sponsors. This "top-down system has given way to a complex network of interrelationships between stakeholders in which different groups exert power in different ways and in different contexts by drawing on alliances with other stakeholders" (p. 191).

North American and Australian Model

The second model that Morgan (2002) referred to is what he suggested is a distinctive North American cartel structure, although the model can also be seen in countries like Australia. Unlike more traditional industries, the sport industry in North America and Australia is often allowed by government to pursue what are effectively anticompetitive practices (Szymanski, 2003). This system arises from tacit agreement that a variety of restrictive practices are essential for the sport leagues to sustain public interest and long-term viability. It has been argued that a completely unregulated sport league would be unsustainable because a few clubs would use their superior fan and revenue bases to capture the best players and dominate the competition. This argument claims that although the resulting conduct may be anticompetitive (or a restraint of trade), it is not unreasonable, nor is it against the public interest (Ross, 2003). Consequently, in North America and Australia, free market capitalism is limited.

In North America and Australia it is argued that sport leagues perform poorly under competitive or free-market conditions and that some form of self-regulation is essential to produce the outcome uncertainty that attracts fans, sponsors, and media interest (Szymanski & Kuypers, 1999).

In North America and Australia professional sport leagues operate as joint ventures or **cartels**. A cartel can be defined as a collective of individual clubs, firms, or organizations that by agreement work collectively to maximize benefits to each. A cartel has a complex set of rules and practices designed to restrict business competition among its members and divide markets among firms in the industry. The agreement on joint policies allows cartels to minimize competition, restrict the entry of new firms, control the supply and cost of their products, coordinate advertising and promotion, set prices, and, most fundamentally, protect the interests of member organizations (Stewart, Nicholson, & Dickson, 2005).

Continued domination by one team in a league would theoretically lessen the dramatic value of the contests and inevitably lead to a lack of interest in games, thereby reducing the league's ability to command high prices in exchange for its events. A league therefore operates to disperse playing talent and instill public confidence in the honesty of the game. The three major types of restrictions that are imposed relate to competition among teams for player services, sale of broadcasting rights, and the location and licensing of teams. Stewart et al. (2005) suggested that the success and effectiveness of a cartel hinge on its ability to restrict the conduct of its members and secure member compliance to the rules and regulations of the cartel. Violations of these rules and regulations will ultimately lead to sanctions and penalties against the offending team. Moreover, Stewart et al. suggest that to be successful and effective, sport cartels adopt particular structures, policies, and strategies. These include (a) establishing a centralized decision-making organization that regulates member teams and clubs and disciplines members who breach the leagues' rules and regulations; (b) aiming to expand profits by implementing various cost minimization regulations that restrict competitive bidding for players and set ceilings on total player wage payments; and (c) aiming to increase revenue by extending the market for their sporting product, improving its overall attractiveness, and enhancing the community standing and status of the league.

Sport cartels can also work collectively to improve the attractiveness of their sport and hence the marketable product. Cartels can be instrumental in developing player skills, improving sporting facilities, and ensuring that the outcomes of games are uncertain, which, it is argued, is a key component to success for sport. Cartels employ two strategies—**drafts** and **salary caps**—to achieve this goal. A draft is a process generally used in North America and Australia in which players are allocated to teams within the professional sport league. A draft allows teams to select players in turn from a pool and then receive exclusive signing rights to that player for a specified period. Salary caps place a limit on the amount of money that a professional sport team within a league can spend on player salaries, as either a per-player limit or a total limit for the team. The drafting process and salary cap restrictions help create uncertain outcomes and consequently raise spectator and television interest. This system coupled with the collusive market power that sport cartels possess by negotiating as a single entity maximizes broadcast rights fees for the league. These broadcast revenues are subsequently subject to an **equalization policy** and redistributed to the clubs within the league. Equalization policies aim to ensure that fiscal inequities between professional sport teams do not allow some teams to become so dominant within a league that they eliminate competition. Less successful clubs are thus able to maintain a level of financial security and remain viable entities (Stewart et al., 2005).

The popularity and status of a sport league can also be heightened by centralized advertising and promotion campaigns that aim to improve the integrity, public image, and overall reputation of the sport. Rules are put in place to regulate the conduct and behavior of team administrators, coaches, and players. This high degree of discretionary decision making and monopoly power, which is used to regulate members and reduce competition among teams for resources, aims to control costs and increase revenue for all members of the cartel (Stewart et al., 2005). **Monopoly power** refers to the exclusive control by a professional sport league or organization over the means of producing or

selling that sport. Some of the actions that professional sport leagues employ to operate as a cartel include restricting competition by controlling the admittance of new teams, controlling the number of sporting events through central scheduling, and limiting player movement and pay through drafts and salary caps. Although the preceding description is a good representation of the United States and Australian models in general, emerging globalization factors (see the case study Globalization of the NFL) provide a glimpse into how professional sport leagues may evolve in the future.

European Model

The third model that Morgan (2002) outlined is the oligarchy model, which can be highlighted through reference to the Premier League in England. To understand this model, recognize that almost no intervention occurs in Europe. Ensuring competitive balance is difficult because European Union antitrust legislation is applied to sport as it is to any other industry. European law requires sporting competitors to be economic competitors. Each team is treated as an economic unit (Edwards & Skinner, 2006). For example, English Premier League clubs are not constrained by salary caps, and they can offer players whatever money it would take to lure them away from another team. Premier League clubs do not have to abide by a draft system or share their broadcast revenues equally among themselves, as do NBA and NFL teams in North America, whose least successful clubs receive as much cash as the most successful ones. The big Premier League teams such as Manchester United, Arsenal, and Chelsea earn more money from broadcast rights because they appear more often. Those teams can spend their larger broadcasting revenue returns and merchandising income on expensive players, which in turn widens the gap between themselves and other clubs in the league.

In the broader European context, attempts to redistribute television revenues equally among all league teams have resulted in conflict. For example, the top four clubs in Holland (PSV, Ajax, Feyenoord, and Vitesse Arnhem) broke away in 1997 from their national league association and signed a separate television deal with Canal Plus. The European commissioner Karel van Miert supported the strategy on the grounds of free-market competition (Giulianotti, 1999). In North America and Australia, it is argued

CASE STUDY

Globalization of the NFL

The National Football League (NFL) was established in 1920 as the American Professional Football Association (APFA), and it became the NFL in 1922. Since then the international business of American football has grown spectacularly; regular-season games are now being played in the United Kingdom and Mexico. The NFL has been playing games at Wembley since 2007, and in November 2016 the league hosted the first regular-season game in Mexico since 2005. Sellout crowds and a surge in public interest make it no surprise that the NFL announced a return to Mexico City in 2017 and signed a 10-year agreement with English Premier League club Tottenham Hotspur to play at least two regular-season games in London from fall 2018 onward. With over 80,000 spectators attending each of those international games, the NFL appears to have a market to expand its reach abroad. The focus on international business is nothing new for the NFL, because the league has a long history of trying to grow the game internationally. From 1986 to 2005 the NFL played an extra preseason game, referred to as the American Bowl, which took place in various international locations. Near the end of the 2007 season, however, NFL commissioner Roger Goodell announced that NFL Europe would discontinue after 15 seasons, citing yearly losses in excess of $30 million and limited success with player development. This timing coincided with the start of the new NFL International Series scheduled to kick off at Wembley later that year. Because this competition has consistently taken place in London, the NFL has signaled a different strategy than other U.S. leagues like the National Basketball Association (NBA), which has instead decided to hold regular-season games in various countries around the world (Swanson, 2015). Some speculate that the NFL might soon have a London-based franchise, which would make it the first American sport league with a team located outside North America. In 2013 the International Olympic Committee (IOC) gave the International Federation of American Football (IFAF) provisional recognition and thereby increased the chances that the game will become an Olympic sport by 2024. But some challenges still need to be overcome before American football can be included in the Olympics, as the recent exclusion from the 2020 Summer Olympics in Tokyo proves. Some of the restrictions preventing the game from being an Olympic sport might be the name of the sport (American football) and the resulting strong association with one culture, the need for specialized equipment, risk of brain trauma, and IFAF's apparent lack of clear purpose and direction. In 2005 the IFAF became a full SportAccord member, and by 2018 27 nations from five continents (North and South America [10], Europe [13], Asia [2], Africa, and Oceania [2]) obtained member status by the IFAF (IFAF, 2018). There are three types of men's and women's American football—tackle, flag, and beach. The IFAF currently appears to be aiming at the same path as rugby (sevens), whose global presence has steadily grown over the past years and ultimately made it an Olympic sport in 2016.

---

that sport leagues perform poorly under competitive, or free-market, conditions and that some form of self-regulation is essential to produce the outcome uncertainty that attracts fans, sponsors, and media interests (Szymanski & Kuypers, 1999). Ultimately, however, the primary beneficiaries of this regulation are the leagues themselves (Sage, 1998).

Smith and Stewart (2010) indicated that league structures can also highlight the differences between the North American and European governance models. North American leagues are characterized as closed systems. The makeup of the league is predetermined; the same teams participate regardless of their league standing in the previous year. By contrast, the European governance model employs a promotion and relegation system. This system, it is argued,

> can bolster interest in championship standings at the top and bottom of the competitive ladder, provide the opportunity for numerous teams from a single city to compete for a place in the highest league, and remove incentives for team relocation given that it is less expensive to buy more talent in order to win promotion. (p. 8)

Promotion-Led Model

The fourth and final major transnational model for the governance of sport, as described by Morgan (2002), is the promotion-led structure. This structure can be seen in sports such as boxing. This form of governance is market led and fragmented. Contests are arranged as one-off events in which a promoter brings together the participants, organizes the venue, and arranges broadcasting rights and sponsorship opportunities. The promotion-led model remains a threat when the established hierarchy no longer meets the needs of the stakeholders. The threat of a breakaway rugby union competition in the Southern Hemisphere was one of the factors that precipitated the International Rugby Board's support of the introduction of professionalism. Morgan, however, suggested that "such breakaways are usually followed by a renegotiated rapprochement with the traditional authorities, as the appeal of the sport depends on offering a legitimate and therefore significant championship rather than a travelling circus" (p. 50).

Emerging Models of Sport Governance

Although the models presented by Morgan (2002) are the most commonly referred to in the literature, as sport becomes increasingly globalized new models of economic governance are emerging. These new models are shaped by "local histories, local political and sporting cultures and local economic conditions" of a country and "reflect the local adaptation to global pressures in sport business" (Amara et al., 2005, p. 189). Examples from three countries follow.

China

In the 1980s China adopted the policy by Jvguo Tizhi to enhance national pride, improve elite sport performance, and increase the number of medals won in global competitions (Peng, Skinner, & Houlihan, 2017). During this time, and until recently, the state's intervention in the development of sport, as well as other industry sectors, remained high. Despite the increased levels of popularity, the performance of the Chinese national football team had not improved, which prompted a reform of the Chinese Football Association (CFA). The governing body of Chinese football, the CFA, was founded in

1992 and has undergone several reform attempts since then. The most recent organizational reform, started in 2015, has seen the change from a system previously referred to as "state-sponsored restricted capitalism" (Amara et al., 2005, p. 194) to a more market-driven model. Still, it has yet to be proved whether the strong links to the state have been attenuated.

Some of the governance practices employed by the league have similarities with the cartel system that exists in North America and Australia. For example, under this system, clubs are franchise controlled, and the CFA has taken responsibility for negotiating and controlling the sale of television rights at the national level, although at the local level broadcasting rights are owned by the clubs, which have the power to negotiate locally. Salary levels for the league ranged between 80 and 100 times the average salary, and the CFA sets transfer values. Therefore, to a large degree the transfer market is a controlled environment. Even so, the number of foreign players playing in the Chinese Super League (CSL) is growing (Amara et al., 2005). Numerous foreign players, most of whom are from Serbia or Latin America (although the number of European players is increasing), have been signed by the CSL.

With this rapid rise to professionalism, problems have emerged. Allegations of corruption and match fixing have arisen, and the ability of some clubs to retain their financial viability has been called into question (Amara et al., 2005). The system of governance in Chinese football is still evolving and perhaps can be best described as "a hybrid between traditional centralized control of vertical government of the game and the network system of governance evident in the European context" (p. 195), discussed earlier.

Japan

Two sports that have established high-profile professional leagues in Japan are baseball and football. Professional baseball in Japan has a longer history than football. The first professional baseball league began in 1936. By contrast, the professional football league, known as the J1 League and consisting of 18 teams, was formed in 1992 (Daly & Kawaguchi, 2003). This league will be the focus of discussion here.

The J1 League was launched on the back of a £20 billion injection of funds and the imposition of conditions on clubs who wished to be part of the league. According to Amara et al., (2005, p. 199), these conditions included the following:

◆ Clubs had to be registered corporations that had football as their core business function rather than the club being a subsidiary of another business.

◆ Teams were not allowed to be based in Tokyo initially because the league wished to decentralize the distribution of teams.

◆ Stadiums had to have a minimum of 15,000 seats, and floodlighting was required.

◆ Clubs were required to field a reserve team.

◆ All coaches were required to be licensed, and teams had to have a minimum of 18 players under contract.

Two conditions were clear departures from the Nippon Professional Baseball League in Japan. First, the requirement that clubs be named not after their owner or sponsor but on their location removed the possibility that team ownership was undertaken mainly as a means of corporate advertising. Second, the decision to share broadcast rights equally between the clubs established a relatively even distribution of major revenue sources, similar to what is done under the cartel system. It soon became clear that if the J1 League were to survive, strong local government support as well as corporate backing would be needed because only a small number of clubs have been able to operate with a profit. The remainder relied on other sources of funding (Amara et al., 2005). As a result, in Japan the professional football system is "built on coalitions of public–private interests serving local markets" (p. 200).

Learning Activity

Compare and contrast the Nippon Baseball League of Japan with Major League Baseball in the United States. Identify the similarities and differences between how the leagues are structured and governed.

Algeria

The model of professional sport under development in Algeria is similar to that of China in that it is state designed and is experiencing implementation problems (Amara et al., 2005). In the 1990s Algeria began to experience economic problems, so the government started to encourage a shift from amateur to professional sport structures to reduce its public financial commitment. This change resulted in a "partial government disengagement from football in 1999 with the intention of total disengagement to occur within a three- to five-year period" (p. 197).

The status of football in Algeria was beginning to change. Government disengagement was identified as the first stage in a shift toward the professionalization of a number of sports within Algeria. If this shift was successful, the practice would be extended to sports such as "handball, volleyball and basketball" (p. 197). It was hoped that this reorientation of sport structures in Algeria might also present other commercial opportunities and lead to the presence of players' agents, the formation of players associations, greater television revenue, and growth in employment both directly and indirectly associated with professional sport (Amara et al., 2005).

The first season of professional football in Algeria was in 1962. The structure adopted was based on the Swiss football system, which was a fusion of amateurism and professionalism. The Swiss league was similar to the system adopted in Tunisia, and it involved two divisions using a promotion and relegation system (Amara et al., 2005). This model did not succeed, and key stakeholders including government representatives, the presidents of the professional clubs, and representatives from the governing body and both divisions of the league decided that reorganization of the system was necessary. A new professional league was formed in 2010. The league was composed of 16 clubs who "would be managed by an autonomous structure known as 'le groupement professionel' (GPF)" (p. 197). The GPF was to take responsibility for organizing the planning and management of the professional league now named the Algerian Ligue Professionnelle 1, or Ligue 1 for short, and on behalf of the club presidents, it negotiated television broadcasting rights. The relegation

Learning Activity

Conduct research on a professional sport league in South Korea. First, discuss the unique economic, political, and cultural characteristics of South Korea. Second, identify key governance features of the league. Finally, determine whether these unique characteristics are linked to the model of governance that is being applied to the league.

Learning Activity

Pick an action sport (e.g., mountain biking, skateboarding, snowboarding) and discuss its cultural origins. What are the implications of this background for corporate or media sponsorship?

system would not be used for the first two years to allow clubs a period of transition to the new environment (Amara et al., 2005). This change required relinquishing some of the governance practices that characterize the oligarchy model, in particular promotion and relegation, for the cartel practices of collective negotiation of broadcasting rights.

Accompanying the shift to Super Division were several financial problems—the steady growth of players' wages, budgeting problems, poor performance, the absence of clear judicial procedures regarding transfer of players, the lack of a taxation system for professional players—all of which, together with the internal lobbying and conflicts inside the AFF and GPF and the lack of external financial investors, rendered the survival of the new professional system problematic (Amara et al., 2005, p. 198).

These factors were confounded by the fact that the major sponsor, the Khalifa Group (which had interests in airways, banks, medicines, TV, and radio), who sponsored a large percentage of the Super Division clubs as well as Olympic Marseille in France, and the Algerian Football Federation terminated their sponsorship arrangements because of financial concerns (p. 198).

Occurrences like these leave leagues and clubs in a precarious financial position, and the experience of professional football in Algeria has yet to assume "a clear final form" (p. 198) of governance.

Revenue Sources

The most significant factors in revenue generation for professional sport leagues include ticket sales attributable to spectator attendance (Burton &

Cornilles, 1998), broadcasting rights, merchandising sales, and sponsorship (Zhang, Pease, & Smith, 1998). Sponsorship involves an organization or corporate identity financing part or all of a league, team, or athlete as a business enterprise to obtain access to the exploitable commercial potential associated with that league, team, or athlete. The objectives for making such an investment for the organization or corporate identity are the potentially huge financial gains. For the professional league, team, or athlete, the reasons (apart from financial) may vary, but the two most widely cited are increasing public awareness of the league, team, or athlete and changing or enhancing the image of the league, team, or athlete (Meenaghan, 1991). Other reasons for entering into a sponsorship agreement may include the forging of links with business and political communities and the entertaining of corporate customers (Shaw & Amis, 2001). Irrespective of the rationale for entering into a sponsorship agreement, measuring its effectiveness is extremely difficult because separating the effects of a particular sponsorship investment from the effects of other marketing strategies is complicated.

Perhaps the greatest potential for achieving some of these objectives exists in China. Amara et al. (2005) point out that in 2003 the league was sponsored for one year by Siemens for €10 million (2017 valuation of US$11.96 million). This amount was €2 million (2017 valuation of US$2.39 million) less than it was paying for the sponsorship of the Spanish football giant Real Madrid in the same year. Furthermore, Amara et al. suggested that

> the potential value of the league, in sponsorship terms, is reflected in the fact that its television audience is estimated at just less than 4 billion per year, and that Siemens as a mobile phone producer is attacking the Chinese market, which is estimated as the world's biggest market with 200 million subscribers. (p. 195)

Clearly, tremendous opportunities are available to generate commercial incomes.

Broadcasting rights and ticketing also provide revenue-generating commercial opportunities, but these elements vary depending on the location of the club and the market in which it operates. For example, in North America and the United Kingdom, News Corporation and other media giants have not ignored the dominant role that the acquisition of broadcast rights continues to play. Law, Harvey, and Kemp (2002) pointed to the increase for the rights to broadcast American football (NFL) to US$395 million and to the right of the National Football League to renegotiate its contract after just five years rather than after eight years. Moreover, they point out that

> News Corporation's worldwide coverage continues to expand as they add the exclusive broadcasting rights for the Super Bowl, NHL games, and the MLB World Series, as well as the World Cup of Cricket and English Premiership football to their broadcast rights stable. (p. 284)

CASE STUDY

English Premier League Tours

The English Premier League (EPL) has become a global phenomenon. Games are being broadcast on television to over 650 million homes in 175 countries. In conjunction with this globalization process, international preseason tours by EPL football (soccer) teams have become a way to position themselves strategically by gaining revenue and additional supporters around the world. Clubs have been engaged in preseason friendlies for decades, but in the last 10 years the reasoning behind their participation seems to have shifted from player and fitness development to capturing commercial opportunities. Scheduling preseason tours is a strategic decision. Millions can be made on appearance fees, merchandising, and TV subscriptions. Clubs can benefit for the rest of the season by traveling to popular destinations such as China, Australia, Singapore, Hong Kong, and the United States ahead of the regular match schedule. For example, participation in tournaments such as the Premier League Asia Trophy and the International Champions Cup is a common choice for English, German, and Spanish football teams. Since 2003 the former tournament has been hosted every two years in Asia, and the Premier League has considered establishing similar competitions in other continents, such as Africa and North America. This trend has led to the formation of the International Champions Cup (ICC). The first ICC tournament was held in the United States and Spain in 2013, and other host countries have included Australia, Mexico, and China. Clubs like Real Madrid, Manchester United, and Barcelona receive around $20 million just in appearance fees to participate in the preseason tournament, making it a lucrative business opportunity. In addition, with British broadcasting rights for the Premier League at a saturation point, overseas rights are the next big growth market, and over £1 billion per year is already being made. From a club's perspective, beyond revenue creation the opportunity to build a long-term global fan base is appealing. A record-setting crowd of 110,000 at the Manchester United versus Real Madrid match in Michigan in 2014 is symbolic of the enthusiasm of international fans wishing to see their teams live in their home country. Whereas Chelsea seems to have its focus set on growing a presence in the United States, Manchester United has its biggest international fan base in Asia. The number of Manchester United supporters has increased continuously from around 10 million fans in 1990 to over 325 million in the Asia Pacific Region and 108 million in China in 2013. This huge increase can be attributed to the allure of the Premier League worldwide and particularly to the large number of international preseason tournaments played in that interval. But managers have lately started to critique the preseason tours to Asia because they had to deal with increased injury rates resulting from bad weather and poor quality of the pitches. Although there has been talk of playing a 39th (extra) match in international venues, English clubs, unlike teams in some American sport leagues (e.g., NBA and NFL), have yet to integrate international competition into their regular-season schedule.

Contrast this to the broadcasting amounts paid in Algeria. Algeria's sole terrestrial channel paid €2.5 million for the broadcasting rights for the first year of operation in 1999. Similarly, in Japan, the major source of revenue shifted from merchandising rights (€26.3 million [2017 valuation of US$31.46 million], or 40 percent of income) in 1993 to broadcasting rights (€36 million [2017 valuation of US$43.06 million], or 46 percent of income) in 2001 (Amara et al., 2005, pp. 198-199).

The amounts are relatively small compared with the amounts in the more developed sport media economies of North America and the United Kingdom.

This variation in price and demand is also evident in ticket prices. Amara et al. (2005) noted that ticket prices in China are set by clubs and have been subject to agreement by the local Price Management Department of the state. Clubs are required to pay either 5 percent (Jia A League) or 2.5 percent (Jia B League) of their ticket income to the CFA. In France, live spectating demand for football can vary noticeably from 88 percent and 85 percent for Marseille and PSG (the biggest football clubs in the French league) to only 48 percent for Strasbourg, also competing in the top flight. Ticket prices are at one-third the average level for the English Premiership, reflecting the variable nature of this demand (p. 200).

This discussion indicates that in some instances the very rules and regulations that seek to protect the members of a league can work against the maximization of financial benefits and perceived growth of popularity of the sport itself. Jane-Anne Lee (2001) reported that the Association of Surfing Professionals (ASP) had turned down a lucrative broadcasting deal worth an estimated US$50 million over five years because of industry fears that control of the sport would be lost. This decision occurred at a time when sponsorship of surfing in the 1990s had begun to wane. Arthur (2003) believed that lack of a television profile was part of the reason for this. Besides the revenue sources listed earlier, international tours are proving to be lucrative for professional sport clubs (see the case study English Premier League Tours).

Competition Among Leagues

Although rival leagues have arisen from time to time to challenge established and official leagues, the history of rival leagues suggests that they often either fail or eventually merge with the established leagues. For example, four teams in the World Hockey Association (WHA) joined the National Hockey League (NHL). Similarly, as previously discussed, in Australia in early 1995 Rupert Murdoch's News Limited introduced its Super League competition in an attempt to control the administration of rugby league worldwide and provide a product for cable and pay television (Fitzsimons, 1996). Two separate national rugby league competitions were played in 1997, but because of mitigating factors, the two rival leagues established a joint venture and formed one professional league known as the National Rugby League. World Series Cricket in Australia lasted only two years before an agreement was reached with the traditional governing body, now known as Cricket Australia, for the rebel players who joined World Series Cricket to return to Cricket Australia. Players from both leagues received increased pay and benefits. The traditional governing body also achieved greater financial gain because of a restructuring of broadcasting rights.

Competition among leagues has emerged recently in India. The battle of the Indian Cricket League (ICL) against the Board of Control for Cricket in India (BCCI) and International Cricket Council (ICC) backed Indian Premier League (IPL) is currently being played out in the courts. The rebel ICL is seeking recognition as unofficial cricket, and the BCCI and ICC support the continuing sanction of

Learning Activity

The Indian Cricket League and the Indian Premier League currently have separate Twenty-20 cricket professional leagues. Determine which league you believe will be the most successful and justify your decision.

players who are participating in the rebel league. With the popularity of the sanctioned IPL growing, and sponsors such as Coca-Cola, Honda, and Vodaphone on board, the ICL looks set to follow the route of its rebel-league predecessors.

Besides competition among rival leagues, the global sport environment also provides challenges for sport clubs to balance international and domestic competitions (see the case study National and European Handball).

CASE STUDY

National and European Handball

The sport of handball is governed globally by the International Handball Federation (IHF), founded in 1946. The international handball world is divided into five regional federations—Africa, Asia, Europe, Americas, and Oceania. In line with the pyramidal hierarchical model, discussed earlier in this chapter, the IHF sits on top of the pyramid and is responsible for the organization of major international tournaments such as the World Handball Championship. To become a member of the IHF, national federations must be part of one of the regional confederations, such as the European Handball Federation (EHF). Founded in 1991, the EHF is the umbrella organization for European handball and currently hosts two club competitions at the European level, namely the EHF Champions League and the EHF Cup. Two years after the foundation of the EHF, the federation took over the running of the Champions League, which was played for the first time in 1993-1994. Each year the leading teams from top European nations compete in the tournament. Currently, 28 teams from 18 countries compete in four groups (8 teams in Groups A and B, and 6 in Groups C and D). The most successful teams of Groups A and B directly enter the quarterfinals, and teams in positions 2 through 6 each proceed to a knock-out round of the last 16. Since the 2009-2010 season, the best four teams emerging out of the group and knockout phases advance to the EHF Final 4, hosted in Cologne, and compete over a single weekend. Although the beginning of the EHF Champions League was fairly modest, with only 5,000 spectators witnessing the games, 25 years later the competition has become a major international event with over 800,000 visitors per season and TV viewership of over 383 million in 2015-2016. The pinnacle weekend of the competition has attracted sell-out crowds of 40,000 fans each year. But critics have started to question whether participation in regional competitions could affect the performance of clubs on a national level. Currently, 50 member federations and 2 associated federations belong to the EHF and compete in their respective national leagues. For example, the German Handball Association (German: *Deutscher Handballbund*) (DHB) has been a member of the IHF since 1950 and the EHF since 1991 and is responsible for the organization of handball within Germany. From the very beginning of the EHF Champions League, German teams have participated in the tournament and have traditionally been fairly successful. Therefore, teams always had to manage regional as well as national competitions. Research conducted by Picazo-Tadeo and Gonzalez-Gomez (2009) on Spanish professional football clubs suggests that although elimination from regional tournaments could result in increased availability of resources in domestic league competitions, it may simultaneously cause a loss of confidence and in turn negatively affect league performance. More generally, however, although participation in multiple official competitions (e.g., the EHF Champions League) could negatively affect club standing in national leagues (e.g., the Handball-Bundesliga), performance benefits may result from competing against top-caliber international competition.

Summary

Professional sport leagues in North America and Australia use their rules and regulations to encourage competitive balance so as to maintain fan enthusiasm by keeping fans in suspense. In the European Union, which applies antitrust legislation to football just as it would to any other industry, such actions would constitute illegal collusion among members of a cartel. In Europe the best-run and most financially viable leagues and teams are successful. This scenario is desirable in free-market economies but not necessarily in sport. In countries such as China, Japan, and Algeria, the governance of professional sport leagues is being shaped by local factors such as history, political and sporting cultures, and the prevailing economic conditions. Although sport management academics argue that sport is a business, some would accept the fundamental principle that equality of outcomes (at the expense of overall standards) is a desirable way to maintain spectator support, league financial viability, and the infusion of sponsorship.

The examples of American football, handball, and football used in this chapter indicate that in the international arena the ongoing viability of professional sport leagues and tours is subject to specific and unique circumstances. The infusion of sponsorship into professional sport leagues and tours continues to be the key to ongoing financial stability, but their long-term viability depends on the ability of their administrators to formulate business strategies that appeal to current and future fans while enhancing the public perception and image of their sport product. Success within a professional sport industry underpinned by this relationship depends on management's ability to respond to the needs of sport consumers—the media, sponsors, and spectators—and to provide a platform for promoting continued interest.

? Review Questions

1. Identify and provide examples of how sport is governed at the international, regional, national, and local levels.

2. List and discuss the key features of the four major transnational models for the governance of sport leagues.

3. Identify the key characteristics of a country that can influence the governance models used in its professional sport leagues. Provide an example of how these characteristics could influence the application of the model.

4. Outline the major revenue sources available to professional sport leagues and the way in which those revenues are managed.

Youth Sport Events and Festivals

Anna-Maria Strittmatter, PhD
Norwegian School of Sport Sciences

Milena M. Parent, PhD
University of Ottawa

Chapter Objectives

After studying this chapter, you will be able to do the following:

- Know about the various youth sport events and festivals hosted around the world.
- Gain an appreciation for the differences in their aim, philosophy, and overall governance.
- Gain a critical view of the value of those events.
- Learn about the benefits and challenges of youth sport events for athlete and coach development.
- Gain insights on marketing opportunities and brand implications related to youth sport events.
- Understand the implications of such events for sport managers and researchers.

Key Terms

Asian Youth Games
Australian Youth Olympic Festival
European Youth Olympic Festival
Commonwealth Youth Games
governance
International Children's Games
International Olympic Committee

international sport federation
Parapan American Youth Games
stakeholders
youth-based events
youth sport events
Youth Olympic Games

Competition opportunities for young athletes have grown in the past decades at the national and especially at the international level. In this chapter, we examine the various **youth sport events** and festivals that have emerged. Although *youth* can be defined in different ways, we use the term to denote events for preteens and teens—events in which the majority of competitors are under the age of 20. In addition, given the international focus of this textbook, we exclude university or college events (e.g., National Collegiate Athletic Association [NCAA] and International University Sports Federation [FISU] events), given the age ranges from late teens to late 20s. Nevertheless, these events are worthy of examination in their own right.

The forerunners regarding international youth competitions were the **international sport federations (IFs)**, such as the football (FIFA), track and field (IAAF), and cycling (UCI) IFs, the latter launching its Junior World Road Race in 1975. Just as in the case of single-sport youth events, the concept of youth multisport events emerged, though more recently, with events such as the **International Olympic Committee's (IOC) Youth Olympic Games**, the Commonwealth Games Federation's (CGF) **Commonwealth Youth Games**, and the Australian Olympic Committee's (AOC) **Australian Youth Olympic Festival (AYOF)**. Based on our cursory overview of the creation dates of various single-sport and multisport events, 21 events were created before 1980 and 50 events were created between 1980 and 2016. Examining the multisport event category more closely, we find only the **International Children's Games** created pre-1980, followed by the **European Youth Olympic Festival (EYOF)** created in the 1990s, and all other multisport events or festivals created in the 2000s (see table 16.1). Thus, the number of international competitions for teenagers has increased exponentially in the past decades and has spread worldwide. Table 16.1 provides an overview of the most prominent international youth elite multisport events and festivals.

Sport federations as well as national Olympic committees (NOCs) argue that elite youth sport events provide young athletes with event experience and practice for their athletic careers at the senior level. Sport governing bodies, such as the

Learning Activity

Examining table 16.1, what do you notice about youth sport events and festivals compared with the senior events (e.g., Olympic Games or Commonwealth Games)? If you were the mayor of your city, would any of these events be appealing to you? Why or why not?

IOC or AOC, also argue that these youth events help promote sport among youth in general. But as many researchers have pointed out (e.g., Digel, 2008; Judge, Petersen, & Lydum, 2009; Loland, 2014; Parry, 2012; Strittmatter, 2017a, 2017b; Wong, 2011), these goals remain problematic and lofty. Still, some researchers see benefits for the young athletes' athletic development (e.g., Hanstad, Parent, & Houlihan, 2014; Parent, Kristiansen, & MacIntosh, 2014). To investigate youth sport events and festivals more closely, we provide an overview of their governance and stakeholders, examine the value of these events, and conclude by providing implications for event managers and researchers.

Governance and Stakeholders

Most research on sport event **governance** has occurred with senior-level Games, such as the Olympic (Winter) Games, the Pan American Games, and the Commonwealth Games. From these studies, researchers have come to understand organizing committees' basic structure, design, and decision making (e.g. Parent, 2008, 2010, 2016a; Theodoraki, 2001, 2007), the event rights holder governance of the Games system and movement (e.g., Chappelet & Kübler-Mabbott, 2008), stakeholder network management and governance (e.g., Naraine, Schenk, & Parent, 2016; Parent, 2013, 2016b), and Games legacy (e.g., Girginov, 2012; Leopkey & Parent, 2015).

Although the process of moving from planning to implementation to wrap-up, as well as having to manage a variety of stakeholder groups—namely, the organizing committee's paid staff and volunteers, the host governments, the media, sponsors,

Table 16.1   Youth Elite Sport Events on World and Continental Levels

Event	Part of world covered	Governing body	First edition	How often	Sports*	Number of athletes**	Age of athletes***
Youth Olympic Games (YOG)	World	International Olympic Committee (IOC)	2010	Summer and winter edition, biennial	Summer: 31 Winter: 15	Summer: 3,579 Winter: 1,067	15-18
European Youth Olympic Festival (EYOF)	Continental	European Olympic Committee (EOC)	1991	Summer and winter edition, biennial	Summer: 9 Winter: 8	Summer: 3,304 Winter: 600-1,519	14-18
Australian Youth Olympic Festival (AYOF)	World	Australian Olympic Committee (AOC)	2001	Summer edition, biennial	17	1,700	13-19
Asian Youth Games (AYG)	Continental	Olympic Council of Asia (OCA)	2009	Summer edition, quadrennial	15	2,404	15-16
Commonwealth Youth Games	Commonwealth countries	Commonwealth Games Federation (CGF)	2000	Summer edition, quadrennial	9	1,000	14-18
International Children's Games	World	IOC	1968	Summer and winter edition, biennial	9	Summer: 1,662 Winter: 500-800	12-15
World Youth Championships	World	International Sport Federations (IFs)	Earliest is 1947 for the Little League World Series	Summer and winter		Varies by sport	Varies by sport
Parapan American Youth Games	Continental	America's Paralympic Committee	2005	Summer	20	1,000	12-21
Asian Youth Para Games	Continental	Asian Paralympic Committees	2009	Summer	14	466-1,200	15-19

*The number of sports varies from one edition to another; we chose the number for the most recent edition (as of March 2017).

**Unlike in the Olympic Games, the number of participating athletes differs from one edition to the next. The numbers are approximate.

***Can vary from edition to edition.

Data from AOC (n.d.); Asian Paralympic Committee (n.d.); AYG (2013); CGF (2014); EYOF (n.d.); ICG (n.d.); IOC (2015); IPC (n.d.); Kristiansen, Strittmatter, and Skirstad (2016); Little League (n.d.); Parent et al. (2015).

the community, sport organizations, and delegations—appears consistent across different types of events, the size and complexity of managing these events varies, as does relative stakeholder salience and specific issues, risks, and legacies. Each of these studies often ends with caveats related to transferability issues between Games as well as between countries and cultures. Thus, what we know for the senior-level sport events cannot be automatically transposed to youth sport events and festivals. As such, we now delve deeper into what we do know about these various youth sport events and festivals, and compare this knowledge to the senior-level events.

Youth Olympic Games (YOG)

The concept of the YOG was introduced by the former IOC president, Jacques Rogge, in 2007 as part of the Olympic Movement's youth strategy. The YOG is the newest member of the Olympic family and organizes summer and winter editions in an alternating manner every two years (i.e., summer, then winter, then summer). The first Summer YOG were staged in 2010 in Singapore. Two years later, Innsbruck was the host for the first Winter YOG, followed by Nanjing 2014 (Summer YOG) and Lillehammer 2016 (Winter YOG). Buenos Aires 2018 (Summer YOG) and Lausanne 2020 (Winter YOG) constitute the third editions of these Games. The IOC's vision for the YOG is as follows:

> The Youth Olympic Games (YOG) vision is to inspire young people around the world to participate in sport and encourage them to adopt and live by the Olympic values and become ambassadors of Olympism. The idea behind the YOG is to organize an event and to educate, engage, and influence young athletes and other young participants, inspiring them to play an active role in their communities. (IOC, 2015, p. 1)

Although some researchers have criticized these Games, as noted earlier, other researchers are finding positive aspects to the Games, such as its values being closer to those of the Olympic Movement than the Olympic Games themselves, and the athletes' experience (e.g., Hanstad et al., 2014; Parent et al., 2014).

The governance of the YOG is similar to the Olympic Games in that the IOC and the local organizing committee (here, the YOGOC) hold the rights to host the event. The YOGOC's board includes representatives from the host country's NOC, as well as local, regional, and national host governments. The YOGOC receives an event manual from the IOC and works with the IOC and other **stakeholders** to prepare the Games. The featured sports' respective IFs are responsible for overseeing the rules and implementation of their sport competitions, assisted by the YOGOC (Lesjø, Strittmatter, & Hanstad, 2017).

Figure 16.1 illustrates a generic YOG's organizing committee structure. Hanstad, Parent, and Kristiansen (2013) identified 23 specific stakeholders for the YOG organizing committee, which can be categorized into four groups:

1. host core stakeholders (host governments and the community);
2. international core stakeholders (IOC, IFs, NOCs, athletes, delegation support staff);
3. sponsors and media; and
4. parents and other stakeholders (e.g., consultants).

Even though the YOG were supposed to be created with the young athletes in mind, Parent et al. (2015) found that athletes are present but not the most important stakeholder. Hanstad et al. (2013) argued that the YOG's salient stakeholder groups are different compared with the Olympic Games, in which the media and sponsors play more important and prominent roles. Much of the costs associated with the YOG are borne by the IOC and the host governments, thereby explaining their high salience. In addition, the YOG lack the degree of international media attention seen in the Olympic (Winter) Games (Hanstad et al., 2013; Judge et al., 2009). As such, the IOC decided to focus on social media platforms, explaining that these were the media preferred by their target market, the youth, and thereby explaining the decreased salience of the media for the YOG relative to other stakeholder groups. Finally, we know that other differences exist between the Olympic Games and the YOG, such as for knowledge management and transfer, as the YOG knowledge management case study demonstrates.

Continental Youth Olympic Games and Festivals

Youth Olympic events and festivals at the continental level were also introduced by an initiative of the former IOC president Rogge to promote Olympism among youth. The first continental youth Olympic event was launched in Europe with the European Youth Olympic Festival (EYOF). Later, youth Olympic events were introduced in Australia and Asia. The vision of the continental Olympic festivals is to promote "sport and physical activity and *inspires* young people to take up sport. [By] following the *Olympic principles*, it fosters the spirit of *friendship, fair play* and *tolerance*" (EOC, 2017, para. 2-3, emphasis in original).

Because the exclusive rights to the event are given to the respective continental Olympic committee or NOC (such as the European Olympic Committee for EYOF and AOC for AYOF), the IOC serves only as patron for those events. But in the case of EYOF, for example, the Olympic Charter, which provides the rules and guidelines for the organization of Olympic Games and YOG, does not apply. In addition, continental event organizing committees are not required to follow event manuals from the continental committees (e.g., from the EOC). Compared with the YOG, the continentally-organized events are even more scaled down in terms of budget, number of sports, service level, and public interest.

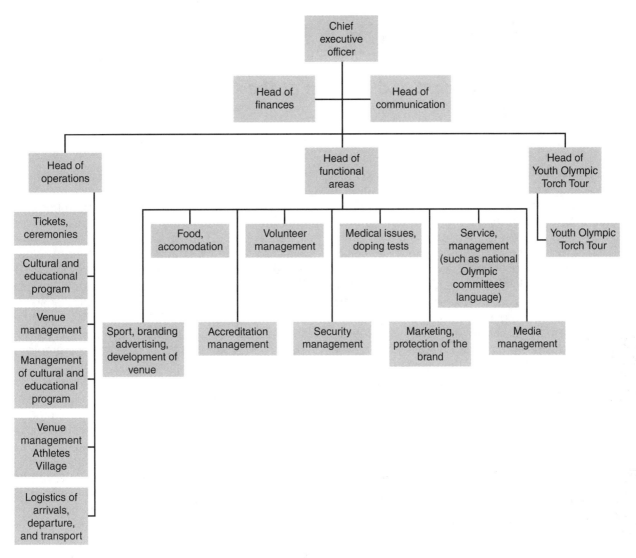

Figure 16.1   Example of an organizing committee of the Youth Olympic Games.
Based on Lillehammer (2016).

In the continental youth Olympic events, the host community and local companies become more important because the Olympic (Winter) Games' TOP (the Olympic Partners) sponsors are not bound to these events. These events also have lower budgets because stakeholders, such as international sponsors, media, and spectators, are rarely present (Kristiansen, Strittmatter, & Skirstad, 2016). A youth Olympic village, as is required at the YOG, is not mandatory for the continental events; local hotels are used for hosting the delegations (i.e., athletes, coaches, and support staff). We could surmise, however, that these events garner higher economic impacts and returns on investment compared with the YOG given the greater reliance on local infrastructure such as hotels, restaurants, and public transportation.

Commonwealth Youth Games (CYG)

The first edition of the Commonwealth Youth Games (CYG) was held in Edinburgh, Scotland, in 2000. The CYG are open to the youth of the 71 countries of the Commonwealth. Similar to the youth Olympic events and festivals, the CYG are a scaled-down version of the senior Commonwealth Games.

As in the Commonwealth Games, all athletes stay in athletes' village-style accommodation and events comply with the relevant sporting federa-

CASE STUDY

Knowledge Management and Transfer at the Olympic Games Versus the YOG

In 1999, the IOC developed the Olympic Games Knowledge Management (OGKM) Programme to foster knowledge management and transfer between Olympic Games organizing committees. This system notably includes an extranet complete with all relevant documents and archival material of all Games since Sydney 2000, relevant Games reference and technical manuals, workshops, Games time observations and shadowing, and a debrief about six months post Games (for more information, see IOC, 2017). The IOC also creates a coordination commission for each of its Games to track the organizing committee's progress.

This system works well with the seven-year lifecycle of Olympic Games organizing committees. On average, they have already had three years of planning time since having been designated the host of the next Games when the current Games takes place. As such, they have recruited their senior executives and perhaps even some midlevel managers, and created their business and operational plans. But they have time to adjust their plans and implementation based on what they learn from the observations, shadowing, and debrief sessions.

In contrast, YOG organizing committees have five-year lifecycles, so the host city has only been named about a year before a YOG takes place. The leader may have been hired, but the senior executive is unlikely to have been hired, and the midlevel managers are even less likely to have been hired. In addition, the business plan may be in the process of being developed, but the operational plan has likely not been started. As such, the quality of the knowledge transfer experience through shadowing and observations is significantly diminished. YOG organizing committees are too early in the planning to understand or gain significantly from operational-level

knowledge transfer; they are still at a strategic-level of thinking.

Therefore, the approach and timing of knowledge management and transfer is different when comparing the Olympic Games and the YOG. For example, when Rio 2016 took place, Tokyo 2020 staff and stakeholders attended the Games for various OGKM activities. Five hundred Tokyo 2020 staff and stakeholders hosted Rio 2016 staff in November 2016 for the 2016 Games debrief (IOC, 2016). In contrast, in the case of the 2016 and 2010 Winter YOG, when Lillehammer 2016 took place, the YOG 2020 leader had just been selected but not even officially confirmed yet (i.e., the YOG 2020 organizing committee had one employee when YOG 2016 took place).

The IOC's approach therefore needs to be different, especially because the YOG is a relatively new event whose elements are still being developed, created, and crystallized. As Parent, Kristiansen, and Houlihan (2017) noted, the IOC appears to be more involved in the YOG event planning and implementation than it is for the Olympic Games. The IOC follows an event co-construction logic with the YOG organizing committee and attempts to be pedagogical in its approach to help guide the YOG organizing committee, given the relative newness of the event as well as the lifecycle timing issue. As such, as Lausanne 2020 completes its planning and enters implementation mode, it will be continually discussing its progress with the IOC to glean the IOC's knowledge and experience, and will communicate with former staff members of Lillehammer 2016 for advice. The presence of the IOC coordination commission for Lausanne 2020 led by the former chief executive officer of Lillehammer 2016 will assist in this regard.

tion's technical rules and regulations, thus giving many competitors their first taste of an international multisport Games. World anti-doping standards also apply. Off the field of play, the Commonwealth Youth Games nurture new sporting global citizens by focusing on friendship, integrity, and cross-

Commonwealth intercultural exchange by learning and living the CGF's values of humanity, equality, and destiny (CGF, 2014, para. 6).

Under the patronage of the CGF, the CYG are meant to embrace competition and cultural activities for athletes and team officials (MacIntosh, 2017).

The CYG are also similar to the YOG and senior-level events in terms of governance structure, having an organizing committee constituted of a board of directors overseeing paid staff and volunteers (see figure 16.2). The CYG's budget is largely composed of public funding, with some sponsorship support. In-house Games services also mirror the YOG with an athletes' village and Games-funded transportation and food services (cf. Samoa 2015, 2015). Thus, we can see that the CYG's governance is more akin to the YOG than to continental youth events and festivals.

A deeper analysis of the CYG's governance and stakeholders, however, is lacking in the sport event management literature. One exception to this is MacIntosh's (2017) examination of the young athlete stakeholder group and its experiences at the CYG. He argued that CYG event organizers, as well as the CGF, need to be aware that the quality and level of services they set for the CYG will affect the young athletes' experiences at the Games and, in turn, affect the Commonwealth Games brand.

International Children's Games (ICG)

The International Children's Games (ICG) is a multisport event in which young participants compete in sport, educational, international trade and commerce, and cultural and arts events. The ICG originated in Celje, Slovenia (then Yugoslavia), in 1986 to promote peace and friendship through sport and are now held in communities around the world. The goal of the ICG, according to its statutes, is

> To enable, develop and advance the meeting, understanding and friendship of students from different countries, and to advance the Olympic idea. In this sense, sports competitions are arranged for students. The International Children's Games pursue their goals in a non-political, non-denominational and non-racist way. (ICG, 2013, para. 2)

Given its extensive nature, the ICG was granted an annual Olympic Games recognition by the IOC (New Taipei City 2016, 2016a). The organization and funding of the Games, however, remain the responsibility of the host city.

The members of the ICG General Assembly are 36 cities from 36 different countries (ICG, 2016). The regulations for the organization of the event are resolved by the ICG General Assembly. A jury, headed by a member of the committee of the ICG for each event, acts as supervising and controlling body of the organization of events (ICG, 2013).

Although Slovenia hosted the first ICG, it also hosted the first winter edition in 1994. So far, over 10,000 children from 555 cities in 95 countries

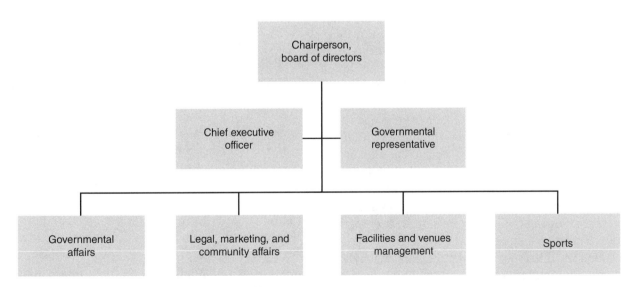

Figure 16.2 Example of an organizing committee of the Commonwealth Youth Games.
Based on Bahamas (2017).

have participated in the ICG (ICG, 2016). The 50th edition of the ICG was held in New Taipei City, Taiwan, in 2016.

Staff and volunteers were divided into five major divisions (general administration, reception, marketing, competition, and service) and 21 units (e.g., general accounting, athletes' village services, media, ceremonial, and medical care units) (New Taipei City 2016, 2016b).

World Youth Championships

World youth championships are age-group specific international championships hosted under the auspice of the IF for a particular sport. For example, FIFA is the international governing body for football (soccer), FIBA (Fédération Internationale de Basketball) oversees and regulates the sport of basketball, the IAAF (International Association of Athletics Federations) governs track and field and athletics, and so on. Refer to chapter 13 for a detailed discussion of IFs. In this chapter, we use the World Junior Alpine Skiing Championships as an example of the governance of these types of events.

World Junior Alpine Skiing Championships

In the World Junior Alpine Skiing Championships, athletes between the ages of 16 and 20 can compete in every alpine discipline—downhill, super-G, combined, the team event, giant slalom, and slalom. The inaugural event of the World Junior Alpine Ski Championships was hosted in the French resort town of Auron in 1982. At the 2019 edition in Val Di Fassa, Italy, more than 500 skiers from 50 countries will participate (Val Di Fassa 2019, 2018). FIS awards junior world titles in different skiing disciplines.

The national ski federation applies to stage the event together with the host city. Generally, for world youth championships, the national federation (NF) of the host country develops a local organizing committee at the site of the championships to complete the hosting, marketing, and fundraising details following the IF organization and competition regulations.

One key difference between the previous multisport events and these single-sport championships is the complexity. The single-sport championships

have only one sport to consider, one type of field of play, one set of athletes' needs, one set of officials' needs, and so on. With multisport events, these needs multiply by the number of sports. Moreover, the IFs are stakeholders of the organizing committee, not event rights owners for these multisport events. Figure 16.3 provides a generic example of the governance of such events.

Rugby Under 20 Championship

With a growing interest in junior competitions, the sport of rugby established world junior championships in 2008. Internationally, rugby is played at amateur (junior as well as senior) and professional levels. The sport has its origins in northern England in the late 19th century, and is especially popular in Great Britain, France, Australia, New Zealand, Argentina, Italy, and South Africa.

World Rugby is the international sports governing body for the sport. The federation organizes two competitions for under-20 national teams, the so-called World Rugby Under 20 Championship and the World Rugby Under 20 Trophy. The World Rugby Under 20 Championship is the upper level of the World Rugby tournament structure for under-20 national teams, and the Under 20 Trophy was launched as a second-level competition featuring eight teams ("World Rugby Under 20 Championships," n.d.).

The World Rugby Under 20 Championship (which was known as the IRB Junior World Championship until 2014) is contested by 12 men's junior national teams with an under-20 age requirement. The inaugural tournament was held in June 2008 in Wales, with 16 teams participating. The number of participating nations was reduced to 12 before the 2010 tournament.

Although rugby's popularity may increase because its seven-a-side format has been included in the Olympic Games since 2016, concern is growing about the effect of this sport on youth's health, especially related to the risk of concussions and severe injuries. In fact, rugby club insurance costs have increased in various jurisdictions, such as in Ontario, Canada, because of the increased rate of injuries. Rowan Stringer, a 17-year-old Canadian, died in 2015 following a concussion suffered during a girls' high school rugby game, her second in a week. Rowan's death

Figure 16.3 Example of governance of world youth championships.

Learning Activity

Compare the governance and stakeholders of the various youth sport events and festivals. What are the similarities and differences? What are the implications for host cities and organizing committees? How would you design the organizing committee of a youth sport event or festival and why?

resulted in a new law, Rowan's law, passed in the province of Ontario in 2016 to attempt to protect Ontario youth from the "ravages of concussion" (Hall, 2016, p. 1).

Little League World Series

One of the largest and most famous youth tournaments is the Little League Baseball and Softball World Series. Little League was founded in 1939 by Carl Edwin Stotz in Pennsylvania, United States, because he wanted young boys to be able to play organized baseball, which at that time was limited to adults. The first tournament was organized in 1947. Originally called the National Little League Tournament, it was later known as the Little League Baseball World Series. Because of its increasing popularity, the league expanded to include girls in the program with softball. Today, more than 2.4 million children between 11 and 13 years old participate in Little League in more than 80 countries (Little League, 2017). Twelve Little League World Series tournaments, sponsored by Little League International, in 12 different locations are now played every year. Each event brings community teams from Little League International regions around the world together in baseball with five age divisions, girls' softball with four age divisions, and boys' softball with three divisions ("Little League World Series," n.d.). Each event operates under different tournament formats, and varying

numbers of teams from regions all over the world participate (Little League, 2017). The tournament attracts audiences worldwide, but especially in the United States, where games from the World Series and even from regional tournaments are broadcast by the ESPN television network.

Value of Youth Sport Events

International sport organizations and governments argue that youth sport events and festivals offer value because they bring young people from around the world together to teach principals of friendship, tolerance, fairness, and integrity through sport competitions and educational programs. But tension occurs between the competitive youth elite sport factor on the one hand and the non-sport objectives on the other hand. In addition, some researchers and practitioners question the value of the youth multisport events and festivals beyond the potential health risks that a given sport may pose (such as rugby and concussions). Concerns range from the timing of the event to perceived weak competition structure, lack of specialization, and limited entry team or squad numbers for some sports (Skille & Houlihan, 2014). Thus, for whom are these events actually beneficial, and what is their value? We offer several discussion points below.

Benefits and Challenges for Athlete and Coach Development

Although organizers and politicians promote the wider social impacts of such events for the youth of the world, athletes' and coaches' focus is on winning medals and gaining experience for their professional careers (Kristiansen, 2015).

Athletes focus on competition and performance, but youth elite sport events often include educational and cultural elements. Multisport event rights holders argue the coming together of youth from around the world allows young people to exchange ideas and learn about cultural experiences different from their own. Lectures and workshops on training, food and health, anti-doping, burnout prevention, and so on are designed to help young people's career development as professional athletes. Athletes, however, seem to emphasize the athletic component, focusing on athletic development and learning, although they also appreciate the social environment of meeting new (young) people from around the world (Parent, MacIntosh, Kristiansen, & Naraine, 2016). For many athletes, these youth events constitute the pinnacle of their careers as athletes (MacIntosh, 2017). Therefore, the interaction between skills, knowledge, and cultural exchanges among the athletes provides a learning opportunity of high value for youth athletes for their athletic development as well as their progress to becoming productive individuals in society.

The educational and cultural programs at such events, however, often create an overly busy Games environment, which athletes perceive as challenging and unwanted, according to studies on athletes' perceptions of the YOG (Kristiansen, 2015) and the CYG (MacIntosh, 2017).

The welfare of the young athletes was a priority for the 2011 CYG organizing committee, which launched the Games Welfare Plan, developed in cooperation with the Isle of Man Child Safeguarding Board (MacIntosh, 2017). The objective of the plan was to keep the risks at a minimum for children and young people taking part in the event so as to maximize the enjoyment and safety of the experience (MacIntosh, 2017).

In addition, the sport competitions in these youth sport events and festivals are designed in a more flexible or creative way than the senior editions. The YOG, for example, developed the three-on-three basketball tournament concept. The YOG also includes mixed-gender and mixed-NOC team competitions. This setup helps coaches and athletes develop athletic skills, communication and inter-

relationship skills, and team spirit in a different way. The International Ice Hockey Federation, for instance, incorporated a skills competition in the YOG that included contests in shooting accuracy, skating agility, passing precision, and other skills. Including skills tests in an international competition might allow youth athletes to develop basic movements that are important in the play itself, as well as allow individual athletes to participate in the event when a given country might be unable to field a full team.

Experiencing an international youth event is also beneficial for coaches lacking international experience, helping them gain experience in athlete career development and management generally and in international elite youth sport more specifically. The increasing number of youth sport events at national and international levels, however, can create challenges regarding the funding, scheduling, and traveling of coaches and young athletes.

Events for Youth Created by Institutions Versus Events Created by Youth

We differentiate between events for youth created by institutions (institution-based events) and events created and driven by youth (youth-driven events, sometimes called lifestyle sport events). The former include the YOG, CYG, and so on, which were created as additions to the senior events held by those institutions. In contrast, youth-driven events are events established by youth culture and governed either by looser organizational cultures or by media and industry. Examples of these youth-driven events include the X Games, Red Bull events, and the Dew Tour. Although we presented the institution-based events in the previous section, here we focus on how they differentiate from youth-driven events and look further into what makes these youth-driven events attractive for young people.

Contrary to institution-driven events, which have highly institutionalized practices (Strittmatter et al., 2018), structures, and rules within organized sport, youth-driven events represent international competitions with core values of self-organized activity shaped by the athletes, industry, and the sport's culture. These events developed an antiestablishment culture, in which the focus is on participation and spectacular show rather than competition.

In the beginning, these events were organized by loose or informal groups deciding on their own how to build the event's identity and values, as well as to develop techniques and skills in relatively young sports, such as action sports. Today, however, events such as the X Games and Red Bull Crashed Ice are highly commercialized, run and governed by large media companies—the powerful American television channel and producer ESPN and Red Bull Media, respectively.

Action sport athletes count the X Games as one of today's most important and influential competitions in their disciplines. The participating athletes receive large sums of prize money and prestige when they reach the podium. These youth-driven events are characterized by a non- or less institutionalized and organized context that focuses less on performance and more on social aspects and new experiences. They represent freedom from or opposition to the dominant sport culture (Strittmatter et al., 2018).

One significant difference is that in such events, rules can be made, adopted, and changed by the owner from event to event, often independent of the rules from IFs, anti-doping agencies, or other related organizations. These youth-driven sport events and festivals attract the desirable youth market in a way that institution-based events created for youth seem unable to do.

An example of this was the Norwegian junior national freestyle snowboard team which decided not to take part in the first ever Winter YOG staged in Innsbruck in 2012 because they preferred to compete at another international snowboard event in Livigno, Italy, called the World Rookie Fest. The event was part of the first-ever global snowboard league established solely for under-18-year-olds. The event was established in 2004 by a group of snowboarders who have since hosted the event as a private event organizer or promoter. The event was established because, at the time, a platform for young people to compete at the international level was not offered by governing institutions; therefore, snowboarders filled the gap themselves.

Both events—the YOG and the World Rookie Fest—create a base for high-level competition, but they also include cultural and educational aspects.

In institution-based events, however, teams and coaches seem more focused on winning, rather than participating and enjoying the sport's subculture lifestyle and creativity as do the athletes in youth-driven events.

The youth-driven events are popular among young participants because they are often established out of the interest and needs of the youth participants themselves (bottom-up), in contrast to the institution-based events, which are initiated and designed by elite, white, older men from the international institutions (top-down).

International institution-based youth sport events seem to provide interest mostly for youth elite athletes rather than the mass of young people. In the following sections, we discuss the marketing and branding of these events, as well as the role that youth sport events and festivals play in the development of youth elite athletes.

Marketing Opportunities and Brand Implications

Institution-based youth events can be considered brand line extensions for the institutions (MacIntosh, 2017; Séguin, Ferrand, & Chappelet, 2014). Including new sports, especially those popular with the younger demographic, and giving upcoming sport stars the opportunity to compete internationally is a strategic decision by institutions to appeal to youth audiences.

These events enable institutions such as the IOC and CGF to use youth sport events to enhance their brand promises. For example, the IOC's brand promises of friendship, excellence, and respect appear better delivered by the young athletes participating in the YOG as "co-creator[s] of the brand" (see also MacIntosh, 2017, p. 440) than by the more senior athletes at the Olympic Games (cf.

Learning Activity

Compare the YOG to the X Games. Why do you think the X Games are more popular with young people? What can the YOG learn from the X Games in terms of event approach or philosophy, organization, and marketing?

Loland, 2014). The experience of the athletes during the event is important for the organizing committee in creating a positive brand image; therefore, youth sport event athletes must be recognized as a critical resource, because they act as brand ambassadors who share their experiences and opinions as so-called external brand communicators (MacIntosh, 2017). This, in turn, has implications for the senior Games' brand, because it will be positively or negatively affected by the line extension's (the youth event's) success (MacIntosh, 2017; Séguin et al., 2014). For example, how young athletes experience the CYG can affect the reputation of the Commonwealth Games.

Through the establishment of youth sport events, institutions enable conditions for their main sponsors to create lasting brand loyalty by engaging with a younger audience. Our observations of the 2012 and 2016 YOG, however, indicated that most of the IOC's TOP sponsors at the time (e.g., Coca-Cola, McDonald's) were rather absent compared with their presence at the Olympic Games, a notable exception being Omega. We surmise that this absence may have to do with the sponsors' perception of the potential backlash of promoting their somewhat unhealthy products to the youth target market.

The IOC also claims that the YOG has promotional capacity for the fight against obesity among youth. The YOG can be seen as a positive marketing tool for sport, physical activity, and Olympic values, as Judge et al. (2014) argued:

> While these Games may never prove to help locate and develop the next world-class archer, they may have positive physical, psychological, and social effects for a few young, aspiring athletes. Even if the world-wide spectators of this event never pick up a racquet, or slip on a pair of ice skates after watching this new Olympic event, any exposure to positive sportsmanship, teamwork, and dedication to excellence should prove to have a positive impact for its viewers. (p. 9)

But, because of the lack of awareness of these events among the public, institution-based youth sport events, such as the YOG or CYG, will need to boost their marketing and promotion efforts of the events themselves if they want such potential positive benefits to accrue.

Benefits and Challenges for Host Organizations

Many youth sport events serve as innovation labs for institutions to establish and test new disciplines, rules, sports, and trends for their suitability for the senior events. At the same time, hosts have the opportunity to gain experience in organizing international events and to test and develop knowledge and skills for staging future senior events. In this respect, cities and countries have the chance to maintain, renovate, and build new venues and training facilities. At such events, management usually employs young people with experience from previous Olympic events (Sand, Strittmatter, & Hanstad, 2017).

The host organizations, such as NFs and NOCs, can establish closer relations to their respective international governing institutions, such as the IFs and the IOC. Therefore, hosting youth sport events might also be connected to political agendas (see also Strittmatter, 2016; Strittmatter & Skille, 2017).

Although the Lillehammer 2016 case study showed that youth sport events can be connected to a political agenda, their hosting draws attention to young people and youth sport for local, regional, and national stakeholders, such as governments, the public, sponsors, and the media. This focus on youth and sport behavior among youth can be a starting point for state campaigns aiming to promote healthy living, physical activity, and sport among teenagers. This goal is often a stated legacy of youth sport events and festivals. Such legacies, however, need to be planned by stakeholders from the outset; they do not automatically happen. Here are some key considerations for event hosts:

◆ Young volunteers with leadership tasks need to be trained for their duty.

◆ Event volunteering experience is not automatically the same as volunteering in a local sport club and its day-to-day work.

◆ Long-term youth sport participation goals through youth sport events must be actively leveraged by all key stakeholders from the beginning. These goals are not attained automatically.

CASE STUDY

How National Olympic Committees Try to Leverage Youth Olympic Events for Increased Youth Sport Participation

The Norwegian Olympic and Paralympic Committee and Confederation of Sports (the Norwegian NOC) emphasized the social benefits for Norwegian organized sport when bidding and organizing the Lillehammer 2016 YOG. As one of the main arguments for hosting Lillehammer 2016, the NOC noted the Games would increase young people's engagement in organized sport in Norway. This argument was connected to the NOC's youth sport policy (YSP) aimed at recruiting more young leaders, young coaches, and young athletes into sport teams and clubs, and to counter young people's dropout from sport teams and clubs in their teenage years. This YSP was also supported by the Norwegian government, which demanded the leveraging of YSP goals when agreeing to deliver the state's financial guarantee for the hosting of Lillehammer 2016.

The NOC gave the responsibility to execute the YSP goals to "implementing agents," who created a young leaders' program, a concept that already existed in the NOC but now became explicitly connected to the YOG. In this program, 223 young people from clubs and sport associations all over Norway were recruited to participate in six gatherings, from 2014 until the event in 2016, to be trained as leaders and to learn about Olympism and the YOG. The aim was to see these 223 young people become volunteers with leadership positions during the event and then, after the Games, apply their leadership knowledge in their sport teams, clubs, or associations, which would increase the number of young people in Norwegian organized sport.

These young leaders looked forward to the responsibility they would have during Lillehammer 2016,

as they had been promised. But when the event organizing committee distributed the tasks among the volunteers, organizers argued that they could not give any responsibilities to the young leaders because they were too young and inexperienced. One hundred and fifteen young leaders were volunteers at the event, but only 15 were given leadership tasks during Lillehammer 2016.

Therefore, questions have been raised about whether the program helped get more young people involved in organized sport in Norway because the young leaders could not link their own engagement at the (organized) grassroots level with their volunteer tasks in Lillehammer 2016.

Creating a huge event and, at the same time, creating large, positive social outcomes for youth sport was arguably not realistic. Two leveraging projects (the young leaders' program and the torch tour) reached out to young people who were already motivated to be part of sport, in itself a small group. The initiatives did not, however, include young people outside the Norwegian sport structure. Therefore, the successful leveraging of Lillehammer 2016 to increase youth involvement in organized sport was not realized. Still, we can say that Lillehammer 2016 mattered locally—the event was reported to be "fun" and "great," many young people attended and contributed to organizing the Games, and it generated a 20 million NOK (US$2.4 million) surplus to be distributed to the community. This positive outlook, however, is based on short-term enthusiasm rather than long-term increased youth sport engagement.

◆ Youth sport events are good opportunities for creating valuable networks and synergies among sport clubs, schools, and other community organizations.

◆ Institution-based youth sport events do not automatically attract a young audience.

Is the Event Schedule Saturated?

The case of the Norwegian snowboarders discussed earlier in the chapter leads to another topic of discussion, that is, whether the number of events for

Learning Activity

Think about your city, country, and sport system. What value would there be for your city, country, or sport system in hosting a youth sport event or festival compared with a senior event?

young people throughout the competition schedule is excessive. The emergence of more and more such youth elite sport events leads us to ask the question: Is the event schedule saturated?

Taking the Innsbruck 2012 snowboarders example again, many of the top snowboarders did not attend Innsbruck 2012 because of the presence of another competition occurring at the same time that offered attractive prizes (e.g., filming with a professional firm, invitations and travel to higher-level competitions, and financial rewards) as well as prestige for the winners. The question becomes the degree to which the emerging youth sport events and festivals are desirable events for young athletes. Certainly, more recent events, such as the YOG, could have less prestige than more established events such as AYOF. This suggestion is supported by Skille and Houlihan (2014), who found a general lack of interest by Norway and Great Britain in attending the YOG.

For example, Great Britain decreased its delegation size between editions, sending 40 athletes to the first summer edition (Singapore 2010) but only 33 to the second (Nanjing 2014), and sending 23 athletes to the first winter edition (Innsbruck 2012) but only 16 to the second (Lillehammer 2016). The decrease in summer delegation size stands in stark contrast to the delegations that the country sends to AOYF, "over 100 athletes to each of the last three AYOFs" (Skille & Houlihan, 2014, p. 45; McDaid, 2016). In turn, Norway sent only five athletes to Singapore 2010, although after the country was awarded the second edition of the YOG, Norway's delegation sizes increased: 28 for Innsbruck 2012, 31 for Nanjing 2014, and 73 as the hosts of Lillehammer 2016 (Kristiansen, MacIntosh, Parent, & Houlihan, 2018). Although Norway, arguably *the* winter sport nation, had the largest delegation for Lillehammer 2016, Canada, Sweden, and the United States far exceeded their numbers for

Innsbruck 2012, sending 52, 35, and 57 athletes, respectively ("2012 Winter Youth Olympics," n.d.). The issue seems to remain one in which NFs vary in their perception of the value of such events; each NF has its own talent development plan and has already identified or targeted key competitions that offer the appropriate level and intensity of athletic competition for their athletes' development (Skille & Houlihan, 2014). British Swimming, for example, prefers to send its athletes to the Commonwealth Games or FINA-organized European events instead of the YOG, whereas British Cycling favors UCI-based European and junior world championships instead of the YOG, AYOF, or EYOF (Skille & Houlihan, 2014).

Given the plethora of existing events, we wonder why organizations continue to create new youth sports events. Taking the British example again, British Swimming and British Cycling now must choose which events to send their athletes to, balancing athletic development needs with

◆ young athletes' capabilities (e.g., not having too many events to burn out athletes),

◆ timing (e.g., which events fit in the schedule, allowing for appropriate recovery between events),

◆ competition structure and event specialization (e.g., whether the competition fits the athletic specialization of the young athlete, such as not asking a specialized track cycling athlete to compete in mountain biking), and

◆ organizational resources.

Spending by NFs and governments for the development of international youth events, including travel costs for junior teams, is increasing. The actual contribution of many institution-based events to youth sport development should be questioned, because the supply of Olympic events (especially for youth at the European level) is considerably higher than the public demand. With finite resources, NFs end up choosing one youth event over another, depending on its characteristics.

Finally, for certain events such as the YOG, only a limited number of athletes in a country can attend, such as only one male and one female in skiing. The presence of the coach is required for the full 10 days, just as it is for the athletes, regardless of the number of actual practice and competition days.

Learning Activity

Think of your favorite sport. Now look at table 16.1 again. Do you think that the number of youth sport events and festivals for your sport is excessive? If not, why not? If so, why? Which events are the best events to attend for your sport, and which are not? Why? Are any events redundant? If so, why?

What happens to the rest of the coach's athletes at home during that period? Should the coach favor one athlete over the others? Should the coach remain at home with her or his other athletes, resulting in the YOG athlete having a new and different coach for her or his first international multisport competition experience? These issues also need to be considered.

Implications for Sport Managers and Researchers

A number of implications can be derived from the foregoing discussion for both managers and researchers. For managers, table 16.1 demonstrates a certain flexibility in the size of the event to be hosted. Moreover, their generally smaller size is complemented by usually lower service expectations and standards; the services provided at the YOG are not as developed or extensive as those at the Olympic Games. Thus, these youth sport events and festivals can be considered more practical for the host city. If the event or festival is planned, cities can mold it to their needs. The event can be leveraged by the city (and other local stakeholders) to act as a vehicle for pre-identified strategic, legacy, and sustainability needs. Youth sport events can also act as testing grounds for new event innovations, such as new sports, new disciplines, or the cohosting of a sport event by two countries, as described in the EYOF case study.

In addition, given the lower degree of media exposure (and arguably less general awareness), these events appear to be of lower risk, where new managers can gain skills in a less stressful environment. These new managers are more likely to be younger (20 to 30 years of age), offering them an excellent opportunity to build skills, network, and boost their curriculum vitae. These younger managers fit into the scaled-down budget of youth sport events and festivals, because their contracts require a lower salary than those of senior event managers. Staff for events are often hired as secondees, that is, borrowed from other sport organizations for a certain period. Of course, those sport organizations, such as NFs or NOCs, have to compensate for the loss of those resources for that period.

For NFs, the plethora of new youth events offers more options to pick developmentally appropriate events for their athletes. NFs, however, are constrained by limited resources, so they need to make choices. But these choices can be made for them, as in the case of event rights holders or owners telling NFs they must attend a certain event or face economic or future participation retribution.

For researchers, a number of future directions can be identified. First, ethical and philosophical questions remain regarding youth sport events and festivals. What is the long-term athletic and health effect of these increasingly numerous elite competitions for young athletes? Will these packed schedules cause them to burn out more quickly? Increase the likelihood of injury? Increase early specialization and development at the expense of long-term athlete development? Are all these events truly needed given the variety of sports and young athletes' developmental needs?

Second, while researching information for this chapter, we found differences in the organizational setup for hosting between the various single-sport events, as well as with the multisport events. Whereas the event rights holder or owner of multisport events usually awards the hosting of an edition of the event to a host city, which in turn creates an organizing committee to prepare and host the event, single-sport events are often awarded to the NF, which prepares and hosts the event on its own or with the help of a local organizing committee (e.g., for local logistics). FIFA, however, has an organizing committee for each event (e.g., Organizing Committee for the FIFA U-17 World Cup India), which reports to the Organizing Committee for FIFA Competitions standing committee, which in turn reports to the FIFA Council (see FIFA, n.d.). These varying governance structures warrant deeper analysis.

Finally, while examining these governance differences, we see a trend of two types of event

CASE STUDY

Cohosting Olympic Events as Future Hosting Model

The 12th edition of the Winter EYOF in 2015 was the first-ever Olympic event co-hosted by two countries, Austria and Liechtenstein. Cohosting is one of the issues encouraged in the IOC's Agenda 2020, after an ongoing debate on costs versus benefits in public and the Olympic Movement (Kristiansen, Strittmatter, & Skirstad, 2016). Besides gaining economic advantages, the 2015 organizing committee faced some challenges.

The organizational chart represented two countries in the top management. The setup was more complex than it would have been had there been only one host country. During the event, the dual-country aspect was apparent during the opening ceremony; two national anthems were played, two official opening speeches were given, and artists from both sides of the border performed.

But the two NOCs had very different powers. The more experienced winter sport (event) country, Austria, took a leading role in the execution of the event (Kristiansen, Strittmatter, & Skirstad, 2016). Liechtenstein's NOC seemed to have a more passive role in the organization, being guided by the Austrian NOC. This model helped the more inexperienced Liechtenstein, which does not have the space or capacity to host an Olympic event by itself, gain expertise in being an Olympic host.

EYOF 2015 represented a great opportunity for the Olympic family to test a cohosting model, which might be relevant experience for future senior Games (Kristiansen, Strittmatter, & Skirstad, 2016). Other opportunities identified were the positive effect of cross-border relationships between the host governments and host NOCs.

Cohosting also brought some challenges for the organizing committee, such as handling two currencies and transportation across the border. The two currencies were an issue in addition to the normal issues with event budgets. Austria operates with the Euro, Liechtenstein with the Swiss Franc. In addition, shortly before the event, the Swiss National Bank changed the fixed currency rate, which created challenges for the CEO in terms of calculating expenses and liquidity. Transportation became an additional issue because participants had to cross a border between Austria and Liechtenstein, which was not part of the European Union, resulting in customs issues (e.g., additional paperwork not normally faced by an organizing committee).

governance: those mirroring the senior events in terms of approach and services (e.g., YOG, CYG) and those more participant-based events with fewer Games in-house services, which mirrors other participant-based events like the Masters Games (e.g., continental Olympic events and festivals). A logical hypothesis deriving from this is that the latter approach could have greater local economic impact, although this hypothesis has yet to be tested. The other issue is which type of event the youth prefer. Thus, the effectiveness of these varying governance structures merits further examination.

Summary

Youth sport events and festivals have grown in popularity worldwide, but they come with their own list of characteristics, benefits, and challenges. Although institution-based youth events are governed under strict rules and regulations by international sport governing bodies, these events provide more freedom and creativity in their sport program and hosting than their senior sport event counterparts. Yet institution-based events do not seem to be as successful at targeting the younger demographic as **youth-based events** are.

Still, youth sport events create opportunities for positive athlete and coach development, as well as for marketing and brand extension if managed correctly. Youth sport events and festivals can be considered more practical for the host city than the larger senior events. On the other hand, the increasing number of such events needs to be seen in a critical light, because NFs and governments face an increase in costs and other resources if they host or participate in such events, as well as because of the low public demand for these events.

? Review Questions

1. Why do international sport organizations establish youth sport events and festivals?

2. What are the differences in the governance structures between youth multisport events and youth single-sport events?

3. What role do youth sport events and festivals play in athlete development?

4. Discuss the benefits and challenges of a multisport youth event for the host city and host country.

5. What ethical dilemmas may be connected to the growth of youth sport events and festivals?

6. Why do youth-driven sport events appeal more to young people than institution-based youth sport events?

7. Discuss the marketing opportunities and challenges of youth Olympic events for the Olympic Movement.

Part IV

Management Essentials in International Sport

Tharaka Basnayaka/NurPhoto via Getty Images

Indian cricket captain Rohit Sharma during the fifth Twenty-20 or T20 cricket match between Bangladesh and India played in Sri Lanka on March 2018. T20 is a form of cricket that is shorter and faster paced which appeals to television viewers and spectators. In 2018, India ranked second in the world ranking of T20 and Bangladesh was tenth.

Intercultural Management in Sport Organizations:
The Importance of Human Resource Management

Eric W. MacIntosh, PhD
University of Ottawa

Gonzalo A. Bravo, PhD
West Virginia University

Chapter Objectives

After studying this chapter, you will be able to do the following:

- Describe the concept of intercultural management.
- Identify characteristics of national cultures that can affect sport organizations and management.
- Understand the concept of organizational culture.
- Discuss ways in which managers can socialize employees into an intercultural organization.
- Discuss why a human resource management approach to international sport management is important.
- Identify the various ways in which a manager can promote a sense of community in a diverse international workforce.
- Work more effectively in an intercultural environment.

Key Terms

human resource management (HRM)
intercultural management
culture shock
national culture

ethnocentric
organizational culture
organizational socialization

The plethora of sporting opportunities today that involve multicultural, multilingual, and diverse exchanges is far greater than ever before. Mega sport events like the Olympics, major athletic competitions of both multi- and single-sport variety, and minor global exchanges such as training camps require people from different backgrounds to work together to operate and run successful ventures. Yet working with people from different backgrounds is not an easy matter. Understanding oneself is difficult enough, but having an appreciation for different ways of seeing the world, organizing, managing, and communicating is a substantial challenge when working in an intercultural setting. Arguably, **intercultural management** is one of the most important and timely topics in the world of sport management today.

The purpose of this chapter is to help the reader develop an understanding and appreciation for cultural differences and diversity that exist within a global business environment. This chapter provides sport management examples to highlight the various ways in which today's workforce must consider differences and diversity, and incorporate them into daily organizational practice. Although few universal principles of management are germane to all situations, we have attempted to identify ways in which an intercultural manager or employee can embrace the myriad differences that exist in sport management today.

Why Intercultural Management Matters

As the movement of people between countries becomes more fluid and the power of the Internet continues to blur operational boundaries for organizations and create enhanced opportunity for cross-cultural consultation and business, the appreciation of intercultural management becomes ever more important in sport management. Intercultural management is a concept that requires careful consideration and deliberation, and its application is highlighted in many chapters of this textbook in various capacities. Here, we further discuss the notion of its importance.

Today's sport leagues around the world are filled with coaches, players, and even team owners from various backgrounds (Hardman & Iorwerth, 2014; Maguire, Jarvie, Mansfield, & Bradley, 2002; Zhou

et al., 2017). This characteristic is particularly true in the sport of football in Europe, where coaches and players from different parts of the world make up the team composition. Interestingly, in recent years, foreign ownership has increased within football in England and parts of Europe, particularly from oil-rich countries like the United Arab Emirates. In North America, the proliferation of player talent in the sports of basketball (NBA), baseball (MLB), and ice hockey (NHL) continues to increase, in no small part by the addition of players of different birth origin. Although all four of the major professional North American leagues (NBA, NHL, MLB, and the National Football League) have an international strategy to grow their game, coinciding with this strategy has been an influx of player talent coming into the North American marketplace, particularly within the NBA, NHL and MLB. Although this sport labor migration is highly evident in the more developed sport markets like the United States and Europe (e.g., EPL, Bundesliga, La Liga), it is also occurring at a fast pace in many other areas around the world where qualified and skilled professional sport workers are needed both in the amateur (e.g., sport megaevents like the Olympics, Commonwealth Games, Asian Games, Pan American Games, and others) and professional sectors of the industry. To illustrate, tables 17.1, 17.2, and 17.3 provide examples of coaches, players, and owners who have worked or invested abroad. Their movement reflects the trend of increased global mobility within professional and amateur sport and further highlights the need for effective intercultural management.

Concomitantly, although the major leagues and high-level amateur competitions continue to provide examples of intercultural talent composition, sport employees working abroad is an expanding phenomenon. Sport labor migration raises a series of challenges not only for the sport system that embraces the migrant athlete and coach but also for the home country that loses qualified sport personnel to more attractive and financially stable sport markets. Among other challenges, host leagues must integrate these people into a new culture through socialization and training. For their part, the new person coming into the organization must adapt and have fair expectations.

Intercultural management in sport affects multiple layers of the organization, such as human resource practices (e.g., recruitment, training,

Table 17.1 Selected Athletes Working Abroad (2018)

Name	Sport	Country of origin	Team	Host country
Ziggy Ansah	American football	Ghana	Detroit Lions[1]	United States
Giannis Antetokounmpo	M-Basketball	Greece	Milwaukee Bucks[2]	United States
Zdeno Chara	Ice hockey	Slovakia	Boston Bruins[3]	United States
Yu Darvish	Baseball	Japan	Chicago Cubs[4]	United States
Edwin Encarnacion	Baseball	Dominican Republic	Cleveland Indians[4]	United States
Manu Ginobili	M-Basketball	Argentina	San Antonio Spurs[2]	United States
Sebastian Giovinco	M-Football	Italy	Toronto FC[5]	Canada
Erik Karlsson	Ice hockey	Sweden	Ottawa Senators[3]	Canada
Gary Lo	Rugby	Papua New Guinea	Castleford Tigers[6]	United Kingdom
Leo Messi	M-Football	Argentina	FC Barcelona[7]	Spain
Timofey Mozgov	M-Basketball	Russia	Brooklyn Nets[2]	United States
Eric O'Dell	Ice hockey	Canada	HK Sochi[8]	Russia
Alexander Ovechkin	Ice hockey	Russia	Washington Capitals[3]	United States
Kristaps Porzingas	M-Basketball	Latvia	New York Knicks[2]	United States
Bruno Mossa de Rezende	M-Volleyball	Brazil	Azimut Modena[9]	Italy
Arjen Robben	M-Football	Netherlands	FC Bayern Munich[10]	Germany
Alexis Sanchez	M-Football	Chile	Manchester United FC[11]	England
Ricardo Sugano	Sumo	Brazil	Japan Sumo Association	Japan
David Villa	M-Football	Spain	New York City FC[5]	United States

[1] National Football League; [2] National Basketball Association; [3] National Hockey League; [4] Major League Baseball; [5] Major League Soccer; [6] Rugby Super League; [7] Spanish La Liga; [8] Kontinental Hockey League; [9] Lega Pallavolo Serie-A; [10] Deutsche Fußball Bundesliga; [11] English Premier League

labor laws), communication departments (e.g., languages, media handling), and finance (e.g., currency exchange, tax laws). MacIntosh, Couture, and Spence (2015) found that dealing with finance and human resources was a particular challenge and obstacle to overcome when working in intercultural management settings such as international sport for development programming. Their findings highlighted two particular sources of stress, namely financial and human resource challenges that impeded operations and programmatic success. In an earlier study, MacIntosh and Spence (2012) demonstrated that part of the strain in program operations and outcomes is attributed to how people ascribe meaning to sport, which is shaped in part through their own cultural lens of values and beliefs. As MacIntosh and Spence explained, what may be the best practice in one context may falter in another because of both agency of the stakeholder and the way in which his or her values shape decision making itself. Hence,

when considering intercultural management in both sport for development and sport development programs, people (management) must spend time upfront before launching programming efforts to understand their colleagues and obtain a sense of common values that can shape the program itself. This process can occur only through much discussion to shape the strategies and ensure that any concerns are discussed preprogram to alleviate ambiguity and ensure that the local context is heard and appreciated. Chun, Gentry, and McGinnis (2004) provided an example whereby Americans and Japanese fans experience the game of baseball in different ways that in part reflect their cultural preferences. This difference can be seen clearly in the World Baseball Classic. Cheering and singing for their team are part of Japanese baseball upbringing (see the documentary *Kokoyakyu* by Eng & Shear, 2006), a marked difference from most of the North American marketplace (save the seventh-inning stretch in MLB) that does not have cheer squads

Table 17.2 Selected Coaches Working Abroad (2018)

Name	Sport	Country of origin	Team	Host country
David Blatt	M-Basketball	United States	Darüşşafaka SK[1]	Turkey
Jan Bartu	Modern pentathlon	Czechoslovakia	Great Britain National Team	England
Mihai Brestyan	W-Gymnastics	Romania	Australia Women's National Team	Australia
Antonio Conte	M-Football	Italy	Chelsea FC[2]	England
Jim Cotter	Curling	Canada	South Korea Olympic Curling Team	South Korea
Jill Ellis	W-Football	United Kingdom	U.S. Women's National Team	United States
Thomas Tuchel	M-Football	Germany	Paris Saint-Germain FC[3]	France
Yuko Fujii	Judo	Japan	Brazil Women's National Team	Brazil
Ottis Gibson	Cricket	Barbados	South African National Cricket Team	South Africa
Joseph "Pep" Guardiola	M-Football	Spain	Manchester City FC[2]	England
Irina Illiashenko	W-Gymnastics	Ukraine	Brazil Women's National Team	Brazil
Hidenori Irisawa	W-Volleyball	Japan	Vietnam Women's National Team	Vietnam
Claude Le Roy	M-Football	France	Togo Men's National Team	Togo
Damian McGrath	Rugby	United Kingdom	Canada Men's National Team	Canada
Manuel Pellegrini	M-Football	Chile	West Ham United FC[2]	England
Vitaly Potapenko (assistant coach)	M-Basketball	Ukraine	Cleveland Cavaliers[5]	United States
Diego Simeone	M-Football	Argentina	Atletico Madrid[6]	Spain
Ognjen Stojaković (assistant coach)	M-Basketball	Serbia	Denver Nuggets[5]	United States
John Walters	Rugby	New Zealand	Korean Rugby Union	South Korea
Unai Emery	M-Football	Spain	Arsenal FC[2]	England
Indra Wijaya	M-Badminton	Indonesia	Badminton Association of Malaysia and South Korea Men's National Team	Malaysia and South Korea

[1] Turkish Basketball Super League; [2] English Premier League; [3] French Football League; [4] Chinese Super League; [5] National Basketball Association; [6] Spanish La Liga

in baseball or fans that engage to the degree found in Japanese games with specific cheers and songs.

The critical value of the role of culture in conducting sport business is also illustrated by Sofka (2008), who noted that business practices that are successful in the United States might fail in China. He noted that franchise apparel companies like Adidas and Nike have decided to end their traditional retail strategy in China because most retailers tend not to follow multinational standards and directives from a foreign company. Instead, these multinational companies have moved into a vertical model of expansion by taking total possession of their businesses through their company-owned stores. In a similar vein, Lombardo (2010), when discussing the state of the NBA in China, pointed out that although the market in China for sport business presents numerous opportunities, it also presents great challenges not only because of the protectionist role and direct involvement of government but also because a completely different business culture is in place. Marc Ganis, a sport

Table 17.3 Selected Foreign Owners and Main Investors in Professional Sport Teams (2018)

Main investor or group	Sport	Country of origin	Team	Host country
Abu Dhabi United Group Investment and Development	M-Football	United Arab Emirates	Manchester City FC[1]	England
Roman Abramovich	M-Football	Russia	Chelsea FC[1]	England
Ali al-Faraj	M-Football	Saudi Arabia	Portsmouth FC[2]	England
Fenway Sports Group	M-Football	United States	Liverpool FC[1]	England
Shahid Khan	American football	Pakistan	Jacksonville Jaguars[3]	United States
King Power International Group	M-Football	Thailand	Leicester City FC[1]	England
Stan Kroenke and Alisher Usmanov	M-Football	United States and Uzbekistan	Arsenal FC[1]	England
Grupo Pachuca	M-Football	Mexico	Everton de Viña del Mar[4]	Chile
Hasso Plattner	Ice hockey	Germany	San Jose Sharks[5]	United States
Mikhail Prokhorov	M-Basketball	Russia	Brooklyn Nets[6]	United States
Qatar Sports Investments	M-Football	Qatar	Paris Saint-Germain FC[7]	France
Vivek Ranadivé	M-Basketball	India	Sacramento Kings[6]	United States
Ekaterina Rybolovleva	M-Football	Russia	AS Monaco FC[7]	Monaco
Flavio Augusto da Silva	M-Football	Brazil	Orlando City SC[8]	United States
Riccardo Silva and Paolo Maldini	M-Football	Italy	Miami FC[9]	United States
Trillion Trophy Asia	M-Football	Hong Kong	Birmingham City FC[1]	England
Tony Jiantong Xia	M-Football	China	Aston Villa FC[1]	England
Chen Yansheng	M-Football	China	RCD Espanyol[10]	Spain

[1] English Premier League; [2] English Football League One; [3] National Football League; [4] Chilean First Division; [5] National Hockey League; [6] National Basketball Association; [7] French Football League; [8] Major League Soccer; [9] North American Soccer League; [10] Spanish La Liga

executive who has done business in China, stated, "The expectation of walking in with a great business card and a battery of attorneys may work in the U.S., but it doesn't work in China" (cited in Lombardo, 2010, p. 43). In an interesting anecdote about the challenges of working in a different market, in early 2018 the Dallas Mavericks of the NBA announced their new official Chinese name after two decades of using the name "Little Cows," the translation of "Mavericks" in Chinese. A new name has been selected that translates roughly in English to "Lone Ranger Heroes" (Ahmadi, 2018).

Another example that illustrates the complexity of doing business in China is shown in the documentary *Bird's Nest: Herzog & de Meuron in China* (Schaub & Schindhelm, 2008). The film shows how two distinct cultures clashed when dealing with the construction of a landmark building for China—the Olympic Stadium for the Beijing Olympics in 2008, or the Bird's Nest, as the Chi-

nese media renamed it. The movie documents how a Swiss firm dealt with the challenges involved in putting in place a monumental architectural masterpiece in a foreign culture. Throughout the construction process, the firm had to reconcile and tactfully negotiate all sorts of challenges with the Chinese authorities, ranging from dealing with a reinterpretation of their original ideas to applying various criteria to reduce construction costs (Dawson, 2008).

The understanding of culture also plays a critical role in sport television commercials, as shown by Jackson, Brandl-Bredenbeck, and John (2005), who found that violence related to sport advertisements took on different meanings for people in Germany, New Zealand, and Japan. An advertisement that showed a prominent cricketer with a chainsaw was not interpreted as violent by people in New Zealand, but those from Germany and Japan thought that the commercial contained a high degree of violence.

CASE STUDY

Adjusting to the Curve in Minor League Baseball: The West Virginia Black Bears' Efforts to Acclimate International Players

Because baseball flourishes outside the United States, international players maintain a substantial presence in Major League Baseball (MLB) and its minor league farm system. The West Virginia Black Bears, a Class A short-season affiliate of the Pittsburgh Pirates, located in Morgantown, West Virginia, are accustomed to hosting foreign players. At the Class A short-season level, teams function as the first developmental platform for new draft picks and international players to grow, physically and mentally, in preparation for competition in MLB. In accordance with standard minor league policies, the Black Bears have implemented procedures and programs to aid international players learning English as a second language and to acclimatize them to American culture.

In an average season, the Black Bears receive five to eight international players. Because transitioning to a different environment can be distressing, the Black Bears typically house international players together. These arrangements provide some level of familiarity through shared language, as well as shared experience from learning a new language and culture. Players from countries where English is not the primary language are placed in English service-learning classes several days per week, depending on need. These classes use a pedagogical approach that incorporates real-world experiences to improve the players' absorption of the material in a meaningful way. Teachers (professors of intensive English language from nearby West Virginia University) not only provide instruction in the English language but also help players overcome cultural differences beyond the language barrier, including teaching them tools that

can help them assimilate to their new environment, like basic conversational and applicable life skills. These lessons are meant to foster players' growth beyond the field. Some players begin these rigorous courses before arriving in the United States, like those from the Dominican Republic, where the Pirates have an established baseball academy in El Toro. Generally, players in the Pirates' farm system are prepared to "graduate" from the classes by the time they reach the Double-A level in Altoona, Pennsylvania, although tutors exist at every level of the minor league hierarchy to assist those who need more intensive guidance.

In addition to offering the English service-learning courses, the Black Bears acclimate their international players by providing a local support system. Through the use of the "Adopt-a-Player" program, international players receive support and guidance from Morgantown residents. Each international player is assigned to an "adoptive" family, who spend a few hours per week with their adopted player. These visits vary from afternoons spent with adoptive families at their homes to aiding players with basic tasks, like grocery shopping and laundry. The Black Bears find that having an adoptive family provides international players with a sense of belonging and normalcy, making their cultural transition less stressful. Currently, many short-season minor league teams use this type of cultural immersion by hosting similar programs, because they are among the most effective methods for international players to learn local language and customs over the summer.

Leighann Sainato, JD
West Virginia University

Conversely, an ad that showed a well-known football player competing with all sorts of evil forces during a football match was not perceived as violent by Germans, but it was considered violent by people in New Zealand and Japan. Findings of this study suggest the importance of recognizing not only the critical role of culture but also the popularity of

particular sports in different cultures. The bottom line, then, is that a commercial from a multinational business that uses sport must always consider the cultural context in which that ad will be shown. This simple illustration displays just one way in which sport managers must be knowledgeable about the environment in which they operate.

Intercultural management, therefore, is concerned with the various ways in which people from diverse backgrounds can work together in an efficient and effective manner. Sport managers must come to understand and appreciate intercultural management in part by reflecting on how their personal value system shapes their attitudes and behavior. This skill, personal reflexivity, is an essential aspect of working within any intercultural environment. Further, understanding how things are done in an organization plays an important role in fostering a successful intercultural environment (MacIntosh & Spence, 2012). For instance, expectations about punctuality, leaving early, working late, working from home, and work attire are ways in which work environments may differ from country to country, yet all are important ingredients to successful integration into an organization. Understanding these elements, combined with some cultural research and sensitivity training, can go a long way in promoting positive intercultural relationships.

One of the most important elements to consider when working within an intercultural setting is the notion of avoiding **ethnocentric** behavior. A person who is ethnocentric evaluates people of a different race or culture by criteria that are specific to his or her own. Hence, assuming that one's own way of doing things is the correct way has the potential to cause serious conflict and misunderstandings when working in intercultural settings (Chaney & Martin, 2004). Indeed, this type of behavior can cause people to resent their new colleague's way of doing things. Poor working conditions and failed projects are often the outcome.

Therefore, one key aspect of working in diverse settings is avoiding ethnocentric thinking. Integrating a talent pool of athletes, trainers, and coaches from different countries into one organization or team can create many types of conflict. The false notion that there is one best way to do things can certainly impede progress. One of the worst things that managers or employees can do is to believe that their own ideas, ways of doing things, and answers to questions are the only right way or right answer to accomplishing tasks. Indeed, such ethnocentric views can create an inordinate amount of conflict and misunderstanding between colleagues. Evaluating people from different cultural backgrounds based on one's own specific beliefs, or lens, may be the most detrimental aspect to intercultural management other than outright deceit and fraudulent behavior. Additionally, xenophobia, an intense dislike or fear of a person from another country, shows ignorance and an irrational understanding of human behavior that will likely cause major communication and operational challenges, leading to inefficiency and failure. Unfortunately, both ethnocentric behavior and xenophobia are a reality of the work environment. Creating awareness and suppressing this mind-set is a critical feature of intercultural management (see the sidebar Tips for People Working in an Intercultural Environment).

Tips for People Working in an Intercultural Environment

- Keep an open mind in all situations; avoid ethnocentric and xenophobic behaviors.
- Know your personal strengths, beliefs, attitudes, and preferences for behavior.
- Be patient when working within a new context and fully engage in listening.
- Know how to leverage diversity and potentially different opinions.
- Be able to put yourself in the other person's position when making decisions.
- Ask open-ended questions (e.g., who, what, why, where).
- Ask closed questions (e.g., invite a yes or a no response).
- Be observant of how things operate, be curious, and be sensitive.
- Clear up any misunderstandings right away (avoid ambiguity).
- Do not jump to hasty conclusions about a new person and her or his culture. (Carte & Fox, 2004; Rabotin, 2008)

Sport business organizations and sport governing bodies that are multicultural and conduct multinational operations (e.g., Nike, Adidas, Rawlings, Reebok, IOC, Commonwealth Games Federation, FINA, FIFA, and so on) face challenges such as language differences (written and oral), business laws, taxation laws, immigration laws, and regulatory impediments sanctioned by local or regional trade organizations that complicate business. Multinational organizations are also influenced by local customs and idiosyncratic factors (Dunning, 1989; Samiee, 1999). Thus, the challenge of a multicultural workforce wherein personal values and ways of doing things may drastically differ complicates matters of integration, socialization, and daily work life. What may be valued and work in one country may fail in another. Making business deals through technology is one example. In some areas of the world, making decisions face to face is considered important, whereas in other areas doing things over the phone or by email is common. Hence, the value associated with one-to-one communication and interpersonal feelings may be higher in one country than in another.

National Culture

Although the concept of a **national culture** is different in many important ways from the concept of organizational culture, it is nonetheless an important consideration because it can inform general business understanding in foreign markets for newcomers. A systematic investigation of a national culture within a discrete set of variables will not describe the whole picture of a country, and in some cases it may not apply at all. Yet for the intercultural manager or employee set to embark on new relations, examining the national culture is a good starting point toward learning about what he or she may see and experience. This investigation is an important mental-mapping exercise before leaving for a new place of work or study, but it should be performed with a certain level of caution. The seminal work of Geert Hofstede (1980, 1991) provides an informative basis that can add to the understanding of expectations before working with a colleague of a different culture in a new setting. Hofstede's research indicated that countries can be understood based on the following value dimensions:

Power distance, or the level of acceptance regarding the distribution of power in an organization, is a key aspect of national culture. A high power distance score indicates organizations in which persons of lesser power accept and expect decision making from people in positions of authority (e.g., India, Mexico, and Brazil). A low power distance score indicates organizations in which authorities foster a close working relationship with subordinates and include them in decision making (e.g., Austria, New Zealand, and Denmark). Knowing the power distance can inform newcomers of potential organizational practices or management strategies that they may encounter.

Uncertainty avoidance is the extent to which people are comfortable or uncomfortable dealing with unstructured situations. For instance, a low uncertainty avoidance score indicates greater acceptance of having fewer rules, laws, and regulations and more change (e.g., Denmark, United Kingdom, and the United States). Another way to view this dimension is the propensity or intolerance for uncertainty and ambiguity in society. For instance, places with a high uncertainty avoidance score (e.g., France, Japan, and Chile) prefer rules, laws, and regulations, want to minimize risk taking, and are less tolerant of uncertainty and ambiguity.

Individualism–collectivism is the extent to which individual effort and success is valued within a country (e.g., Australia, Canada, and the United States) versus a broader focus and loyalty to the group (e.g., Greece, Indonesia, and Mexico). This dimension highlights the propensity by which people are integrated into groups (e.g., collectivism sees high levels of group integration). The drive for success and the way in which that is defined can differ between people of various backgrounds when examining this dimension.

Masculinity–femininity is the extent to which achievements that are valued have more masculine or feminine qualities. Typical "male" roles characterized by assertiveness and competitiveness (e.g., Italy and Japan) are distinguished from typical "female" roles characterized by nurturing, modesty, and caring (e.g., Denmark and Sweden). Thus, masculinity versus femininity exhibits the degree of assertiveness and competition versus modesty and caring.

Learning Activity

Learning Activity

Consider what *best practice* means to you and reflect on the professional criteria on which you base your everyday management activities. Analyze how many of these activities may be based on your own culture and expectations. How would these criteria differ if you were based in a different culture? How would you adjust if any of these criteria changed suddenly?

Later, a fifth dimension was added, *long-term versus short-term orientation* (Hofstede & Bond, 1984). This dimension refers to an individual's preference to focus and prepare primarily for future events with a longer time frame attached (e.g., Hong Kong and Japan) or to concentrate on the present and the fulfillment of current obligations (e.g., France and the United States). Having a short-term orientation is more representative of fulfillment of social obligations and protection of one's "face" (Hofstede & Bond, 1984).

Knowing that organizational culture can be influenced by the national culture in which it operates, the employee new to an organization in a different country should become acquainted with the national culture and embrace the differences that exist (while also, of course, understanding that generalizations of a national culture may not reflect what her or his experience will reveal and teach). With some caution in interpreting national values, the intercultural employee can ascertain an understanding of the new environment that he or she will be entering.

If you intend to work successfully on an international stage, you will need to develop a particular sensitivity to the culturally based factors that you usually take for granted but that will change, often subtly but sometimes overtly, depending on the culture in which you are currently immersed.

Shenkar, Luo, and Yeheskel (2008) noted that the cultural distance metaphor has popularized culture as a research variable but has also forced the phenomenon into what they called a methodological and theoretical straightjacket that has proved to be counterproductive for understanding culture

in international management. For instance, the premise that a culture clash based on predefined ways of thinking will occur when East meets West in the conduct of business is not always true. Such a simplification has played a central role in the descent of international management scholarship from the already limiting ethnocentric research.

With that said, the ready intercultural manager should be knowledgeable of several aspects of international business based on national customs and include them in her or his repertoire: handshakes, bowing and greetings, dining etiquette, the physical space of offices, gift exchanging, punctuality for business meetings, business attire (casual, formal), meeting expectations (sensitivity to time), idle conversation at work (acceptable topics), conversations deemed acceptable, and a number of other issues.

Although typical practices and behaviors vary from country to country (e.g., handshakes in North America, bowing in Japan), and the behaviors (e.g., firm handshake versus weak handshake) can send mixed messages, managers need to remain open to these types of greetings at all times in a business environment as well as accept that differences in greetings are perfectly fine. People value common courtesy and manners regardless of lines that appear on a world map.

An interesting example that illustrates differences between cultures is the case of presenting a business card (Chaney & Martin, 2004). The practice in the United States of glancing at the business card and promptly putting it in the pocket is considered rude in countries like Japan and China, where the card is often accepted with an attitude of interest and respect. The Japanese and Chinese often take the card in both hands, hold it in front of them, and carefully examine it while making a comment upon its acceptance. Chinese also believe strongly in maintaining a person's status in the most flattering light. Thus, the concept of "face" is important in making a good impression in business dealings. The exchange of business cards is one simple illustration.

Dining practices also vary considerably between cultures. In many parts of the world, such as Spain and Mexico, the main meal is partaken around lunch (2:00 to 4:00 p.m.), but in the United States and Canada, the main meal occurs later, such as at 6:00 p.m., or at "dinner time." Ultimately, this difference can influence a person's natural biorhythms and ability to adapt to another time zone (a luxury or plight of international travel). The time of day when people are accustomed to eating should not be taken for granted. People need to prepare themselves and perhaps even excuse themselves from a meeting to eat a snack.

Another illustration of differences can be witnessed in the consumption of alcohol. Chinese enjoy alcohol with their meals and are known to hold informal meals before having a more formalized business meeting. Having alcohol with business meals is common and accepted in many parts of China. In contrast, business meetings in many Western countries do not include alcohol, particularly during the lunchtime hours and during preliminary meetings. But business people in Western countries do enjoy "happy hour." Business practices in China tend to become more social in nature over time compared with practices in many Western countries, where business relations tend to remain professional and more formal in nature. This difference may illustrate the collective versus individual attitudes noted by Hofstede. Discussion points during business relations in China may include personal information regarding the family, personal feelings, and aspirations. Although these elements can be discussed in Western countries, they are often not encouraged as part of business relations, thus highlighting another difference in business practices. In the United Kingdom, keeping business life separate from personal life is much more common, similar to what may be expected in Canada.

Another example is the role of the company mission statement. In many Western countries the mission statement is acknowledged as an important and potentially binding element of workforce life. In Canada and the United States, the company's mission statement is often used to promote a sense of common understanding and purpose for an organization. Clues to "how things are" in an organization can be found in its mission statement. The existence of a mission statement, however, does not mean that the employee accepts or agrees with the prescribed manner in which work is to be performed. A clear and simple mission statement is one way to come to know about an organization. But a mission statement makes up only part of the picture.

In addition to the aspects of culture immediate to the conduct of business, religion is another aspect that sport managers must take care to respect and accommodate. Although this subject can be difficult to breach, particularly in an intercultural setting where religious rituals and beliefs may present real ramifications to relationships, maintaining an open mind and accepting each person's right to religious freedom are critical when working in a shared environment and space. In some cultures more than others (e.g., Indian culture), discussing religious beliefs is important and is often part of getting to know one another. Embracing family heritage and background is often done in the first meeting with a new person. In many other cultures, however, religion is not openly discussed. Such a topic is breached only after much time and trust building has occurred between people, and even then it may be too personal to discuss.

Learning Activity

You are an employee of an American sport marketing firm that is hosting a reception at the hospitality tent during a major international tennis tournament in Madrid, Spain. Several prominent guests will be attending the reception, including CEOs from multinational enterprises from China, France, Spain, and the United States. Also, the entire board of directors of the International Tennis Federation (ITF), which includes representatives from Great Britain, Italy, Egypt, and India, is expected to attend. In addition, invitations were sent to people from the local media, artists, and politicians in the city of Madrid. One of your responsibilities is to ensure that the food and beverages for the night are not only appealing to this international crowd but also not offensive to anyone and do not prevent people from enjoying the evening. Determine the appropriate etiquette in hosting a business reception in Spain. What type of food and beverages would people expect to be served in Spain? What special considerations would you make for a particular delegation?

Organizational Culture

A shared meaning of work or purpose in any organization is an important way in which people gain a sense of belonging, and this aspect should inform intercultural management practices. The phenomenon of organizational culture is thought to be one of the most important areas of attention for leaders of companies. Generally, **organizational culture** comprises values, beliefs, and assumptions that help guide decision making and describe why an organization is what it is (Martin, 1992; Schein, 1985).

Many scholars believe that organizational culture is a fundamental determinant of behavior. Whereas lower creatures are largely governed by instinct, humans mainly learn their behavior. Given the enormity of different backgrounds within the global sport industry, learned behavior obviously varies a great degree from country to country. For instance, a focus on what is good for the group is an early learned behavior in Japan, which is different from the mentality of a focus on what is good for the individual as found in the United States. Thus, we may expect to see some notable differences in organizational life between Japanese and U.S. organizations based on the differences in learned behavior that occur early in childhood.

A new person (coach, athlete, or staff member) working within an organization for the first time can find ways to understand "how things are done around here" that can inform his or her business behavior. For instance, a person can observe the physical surroundings and the way in which people dress to become informed about whether a business is casual in nature or professional. A person can learn about an organization's culture by observing and ultimately understanding a wide array of symbols, actions, and meanings that take place within the organization. Schein (1985) noted that organizations can be understood based on three progressively deeper levels: artifacts, values and beliefs, and basic assumptions (adapted from Schein, 1985; MacIntosh & Doherty, 2008):

◆ Level 1: Artifacts are the most visible manifestations of organizational culture, including such things as dressing norms, stories, informal codes of behavior and conduct, rituals, ceremonies, company awards, jargon, banter, and jokes that members

of the company would appreciate. Some common characteristics are the following:

Visible signs, such as the pictures on the walls, the statues inside and outside the building, and the retired numbers in the rafters, act as observable features of important history and tell a tale of what is important (e.g., work ethic, teamwork, passion).

◆ Level 2: Values and beliefs are composed of organizational goals, philosophies, mission and vision statements, and the general direction of the organization. Some common characteristics of this level are the following:

Most often, organizations express their important beliefs and values in the form of codified, explicit knowledge. For example, paragraphs may be written on the company mission or a vision statement may appear in the boardroom or office setting. For new employees, these aspects could be highlighted further in their training package or documents. Many sport organizations post these types of guiding statements on their websites. Irrespective of how values and beliefs are formalized into the organization, the leadership and employees tend to adopt patterns of behavior that reinforce these important values and beliefs.

◆ Level 3: Basic assumptions are the underlying expectations of the organization that are taken for granted, act at an unconscious level, and form our general habits of perception. For example, most sport organizations believe in the power of sport for good, that sport can provide aspects of physical health through movement. This taken-for-granted belief is not something that is stated too often, or discussed, but it exists in the mind-set of the majority of people. In a fitness organization, for instance, one deeply held assumption is that physical activity matters because it can enhance a person's health. Any challenge to a basic assumption, such as a fitness trainer smoking on her or his break, can create dissonance and potential conflict with the general idea of working for the organization.

Consequently, these various levels of organizational culture can act as guide posts or reference points for a person coming into an organization and seeking to learn about the job role, tasks, and working environment. Accurately deciphering an organization's culture can take time. Initial inspection at the level of artifacts can provide a general idea about the company, but values form the central aspect of the culture (MacIntosh & Doherty, 2008). "Values are social principles, goals, or standards accepted by persons in a culture. They establish what is proper and improper behavior as well as what is normal and abnormal behavior" (Chaney & Martin, 2004, p. 46). In an intercultural setting, values are important to understand for several reasons, not the least of which is to have a more complete understanding of what is most important to the organization. Consider the differences between a culture that focuses on the group versus a culture that focuses on individual achievement. Such values tend to focus decision making. As a result, working in an intercultural setting can be a challenge to a person's basic assumptions about what is the right or wrong focus of attention.

If you, as a sport manager, encounter problems in understanding the culture of the organization or the ways of doing things within another country, ask someone who understands the local culture. Using this commonsense approach is an excellent way to gain an appreciation for the ways in which business works in the environment and a way to build a network through establishing a relationship with a mentor.

Organizational culture can also be shaped by geography. For instance, in some Latin American countries, having a siesta (a short afternoon nap) is common practice because of the uncomfortably hot afternoon temperatures. Allowing workers to rest and modifying working hours to accommodate this felt need can alter the common work environment. Further, religious customs can change the manner of work. For instance, Muslims have an afternoon prayer session when all work stops for a time to conduct the religious ceremony. How to dress when doing business also varies from place to place. For example, in Hawaii, men, even those who do not reside in the islands, can conduct business wearing a traditional Aloha shirt instead of a suit and tie. These examples constitute practices that would not be adopted in every country because they are shaped by tradition or climatic factors specific to certain areas of the world.

Culture Shock and the Role of Human Resources

In the world of elite sporting competition, both professional and amateur sport organizations are interested in developing and enhancing various skills to enable athletes and teams to compete and win important events. The importation of skill, expertise, and knowledge is common in sport. For instance, within the Olympic sport system, a coach from one country who has experienced success on the international stage is often offered employment in another country to help grow that sport. This practice may be observable in the composition of coaches for your national teams (e.g., bobsleigh, rowing, football, hockey, swimming, and several other sports); coaches have likely been brought from other countries because of their skills and international success in the expectation that they can transfer their technical expertise. The challenges of working and living in another country affect sport managers and other sport organization staff working internationally. Moving to another country (e.g., Canada to Australia) or even within a country to a different province or state brings with it a set of unknowns that need to be addressed. Table 17.2 illustrates many examples of coaching expertise on the move globally.

Indeed, the aspect of **culture shock** is a real phenomenon that the sport manager, coach, athlete, or employee must consider when engaging in any intercultural management setting. Smith (2008) indicated that "culture shock may be viewed as travel anxiety, and it is nothing more than the experience of dissonance brought about by unfamiliar people and environments" (Smith, 2008, p. 42). Smith (2008) suggested that people could avoid culture shock by studying the country using such tools as Google Earth to help visualize it; by developing an understanding of the history, climate, and monetary system; and by using MapQuest as a resource to learn the geography of the new destination. These simple strategies help a person not only develop a mental map of the new place but also manage the anxiety that typically arises when going to a place where life is not exactly the same as it is in the place of origin. Another important consideration that may help with transitioning into a new place is finding a person to act as a mentor before leaving so that on the other end, he or she can greet the newcomer, help in settling in, and answer questions that may help alleviate some of the anxiety of travel and working in a new setting. Although these tactics may not eliminate culture shock, they can help a new person feel a greater level of comfort about a new situation earlier in the period of transitioning.

In this regard, the critical role of **human resource management (HRM)** and the people involved in the department that effectively manages personnel cannot be overstated. HRM encompasses many aspects of working with people in the organization, from recruiting new entrants to hiring, training, developing, and nurturing a person's skill set and attributes for the good of the person and the organization. The HRM role is a critical one, especially in creating a welcoming environment that can foster and grow talent.

The person or persons in the HRM department of a sport organization responsible for managing and overseeing the personnel need to have an appreciation for the individual, the organization, and the interaction with the external environment. Consequently, these people need to have a sophisticated communication skill set that includes knowledge of how to integrate and socialize people (coaches, players, new employees) into a new culture. Typically, the HRM department is involved in a number of activities designed to ease the transition for the new person.

The traditional HRM process model includes planning, recruitment, screening, selection, orientation and organizational socialization, training and continuous development, feedback and performance appraisals, recognition and reward systems, compensation, retention, and replacement. These aspects are important in both domestic and international affairs. But when it comes to intercultural management in particular, what is taken for granted in domestic affairs cannot be overlooked when an international person goes through these various processes.

Within an intercultural management context, the HRM department must recognize that what works within the organization in the home country in terms of procedures, labor laws, taxation, and other elements may not work the same way in another setting. The HRM people must have a global mind-set to succeed in the international marketplace (Chaney & Martin, 2004). Language, sensitivity to time, motivation, and emphasis on goal orientation are some of the important elements to consider related to work life.

Employee Socialization

Allen (2006) noted that socialization tactics enable organizations to equip new employees with the proper tools and knowledge of the important values needed to succeed in their work. Well-thought-out employee socialization programs can provide new people with a sense of what may be expected when moving to a new country to perform work, thus helping to prepare them for the new work experience to come. Indeed, we know from research that well-implemented programming at the front end of a new experience can reduce turnover at the back end through job satisfaction. Therefore, a manager should put her- or himself into the proverbial shoes of the new person as early as possible, well before the official work or contract begins.

Although employee socialization is typically conceived of within enduring organizations, as Parent and MacIntosh (2013) found, for temporary organizations such as the local organizing committee of an Olympic Games, new employees and volunteers have a profound need to understand aspects such as the basic philosophy, guiding principles, and the way in which their task performance integrates with the rest of the team. This requirement speaks in part to the importance of the Olympic Games Knowledge Management program but also to things like liminal spaces, expert leadership, and the need of top and middle management to instill important values in the local organizing team. As Parent and MacIntosh explained, "We see that for temporary organizations, there is an urgency to infuse guiding principles, values, and philosophies. The socialization process then becomes critical to the ongoing

CASE STUDY

Olympic Games Knowledge Management Program

In the late 1990s the International Olympic Committee (IOC) recognized the need to capitalize on the vast knowledge accrued when hosting the Olympic Games. Therefore, an early version of a knowledge management program was implemented during the Sydney 2000 Olympic Games, which by 2005 came to be known as the Olympic Games Knowledge Management (OGKM) program. The main purpose of this initiative was to support existing local organizing committees (LOCs) and other stakeholders involved with the bidding and organization of the Olympic Games by providing them with information and knowledge about previous experiences regarding the planning, organization, and evaluation of the Games. As noted by Phillipe Blanchard (n.d.), director of information management in the IOC, the main purpose of the OGKM was to "reduce organizational risks, reduce organizational costs and complexity, enhance productivity, maintain and improve quality of the product, and improve service levels to stakeholders" (p. 36). Through the use of technology and training, the OGKM provides access to critical data and information and conducts workshops on a range of topics to people who are directly involved with the organization of the Games (Xi & Duncombe, 2016). Considering that the planning and organization of the Games involve relationships with an array of international organizations and people from all backgrounds and nationalities, training these professionals and volunteers requires not only transferring technical knowledge but also providing them with socialization and acculturation skills through cross-cultural awareness activities.

Over the course of seven years, most LOCs recruit several thousand professionals, many of whom are expatriates from all over the world. For example, the volunteer program in Rio 2016 included 36,000 volunteers from 100 countries, and in Pyeongchang 2018 there were 17,300 volunteers from 62 countries. Because a vast amount of knowledge is gained from organizing sport megaevents, LOCs treat the transfer and acquisition of this knowledge as a part of the legacy of the Games in the form of human capital (Holt & Ruta, 2015). Despite these efforts, critics of the OGKM program question the efficacy of some of the strategies used to transfer knowledge. Scholars from Oxford University complained that most of the information transferred to other LOCs "is often presented to host city staff in a language that is unfamiliar to them" (Boyes, 2016, p. 10). Other critics pointed out that some of the strategies transferred to train volunteers were based on the assumption that different countries and cultures embrace a similar volunteer culture. This problem arose for the Sochi 2014 Games when organizers found that strategies to recruit volunteers that worked in Australia did not work in Russia (Lockstone-Binney, Holmes, Shipway, & Smith, 2016). Although the OGKM program has not yet reached maturity, this initiative is undoubtedly going in the right direction. Preparing and training a diverse workforce involved in the operation of global venture is not an easy task, and it can be even more complex when the venture occurs in a relatively short time span.

---

negotiation and interaction of members throughout the temporary organization's management processes" (p. 233).

For both enduring and temporary organizations then, the aspect of organizational socialization becomes an important part of their job.

Three important stages mark the **organizational socialization** process for new employees: (1) anticipatory socialization (occurs before organizational entry), (2) encounter or accommodation (as the newcomer enters the organization), and (3) adaptation or role management (as the new-

Learning Activity

Conduct some research on the web and expand your understanding of what transfer of knowledge in sport events is about. Pay attention to the difference between information and knowledge and between tacit and implicit knowledge. Provide examples of the last two concepts in the context of a sport event.

Learning Activity

Discuss whether it is fair for an international sport organization to require all athletes to speak the same verbal language. Do they already share all the etiquette and rules of the game? Do you think that the inclusion of foreign athletes in professional leagues (e.g., the English Premier League in England or the National Basketball Association and the National Hockey League in the United States and Canada) hurts a league or makes it stronger?

comer adapts and settles into the job). Knowing these three important stages and the importance of organizational culture, HRM departments can use particular strategies to promote the message. The following activities are potential tools that management can use for these purposes (Cable & Parsons, 2001):

1. Collective socialization helps provide a common message about the organization, role clarity within various jobs, and appropriate responses for the new employees to be aware of. These elements are instructive right from the beginning. This activity helps reduce uncertainty concerning roles and can lead to a greater sense of shared values among people within the organization.

2. Formal tactics help provide a consistent message to new recruits and signal the importance of adapting to the new organizational environment, which may lead to shared values and reduce uncertainty about the job.

3. Sequential tactics provide information on the sequence of learning activities and experiences, which also help to reduce uncertainty about job tasks and responsibilities. Newcomers want to establish routines and a sense of personal control. This tactic can reduce the anxiety and stress associated with adjusting to a new environment and a different organizational culture.

4. Fixed tactics help provide information on the timing associated with completing each socialization stage. This tactic is similar to sequential

tactics in that it can reduce anxiety about the job as well as help newcomers develop a sense of control over their new environment.

5. Serial tactics provide experienced organizational members as role models or mentors who can help newcomers make sense of their environment and provide resources that they can turn to when in need of assistance. This tactic can help newcomers attain a sense of competence and task mastery.

6. Investiture tactics provide newcomers with positive social support from experienced organizational members. An important aspect of newcomer adjustment is gaining a sense of competence and confidence. Tactics that invest in newcomers by providing positive social feedback may help newcomers develop this sense of competence.

In essence, these tactics can provide common messaging and communicate the critical values and beliefs that shape organizational culture. Using such management strategies can ultimately lead to a better fit between the person and the organization. Further, when experienced organizational insiders are used in the socialization process as role models or mentors, turnover can be reduced. Including such tactics into the socialization process of new members can help the intercultural manager or employee avoid culture shock.

LPGA Requirement of English Test

In 2003 former Australian star at the LPGA (Ladies Professional Golf Association) Jan Stephenson said to *Golf Magazine*, "The Asians are killing our tour. Absolutely killing it. Their lack of emotion, their refusal to speak English when they can speak English. They rarely speak" (Blauvelt, 2003, p. 3). Although Stephenson publicly apologized for her comments, she exposed one of the challenges that foreign athletes face when they have to adapt to a new culture and communicate effectively with the media, fans, coaching staff, and teammates.

One of the most controversial policies regarding foreign athletes surfaced in August 2008 when the LPGA decided that foreign players who had been in the league for two or more years had to pass an oral English test. Failure would result in revocation of their membership. The LPGA, an American-based organization that in 2008 included 121 international players from 26 countries, including a large contingent of Korean players, believed that the proposed language policy was in the best interest of the league, players, and fans. The LPGA executives stated that in their business what really mattered was the player as a whole, not just the athlete. Accordingly, the LPGA claimed that if players were not able to communicate effectively in English with sponsors, media, and amateurs who paid big dollars to be with them during the pro-am tournaments, the entire business of the LPGA would suffer.

Critics pointed out that no other professional sport had implemented such a rule. Moreover, LPGA sponsors, such as insurance company State Farm and Choice Hotels International, openly condemned the measure (Wilson, 2008). For many, success in high-performance sport was to be accrued by merit of pure skill in the sport, not by any other means. After weeks of hot and controversial debate with lawmakers, sponsors, and other stakeholders, and after recognizing that a public relations disaster had occurred and that civil rights groups might sue, the LPGA overturned its original plan. Instead, the LPGA proposed a plan to provide and expand its cultural support to players who could not effectively communicate in English. Although the LPGA's original idea to establish an English language requirement was overthrown and today is part of history, this incident shows how the lack of cultural awareness can result in a major public relationship fiasco.

Reflecting on the global reach of the LPGA, Brian Carroll, vice president for television and emerging media for the LPGA, commented in 2014,

> We have tournaments in Australia, Thailand, Singapore, France, the UK, China, Canada, Mexico, Malaysia, Korea, Japan, and Taiwan. And our players are from all over the world, too. We have language-specific sites for Chinese, Korean, Spanish, German, and Japanese, with another one to be announced soon. (Gregg, 2014, pp. 53-54)

When asked about the infamous English-speaking test, he said, "I think we're past that. Many of our players (voluntarily) learn other languages. We have a Language Training Center onsite each week for those who want to do that" (p. 54).

Summary

Today's sport managers need to understand the various ways in which people from different countries and diverse backgrounds can work together in an efficient and effective manner. As a result, when working with foreign personnel, sport managers must first strive to understand who they are and what values they hold. The sport manager involved in human resources, coaching, or instruction of any kind must demonstrate a genuine sense of appreciation and sensitivity for the person who, while bringing superb technical skills, might also bring a set of values that challenge the status quo. Consequently, sport managers who are involved with an international workforce need to have sophisticated communication skills to work well with others.

Although people make the difference within organizations, the culture of every organization is built from an array of influences not always directly initiated by people within it. Influences include various institutional forces that have been shaped over a long period not only within the organization but also from the wider environment. Because organizational culture is essentially made up of the values, beliefs, and assumptions about why an organization is what it is, it plays a critical role in informing intercultural management practices. By simply observing how things are done in an organization, a new employee can obtain valuable information about what is appropriate and what is not in terms of business behavior. But to gain a true understanding of work behavior, the person must engage deeply with the people in the organization to determine work expectations and objectives. In addition, knowing that an organizational culture is also influenced to some degree by the national culture, the new employee working overseas should become acquainted with the national culture to learn how it might influence the way that business is conducted in that country (e.g., greetings, meetings, socializing outside work, general values).

Intercultural management practices can also be facilitated through a series of socialization tactics, which typically occur in three stages. By including formal tactics of socialization within the overall strategy of intercultural management practices, sport managers can significantly help new employees become better acquainted with the new environ-ment. Socialization tactics can reduce stress and culture shock and facilitate a better fit between the employee and the organization.

Carte and Fox (2004) noted that misunderstanding and conflict between people of different cultures and between compatriots occur when people focus exclusively on their own agendas and do not consider others in their decision making. Sport managers who travel to foreign countries to do business knowing that they will encounter misunderstandings and communications challenges can alleviate some unnecessary conflict. Being alert to interpersonal obstacles can make or break a business transaction. Successful people, whether in business, industry, government, or science, know that in their relations with other cultures no specific values or behaviors are universally right. A successful global sport manager must remain flexible and open to accept differences in values, beliefs, and ways of doing things. In addition, she or he must be sensitive to verbal nuances and nonverbal signals, and be knowledgeable about religious, business, and social practices of other cultures. These and other steps will assist the sport manager in reducing the frictions, challenges, and confusion that typically emanate from poor intercultural management practices.

Review Questions

1. What factors does a sport manager need to consider when involved in an intercultural management setting?
2. Describe what is meant by ethnocentric behavior.
3. Define national culture and organizational culture. In what ways might these two types of culture overlap in a sport management setting?
4. Which aspects of organizational culture can be readily identified as describing what is valued within an organization?
5. How can a human resource manager ease the transition of a new person (e.g., athlete or coach) into the organization?
6. What strategies might you consider using if you are to host a new employee who has relocated from another country?

Macroeconomics of International Sport

Holger Preuss, PhD
University Mainz, Germany

Kevin Heisey, PhD
American University in the Emirates

Chapter Objectives

After studying this chapter, you will be able to do the following:

- Explain the general importance of sport in the economy.
- Identify the fundamental ways that sport influences the macroeconomy.
- Distinguish between tangible and intangible benefits.
- Determine the primary economic impact of sport on an economy.
- Explain the induced impact, or multiplier, effect.
- Discuss short-term, long-term, and legacy effects of international sport events.

Key Terms

consumer surplus

crowding out

induced impact

intangible benefit

legacy effect

multiplier effect

Pareto improvement

Pareto optimal

primary impact

tangible benefit

In the science of economics, the macroeconomic perspective is the broad perspective, considering the economy of a nation (or other defined political or geographic area) as a whole. This viewpoint is distinct from microeconomics, which considers the economic situations and decisions of a firm or a household to allocate limited resources. Macroeconomists study aggregate indicators such as the national production and income measure gross domestic product (GDP), import and export, unemployment rates, and price indices to understand how the whole economy functions and develops over time (that is, business cycles in the short run and economic growth in the long run). For this purpose, a focus of macroeconomic investigation is the interplay of aggregate supply (production) and demand (consumption) of the whole economy and on its submarkets (on the one hand, collective sectors of similar production and single industries, and on the other hand, final demand of private consumers and corporate demand of primary and intermediary products). The relevant data that macroeconomists need for their work are collected in detail by the national accounting in terms of the monetary values composing the GDP calculation. The key message of macroeconomics is that (developed) economies are huge, complex, and highly interconnected structures of a multitude of individual decisions that, additionally, are closely linked with the rest of the world by international trade. The ultimate aim and result of macroeconomic analysis are therefore to provide knowledge, data, and advice for political and corporate decision makers to cope effectively with this complexity.

This chapter focuses on the role of sport in a country's economy. The economic importance of sport relative to the rest of a country's economy is discussed first. Next comes an account of the fundamental ways in which sport influences an economy through the creation of sport-related goods and services. Important distinctions are made between tangible and intangible economic benefits associated with sport and the ways in which both types of benefits affect an economy. A focus on mega sport events such as the Olympics and the FIFA World Cup is used to illustrate the process of how primary economic impacts of sport can work through an economy, leading to potentially greater total impacts. Shown as well are the characteristics of an economy that make induced economic impacts

more likely. These megaevents can be economically significant and provide comprehensive examples of the effects of sport on the economy because they are temporary. Using megaevents as examples, we can see how an initial intervention of spending on sport builds up and works its way through the economy. Finally, long- and short-term economic benefits from sport and the legacy effect that remains after a sport event has concluded are discussed.

Role of Sport in a National Economy

From the macroeconomic perspective on sport an important question arises: Does sport contribute to increases in economic well-being in the overall economy, and if it does, how significant are the increases or how many jobs does sport create? In absolute terms, the economic impact associated with sport appears quite large, but relative to the economy as a whole the economic significance of sport is rather low.

In Europe some countries measure the economic importance of sport in their economy as is required by the European Union. Table 18.1 illustrates the magnitude of sport in selected European national economies.

Global spending on sport events (including tickets, media rights, and sponsorship), for instance, was US$80 billion, and adding in sport equipment, apparel, footwear, and fitness brings the total spent on sport to nearly US$700 billion in 2014, representing almost 1 percent of the global GDP (A.T. Kearney, 2014). Developed countries typically spend from 1 to 4 percent of their GDP for sport. Indeed, such minor relative figures are found for most economic sectors and industries, but they may not necessarily be insignificant for the functioning and growth of the economy as a whole, given the interconnectedness within the economy. Keep in mind that large national economies account for trillions of dollars. Thus, even big multibillion-dollar businesses account for only an extremely small percentage of a country's total economy.

When considering the role of sport in the economy, differentiating between benefits that accrue to a particular group and benefits that accrue to the economy as a whole is important. Economists use the term *Pareto optimal*, which is an outcome or state in an economy in which no member of the

Table 18.1 Sport Figures for Selected European National Economies

	Austria	Cyprus	Poland	United Kingdom	Netherlands	Germany
	2005	2004	2006	2010	2010	2010
Employment (millions)						
Sport related	0.242	0.007	0.225	0.639	0.15	1.847
Percent of total	6.4	2.2	1.54	2.2	1.7	4.6
Gross added value (billions Euros)						
Sport related	10.7	0.3	5.3	39.4	5.4	77.4
Percent of total	4.9	2.4	2	2.7	1.0	3.5
Household consumption (billions Euros)						
Sport related	4.9	0.3	3.5	31.0	7.5	92.2
Percent of total	3.6	3.7	2.1	3.0	2.7	6.8

Data from European Commission (2011); Statistics Netherland (2015); Department of Culture, Media, and Sports (2015); Ahlert and an der Heiden (2015).

economy can be made better off without making another member worse off (Pareto, 1971, p. 261). A Pareto optimal outcome means that for a given amount of resources (natural resources, knowledge, talent, number of people, or any other productive resource) the economy is producing as much benefit as possible. No unexploited opportunities remain that could make somebody better off. When the economy is at a Pareto optimal outcome, the only way that a person can improve his or her situation occurs at the expense of somebody else.

Applied to sport, consider an economy that hosts a sport event and assume that the people who spend money to attend the event would have otherwise spent the same amount of money on dinner and a movie if the sport event had not occurred. The organizers of the sport event are better off, but only at the expense of the restaurant and movie theatre owners. In this case, overall well-being in the economy has not improved; the reallocation of money has simply caused a shift of economic activity between sectors. An enhancement of overall well-being in an economy is called a **Pareto improvement**, an improvement in economic well-being that does not come at the expense of others (Varian, 2010, p. 17). When considering the economic impact of sport on an economy, we have to be able to distinguish an increase in well-being in the overall economy (Pareto improvement) from a shift of well-being between sectors or individuals within an economy.

The benefits of sport to an economy can be categorized as either quantifiable (**tangible benefits**) or nonquantifiable (**intangible benefits**). It is possible to measure the amount of tangible economic activity related to a sport event, team, or facility in monetary terms. As noted earlier, the tangible impact of sport is relatively low compared with that of other sectors of the economy. Sport, however, brings many nonquantifiable (intangible) benefits that often lead to indirect economic benefits. For example, if a sport event motivates children to increase participation in sport, overall health costs may decrease. If people reduce stress by watching sports, productivity at work may increase and the illness rate may decrease. Vice-versa, a Super Bowl final or a FIFA World Cup winner can decrease productivity because of distraction from work. Nations rally around and take pride in their sport teams, facilities, and the events that they host. Most Germans will never forget the 2014 FIFA World Cup, whereas they probably have no recollection of how top retailer Edeka fares from year to year.

It is often said that hosting a mega sporting event like the FIFA World Cup or the Olympic Games puts a city or country "on the map." In the United States, having a major professional sport franchise is often seen as making a community a "big-league city." Measuring the monetary value of the benefits of being on the map or being a big-league city is difficult, but the benefits clearly exist, are likely to be significant, and could far outweigh any tangible benefits that can be more easily measured.

But sport should never be seen as an economic panacea or as a major component of an economic development policy. Although hosting an international mega sport event can bring tangible economic benefits, they are small relative to the economy as a whole and their impact is short lived. The 2014 FIFA World Cup in Brazil increased the Brazilian GDP by only 0.09 percent that year (Preuss, 2014). The intangible benefits of hosting such an event are likely more significant. Increased happiness, improved image of the city or country as a place to visit or do business, education of people, emotional consumption, and the investments that some hotels and restaurants make are among the intangible benefits that seem to make up the major effect of hosting a megaevent. The unique quality of sport and competition is its universal nature. Little else in society has an appeal as broad as that of a major sport event such as the great marathons in the cities of Berlin and New York, or international football or Olympic competition. People across cultures and ages can enjoy, appreciate, and celebrate the excitement of athletic competition. This effect is a major benefit of a sport event.

Macroeconomic Effects of Sport

A useful practice is to examine and categorize the ways that sport influences the macroeconomy. What are the goods and services provided by sport? (See table 18.2.) Goods are physical items that are sold. The goods that make up sport's influence on the economy are consumption goods and investment goods. Examples of services related to sport are entertainment; instruction, coaching, and officiating; and sport travel and tourism.

Consumption Goods

A consumption good is something that an individual consumer purchases for use, such as a sports drink, which he or she physically consumes, or sportswear and equipment that is consumed over time. If the good is directly related to the sport, we call it a direct consumption good. Table 18.3 presents global sales of major categories of direct consumption goods. Sport also contributes to indirect consumption spending, which is spending on consumption goods that are not directly sport related but would not have been made without

Table 18.2 Examples of Goods and Services in Sport

Type	Examples
	Goods
Consumption, direct	Equipment, apparel, nutrition, sports drinks
Consumption, indirect	Transportation, lodging, concessions
Investment, direct	Facilities: golf course, tennis court, stadium, arena
Investment, indirect	Parking, clubhouse, ski lodge
	Services
Professional sport	Coaches, personal trainers, referees
Tourism	Travel and tour agencies, skiing instructors
Entertainment	Spectator sport, media broadcasts, sport shows

Table 18.3 Global Sales of Sport Direct Consumption Goods

Direct consumption good	Global sales
Sporting goods—apparel, footwear, equipment, health and fitness	US$619 billion (2014)
Licensed sport products	US$24.9 billion (2015)
Sports drinks	20.68 billion liters (2014)

Data from A.T. Kearney (2014), International Licensing Industry Merchants Association (LIMA) (2016).

the sport event. Transportation to and from sport events is an example of indirect consumption spending that is generated by sport. Other examples of indirect consumption expenditures that are significant to sport are spending on food, beer, soft drinks, and lodging that occurs because of sport events and tournaments. Sport-related spending on consumption goods is often linked to the heavy sport sponsorship and advertising spending by the companies in industries such as beer and sport apparel companies.

Investment Goods

Investment goods are items to be used by many consumers over a long period. Their key feature is that they are designed to result in increased future productive economic activity. All the for-profit facilities or parks where sport is played are considered direct investment goods. Prominent examples are stadiums such as Emirates Stadium in North London, which cost £430 million (US$790 million) (Arsenal Holdings plc, 2007) and the O_2 World Arena in Berlin, which cost €165 million (US$260 million) (Nolan, 2008). Over 13 billion ZAR (US$1.6 billion) was spent on new stadiums and upgrades to existing stadiums before the 2010 FIFA World Cup in South Africa (Bayoli & Bekker, 2011). But sometimes sport facilities for megaevents are not used afterward and therefore the investment was unsuccessful. Examples are the Green Point stadium in Cape Town and the football stadium in Manaus (Brazil). We can often see what kind of sports are popular in an area when flying in an airplane by looking down at the golf courses, baseball fields, tennis courts, football pitches, and swimming pools, all of which would be considered small-scale sport investment goods. Sport equipment may also be considered investment goods in the case when it is used to earn money. For example, a tennis trainer's racket or a professional golf player's equipment is an investment good because the person uses it for financial returns, whereas the same equipment used for leisure sport is considered a consumption good.

Examples of indirect investment goods that can be attributed to sport are parking areas, transportation hubs, lodging at ski resorts, and clubhouses that are built as part of or next to sport facilities in many parts of the world. Other indirect investment goods are all the machines that produce sport equipment and apparel. Although none of these expenditures are directly caused by sport, they would not exist without sport.

Services

Sport-related services that are sold can be directly related to a sport, such as tennis instruction, coaching, umpiring or refereeing, personal training, and setting up and managing a recreational sport league. Tourist agencies that focus on sport-related tours are another example of a sport-related service. Backroads, an outfitter based in Berkeley, California, that specializes in active holidays, led approximately 30,000 people on 2,500 biking, hiking, and multisport tours worldwide in 2014 (Olmstead, 2015).

The final service is entertainment, which is the raison d'être for spectator sport. People pay to attend and follow sport events so that they can be entertained, and entertainment is the product that sport leagues sell. The media, whether it presents events, reports results, presents highlights, recaps and discusses past events, or predicts the outcome of future events, is also selling entertainment. Modern events are packaged and presented through various media so that millions of people worldwide can enjoy them simultaneously. Television, radio, live Internet video streaming, and other new media allow major sport events to entertain people around the globe. The next several sections focus on international sport megaevents. Study of these short-term interventions in an economy can increase our understanding of the macroeconomic effects of sport.

Tangible and Intangible Effects

An additional characteristic that is a key to understanding the macroeconomic effects of sport activities is the distinction between tangible and intangible effects. Tangible economic effects are often defined as those that can be measured in monetary terms, but it is more accurate to define them as those that can be easily measured in units. Clearly, if an event drew 50,000 nonregional visitors to the region and those visitors spent on average $200 each attending the event, then a measurable $10,000,000 of spending was brought into the regional economy by the visitors who came to the event. And we can also measure air quality, noise levels, and traffic counts that are affected by the existence of a sport event. All those elements contribute to the overall

CASE STUDY

Manchester United: Superstar Effect and the Global Sport Economy

In recent years technology has redefined the potential export market for sport. American baseball games can be watched live on the Internet by streaming video for a relatively modest fee on MLB.com. Likewise, American soccer fans have affordable access through cable or satellite television to the Spanish La Liga de Futbol Profesional, the German Bundesliga, and UEFA Cup qualifying matches. The NBA attracts a television viewing audience in China that may soon rival its audience in the United States.

The access and affordability that arise from technology contribute to what economists call the superstar effect. The logic behind the superstar effect is that, all things being equal, consumers want to consume the very best of a product if they have the option. It follows, then, that because sport is mostly consumed by live video, consumers who have affordable access to many viewing options will likely choose the highest quality sport. If sport fans at home, with a click of the remote, can watch the best leagues, teams, and athletes in the world, those leagues, teams, and athletes will become increasingly popular globally. Therefore, the potential target market and audience for the most successful entities in sport is enormous.

The popular English Premier League powerhouse Manchester United is a great example of how large a sport club's export market can be. According to a survey of 54,000 people in 39 countries conducted by market research company Kantar, the club was identified as the favorite team of an estimated 659 million fans around the globe (Manchester United FC, 2012). U.S.-based businesses like General Motors and 20th Century Fox do not enter sponsor partnerships with Manchester United to reach the relatively minor United Kingdom market or the 76,000 fans who pack Old Trafford for each home match. They do it to reach a global audience. After signing a record jersey sponsorship deal with the club, General Motors director of global marketing Megan Stooke said, "Chevrolet as a global brand is really trying to strengthen its position in the emerging markets. When you look at the fan base of Manchester United, one of the world's most popular sports brands, we saw a great alignment in those markets" (Baxter, 2014). Manchester United, through the superstar effect, is using technology to export its product to the entire global market, while bringing additional autonomous spending to the United Kingdom economy.

---

impact on the economy, so a more inclusive definition that includes a greater number of effects that can be measured in units is a more accurate definition of tangible economic effects.

Intangible economic effects are those that cannot be measured in units, but they are important because they often make up the most significant economic impact of a sport event. Examples of intangible effects are local pride (either in the success of a local site or the ability of the city to host a major event or both), happiness, motivation and other psychological effects, local image, cultural identity, increased know-how, reduction of crime, changes in pollution levels and environmental quality, or option value (the benefit of knowing that you, your family, friends, or offspring have the option to use and benefit from a resource, even if you currently choose not to) (Asafu-Adjaye, 2005, p. 111).

Intangible benefits can be enormous for individuals and for societies as a whole. As an example, for the 2010 FIFA World Cup in South Africa, the South African team's multiethnic roster and the country's hosting the world helped heal racial divisions (Cornelissen et al., 2011). Evaluating the extent of the intangible benefit derived from 2010 World Cup showed that it was clearly significant (Knott et al., 2012).

Because intangible effects are difficult to measure and, as stated earlier, are often the most significant benefits that an economy derives from sport, devising ways to estimate intangible benefits is a growing area of research in the field of sport economics. This effort is all the more important when considering that substantial intangible benefits may even arise in economic market transactions by exchanging dollars between sellers and buyers of a sport com-

Estimating the Intangible Economic Benefits of Sport

The intangible benefits associated with sport are clearly significant and may overshadow any tangible economic benefits. Residents of a city that hosts a major event do not have to spend money on the actual event or even consume it to enjoy its benefits, whether it is through the excitement generated by the event or civic pride in the successful hosting effort. A movement has developed among economists to estimate the magnitude of the intangible benefits.

An increasingly common method of evaluating indirectly intangible benefits associated with sport is the contingent valuation method (CVM). The CVM was originally developed as a way for environmental economists to estimate the value of the benefits of environmental goods, like water quality or air quality, not normally bought and sold in a market. The essence of the CVM is for researchers to create a hypothetical market scenario that describes varying levels of the intangible good being studied and provides a payment method used to attain more of the good. A statistically significant number of people are chosen by a random sample in the appropriate geographic area and are asked how much they would be willing to pay for increased levels of the good. For example, respondents could be asked how much additional sales tax they would be willing to pay for an increased level of air quality.

Some examples of studies that used the CVM to estimate the intangible benefit enjoyed by host citizens as the result of an international megaevent are Atkinson, Mourato, Szymanski, and Ozdemiro-glu (2008) and Heyne, Maennig, and Suessmuth (2007). Atkinson et al. interviewed 602 residents of London, 152 residents of Glasgow, and 151 residents of Manchester to estimate the intangible benefit experienced by United Kingdom residents of London's hosting of the 2012 Olympic Games. They estimated that the willingness to pay in increased taxes (among Londoners) and donations (for the rest of the country) is just short of £2 billion (US$3.98 billion), which roughly approximates the planned public expenditure of £2.375 billion (US$4.726 billion) at the time of their study.

Heyne et al. surveyed German residents before and after the FIFA World Cup 2006. Their hypothesis was that any increase in willingness to pay after experiencing the event could be described as the money value of the intangible experience. They found that the difference between residents' willingness to pay before and after the event amounted to €495 million (US$634 million) for the entire country. The result is interpreted as an additional intangible benefit on top of the €351 million (US$449 million) that people were willing to pay before they experienced the event.

Countries and cities that are considering hosting events should consider all the relevant benefits and costs associated with the events so that they can make sound policy decisions. The intangible benefits are clearly significant for major international events; therefore, efforts to measure and quantify those benefits can play a key role in providing criteria to key decision makers.

---

modity or service. An example of such an intangible effect is the change in a consumer's surplus associated with sport. Simply defined, **consumer surplus** is the net benefit from consuming a discrete good or service (Varian, 2010, p. 253). For example if a cricket fan is willing to pay $100 to attend a test but is able to purchase a ticket for $75, economists say that she enjoys $25 of consumer surplus, because attending the match is worth $100 to her but she paid only $75. If a person freely makes a purchase, then it can be assumed that she is enjoying consumer surplus greater than or equal to 0. Except when a person is paying exactly the maximum that she is willing to pay, consumer surplus will be positive. In another example, suppose that a person pays $100 for a ticket with a $20 face value to attend a sold-out event. The person was not forced to pay an exorbitant price to attend the event, because he could have chosen not to purchase the ticket. Attending the event is clearly worth at least $100 to him. If he buys a ticket for $20, he would enjoy at least $80 worth of consumer surplus.

Why is consumer surplus significant in examining the macroeconomic effect of sport? When measuring tangible benefits, economists normally do not consider expenditures on sport made by people who ordinarily spend their money in the economy as additions to tangible economic benefit. Logically, those people normally spend their money in the economy anyway, so the existence of a sport option only causes their economic activity to shift within the economy, not add expenditure to the economy. But when considering overall economic well-being or welfare through the framework of consumer surplus, if people are choosing to spend their time and money on sport, we can assume that they are enjoying greater consumer surplus than they otherwise would have. For simplicity's sake, if we assume that all entertainment options cost the same, although we cannot readily measure consumer surplus (unless consumers are willing to tell us their maximum willingness to pay to attend each event), we can infer from their choices which event gives consumers the most surplus—it is the event that they choose to attend. So, if members of the local economy are choosing to attend sport events rather than other entertainment options available to them, although their actions do not represent a net increase in spending in the economy, they do represent an increase in consumer surplus and therefore an increase in economic well-being.

Therefore, a macroeconomic income measure like the GDP does not completely reflect the welfare of a nation, although in the public debate it is often seen and used as an indicator of well-being. But this notion refers to the microeconomic concept of utility like the consumer surplus, which is difficult to measure and is not an explicit object of macroeconomic analysis. In contrast, the GDP may rise while the social utility falls and vice versa. For instance, sport injuries can be clearly qualified as undesirable and as causing diminished welfare. Yet an injury enhances the sport-related GDP by expenditures for doctors, medicine, surgeries, and so forth. Such unpleasant incidents that increase total income are called "bads" in macroeconomic national accounting. The opposite effect can also occur if, for example, prices tend to fall because of enhanced competition from foreign companies in the sports shoe industry. The buyers benefit from a rise in their consumer surplus, whereas the increase in imports reduces the GDP. Thus, the GDP is simply the aggregated reflection of all money flows in the economy at current prices that are observable in the market place and recorded in the national accounting. The GDP does not incorporate any judgment or (normative) evaluation of the underlying occurrences as being positive or negative for society. Likewise, the national income could be extremely unevenly distributed among individuals, which may be perceived as unjust. Ultimately, the GDP can only tell us whether a country is rich or poor in terms of money circulating in the economy (that is, the part of social utility that actually materializes in monetary values) or whether an economy is growing or shrinking during a certain period.

Primary Impact of a Sport Event

It is useful to think of the economic impact of sport in terms of a simplified version of Keynes' circular flow model of an open economy (Mankiw, 2015, p. 141). For simplicity's sake, we assume that government is neutral in this example.

$$Y = C + I + (X - M)$$

Where:

Y = the size of the economy measured as total income

C = total consumption spending in the economy

I = total investment spending in the economy

X = total export spending in the economy, or the sale of goods produced in the economy to people outside the economy

M = total import spending in the economy, or the purchases by people in the economy of goods produced outside the economy

(X − M) = net exports

Using this model we can think of changes to total consumption spending (C), investment spending (I), or net exports (X − M) resulting in changes to the overall size of the economy. As mentioned before, changes in the patterns of consumption or investment spending that amount to a shift in spending among sectors in the economy would not result in a change in the size of the economy. Changes in net exports, however, would directly result in changes to total income level for the economy.

For a closer look at net exports, consider the Olympic Games, which trigger economic impacts

Learning Activity

Research the security expenditures for the 2016 Rio de Janeiro Olympics. List three ways in which those expenditures affected the Brazilian macroeconomy and three ways in which they affected the South American macroeconomy.

all around the world but cause the strongest impact in the host nation and the host city. The **primary impact** is the change in consumption, investment, and export spending that can be attributed directly to the sport event. Obviously, the calculation of the impact of the Rio de Janeiro 2016 Olympics on Brazil or the city of Rio does not include the payments of national sponsors in Australia or expenditures to dress and equip the South African Olympic team. But the calculation becomes complex when indirect effects, such as the change of infrastructure in Beijing for an Olympic Training Centre itself, have to be considered. To isolate the primary regional economic impact from the total primary impact, each flow of money has to be analyzed.

A matrix of four variables can be used to calculate the regional primary impact and Olympic expenditures for a sector in the economy or category of expenditure. The origin of spending can be autonomous (coming in from outside the area) or regional (from people already living in the area), and the money can be spent regionally (stays in the area as income) or on imports (leaves the region). For example, an Australian Olympic tourist spends money in a local restaurant during the Olympics in Rio 2016. The tourist's expenditure is considered autonomous spending (a) and therefore creates a regional benefit, because fresh money enters the city (R). The origin, autonomous (a) or regional (r), and destination, region (R) or import (I), of each expenditure determine whether a regional economic impact occurs (Preuss, 2004). Each expenditure can create one of the four following effects:

1. Benefits: Autonomous spending means that fresh money from outside the region is spent and stays in the region (a × R).

2. Costs: Regional spending used for imports and that leaves the region (r × I).

3. Reallocations: Regional funds that are spent in the region (r × R). To be precise, reallocations also can create economic costs and benefits. If regional funds are spent in another industrial sector than they would have been without the sport event and if that sector has stronger (weaker) "creation of value," benefits (costs) will occur. For example, spending on a product that was produced in the region creates more value in the economy when compared with spending on a product that was imported. The economy will always have winners and losers even though the size of the total economy may remain unchanged. Recall from earlier that although the reallocation of money is neutral to the macroeconomy in monetary terms, it may result in higher consumer surplus.

4. Neutrals: Autonomous funds that are used for imports (a × I). To be precise, neutrals can indirectly create economic costs and benefits. The streams of money are neutral because the autonomous money is directly spent for imports and does not remain in the region as income. Something was imported, however, and that can create follow-up costs or benefits. For example, a sport arena financed by the state government and constructed by a foreign company for the Olympics is a neutral stream of money for the host city. After the Games the arena hosts other events that entertain citizens, but it has to be maintained. So those effects are considered postevent costs and benefits.

Each sport-related stream of money therefore will be split into four parts: (1) direct benefits, (2) direct costs, (3) reallocations within the economy to value-increasing sectors or value-decreasing sectors, and (4) neutrals. The sum of these effects forms the primary regional impact for the period considered.

Note that the primary regional impact can be negative. If net exports to the region are negative, which means that the region imported more than it exported for the event, and spending is reallocated from value-increasing sectors within the region to sectors outside the region, the event will lead to a negative economic impact, even if gross spending is significant. If a self-sustaining extreme sport festival comes to town—that is, the promoters provide their own setup, teardown, ticket and refreshment sales, and so forth—the economic impact of the festival would be to generate spending that is removed from the local economy and taken with the promoters, performers, and staff. In other words, despite generating a great deal of economic activity, the festival would take money from the economy and the direct economic impact would be negative. This effect is often a concern for cities that host professional sport teams that generate a lot of the money from regional spectators. The money goes to the team owner and the players, who may not spend the money in the region.

Export of Services

Tourism spending as a result of hosting a sport event is considered an export of service and a benefit to the regional economy. The service being exported is the entertainment of the event or other tourist attractions associated with the event. The nonlocal or foreign visitors literally take the service back home; that is, they import it to their region or country of origin, in the form of consumed food, memories, good feelings, and photos. This service is considered an export because it is created within the region and is paid for and enjoyed by people from outside the regional economy. The result is autonomous money entering the region from outside and an increase in economic benefit to the host region. But it is important to consider whether the tourist would have visited the region if the event had not taken place (Preuss, 2005). The proper calculation of the primary impact of tourist spending has to be done with great care to avoid double counting of visitor spending as well as to avoid erroneously counting the spending of those who do not bring fresh money into the region.

Import Spending

Money paid to outside construction firms hired to build sport facilities and event infrastructure is considered import spending. To the extent that Qatar uses foreign construction companies in its buildup to hosting the 2022 FIFA World Cup, it is importing services from outside its economy (the manpower and know-how of architects, civil engineers, skilled construction workers, and others coming into the country). That spending can be a cost to the host economy if Qatar's spending is leaving the country, or it can represent money passing through the economy because of the event. If sponsorship money originating from outside the country was used on construction provided by firms from outside of the country, then the direct monetary effect passed through the host economy. Recall, however, that the existence of the new facilities and infrastructure will result in future benefits and costs for the host economy. Moreover, wages for local construction workers or expenses for local subcontractors paid by the foreign company will stay in the economy and thereby create an inflow of money.

Import Substitution

The final example explains the case of import substitution (Cobb & Weinberg, 1993). Coca-Cola, which has its headquarters in Atlanta, Georgia, host of the 1996 Olympics, is one of the major sponsors of international sport events. Because Coca-Cola is an Atlanta company, we might think that any of its sponsorship dollars that ended up with the Atlanta Olympic Organizing Committee could not be considered a net gain in spending for the Atlanta regional economy. But this special case of import substitution represents additional spending in the local economy. As a primary Olympic sponsor, Coca-Cola spends dollars sponsoring the Olympics no matter where they are held. If the 1996 Games had been awarded to Athens, Greece, the runner-up in the selection process, Coca-Cola sponsorship dollars would have been spent in Athens rather than Atlanta. In effect, for the typical Olympic Games, Coca-Cola is importing an association with the Olympics from the host city. When the Games were held in Atlanta, the sponsorship money stayed in the region instead of being spent elsewhere. Coca-Cola's typical import spending on the association with the Olympics stayed at home in 1996 and resulted in a gain in spending to the local economy because had the Games not been held in Atlanta, Coca-Cola's dollars would have gone to the alternate host city.

Multiplier Effect

Besides the primary regional impact of an event on an economy, we must also consider the **induced impact**, which is the additional change in consumption, investment, and export spending that results from the initial change in spending working its way through the economy. To understand induced impact, we must recognize the concept of the **multiplier effect**. The multiplier effect can be described as an increase in spending that leads

CASE STUDY

Economic Impact of a FIFA World Cup Stadium in Manaus, Amazonas

The Amazon Arena built for the 2014 FIFA World Cup in Manaus, Brazil, is an interesting case of the immediate and long-term economic impacts of megaevent facilities. Manaus was the most geographically remote World Cup site, located in the heart of the rainforest in the state of Amazonas. The city is primarily accessible by airplane or boat. The case is an example of Brazil internal power politics and meeting FIFA requirements to spread match sites around the host country and provide stadiums that seat more than 40,000 spectators. The city and in particular its governor saw the event as an opportunity to develop the infrastructure of Manaus (airport, roads) and to promote tourism and demonstrate accessibility in what they see as an undervisited region. Although Brazil is well known for the Amazon, only 10 percent of visitors to the country travel to the region (CCTV.com, 2014).

Despite the fact that the local professional soccer teams competed in lower-division leagues and typically drew fewer than 1,000 spectators per match (Ormiston, 2014), US$300 million was spent building the new stadium on the site of a demolished old stadium (Manfred, 2015). The clear benefits were the local construction jobs provided and investments in indirect World Cup infrastructure (airport and so on), the influx of tourists in 2014, and the global media exposure during the World Cup, when five European countries (Croatia, England, Italy, Portugal, and Switzerland) and the United States played in the four games hosted by Manaus. The state authorities hope that the attention "will persuade a whole new generation of travelers that you don't have to be especially adventurous, or rich" to visit there (CCTV.com, 2014).

A key issue, however, is the ongoing cost of maintaining the stadium and its post–World Cup use. Estimates of the monthly maintenance and operating costs range from US$233,000 to US$250,000 (Garcia-Navarro, 2015; Ormiston, 2014). These costs are out of reach for the local, lower-level professional soccer clubs. The clubs in the Amazon not only draw small crowds compared with those in other Brazilian states but also have lower family overall expenditures and typically pay higher prices for household staples because of transportation costs and the remoteness of the region (TechinBrazil, 2015). The local population is likely unable to afford the level of ticket prices and leisure expenditure that would make the stadium feasible long term. Low spectator figures also bring into question the amount of fresh money that will enter the city.

Although the stadium hosted Rio de Janeiro 2016 Olympic matches, some national team friendlies, and FIFA World Cup qualifiers, it has seen little use since the 2014 World Cup (Manfred, 2015). The initial plan was for the state to sell the facility to private operators, but so far, there have been no takers. The initial construction spending (with a majority of money from the central government), 2014 visitors, and any that follow in the coming decade were a positive economic impact for Manaus, but that benefit doesn't represent a net impact for Brazil. It represents shifting of economic activity within the country. Although the city of Manaus benefits from these shifts, Brazil as a country does not. It remains to be seen whether the long-term maintenance and operating costs of the stadium will outweigh any benefit that the region enjoyed. Today, the proposition looks questionable at best.

to an increase in the size of the overall economy that is a multiple of the original increase (Mankiw 2015, p. 483). The basic reason that the eventual change in the size of the economy is a multiple of the initial increase in spending is that one person's spending is another person's income. When visitors spend their money in the local economy, the spending results in increased income for members of the local economy, who in turn increase their spending, which further increases other peoples' incomes, and so on. In its most basic form, the multiplier is determined by the propensity of people to consume the additional money that they receive. If they are more likely to save their extra money or spend it outside their region, the multiplier effect will be smaller. If they are more likely to spend it, the multiplier effect will be larger.

Learning Activity

Investigate the general economies of the Republic of South Africa or Brazil and Germany to determine how the economic impact of the 2010 or 2014 FIFA World Cup differed from the economic impact of the 2006 FIFA World Cup on the respective host nations.

The total economic impact of a sport event on a region consists of the primary regional impact (the direct effect) times the multiplier (the induced effect). In the usual case of a positive total effect, the value of the multiplier is at least larger than one. A neutral effect would give a multiplier that is equal or close to unity because the initial economic injection to the region would remain (nearly) the same, even after the circular process described earlier. Note that the multiplier is influenced by many factors, particularly the characteristics of the local economy. UK Sport, which conducts economic impact studies of sport events hosted in the United Kingdom, does not consider the multiplier effect when reporting results. Because the purpose of their studies is to compare the economic impact of many hosted events and because the multiplier is a characteristic of the regional economy and not the event, UK Sport focuses only on the primary regional impact and therefore is underestimating the total impact.

The main factors influencing the magnitude of the multiplier effect are the diversity and size of the economy. A mature, diverse economy will have a greater multiplier effect than a developing economy because more of the spending can be captured in a diverse economy and therefore the leakage is smaller. Such economies provide more productive opportunities to spend money that is earned from the initial injection or from induced income in the following rounds of spending. So, the medium- and long-term productivity of economic activities where the funds go is an important determinant of the multiplier.

The multiplier effect is similarly influenced by the breadth of the definition of the regional economy. The extra spending that makes up the primary regional impact is much more likely to stay in the region if the defined region is large. In other words, the mentioned leakages are smaller. Only diversified national economies have the potential to create multiplier effects as large as 2.5 to 3.0.

The economic situation affects the multiplier as well. If the economy is close to full employment, the multiplier will be lower than it would be if many resources were underemployed (unemployed labor, idle equipment, unused building materials). For an economy close to full employment, additional economic activity is more likely to result in **crowding out** of existing economic activity (Mankiw, 2015, p. 486), resulting in less induced impact and a lower multiplier. In contrast, if many resources are underemployed and crowding out does not occur, the multiplier will be much higher. Therefore, the multiplier depends on the macroeconomic business cycle (how close the regional economy is to full employment) at the time of the highest event expenditures as well as the overall maturity, diversity, and productivity of the economy and the productivity of the activities on which the money is spent.

The total economic impact (primary regional impact times the multiplier) for all one-off projects, such as mega sport events, is short lived. Figure 18.1 shows the annual net benefits simulated for an Olympic host city in 2012.

The yearly net benefits peak during the event and lose power after the event. Depending on the legacy created through the event, a city can experience annual positive net benefits following the event (e.g., through stimulated postevent tourism) but also net costs (e.g., through high cost for maintaining the event facilities). To understand how the event-driven economic impact fades away, we go back to the Keynes model and add government to the model. Injections to the circular flow of money in the economy are investment, government spending on goods and services, and exports (tourist consumption). Leakages are savings, taxes, and imports. The primary regional impact occurs through the injections; the host city may have spent money on facilities construction (investment) assisted by government subsidies (government spending on goods and services), and tourists came and spent money while they enjoyed the event (exports). Most of the injections occur before and during the event. The

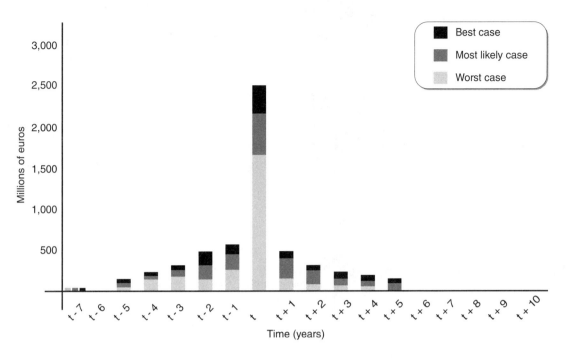

Figure 18.1 Discounted net benefit of an Olympic Games for a host city.

Injections and Leakages Associated With a Major Sport Event

Injections

Autonomous investments

Government spending on goods and services (if local region)

Exports (e.g., tourism)

Consumption of the organizing committee (funded by autonomous money)

Import substitution

Leakages

Savings

Taxes

Imports

---

sidebar lists examples of injections and leakages associated with a major sport event.

Although leakages also occur before and during the event, after the event they dominate. The amount that made up the primary regional impact and its induced effect quickly dwindles away because of people saving (rather than spending), paying federal taxes that leave the region, and importing goods and services from

outside the economy. The impact created through the event necessarily returns to its preevent state, and the direct, total economic impact has run its course. Only if the new infrastructure permanently attracts new money to the economy will the regional economy reach a higher level (Spilling, 1999). This result may occur because of a permanent increase in tourism to the former host city or the staging of future events in

Learning Activity

In a small group, identify three specific examples of ways in which the initial amount of increased money brought into an economy by a sport event leaks from the economy over time. What strategies can slow these leakages and extend the benefit of the event?

existing facilities. This effect is called a positive event **legacy effect** (see Preuss, 2015).

Long- and Short-Term Benefits From Sport and the Legacy Effect

Few past megaevent impact analyses have recognized the clear limitations of the multiplier, namely that the effect of a nonrecurring expenditure weakens over the course of time and then vanishes completely. The increase in income declines with every new period, and in the long run falling demand leads back to the equilibrium income that existed before the event if there is no positive legacy effect. Typically, the multiplier impact over time for a nonrecurring autonomous expenditure can be calculated using this equation:

$$c^n \times \Delta A$$

where ΔA is the initial direct and indirect impact and where c (where 0<c<1) represents the level of induced impact. As n (the number of periods) increases to infinity, the value of the induced impact tends toward zero. But the Olympic Games are a special case. The increased demand lasts for many years. During this period, autonomous expenditures are made so that the equilibrium income will not immediately return to the starting point following the event. Caused by varying autonomous injections (ΔA), permanently changing demand functions will exist during the remaining time. Long after the Games, increased demand will persist, depending on the type of long-term infrastructural changes. For example, the operation and maintenance of sport facilities will continue and the number of visitor will

remain high because of improved attractions and the Olympic image. The sport facilities and the changed structure of the city can enhance the attractiveness of the city, as seen in the example of the Munich Olympic Park, and lasting income increases can be the consequence.

Because the direct economic impact dwindles quickly because of leakages that cause the primary impact to lose power over time, a one-time event cannot directly improve the economic welfare of a region in the long run.

But the event can create intangible effects, in particular changes of location factors such as infrastructure or knowledge, and leave a so-called positive legacy. If the event improves the normal economic structure, which is called event legacy, then it can indirectly increase economic activity in the region in the long term.

Overall, six types of event structures are usually preserved after a megaevent. Four of these are related to "soft legacy"—policy and governance, human development (skills, knowledge, networks), intellectual property, and social development (beliefs and behavior)—and develop people. A further two—urban development and environmental enhancement—change the space (Preuss, 2016). Each of these six structural changes caused by the event transforms the location factors of the host city and thus can help create new economic activity.

Figure 18.2 shows six structural changes that affect a city by a change of location factors, but only when the changed structure is used. When hosting a megaevent, decision makers are wise to plan with the legacy in mind by investing not only in the event but also in additional infrastructure needed to change location factors. For example, the tourism product at a destination is affected by the following event structures: new physical tourist attractions, upgraded and new hotels, better public transportation, a better and more interesting image, more knowledge in the tourism service industry, a more interesting cultural presentation, and enhanced cultural identity (see Solberg & Preuss, 2007). Another example is a better business destination developed through event infrastructures such as an upgrade of the general infrastructure (particularly traffic systems), knowledge (e.g., organiza-

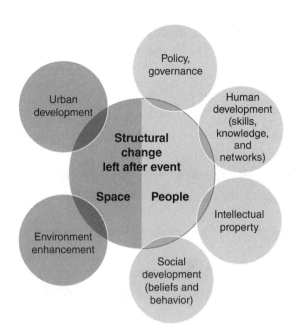

Figure 18.2 Impact of event structure on location factors.

tional and service skills, security), skilled labor, image as a business location, and political and business networks.

Increased tourism activity in the city may lead to long-term economic growth and additional jobs. But such economic growth based on event-related improved location factors does not obviously appear in many evaluations as being event related.

For example, new and improved infrastructure and facilities could result in the hosting of future events that attract visitors and again bring autonomous money into the economy. Museums and parks built for the Olympic Games could become a permanent tourist attraction that leads to a long-term increase in the number of visitors to the region. This result certainly occurred after the Barcelona 1992 Olympic Games (Preuss, 2007). Additionally, the knowledge gained by local organizers in hosting the event could become a future export good as they become consultants for future hosts. Although the direct economic impact of an event on a region is short lived, the indirect, long-term impact can potentially be quite large if the legacy effect of the event results in useful permanent changes in the region, such as an enhancement of its image, an increase in the skills and knowledge base of its

Learning Activity

Compare the long-term legacy benefits of the 2008 Beijing Olympics and the 1994 Lillehammer Winter Olympics to the respective host cities. Consider the size, location, and economic characteristics of the host cities.

workforce, or a greater ability to attract and host future large-scale events.

Summary

This chapter explained the macroeconomics of sport by using the economic impact of mega sporting events on a host region or country as an example. The same mechanisms hold for the economic impact of other sport-related activities in a region, even small local events. Consider a new sport equipment manufacturing plant, a newly constructed arena, or an increase in participation in active sport and health clubs. The economic effects of all these actions must be seen as attracting autonomous money to the region and creating jobs, taxes, and income in the same way as was explained in the example of hosting a mega sport event. The macroeconomic effect, however, will be long term as long as the manufacturing plant or arena are operating and as long as people maintain their increase in athletic activity. Unlike the mega sport event, the macroeconomic effects in these examples will probably not create any legacy that induces economic activity after they end.

From a macroeconomic perspective the key welfare issue is whether a sport event achieves efficient outcomes given the potentially incompatible aims of various stakeholders. Invariably, these differences lead to some debatable investments of scarce public resources. An enormous intervention such as an Olympic Games always affects the location where it takes place. Any structural change of a location means that in the long term other industries are stimulated that would not have been developed without the event. For example, a larger number of tourists increases demand in the tourism industry, or new transport infrastructure increases the number of corporations that settle in the region.

Note that the smaller the event or sport intervention is, the smaller the macroeconomic impact is.

Whatever sport intervention takes place, some stakeholders will not be interested or will not want the event or sport activity. Each decision for a major sport activity will satisfy demand for some, which can be seen as beneficial, but others will claim that the resources would have been better used for other activities. These people can be seen as losing economic benefit because of the sport event.

? Review Questions

1. What are some of the intangible economic benefits associated with sport? Are the intangible economic benefits more significant than the tangible benefits?

2. What are the differences between direct and indirect investment goods in sport?

3. How does public spending on direct and indirect investment goods affect the larger economy?

4. What is the overall significance of the team to the economy, and what tangible and intangible benefits are generated by the franchise?

The Business of International Sport

David J. Shonk, PhD
James Madison University

Doyeon Won, PhD
Texas A&M University–Corpus Christi

Ho Keat Leng, PhD
Nanyang Technological University, Singapore

Chapter Objectives

After studying this chapter, you will be able to do the following:

- Understand the global impact of both participant and spectator sport.
- Describe how sport leagues operate around the world.
- Discuss the differences between various models of sport.
- Explain the transfer of players in European football.
- Differentiate participant and spectator sport around the world.
- Understand how revenues are generated by sport leagues around the world.
- Explain the posting system in baseball.
- Identify how sport differs between countries.

Key Terms	
action sports	single-entity structure
reserve clause	posting system
free agency	tanking
reverse-order draft	promotion and relegation
league structure	transfer fee

Sport is receiving increasing emphasis in countries around the world. According to Plunket Research (2018), the size of the global sports industry was estimated at US$1.3 trillion. Depending on where you are from, definitions of sport may vary. For example, jogging in some parts of Europe is considered sport, whereas it is classified as a recreational activity in the United States. This chapter focuses on the business of international sport. The chapter is divided into two sections. The first section discusses amateur participant sport, focusing on nonprofessional participants who engage in a wide range of activities. The second section focuses on spectator sport, which mostly involves watching professional and amateur athletes competing in various types of sport. We discuss various structures and differences between models of sport throughout the world.

Amateur Participant Sports

Although many students are enamored with spectator sport, Chelladurai (2014) points out that participant sport is the core of the industry that spawns spectator sport, which in turn is supported by other industries. Chelladurai notes that more than half of the sport industry is engaged in participant sport. Thus, students have numerous job opportunities around the world, and they have much to learn about the business and idiosyncrasies of the various activities within participant sport. In this section, we focus on golf, action and adventure sports, marathons and road races, the health and fitness industry, and youth sport in the United States.

Golf Facilities

According to the National Golf Foundation (2018), in 2017 a total of 32,737 golf facilities existed in 208 of the world's 249 countries, and the United States was home to 45 percent of the courses. In 2017 there were 306 courses in planning and 199 under construction, and 108 countries had active golf projects, up from 103 in 2016. A report by the R&A (2017) stated that Africa had 51 new projects underway in 19 countries in 2016. Europe had 124 new golf course projects underway, and a shift to the east was occurring as countries like Hungary, the Czech Republic, and Kazakhstan were developing new courses. Asia, including the Middle East, was in

the process of developing 176 new courses, Vietnam was adding 32 new courses and India another 28 courses. North America, including Central America and the Caribbean, had 156 new course projects underway. Oceania (Australia and New Zealand) had 29 new course projects during this time, and South American countries were developing 20 new courses.

Although soccer is generally considered the world game, Stoddart (1990) suggests that the title arguably belongs to golf. The number of courses worldwide has grown substantially over the last 25 years despite slowing in recent years. In 1990 there were over 25,000 courses with 25 million registered players in the United States, Scotland, and Australia. Participation in golf, particularly in the United States, continues to evolve as the definition of golf expands. In 2016 the National Golf Foundation expanded the definition of golf to include engagement in golf at facilities other than traditional courses. For example, Top Golf and golf simulators are popular ways that people can engage in golf outside of playing on a course. Research by the National Golf Foundation (2018) suggests that golf participation on courses in the United States peaked in 2003 at 30 million participants and has since dropped to 24.1 million on-course participants in 2015 and to 23.8 million in 2016 and 2017. Under the new definition, however, which considers both on-course and off-course participation, golf saw an 11 percent increase in participation to 32 million. According to Matuszewski (2017), golf generates almost $70 billion in annual economic impact in the United States, is responsible for about 2 million jobs, and contributes more than $4 billion to charity.

Learning Activity

After reading the section on participant sport, choose one or more of the sports in which you have participated. Create a short video that describes the following: when and where you participated in the activity, your motivations for participating in this activity, and statistics germane to the sport and relevant to the site where you participated.

Action and Adventure Sports

Action and adventure sports (AAS) are on the rise, but attempting to discuss the business and finance of AAS, especially from a global perspective, is as difficult as trying to define them. Although we will refer to them here as AAS, sometimes the terms *extreme sports* or *individualistic sports* are used interchangeably. The term **action sports** has been used to describe sports that are not traditional or mainstream and often include risk, danger, or unconventional rules or techniques, and athletes often compete on an individual basis (Bennett, Henson, & Zhang, 2002). Just a few examples of action sports are climbing, mountain biking, skateboarding, inline skating, and snowboarding (Puchan, 2004). Adventure sports are sometimes not regarded as sports because the competition is often between an individual and nature, not between individuals. Puchan describes adventure sports as lifestyle sports that include an element of leisure time, weekend diversion, physical exercise, risk, and sometimes even a spiritual journey. Page, Steele, and Connell (2006) suggest that the landscape of these adventure activities may include water (e.g., kite surfing, open canoe, power boating, sea kayaking, surfing, white-water kayaking and rafting, and wind surfing), earth (e.g., hill walking, mountain biking, rock climbing, and scrambling), adrenaline (off-road driving, quad biking, and sphereing), ice (e.g., skiing, snowboarding, and winter mountaineering), and air (e.g., microlight flying and paragliding).

Finding exact figures regarding participation in extreme sports and their business models is difficult. Most literature, however, suggests that participation in extreme sports has steadily risen over the past 10 to 20 years. The Youth and Sports Ministry in Malaysia began organizing and promoting extreme sports events in 2010 (Star Online, 2010). A report by Sandler Research (2016) suggests that the global adventure tourism market is expected to increase at a compound annual growth rate of nearly 46 percent between 2016 and 2020. Europe dominates the adventure tourism market, accounting for more than 40 percent of the total market, and countries such as France, Germany, Spain, and Iceland are the most preferred adventure tourism destinations. The most popular adventure sports attracting tourists in Europe include para-gliding, kite surfing, and hiking on mountains and glaciers. An increasing number of tourists are visiting countries such as Albania, Serbia, Hungary, Latvia, and Romania. Benedictus (2016) claims that the number of first-time jumps reported by the British Parachute Association rose from 39,100 in 2006 to 59,679 in 2016. Membership in the British Mountaineering Council rose from 25,000 in 2000 to 55,000 in 2016. Within the United States, skateboarding is the most popular action sport; 12 million Americans participate each year, and 4.7 million participants skate more than 30 days per year. The Outdoor Foundation (2017) reports that surfing participation in the United States rose from 2.17 million in 2006 to 2.79 million in 2016. The global body board market is expected to grow at a compound annual rate of 7.51 percent from 2016 to 2020 (Technavio Research, 2016). According to contributors to FutureOf.org, some of the interest in extreme sports is fueled by easy recording and uploading technology like GoPro and YouTube. Although the business of action sports in the United States does not compare with professional sport, interest is increasing. For example, the owners of the Boston Celtics and San Francisco 49ers recently invested in Street League Skating.

Road Races and Marathons

Road races and marathons continue to gain in popularity. Wahba (2015) reports that road racing is estimated to be a $1.4 billion industry that is growing and feeds a $3 billion running-shoe sector. As proof, Wahba reports that Providence Equity Partners sold ownership of the Ironman series of triathlons to China's Dalian Wanda Group for $650 million, reportedly for four times its initial investment. According to *Runner's World* (2016) the largest marathons in 2016 based on the number of finishers are located in New York (51,388), Paris (41,708), Chicago (40,608), London (39,072), and Tokyo (36,150). With the large number of participants come an increasing number of sponsors.

Although the top athletes competing in road races make little in comparison to the top professional athletes in the major sports in North America, the prize money continues to get better. Haile Gerbilaria from Ethiopia has earned more than $3.5 million in his career; on the women's side, Mary Keitany Choosey from Kenya has lifetime earnings of over $2.7 million (Association of Road Racing Statisticians, 2018). Wade and Fuehrer (2014) reported the payouts to the winners of the highest paying road races: the Dubai Marathon ($200,000), Boston Marathon ($150,000), Chicago Marathon ($100,000), New York City Marathon ($100,000), and Seoul International Marathon ($80,000). The highest possible payout to one runner is $580,000 at the Seoul International Marathon, based on a combination of the guaranteed winner's purse and time, course, and world-record bonuses. The total prize money distributed among the top finishers in the 2017 Boston Marathon was $830,500, and an additional $220,000 if records were broken in the open, masters, or push rim wheelchair division (Boston Marathon 2017).

Health and Fitness Industry

According to the International Health, Racquet, and Sportsclub Association (IHRSA) (2018), the global health club industry was worth over US$84 billion in 2014 as compared with US$67.19 billion in 2009. The health club industry accounted for US$35 billion in 2014 as compared with US$31.37 billion in 2009. The IHRSA reports that the Asia–Pacific region is the third largest region for health

CASE STUDY

Tokyo Marathon

Tokyo, Japan, hosts one of the largest marathons in the world, with 36,000 runners, 10,000 volunteers, and 1.6 million spectators. Formed in 2006, the race is organized by the Tokyo Marathon Foundation and has traditionally been held on the last Sunday in February. Beginning in 2019, however, the race will be run on the first Sunday in March. The race serves as a selection trial for the 2018 Asia Jakarta Marathon Grand Championship Series and the Abbott World Marathon Major Series (WMM). Started in 2006, the WMM is a marathon grand slam series in which participants compete in races in six cities: Tokyo, Boston, London, Berlin, Chicago, and New York City. A $1 million pool of prize money is split among the top male and female finishers in these races, and the race directors from each of these locations contribute equal amounts. The Tokyo Marathon has two types of events:

◆ Marathon events (categories include men, women, wheelchair men, wheelchair women)

◆ A 10K race (categories include men and women for junior and youth, visually impaired, intellectually challenged, organ transplant recipients, and wheelchair)

Although up to 300,000 people have applied to run in either the marathon or the 10K race, the races are capped at 35,500 runners for the marathon and 500 runners for the 10K race. For example, 308,810 people applied to enter the race in 2015, which was 11.3 times more than could be accepted. Entry fees for Japanese residents are 10,800 yen (about US$100) for the marathon and 5,600 yen (about US$50) for the 10K race. Entry fees for nonresidents are 12,800 yen (about US$120) for the marathon and 6,700 yen (about US$60) for the 10K race. The prize money distributed for the 2018 race was $1.26 million.

The Tokyo Marathon has over 30 partners that sponsor the event, including BMW Japan, Seiko, Mizuho Bank, Seven-Eleven Japan, Yamazaki, Asics Japan, Dole Japan, Starts Corporation, All Nippon Airways, and McDonald's. Although the marathon is its primary focus, the Tokyo Marathon Foundation also manages and organizes other activities, such as their official running club ONE Tokyo; the Sports Legacy Program, which focuses on charity; the official volunteer club called VOLUNTAINER; and their runner support facility, JOGPORT ARIAKE. More than 100,000 visitors attend the Tokyo Marathon Expo, which has more than 130 exhibition booths at the Tokyo Big Site during the three days leading up to the event.

Security at the Tokyo Marathon is tight in lieu of concerns about terrorist attacks. Security at the event entails the involvement of more than 10,000 personnel, including 6,000 employees of private security firms and volunteers. Security personnel conduct baggage and body checks at the start and finish lines. Participants are not permitted to bring in plastic beverage bottles, cans, glass bottles, or other water containers. Only unopened paper packages of drinks are allowed. Numerous metal detectors and 1,200 street security cameras are on the course, and police officers run alongside race participants.

clubs, accounting for US$26.8 in revenue in 2014. Of this amount, the most revenue is generated in Japan, Australia, China, and South Korea. In 2014 the industry in Latin America generated about US$6 billion; Brazil was the largest individual market with more than 30,000 fitness centers that generated over US$2.4 billion in revenue. Note that the largest number of health and fitness clubs are located in Latin America; almost 56,000 of the 183,000 centers worldwide are located in this region. More than 50 percent of those in Latin America are found in Brazil, and Argentina and Mexico each have about 15 percent of the total. The IHRSA reports that Europe is the second largest region with more than 51,000 fitness centers. Germany accounts for around 15 percent, Italy around 13 percent, and the UK about 12 percent. The North American market has approximately 40,710 health and fitness clubs, the majority of which are located in the United States.

Youth Sport in the United States

Although classifying youth sport in the United States is difficult, an article by Gregory (2017) in *Time Magazine* recently suggested that it is a $15 billion industry. Youth sport drives the market for amateur sport events that travel from market to market, and spending per athlete in 2016 averaged $894.90 per event (O'Connor, 2017). Many families spend more than 10 percent of their income on registration fees, travel, camps, and equipment (Gregory, 2017). Sports facilities in each town or municipality across the United States now compete against each other to attract the next youth event. The LakePoint Sporting Community in Cartersville, Georgia, boasts 5 sporting venues with 8 baseball fields, 3 multipurpose fields, 10 beach volleyball courts, 3 cable wakeboarding pools, and a 170,000-square-foot (16,000 sq m) indoor facility with 12 basketball courts that can convert into 24 volleyball courts. Across the country are many venues similar to this one.

Although the state of youth sport in the United States appears on the surface to be strong, it does not come without many critics and serious problems. The Aspen Institute's *State of Play* report (2017) describes data provided by the Sports and Fitness Industry Association from more than 24,000 individuals and households. The data from this report suggest that the number of kids playing at least one team sport on a regular basis has declined from 41.5 percent in 2011 to 36.9 percent in 2016. Furthermore, youth participating in individual sports has dropped from 53.2 percent in 2011 to 49.8 percent in 2016. The National Physical Activity Plan Alliance (2014) recommends that youth sport participants obtain 45 minutes of moderate to vigorous physical activity on average during practices. Between 2008 and 2013, statistics from SFIA suggest that less than one in three children between the ages of 6 and 12 participated in a high-calorie-burning sport or fitness activity three times a week. As Lee (2015) points out, this finding is troublesome because research suggests that children who enter sport at an early age are 1/10 as likely to become obese, 15 percent more likely to go to college, and more likely to be productive adults than children who do not play sports.

Declining participation and a rise in sedentary behavior are just two of the many issues facing youth sport. The increasing costs of participation make it difficult for children from low-income households to participate. Bogage (2017) suggests that children from low-income households are half as likely to play a day of team sports than children from households making at least $100,000. According to Dilworth (2015) with the National Alliance for Youth Sport, 70 percent of children will drop out of sport by the age of 13. The dropout rate can be attributed to an overemphasis on winning, longer practice times and seasons, specialization in sport at an early age, stress to perform at a high level often coming from parents, injury, expenses (e.g., travel teams, camps, equipment), unqualified coaches, and earlier starts in youth sport that cause burnout (Woods, 2011).

Spectator Sports

Most spectator sports are organized into a hierarchy of leagues, containing a major league, premier league, or first division, followed by minor leagues or lower divisions. The supply of athletic talent for professional sport in North America comes from two primary sources: (1) minor league farm systems or tours (e.g., tennis and golf) and (2) colleges and universities. Professional sport leagues, particularly in the United States, implement ownership restrictions that affect the employment of players and their distribution across teams (Rosen & Sanderson, 2001). European models of sport are built around club systems that develop players from a young age. Whereas, Asian sport employs both North American and European models of sport. Professional and college sport in North America attracts millions of fans to both live events and broadcast viewership. European football draws millions of avid fans who are members of their clubs. Finally, spectator sport continues to grow in Asia in places such as China, Korea, Japan, and Singapore.

European Sport

The European model of sport is characterized by its pyramid structure. The European Commission (1998) describes this structure in the following ways. Imagine a pyramid at the bottom of which are the clubs that form its base. The clubs allow everyone the opportunity to participate in sport and help to develop sport for all with unpaid participation. Forming the next level above the clubs and moving toward the apex of the pyramid are the regional federations, of which the clubs are members. The federations are responsible for

CASE STUDY

Real Madrid

Cristiano Ronaldo is one of the most famous football players in the world on one of the most famous teams in the world. Real Madrid plays in La Liga Spain and has won 64 trophies, including a record 33 La Liga titles, 19 Copa del Rey, 10 Super Copa de Espada, a Copa Eva Duarte, and a Copa de la Liga. Real Madrid has over 100 million social media followers, sells millions of dollars in merchandise each year, and has a number of major sponsorship deals, including Adidas (£34 million [about US$46 million] per year) and Fly-Emirates (£20 million [about US$27 million] per year).

In 2017 *Forbes* valued Real Madrid at $3.58 billion, ranking them third in value behind Manchester United ($3.69 billion) and Barcelona ($3.64 billion) and second in sponsorship rights, worth $216 million. Real Madrid benefits from the fact that Spain mandates that football clubs individually negotiate broadcasting deals. This structure is vastly different from the collective bargaining agreements seen in England and Germany. Operating income during the 2016-2017 season was £675 million [about US$905 million], including revenues from the stadium, international and friendly matches, broadcasting, and marketing.

The club has official stores that are operated by Adidas and promote officially licensed products. Nine stores are located in Spain, two in Mexico City, and one in Doha, Qatar. The club operates four restaurants and hosts more than 200 corporate events that take place in their facilities. New corporate offices located in Real Madrid City, Spain, were built during the 2016-2017 season with a focus on environmental sustain-ability and energy efficiency. This site is located next to the airport, about 10 miles (16 km) from the center of the city.

Although football receives much of the attention, the club has had basketball since 1931 and won their 10th European Cup in 2018. Basketball is played at the Palacio de los Deportes. During the 2016-2017 season, the club had 7,647 season ticket holders and total attendance of 350,000. The football team plays its games in front of more than 81,000 fans at the newly renovated Santiago Bernabéu Stadium in Madrid, Spain. During the 2016-2017 season, the team had 61,817 football season ticket holders. Anyone wishing to be a season ticket holder must be a socio, or member, of the club.

The structure of Real Madrid is unique because fans own the team. In 1992 the government in Spain passed a law that made it mandatory for professional football clubs to be privately owned PLCs. But because it was able to show that it turned a profit for the previous five years, Real Madrid was able keep their fan ownership model. The club has over 90,000 members who control all aspects of the club, including voting for the president and board of directors. Prospective members must be recommended by two existing members, and membership benefits include the right to vote and easier access to tickets. The members hold an election to form a member assembly made up of about 2,000 members elected by the socios for four-year terms.

coordinating sport on a regional level or organizing regional championships. Moving further up toward the apex of the pyramid are the national federations for each discipline, whose membership comprises the regional federations. These national federations regulate all general matters within the discipline, provide representation within the European and international federations, organize all national championships, and serve as regulatory bodies. Finally, the apex of the pyramid is formed by the European federation, which is organized similar to the national federations. Only one national federation from each country is allowed to be a member. The European federation may invoke sanctions for those taking part in championships that have not been recognized or authorized by the international federation. Blackshaw (2017) describes the pyramid structure in the following way:

> The pyramid structure implies interdependence between the levels, not only on the organisational front, but also on the competitive side, because competitions are organised on all levels. This can be compared very specifically with the "horizontal structure" of U.S. sport, where there is little connection between the professional leagues and the lower echelons of any particular sport. (p. 6)

Financing European Sport

Football is the predominant sport in Europe, and most teams are individually owned. According to Deloitte (2018), the European football market produced revenue of €25.5 billion (about US$30.5 billion) in 2016-17. Revenues of the "big five" leagues in England, Germany, Spain, Italy, and France generated €14.7 billion (about US$17.6 billion), or 58 percent of the total. The European football industry generates income in the following three ways: (1) media rights (i.e., the value paid by media companies to broadcast sport events); (2) commercial income (e.g., sponsorships from placing the brands on T-shirts, around the stadium, media broadcasting) and other business income (e.g., marketing activities, conference services, catering); and (3) **matchday revenue** (e.g., money from ticket sales including season tickets subscriptions) and supporters' expenses inside the stadium (promotional items, services).

The Big Five European Leagues

The big five European Leagues include England's Premier League, Spain's La Liga, Germany's Bundesliga, Italy's Serie A, and France's Ligue 1. The English Premier League (EPL) is the market leader. The total revenue of the European professional football market in 2015-2016 was £24.6 billion (about US$33 billion). The EPL generated £4.5 billion (about US$6 billion) from the 2016-2017 season, and every one of the 20 clubs in the league set a personal annual revenue record. In 2016-2017, the collective revenues of the big five leagues grew by €1.3 billion (about US$1.6 billion) because of increased broadcasting rights revenue. Broadcast revenues drive La Liga's revenues in Spain; total revenue was a record €2.9 billion (about US$3.5 billion) in 2016-17. Thus, La Liga overtook Bundesliga to become the second highest revenue-generating league in the world. Earning €1.6 billion (about US$1.9 billion) in 2016-17, France's Ligue 1 generates the least revenue of any of Europe's big five leagues. UEFA also distributes €1.2 billion (about US$1.4 billion) to clubs from the big five participating in the Champions League and Europa League and plays a significant role in their financial performance. Premier League clubs received more than €300 million (about US$360 million), the most revenue distributed by UEFA, whereas Ligue 1 clubs collectively earn the least of the big five leagues (Deloitte, 2018).

Differences Between North American and European Sport

North American sport differs from European sport in significant ways. Fort (2000) highlights three fundamental differences between North American and European sport organizations. First, different organizations are involved in oversight of sport. One of the primary differences is that North American clubs do not compete in international competition in the same manner as European clubs do. In the North American model, although the New England Patriots in the National Football League (American football) may be called "world champions," they do not compete in any real international-level competition. In contrast, the European oversight structure for football is as follows. The Fédération Internationale de Football Association (FIFA) is responsible for governing world football; the Union of European Football Associations (UEFA) governs football in Europe; and national associations are responsible for their own members. Second, North American sport does not have a system of **promotion and relegation** like that characterizing European sport. Noll (2002) points to on-field success as the primary criterion for promotion and relegation, whereby the best minor league teams are promoted to the major league and the worst major league teams are reassigned to the minor league. Several lower leagues are organized hierarchically in larger countries. For example, Noll (2002) states that English football (soccer) involves seven levels of leagues, with the bottom two levels further divided into hierarchical divisions. The third and final difference between North American and European sport noted by Fort (2000) concerns funding. In the North American model, funding does not flow from high-revenue, premier-level, and international play to the lower levels of sport. For example, in MLB and the NHL the lower levels are integrated, either through direct ownership or contractual arrangements.

Humphreys and Watanabe (2012) note some additional differences between the North American and European model. North American leagues are predominantly static (i.e., closed) leagues, whereas European leagues use an open (i.e., promotion and relegation) system. European leagues do not use a reverse-order entry draft. Instead, they operate youth academies that identify the best players at a young age, sign them to contracts, and train them. In North America, leagues such as the NBA and NFL primarily use colleges and universities as their farm systems. In Europe the individual clubs develop the players very early in life and bear all scouting, training, and development costs. Another important difference is that European leagues do not trade individual players, groups of players, or draft picks. Instead, they use transfers, whereby a club pays another club a **transfer fee** to purchase the rights to a player. In 2017 the most expensive transfer fee in the history of football occurred when Paris Saint-Germain (PSG) paid $263 million for the rights to Neymar from Barcelona (Gaines, 2017).

North American Sport

In North America, professional sport teams operate within a **league structure**. Teams may be privately owned, publicly owned, or owned by nonprofit organizations. Leagues are predominantly structured as a type of unincorporated joint venture among individual teams. The predominant professional leagues in North America include the National Football League (NFL), Canadian Football League (CFL), National Basketball Association (NBA), Women's National Basketball Association (WNBA), Major League Baseball (MLB), National Hockey League (NHL), and Major League Soccer (MLS). Teams may have an individual owner or a group of owners. The leagues often operate as monopolies and are vulnerable to federal antitrust liability under Section 1 of the Sherman Act. Although not as common today, some leagues (e.g., WNBA and MLS) have attempted to avoid antitrust legislation by organizing as a **single-entity structure**, whereby the league owns all the teams, holds players' and coaches' contracts and pays their salaries, and maintains sponsorship deals and broadcasting rights (Kaiser, 2004). Stadium lease arrangements, monopolistic bargaining for broadcasting rights, and territorial rights in predetermined geographic markets are all distinguishing factors that differentiate professional sport from other businesses (Mason, 1999).

Because uncertainty of the outcome is crucially important in sport, one of the distinguishing features of professional sport leagues is the concept of competitive balance. Often, this characteristic equates to a distribution of wins versus losses for each team. But determining how to measure competitive balance in sport is difficult (Zimbalist, 2002). Unlike the model used in places like South America and Europe where talented young players are developed through an academy system and then play for the club, the best players in North America go to the worst professional teams using a **reverse-order draft**. One of the primary criticisms of the reverse-order draft is that it promotes **tanking**, which has been loosely defined as the "systematic writing-off of entire seasons by franchises hoping to rebuild for future success through the draft" (Sheinen, 2018).

Revenue sharing is common in many professional sport leagues across North America. Revenue sharing has been used for purposes such as supporting small-market teams, assisting with creating league parity, and improving team profitability by suppressing player salaries (Rockerbie & Easton, 2017). According to Brown, Rascher, Nagel, and

McEvoy (2017), two models of revenue sharing are commonly used in North American professional sport. In the first model, used by MLB and the NBA, the leagues provide increased revenue allocations to teams with low local revenues. In contrast, in the second model for revenue sharing, the league allocates equal amounts to each team in the league. This model is currently used by the NFL. During the 2016-2017 season, the NFL shared US$7.8 billion in national revenue; US$6 billion came from league television contracts with NBC, CBS, Fox, ESPN, and DirectTV (Weinstein, 2017). Zegers (2017) reports that MLB has the widest disparity between the large- and small-market teams, or the haves (high-revenue teams) and have nots (low-revenue teams). All teams in the league pay 31 percent of their local revenue into a shared fund, which is divided equally among all teams. Additionally, monies from national sources such as network television contracts go to lower-revenue clubs. MLB also has a **luxury tax system** whereby teams with high payrolls pay a dollar-for-dollar penalty, which goes into the MLB Industry Growth Fund that is used for marketing programs. In the NBA, all teams pool their money and distribute it from low-income teams to higher-income teams. Even so, nine NBA teams lost money during the 2016-2017 season after sharing revenues (Wood, 2017). In the NHL, the top 10 moneymaking teams contribute to a revenue-sharing pool, and the bottom 15 teams are eligible to collect from the pool. These bottom 15 teams, however, must reach at least 80 percent capacity in home attendance

CASE STUDY

Washington Nationals

Baseball officially came back to Washington, DC, in 2005 when the Montreal Expos moved to the city and took the name Washington Nationals. The new team in Washington was a long time in coming because the city had gone without baseball since the Washington Senators left town for Dallas-Fort Worth in 1971 to become the Texas Rangers. The team is owned by Ted Lerner, who bought the franchise in 2006 for $450 million. The Nationals played their first three seasons (2005-2007) in RFK Stadium in Washington before they moved into the new Nationals Park in 2008. Between 2005 and 2017 the Nationals posted a .500 win-loss record and had competed in postseason play five times.

The Nationals' lack of postseason success has been a bit puzzling to their fans, especially because in recent years they have been one of the best teams in the National League. Between the years 2012 and 2017 the Nationals have come in either first or second place in their division each year. Only two years earlier, in 2010, a young slugger named Bryce Harper was the first overall pick by the Nationals in the Major League Baseball draft. Two years later, on April 28, 2012, Harper made his major league debut with the Nationals. Widely considered one of the best players in baseball, Harper was named the National League Rookie of the Year in 2012 and the National League Most Valuable Player in 2015. In 2018 Harper was in the last year of his two-year $35 million contract and was set to become a free agent at the end of the year.

The Nationals on-field success can be attributed to a couple of factors. First, the Nationals were able to attain talented players like Bryce Harper, Ryan Zimmerman, and Stephen Strasburg through the MLB draft and develop them in their farm system. Zimmerman was drafted as the fourth overall pick by the Nationals in the 2005 draft, and Strasburg was selected as the first overall pick in 2009. Second, Nationals general manager Mike Rizzo has been successful in signing some key free agent players. Rizzo came to the Nationals in 2009, and his notable signings include Ivan Rodriquez, Jayson Werth, Max Scherzer, and Daniel Murphy.

Since the start of the Harper era in 2012, the Nationals have averaged over 2.5 million fans per year. Before 2012 the Nationals had never attracted over 2 million fans, with the exception of 2008 when 2.3 million fans came out to witness the new Nationals Park. These statistics are consistent with research in sport that suggests that new stadiums cause a spike in attendance. Attendance then returns to normal unless the team is winning. Revenues for the Nationals grew consistently between 2009 and 2017, and the franchise experienced a large jump in revenues (from $244 million in 2014 to $287 million in 2015) during Harper's MVP season.

and show revenue growth that exceeds the league average (Zegers, 2017).

In the late 19th century, professional teams used a **reserve clause** to try to reserve players to their current teams and thus restrict **free agency**. Players who are allowed to sign a contract with any professional team are considered free agents (Nagel, 2011). Free agents may be unrestricted or restricted. An unrestricted free agent can sign with any team, although a team may have an option on the player's contract. A team may exercise an option whereby they decide to keep a player for another year. A player option allows the player to decide whether to stay for another year or become a completely unrestricted free agent.

Sport in Asia

As the market for North American leagues continues to saturate, the Asian sport market is drawing increasing attention, in part because China is one of the world's biggest economies. Therefore, North American leagues such as MLB are planning to host games in Asia, particularly in Japan. The large population base in China has long been attractive to the NBA, and in 2018 LeBron James had the top-selling jersey in the country. Numerous NBA players have visited China, teams have visited as part of the NBA Global Games, and the league has a partnership with Tencent, which distributes more than 600 games for viewership in China through League Pass. The NBA is also looking to expand its footprint in Southeast Asia into the Philippines, Indonesia, Thailand, Japan, and Australia (Lim, 2018).

Next, we discuss various sport leagues in Asia. The North American and European models of sport are quite distinct, but models of sport in Asia mix and match both North American and European models (Humphreys & Watanabe, 2012). In this section, we focus on baseball in Korea and Japan; football in Singapore, Korea, and Japan; and motor sport in Asia, particularly the Singapore Grand Prix.

Korean Baseball League

Founded in 1982, the Korean Baseball League (KBO) has 10 teams. In the 2016 baseball season, 10 KBO teams collectively made $469 million dollars in revenue, an increase of 10.6 percent from the previous year. Four teams made a profit, and six teams had deficits. Their average net income was $12.3 million, an improvement from an average net loss of $4.8 million in 2015. One of the 10 KBO teams, Nexen, had annual revenue in 2015 of $58.3 million, an increase of 52.3 percent. Nexen's big financial gains were primarily because of player transfer fees from two MLB players (worth $17.9 million), revenues from their new domed ballpark, and increased ticket sales and advertising deals.

Media rights deals were also lucrative for the KBO. In 2017 the KBO and its associated 10 league teams earned about $50 million from television rights (61 percent) and new media (39 percent). Thus, each KBO team received about $5 million from the revenue-sharing system. Although KBO teams' financial balance sheets have seen some positive improvement because some teams made profits, the financial sustainability of the teams is still in question. Unlike other established professional sport leagues (e.g., MLB), KBO has advertisement deals as its primary revenue source, followed by ticket sales. On average, KBO teams make 50 to 60 percent of their revenue from advertisements, mostly from each team's affiliated corporations. For example, in 2013 the Samsung Lions received a sum of $40 million, which is 56 percent of its annual revenue, from advertisement deals with Samsung Electronics, Samsung Life Insurance, Samsung Fire and Marine Insurance, Cheil Worldwide (a marketing company under the Samsung Group), and Samsung C&T Corporation.

In 2015 the Lotte Giants had a net deficit of $15 million and total revenue of $34.2 million. The revenues for Lotte come primarily from gate receipts ($5.2 million), advertisement and sponsorship ($18.6 million), merchandise sales ($1.7 million), membership sales ($4.7 million), and other commercial activities ($8.2 million). Similarly, the

Learning Activity

Write a 400- to 500-word, two-paragraph paper that compares and contrasts sport in Europe, North America, and Asia. Each paragraph should include real world examples. The first paragraph should highlight the differences between North American and European sport. The second paragraph should describe how Asian sport is similar to North American and European sport.

Samsung Lions had a net deficit of $14 million, even though they had the largest total revenue, $54.2 million, among all the KBO teams. Samsung made its revenue from sponsorship and advertisements ($31 million, 57.3 percent), gate receipts ($6.4 million, 11.7 percent), commercial activities ($13.9 million, 25.6 percent), player trades ($2.5 million, 4.6 percent), and facility lease ($0.4 million, 0.7 percent). Although a couple of teams may generate significant annual revenues from ticket receipts, all the KBO teams rely on the financial support of parent companies. In 2014 KBO teams made only $8.50 per game attendee in comparison with MLB's average of $30 per spectator.

Singapore Football League

Football is a popular sport in Singapore. In the *National Sports Participation Survey 2011* conducted by Sport Singapore, 4.4 percent of respondents participated in football, making it the fifth most popular sport in the country. A total of 18.1 percent of respondents watched football, ranking it as the most popular sport watched by Singaporeans on various platforms including television, at the event venue, and online (Sport Singapore, n.d.). Broadcasters in Singapore believe that the English Premier League is so popular that the pay TV operators put in the highest bid among Asian countries of £35.20 (about US$57) per capita for the 2013-2016 period (Harris, 2013). Despite this interest in football, the Singapore Football League (the S-League), has been plagued with poor attendance at its matches.

Before the formation of the S-League in 1996, Singapore footballers competed in the Malaysia Cup and Malaysian Football League. After winning the league and cup double in 1994, the Football Association of Singapore decided to pull out of the competition and launched the S-League as a means to promote and develop sporting talent in the country. Foreign clubs joined the league over the years, including Albirex Niigata FC (Japan), Brunei DPMM FC (Brunei Darussalam), Harmau Muda (Malaysia), Liaoning Guangyuan FC (China), Sporting Afrique FC (Africa), and Super Reds FC (Korea) (Mohan & Leng, 2015; Selvam, 2015). Today, the S-League is highly dependent on donations and grants. It is unable to operate like established European leagues, which rely on a large fan base of spectators for revenue. In addition, broadcasting rights do not generate sufficient revenues because games are broadcast free on the nation's free-to-air broadcaster, MediaCorp.

The average number of spectators in the S-League during its initial years from 1996 to 1998 was 2,450 spectators per match. Attendance declined, however, between the years 2010 and 2012, falling to 1,150 spectators per match (Dan, 2014; Selvam, 2015). In its annual report for the financial year ending in March 2017, the total revenue for the league was $31,001,193, a decrease of 13 percent from 2016. Gate receipts were only $68,456, contributing less than 1 percent to total revenue. The main sources of income came from donations valued at $16,584,022 (53 percent), grants and subsidies valued at $7,400,170 (24 percent), and sponsorship valued at $6,312,759 (20 percent). Advertising and television rights brought in only $2,092, a minuscule amount of income (Football Association of Singapore, n.d.). To help draw some comparisons, the total revenue for the English league in 2010-2011 was €2,515 million (about US$3,370 million), including match-day receipts of €610 million (about US$817 million) (24 percent), broadcast revenue of €1,305 million (about US$1,750 million) (52 percent), and sponsorship and other commercial revenue of €600 million (about US$800 million) (24 percent). The German and Spanish leagues were similar in that match-day receipts constituted a similar proportion of total revenue. Although broadcast revenues account for almost half of total revenues in the Spanish league, they accounted for only 30 percent of total revenue for the German league (Bose, 2012).

K League Football in Korea

Soccer is the most popular sport in Korea, but when it comes to the domestic professional sport league, soccer is the second most popular behind baseball. The Korean Professional Football League launched the K League in 1998, which has grown to 22 teams in two divisions. Corporations own many of the teams. The league suffers from lack of fan interest in terms of low stadium attendance and low television viewership and, consequently, low sponsor interest. The national television networks broadcast only a few live matches. Most games are broadcast by cable channels that offer limited viewer access. According to Duerden (2018), the league is often thought to be boring, and play is considered reactive, physical, defensive, and counterattacking with the same old coaches producing slow football.

According to the K-League Association's budget information (not individual teams), the association had revenue of $70 million and expenses of $68 million (i.e., a net profit of $2 million) in 2017. The association's major revenue items include sponsorship ($31 million), grants ($14 million), lottery ($16 million), media rights ($5 million), and gate receipts ($2.8 million). Similar to the KBO, the K-League depends on sponsorship deals from parent corporations. There is room for improvement in terms of media rights and spectator attendance. In 2011 Daegu FC had a net loss of $1.7 million and revenue of $6.3 million. Daegu made their revenue from sponsorship and advertisement (63.8 percent), player trades (28.1 percent), gate receipts (4.4 percent), and merchandise sales (0.5 percent). Daegu is considered a top- to middle-ranked team in terms of fan avidity and game attendance within the K-League. Similarly, Ulsan Hyundai FC had annual revenue of $14 million from parent companies' sponsorship (73 percent), player trade deals (13.3 percent), advertisement (7.3 percent), and gate receipts (2.7 percent).

Nippon Professional Baseball in Japan

Formed in 1936 as a single league with seven teams, Nippon Professional Baseball (NPB) was Japan's first professional baseball league (Kawai & Nichol, 2015). The league currently has 12 teams that compete in a two-league format (Pacific and Central League) that is similar to MLB. Teams in the NPB include the Hiroshima Toyo Carp, Fukuoka Soft-Bank Hawks, Hanshin Tigers, Saitama Seibu Lions, Yokoham DeNa Baystars, Tohoku Rakuten Golden Eagles, Yomiuri Giants, ORIX Buffaloes, Chunichi Dragons, Hokkaido Nippon Ham Fighters, Tokyo Yakult Swallows, and the Chiba Lotte Marines. The Hiroshima Toyo Carp operate an academy in the Dominican Republic in close proximity to MLB academies. Kawai and Nichol (2015) note the NPB operates an entry-level draft in the same manner as MLB. Free agency was introduced in 1993 not by the league, but by the Yomiuri Giants, who wanted to acquire the best players from other NPB clubs. The success of Japanese players (e.g., Ichirō Suzuki and Matsui Hideki) has created a market for those who now play in MLB. Recently, Japanese players like Yu Darvish, Masahiro Tanaka, Kenta Maeda, Yoshihisa Hirana, Kazuhisa Makita, and Shohei Ohtani have been on MLB rosters.

When Japanese players transfer from the NPB to MLB they do so under a **posting system**, which allows reserved NPB players to transfer to MLB before serving the nine years required to qualify as international free agents. In 2013 NPB and MLB agreed to the following protocols for the posting system. According to Kawai and Nichol (2015), the posting system works in the following way:

- The posting period operates from November 1 until February 1 of the following year.
- The negotiation period is 30 days.
- Before posting a player, the NPB club sets the release fee (formerly the posting fee), and the amount cannot be changed.
- Release fees are capped at $20 million
- Any MLB club willing to pay the release fee may negotiate a contract with the posted player (Kawai & Nichol, 2015).

On December 1, 2017, MLB announced that Shohei Ohtani would be posted by the Hokkaido Nippon Ham Fighters with a release fee set at the maximum $20 million. Beginning on December 1, any MLB team that was willing to meet the Fighters' release fee of US$20 million would be allowed to negotiate with Ohtani and his agent, but only the team that ultimately secured a contract with Ohtani

Learning Activity

Create either a PowerPoint or Prezi presentation that discusses one or two of the professional sport leagues discussed in this chapter. For example, you could talk in detail about the Nippon Professional Baseball League in Japan. Alternatively, you could discuss the J League in Japan and the K League in Korea and describe the differences between the leagues. The presentation should be 10 minutes or less and should include photos.

was required to pay the money. That MLB team was the Los Angeles Angels (Adams, 2015).

J League in Japan

Founded in 1992, the Japan Professional Football League (J League) is the top professional football league in the country. The J1 League has 18 teams, which are subject to relegation to the J2 League. Fan interest in football in Japan has shrunk considerably during the past decade. Fan attendance at J League games has declined by almost 34 percent from 16.5 million in 2009 to 10.9 million in 2017. According to Alyce (2015), J League clubs are primarily owned by corporations and big industrial companies. The average budget for a J League club is between US$30 and $50 million. Ticket sales and sponsorship are the major source of income. The top J2 teams have budgets between US$10 and $20 million. The league has its own licensing system that sets restrictions on club losses and thus prevents them from spending beyond their earnings. Recently, some clubs have started to build their own stadiums in an effort to increase their revenues.

In 2017 the J Leagues signed a 10-year deal with British-based Perform Group worth ¥210 billion (about US$2 billion) to sell digital online broadcasting rights. The contract was the largest commercial deal in the history of Japanese sport. With these monies the J League winner in 2017 was awarded ¥1.55 billion paid in installments of ¥1 billion, ¥400 million, and ¥150 million over three years; the runner-up made ¥700 million over the same period; the third-place team earned ¥350 million over two years; and the fourth-place team received payment of ¥180 million. The team that won the J1 title received a bonus of ¥300 million, and the runner-up and third-place teams were paid ¥120 million and ¥60 million, respectively. The League Cup winner received ¥150 million. All 18 of the J1 teams were given ¥350 million, second-division teams earned ¥150 million, and J3 teams earned ¥30 million. Teams relegated to the J2 division received ¥130 million, and clubs relegated into J3 received ¥90 million (Kyodo, 2017).

Motor Sport in Asia: Singapore Grand Prix

Motor sport in Asia is booming. The Singapore Grand Prix is probably the most important event in Asia, but world championship rounds and other important series are hosted by various countries, including Japan, Malaysia, China, Singapore, India, South Korea, Indonesia, Turkey, and Gulf States like Qatar, Dubai, Abu Dhabi, and Bahrain (Circuitbooking.com, 2018). The inaugural F1 Grand Prix night street race was held in Singapore in 2008, but this was not the first time that the country had hosted a major motor racing event. About a century earlier, Singapore made history by hosting Asia's first motor racing event in 1911, organized by British residents on the island. Because motor racing was then considered an expensive hobby, the number of participants was limited (DeCotta, 2008).

Organizing a major sport event like the F1 Grand Prix can be costly. Besides the usual costs associated with major sport events, the F1 Grand Prix required existing roads to be widened, new roads and a pit building to be constructed, and fences and other temporary structures to be installed. Because the race occurred at night, the track required additional lighting, thus incurring higher costs compared with other F1 Grand Prixes (Henderson, Foo, Lim, & Yip, 2010). Like other large-scale sport events, the F1 Singapore Grand Prix has been augmented with related activities to enhance and broaden the event's appeal to spectators. For example, the 2008 event included an exhibition of a yellow 1926 Rolls Royce, and the event in 2012 featured various races and other marketing activities like race-car simulators, competitions, a gala premiere of the award-winning film *Senna*, and publicity events (Singapore GP, 2013).

The augmented activities that have attracted the most attention, however, are the street parties and live concerts. In 2010 more than 300 performers provided entertainment for spectators, costing the organizer more than S$5 million (about US$3.75 million) (Singapore GP, 2013). Subsequent years featured even more artists, including headline acts like Duran Duran from the United Kingdom, Kylie Minogue from Australia, Bon Jovi from the United States, Mayday from Taiwan, and BigBang from Korea. The cost to organize the event can be high; one estimate was about $130 million per year (Henderson et al., 2010). But over the years, the organizers have managed to reduce the cost of organizing the event. Reportedly, the event is estimated to cost $130 million per year, and the Singapore government pays approximately 60 percent of the cost (Meng, 2017).

In 2008 a standard ticket for the three days cost $168, and a one-day ticket cost anywhere from $38 to $108. By 2018 the cheapest one-day ticket cost $128. Despite high ticket prices, the event attracts an average of 200,000 spectators each year. The event also attracts a large number of tourists to Singapore (Remember Singapore, 2016). Of the 200,000 spectators in attendance each year, approximately 40 percent are tourists. The Singapore Tourism Board reports that the event brought in an additional 450,000 tourists and $1.4 billion in tourism receipts in its first decade. More than 780 million international broadcast viewers watch the event, further promoting Singapore as a tourist destination (Singapore GP, 2017).

Summary

This chapter highlighted the importance of sport in countries around the world and emphasized the sheer size of the global sport industry. The chapter was broken into two sections. The first discussed amateur participant sport with a focus on nonprofessional participants, and the second section focused on spectating of professional and amateur athletics. Various structures and differences between models of sport throughout the world were reviewed. Models of sport in North America, Europe, and Asia were discussed. Some of the fundamental differences between North America and European sport concern structure, promotion and relegation, and funding. Transfer fees and the system of promotion and relegation take place in European football. European sport has a pyramid structure that consists of clubs forming the base and the regional federations, national federations, and the European federation forming the apex of the pyramid. Concepts such as revenue sharing, reverse-order draft, tanking, reserve clause, free agency, and single-entity structures in North America were discussed. Sport in Asia adopts various elements from both North America and Europe.

A large portion of the chapter facilitates better understanding of various sport leagues around the world. North American sport revolves around a league structure with an emphasis on the NFL, NBA, MLB, and NHL. The text highlights the significance of football in Europe and the importance of the big five European football leagues—England's Premier League, Spain's La Liga, Germany's Bundesliga, Italy's Serie A, and France's Ligue 1. Interest in the Asian sport market is growing, especially because North American sport markets are becoming more saturated. Leagues in North America are shifting their attention to marketing in places like China, the Philippines, Indonesia, Thailand, Japan, and Australia. Finally, we focus attention on Asian leagues such as the Korean Baseball League, Singapore Football League, K League Football in Korea, Nippon Professional Baseball in Japan, and the Japan Professional Football League. Motor sport is also popular in Asia, and the Singapore Grand Prix is highlighted as perhaps the most important motor sport event in Asia.

? Review Questions

1. What important business considerations should managers of participant sports consider?

2. Discuss the differences between a player who is drafted and one who is a free agent.

3. Explain how revenue is generated in most professional sport leagues.

4. What geographic regions do you believe will witness the most growth in sport? What sports are growing the fastest in markets around the world?

5. Describe the concept of promotion and relegation in football, and provide some examples of teams that have been promoted or relegated.

6. What structures in sport do you believe are the most lucrative for generating revenue?

Part V

International Sport Business Strategies

Women's field hockey match between Scotland and Malaysia in the 2018 Gold Coast Commonwealth Games. Scotland defeated Malaysia 4-2 for the seventh place. New Zealand took the gold by winning 4-1 to Australia. England won the bronze medal after defeating India 6-0. The 2018 Commonwealth Games included the participation of 4,426 athletes, representing 71 countries, which competed in 275 events in 19 sports.

Matt King/Getty Images

International Sport Marketing

Gashaw Abeza, PhD
Towson University

Benoit Seguin, PhD
University of Ottawa

Chapter Objectives

After studying this chapter, you will be able to do the following:

- Understand the nature and unique aspects of sport business.
- Discuss the basic concepts of sport marketing and apply them to a global setting.
- Identify the unique features of sport product and apply them to a global setting.
- Understand the nature of sport consumption and sport consumers in a global setting.
- Recognize the place of sport sponsorship in a global setting.
- Discuss the concept of brand and appreciate the unique features of the Olympics brand.

Key Terms

sport-marketing uniqueness	sport consumption
sport product	branding
STP	Olympics brand
SWOT analysis	brand equity
PEST analysis	sponsorship

Sport is a common language that breaks down barriers, unites cultures, and crosses borders in society (Westerbeek & Smith, 2002). Over the past decade, sport has become increasingly internationalized and the business of sport is transcending boundaries (Foster, O'Reilly, & Dávila, 2016). Particularly over the past few years, the management of sport business has become more global, more competitive, more digital, and more data centric (Foster, O'Reilly, & Dávila, 2016). At the same time, sport consumption today with rapid technological change is crossing borders and erasing time barriers. Therefore, as the sport industry becomes more complex, and as sport consumers and organizations increasingly cross national borders, an understanding of the dynamics of international sport marketing becomes crucial.

Consider the following examples, seemingly unrelated to each other, and think about how each addresses themes central to international sport marketing:

◆ Star athletes today are seen as global icons (e.g., professional footballer Cristiano Ronaldo).

◆ Players' international movement becomes a norm (e.g., 69.2 percent of the players in the English Premier League are foreigners [Sky Sports, 2017]).

◆ Licensing and merchandising is no longer localized (e.g., Manchester United opened a store in China in 2008 [Man Unitd, 2008]).

◆ North American professional sport leagues are expanding their offices globally (e.g., the NBA has a major international presence with offices in 13 markets worldwide [NBA, 2017]).

◆ Sponsors are crossing borders to partner with sport teams (e.g., the United Arab Emirates' Etihad Airways sponsors the English Premier League club Manchester City FC).

◆ People are traveling abroad to attend sporting events (e.g., the Olympic Games).

◆ Coaches are increasingly being hired in foreign lands (e.g., Spain's Real Madrid hired a French coach, Zinedine Zidane).

◆ Traditional sport events are repackaging their products (e.g., the new approach to track and field events with Nitro Australia).

◆ Sport goods manufacturers are diversifying their geographic reach (e.g., Nike).

◆ Multimedia and broadcasting efforts are expanding their geographic market (e.g., Univision in Spanish has rights to UEFA events through 2022).

◆ Professional sport teams have fans across the world (e.g., Manchester United Football Club fans).

With these dynamics of sport business, it is clear that the makeup of an international sport market is influenced by the political environment, economy, social issues, cultural composition, and legal restrictions of different domestic and foreign markets (Schwarz, Hunter, & LaFleur, 2012). Also, we can appreciate that international sport marketing does not exclusively center on international organizations such as the International Olympic Committee (IOC) and international sport federations (IF). Overall, the advancement of sport business management at a global level, together with sport's cross-cultural ability to appeal to different generations of people in multiple geographic locations (Ratten & Ratten, 2011) highlights the importance of international sport marketing. In particular, an understanding of the basics of sport marketing, appreciation of different values and belief systems of different countries and geographic regions, and recognition of the need to adapt to various situations is necessary for anyone studying sport marketing. Furthermore, Crow, Byon, and Tsuji (2011) identified three reasons that show the value of studying sport marketing from an international perspective:

1. First, it provides students increased opportunities for meaningful employment in the sport industry when national borders are crossed.

2. Second, sport consumers and organizations operate differently in countries around the world, so exposure to a global perspective is crucial.

3. Third, a basic understanding of the topic will be important for the evolution of the continued study of sport marketing from a global perspective.

The purpose of this chapter, therefore, is to build on the foundational knowledge of sport marketing and apply this knowledge in an international sport context. This background includes the unique nature and aspects of the sport business, the basic concepts of sport marketing, the unique features of sport products, the nature of sport consumption and its consumers, the place of sport sponsorship in a global setting, and the concept of brand applied to the Olympics. The chapter is organized in such a way as to gain a background in these topic areas.

Nature and Unique Aspects of Sport Business

Sport takes many forms.

- It can be an individual (e.g., golf, running), dual (e.g., boxing, tennis), or team sport (e.g., basketball, soccer).
- It can be seen as a spectator sport (e.g., basketball) or a participant sport (e.g., mass-participation road race or marathon).
- It can be seen in various contexts such as professional sport, college sport, Olympic sport, or community sport.

Sport can also be taken as fun (for most of us), as work (for professional athletes), as a means of employment (for athletic directors), and as a business (for sport marketing agencies). Regardless of the form sport may take, understanding **sport-marketing uniqueness** (i.e., the features of sport marketing that distinguish it from marketing in other businesses) will be important in the discussion of international sport marketing. Three main unique features make the sport business, specifically the professional sport business, different from mainstream businesses such as airlines, insurance, restaurant, or banking: (1) its product's unique features, (2) its unconventional sources of revenue, and (3) its distinctiveness as a social institution. These three aspects are briefly discussed next.

Unique Features of the Sport Product

As a sport marketer, what do you think makes your product (e.g., a match, competition, or tournament) different from services and products offered by car manufacturers, airline companies, banks, hotels,

grocery stores, and so on? A number of scholars (e.g., Armstrong, 2014; Mullin, Hardy, & Sutton, 2014; Smith & Stewart, 2010) have discussed the unique features of the professional sport product that distinguish it from traditional mainstream products. According to these scholars, a **sport product** (e.g., a football match) is different from other products for these reasons:

- It is simultaneously produced and consumed.
- It is perishable (i.e., people watch games as they are being played).
- It has a fixed supply (i.e., schedules of games are fixed and number of tickets is fixed by the number of seats).
- Production is dependent and interdependent (i.e., teams rely on other teams to produce a game).
- Fans and consumers help produce the product (i.e., the presence of cheering spectators when games are being played is vital).
- A sport product is of variable quality (e.g., the quality of the game can vary).
- A sport product is consumed irrationally (i.e., fans and consumers exhibit irrational passion and a high degree of loyalty).
- The outcome is uncertain and unpredictable (e.g., the outcome of any game is uncertain before it is played).
- Sport teams continually invest in training, unlike businesses that employ people from professions such as engineering, accountancy, and others.

Unconventional Sources of Revenue

Unlike mainstream businesses, a sport performance business (e.g., professional or college sport) generates its revenue not only by selling its main product (i.e., competition) but also by exploiting unconventional sources such as sponsorship sales, merchandise sales, broadcast contracts, naming-rights deals, licensing fees, donations (e.g., NCAA), membership fees (e.g., Cycling USA), parking, and venue rental. Rarely do other businesses generate as much income through the abovementioned sources as sport businesses do.

Learning Activity

Think of a recent sporting game that you attended and identify at least five features of the game (see the just discussed unique features of sport products) that make it different from products that are being sold at a grocery store or at a hotel near you.

Distinctiveness as a Social Institution

Sport is part of the culture of many societies of today's world, from hockey in Canada to baseball in Japan to rugby in New Zealand to football in Brazil. Sport management reinforces social and cultural values (Smith & Stewart, 2010) such as striving for success, willingness to work hard, and valuing victory, teamwork, brotherhood, unity, and friendship. Sport has occupied and will continue to occupy spectator interest across the globe (Stavros & Westberg, 2009). It is an expression of self and social identity, serving as an attraction point for families, neighbors, office colleagues, citizens, and nations (Shank & Lyberger, 2014). Sport fans' loyalty to a sport team is unique and far stronger than any other customer exhibits to other brands; think of the fans of FC Barcelona or Real Madrid (Waters, Burke, Jackson, & Buning, 2011). Besides, sport attracts media attention and is almost always in the public spotlight where, for example, the media cover athletes' actions both on and off the field on a daily basis (Lee, Bang, & Lee, 2013). The social and cultural values of sport in our society, together with media interest, show the uniqueness of the operation of sport business as a social institution unlike other mainstream businesses.

These unique features of sport business make sport marketing both challenging and rewarding, often even more so in a global setting. So what is sport marketing? The next section discusses the definition and components of sport marketing.

Sport Marketing Basics

Sport marketing involves aspects ranging from ticket prices to fans' experience to sponsorship to media rights. Consider the following questions:

- How can Dallas Cowboys enhance their fans' experience?
- How can La Liga (Spanish football) teams develop, maintain, and enhance their fan base?
- What is the appropriate ticket price for IAAF Diamond League meets?
- What teams and athletes should Nike sponsor?
- How can Nippon Professional Baseball (NPB) in Japan increase its TV ratings?
- How much should the U.S. Open charge its official sponsors?
- How can teams in the Bundesliga (German Premier League) sell more tickets? Can teams in Serie A (Italian Premier League) and Ligue 1 (French Premier League) employ the same sales strategy?
- Why are the All Blacks (the New Zealand national rugby union team) well known around the world, and what is the implication of that in terms of the team's global brand?

These and other similar questions fall under the purview of sport marketing. So what is sport marketing? Sport marketing can be defined as the specific application of marketing principles and processes to sport products and to the marketing of nonsport products through an association with sport (Gray & McEvoy, 2005). Pitts and Stotlar (2007) define sport marketing as the process of designing and implementing activities for the production, pricing, promotion, and distribution of a sport product to satisfy the needs or desires of consumers and to achieve the company's objectives. The two definitions encompass the marketing of sport as well as marketing through sport. As Shank and Lyberger (2014) discuss, marketing through sport is the use of sport as a promotional vehicle for companies to reach out to consumers through endorsement (e.g., Roger Federer's endorsement of Rolex watches), naming rights (e.g., AT&T's naming rights fee for the Dallas Cowboys' stadium), or sponsorship (e.g., VISA's sponsoring of the Olympics). On the other hand, the marketing of sport refers to the application of marketing principles and processes to market sporting goods and services to sport participants and spectators (e.g., Swimming Canada's recruiting of kids to join swim clubs).

In contemplating the definition of sport marketing, keep in mind that a sport marketer's job ultimately comes down to one action: creating demand (Shank & Lyberger, 2014). Marketing is about identifying customers' wants and needs, and satisfying them while achieving the company's objectives. The process of designing and implementing marketing activities demands a clear understanding of what are referred to as the 4Cs (consumers, company, competitors, and climate) and the 4Ps (product, price, promotion, and place) of marketing (Shank & Lyberger, 2014). Each of these components of sport marketing is discussed next.

Four Cs of Marketing

In this context, *consumer* refers to a marketer's knowledge and understanding of existing and new consumers. A marketer should have a database that allows segmenting, targeting, and positioning its products in the consumers' minds. This process is commonly referred to as **STP**, the foundation of a marketing strategy. To run an STP, a marketer needs to gather data on factors such as demographics (e.g., age, sex), psychographics (e.g. attitude, opinion), geography (e.g., area, region, country), and behavior (e.g., purchasing behavior, brand usage rate, brand loyalty). An understanding of market segmentation increases effective market selection. Here it will be worth defining the three key elements of STP. According to Shank and Lyberger (2014), segmentation is the identification of groups of consumers based on their common needs, targeting is choosing the segment or segments that will allow an organization to attain its marketing goals efficiently and

effectively, and positioning is fixing the sport entity in the minds of consumers in the target market.

Company is about marketers understanding their own company. An understanding of a company includes being clear in stating its organizational vision, mission, objectives, marketing goals, and organizational culture (Pitts & Stotlar, 2013). For example, any action that marketing managers in the cricket teams of the Indian Premier League (IPL) might take depends on the mission, vision, and objectives of the company. Marketing managers are responsible for aligning their marketing strategies with the company's objectives in an effort to maximize an organization's benefits. For example, World Triathlon Corp. (WTC), a subsidiary of the Chinese Dalian Wanda Group Co. Ltd., had the objective of expanding its running and cycling market worldwide. With that objective, the company pursued a global roll-up strategy in pursuit of a bigger global market share in the highly fragmented mass-participation race business. In June 2017, the company acquired the American based Rock 'n' Roll Marathon series. In the deal, WTC added 29 annual running events, including 7 outside the United States, to its growing participatory endurance properties.

The concept of *competitor* deals with the understanding of what an organization's competitors are capable of doing (Shank & Lyberger, 2014). This subject includes studying competitors' financial strength (e.g., in American professional sport leagues, teams in New York have a large yearly revenue, and other teams in the leagues take that into consideration), studying the market place (e.g., in Dallas, Texas, five professional teams compete for market share in the region), gathering competitors' data (e.g., ticket prices charged by other teams), recognizing a competitive advantage (e.g., having a starting player like LeBron James), and so on. Marketers are expected to run constant competitive analyses to ensure that their organizations stay relevant in their markets.

Climate refers to a marketer's understanding of current situational factors that affect the organization's business (O'Reilly & Séguin, 2013). In this respect, marketers need to study factors such as political (e.g., players' lockout), economic (e.g., English Premier League clubs and the depreciation or appreciation of the pound currency), legal (e.g., suspension of players and scandals), social (e.g., sexual orientation and athletes), and technologi-

---

Learning Activity

Conduct an online search to find demographic data on NBA, NHL, MLB, and NFL sport fans in the United States. Find gender, age (e.g., <17, 18-34, 35-54, >55), race and ethnicity (e.g., White, Black, Hispanic, others), and income (e.g., >US$100,000, 75,000-100,000, 40,000-75,000, 20,000-40,000, <20,000) information. Compile your results and discuss them with your classmates.

Learning Activity

Identify a sport organization in your area and briefly discuss the 4Cs of that organization (i.e., its consumers, the organization's objective, its competitors, and its climate.

cal (e.g., the Arizona Cardinals being the last to join Twitter). This process is commonly known in marketing literature as **PEST analysis** (political, economic, social, and technological). For instance, the potential effect of Brexit on the English Premier League clubs' market should be one factor that a marketer in the league takes into account in her or his analysis of the business climate. Particularly, the Premier League clubs could be concerned about EU players' labor restrictions post-Brexit. In the Premier League 2015-2016 season, more than half of the 647 players were classified as non-British, and the majority of those (208) were from the EU. Therefore, understanding the external factors that affect the global sport environment is an essential part of any sport marketing effort.

Marketers use various approaches to acquire information about the 4Cs in developing their strategies and decision making (O'Reilly & Séguin, 2013). One tool that is commonly adopted by marketers is an analysis of strengths, weaknesses, opportunities, and threats (SWOT). A **SWOT analysis** is a study undertaken by an organization to identify its internal strengths and weaknesses, as well as its external opportunities and threats.

Four Ps of Marketing

The marketing mix refers to controllable variables that the company puts together to satisfy a target group—the recipe for creating a successful marketing campaign, commonly referred as the 4Ps (i.e., product, price, promotion, and place) (Shank & Lyberger, 2014).

Product

In the marketing of sport, a sport product is the actual event plus the benefit that consumers seek from the experience. Sport marketers do not have direct influence over a team's chance of winning a game. Because they have little control over the outcome of a game, sport marketers must focus on

CASE STUDY

SWOT Analysis: Nike and Adidas

Nike and Adidas are American and German, respectively, multinational corporations that engage in the design, development, manufacturing, and worldwide marketing and sales of footwear, apparel, equipment, accessories, and services. The SWOT analysis for Nike in its campaign effort to be number one in the world soccer market is presented here.

SWOT analysis: For Nike, their use of a SWOT analysis in the world soccer market recognizes that they are the most widely known athletic shoe producer and retain the largest market share worldwide, 17 percent, with revenues of $20 billion. Adidas is second with a 12 percent market share. Specific to soccer, however, Nike is second. Nike brought in $2.3 billion in revenue in 2013-2014 (fiscal year ending May 2014), whereas it is estimated that Adidas will procure $2.7

billion in soccer revenue for the same year. Nike has not engaged in the soccer apparel industry as long as Adidas has. Nike did not "do" soccer until 1994, whereas Adidas has engaged in the soccer forum for over 66 years. At the start of the 2014 World Cup, Nike sponsored 10 teams, and Adidas sponsored 9. In the end, it was not a Nike versus Nike or an Adidas versus Nike battle: It was an Adidas versus Adidas final, Germany against Argentina. Nike's best opportunity will be the 2020 Summer Olympics, which will have a vast audience watching on television. The major threat will be Adidas.

Discussion: From this analysis, identify Nike's strengths versus weaknesses, and opportunities versus threats in their effort to be number one in the world soccer market.

external factors surrounding the game that can be managed, referred to as product extension (Shank & Lyberger, 2014). The *extensions* are a variety of tactics used to enhance the consumers' experience of attending beyond the game itself. Extensions include performances during breaks, in-stadium video boards, cheerleading, and so on. Note here that sport products can also include products manufactured by Nike, Adidas, Puma, Reebok, Li-Ning, and others.

Price

Prices could be prices of tickets, satellite TV packages, subscriptions for special information on a sport website, and so on (O'Reilly & Séguin, 2013). Today, increasing evidence indicates that sport fans are not willing or able to pay because of the drastic increase in the price of attending sporting events or matches. The price of a ticket for many events is increasingly separated from the actual ticket price to include premium services such as access to restaurants and waitperson services (Masteralexis, Barr, & Hums, 2015). Fans also consider the entire cost when determining the value of attending a game: Cost = ticket price + parking fee + concessions + personal time, and so forth. Team Marketing Report, an American publisher of sport marketing information, has developed the Fan Cost Index (FCI) tool to determine the average costs for a family of four (two adults, two children) to attend a game for one of the teams of the North American professional sport leagues (NHL, MLB, NFL, NBA). FCI is determined for each team's specific market and comprises four adult average-price tickets, two small draft beers, four small soft drinks, four regular-size hotdogs, parking for one car, and two least expensive, adult-size adjustable caps. The important takeaway message here is that when determining ticket price, marketers must make sure that they balance perceived value and perceived quality.

Place

A typical mainstream product is produced at a manufacturing site and transferred to a location (e.g., a mall) for sale to customers, and it has a shelf life (if it cannot be sold today, it can be sold tomorrow). Neither condition is true in sport. Sporting events are produced and consumed simultaneously, and when the game is over, the ticket cannot be resold. The physical surroundings of the stadium that affect spectators' desire to stay at the stadium are also important factors that are unique to sport. This concept is known as sportscape (Shank & Lyberger, 2014). Key factors to consider are access (transportation, close to cities, and so on), facility aesthetics (retro features in new ballparks, clean facility, and so on), scoreboard qualities, amenities (sport experience is a social one and thus needs bars and restaurants), and the perceived crowding (seating comfort, layout accessibility, proper signage, and so on). For example, the Dallas Cowboys stadium (AT&T Stadium) that opened in 2009 has a size of 3 million square feet (280,000 sq m), 80,000 to 100,000 seats, and 2,900 TV screens.

Two concepts associated with place are distribution of tickets and distribution of event media coverage. Ticket distribution refers to the way in which sport consumers access tickets to games. Most teams today sell their tickets online; for example, Ticketmaster is the official ticketing partner of the NBA. In terms of event media distribution, one good example is the recent effort made by the English Football League (EFL). With the recent evolution in digital media, sport teams are making their products more accessible across borders, reaching out to fans overseas. For instance, the EFL in 2017 launched a new live-streaming service to offer access to overseas fans to watch their favorite team games in action. Overseas fans of most EFL clubs were able to watch live games of the 2017 season on a new digital platform called iFollow.

Promotion

Promotion is what the public often thinks is marketing, because promotions are what the public sees. Promotions are activities designed to get the attention of consumers (O'Reilly & Séguin, 2013). This activity includes advertising (paid messages conveyed through media); personal selling (face-to-face presentation to pursued buyers, from season tickets to corporations); publicity (media exposure through press conferences); and sales promotion (coupons, trade shows, exhibitions, and so on). Some textbooks include **sponsorship**, an investment (in cash or in kind) in activity in return for access to the exploitable commercial potential associated with that activity (Meenaghan, 1991), in this category. In today's international sport marketing, social media is becoming one of the prime promotion outlets. For example, in its expansion of global market reach, Union of European Football Associations (UEFA) launched its "Together #WePlayStrong" marketing

Summary of the 4Cs and 4Ps of Sport Marketing

The 4Cs are factors that marketers need to study to make decisions and develop strategies.

- ◆ Consumer: knowing and understanding existing and new consumers
- ◆ Company: understanding one's own company by conducting a SWOT analysis
- ◆ Competitor: studying what others are capable of doing and developing new strategies
- ◆ Climate: studying the current situational factors that affect the sport business

After information has been collected about the 4Cs, the next step is making decisions and formulating strategies about the marketing mix (4Ps).

- ◆ Product: what you create for the consumer
- ◆ Price: exchange agreement with the consumer
- ◆ Place: getting the product to the consumer
- ◆ Promotion: communication with or getting the attention of the consumer (Pitts & Stotlar, 2013; Shank & Lyberger, 2014)

---

campaign that aimed at stimulating women's sport and making football the number one participation sport for girls and women in Europe by 2022.

Having provided an overall understanding of sport marketing and its various components, we now discuss in more detail the unique features that make the sport product and its marketing distinct from the marketing of other mainstream businesses. The following section, through the lens of the marketing of sport (not marketing through sport) and focusing on professional sport teams, discusses the unique features that make sport products (e.g., professional basketball games) different from other products.

Nature of the Professional Sport Team Product in a Global Setting

A number of scholars (e.g., Armstrong, 2014; Beech & Chadwick, 2007; Mason, 1999; Mullin, Hardy, & Sutton, 2014; Smith & Stewart, 2010) have discussed the unique features of the professional sport team product that distinguish it from the traditional mainstream product. According to these scholars, professional teams in a league compete against each other in a fixed schedule or for a series of games, with an uncertain outcome, in a league-designated home territory of one of the teams. Fans help produce the product (e.g., support in a stadium by cheering for their team playing a game), the competition that can vary in quality (e.g., NBA playoff games), and then consume it as it is produced. A

number of sport fans exhibit a high degree of optimism, and at times their demand may even exceed the available seats. Still, the supply remains fixed in terms of number of tickets or games played. A list of unique features of such a sport product is presented in table 20.1. Given the unique features of sport, its management and marketing demand a customized set of practices to ensure its effective operation (Armstrong, 2014; Smith & Stewart, 2010).

From a financial point of view, as Humphreys and Mondello (2008) state, a distinguishing characteristic of a sport franchise compared with traditional businesses lies in its dependence on intangible assets. These intangible assets include player contracts, television rights, stadium agreements, and relationships with fans. As opposed to the traditional assets such as manufacturing plants and equipment, intangible assets are important factors that contribute to the overall financial status of professional sport teams (Humphreys & Mondello, 2008). In terms of consumers of the professional team sport product, Mason (1999) discusses four distinct groups of consumers: the fans, television and other media, communities that construct facilities and support local clubs, and corporations that interact with the leagues and teams.

Nature of Sport Consumption

Sport can be consumed both as a spectator and as a participant (Shank & Lyberger, 2014). For example, attending a live match between Real

Table 20.1 Unique Features of Sport (What Makes It Different From Other Products)

Features	Studies focused on these features
The outcome is uncertain.	Beech & Chadwick (2007); Mason (1999); Mullin, Hardy, & Sutton (2014); Smith & Stewart (2010)
Consumers help to produce a product—the presence of other customers is vital.	Beech & Chadwick (2007); Mason (1999)
Consumed irrationally—people develop irrational passions.	Beech & Chadwick (2007); Armstrong (2014); Mullin, Hardy, & Sutton (2014)
Sport receives greater media interest.	Beech & Chadwick (2007); Mason (1999)
Differences in judging performance—a heterogeneous and ephemeral experience.	Mullin, Hardy, & Sutton (2014); Armstrong (2014)
Interdependency—a team's existence depends on other teams.	Beech & Chadwick (2007); Mullin, Hardy & Sutton (2014); Taylor (2008)
Sport product (a game or contest) is of variable quality (e.g., playoff series games).	Smith & Stewart (2010); Armstrong (2014); Mason (1999)
It enjoys a high degree of product or brand loyalty—unwavering loyalty.	Beech & Chadwick (2007); Smith & Stewart (2010)
It engenders vicarious identification.	Smith & Stewart (2010)
Sport fans exhibit a high degree of optimism.	Mullin, Hardy, & Sutton (2014); Smith & Stewart (2010)
A fixed supply schedule.	Smith & Stewart (2010); Armstrong (2014)
An intangible, experiential, and subjective nature.	Mullin, Hardy, & Sutton (2014)
Simultaneously produced and consumed.	Mullin, Hardy, & Sutton (2014)
Continual investment in training.	Taylor (2008)

Madrid and Barcelona or watching an Olympic competition on TV is consumption of sport as a spectator. In the same way, someone can take part in a mass-participation road race such as the Dubai Marathon or London Marathon and consume sport. Furthermore, buying team or event merchandise can be considered a form of consumption. These consumption types are captured in figure 20.1.

Today, **sport consumption** is becoming increasingly costly (for instance, entry fees and team merchandise keep rising in cost). At the same time, global sport consumers are confronted with numerous choices (e.g., places and events) on which to spend their time and money. Demanding and sophisticated sport consumers are emerging around the world (Abeza, O'Reilly, Séguin, & Nzindukiyimana, 2017). Successful sport marketers need to have good understanding of the factors that influence consumers' interest in sport and their consumption of sport.

A number of scholars have tried to address questions related to sport consumers, such as the following: Why do some people follow sport with more passion than others? Why do most people jump off a bandwagon faster than they climbed on? Why do people who live in Africa or Asia and have never been to Spain, Italy, or Britain latch onto teams such as Manchester United, Real Madrid, and Juventus rather than a hometown team? As Shank and Lyberger (2014) discuss, sport consumers' consumption can be influenced by a number of conditions or factors. These factors include fan motivation factors (e.g., escape from everyday life issues, gambling or fantasy sport, family ties), game attractiveness (e.g., the Olympics, Opening Ceremony, Premier League), economic factors (e.g., average income of the population), demographic factors (e.g., culture of the sport, age, gender, education, occupation), sport involvement (e.g., the perceived interest in and personal importance

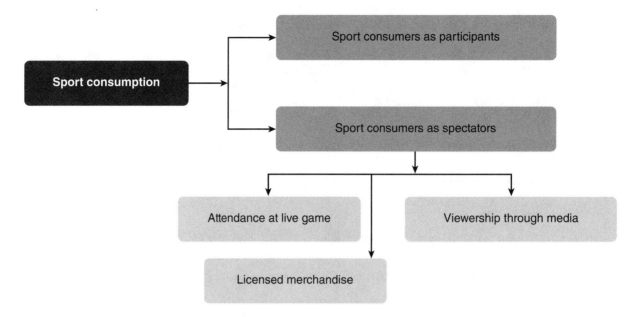

Figure 20.1 Types of sport consumption.

of sport to spectators), and fan identification (e.g., the personal commitment and emotional involvement that customers have with a sport organization). Regardless of the conditions that affect sport consumption, most sport cannot depend only on die-hard fans to fill up seats. For that reason, among others, selling tickets for a losing team is usually challenging (Masteralexis, Barr, & Hums, 2015). This point raises the question about the difference between sport consumer and sport fan.

In the mainstream marketing literature, the people who purchase goods and services are commonly referred to as consumers (Crow, Byon, & Tsuji, 2011). In the sport management literature, the term *consumer* is used, at times, interchangeably with spectators or fans. Although there is not a universally agreed upon distinction between sport consumer and sport fan, the literature offers an understanding of the motivational, behavioral, and attitudinal differences and similarities, and thereby the conceptualization of consumers compared with sport fans and spectators. In this chapter sport consumers are understood as anyone who is consuming sport regardless of the consumption motivation or the level of behavioral and affective attachment to the product (e.g., a cricket team). In this regard, a number of authors (e.g., Foster, O'Reilly, & Dávila, 2016; Funk & James, 2001; Gladden & Funk, 2002;

Hunt, Bristol, & Bashaw, 1999; Stewart, Smith, & Nicholson, 2003; Tapp, 2004; Wann & Branscombe, 1990) contributed to the advancement of this body of literature. These scholars suggested that sport consumers are not only distinct from the consumers of other businesses but also have a varying level of sport consumption attachment, indeed displaying a range of values, attitudes, and behaviors.

According to Wann (1995), the difference between a spectator and a fan is that a spectator is an individual who is observing a sporting event and a fan is someone who is enthusiastic about a particular team or athlete. The difference between a fan and a spectator, by implication, is the difference in the degree of devotion to a sport object (e.g., a team such as Manchester United FC, a player such as Lionel Messi, or a coach such as José Mourinho). According to Anderson (1979), a fan can be defined as an ardent devotee of sport. Similarly, Hunt et al. (1999) described a sport fan as an enthusiastic consumer of organized sport or as a consumer who is motivated to engage in behavior related to sport and has some level of attachment to a sport object. Because there are differences among and between spectators and fans (e.g., the difference from fan to fan in terms of the level of attachment to a sport object, namely, the underlying motivation for consumption of sport and actual sport-related behavior), several authors have attempted to construct precise typologies or classifications of sport fans. Hence, because some may too easily assume that sport fans are not homogenous, it is problematic to view fans as a singular group (Foster et al., 2016; Stewart et al., 2003). Sport fans vary in their allegiance or psychological attachment to a team (Foster et al., 2016; Wann & Branscombe, 1990). In addition, the notion that all sport fans are determinedly and unwaveringly loyal is naive and even idealistic (Harris & Ogbonna, 2008). Lastly, sport fans may not necessarily attend live games all the time, but they often consume sport by watching games on television or purchasing apparel and licensed products (Funk & James, 2001; Gladden & Funk, 2002; Tapp, 2004; Wann, Melnick, Russell, & Pease, 2001).

To offer an example from the abundant literature, in the context of an individual's psychological connection to sport and the temporal process through which that connection moves, Funk and James (2001) proposed the psychological continuum model (PCM) to help outline, among other aspects, the sport spectator and sport fan involvement level with a team. For this purpose, the authors integrated the body of research to examine the differences among and between spectators and fans. According to the PCM, four levels of categories are found along a continuum:

1. awareness,
2. attraction,
3. attachment and
4. allegiance.

Awareness signifies the point when a person is first introduced to a given sport or team (e.g., media, friend, moving to a new city, and so on). To give an example using a team from the National Hockey League, the Montréal Canadiens, the statement "I know about hockey and I know about Montréal Canadiens" illustrates the awareness stage. Attraction designates the point when a person recognizes that he or she has a favorite team or a favorite sport. The statement "I like hockey and I like the Montréal Canadiens" illustrates the attraction stage. Attachment signifies the point when a person manifests a psychological connection with the sport object (e.g., a favorite team). The statement "I am a hockey player and I am a Montréal Canadiens fan" illustrates the attachment stage. Finally, allegiance signifies the

point when a person becomes a loyal (or committed) fan of a particular sport or team. Allegiance also produces influential attitudes that create consistent and durable behavior. The statement "I live for hockey and I live for the Montréal Canadiens" illustrates the allegiance stage. In a separate study on fan behavioral loyalty, Tapp (2004) argued that game attendance is not necessarily the best measure of fan loyalty. According to the author, although fans with low levels of loyalty develop from such factors as team success or recent relocations, high levels of loyalty derive from factors like family history and self-identity.

Contemplating the various ways in which consumers can express their sport interest, a number of authors (e.g., Foster et al., 2016; Funk & James, 2001; Gladden & Funk, 2002; Hunt et al., 1999; Mahony, Madrigal, & Howard, 2000; Stewart & Smith, 1999) proposed multidimensional typologies for sport consumers. These authors based their classification on

- consumption motives (escape, eustress, social interaction);
- emotional commitment (strong, conditional, and fragile);
- economic commitment (strong, moderate, and weak financial interest);
- level of identification—as an extension of self-identity (civic and community pride, or social and cultural identity);
- loyalty (through game attendance, displaying team colors, chatter, and conversation);
- connection point (primary point of connection is a team, a sport or league, or a player); and
- frequency of game attendance (frequent, moderate, and low).

These typologies, in general, differentiate sport consumers based on a number of factors that include emotional attachment to teams, loyalty, and identity, which then link to a specific pattern of consumption, namely game attendance, television viewing, and the purchase of team merchandise. From this list, as Wann, Grieve, Zapalac, and Pease (2008) and Wann et al. (2001) stated, the eight most common factors that motivate people to consume sport (although the list of potential motives is quite

Learning Activity

Write down five reasons that motivated you to consume sport recently and address how you think students in other countries would answer this question. Discuss your answers with classmates.

extensive) are escape, economic (e.g., gambling), eustress (positive level of arousal), self-esteem, group affiliation, entertainment, family, and aesthetics qualities (i.e., artistic).

As Crow, Byon, and Tsuji (2011) pointed out, most of the studies on motives and identification affecting sport consumption have been conducted in the context of North American sport. But the concepts have important dimensions in international sport settings and apply to international sport consumption behavior. For instance, Neale and Funk (2006) found that several motive factors, including vicarious achievement, player interest, entertainment value, drama, and socialization, influenced spectators to attend Australian football games. Spectator motive also was found to be an important driving force for soccer fans of the Japan Professional Football League. Andrew, Kim, Andrew, and Greenwell (2009) also found that motive positively influenced both Korean and U.S. spectators to watch mixed martial arts events.

The sport consumer typologies proposed (and the various factors on which those classifications are based) provide an understanding that the consumption of sport is unique and, as Madrigal (1995) stated, involves considerable emotional significance. Yet these typologies also imply the clearly multifaceted nature of sport consumption. After reviewing a number of scholarly works that attempted to classify sport consumers, Stewart et al. (2003) argued that no single typology is best; all the classifications have both strengths and limitations.

In the discussion of international sport marketing, note the role that sponsorship and media play in the advancement of sport business. Sport organizations, media organizations, and corporate sponsors all depend on each other. Without the support of the media and sponsors, sport might not have reached the global popularity it enjoys today. Sponsors provide support to sport proper-

ties, in kind and in cash, in return for exploitable commercial benefits associated with the sport property. Similarly, sport properties charge corporate partners to be associated with their properties, and that connection allows them to create an emotional connection with sport fans. The media is similarly interested in airing entertaining sporting competitions that draw large audiences. Toward this end, media organizations expect a well-organized sporting event with few financial concerns. Although other reference materials can provide a more in-depth understanding of the three parts of the triangle, particularly the role of media in sport business, a brief discussion of international sport and sponsorship follows here.

International Sport and Sponsorship

In early days of modern sponsorship, the act of sponsorship was not different from philanthropy. The support was reflected as an individual interest of senior management rather than a sensible evaluation of sponsorship benefits. In the 1980s and early 1990s, sponsorship started to be viewed as an alternative to advertising and as a way of obtaining media exposure (Crompton, 2004). Today, corporate sponsorship is one of the fastest growing forms of marketing communication (O'Reilly, Pound, Burton, Séguin, & Brunette, 2015). It is exceeding both media advertising and promotion in terms of year-to-year growth in expenditure. The growth of sponsorship, both in money allocated and in the projection of sponsorship as a legitimate element in the marketing mix, is due in part to the view of sponsorship as a cost-effective alternative to traditional media (Abeza, Pegoraro, Naraine, Séguin, & O'Reilly, 2014).

Sport continues to receive the lion's share of the total global sponsorship expenditure involving mutual benefit to both sponsors and sport (O'Reilly et al., 2015). With the internationalization of sport business today, corporate partners are crossing national borders and partnering with sport teams and events far from their headquarters. For example, traditionally the FIFA World Cup partners have been mostly companies based in Europe and North America, but the World Cup has recently attracted Chinese companies. In early June 2017, FIFA signed a third Chinese World Cup sponsor. FIFA secured a sponsorship deal with smartphone maker Vivo amounting to US$449.6 million.

As Garland, Charbonneau, and Macpherson (2008) stated, sponsors are using the sport product (e.g., events, athletes, facilities, teams, and so on) as the tie or association to influence consumers to form positive brand images or make purchases from the sponsors. Basically, sport sponsorship is attractive to corporations because sporting events provide a highly involved, passionate, and loyal audience that is composed of people with similar demographics (Madrigal, 2001). McCarville, Flood, and Froats (1998) cite various research works that have mentioned public interest, involvement and commitment, emotional attachment, and drama that make sport an ideal venue for sponsorship.

Similarly, Copeland, Frisby, and McCarville (1996) discussed the attributes of sport attractive to corporate sponsors.

- First, specific target groups can be reached in a more direct and cost-efficient manner than by using traditional forms of mass advertising.
- Second, the image of a sponsor can be enhanced as a company associates itself with the positive features of a sport product.
- Third, sport often generates substantial excitement and emotional attachment among its consumers, and such attachment may let consumers be more disposed to sponsors' messages and other marketing initiatives.
- Fourth, sport sponsorship is a flexible channel, leveraging opportunities such as merchandising, cross promotions, and dealer incentives that can be exploited.

Such features make sport sponsorship a unique vehicle for reaching beyond traditional advertising. Note, however, that some corporate partners are expressing their concerns with the crowded sponsorship market in certain sport. For example, when Heineken announced its renewal of the 27-year association with rugby, the Rugby World Cup 2019, Heineken's global sponsorship director stated the concern with the crowded soccer sponsorship market.

Another concern linked to sport sponsorship is known as ambush marketing. Ambush marketing is an expected part of today's international sport marketing and sponsorship landscape that surrounds major sport properties (i.e., players, teams) including sporting events (i.e., Olympic Games, FIFA World Cup, and so on). As Sandler and Shani (1989) noted, ambush marketing occurs when a nonsponsor tries to gain some sort of association with a sport property without having paid for the official rights. This activity is a problem for sport properties that offer product exclusivity to official sponsors. The development of exclusivity means that the sport organization (e.g., EUFA's Champions League) is able both to create and control the sponsorship environment in which its brand is used, thus enabling it, in theory, to control clutter (i.e., a crowded sponsorship market) by limiting the number of available opportunities. This feature makes the sponsorship opportunity rare and consequently provides greater value for corporate

CASE STUDY

Ambush Marketing and the 2020 Japan Olympic Games

You are the commercial rights manager for Japan Olympic Games in 2020 and have a decision to make about what appears to be ambush marketing. A local restaurant, called Olympia, has been a fixture in the community for over 50 years. Their current marketing efforts appear to be contravening the legal protection of Olympic marks because their advertising is suggesting a connection between the Olympics and the restaurant (e.g., the name, Olympia, and the menu, which has gold, silver, and bronze menu choices). The restaurant is not a sponsor on any level of the Games.

Discussion: What do you do? Explain the process you used to come to a decision in this situation about whether to take antiambush action (e.g., legal, cease-and-desist) or leave it be?

partners. But at the same time, the desirability of a property such as the Champions League and the hefty price tag placed on exclusive sponsorship rights ($70 million per year) creates a sponsorship environment that fosters and encourages the development of the practice of ambush marketing. As the cost of sponsorship exclusivity continues to escalate, sport properties have to think proactively in managing the potential damage caused by ambush marketing on its partners. In other words, the property must carefully manage increased expectations of sponsors in this situation.

Olympic Brand

The five interlaced rings are known throughout the world as the symbol representing the Olympic Games. The symbol is the property of the IOC and it signifies the corporate brand. Brand is the name, logo, or other outward symbol that distinguishes a product or service from others in its category (Aaker, 1991). In other words, the brand is closely connected to the IOC and the Organizing Committee of the Olympic Games (OCOG) as it produces the Olympic Games and offers programs (products) that are linked to the brand. The brand plays a central role in the brand portfolio (Olympic Games, Youth Olympic Games, Athletes Career Programme, peace through sport, development through sport, and so on) of the IOC and in the numerous brand alliances spearheaded by the organization (e.g., national Olympic committees or NOCs, OCOGs, commercial partners, IFs, host government, and so on). Consequently, the marketing programs designed by the IOC, NOCs, and OCOGs and the activation programs of its stakeholders are designed to capitalize on the corporate brand and its branding (Ferrand, Chappelet, & Séguin, 2012). Here, **branding** refers to the process of creating a brand with an image that matches the image that the target market seeks association with. According to an international marketing research program conducted in the late 1990s and commissioned by the IOC, the **Olympics brand** has four main propositions: hope and optimism, dreams and inspirations, friendship and fair play, and joy in effort.

A brand enjoys a high level of **brand equity** when the following components are prominent: brand awareness, brand associations (strong, favorable,

and unique), perceived brand quality, and brand loyalty (Aaker, 1991). In the case of the Olympics, a number of assets add to its brand equity such as symbols and properties (e.g., Olympic Oath, the Olympic flame, the Olympic torch relay, and the Olympic mascot). In addition, the Olympic brand promises to provide a set of features (i.e., excellence, friendship, respect) that will provide benefits (emotional, social, symbolic) or experiences (delivered through every interaction that the IOC stakeholders have with the Olympic Games, YOG, and other products and services) that are delivered on a consistent basis (e.g., from one OG to the next). Moreover, the brand connects with its heritage by having a cultural element (in addition to sport) that provides differentiation from other sport properties (Ferrand et al., 2012).

The Olympic Games, the flagship product of the brand, are the pinnacle of sporting achievement—that is, a celebration of sport, cultures, and humanity. By aligning its brand with strategic stakeholders (e.g., sponsors, broadcasters, IFs, governments, athletes, professional leagues, and so on), the IOC has created a system in which stakeholders are an essential part of the brand (Ferrand et al., 2012). In other words, they actively contribute to its value, to its protection, and in the end to its equity, making the Olympic brand one of the most powerful brands in sport.

Summary

Sport has become increasingly internationalized, and the business of sport is transcending boundaries over the past decade. As sport consumers and organizations increasingly cross national borders, the importance of studying the dynamics of international sport marketing has become clear. To help you recognize the value of sport marketing in an international context, this chapter has covered topics such as the nature and unique aspects of sport business, the basic concepts of sport marketing, the unique features of sport products, the nature of sport consumption and its consumers, the place of sport sponsorship in a global setting, and the concept of brand applied to the Olympics.

Although this chapter provides the foundational concepts on the topic area, you should read information beyond this text. You will be able to get up-to-date information on international sport marketing by reading periodicals such as *Forbes, Street and Smith's SportsBusiness Journal Global*, and others. You can also refer to academic journals such as *Sport Marketing Quarterly*; *Sport, Business and Management: An International Journal*; the *International Journal of Sport Marketing and Sponsorship*, and the *International Journal of Sport Management and Marketing*. As a current or future sport manager, it is important to keep up with the fast-paced changes in the world of international sport including the various marketing practices discussed in this chapter.

? Review Questions

1. What are three unique features that make sport business different from any other mainstream business? Discuss each of these features.

2. Define and briefly discuss sport marketing, the marketing of sport, and marketing through sport.

3. List the 4Cs and 4Ps of marketing and discuss briefly each component with an example.

4. Identify and briefly discuss at least five unique features of a sport product (in professional sport context) that differentiate it from products and services of other mainstream business.

5. Identify and discuss the various types of sport consumption.

6. Define sponsorship and give three examples of corporate sponsorship in a global sport setting.

7. What makes the Olympic brand one of the strongest brands in the world (having a high level of brand equity)?

Digital Media in International Sport

Engaging Fans Through Social Media and Fantasy Sport

Michael L. Naraine, PhD
Deakin University

Adam J. Karg, PhD
Swinburne University University

Chapter Objectives

After studying this chapter, you will be able to do the following:

- Understand engagement as a concept related to sport consumption.
- Appreciate the development and use of tools including social media and fantasy sport.
- Understand the impact and implications of use for stakeholders, including sport organizations and consumers.
- Understand challenges for these digital engagement tools.
- Recognize some concepts or digital engagement tools that will enhance the prominence of digital media in sport in the future.

Key Terms

consumer engagement	daily fantasy sport
asynchronous	fantasy sport revenue streams
synchronous	social listening
user-generated content	millennial
emojis	hashtags
fantasy sport	virtual reality
rotisserie leagues	augmented reality
head-to-head formats	

Within the global sport industry, digital and online technologies have provided opportunities to advance communication and engagement between organizations and consumers, or groups of consumers themselves. Although technology allows faster transmission of and access to data, information, images, and video, use of tools for engagement within sport consumption have sought to harness and extend the already high levels of involvement and connection that consumers have with brands and organizations. The removal of barriers to consumption to allow rapid transfer and communication of information has created many opportunities to increase the value that sport fans elicit from consuming sport. In capitalizing on such technological advancement, federations, leagues, teams, brands, and athletes have all sought to leverage tools of engagement to increase consumer value. This chapter focuses on two of these tools—social media and fantasy sport. Both are examples of what are now mainstream facets of engagement that have grown exponentially in sport over the last decade.

The activities underpinning these tools are not new, but they are certainly enhanced by the presence of technology, making them more accessible. For example, organizations and fans have always shared information, but they can now do so supported by rapid transfer of data and social media channels. Likewise, fans have always sought to share their experiences with each other, but they can do so now through digital channels in ephemeral form or in real time. Likewise, fantasy sport using early rotisserie leagues is a concept dating back to the 1960s and 1970s. but it gained mainstream traction only when online or digital versions of games evolved. More recent growth has come through innovation and short-form games such as daily fantasy sport.

After introducing the construct of engagement, the aim of this chapter is to present these tools—social media and fantasy sport—including a description of their growth, value proposition for consumers, facets of their management, and current and future issues relevant to their ongoing development in a globalized context. We frame the concepts under an engagement construct and use such a framework to explain how teams, leagues, and related organizations use them, and sport, to created attitudinal and behavioral outcomes for the sport and its stakeholders around the world.

Engagement

Engagement consists of three interrelated dimensions (Brodie et al., 2011, 2013) in which consumers' cognition, emotions, and behaviors are antecedents for a series of positive outcomes for brands, organizations, and events. Related to consumers, engagement sits within an expanded relationship approach to marketing (Vivek et al., 2012) in which consumers are part of interactive relationships with brands, organizations, and each other. Engagement seeks to describe relationships that extend cognition and "encompasses a proactive, interactive customer relationship with a specific engagement object (e.g., a sport brand)" (Brodie et al., 2011, p. 257). Social media and fantasy sport provide examples of digital tools that help harness and develop such relationship using digital engagement tools.

Sport provides a valuable context to explore and observe engagement given inherent aspects that are emotional, cognitive, and behavioral in nature. Sport is often described as a high-involvement service domain, in which part of the role of sport marketers is to leverage commitment and loyalty toward brands using a range of experiences, tools, and exchanges. Therefore, structuring activities to enhance emotional, psychological, and physical investment in brands is a powerful strategy for sport organizations.

The process of engagement suggests that consumers are motivated by hedonic or utility means to engage in an activity (figure 21.1). From here, a subprocess of engagement that involves sharing, socializing, codeveloping, advocating, and learning is said to develop deeper attitudes, connections, and ultimately relationships within and between consumers and organizations. This chapter will show how both social media and fantasy sport provide ample opportunities to utilize such a subprocess given the design of the tools and exchanges within them.

Consumer engagement processes, as well as antecedents and consequences, can help in developing and strengthening interactive relationships. The construct in nonlocalized or international consumer settings has much to offer, in particular when combined with tools such as social media and fantasy sport that are digitalized in nature and available for use at limited additional costs

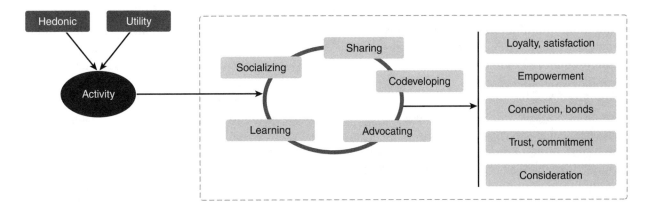

Figure 21.1 The engagement process.
Data from Brodie et al. (2013); Karg and Lock (2014).

to sport organizations, leagues and events. The chapter seeks to present how these tools have developed and how they can be used to engage fans outside the traditional settings such as match or game attendance. By using digital tools that do not limit consumption to geographic boundaries, sport marketers can seek to develop engagement of fans through digital channels and leverage higher and more developed levels of interaction and consumption between organizations and consumers, and between groups of consumers. In the remaining parts of the chapter, we consider social media and fantasy sport as two such mechanisms, which are widely used in sport to development and leverage engagement.

Social Media

Tweets, posts, likes, and (un)friending. Hearing these terms used in casual conversation between people in the modern sport setting is certainly not unusual. Their inclusion into the lexicon of sport marketing and communications professionals also emphasizes the rapid growth of social media over the past decade. As more athletes, leagues, and sport organizations consider social media as an additional avenue to connect with stakeholders around the world (e.g., fans, sponsors, governments), the contemporary sport manager needs to understand the dynamics of this tool, the various platforms available to engage in social media activities, and the importance of analyzing social media data.

Social Media Dynamics

At its core, social media is composed of seven major functional elements (Kietzmann, Hermkens, McCarthy, & Silvestre, 2011):

1. Sharing
2. Networking
3. Identity
4. Presence
5. Reputation
6. Conversation
7. Community

Fundamentally, social media allows users to present a digital identity or profile to others, demonstrating their likes, dislikes, attitudes, and opinions through **user-generated content**. Users may share this content, whether **synchronous** or **asynchronous**, to groups or communities of others linked by family, work, or shared interests, indicative of their willingness to engage and interact with others, and enhance the reputation of their digital persona. Collectively, these elements demonstrate why social media is considered a rich, interactive communications environment unlike any digital media at present or which came before. The tool has been particularly influential on the **millennial** generational cohort, because people from this group have an affinity for computer-mediated technologies and are inclined to adopt innovations in the digital realm. Thus, with its multifaceted nature and a growing demographic that willingly embraces digital media, social media has emerged as a popular engagement method that must be considered by global sport managers to remain competitive and reflect currency to their stakeholders.

Social Media Platforms

Although social media presents a unique ability to share user-generated content, an abundance of platforms enables such activity to transpire. Names such as LinkedIn, Sina Weibo, Periscope, and VKontakte, while popular, pose a significant challenge to sport managers: Which platforms can maximize engagement with stakeholders? Here, we discuss FITS (i.e., Facebook, Instagram, Twitter, and Snapchat), four key platforms that international sport managers need to consider for their social media strategy.

Originally designed in 2004, Facebook has emerged as the quintessential platform in the social media space. For individual users or consumers, the central element of using Facebook is the ability to have a profile page. This element operates functionally as a user's personal website, featuring photos and albums, life events (e.g., work, education, and marriage), and the user's friends (also known as social network), among other features. Profile pages also offer individual users and their friends the ability to post updates about daily activities, popular culture, and **hashtags**, and share content from other sources (e.g., news sites, other social media). The ability to provide these details on a personalized page and develop communal bonds affords users the opportunity to develop and enhance their digital profile. Organizations can also develop Facebook pages with customizable tabs that depict operating hours, location, menus and services, upcoming events, and a comments section for fans and consumers. Additional applications include private messaging (i.e., Facebook Messenger) and live video broadcasts (i.e., Facebook Live). Its wide gamut of functionality coincides with its extensive use by both younger and older demographics: Facebook has over 1.5 billion monthly active users.

Released in 2010, Instagram serves as a photo-sharing service that allows users to submit photos that they take in real time or those stored from previous activity and provide a caption with or without hashtags. Additionally, photos are subject to user alterations, including cropping out unwanted aspects, blurring, sharpening, and brightening, as well as enhancing the image with preset photo-

graphic filters. This sentiment highlights the added value of this platform. Although Instagram shares many similarities with other platforms (e.g., Twitter) in how users create their own content and subscribe to others for aggregation of content, Instagram posts always feature multimedia whereas Twitter posts may not. Now owned by Facebook, Instagram has become a staple platform for all millennials, and it has over 700 million monthly active users.

Twitter's popularity is rooted in short, expedited communication between users. Developed in 2006, the platform serves as a microblog, in which users post messages consisting of 140 characters or fewer to what is referred to as a timeline. Within these posts, users can append pictures, videos, web links, hashtags, and **emojis**, and mention or "tag" other users. Besides creating these messages, users can follow the accounts of other fans, athletes, teams, leagues, and mass media (personalities and organizations) to get real-time updates of scores, statistics, injuries, and transactions. Users can access other user-generated content in the Twitter ecosystem through denoted hashtags. Although the expanse of Twitter has waned in recent years, the polarized nature of sport has helped the platform remain one of the mainstays in the social media discourse. Indeed, many of Twitter's 300 million monthly active users are older millennials and middle-aged users seeking instantaneous communication.

Finally, Snapchat, launched in 2011, has emerged as one of the top platforms among the younger millennial demographic. Snapchat now has over 300 million monthly active users who take over 2 billion "snaps" per day. Those snaps take the form of images or short videos that have temporal limits (usually 5 to 10 seconds), feature unique geofilter and comedic overlay options, and normally disappear after their first viewing. The unique feature of Snapchat is its ability to capture spontaneous or sensitive user-generated content and share it only with those selected by the originating user. Additionally, textual communication can occur by one-on-one, direct messages, normally after a snap has been viewed.

Social Strategy

Having revealed the prominent platforms in the social space, the next step is to identify how sport stakeholders are operationalizing (or using) social media altogether. Because fans, athletes, and sport

A Multiplatform Social Campaign for a Future Major Professional Soccer Team

The rise of social media as a marketing communications platform has begot an abundance of channels for teams and brands to engage with their publics. Each platform has the capability of targeting specific demographic segments based on their age, gender, and location. For example, Pinterest, the popular photo- and idea-sharing site, is known to have more female than male users, whereas XING, the business-focused social network, is particularly popular in German-speaking markets. In essence, organizations can target multiple market segments by developing a multiplatform presence. This approach is important not only for preexisting clubs but also for new and emergent teams that are looking to build their brand equity locally, nationally, and globally.

Recently, Major League Soccer (MLS) has embarked on an ambitious course of expansion. From 2010 to 2017, six new teams began play in the league, and additional cities are being considered for future growth. One of those cities is San Diego, California. MLS had previously considered San Diego a candidate for expansion but focused their attention elsewhere. But with the 2017 move of the San Diego Chargers professional football team to Los Angeles, San Diego has emerged as a viable candidate, backed by former players like MLS veteran Landon Donovan. Situated in close proximity to the United States–Mexico border, San Diego enjoys a favorable soccer climate in an unsaturated professional sport market; with the Chargers leaving, the only other major professional team in the city is the Padres, a professional baseball team. Adding an MLS team in San Diego would align with the region's passion for soccer, exemplified by the multiple teams located in California

(i.e., LA Galaxy, LAFC, and San Jose Earthquakes).

Developing a new brand can be a difficult task because multiple variables must be considered. Managers must consider the market's demographics and competition, as well as the mission, vision, and values of the organization. Producing quality brand visuals and identity can effectively communicate what the organization stands for and help engage with potential fans for the new team. Social media platforms can significantly enhance this engagement, allowing the team to target specific audiences while communicating their brand identity. Although the professional sport market in the city may be favorable, an MLS team in San Diego would experience competition for fan support from both the Los Angeles and Mexican football markets. Knowing the social media platforms on which to develop a presence can mitigate this competitive force and attract fans from beyond Southern California.

In small groups, reflect on the San Diego MLS case study. First, think about a cool, catchy name for a soccer team in the city and what its visuals (e.g., logo, colors) might look like. Then think about a multiplatform social strategy for the club (this strategy could include some, all, or none of the FITS channels). Identify what demographics each platform would target, focusing on channels that can help the club gain more international fans. Finally, think about the content that the club would advance on each of the platforms that your group has identified. Develop a hashtag campaign for the San Diego team; your group should consider the location, fan base, sport, and team identity.

organizations all have different wants and needs, each group will have varying degrees of activity on social media. For sports fans, the gratification sought through social media is connected to interactivity and fandom. Fans have a desire to be part of a community that shares similar interests (e.g., fandom of the team), and they want to be closer to their favorite teams and athletes. Social media provides a voice to fans so that they can collectively

add to the discourse about a sport team, athlete, or topic. But communicating in this manner results in a sporadic strategy, in which fans engage with any and all content from others. For athletes, social media serves to expand their reach to fans and critics, enhancing their personal brand. Unlike traditional media that filters athlete communication, social media provides a direct link for athletes to the masses. Recently, athletes have found value in leveraging their social media profiles on various platforms to endorse products and services such as Serena Williams with Gatorade, Usain Bolt with Puma, and Roger Federer with Mercedes-Benz, to name just a few. For sport organizations, the operationalization of social media is much more difficult because multiple stakeholders view engagements simultaneously. Although social media is a fun, interactive environment, many sport organizations use a formal, structured approach that is confined to reporting, informing, and promoting—the "RIP" method of social media (see figure 21.2). When organizations report, they provide the real-time updates and news items that their publics yearn for. The informational aspect refers to the redirection to other sport organization sites or content, as well as to behind-the-scenes multimedia. Finally, sport organizations tend to use social media as a promotional tool to let their stakeholders know of upcoming charitable events, future competitions, and contests and to promote their brand generally. Operating social media within the confines of RIP allows the organization to remain relevant with this popular engagement medium while reducing the threat of a public relations disaster. Here are some other key facets to consider when developing a social media strategy:

◆ Authenticity: Stakeholders will be conversing with a persona, and an organization must recognize that their social voice represents the whole brand.

Stakeholders will be able to distinguish between an authentic and an inauthentic voice.

◆ Creativity: Social media is a fun, open environment, and engagement is stimulated thusly. Sharing videos and images that showcase behind-the-scenes exclusive content are vital to success.

◆ Innovation: The development and progression of social media is predicated on innovation, and successful sport stakeholders will adopt a similar spirit. Instituting new segments and campaigns is important, even if they are not widely accepted (because ascertaining the content that stakeholders will engage with is difficult).

◆ Integration: Social media operations should not be conducted without integration back into the organization's overall marketing strategy. Understanding the goals and objectives of a marketing plan will affect which hashtags, multimedia, and social interactions are advanced.

◆ Currency: Although the FITS channels have global influence, sport organizations must stay current with new, developing platforms, especially those within their geographic area (e.g., Sina Weibo in China, VKontatke in Russia).

Social Listening and Issues With Social Media

Apart from understanding the intricacies of a social strategy (e.g., where, when, how), the challenge for sport managers is to reflect on their social media output as well as those within the broader social media environment. This undertaking requires the ability to perform **social listening**, or the analysis of content, trends, and communities as they emanate across various platforms. Social listening can be challenging for sport stakeholders to consider, because social media engagement is often considered to be self-driven, based on a strategic plan or anticipated outcome. But this tactic can be intimidating if the organization or individual does not know how to go about conducting such analysis (Naraine & Parent, 2017). Table 21.1 provides a list of several social listening applications and their functions. Although some tools are relatively similar (e.g., Sprout and Hootsuite), testing each platform to determine its applicability to the user or organization is still important.

Figure 21.2 The RIP strategy
Data from Naraine and Parent (2016).

Table 21.1 Common Social Listening Tools

Tool	Description	Applicability in the sport industry
Affinio	Segments users within a social media ego network into groups based on social media activity and demographic information	• Reveals tribes within a sport stakeholder's network (e.g., sport team) • Can assist in the comparison of fans across multiple teams
Echosec	Allows users to search and extract social media data from a particular location in real time	• Provides sport managers with knowledge of social activity at their stadium or stadia elsewhere • Enables comparisons between temporary events (e.g., marathons, multisport games)
Hootsuite	Social media management software that allows users to organize multiple platforms (e.g., timed content releases) but also extract key metrics (e.g., views, retweets)	• Creates a structured approach to social media engagements • Highlights engagements with significant traction among stakeholders
Netlytic	A tool that analyzes various platforms (e.g., Facebook, Twitter, Instagram) and automatically summarizes and visualizes conversation based on keywords or hashtags	• Demonstrates how users are conversing when appending a sport-based hashtag • Explores emerging trends and themes based on stakeholder conversation
NodeXL	A network analysis add-on package to Microsoft Excel that imports social media data for visualization and performs network analyses based on conversation and relationships	• Provides quantitative measures to sport stakeholder network relationships • Identifies clusters of users heavily involved in a given sport network
Pulsar	Besides providing network visuals and content analyses, performs image analyses to recognize key patterns in multimedia	• Can decipher key products and sport paraphernalia in user images • Can extract custom segment conversation from fans, sponsors, and athletes
Sprout	Another social media management software that offers efficient communication across multiple channels and measures the effectiveness of the engagement	• Creates a structured approach to social media engagements • Highlights engagements with significant traction among stakeholders

The measurement of social media data can be especially useful for athletes, sport organizations, and sponsors looking to identify whether a hashtag campaign or specific social media strategy (e.g., contests, promotions) has gained traction among a specific community. Given that social media demands a higher capacity to engage with various stakeholders, the ability to make data-driven decisions beforehand is vital to ensuring that resources are efficiently expended. Moreover, social listening can aid in the monitoring of social campaigns, highlighting whether the goals and objectives of the activity have been met, or if a pivot of strategy or increased engagement (e.g., intervening into the social conversation) is required. Social listening can also be used to attract new partners and corporate sponsorships.

Fantasy Sport

Fantasy sport has undergone exponential growth as an aligned form of sport consumption and is now active in a large range of sports across the world. **Fantasy sport** involves the selection and maintenance of fictional, or fantasy, teams made up of players from within a sport league (Karg & McDonald, 2011). Teams are built by individuals and compete against others in leagues or competitions that can span a single game or day, all the way through to a season or longer. While originally operationalized as paper format games, the majority of competitions are now administered through online formats. Fantasy leagues allow players to build teams drawn from players and athletes across all professional rosters in a league. A player's performance is assessed

CASE STUDY

Social Tribes and the Toronto Raptors

Although basketball has entrenched itself as a global sport, it has not traditionally been popular within the Canadian sport landscape. In a country historically dominated by ice hockey and Canadian football, basketball has only recently emerged in major urban Canadian centers. Part of the explanation for this growth can be attributed to the success of the Toronto Raptors. The Raptors, who compete in the National Basketball Association (NBA), are Canada's lone team in the league after the Vancouver Grizzlies franchise relocated to Memphis in 2001. After several subpar season performances, the Raptors have captured the attention of fans by earning several consecutive playoff berths, including an Eastern Conference finals appearance in 2016 (which they lost to the eventual champion Cleveland Cavaliers). With its on-court success, the popularity of the team (and sport) in Canada has never been higher.

The Raptors occupy a unique position within the professional sport landscape. As mentioned, they remain Canada's only NBA team, and the Raptors are also the only non-U.S. team in the league. This characteristic has allowed the team to become more attractive to international markets, especially players themselves. Over its 20-plus-year history in the league, the Raptors have had multiple players from North America (e.g., Canada and the United States), South America (e.g., Brazil and Argentina), Western Europe (e.g., France, Spain), Eastern Europe (e.g., Lithuania and Serbia), and Africa (e.g., Congo and Nigeria). Even so, the marketing of the Raptors has focused on Canadian nationalism. The most recent campaign (i.e., "We the North") emphasizes the northern characteristics of Canada (e.g., frigid temperatures and snow) and its unique position as the lone Canadian team. Certainly, this form of marketing has been vital for the Raptors to build interest in the team and sport across the nation, but it may constrain the

team's ability to market abroad and tap into basketball fans worldwide.

Figure 21.3 depicts the social network fan tribes within the Toronto Raptors Twitter network. In groups, think about the tribes that exist within this network and how they align or misalign with the present We the North marketing campaign. Afterward, consider developing a plan to market the team internationally, with specific mention of the tribes associated with the global clusters in the plan.

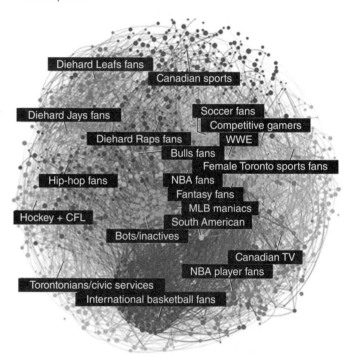

Figure 21.3   Example cluster analysis of the Toronto Raptors Twitter network.

Reprinted by permission from Affinio.

through forms of aggregate scoring based on players' actual competition statistics.

The growth of fantasy sport has accelerated as digital capacity has evolved, and fantasy sport now provides an important piece of the consumption and engagement offering for large segments

of sport consumers. Particularly for sports with global popularity such as the English Premier League (EPL), the activity has allowed existing, committed fans to extend their engagement with the sport, while also providing a platform for new consumers to learn and develop fandom with a sport. This section of the chapter provides an overview of the concept of fantasy sport and its growth, including the key drivers of growth. It then considers various forms of games and business models that sport and nonsport organizations have used to benefit from consumer engagement in fantasy sport. Following this discussion, we consider how fantasy sport consumption affects sport consumption. Finally, we present current issues and commentary around fantasy sport consumption as the industry continues to mature.

Forms of Fantasy Sport

Traditionally, sports high on statistical content such as baseball and basketball have best fit the fantasy sport genre. The increased range of sports operating fantasy sport competitions, encouraged by technological development, has led to fantasy sport becoming a prominent opportunity for consumer engagement. In line with this, table 21.2 provides examples of current sports providing lucrative fantasy sport competitions globally, demonstrating how sports from soccer to fishing have grasped opportunities.

Traditionally, longer form games covered a full season, and players selected and maintained their teams by ongoing trading and recruitment. In such forms, players compete in closed leagues (for example, a league of 10 or 12 players) against an opponent each week. Higher volume games, in which mass numbers of players compete for the best

score, emerged more heavily in the online, digital growth stage of fantasy sport, leading to awarding of game, weekly, and season prizes. Within each form, games may use a draft format in which all available players are divided or selected into teams (i.e., all actual players are assigned to only one team), or an open or salary cap model in which players can select any players they wish from the pool, often resulting in the better players from the league being recruited into multiple and in some cases the majority of teams.

Under emerging shorter forms, or **daily fantasy sport (DFS)** games, players can compete over a single game or a shorter run of games (e.g., one round of games over a weekend). In this format, they may select, for example, six players from single match or from games over a single day and compete for the best overall score. Models might include **head-to-head formats**, playing against only one other player; 50-50 games in which players finishing in the top half double their money; or guaranteed prize pools in mass-entry games in which prize money is distributed in majority to those finishing in a small percentage of the top positions. Therefore, the modern design of daily fantasy sport largely mirrors online poker examples, using differing levels of spend, duration, and scoring systems. In such pay-to-play games, sites themselves benefit from higher volumes of players, taking a small percentage, or "rake," of the total revenue of each game.

Table 21.2 Example of Fantasy Sport Competitions

Sport	Country or region	Sample statistics used in fantasy sport competitions
American football	North America	Passes, catches, tackles, touchdowns, scores against, yards gained
Baseball	North America	Batting average, home runs, stolen bases, saves
Association football (soccer)	Global	Goals, score assists, pass completions, tackles, clean sheets
Australian rules football	Australia	Possessions, marks, tackles, scoring
Cricket	Global	Runs, wickets, catches, team performance
Golf	Global	Overall round scores, hole by hole scores, match play victories
Bass fishing	North America	Size and weight of fish caught by anglers, other bonus structures
Mixed martial arts	Global	Strikes, takedowns, knockdowns, finish to a fight
Auto racing	North America	Wins and place by drivers, other bonus structures
Horse racing	Australia	Wins and place by horses, other bonus structures

Growth and Development

Fantasy sport leagues, known as **rotisserie leagues** in early formats, date back to the 1960s and 1970s. Golf and baseball were among the first sports reported to develop versions of fantasy sport and were most commonly administered in paper format. These mirror the predominant original design of fantasy sport games of the 1960s and 1970s, in which paper or physical records and calculations would be kept to manage leagues. A league table would be maintained throughout the season, and a finals or playoff system could follow a regular season of play. Fantasy sport would remain a niche activity for decades, but around it would develop an industry in which dissemination of statistics, information, and strategy would become increasingly prevalent. In the 1980s the *Bill James Abstract*, *Fantasy Football Index*, and *Fantasy Sports Magazine* were publications that covered one or multiple sports, which helped to grow the activity. This developing interest in statistics and analytics has become important to sport consumers today.

Undoubtedly, the driving factor in the growth of fantasy sport was the proliferation of use of the Internet and computers. The removal of barriers to entry and facilitation of faster transfer of information quickly positioned fantasy sport for a period of exponential growth over the 1990s and 2000s. As fantasy sport businesses, in both start-up form and as extensions of media sites, appeared over this time, games with strong followings started to realize commercial value. Promotional opportunities for companies to leverage early online versions slowly developed as both media and commercial organizations accelerated interest in fantasy sport activities. In 1996 Canada's Molson Breweries won an international award for its digital site based on fantasy hockey; statistics, content, and an in-site fantasy game were part of the design. In doing so, Molson leveraged fantasy sport to develop significant opportunities for its brand, as well as help develop consumer interest in fantasy sport in much the same way as media organizations do. Around the same time, media organizations including Yahoo developed fantasy sport competitions, and online brands like Commissioner.com were acquired by media brands that began to recognize value in the activity.

The popularity of fantasy sport continues to grow, turning it from a niche activity toward one with mass appeal. Innovations continue to emerge in fantasy sport products, games formats, and delivery. The growth in the analytics domain within sport played a role, as exemplified by the popular book and movie *Moneyball* (based on a MLB team's use of statistical information to help select players), and the more prominent role of statistics in sport consumption. Data transfer capabilities and cloud computing systems and apps helped facilitate faster transfer of information and real-time access to statistics and scores. Concurrent increases in the volume and accessibility of televised sport, the increased accessibility of sport and statistics on the Internet, and the number of fantasy sport services offered likewise increased. In the last five years, smartphone apps have made fantasy sport more mobile, increasing the portability of competitions. Related to this, short-term or daily fantasy sport (DFS) emerged, created another wave of growth, including a three-fold growth in DFS entry fees in North America in 2015 to over US$3 billion.

Player numbers underwent continual growth in key markets, and the number and size of businesses providing fantasy sport or related services likewise increased. FSTA surveys have highlighted growth in North American markets. Estimates in 2003 suggested that 15 million players shaped a US$1.5 billion industry. Later, figures would swell to 27 million fantasy sport players generating economic activity of US$4 to 5 billion annually in 2010. By 2015 nearly 57 million people were playing fantasy sport. Besides the increase in the number of players, figures on turnover by player suggest

Learning Activity

Use web searches to identify examples of fantasy sport competitions that run in your region across a range of sports. What sorts of organizations run these existing competitions, and how do they differ? Finally, what opportunities (both locally and globally) might exist for sports that do not currently appear to run fantasy sport competitions?

a staggering development, largely driven by DFS formats. Although such players spent only $5 a year on average in 2012, they spent over $250 per year in 2015. The percentage of fantasy sport players who played some form of daily fantasy sport rose to 64 percent in 2015 (Legal Sports Report, 2016). In terms of daily games, projections are that daily fantasy games will generate around $14.4 billion in entry fees by 2020 (Time, 2015).

Business Models

With the proliferation of fantasy sport games, a range of differentiated business models have emerged for the delivery and commercial exploitation of fantasy sport competitions. Such models are based on the benefits that fantasy sport offers organizations from a commercial perspective, through either subscription or advertising models. The majority of fantasy sport organizations available for play are operated under one of three structures: league owned, media owned, or privately owned.

Media companies and leagues themselves are among those that offer fantasy sport services. Leagues can operate and own their own fantasy sport competitions; for example, the English Premier League promotes and runs a competition with millions of competitors from around the world playing weekly. In this case, the league itself can leverage the activity, providing ample opportunities for league branding and messaging, and cross promotion and integration of partners and sponsors. Large media companies have also had strong interest and involvement in owning and operating FS competitions. Yahoo, ESPN, and NBC are examples of large North American media organizations who deliver fantasy sport competitions. In Germany, *Bild*, a major newspaper, runs a large competition based on the Bundesliga, the major football league. In these examples, fantasy sport competitions offer extensions to other business lines, offering synergies between statistics and other sport-related news and content. Organizations seek to realize commercial returns by attracting and leveraging consumption of fantasy sport players through their media sites. For example, media companies may seek to leverage fantasy players' online activity toward click-through traffic for advertising content and consumption of other news, statistics, or related products. Globally, there are examples of online media subscriptions, merchandise, premium statistical content, and live stream sport access being sold through media sites to fantasy sport players.

In a related but distinct version of ownership, new organizations have started with a sole or majority aim to develop and grow fantasy sport competitions. Most prolifically, these have arrived in the form of DFS. Companies such as Draft Kings and FanDuel are examples of start-up companies undergoing exponential growth in their early years. Although media companies have generally offered both free and pay-to-play versions, DFS models run primarily pay-to-play games, deriving revenue from a share of the revenue spent on the site, as well as through associated advertising and sponsorship with commercial partners.

The rationale for involvement differs for the models, but it largely mirrors online business models in which subscription revenue can be extracted from users, complemented by advertising revenue in which player numbers, visits, and volume of time spent on site (all behavioral measures of engagement) are critical. Although fantasy sport is highly attractive in its ability to offer a unique online product, this attribute is combined with the high-involvement context of sport, often within the attractive demographic market for fantasy sport (skewed toward professional males with high levels of disposable income). Not surprisingly, competition has intensified as organizations seek to develop platforms and brands that will attract and retain players across the growth and maturity stages of fantasy sport.

Specific **fantasy sport revenue streams** for sites can be driven by many channels, including but not limited to the following:

- Pay-to-play or daily fantasy sport models, in which sites take a percentage (or rake) of any fantasy sport pools or collected player revenue
- Site advertising by click-through or banner advertising or where sponsors, advertisers, or third parties may have direct marketing opportunities to access player databases
- Sponsorship for naming rights to the competition
- Premium statistics access in which players pay extra to receive a higher or more sophisticated level of statistics to aid their game play

CASE STUDY

Adoption of Fantasy Sport in Australia

Leagues and competition owners who run fantasy sport gain value from consumers who spend a high volume of time on digital sites and apps, particularly when patterns of visitation are regular and consistent. Therefore, sites with more users and high volumes of use are best placed to leverage the benefits of fantasy sport commercially. The nature of this value places a strong emphasis on the adoption processes for owners and managers of fantasy sport, focusing attention on achieving quick growth and capturing market share. Such a scenario was highlighted in the early stages of fantasy sport in Australia in the 2000s. Until that time, although some fans were already engaged in overseas games and platforms for sports like soccer (through English Premier League competitions) and basketball (through National Basketball Association competitions), fantasy sport was a relatively rare activity. In line with themes in this chapter, growth would develop in the 2000s, and Australian rules football was one of the sports seeking to drive growth and consumption of fantasy sport with its own game.

Within this market, the adoption and growth stages for fantasy sport for the games transitioned into a battle for market share between two major organizations, offering distinct and competing alternatives for the sport. The league itself, the Australian Football League (AFL), developed and marketed its own game, called AFL Dream Team. Meanwhile, a major media organization (News Corp) developed its own version, called Super Coach. The games were fundamentally similar (and both were free to play at the time), but each sought competitive advantage through differences in branding, scoring systems, and access to levels and types of additional content and information. Seeking to leverage ownership of statistics and information, the AFL for some time ensured that only its game offered live scoring through its platform; in contrast, the media version updated only four times during the game, at the conclusion of each quarter or period of the game.

The battle for higher player numbers in the adoption stages of the activity was seen to be critical because once adoption happened and fantasy leagues between social groups of consumers had formed, consumers would likely stay loyal to that particular game format or competition. Managers of fantasy sport competitions spent heavily on advertising and raced to get their games promoted and launched earlier than competitors, which in key years of growth equated to the capture of thousands of users who were adopting fantasy sport for the first time. The aggressive strategies of both organizations allowed them to gain significant traction and gain a share of the 1.2 million users of fantasy sport games around 2011 in the peak period of fantasy sport participation in the region. Although the number of fantasy sport users in Australia has plateaued in recent years, both organizations have continued to build their audience and player bases. Their aggressive early approaches to capturing market share are considered essential to their current positions.

◆ Revenue generated by product extensions including podcasts, books or guides, magazines, or trophies as complementary products to fantasy play

Besides revenue and traffic, additional benefits can be leveraged by organizations. For all versions of fantasy sport, sign-up processes and social integration allow the capture of data for targeted and customized marketing, allowing organizations to use consumer data to improve their understanding of highly involved consumers or build commercial-ized databases. A major benefit for media organizations in particular is the linkage to other news and content they can offer alongside fantasy sport participation. For example, content pieces, news, or stats access can be bundled with subscriptions to newspaper or online sales models. The growth of Australian fantasy sport provides an interesting case to compare competition and marketing strategies over a period of exponential growth. As with many products, developing a strong brand has been vital in local and global markets, and innovative campaigns have been used to capture and maintain early market share in an increasingly crowded space.

Consumer Impact and Sport Engagement

Besides the clear commercial impact and opportunities that fantasy sport has provided to organizations, the influence on consumers has likewise developed as a key theme for sport organizations. Although primarily presumed as positive, one question in the growth stages of fantasy sport markets concerns the extent to which fantasy sport is a complementary or competitive activity, and as such whether leagues and teams should encourage it.

According to the opening section of this chapter, this interaction can be framed and explained under an engagement framework. Fantasy sport offers an additional level of interaction between a sport and fans, and it can be used to develop and maintain levels of consumption and engagement in emotional, cognitive, and behavioral settings.

From a learning or cognitive perspective, fantasy sport can play a key role in educating consumers about a sport. Whether by extending knowledge around basic concepts such as the number of players required on a team, rules and their interpretation, and game or team strategies, playing fantasy sport can deepen the sport fan's level of understanding. In addition, players develop deeper knowledge about individual players, player types, and the core actions and statistics within a certain sport. The combination of such knowledge is a key part of the attachment processes associated with fandom. Although the majority of players of fantasy sport are highly engaged and differ significantly in their sport consumption patterns compared with nonplayers, the learning process associated with sport is one area in which those with low or moderate levels of fandom can be influenced positively by fantasy sport participation.

Fantasy sport also has clear behavioral effects. For example, fantasy sport induces players to watch additional games that do not include their favorite or supported teams or players. Fantasy players are also likely to broaden their league viewership to include both teams they support and games in which their "owned" or fantasy players participate. Although one-sided contests are not attractive to many sport fans, fantasy players want to see how their owned

players perform in those games, thereby increasing both the duration of viewership of individual games and the number of games watched. Players also consume more associated content for a sport, including articles, news, and statistics. In a recent study, more than 60 percent of players reported watching and reading more about sports because of fantasy versions (Legal Sports Report, 2016).

Within these behaviors, players in weekly or season-long competitions in particular develop rituals to their sport and fantasy sport behavior that embed attitudes and outcomes toward their consumption and related patterns. In addition, fantasy sport provides additional social interaction between players. In line with the engagement subprocess shown earlier in the chapter (figure 21.1) and in addition to the learning behaviors noted earlier, fantasy sport provides a base for sharing and socializing behaviors. This aspect is particularly significant when players compete in teams and leagues with friends or engage with other players through social or completion-related channels.

Although predominantly positive, fantasy sport participation can distract from traditional sport behaviors. Fantasy sport can be seen as a tool to increase knowledge of the sport and raise involvement levels, potentially driving behavior related to the sport (e.g., game attendance and TV viewership). At the same time, participation in fantasy sport could compete for consumers' time and reduce other forms of consumption of the same sport, potentially creating tension in consumption behaviors. For example, a player may be consuming fantasy sport and games of the league through media channels, hence driving revenue and engaging with fantasy sport sites. But this activity could result in less loyalty to the person's supported team, lower direct revenue through attendance at fewer games, and less interest in the supported team. The scenario is realistic, and the increasing sophistication of the televised or lounge room experience has shaped this as an area of concern for marketers, in particular in local markets for a team. Increasingly, consumers have more control over games watched (e.g., NFL RedZone), more access to stats (e.g., ESPN Data Center), and better access to the Internet—all of which position the at-home experience as a preferred match-day environment.

Although evidence has suggested that fantasy sport consumers have widened their interest across a sport to more players, teams, and games watched, little empirical evidence indicates a negative impact. Nevertheless, organizations, teams, and venues themselves have taken steps to embrace and reposition the match-day experience, in part tailored to trends in fantasy sport consumption. The NFL in particular has to deal with this issue because many games are played in the same time slot on the same day. The development of fantasy sport lounges within stadiums, where consumers can arrive early to watch games and access detailed information across the league in real time, and adjustments to stadiums to increase Wi-Fi or network access to encourage additional content consumption are examples of how organizations have proactively sought to adjust their offering to appease fantasy sport players.

Overall, fantasy sport can influence the cognition around sport, behaviors, and levels of consumption, as well as how and why people consume sport. In sum, fantasy sport can be used as an education tool about the sport, teams, and players and can also serve to increase the commitment and interaction of consumers with a sport. Therefore, a series of positive outcomes motivated by the learning, socializing, codeveloping, and sharing behaviors are undertaken within the engagement subprocess. Although benefits of game attendance are specific to local teams, the encouragement of socialization, learning, and media consumption as fantasy sport outcomes adds significantly to the outcomes of sport marketers seeking to influence international consumers of their brands or build the interest and engagement of fans in new markets.

Issues and Future Directions

This chapter has considered the growth, business structures, and influence of fantasy sport, positing it as a tool for engagement. In addition, much attention has been focused on legal, sociological, and economic issues surrounding fantasy sport, which present implications and challenges for fantasy sport stakeholders and sport stakeholders more widely.

Fantasy sport has long been discussed in terms of its relationship and overlap with gambling. The legal extent to which pay-to-play fantasy sport represents a form of illegal gambling is determined by the extent to which it is considered a game of chance versus a game of skill. Within North America,

where legal activity around fantasy sport is most commonly discussed, this factor, and specifically the interpretation of chance, is generally the key test as to whether fantasy sport is considered the same as or separate from sport betting or lottery products. The focus on the legality of fantasy sport has increased with the growth of DFS games, which have narrowed the differentiation between fantasy sport and proposition, or prop, betting.

In countries where state or regional laws differ, such as the United States, fantasy sport is considered by some states or regions (e.g., Kansas, Michigan) as a game of skill, so it is legal or permitted. In other areas (e.g., Nevada), fantasy sport has been deemed a form of sport gambling, so companies have been forced to withdraw activities if they do not hold a specific gaming license for the region. Pertinently, organizations that drive their growth with daily fantasy sport games but lack licenses have been restricted in their operations and have been forced to seek clarity in existing and potential new regions. For the time being, legal challenges have been less prominent in Asian, Australian, and European markets, but legal definitions of fantasy sport and related regional laws have emerged as a key consideration for the growth, promotion, and management of fantasy sport games. In particular, the ability of consumers across the world to engage in the same competitions (or compete against each other) is complex when the activity is governed by different legal systems.

Legal aspects have also been prominent for internal organizations and stakeholders within the fantasy sport industry. The growth of fantasy sport has provided cases concerning intellectual property (IP) rights of players, extending to challenges to the use of player profiles and statistics, which have

---

Learning Activity

Explore some of the online media regarding the legalization of fantasy sport in your region. Where might fantasy sport and gambling overlap, and what issues might this present for sport organizations and fantasy sport providers? In particular, how does legislation in your area affect the opportunities of fantasy sport at the global level?

involved player associations, leagues, and fantasy sport companies. Major sport leagues (including MLB and the NBA) have mounted cases to prevent or limit statistics providers from distributing in-game score information in real time, use devices to do so, or use the likeness and details of players, in challenges to protect players' IP from use within fantasy sport platforms. In legal cases, the majority of rulings have aligned with the fantasy sport industry, citing IP, copyright, and right of publicity laws to rule that statistics are public and available for use. Although these cases have the potential to cause significant changes to the flow of information and access to it that underpin the fantasy sport games industry, decisions have maintained accessibility to real-time statistics that are required for growth and continuation.

The role of fantasy sport in cultivating consumer benefits was outlined earlier and is representative of the growth of sport analytics and the focus, by organizations and consumers, on data and statistics as part of developing or consuming sport products. In the last section, we saw how stadiums and leagues are adapting the sport experience to align with fantasy sport usage. Likewise, broadcasters and media organizations are enhancing the real-time experience, adding statistical content, interactive experiences for consumers, social and gamification features, commentary, and in some cases new television shows and channels. Fantasy sport has generated new ways of consuming and deriving value from sport and in many ways has become an industry of its own. Within this sector, podcasts, publications, and even fantasy sport player trophies have formed part of a burgeoning range of fantasy-sport-related products.

Within the industry, intensified with the birth of shortened form DFS games and the overlap with gaming, questions have emerged around appropriate advertising by fantasy sport providers. Although much advertising has focused on prospects for winning large cash prizes, research has shown that much of the financial reward flows to a small percentage of players. Combined with social and economic work about consumption and consumption attitudes, calls have been made for a tempering of the advertising used to attract fantasy sport players.

With the caveat of social and legal issues noted earlier, the fantasy sport market is maturing, aided by the emergence of products and innovations.

Player numbers in markets such as Europe and Australia have plateaued, in particular for longer forms of fantasy sport games. Future growth will be driven by further focus on daily or shorter form game providers and the continuation of overlap with media and private equity investment in those formats. Online gaming, e-sport, and gambling will continue to play a role in strong e-commerce and digital consumption markets, and sport advertisers will become a key stakeholder here. Although the major growth phases may have already occurred in the industry, the benefits of fantasy sport appear well understood by sport organizations, which will need to continue to modify practices in how they promote and offer both sport products and fantasy sport games. For example, opportunities will exist as leagues and teams become more global in nature. Marketing activities as well as continuing movement to international streaming and broadcasting will provide increased opportunities to grow fan bases. Here, fantasy sport will continue to provide managers with a tool for additional engagement in these markets.

Future of Digital Media Engagement

Both social media and fantasy sport demonstrate how technological advancements in the broader environmental context have brought about new digital tools to engage with stakeholders, especially fans. With the expanse of the Internet and the World Wide Web, social applications and sites have enabled stakeholders to socialize, share, codevelop, learn, and advocate with greater intensity than they could before those innovations appeared. This development does not discredit the engagement activities engaged in previously, such as gathering at bars, offering commentary on a sports-talk radio program, or even participating in online sports forums; these activities did, and in many cases still do, connect fans with athletes and sport organizations. Social media and fantasy sport, however, serve as hyperconnective engagement tools, harnessing the power of digital technology to immerse stakeholders in an online environment.

The development of social media and fantasy sport provides a window to the future of digital media as engagement tools in a sporting context. Specifically, the global sport manager should heed two swiftly rising phenomena in the next 5 to 10 years. The first is the development of **virtual reality (VR)** technology. Whereas social media and fantasy sport are tools to engage as a third party to the sporting activity (e.g., fans using social media to comment on their sport viewing or to learn about teams and players through fantasy games), VR adopts a first-person perspective, placing users directly into the sporting experience. Whether sitting in the front row at the FIFA World Cup, snowboarding down the course at the Winter Olympic Games, or interviewing a star player during a postgame news media scrum, VR truly immerses the user, providing an opportunity for an experiential engagement that builds fan loyalty and commitment. Moreover, it provides an additional outlet by which users can interact and share, including the codevelopment of new experiences that may not have occurred in real life. In the past five years, VR technologies have evolved to become more consumer friendly, allowing users to affix smartphones with VR headset hardware to partake in the experience. Although VR experiences to date have been focused on gaming (e.g., first-person shooters, role-playing games) and exotic leisure activities (e.g., rock climbing, skydiving), professional sport teams and leagues have been advancing partnerships to activate in this space. The NBA has partnered with the firm NextVR to offer users select games and highlights from the regular season in VR. Other leagues, like the NHL, have deferred to their preexisting media partners, like Rogers in Canada, which offers games in VR from various vantage points (e.g., above the penalty box, behind the net). As VR grows in the sporting industry, so too will the ability to share these experiences with others in an **augmented reality (AR)** sport setting. Imagine watching the Ashes cricket series from the perspective of the bowler, as another user watches simultaneously from the role of batsman. Exposing consumers to these experiences continues the accelerated engagement that social media and fantasy sport currently provide.

The second future trend in this area is referred to as e-sport (electronic sport). E-sport can be defined as the organization and professionalization of video gaming, whether those games have a real-world sport focus (e.g., EA Madden NFL, EA Sports FIFA, NBA2K) or otherwise (e.g., Halo, Call of Duty, League of Legends). Video gaming has always existed as a form of digital engagement, offering multiple-player experiences and the socialization element well before the first wave of social media occurred. But as social media has expanded to create and share various experiences (including video games), a recent development has enabled video gamers to live-stream their gaming experience to their social networks. The result of these live projections has been increased demand for viewership of video games, eventually spawning professional leagues involving expert players. As such, the e-sport phenomenon mimics the traditional professional sport experience in that fans consume by in-person attendance and may also engage simultaneously by social media. Similar to VR, however, e-sport can provide experiential engagement opportunities that traditional sport may not, given the low barriers to adoption. For example, users can join amateur leagues or e-sport competitions through a gaming system and controller, an opportunity that conventional sport cannot provide. So although a consumer may not be able to get a tryout with the Golden State Warriors based on her or his abilities, the person may be able to try out for the NBA2K e-sport league using the digitized version of the Warriors. For this reason, professional sport leagues and teams are embracing the e-sport trend. Sport organizations have recognized the value that e-sport can provide because it enhances fan loyalty and commitment. Although traditional viewership may be of interest to fans, others may want to partake in the outcome (akin to the notion of AR) and even broadcast that experience to the masses. Both VR and e-sport highlight the continual advancement of technology not just to refine preexisting tools (e.g., social media, fantasy sport) but

Learning Activity

Globally, a number of professional teams and organizations have formed partnerships with e-sport brands. Consider an example of an existing traditional professional sport team or brand that has invested or aligned its activities with a form of e-sport. In the chosen case, and using online media sources to assist, compile a list of the advantages that might exist for the sport brand and the e-sport brand by engaging in such a partnership.

also to develop new tools that can be embraced and used to grow engagement.

Summary

In this chapter, we have focused on the idea of engagement, showcasing two prominent digital media tools used to achieve engagement that have benefitted from digitalization and low barriers to global consumption of their medium. Social media and fantasy sport have undoubtedly transformed the way in which sport is consumed, but they have also transformed the predisposition of organizations that produce content and consumption experiences. For social media, the user (whether a fan, athlete, or organization) generates the content for dissemination by other users. This sentiment is reshaping how actors within the sport industry market themselves, including how they interact with their publics and what tools are embraced and operationalized to maintain consumer interest. In the case of fantasy sport, users are able to extend their engagement with sport, whether they have an existing connec-tion or are new to the league or event. At the core are enhanced opportunities for consumer learning, socializing, and sharing processes, which happen in an online environment not limited to the local context. As access to sport continues to grow across international boundaries, social media and fantasy provide ways for marketers to complement and extend sport consumption on a global scale.

But both social media and fantasy sport are not without their challenges. As digital technology improves, providing adequate resources or deriv-ing significant value from these tools remains a challenge because their saliency can change at any moment (especially as new tools like VR and e-sport emerge). Global sport managers must recognize the potential of these digital media tools for engagement but demonstrate the ability to adapt and pivot as new platforms and tools come to light. Success for global sport managers, therefore, is predicated on their ability to seek out, learn about, and incor-porate new or enhanced engagement strategies, thereby gaining competitive advantages for their organizations.

 Review Questions

1. Describe the engagement process. Why is engagement important in the sport industry?

2. What key facets should a global sport manager consider when creating a social media strategy?

3. What is social listening? Why is social listening vital for the success of a social media strategy for a sport organization?

4. In your view, what characteristics within a particular sport translate to make it a good fit within fantasy sport as well?

5. Provide examples of how fantasy sport might be viewed as complementary or positive as a mar-keting tool. In your response, consider how fantasy sport might affect both attitudes and behaviors within the sport setting. Does fantasy sport consumption have any negative outcomes?

6. Maximizing engagement through social media and fantasy sport services requires consumers to be connected to devices as they attend sport events and consume sport experiences. What implica-tions does this have for managers of live events, leagues, and stadiums?

7. How do VR and e-sport differ from social media and fantasy sport?

International Sport Tourism

Kamilla Swart, EdD
American University in the Emirates

Douglas Michele Turco, PhD
Sport Business School Finland

Chapter Objectives

After studying this chapter, you will be able to do the following:

- Describe the components of the sport tourism industry.
- Differentiate the three main segments of the sport tourist market.
- Identify constraints to sport tourism participation.
- Describe the economic, sociocultural, environmental, political, and legacy effects of sport tourism.
- Introduce the steps and considerations for strategic sport tourism planning.

Key Terms

tourist	excursionists
tourism	day trippers
sport tourists	serious sport tourists
sport tourism	constraints
visiting friends and relatives (VFRs)	sport commissions
watching friends and relatives (WFRs)	destination marketing organizations

Sport is big business. Cities wager millions to stage an Olympic Games, Formula 1 races, World Cup events, and other types of sport. In return, cities expect millions more from sponsors, developers, and visitors. The sport market in North America was worth $60.5 billion in 2014 and is expected to reach $73.5 billion by 2019 (Heitner, 2015). The estimated size of the global sport industry is $1.7 trillion (Plunkett Research Group, n.d). Furthermore, global sponsorship spending grew 4.6 percent in 2016 to $60.1 billion, according to IEG, a sponsorship consultancy company (ESP Properties, 2017). Given the influence of globalization in emerging markets, it is not surprising that sponsorship spending in the Asia-Pacific region was the fastest growing of any region in 2016 at 5.7 percent (ESP Properties, 2017).

According to the UN World Tourism Organization, 2016 was the seventh consecutive year of sustained growth following the 2009 global economic and financial crisis (UNWTO, 2017). Consequently, 300 million more international tourists traveled the world in 2016 as compared with the precrisis record in 2008. Similar to the sport industry trends, Asia and the Pacific (+8 percent) led growth in international tourist arrivals in 2016 (UNWTO, 2017). This growth may be because of the legacy effects of the 2008 Beijing Olympic Games, as well as events in the lead-up to the 2018 Pyeongchang Winter Olympic Games and 2020 Tokyo Olympic Games.

Sport-related **tourism** is now presenting major opportunities for both emerging and mature destinations (UNWTO, 2016). According to the National Association of Sports Commissions (NASC, 2015), visitor spending associated with sport tourism in the United States was $8.96 billion, with 25.65 million sport visitors. According to the UNWTO (2016), Eurosport has recently estimated that sport tourism is worth US$800 billion, constituting more than 10 percent of international travel and tourism receipts. Furthermore, sport tourism accounts for 25 percent of all tourism receipts, rising to as much as 55 percent in Australia and parts of New Zealand.

People travel for a variety of reasons: visiting friends and relatives, business, and leisure. Sport tourism is a major segment of the broader leisure travel market. Sport tourism resides at the intersection of the sport and tourism industries and is dynamic and filled with intrigue, challenges, and opportunities for research and business practice

(see figure 22.1). Sport tourism combines the best and worst of both the sport and tourism industries. Sport is a universal language, involving competition, conflict, emotion, and often-entertaining drama. Tourism by its very nature is invasive, involving host-guest interactions and impacts. It is not always about happy tourists and their spending. At times it can lead to crowding, queuing, environmental degradation, price gouging, and resentment by locals.

Sport, tourism, and leisure are closely related concepts. Broadly, leisure can be defined as that portion of an individual's time that is not directly devoted to work or work-connected responsibilities (Kraus, 2001). **Sport tourism** has been conceptualized to mean a leisure-based tourism that takes people temporarily outside of their home environment to participate in, watch physical activities, or venerate attractions associated with physical activities and sport (Gibson, 1998). In 2009, Weed and Bull broadened the definition by underscoring that sport tourism is a social, economic, and cultural phenomenon arising from the unique interaction of activity, people, and place. Consequently, several activities are associated with sport tourism.

Sport tourism as an academic discipline has evolved considerably in the past two decades. Textbooks, academic conferences, undergraduate and graduate degree programs, and a scientific journal, *Journal of Sport and Tourism*, now exist. This chapter examines the current body of knowledge devoted to sport tourism and identifies patterns of sport tourist behaviors, impacts, issues, and future areas for best practice and further study. Focus areas covered include event economic impacts, active and serious **sport tourists**, prestige-worthy sport tour-

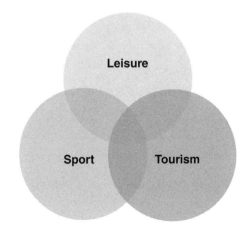

Figure 22.1 Sport and tourism intersection.

ism, social impacts, residents' perceptions of events, and **watching friends and relatives (WFRs)**. It is intended that through this analysis and knowledge sharing, the evolution of sport tourism studies may continue to prosper for the next 20 years.

Core Principles and Terms

A number of operational definitions pertinent to sport tourism are provided before we proceed further. For this chapter, a **tourist** is defined as a visitor for at least one night but not more than six months and whose main purpose of visit is other than the exercise of an activity remunerated from within the place visited.

Sport tourism is simply defined as travel to a destination to experience sport. Sport tourists are visitors to a destination for the purpose of participating, viewing, or celebrating sport (Turco, Riley, & Swart, 2002). **Visiting friends and relatives (VFR)** are a tourist market segment referring to nonresidents in the host community whose primary motive is to visit friends or relatives. In sport tourism, WFRs are VFRs with associates participating in a sport event.

The sport tourism industry involves all the people, places, and things that support, influence, and are affected by sport tourists. It is the collection of businesses, institutions, resources, and people who service sport tourists. They include tourists, host residents, and goods and services providers in the broad tourism categories of transportation, accommodations (i.e., hotels, bed and breakfasts, resorts, and eating and drinking places), and shopping. Sport serves as the focal or secondary attraction.

Figure 22.2 illustrates the sport tourism system, the interactions of the sport tourism industry within the marketplace. Natural resources form the bases for the sport tourism system. Many participatory and event-based sport tourism experiences occur in natural resource settings. Fishing, nautical, marine, and aquatic sports are enjoyed on water; climbing, snowboarding, skiing, snowshoeing, snowmobiling, and hunting are done in forests and fields. The natural environment adds to the challenge and allure of a sport tourism attraction. For example, the presence of red sandstone formations has made Moab, Utah, the mountain biking mecca. Sipadan Island in Malaysia is world-renowned for the diving it offers,

but it takes place in an environmentally sensitive area. Tourism's infrastructure of transportation, communication, accommodations, and attractions is built on natural resources. Governmental policies including immigration and travel requirements, security, trade, tariffs, currency values, and international relations influence the tourism supply and tourist demand. Communication of sport and tourism information is critical because people obviously do not travel to places they don't know about. **Destination marketing organizations** (e.g., convention and visitors bureaus, governmental travel offices), sport and tourism suppliers (sport tourism attractions such as museums, halls of fame, and stadia), and sport organizers and managers (tour operators, travel agents, and so on) use an array of methods and mediums to communicate to potential and current travelers including websites, trade shows and events, periodicals, advertisements, and, increasingly, digital and social media platforms.

Sport Tourists

Three primary types of sport tourists have been identified: participatory, event-based, and celebratory sport tourists. Participatory sport tourists travel to destinations to play sport. They may include golfers playing a round at Royal St. Andrew's Golf Club in Scotland, skiers at St. Moritz in Switzerland, runners in the Berlin Marathon, or surfers in Bali. Participatory, or active, sport tourists may be elite professionals or rank amateurs; the qualifiers for participatory sport tourists are that they are visi-

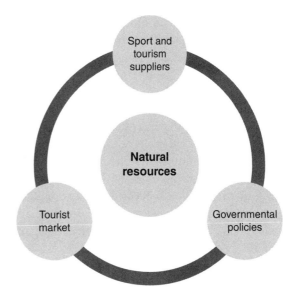

Figure 22.2 Sport tourism system.

tors to the host destination and they are engaged in sport. The concept of active sport tourists has been expanded from a serious leisure perspective, which is explored later in the chapter.

Some participatory sport tourists play a dual role in the sport tourism industry. As visiting sport competitors, they require transportation, accommodations, and other tourist services, while simultaneously serving as the attraction for event-based sport tourists. Event-based sport tourists are those who travel to a destination to watch others participate in sport. Examples of sport events witnessed by tourists (and researched by scholars) range from A to Z: America's Cup to the Zagreb Open tennis tournament. Consider the Little League World Series (LLWS) in tiny Williamsport, Pennsylvania. Held annually in August, the LLWS is the pinnacle of athletic achievement in baseball for boys up to 13 years of age. Teams from around the world compete in round-robin and elimination play, attracting over 500,000 spectators and live television coverage worldwide on ESPN. Lodging accommodations are sold out within a 60-mile (100 km) radius of the city. The athletes, coaches, and officials are participatory sport tourists to Williamsport for the 10 days of the LLWS. Parents, friends, and relatives of the participants are event-based sport tourists.

Celebratory sport tourists travel to destinations to visit halls of fame, museums, stadiums, and other places of remembrance. Numerous celebratory sport tourism attractions exist. Thousands of people each year pay their pounds to tour an empty Wimbledon Tennis Centre. The National Olympic Stadium of the 2008 Beijing Games, known as the Bird's Nest, has become a regular stop on domestic tourist itineraries and will host the opening ceremony of the 2022 Winter Games. The Basketball Hall of Fame in Springfield, Massachusetts, attracts 250,000 visitors each year, of which 20 percent are from outside the United States. The Hillerich & Bradsby Company, makers of the iconic Louisville Slugger baseball bat, receives 300,000 paying visitors annually to see the manufacturing process in its factory. Table 22.1 contains examples of sport halls of fame and sport museums in North America and other parts of the world.

Constraining factors may limit a person's travel behavior to participate in a sport tourism activity, irrespective of type (Hinch et al., 2006). For

Table 22.1 Halls of Fame and Sport Museum Names and Locations

Hall of fame or sport museum	Location
British Golf Museum	St Andrews, United Kingdom
California Surf Museum	Oceanside, California
Hockey Hall of Fame	Toronto, Canada
National Baseball Hall of Fame and Museum	Cooperstown, New York
Negro Leagues Baseball Museum	Kansas City, Missouri
FIFA World Football Museum	Zurich, Switzerland
Gilles Villeneuve Museum	Montréal, Quebec
Holmenkollen Ski Museum	Oslo, Norway
MCC Museum	Lords, United Kingdom
Olympic Museum	Lausanne, Switzerland
Springbok Experience–South African Rugby Museum	Cape Town, South Africa
Wimbledon Lawn Tennis Museum	Wimbledon, United Kingdom
World Rugby Museum	Twickenham, United Kingdom

example, event-based tourism is often associated with overcrowding and price gouging, whereas for active sport tourists the **constraints** may be closely related to fitness and health. Hinch et al. highlight that participation in nostalgia sport tourism may be limited by a lack of awareness or a limited supply of such opportunities. External constraints include a lack of time and money, geographical distance, and a lack of facilities, whereas internal constraints refer to factors such as personal capacities, abilities, knowledge, and interests (Francken & van Raaij, 1981). Jackson and Searle (1985) refer to blocking constraints that preclude participation and inhibiting constraints that moderate participation to a degree, depending on the situation. Although the application of constraints research is limited, Hinch et al. underscore that understanding the constraints facing sport tourists is important, especially in relation to constraints preventing nonsport tourists from becoming sport tourists. This topic represents a gap in consumer behavior research applied to tourists.

Learning Activity

Review some of the sport halls of fame and museums around the world for the unique features that help them attract celebratory sport tourists year in and year out. If you had an opportunity to develop a sport hall of fame or museum in your hometown, what would it be?

Within a crowd of sport event spectators are distinct market segments with respect to their consumer behaviors. Their places of origin and local spending influence the economic impacts of the event. Among sport event spectators, several distinct market segments were identified by Preuss (2005). Casuals are visitors who attend a sport event but were in the host community primarily for other reasons (i.e., VFRs, business, and so on). **Day-trippers**, or **excursionists**, are visitors who do not stay overnight in the host community. Primary sport event tourists are those visiting the host community specifically because of the sport event in question. Residents are sport event attendees in their home community. Resident spending represents a switching of transactions from one local business (i.e., dining out, cinema, theatre, and so on) to another, in this case the sport event. Time switchers are those who purposely schedule their visit to coincide with the sport event but who would have visited at another time anyway. Runaways are residents who purposely leave the host city during the event because of the event. Homestayers are residents who purposely stay in the host city during the event because of the event. Preuss and Schutte (2008) suggest that primary sport event tourists spend at higher levels than the overnight visitors they displace in hotels and other paid accommodations. In such cases, the value-added of primary sport event tourists must be factored in this crowding-out effect.

Sport Tourism Suppliers and Consumers

Figures 22.3 and 22.4 (based on information from Turco et al., 2002) provide an illustration of sport tourism suppliers and consumers based on the level

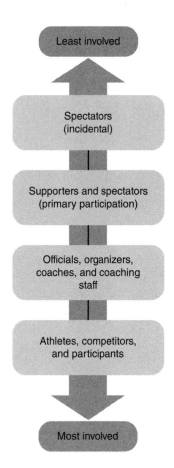

Figure 22.3 Sport tourism consumers.

of intensity at which people partake in sport tourism. Those who are most involved are the athletes, competitors, and participants as well as the officials, organizers, coaches, and coaching staff. These sport tourists are required the most for sport tourism to occur. Fans and general spectators are less involved because they may have alternative activities that can draw their attention, interest, and time away from the sport tourism activity. Spectators can also participate in sport tourism incidentally if they travel to a destination for other leisure-related purposes.

The range of sport tourism suppliers is presented next. Note that participants are demanders and suppliers of sport tourism services, because without them no one will be organizing or observing (Turco et al., 2002). Sport museums and halls of fame also serve as primary attractions. The organizers, managers, and marketers of the sport tourism opportunities serve as the link between the sport and other tourists. They are directly involved in the production of the sport attraction, and include sport associations, **sport commissions**, and government

Figure 22.4 Sport tourism suppliers.

sport ministries. Sport tour operators and travel agents provide travel and hospitality requirements to the sport tourist. Sporting goods manufacturers and sport retailers of equipment, apparel, and memorabilia are found at the next level because they are not directly involved in promoting travel opportunities. But they could also serve as primary attractions or secondary attractions if their factories or stores are set up in this manner (for example, the Louisville Slugger factory and Niketown). Sport-themed restaurants are peripherally involved in the supply of sport tourism services because their revenue is mainly generated by nonsport tourist clientele. Government, at all levels, provides basic infrastructure such as transport, health, and safety services. In addition, governments could provide sport tourism policy planning and financial support as well as maintain the natural resources required for many sport tourism activities. They are less involved but are a significant supplier of sport tourism.

Economic Impact

Economic impact studies are one of the most common forms of evaluating sport tourism events. Despite their widespread use, sport event economic impact research has been met with growing skepticism, in part because of faulty studies and inflated findings (Crompton, 2006; Li & Jago, 2013). Inaccuracies occur for several reasons, including purposeful falsification. Crompton (2006) argues that some event studies are inflated for political reasons, such as to sell or justify public investment in sport, to improve public relations, or to further an election campaign. In a study conducted on all the Olympics Games from 1964 to just before 2016, the most expensive Olympics was the Sochi 2014 Winter Olympics at $21.9 billion. The cost overrun for Sochi was 298 percent, compared with the second highest cost overrun for the London Games at 76 percent (Flyberg, Stewart, & Budzier, 2016).

Mega events are bid on primarily for the expected value added to the host city. An economic impact study essentially measures how much value the event adds to the city. Put another way, what would be missing from the economy without the event? A sport tourism event's pull, or drawing power, is measured by its ability to attract nonresidents and induce consumer spending at and near the event venue (Yu & Turco, 2000).

Visitors drawn by a major sport event may displace others who would have visited but did not because they could not secure accommodations or they were not willing to deal with the crowds attracted by the event. Other tourists and residents avoid the mega event or are priced-out, so the host city loses money that would have otherwise been spent. Crompton (2006, p. 76) contends, "If each of these visitors merely replaces another potential visitor who stayed away from the community because of the congestion associated with the tourism event, there is no new economic impact."

Event economic impact totals are often compared as if a larger amount implies greater import or success. Events vary by edition. Host cities change, economies change, competitors change, and spectators change. Despite a plethora of studies, the need remains for a refined and agile model to predict a sporting event's economic impact. Many studies fail to account for variances in consumer behaviors among spectator market segments and the crowding-out effect. Distinguishing sport event tourists by their spending behaviors (as Preuss and others have done) will lead to more accurate economic impact estimations.

The case study Cricket World Cup illustrates the importance of cricket in several countries and the consequent economic benefits of hosting these kinds of sport tourism events. The case also points to the future of cricket and further demonstrates that economic impacts cannot be viewed in isolation and that the political ramifications of sport tourism should be considered. A global battle for supremacy is occurring in the world of cricket. The balance of power appears to have shifted from England to the West Indies and to Asia, in particular, India, Pakistan, Sri Lanka, and the UAE.

Behaviors of Sport Tourists

How much does the average sport event tourist spend per trip? The answer depends on the nature of the sport event, the spectator market, and the characteristics of the host economy.

Where sport tourists live in relation to the host economy and whether they are first-time visitors influence their spending. Event visitors from communities nearer the host economy typically spend less money than those from greater distances. International visitor groups to the 2005 LLWS spent, on average, US$700 more in the Williamsport economy than domestic visitor groups did, after adjusting for group size and length of stay (Scott & Turco, 2007). Because the geographic

---

CASE STUDY

Cricket World Cup

Cricket is a global and lucrative sport whose balance of power is now shifting to Asia. According to a brand valuation report, the Indian Premier League had a value of $2.99 billion in 2012 whereas the England and Wales Cricket Board (ECB) had an annual turnover of $100 million (Glover, 2013). Television revenue generates 70 to 75 percent of ECB's income, and the Asian market is the most important. Concerns have been expressed, however, at the level of corruption emerging in developing markets, such as episodes of spot fixing in Pakistan and India.

The International Cricket Council (ICC) Cricket World Cup (CWC) tournament is one of the world's largest sporting events. CWC matches officially began in 1975, and a tournament has taken place every four years since then. The ICC CWC 2015, hosted by Australia and New Zealand, provided a major positive boost to the local economies. PricewaterhouseCoopers estimated that the tournament generated more than AU$1.1 billion in direct spending, created the equivalent of 8,320 full-time jobs, and had a total of 2 million bed nights across both countries (ICC, 2015). About 145,000 international visitors came to Australia and New Zealand for the tournament, and the largest number of overseas visitors came from Asia. The tournament was watched by more than 1.5 billion people

worldwide. ICC chief executive David Richardson said that cricket was not only popular across both countries but also an important contributor to the local economies. The Australian sports minister added that the Australian and New Zealand governments had worked closely with the World Cup organizers to ensure the greatest spectacle for sport fans while also maximizing the trade and tourism opportunities created by the tournament. The CWC 2015 Ltd. chief executive officer John Harnden said that the introduction of a single visa for the event was a significant initiative that made it easier for international guests to visit New Zealand and Australia. Additionally, both countries provided a safe, warm, and welcoming experience for all fans from around the world and provided them with an experience they would not forget.

The next major ICC tournament after the 2015 CWC was the ICC Champions Trophy in 2017, which was won by Pakistan, who trashed India in the final. The dominance of Asia in the global cricket context was again underscored. Note that at the time Pakistan had not played a home game since 2009 (home games have been played in the UAE) because of the devastating terrorist attacks, including the attack on the Sri Lankan team in 2009. There is renewed hope that matches will return to Pakistan.

origins of event spectators changes from year to year, so too will their economic impacts on the host economy. Where the competing athletes are from influences who and how many will travel to watch the competition and how much they will spend (Tang & Turco, 2001). Greig and McQuaid (2003) conducted spectator interviews at two one-day rugby international matches in Edinburgh, Scotland (Scotland versus England and Scotland versus France), to estimate the economic impact on the region and city. The study revealed that the origin of spectators differed between matches, naturally reflecting the origins of the visiting teams, and a clear association was found between the distance spectators came to watch the match and the amount they spent.

The prestige of a sport tourism experience as perceived by the sport consumer also influences the size of the visitor group and their spending. Competing in a world championship is for most a once-in-a-lifetime opportunity, and such events often attract large numbers of spectators who are relatives or friends of the athletes. The Olympic Games and world cups are the most prestigious events in the world for the sports they cover because of their global nature, scale, and infrequency. Grand Slam events in tennis (Australian, French, and U.S. Opens and Wimbledon) and golf (Master's, British and U.S. Opens and PGA Championship) are more prestigious than other events. History, prize money, media coverage, scarcity, and the field of competitors influence perceived prestige. The composition of a tournament field and its "star power" influence the media

attention, gallery size, and economic impact. An annual event such as the U.S. Open golf championship may experience significant fluctuations in attendance, spectator market segment proportionality, and spending from year to year. A case in point is what became known as the Tiger Woods effect, whereby weekend ratings were 58 percent higher in tournaments in which Tiger played (Sandomir, 2008). Even today he draws a following when he plays.

Watching Friends and Relatives

Relatively little attention has been devoted to tourists who travel to watch relatives or friends (WFR) participate in sport events. As previously alluded to, spectators with a player association spent more time and money in the local economy. It was surmised that watching a friend or relative in the LLWS was a once-in-a-lifetime experience, so spectators were willing to spend money on the event accordingly. A comparison of consumer behaviors among domestic and international WFRs and other tourists at the LLWS is provided in table 22.2. Note that domestic WFRs spent more than three times more money in comparison with other spectator market segments, although it is contended that per trip spending by WFRs would diminish as they attend more sporting events in which their friends and relatives participate. A study conducted on the Old Mutual Two Oceans Marathon in 2016 found that 97 percent of participants were accompanied by WFRs and predominantly traveled in parties of sizes of one to five people (Western Cape Government, 2016), thus under-

Table 22.2 Characteristics of WFR and Other Tourists at the 2005 LLWS

	Travel party	Sessions attended	Length of stay	Spending
Domestic WFR sport tourist	3 persons	6 sessions	7 nights	$2,337; $1,215 for travel
Domestic sport tourist	4 persons	4 sessions	3 nights	$668; $175 for travel
International WFR sport tourist	4 persons	9 sessions	11 nights	$4,550; $1,600 for travel
International sport tourist	2 persons	6 sessions	7 nights	$3,200; $700 for travel

Data from Scott and Turco (2007).

Learning Activity

Choose several different types of sport events hosted in your area. What are the some of the similarities in relation to length of stay and spending in relation to the type of sport tourist (domestic and international and WFR)?

scoring the value of the WFR segment to sport tourism events.

Serious Sport Tourists

Serious sport tourists take sport participation to another level. They are focused on and highly committed to participating in their sport. To the less committed, their dedication borders on obsession. Elite gymnasts and their families sacrifice normalcy for specialized and intense training that often comes with high social, psychological, and financial costs. Although they are mere children, elite gymnasts undergo a daily regimen of training and diet that can make sport a work-like obligation. Serious youth sport tourists are often accompanied to competitions by their serious parents. They spend more money on sport-related goods and services, travel more frequently, and stay longer and spend more per night than other tourists do (Getz, 2008). For those reasons, the Walt Disney World Company built the Wide World of Sports complex in Orlando, Florida, in 1997.

Elite athletes are not the only serious sport tourists. In fact, the vast majority are amateurs. The physical demands to prepare for and compete in an Ironman Triathlon imply a serious commitment to sport. To earn the title of Ironman finisher, a participant must swim 2.4 miles (3.9 km), cycle 112 miles (180 k), and then run a marathon (26.2 miles, or 180 km). Nearly 40 Ironman races are held worldwide at a capacity of 2,000 to 2,500 athletes. The demand is so high for some Ironman events that entries sell out on the first day of open registration.

Distance running is another popular activity for serious sport tourists. The 50-States Marathon Club is composed of runners who have completed a marathon in each state in the United States. Besides the serious time, financial, and physical demands required to run a marathon, the added time, travel, and accommodations costs to run in every state demonstrate the high level of commitment these athletes have toward their chosen endeavor.

Serious leisure is the systematic pursuit of an amateur, hobbyist, or volunteer core activity that people find so substantial, interesting, and fulfilling that, in the typical case, they launch themselves on a leisure career centered on acquiring and expressing a combination of its special skills, knowledge, and experience (Stebbins, 2007, p. 3).

Serious leisure participants distinguish themselves by the (1) need to persevere at the activity, (2) availability of a leisure career, (3) need to put in effort to gain skill and knowledge, (4) realization of various special benefits, (5) unique ethos and social world, and (6) an attractive personal and social identity (Stebbins, 2007). Serious leisure can be contrasted with casual leisure by a key defining characteristic of providing a sense of social identity (Green & Jones, 2005). Travel to participate in serious leisure falls within the domain of serious sport tourism.

Serious sport tourists include spectators who follow their favorite team to attend away matches. In some cases, visiting sport event tourists outnumber (and outcheer) home fans, negating the home field advantage. Consider the legions of football fans who travel throughout the year to witness their teams in action. The package for the 2018 UEFA Champions League Final in Ukraine is $4,765 per person (based on double occupancy) for a first-class, two-night stay, ticket, and transfers excluding airfare. With Real Madrid's sublime performance in 2017 when they beat Juventus 4-1, this package is likely to be sold out quickly. Therefore, serious sport tourists can be both participants and spectators.

Social Costs and Benefits

A range of social costs and benefits attributed to events is explored in the generic survey statements developed by Fredline et al. (2003) to measure sport tourism social impacts.

Costs of the Cancellation of Ironman New Zealand

The Ironman New Zealand (IMNZ) is one of the older events on the Ironman calendar, but its organization has been affected by poor weather on several occasions. In 2012 the organizers announced a postponement of the event, although a substitute half-distance event was hosted. Many considered the event canceled because they did not have the opportunity to complete their goal of racing the full distance. Besides the intensive physical training undertaken to prepare for the event (weekly average of 4 hours swimming, 11 hours cycling, and 5.5 hours running for about 15 weeks), serious sport tourists also invested significant personal resources for travel, accommodation, registration, and training. Therefore, it is not surprising that many of them were upset and disappointed at having to wait a year for the next opportunity to compete. The postponement was even more devastating for first-time entrants. Although people recognize the risk associated with outdoor sport events, the findings revealed that if the risk was considered too high

(further cancellations and associated travel costs), then a future avoidance strategy could be invoked. Although some considered contingency planning by opting to enter another Ironman in their home country as a backup, others were reconsidering their commitment to overseas events because of the financial risks. But the cancellation did not deter some serious sport tourists' participation in other Ironman events because they chose different destinations as a way to see the world rather than regularly return to the same event. Scaling back participation appeared to be the most extreme behavioral response adopted by a few interviewees who experienced great disappointment with the cancellation of IMNZ.

For more information, refer to the following study: Lamont, M., Kennelly, M., & Moyle, B. (2014). Costs and perseverance of serious leisure careers. *Leisure Sciences*, 36(2), 144-160.

Measures to Assess Residents' Perceptions of Sport Event Social Impacts

[Responses: agree, disagree, don't know]

Entertainment

Residents have an opportunity to attend an interesting event with their family and friends, and interact with new people.

Economic Benefits

Visitors spend money at the event, which helps to stimulate the economy, creates employment opportunities, and is good for local business.

Community Pride

Local residents feel more proud of their city, and the event makes them feel good about their community.

Regional Showcase

The event showcases the destination in a positive light and encourages future tourism or business investment.

Public Money

Too much public money was spent on the event that would be better spent on other public activities.

Disruption to Local Residents

The lives of local residents were disrupted because the event caused problems like traffic congestion, parking difficulties, and excessive noise.

Community Injustice

The costs and benefits of the event were distributed unevenly across the community.

Loss of Use of Public Facilities

Public facilities and public transport were less available to locals because of closure or overcrowding.

Bad Behavior

The event attracted people who behaved inappropriately, in a rowdy and delinquent way.

Environmental Impact

The environment was negatively affected by the event because of excessive litter, pollution, and damage to natural areas.

Prices

Prices increased for goods and services, and property values rose because of the event.

Learning Activity

Evaluate an existing event in your community and identify some of the costs and benefits of hosting the event from a resident's perspective. What are some of the steps you would take to mitigate negative impacts?

For more information, refer to the study by Fredline, L., Jago, L. and Deery, M. (2003). The development of a generic scale to measure the social impacts of events. *Event Management*, 8(1), 23-37. (Measures are not listed in order of importance.)

Unfortunately, examples of fan violence abound, particularly in football. Crime (or the perception of crime) is a major deterrent to sport tourism. The regional showcase element in the preceding list addresses this issue. For both South Africa and Brazil, whose destination images are plagued by perceptions of crime, the megaevents hosted in those countries recently did much to enhance those images. At the same time, residents believed that those efforts should be sustained in the long term and focused not only on the tourism precincts.

Price inflation may occur in cities hosting megaevents well before the event begins. After London won the bid to host the 2012 Olympic Games, home prices in the districts where Olympic venues were sited rose as much as 33 percent, well above the city's 24 percent average (Johnson, 2012). On a more positive note, sport may provide entertainment for many locals (in addition to tourists), and civic pride may be elevated from hosting a megaevent. In advance of their city's hosting of the Tour de France stage 1 race, the vast majority of residents in Canterbury were aware of the event and many planned to watch the race or participate in related activities (Bull & Lovell, 2007). Despite the potential for various negative impacts, support for the decision to host the event was overwhelming.

Greater attention has also been paid to environmental impacts, which in combination with economic and social impacts call for consideration of a triple bottom-line perspective. Issues of climate change and global warming affect all forms of sport tourism. One such example applicable to

CASE STUDY

Carbon Footprint of Skiers and Boarders

Transport and travel contribute to increasing greenhouse gas emissions, leading to negative environmental impacts such as climate change and global warming. The melting of snow and ice is one consequence of global warming, which has an adverse effect on snow sport tourism. For example, Alpine Skiing World Cup races had to be canceled in several European countries in the 2015-2016 season. A lack of snow affects both competitive and recreational skiers with a negative knock-on effect because these snow sport tourists in all likelihood need to travel farther to reach operational ski areas. Carbon footprint analysis is used to measure greenhouse gas emissions and is generally obtained from travel survey information. A study conducted in Germany with snow sport tourists revealed that 40 percent were skiers, 38 percent were boarders, and 22 percent did both sports. In terms of their snow sport travel-related behavior, 92 percent were on skiing or snowboarding vacations, 46 percent took day trips, 25 percent participated in training courses, and 5 percent traveled to competition during 2015. The annual carbon footprint of boarders was higher than that of skiers. People involved in both sports and those involved in competitive sport had higher carbon footprints than recreational snow sport tourists did. Furthermore, active and regular sport participation seems to be associated with higher carbon footprints than passive sport consumption of one-off events such as the 2004 Wales Rally and the UK stages of the 2007 Tour de France. The findings also highlight the challenges with respect to sustainability of the snow sport tourism industry because these tourists, who consider themselves environmentally conscious, do not necessarily produce fewer carbon dioxide emissions. For more information, refer to the study by Wicker (2017).

both event-based and active sport tourism is that of snow sport tourism, as highlighted in the case study Carbon Footprint of Skiers and Boarders.

Residents and Mega Sport Events

Residents in host cities experience firsthand the impacts of mega events during the event lifecycle: application and bidding, preparation, operation, and legacy stages. For an Olympic Games, residents may have encountered sport tourists directly or been affected indirectly by their presence during the Games. Following the Games, residents may use new or improved transportation systems, accommodations, and other infrastructures in the host city or region. They are therefore in a unique position to evaluate the event as taxpayers, hosts, consumers of infrastructure, and possible consumers of Olympic sport venues. Residents may experience sport side by side with sport participants and spectators. Among the 40,000 runners in the Berlin Marathon are a mix of Berliners and visitors.

The Olympic Games lifecycle includes bid (application and candidacy), preparation, operation, and legacy stages. The length of each stage varies considerably: 2 years for bidding, 7 years for preparation, 17 days for operation, and a lifetime for the legacy. Public perceptions of the event shift across the lifecycle, from elation and euphoria at the bid stage; concerns over readiness, costs, and anxiety and a wait-and-see attitude in the preparation stage; relief and joy during operations; and pride, appreciation, and satisfaction following the Games. This rollercoaster pattern of resident perceptions is illustrated by Lohman et al. (2017) in their study of residents in relation to the 2016 Summer Olympic Games in Rio (see table 22.3). Rio residents were asked to evaluate their perceptions of hosting the Olympic Games before, during, and after the Games. Table 22.3 shows that over the first two periods, some aspects were perceived more positively, whereas others were perceived more negatively. Residents perceive the hosting of a mega event across the event's lifecycle as having ups and downs. This perception is also influenced by the political and economic climate of the day, as in the case of Brazil. As the sport event evolves, so too do the opinions of

Table 22.3   Residents' Perceptions of the Positive and Negative Impacts of the 2016 Olympic Games (in Percent)

Impacts	Before	During
Cultural exchange	2	16
Legacy	39	22
Infrastructure	23	32
Inaccurate expenses	25	31
Traffic	13	19

Data from Lohman, P. et al. (2017).

host residents toward the event. Therefore, the sport event organizing committee should conduct periodic assessments of residents across the event lifecycle.

Impacts on Nonhost Cities

Although much is made of the primary host cities for an Olympic Games, FIFA World Cup, or UEFA EuroCup, other smaller cities serve as hosts for preliminary matches, training, or team base camps. The impacts of a mega sport event may be more pronounced in these satellite cities because of their relatively small size and the large numbers of spectators they must host. For major international football competitions, teams often establish base camps away from major cities to prepare for matches and avoid the distractions of larger cities. Spreading the benefits beyond the host cities for the 2010 FIFA World Cup in South Africa was a strategy used by various regional governments. For example, the Western Cape government was successful in their base camp bids to host three national teams in George, a much smaller town, in addition to having others considered as satellite accommodation areas.

Destination Branding

The overall impression that the destination creates in the minds of tourists can be described as the destination brand (Chalip & Costa, 2006). Sport tourism events are a critical component for the branding of destinations as desirable locations for tourism and investment. Not surprisingly, place marketers are increasingly using sport tourism events (and the associated attractions and activities) to enhance the destination brand of the host city (region or country) or use it as a differentiating strategy. One way of doing this is through cobranding, which occurs when the event brand is paired with destination brand to reinforce or change a brand image. The 2010 FIFA World Cup is a case in point. Because the FIFA World Cup is a global brand, South Africa was in a position to leverage its association with this brand to enhance its tourism and investment profile and stature. Similarly, FIFA used the opportunity to improve its global footprint and image by hosting the first World Cup in Africa. For this positive transfer to take place, however, a properly managed event communication strategy is required. Higham (2005, p. 154) highlights that "the role of the media is critical to achieving destination branding outcomes." This aspect is particularly challenging for South Africa (and Africa generally) because the destination is often associated with negative images. Dimeo and Kay (2004) underscore that developing countries are less able to control images projected by the media because of preconceived notions and prejudices of the Western media. Therefore, working with the event promoters, sponsors, and media becomes critical to ensure that the destination is portrayed in the way that it wants to be perceived. For South Africa, perceptions of the destination changed in a positive direction as a result of hosting the World Cup.

Sport can create immediate name brand recognition for its host and vice versa. When sport and destinations are highly successful at cobranding, thinking of one (sport) without the other (destinations) is nearly impossible. Consider the following: Innsbruck or Lake Placid (Winter Olympic Games), Indianapolis (Indy 500), Pamplona (San Fermin Festival, Running of the Bulls), Dakar (Rally). Chalip and Costa (2006) argue that some sport brands are so closely associated with the host destination that the link goes beyond cobranding and the sport tourism event can be viewed as an extension of the destination brand. The Cape Town Cycle Tour, which has attracted about 35,000 cyclists to the city annually since 1978, can be considered a brand extension, to the point where the organizers renamed the event. The race route features 68 miles (109 km) of the scenic Cape Peninsula.

A portfolio of sport tourism events is required to sustain the impact of events on the destination brand and to enhance the reach and frequency of destination-specific messages. But only sport tourism events most suited to building the destination brand should be included (Chalip & Costa, 2006). Furthermore, other sport tourism attractions and activities that complement events in the overall destination marketing communications mix should also be considered (Chalip, 2005).

The perceived attractiveness of the host community (i.e., alternative attractions, climate, culture, nightlife, shopping, proximity to relatives and friends, and so on) elicits larger visitor groups and stimulates relatively more spending from sport tourists. A sport event destination may not possess warm, sunny weather, snow-capped mountains, or white sand beaches, but other regional attractions, in aggregate, could encourage sport tourists to extend their stays. For example, aside from the LLWS, Williamsport, Pennsylvania is not known for or marketed as a tourism destination. No distinguishing natural resources or other unique attractions are located in the area. Little League officials have staged a parade and developed a self-contained entertainment complex with a museum, conference facility, recreation center, park, and lodging accommodations, in addition to the sport stadiums and practice and training facilities, to keep visitors longer.

Sport Tourism and Universal Accessibility

A potential growth segment for sport tourism is that of the disabled population. The World Health Organization's *World Report on Disability* (2011) estimates that 15 percent of the world's population is made up of persons with disabilities and that this number is set to increase because of aging populations and the global increase in chronic health conditions such as diabetes, cardiovascular disease, cancer, and mental health disorders. The *Brettapproved Report on the Disabled Travel Market* (2015) projects that by 2050 the number of persons over 60 years will increase to 20 percent of the world population, with one-fifth of this group being over 80 years old. Furthermore, they project that by 2030 nearly 24 percent of the U.S. population, approximately 84 million people, will be disabled. Accessible travel is also reported to be the fastest growing market sector and was valued at US$15 billion per annum, with an expected increase because of aging boomers (TravelAgentCentral, 2012, cited by Brettapproved, 2015).

The 1990 Americans with Disabilities Act (ADA) and other similar policies globally have enabled people with disabilities to travel more as well as lead more physically active lifestyles. Similarly, an upward trend is occurring in senior participation in leisure activities such as travel and sport (Delpy Neirotti, 2003). Besides the elderly, parents with children and those who are clinically disabled will benefit from a more accessible environment and create a more diverse audience. An inaccessible event could result in a lost opportunity in attendance, causing an adverse effect on the event organization and host community economically. Therefore, sport tourism managers need to consider these possibilities when planning a sport tourism event.

By implementing successful universal accessibility strategies and measures, a destination will be able to attract future sport tourism events that offer universal accessibility in general and disabled sport in particular. A number of events such as the Commonwealth Games, Deaflympics, Special Olympics, and Olympics and Paralympic Games cater to many athletes with disabilities, offering possibilities for future business. Moreover, such approaches can position the host city or region as an accessible tourism destination. Improvements to accommodations, facilities, transportation, and infrastructure will encourage general tourism among people with disabilities in the future. This development, in turn, will positively affect the residents of a host destination by creating a more knowledgeable and supportive society for people with disabilities.

Legacy Effects

Sustaining sport tourism is a primary management challenge in the face of finite natural resources, financial market uncertainty, and fierce competition from other destinations and competing leisure interests. Major sport events can be footloose and offer their event to the highest bidder. Some events lead to flow-on investments, increased tourism, relocated headquarters by associations and corporations, or improvement of social issues in the community. Such impacts may take years following an event to materialize. Indianapolis developed a strategy involving sport as a catalyst for economic development in the late 1980s and has adhered to its plan of establishing itself as the capital of amateur sport. Several national sport governing bodies, including the National Collegiate Athletic Association (NCAA), relocated to Indianapolis. Enduring sport and destination image and brand are also components of a sport tourism legacy. As noted earlier, sport and destinations may become inextricably linked, such as Manchester, England (Manchester United and Manchester City Football Clubs), Kenya (distance running), and Brazil (football).

Legacy is no longer a desirable extra but an essential priority for any host destination, sport federation, or organizing committee responsible for bidding, winning, and delivering a major sport tourism event. Preuss (2007) defines legacy as "all planned and unplanned, positive and negative, tangible and intangible structures created for and by a sport event that remain longer than the event itself" (p. 211). Examples of planned legacy structures may be museums or halls used for meetings or exhibits after the event; an unplanned structure would be a terrorist attack that tarnishes the city's tourism image. What constitutes a positive or negative legacy structure may be in the eye of the beholder. An increase in the number of visitors may be positive for tourist-dependent business owners but a negative for residents who deplore mass tourism and its consequences. Some legacy structures are long-lasting, take years to develop, and occur during the build-up to an event (e.g., infrastructure); others may occur during the event, such as viewers' impressions of Chinese culture gained from watching the 2008 Beijing Olympic Games Opening Ceremony.

Sport tourism event planners may have a range of legacy imperatives such as improved accessibility for persons with disabilities, youth sport development, improved tourism image, environmental neutrality, and economic stimulus, among others. From a universal accessibility perspective, the Australian Sports Commission (1998) predicted the following legacies from the Paralympic Games in Sydney 2000:

◆ Raised awareness and appreciation of athletes and all peoples with disabilities
◆ More trained officials

◆ Improved infrastructure
◆ Improved capacity to meet the needs of large numbers of travelers with disabilities

For Beijing and the 2008 Olympic Games, the goal was to portray a green Games and an open modern society embracing the world. The organizing committee for the 2008 Beijing Olympic Games adopted the motto One World One Dream to convey an Olympic ideal shared by all. The motto may also apply to China's ambitions to be the world's economic superpower. Judging by its strong foreign trade position and financial stability relative to other nations, China is in a strong position to capitalize on the 2008 Olympic Games for years to come. Although its environmental legacy is questionable, Beijing will make use of venues and infrastructure from the 2008 Games for the 2022 Winter Games.

Because of major corruption scandals plaguing both FIFA and the IOC, residents have given less support to hosting these mega events (Osborn, 2017), and sponsors have been more difficult to entice (Menarey, 2017) because of ethical concerns (Crafton, 2017). Cities and countries now approach the bidding and hosting of mega events with more caution and greater attention paid to the concept of legacy.

Planning and Evaluation

Major cities prepare years in advance to vie for the most coveted sport events: the Olympic Games, FIFA World Cup, Commonwealth Games, and so on. Smaller cities compete for relatively smaller events, including the World Games, Deaflympics, Ryder Cup, and World Figure Skating Championships. Despite the potential that sport tourism offers, cases of strategic planning in sport tourism are rare (Higham, 2005), probably because of the focus on short-term gains with respect to the hosting of sport tourism events and less concern for the long-term consequences for a host destination. Sport tourism planning includes planning for sport tourism events and event-related infrastructure as well as planning for other sport tourism facilities such as halls of fame and museums. Sport tourism planning has generally been geared to the tourist, and little attention has been paid to local use. Planning for sustainable sport tourism development must take into account the interests of local residents. Plan-

ning for dual use is further exacerbated by the fact that sport and tourism policy and planning usually reside in different government departments. Institutional arrangements therefore affect how sport tourism is planned at various destinations.

With large amounts of funds, especially public funds, being invested into the bidding and hosting of sport tourism events, greater accountability is required. Monitoring and evaluation of sport tourism initiatives should include triple bottom-line assessments (economic, social, and environmental) as well as studies of sponsorship effectiveness, marketing effectiveness, and media impact.

Summary

We have introduced sport tourism—its definition, industry segments, and impacts—and offered examples of sport tourism practices. This section summarizes the key points made earlier in the chapter and offers suggestions for future study in sport tourism.

Participatory sport tourism induces event-based sport tourism and subsequently celebratory sport tourism. To what extent does celebratory sport tourism influence participatory and sport event tourism, if at all? For example, are those who visit the National Basketball Hall of Fame in Springfield, Massachusetts, more (or less) likely to travel to watch or compete in basketball events? Are those who visit Wimbledon or Old Trafford more (or less) likely to watch or compete in tennis and football (soccer) events? Similarly, to what extent does sport event tourism influence participatory sport tourism? For example, are visitors to the 2017 U.S. Open Golf Championship at Erin Hills, Wisconsin, more (or less) likely to travel to play golf? Are residents who witness the Cape Town Cycle Tour more (or less) likely to participate in this event or travel to other cycle events around the world?

What inhibits or constrains people from experiencing sport tourism? How do they negotiate these constraints? Typically, a lack of time, money, opportunity, or self-concept is the constraint. A vast body of knowledge already exists on constraints to leisure (Jackson, 2005), and it can be extended to sport tourism environments. Constraints to sport tourism for persons with disabilities, which include the aforementioned constraints as well as transportation and architectural barriers, inaccessible communications, inflexible sport rules, and lack of adaptive sport equipment, offer another intriguing research opportunity.

Serious sport tourists were introduced as those who travel to pursue their leisure sport "careers." Further understanding of serious sport tourists is warranted to gain insights into their sport involvement, time and financial management priorities, and consumer behaviors. The commitments of time and financial resources for elite and less skilled serious sport tourists may be compared. Elite athletes are hypothesized to spend less time and money on training and equipment because their exceptional skills and performance are enough for success, whereas less skilled athletes attempt to compensate by investing in training and expensive equipment.

Event-based sport tourism involves sport participants as the focal attraction and, typically, spectators, some of whom may be visitors to the host city. Most research on sport tourism involves megaevents in developed countries, but the body of knowledge about developing countries is growing because of the increasing proliferation of these events in recent years. Sport event tourism managers in developing countries, including central European countries new to democracy, market-driven economics, and sport governance systems, face unique challenges. Their communities often lack appropriate sport venues, adequate transportation systems, and sufficient accommodations at various star ratings for large numbers of fans. They may have limited available capital, political instability, perhaps a one-sport culture, a male-dominated culture, and so on. People may argue that all countries are developing or redeveloping because of globalization, population shifts, immigration, changes in political ideology, adaptation to a market economy, limited food and water supplies, changeable oil and energy supplies and demands, and climate change. Each of the aforementioned change factors presents a unique research avenue for scholars interested in sport tourism in developing countries.

Some sport events appear to attract high-end consumer groups because of the relative cost to entry (e.g., America's Cup yacht race, Masters Golf Tournament, Singapore Formula One), and others attract more thrifty visitors (Yu & Turco, 2000). We would surmise that per day and per capita spending would be higher among spectators and participants who attend upscale events, but this is not always the case. Investigations into the sport lifestyles of the rich and famous (as well as the poor and unnoticed) may shed light on this question. Few published studies have provided glimpses into the world of sport's super rich in polo, yachting, or fox hunting, likely because of participant privacy issues.

Lastly, the watching friends and relatives market at sport contests should be studied in relation to event prestige. As WFRs are often seasoned, repeat consumers of sport events, they have devised ways to keep travel costs in check. Some have hypothesized, however, that greater event prestige will negate the downward spending effects associated with repeat visitors.

? Review Questions

1. Review the bid specifications for a major sport event from the website of a sport governing body (e.g., FIFA, Olympic Games, UEFA, Formula One, ICC). Which city in your country would be most suited to host the event and why?

2. Analyze a (relatively) large sport event from a tourism perspective. How many overnight stays are attributed to the event? What are the tourist impacts on the host city?

3. Select a hall of fame, sport museum, or other celebratory sport tourism attraction and describe the trends in visitor demand over the past 10 years. What are the primary consumer markets in terms of their geographic and demographic characteristics?

4. Perform an accessibility audit on a sport tourism venue and the primary transportation systems that people would use as sport tourists. What score would the venue and transportation systems receive?

5. Access the economic impact figures for a recent NFL Super Bowl. How was the economic impact determined? How does the economic impact compare with a previous Super Bowl when adjusted for inflation? Analyze the same for a UEFA Championship.

6. Because events vary by edition, choose a recurring event (annual or quadrennial) and review how sport tourism consumer spending patterns have changed from one edition to the next.

7. Discuss the specific steps that governmental officials are taking to address climate change, especially in relation to accelerating sustainability and the green economy, for the 2020 Tokyo Olympic Games.

Part VI

Frontiers and Challenges in International Sport

Mark Kolbe/Getty Images

Rugby Sevens match between New Zealand and Kenya on day 10 of the Gold Coast 2018 Commonwealth Games.

Corruption in International Sport

Samantha Roberts, PhD
Texas A&M University–Commerce

Clayton Bolton, EdD
Texas A&M University–Commerce

Chapter Objectives

After studying this chapter, you will be able to do the following:

- Define corruption in sport.
- Discuss the different types of corruption in sport.
- Understand how and why corruption can occur in international sport.
- Understand the impact and implications of corruption on the sport industry's main stakeholders.
- Discuss the complexities in addressing corruption in international sport.
- Discuss the gray area of corruption in sport.

Key Terms

bracket fixing	Skategate
closed league structure	spiral of pressures
competition corruption	sporting transgression
Crashgate	spot fixing
doping	tanking
management corruption	uncertainty of outcome
match fixing	zone of tolerance
open league structure	

Imagine it is the final of the FIFA World Cup and your national team has just lifted the treasured trophy after winning the tournament. How would you feel? Proud? Euphoric? Excited? Then you find out that payments were made to your opponents earlier in the tournament to ensure your team's safe passage through the competition. How do you feel now? Has the victory been tarnished? Has the integrity of the competition been affected? What about your team? Has their integrity been tarnished too? For some, it will have been. For others, winning the World Cup is worth it. Herein lies the problem with corruption in sport.

Sport has long had a history of corruption, ranging from executives in some of sport's most high-profile governing bodies taking bribes to referees betting on the games they were officiating, from athletes using performance-enhancing drugs (PEDs) to players taking payments to lose or perform in a certain way. Names once synonymous with sporting excellence and achievement, including American sprinter Marion Jones, soccer club Juventus, and cyclist Lance Armstrong, are part of a history tarnished by cheating and the overwhelming desire to win. Some of the earliest examples of such behavior can be traced back to ancient Greece, where athletes used special diets and herbal concoctions in competition to gain an edge and where wrestler Eupolos of Thessalia paid rivals to lose in an Olympic tournament. Canadian sprinter Ben Johnson all but destroyed his career in 1988 by failing a drug test after breaking the world record in the 100-meter final at the Olympic Games in Seoul, South Korea. That blue-ribbon race became known as the dirtiest race in history (Moore, 2012) because six of the eight finalists faced accusations during and after their careers of using PEDs, failing drugs tests, or being banned from the sport for supplying illegal substances to other athletes. More recently, Crashgate in Formula One, the salary cap breaches in the National Rugby League (NRL) in Australia by the Melbourne Storm and Parramatta Eels clubs, and the spot-fixing scandal involving three members of the Pakistan cricket team have ensured that sport has moved from the back pages of the newspapers to the front. Sport is also littered with examples of athletes and teams taking money to lose sporting competitions, like South African cricket captain Hansie Cronje (pronounced cron-YEAR) and the Chicago White Sox in 1919, the team that purposely lost the World Series in that year and became known as the Chicago Black Sox. Animals, particularly race horses, have also been given substances that prevent peak performance, thus manipulating race results. The reputations of the individuals or organizations involved are questioned, and the history of sporting achievements can be tarnished by the decision to cheat. But the guilty-by-association tag can be just as damaging for stakeholders, including governing bodies, fans, and sponsors.

This chapter examines corruption in international sport, discussing the types and prevalence of this behavior and analyzing the issues involved in defining and tackling corruption in sport. More specifically, the chapter highlights the implications and impacts of such behavior for the sport industry as a whole and discusses some of the issues faced in trying to address corruption in international sport.

Defining Corruption

At the outset, understanding the terminology used when discussing corruption in sport is important. Because of the rather limited academic focus that this area of sport management has received to date, providing a definition of corruption in sport relies on a much broader analysis of extant literature, particularly in the fields of business and politics. But first, it is vital to discuss one of the main reasons, or factors, that separate sport from other industries, one of the unique features (Smith & Stewart, 2010) of the sport industry that keeps stakeholders, like the media, sponsors, fans, and academics, interested in sporting competition—the principle of **uncertainty of outcome**. In a speech at the 2012 Olympic Games, Lord Sebastian Coe, chairman of the London Organizing Committee of the Olympic Games (LOCOG), said, "There is a truth to sport, a purity, a drama, an intensity, a spirit that makes it irresistible to take part in and irresistible to watch" (BBC TV, 2012). Whannel (1992, in Mason, 1999, p. 405) further suggests that

> like other forms of entertainment, sport offers a utopia, a world where everything is simple, dramatic and exciting, and euphoria is always a possibility. Sport entertains, but can also frustrate, annoy and depress. But it is this very uncertainty that gives its unpredictable joys their characteristic intensity.

This uncertainty is based on the premise of *ceteris paribus*, or "all things being equal"—opposing players or teams playing to the best of their ability in pursuit of victory. After all, as Westerbeek and Smith (2003, p. 53) suggest, "There can be no sport unless there is a chance of either victory or defeat."

Developing from Neale's (1964) Louis–Schmelling paradox, with a foundation of Rottenberg's (1956) theory of competitive balance, the uncertainty-of-outcome hypothesis is based on the principle that the more unpredictable the result of a sporting competition is, the greater the demand will be for that competition (Alavy, Gaskell, Leach, & Szymanski, 2006). Think about the dominance of Manchester United in England's Premier League over the last 25 years or Glasgow Celtic in Scottish football over the same period; the argument here is that if this dominance continues, eventually this predictability, or a perceived lack of competitive balance, will cause spectators to lose interest in the competition (Szymanski, 2001). With no one viewing these competitions, media companies have no audience and sponsors have no target market to sell their products or services to; they would no longer derive any value from being associated with the sport industry and would withdraw from it.

Literature suggests that there are three types of outcome uncertainty—the uncertainty of match outcome, the uncertainty of seasonal outcome, and the uncertainty of championship outcome—with the significant difference between the three being

Learning Activity

Investigate other sporting dynasties, when teams or athletes enjoyed regular and long-term success, and the effect that those dynasties had on other teams and viewing figures. Did attendance go up or down when a team was playing the dynasty? What are the implications for the teams and the league as a whole? Were the viewing figures for Formula One affected during Schumacher's dominance in the 1990s? What happened during Sebastian Vettel's four championships in a row? What are the implications for a sport like Formula One?

time (Cairns et al., 1986, in Czarnitzki & Stadtmann, 2002). The latter refers to the long-term dominance of a league competition by one team, as previously highlighted. The former, however, provides some of the contextual background for this chapter—the argument being that attendance will be higher if the probability of either a home team or away team victory is equal, thus leading to higher tension. The result of this type of competition, or match, is much easier to manipulate or fix than a 10-month English Premier League season or a 162-game Major League Baseball (MLB) season. So, although sport is based on uncertainty of outcome, corruption in sport undermines this principle. Match fixing removes this unpredictability, or uncertainty, of the outcome of a sporting competition. The use of PEDs by athletes may do the same, but perhaps in a more subtle way. Even the measures put in place by leagues in North America to try to ensure a level of competitive balance have contributed to the development of a form of match fixing, known as tanking, designed to take advantage of certain strategies.

What we have discussed here is what Gorse (2014) calls **sporting transgression**, "any illegal, immoral or unethical activity that attempts to deliberately distort the outcome of a sporting contest, or an element within that contest, for the personal material gain of one or more parties involved in that activity" (p. 67). This definition builds on the thinking of Maennig (2005), who used the term *competition corruption* to describe

> behavior by athletes who refrain from achieving the level of performance normally required in the sport in question to win the competition and instead intentionally permit others to win, or behavior by sporting officials who consciously perform their allocated tasks in a manner at variance with the objectives and moral values of the relevant club, association, competitive sports in general and/or society at large. (p.189)

Note, however, that Maennig (2005) does not acknowledge doping as a form of corruption, arguing that corrupt activity involves behavior that prevents an athlete from performing to the best of his or her ability, whereas the use of PEDs leads to what he calls a "super performance" by an athlete. He also argues that because doping does not include any financial transaction, it cannot be a form of corruption. It could be argued that this view is flawed; athletes are paying for these substances and, as a result of using them, are potentially earning millions of dollars in sponsorship and endorsement revenues as well as winning and appearance fees. The definition provided by Gorse (2014) is used to underpin the discussion of this type of cheating behavior in this chapter.

The concept of **management corruption** is discussed by Maennig (2005) to describe activity by sporting officials and governing bodies that can be considered nonsporting, in that they do not affect a match or sporting competition. It is more about the decisions made by governing bodies or event

hosts to, for example, award construction contracts for major stadiums, sell media or marketing rights, or award host-nation status for megaevents. The awarding of the 2002 Winter Olympic Games to Salt Lake City in Utah is one such example, when International Olympic Committee (IOC) members were alleged to have received bribes and other gifts from the Salt Lake Organizing Committee (SLOC). It has also been alleged that Fédération Internationale de Football Association (FIFA) officials have systematically accepted bribes to award contracts. Many of them have been indicted by U.S. federal authorities for such criminal activity as money laundering, wire fraud, and racketeering.

Running From the Rules?

The International Association of Athletics Federations (IAAF) has long been at the forefront of anti-doping practices by subjecting athletes to what were perceived to be stringent testing schedules and severe sanctions for failed tests. A four-year ban for athletes using PEDs (for a first offence) was reintroduced in 2015, after bans were reduced from four to two years in 1997 to be in line with penalties imposed by other international sporting organizations. Some of the sport's biggest names called for the ban to be increased from two to four years. Current IAAF president Sebastian Coe stated, "We have to go back from two years to four years. The move down to two did a lot of damage to my sport" (BBC, 2013, para. 16). From reading the newspapers or websites, it is clear that some high-profile athletes were calling for longer bans but others were running from the rules.

Sprinters Asafa Powell from Jamaica and American Tyson Gay were banned for doping offenses in 2013, and home favorites Konstantinos Kenteris and Ekaterini Thanou were sanctioned for evading doping control in the run-up to the Olympic Games in Athens in 2004. New and improved testing methods have led to dozens of athletes being punished for violations of anti-doping rules stretching back to the 2008 Olympics in Beijing, including Nesta Carter, a member of the world-record-holding Jamaican 4-by-100-meter relay team; his failed test led to arguably the greatest sprinter of all time, Usain Bolt, being stripped of his relay gold medal from Beijing, which took away

his treble-treble (winning 100-meter, 200-meter, and 4-by-100-meter gold medals at the 2008, 2012, and 2016 Olympic Games).

The spotlight continues to be on the IAAF as allegations of systematic doping in Russia plague track and field and many other sports. More alarming are the allegations of corruption targeted at those responsible for the governance of the sport—members of the IAAF Executive Board and even its former president, Lamine Diack, who, according to an independent WADA report, was "responsible for organizing and enabling" corruption (Hodgetts, 2016, para. 3).

When Sebastian Coe became president in 2015, he faced, and continues to face, massive challenges in both restoring the integrity and credibility of the IAAF and dealing with doping in the sport. This challenge was evident at the IAAF World Athletics Championships in Beijing in 2015. The men's 100-meter final saw Jamaican Usain Bolt face American Justin Gatlin, who had served two drugs bans in his career. The media portrayed the race as good versus evil, and much of the build-up focused not only on Bolt's reputation but also the reputation of the sport (the Russian scandal had broken in the weeks leading up to the event).

The sport of athletics is in turmoil. Can we trust the competition we see before us? How can those responsible for the governance of the sport address the issues of its recent past? Do stakeholders really care?

Types of Corruption

Within the parameters of the two main concepts of corruption in international sport, sporting transgression and management corruption, a number of different types of behavior fall into each category. Figure 23.1 shows these types of behavior against a gray area, which will be discussed later in this chapter.

Some of these types of behavior, or terms, you will no doubt be familiar with. **Doping**, the use of PEDs, is prevalent across sport and around the world. Athletes and coaches look for any advantage over their rivals, and many look to the world of science for help. Substances and medical procedures are developed and used to get an edge, or gain an unfair advantage, over competitors. The creation of the World Anti-Doping Agency (WADA) and the mechanisms in place to try to manage the threat of PED use in international sport is addressed in chapter 14 of this book. As Maennig (2005) suggests, doping leads to a "super performance" by an athlete, cheating to win, unless, of course, we consider sports involving animals. In horse racing, for example, substances can be given to horses either to enhance or to hinder performance. **Match fixing**, on the other hand, is usually about cheating to lose, particularly when it involves gambling, and it is designed to fix the result, or an outcome, of a sporting competition. It is commonly accepted that match fixing is of two main types—betting-related activity and non-betting-related activity. Betting-related match fixing occurs when results are manipulated to secure financial reward through betting operators for those involved. Point shaving is a type of betting-related match fixing in which one or more players on a team, paid or manipulated by gamblers, purposely try to prevent their team from covering a point spread. A point spread is determined by odds makers who look at a team's win-loss record, injury reports, and even the weather to predict who will win and by how many points. For example, let's say that the Boston Celtics are scheduled to play the Los Angeles Lakers. Based on these previously mentioned factors, the point spread has been determined to be the Celtics favored by seven points, or expected to win by more than seven points. In gambling terms, if the Celtics

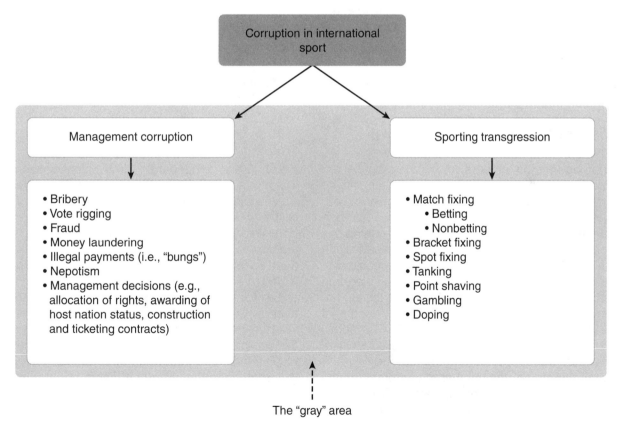

Figure 23.1 Types of corruption in international sport.

win by eight points and you bet on the Celtics, you would be a winner. If you bet on the Lakers and the Celtics win by six points, you would still win your bet because the Celtics didn't cover the spread; the spread basically gives the Lakers a seven-point lead going into the game. To manipulate the spread, a basketball player could intentionally miss shots. In American football, a quarterback could throw bad passes, thus purposely preventing his team from scoring. Gambling is also included as a form of sporting transgression. Most governing bodies around the world have regulations that prevent athletes, coaches, officials, and others from gambling on sporting competition, particularly those in the sport they are involved in. This betting might not be to try to fix a match, but people might use information they have about injuries, team sheets, or pitch conditions to win substantial amounts of money from betting operators. This activity is what we would call the misuse of inside information.

Non-betting-related match fixing ensures a match or league victory over a rival or influences the actions of officials to ensure victory for one party. It can also be used in competitions in which a round-robin format leads to knockout stages. In the FIFA World Cup and UEFA Champions League, teams are placed in groups that play each other. The top

two in each group, based on the number of points accrued in these first sets of games, progress to the next round. In an ideal world, a team doesn't want to play Germany or FC Barcelona early in the competition, so they look to do what they can, what they can control, to avoid those opponents in the knockout stage. If that means intentionally losing a game, or fielding a weaker team, then that is what they may do. The **Crashgate** scandal in Formula One is another example of this type of match fixing; it is not betting related but is based on doing something to allow a teammate to win a race (see the case study You Want Me to What? Crash?).

Spot fixing occurs when a component, or element, of a game on which a person can place a bet is fixed but has no effect on the outcome of that game. So, for example, a player might bet on when the first throw-in might occur in a soccer game in which he or she is playing. The player just happens to have the ball at his or her feet at the gambled-on time, so the player might kick the ball out of play, giving away a throw-in but winning the bet. This action would have no real effect on the final result of the match and is therefore difficult to detect. But people have been caught (see the case study Catching the Spot Fixers, later in this chapter). This type of fixing is of particular relevance in the sport

CASE STUDY

We Don't Want to Play Them!

Eight badminton players from four teams were expelled from the London 2012 Olympic Games after being found guilty of "not using best efforts" and "conducting oneself in a manner that is clearly abusive or detrimental to the sport." Chinese world champions Wang Xiaoli and Yu Yang, Greysia Poli and Meiliana Jauhari of Indonesia, and two South Korean pairs, Jung Kyung-eun and Kim Ha-na, and Ha Jung-eun and Kim Min Jung, were disqualified from the tournament following an emergency disciplinary hearing of the Badminton World Federation (BWF). This action appeared to be the first mass disqualification in Olympic history. It was reported that the Chinese pair, Wang and Yu, "were accused by other players of attempting to throw their 'dead rubber' in order to avoid playing China's no. 2 ranked pair before the gold-medal

match" (Kelso, 2012, para. 2). The Chinese coach, Li Yongbo, suggested at the time that, although there was no excuse, new rules that had been put in place in the run-up to the Games facilitated his players' behavior. Their play allegedly led to a response from the other pairs, who deliberately threw their games to try to upset the Chinese plan. The players were subjected to booing and jeering from the packed crowd at the event, and commentators spoke of their dismay at the way the matches were being played. Each team was making basic errors—deliberately serving into the net, hitting the shuttlecock long or wide (out of play), and purposely missing the shuttlecock to limit the length of any rally; in one match, the maximum rally was just four shots!

industry today given the increasing availability and use of Internet betting sites. People can now gamble on so many different components within a game that this type of behavior will almost inevitably become more common.

In 2013, three years after the Pakistan spot-fixing scandal, former Australian cricket captain Steve Waugh suggested that **bracket fixing** was the next big threat to the integrity of cricket. The contention here is that a section of a game may be affected rather than just one component of it, as in spot fixing. For example, in cricket, matches are played over a five-day period (a test match), 50 overs, or the new, faster version of the sport, Twenty-20 cricket. In a Twenty-20 match, each team has 20 overs (an over is made up of six deliveries, or the bowler will bowl the ball six times, unless no balls or wide deliveries are bowled) to score the most runs they can. Each team, when they bat, has three power plays, when fielding restrictions are different from convention. In bracket fixing, one or more of these power plays could be manipulated, or fixed, to score a certain number of runs or bowl a number of no balls. If the captain of the team is involved in any scheme, this result could be achieved with limited suspicion, especially given the fast-paced nature of the game.

Tanking, a form of match fixing, can occur in numerous sport environments. The badminton scandal described in the case study We Don't Want to Play Them! could be considered a form of tanking, or cheating purposely to lose. Most examples of this type of behavior, though, tend to be found in North American sport (all you need to do is look at the Philadelphia 76ers' recruitment strategy in recent years!) and occur because of how the sport system is designed. Across Europe, particularly in

Learning Activity

Table 23.1 includes examples of management corruption. Investigate the history of corruption in FIFA and in soccer more generally. How many of these examples of corruption can you find? How have authorities tried to deal with each? Andrew Jennings' book *Foul! The Secret World of FIFA: Bribes, Vote Rigging & Ticket Scandals* (2006) would be a great starting point.

soccer, an **open league structure** that includes the threat of relegation and the associated financial losses is enough to ensure that teams play every game to win. Moreover, the benefits of promotion, particularly to the English Premier League, can be incredible. The North American system operates with a **closed league structure** that does not relegate teams from a league and that includes a draft system that may offer benefits to finishing last. This setup potentially gives teams the opportunity to tank, to lose on purpose, to gain, for example, a better draft pick, facilitating long-term development and growth for a team or franchise.

To Cheat or Not to Cheat?

Or should that be To Cheat or Be Cheated?

According to Tanzi (1998), causes of corruption are both direct and indirect; both are important in the understanding of corruption in international sport. Tanzi (1998) suggests that the quality of and the examples set by leadership are among the indirect causes of corruption. Clearly, in sport, leadership and governance have led to examples of

Table 23.1 Causes of Corruption

Cause	Example
Low income (search for alternative sources of income, even illegal)	Attempt to seek personal gain by delaying or harassing people by an arbitrary application or interpretation of law
Inequitable distribution of wealth	Weak legal system, particularly in many developing countries
Government subsidies	Poor quality of government officials
"Scarcity is the father of corruption"	People will do whatever it takes, including illegal activity, to survive

Learning Activity

Look at how Major League Baseball has dealt with the use of PEDs in the sport. How did this change after the Mitchell Report was published in 2007? What were the circumstances that led to the *Report to the Commissioner of Baseball of an Independent Investigation Into Illegal Use of Steroids and Other Performance Enhancing Substances by Players in Major League Baseball?*

both management and competition corruption. The doping scandals in cycling are one such example; the manner in which the governing body, the UCI, has dealt with the use of PEDs in the sport may have been perpetuated by the sport's leaders. The mechanisms used to manage the use of PEDs in a sport largely reflects "the attitude of the political body [or in this context, a sport's governing body] toward this problem" (Tanzi, 1998, p. 575) of corrupt behavior.

The transparency of these mechanisms as well as rules and laws is also vital—"the lack of transparency in rules, laws, and processes creates a fertile ground for corruption" (Tanzi, 1998, p. 575). In sport, a lack of transparency is apparent despite the establishment of organizations such as the World Anti-Doping Agency (WADA) that try to regulate corrupt behavior, in this case the use of PEDs. In particular, although WADA is charged with testing for the use of PEDs and punishing those caught, the penalties or sanctions imposed for such offenses vary by sport, by nation, and by substance (Gorse & Chadwick, 2010). Tanzi (1998) also argues that "relatively few people are punished for acts of corruption, in spite of the extent of the phenomenon" (p. 574). This definitely appears to be the case in sport. Drug manufacturers are perceived to be one step ahead of testers, and many cases of match fixing go unnoticed and therefore unpunished by governing bodies and other authorities. In some cases, officials or referees in sporting competitions have succumbed to the perceived benefits of this type of activity. The ice-skating scandal at the Winter Olympics in Salt Lake City in 2002, known as **Skategate**, is one such example. After what many

considered a flawless routine in the pairs' competition, Canadian skaters Jamie Sale and David Pelletier looked set to take the gold medal, but the judges' scores gave them a second-place finish. An investigation revealed that one of the judges had been in collusion with another judge to ensure that one country's pair won the competition in return for another winning the solo event. Former NBA referee Tim Donaghy was sentenced to 18 months in a federal prison after he was found guilty of betting on games that he officiated during his last two seasons and that he made calls affecting the point spread in those games.

Another cause of corruption, according to Tanzi (1998), is the level of wages paid to public-sector workers. This issue can be clearly applied to the sport industry. The wage disparity in soccer, for example, between leagues across Europe is so marked that, in certain circumstances, players from lower-paid leagues (e.g., from across Eastern Europe) may seek opportunities to supplement their earnings, just as public-sector workers may choose to do. Likewise, this issue occurs in cricket because professional cricketers in countries like England, South Africa, and Australia earn significantly more than players from places like Pakistan. Sport as an industry has benefitted greatly from internationalization, but it is acknowledged that "the worldwide spread of corruption has been recognised as one of the darker sides of globalisation" (Park, 2003, p. 29).

Being successful in sport can and does lead to other benefits, like bonuses and sponsorship agreements, and many athletes choose to pursue questionable activities to achieve them. Athletes may have a desire to be the best in their sport or win gold medals; Schweitzer, Ordonez, and Douma (2004, p. 422) suggest that "people with unmet goals were more likely to engage in unethical behavior." Sociologists Hughes and Coakley (1991) suggest that corrupt behavior in sport occurs when athletes overconform to the sport ethic; by being a success on the track or field of play, the individual is seen as an athlete by teammates, competitors, spectators, and wider society. Athletes may decide to use PEDs as a means of achieving this status, and because they may view their behavior as in some way assisting their team to be more successful, they do not view their behavior as deviant. In fact, "through positive deviance people do harmful things to themselves and perhaps others while motivated by a sense of duty and honour" (Hughes & Coakley, 1991, p. 311).

One of the most interesting concepts that can be applied to corruption in international sport is the work of Den Nieuwenboer and Kaptein (2008). They argue that three downward spirals of corruption can exist or occur within an organization (see figure 23.2).

The first spiral, the spiral of diverging norms, suggests that people involved in corrupt behavior justify their activity by refusing to accept it as their own doing and blaming others. Employees may not think that they are breaking ethical rules or values and would argue that because no one is harmed, the act is not corrupt or that the violated party deserved what occurred. The Chicago Black Sox scandal in 1919 could be used here as an example of this spiral becoming evident in the field of corruption in sport. Players involved in the match-fixing scandal of the 1919 baseball World Series accepted money from gamblers to fix the result of games played. It was later discovered that the owner of the team had promised the players substantial bonuses that had failed to materialize, which the players then cited as their reason for their behavior.

The second, the **spiral of pressures**, suggests that "high pressures on performance . . . seduce people to engage in any type of corruption that increases one's performance" (Den Nieuwenboer & Kaptein, 2008, p. 138). For example, in busi-

ness, the pressure to achieve profit margins, sales figures, and market share percentages puts a great deal of stress on both employees and management, and to justify those pressures, organizations offer incentives to reach and maintain a certain level of achievement. To maintain this level, people may believe that they have to break or continue to break the rules. The argument then becomes that "performing well through corruption will automatically increase the threat to identity, starting a self-perpetuating spiral of increasing pressures to commit corruption" (Den Nieuwenboer & Kaptein, 2008, p. 138). Then, as new employees join an organization, they will be exposed to this type of behavior and come to view it as the prevailing norm. These two factors have particular significance when discussing sporting transgression. Athletes accept that being at the pinnacle of their sport, or at least being successful at it, provides them with a wealth of opportunities, both on and off the field of play. If athletes use PEDs to achieve all this success, the problem then becomes the measures they have to take to maintain this level. Athletes may have to continue to use the substances to maintain their status and thus begin a self-perpetuating spiral of pressures. Davis & Ruhe (2003, p. 280) state that "an organisation that perceives a country is corrupt, or has a reputation for corruption, will behave according to that perception." Again, doping scandals in cycling provide a possible example of

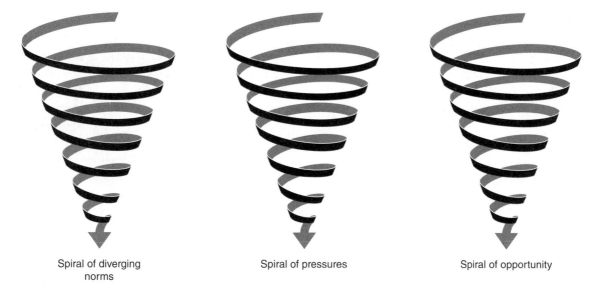

Spiral of diverging norms   Spiral of pressures   Spiral of opportunity

Figure 23.2 Three downward spirals of corruption.
Based on Den Nieuwenboer and Kaptein (2008).

this circumstance. The argument that "everyone else is cheating so I should too" becomes the norm in the sport and becomes difficult to manage unless, of course, management is complicit or ignorant to that behavior. In addition, the history of cycling shows that PED use in the peloton appeared to be the norm; riders were seemingly ostracized when they chose not to partake in this activity.

The final spiral, the spiral of opportunity, suggests that "the risk of getting caught and/or punished is such that it does not deter (potential) perpetrators" (Den Nieuwenboer & Kaptein, 2008, p. 139). If managers in an organization are failing to recognize or punish those involved in a corrupt activity, or are involved in that corrupt activity themselves, there is no reason for that behavior to stop. This reasoning may be applied to examples in which the managers of sporting organizations are failing to recognize, acknowledge, or deal with corrupt activity within their sports, thus providing athletes within those sports the opportunity to cheat. Indeed, management may perpetuate the problem by actually providing an environment in which athletes, teams, and officials can cheat. Den Nieuwenboer and Kaptein (2008) state that "the more corruption has been tolerated and is prototypical, the greater the difficulty to punish it" (p. 139). Does this explanation describe Major League Baseball's current struggles in ridding the sport of the culture of steroid use that has permeated baseball since the 1970s? Or the use of PEDs, like erythropoietin (EPO), in cycling? Or the cycles of allegations of corruption in organizations like FIFA? Crittenden, Hanna, and Peterson (2009) argue that a much bigger issue facing society is a cheating culture that is allowed to develop and become ingrained in that society. People become tolerant of cheating behavior and believe that cheating is needed to achieve goals. The perception that everyone else is cheating is the pervading attitude.

Implications for Stakeholders

Much has been written in academic literature about the effects of PEDs on athletic performance and the various cases of corruption across both business and politics. A gap in understanding in this area of research, particularly in the sport industry, is the implication of such activity for stakeholders. What

does it mean for sponsors to be associated with someone who cheats? How might it affect them, in terms of both image and profitability (especially because the two are linked)? How do fans feel? Indeed, how should they feel? If fans are paying substantial amounts of money over the course of a season to watch their favorite team play or to take a once-in-a-lifetime trip to the Olympic Games and they find out about match fixing or systematic PED use, what should they do? What about media companies? Should they continue to show sporting competitions that are proved to be corrupt?

Those questions have no easy answers. Much depends on the scope and severity of any case, its prevalence in a particular sport, the people involved—so many issues are involved that a wait-and-see or "it depends" mentality is apparent. One of the key components of this "it depends" mentality is how much a stakeholder is willing to tolerate in conjunction with the risks associated in making the wrong decision (for example, withdrawing from a sponsorship agreement or punishing an innocent athlete). The concept of the **zone of tolerance** is important in any decision-making process. As Schurr, Hedaa, and Geersbro (2008) suggested, "Tolerance zone differences explain why one actor [or stakeholder in this context] perceives positive outcomes from an interaction episode [or case of transgression] while the other perceives negative outcomes" (p. 882). This difference in perception can lead to different stakeholders responding in different ways to exactly the same case. For example, sponsors in the sport of cycling took different courses of action in light of the U.S. Postal investigation in 2012. Some withdrew from the sport completely, including Rabobank; others adopted a clear zero-tolerance policy to the use of PEDs in cycling; a small number took a very strong stance in trying to force or drive change in the governance of the sport; and others took advantage of the scandal to enter into a sport whose signature race was going to have a significantly larger profile in 2013 than it did in previous years because of the U.S. Postal investigation and the subsequent effect on the value of sponsorship agreements.

Expectations about the behavior of sports people within certain sports differ—how stakeholders in some sports respond to corrupt behavior may differ from how those same stakeholders would perceive a case in a different sport. For example, a zone of tolerance that exists within sports that are deemed to have lower morals, like international soccer, may be more accepting of certain types of behavior that in other sports would be punished. An example of this could be the use of PEDs. Rarely are cases of failed drugs tests reported in soccer, and given the fact that substances like cocaine, cannabis, and even caffeine appear on WADA's prohibited list, it would seem unlikely that soccer is a clean sport. In athletics, an athlete who tests positive for cannabis would be punished in some way, either with a public warning or a ban. Differences in the zone of tolerance are also seen between sporting nations. What is deemed acceptable behavior in one country would be classed as corruption in another. This may be more applicable to what Maennig (2005) classes as management corruption, corrupt behavior by those responsible for the governance of sport, but in sporting transgression, the rules and regulations governing the management of such behavior varies significantly between nations. Finally, the zone of tolerance of consumers may vary between sports. As cases of sporting transgression occur in a sport, the fans may react in a certain way based on how accepting they are of certain types of behavior.

The question becomes, How would you deal with it?

Sponsors

> Cyclist Lance Armstrong's doping scandal is causing sponsors to question their future in a sport that allows them to reach mass audiences at a moderate price, but risks tainting their brand.
> Weir (2012, para. 1)

The reputation of professional cycling and the credibility of the sport's showcase race, the Tour de France, has repeatedly been brought into question by scandals involving the use of PEDs. Because of these scandals, sponsors have been forced to reevaluate their involvement in the sport, recognizing that doping allegations can instantly tarnish a sponsor's reputation and image. Since 2006, sponsors including Deutsche Telekom, Audi, Adidas, Nissan, Enovos, Liberty Seguros, Phonak, and Rabobank have all pulled out of the sport, many citing the continuing threat of doping scandals as the primary reason for their withdrawal. In light of the USADA investigation that revealed the "most sophisticated, professionalized and successful

doping program that sport has ever seen" (USADA, 2012, para. 1), many of these sponsors might think that they have been justified in their decision. The Tour de France remains, however, a massive event, attracting millions of spectators every year. Commonplace in media coverage are images of crowds of people lining the route in every stage of the race, particularly in the iconic Alps stages. This evident popularity means that sponsors are still attracted to the event, investing a lot of money in deals with teams and the race itself. It is suggested, however, that cycling now represents "a much better deal than other sports—the doping problem instituted a discount on the pricing" (Reuters, 2013, para. 6) of a sponsorship agreement. Before their withdrawal from cycling in 2006, the founder and CEO of Phonak, Andre Rihs, stated that "he was glad that doping was an issue in cycling, because it scares off big corporations from becoming sponsors, allowing smaller companies like his to afford to be involved" (Day, 2006, para. 6). Other sponsors, BSkyB, for example, have taken a firm stance against doping in cycling and have adopted a zero-tolerance policy toward the use of PEDs. This approach has allowed these organizations to benefit from the exposure gained by being involved in the sport while promoting their brands as honest and open. Note, however, that after what can be described as a chaotic election in 2013 of a new president of the Union Cycliste Internationale (UCI), cycling's governing body, in which Brian Cookson, the former head of British Cycling and staunch supporter of clean sport, beat Pat McQuaid to the position (after McQuaid's time in charge had been beset with doping scandals), the first cyclist to fail a drug test was both British and a member of Team Sky!

Sponsors involved in other sports have also been forced to reevaluate their investment because of corruption in sport. The Dutch financial services provider ING immediately terminated their association with the Renault team because of the Crashgate scandal that occurred at the 2008 Singapore Grand Prix in Formula One, as did fellow major team sponsor Mutua Madrilena, suggesting that the scandal, while not only compromising the integrity of the sport and the safety of spectators, marshals, and drivers, "could affect the image, reputation and good name of the team's sponsors" (Reuters, 2009, para. 4). The Pakistan team equipment supplier, BoomBoom, severed ties with brand ambassador

Mohammed Amir as his involvement in the cricket spot-fixing scandal in England in 2010 became clear, stating that they couldn't allow their brand to be "associated with any whiff of corruption or suspicion of foul play" ("Major Sponsor," 2010, para. 6).

Fans

The Indian Premier League (IPL), the biggest Twenty-20 cricket tournament in the world, has been rocked by numerous match-fixing scandals in recent years, leading to the Chennai Super Kings and Rajasthan Royals being banned from competition. The IPL operates as a franchise league, and every year an international player auction is held, allowing teams to recruit some of the highest profile players from England, Australia, New Zealand, and South Africa, among others, to build strong teams and attract an international audience. Although Indian cricket authorities have made it clear that these international players have not been implicated in any investigations, questions no doubt remain about the integrity of the competition. Despite this uncertainty, however, millions of people attend games and millions more watch on television.

Athletes

Today's generation of cyclists are also continuing to battle the proverbial demons of the past; some are being accused of using PEDs primarily because they are successful. Four-time Tour de France champion (at the time of writing) Chris Froome had a cup of urine thrown in his face and the word

CASE STUDY

You Want Me to What? Crash?

When Nelson Piquet Jr. crashed on the 14th lap of the Singapore Grand Prix in 2008, the crash was initially considered a racing incident—he spun coming out of a corner and crashed into a wall. Because of the crash, the safety car was deployed and Piquet's teammate, Fernando Alonso, took advantage of the situation and won the race.

The story changed after Piquet Jr. was dropped from the Renault team after the 2009 Hungarian Grand Prix. Piquet Jr. then alleged that he had been asked by the team to crash deliberately to improve the race situation for Alonso, sparking an investigation of Renault F1 for race fixing by the Fédération Internationale de l'Automobile (FIA), Formula One's governing body. Initially, Renault F1 began criminal proceedings against Piquet Jr. and his father, a three-time F1 World Champion, for making false accusations and allegedly attempting to blackmail the team to allow Piquet Jr. to drive for the team for the remainder of the 2009 F1 season. Renault F1's efforts proved futile because the Piquets won the case and received substantial damages from the Renault team. Because the allegations made were not proved false, investigators turned to the team management, executive director of engineering for Renault F1 Pat Symonds and team boss Flavio Briatore.

After a 90-minute hearing of the World Motorsports Council (WMC), a disqualification was imposed on Renault, suspended for two years, meaning that if a similar incident occurred before 2011, Renault would be banned from Formula One. Briatore was banned indefinitely from any FIA-sanctioned event, and Symonds received a five-year ban.

Despite the narrow sanctions handed out by the WMC, the Crashgate scandal, as it became known, cost the Renault team substantial amounts of money. ING, the Dutch financial services provider, immediately terminated their association with the team, closely followed by fellow major team sponsor Mutua Madrilena.

Briatore and Symonds both had their bans overturned on appeal and were both free to rejoin Formula One in 2013. Symonds became chief technical officer for the Williams F1 Team and then, in 2017, joined the Sky Sports Formula One team as a technical expert and commentator. For Piquet Jr., however, the path forward has been more difficult. Despite the fact that he never received a sanction for his part in the scandal, which irritated some because his action was tantamount to race fixing, he hasn't driven in Formula One since he was dropped in 2009. He joined the NASCAR series in North America and has since become Formula E World Champion.

"doper" yelled at him during a mountain stage of the 2015 Tour. Many believe that because of his extraordinary talents on the bike, something about his performances to date is suspicious. To keep his name clean, Froome has been very open with his biological passport data and testing results. It could be argued that it is a shame that athletes have to take those steps to try to keep their names clear from negative associations with former cheats, but unfortunately this is the world that many of today's athletes operate in.

Media

Media organizations around the world enjoy a good scandal! Think about the hours of television exposure surrounding the U.S. Postal investigation and Lance Armstrong—it was breaking news and the lead story for days after the report was published. The FIFA investigations were covered by many major international news networks, and the Russian doping scandal is always in the news. As seen in the case study Catching the Spot Fixers, it was a reporter from the *News of the World* newspaper in the United Kingdom who uncovered the spot-fixing scandal involving three members of the Pakistan test cricket team. These media organizations have an image and a reputation to consider not only when exposing these scandals but also when broadcasting the events or sports in which these corrupt behaviors have occurred.

We also have to consider the influence of social media on this issue. If something happens, fans around the world can hear or read about it almost instantaneously. If an allegation is made, the same is true. Social media can cause huge problems for all concerned when rumors start to circulate; even if those rumors prove to be false, the accusations are available for all to see. Again, the guilty-by-

---

CASE STUDY

Catching the Spot Fixers

A test match series in 2010 between England and Pakistan became front-page news around the world when it was found that three members of the Pakistan team—captain Salman Butt, bowler Mohammad Asif, and bowler Mohammad Amir—received payments for manipulating elements of a match between the two sides at the home of international cricket, Lord's Cricket Ground in London. Investigative reporters from the *News of the World* newspaper secretly videotaped a bookmaker, Mazhar Majeed, informing them that fast bowlers Asif and Amir would deliberately bowl no balls at specific points in an over and accepting payment for that information. Gamblers would place bets based on this inside information. This activity is an example of spot fixing; bowling the no balls would have had no real effect on the result or outcome of the match, but those components of a competition can be gambled on and can be very lucrative if you can manipulate what is going to happen.

As a result of the investigation, British police arrested Majeed, and the International Cricket Council (ICC), cricket's governing body, banned the three players for between 5 and 10 years. In November 2011, Butt and Asif were found guilty by a London court, after Amir and Majeed had entered guilty pleas on criminal charges relating to spot-fixing conspiracy to cheat at gambling and conspiracy to accept corrupt payments. All four were given prison sentences, ranging from 6 to 32 months.

This case put cricket back in the newspapers after the notorious case involving South African cricket captain Hansie Cronje. As with the Pakistan spot-fixing scandal, Indian gambling syndicates were allegedly involved in the funding of match fixing by Cronje and three of his teammates. As a result of an investigation by the King Commission and a tearful admission in front of members of the international media, Cronje was banned from all cricket involvement for life.

Hansie Cronje's life was cut short by a plane crash in 2002. Conspiracy theorists questioned the circumstances surrounding his death. These questions were raised again after former South African cricket coach (and coach while Cronje was captain) Bob Woolmer died in the West Indies in 2007. A former colleague of Woolmer's in English county cricket insisted that both Woolmer and Cronje were murdered on the instructions of betting syndicates (Drake, 2007).

association or guilty-until-proven-innocent tags can be hard to shake.

Tackling Corruption

International governing bodies and other global organizations have been realizing the potential effect of corruption for individual stakeholders and the wider sport industry. Chapter 14 of this text discusses the introduction of the World Anti-Doping Agency (WADA), designed to tackle the growing and continuous threat of PED use in sport. Besides WADA, organizations like Interpol, the IOC, and the European Union (EU) have established monitoring mechanisms and investigative units to tackle the threats posed. This task is not easy, however, because balancing the needs of all stakeholder groups is incredibly difficult.

Interpol runs a number of initiatives to raise awareness of the issues presented by corruption in sport while serving to facilitate the sharing of information, intelligence, and best practices among member countries. They also conduct joint investigations and operations that aim to dismantle the organized networks behind crimes in sport. The EU Expert Group on Good Governance produced the report *Principles of Good Governance in Sport,* which highlighted the importance of good governance in sport and included this definition:

> The framework and culture within which a sports body sets policy, delivers its strategic objectives, engages with stakeholders, monitors performance, evaluates and manages risk and reports to its constituents on its activities and progress including the delivery of effective, sustainable and proportionate sports policy and regulation. (European Union, 2013, p. 5)

Good governance is of paramount importance in sport. You only need to look at organizations like FIFA, the IAAF, and the UCI to see what happens when those in positions of power are less than credible!

Much of the focus on tackling the threat of match fixing started in the 2000s when many governing bodies established monitoring mechanisms to keep a particular proverbial eye on gambling. FIFA introduced the Early Warning System in 2007, a company set up to monitor betting on FIFA tournaments, and the IOC established its own Integrity Betting Intelligence System (IBIS). The IOC also adopted the Olympic Movement Code on the Prevention of the Manipulation of Competitions, which aims to define match fixing and to harmonize standards, disciplinary procedures, and sanctions. The International Tennis Federation (ITF) set up the Tennis Integrity Unit in 2008, and the International Cricket Council (ICC) established their Anti-Corruption Unit (ACU) as a direct result of the Hansie Cronje case in 2000.

With so many anticorruption codes across many sports, knowing who has responsibility for monitoring activity might be confusing. For example, for a soccer tournament at an Olympic Games featuring FIFA-sanctioned teams, is the IOC responsible for monitoring the betting market? Or FIFA? Or should these organizations work together? If they work together, whose regulations or practices do they use? If they don't work together and monitor the betting markets separately, who decides when a violation has occurred?

Just as with defining corruption in international sport, a broad gray area is present in the tackling of it.

Gray Area

In figure 23.1, the different types of behavior that constitute corruption in sport are shown, surrounded by a gray area that represents those behaviors that some see as cheating and others do not. This area presents potentially a vast number of problems for the governance of sport and all of its stakeholders.

Take the example of a soccer player taking a dive or a basketball player flopping—is this cheating? Some would argue yes; others would say it is part of the game. Should this type of behavior be seen as corruption? It could be argued that as with stakeholder responses to corruption, it depends. The answer might depend on whether the player who committed the alleged foul that led to the dive is sent off or ejected from the game. At what point in the game did it occur? Does it matter? If you think that taking a dive in a soccer game is just part of the game, that is fine. But would your view change if an opposing player took a dive in the penalty box in the 89th minute of a World Cup final and your team lost?

Another example is the design of specialist equipment. The full-body coverage LZR Racer swim suit has been one of the most discussed and debated technological developments in recent years. Although the suit is now banned, many swimmers wore these suits at the Olympic Games in Beijing in 2008 and the World Swimming Championships the following year and were successful. The suit allowed better oxygen flow to the muscles, held the body in a more hydrodynamic position, and trapped air to add buoyancy. Some argued that the technology involved in making the suits was tantamount to technological doping. But if everyone had access to the same technology, is it cheating? In this case, not everyone could use the suit—some because of the limited resources available to their national swimming teams and others because they weren't sponsored by the company that made them.

When cities want to host the Olympic Games or the FIFA World Cup, the rules of the bidding process prohibit the offering of gifts to the executive committees of those sport organizations because such gifts are, or at least can be seen as, a bribe (and this has happened in the past many times). But in some countries, like China, giving gifts is a customary part of any business dealing. So, are international sport bodies going to dictate tradition and cultural norms? If decision-making committees do accept gifts from these nations because of traditions, then ethically should they accept gifts from all bidding nations? Does the process then become an arms race about who can afford the priciest gift? Would giving a more expensive gift be more persuasive in any voting process?

This gray area, for the most part, comes down to each person's zone of tolerance. We all have our own views, norms, values, and opinions when it comes to the issue of corruption in sport. How we deal with corruption in international sport moving forward will all depend on the people in charge!

Summary

The integrity of sporting competition and those in positions of power in sport's governing bodies is clearly being questioned. This chapter has sought to introduce some of the key issues in corruption in sport, the various types of corruption, and some of the challenges of dealing with this type of behavior. Crucially, it has also highlighted the effect of corruption on the many stakeholders in the sport industry. As the next generation of sport managers, you must try to address the issue. What are you going to do about it?

? Review Questions

1. What is the main difference between the definitions of corruption in sport and sporting transgression, offered by Maennig (2005) and Gorse (2014)?
2. Describe how sport is built on the premise of *ceteris paribus*.
3. What does overconformity to the sport ethic mean in the context of this chapter?
4. How does a closed league structure facilitate tanking?
5. What does the gray area mean when it comes to sport corruption? Provide an example.

Corporate Social Responsibility, Sport, and Development

Mitchell McSweeney, MA
York University, Canada

Bruce Kidd, PhD
University of Toronto Scarborough, Canada

Lyndsay Hayhurst, PhD
York University, Canada

Chapter Objectives

After studying this chapter, you will be able to do the following:

- Define corporate social responsibility.
- Describe the emergence and evolution of corporate social responsibility.
- Describe and interpret corporate social responsibility using both managerial theory and critical theory.
- Understand the efforts of workers and NGOs to win fair labor conditions and responses of corporations.
- Examine how corporations are responding to the call to conform to basic human rights.
- Describe and critically analyze the role of corporations in international development.

Key Terms

capitalism
corporate social responsibility (CSR)
critical theory
development
human rights
NGOs

philanthropy
sport for development and peace (SDP)
United Nations Global Compact
United Nations Sustainable Development Goals (SDGs)
Universal Declaration of Human Rights

Corporate social responsibility (CSR) has become increasingly important to businesses in recent years because of growing expectations from various stakeholders for firms to act in an ethical and socially responsible manner. Global corporations, such as oil and gas companies Exxon Mobile and BP Oil, have specific pages on their websites outlining their approach to social responsibility and community involvement. Telecommunications conglomerate Samsung Mobile publishes individual public reports on each component of its social responsibility, including society, environment, people, and business conduct guidelines (Samsung C & T, 2016). McDonald's publishes reports annually on its sustainable and community **development**, outlining the amount of funds the corporation spends on protecting the environment, the community, and its philanthropic activities. Likewise, the multinational extractive corporation Rio Tinto emphasizes its commitment to ensuring environmental sustainability, and lists various commitments it has to the community, its workforce, its sustainability approach, the government, climate change, and the way in which they work to be responsible to various stakeholders.

Many of these companies involve sport within their CSR activities. For example, McDonald's sponsors a variety of sporting events globally, and Rio Tinto contributes in multiple forms to the communities in which it works, such as funding track and field courses in Indigenous communities, developing super soccer programs, and supporting healthy lifestyle initiatives within local areas where they work. Samsung Mobile, through various community initiatives that it sponsors and funds, lists sport as one of the firm's core focus areas of CSR practice and program areas. Many of these firms pursue the achievement of social responsibility by partnering with sport organizations that implement or run sport programs and initiatives.

Sport organizations and companies also pursue CSR through various means. Companies involved in the sport marketplace such as Nike, Adidas, Under Armour, and Reebok have constructed policies and conduct socially responsible practices that in large part can be explained as a corrective response to their past involvement in exploitable practices, one example being Nike's history of operating sweatshops in various areas of the world. CSR is a way for corporations to legitimize themselves in the eyes of consumers and the public, and respond to institutional pressures of the marketplace. Indeed, CSR is a crucial part of organizations and companies in contemporary society.

What are the origins of CSR, and why has it emerged as such a pressing social issue? How is CSR regarded by the companies themselves, their workers, consumers, and social scientists who study the modern corporation? What are the links between CSR, **human rights**, sport, and international development? How has CSR shaped the growing **sport for development and peace (SDP)** movement? The purpose of this chapter is to respond to these questions.

Throughout this chapter, we will use the terms *one-third world* (to refer to the advanced economies of Europe, North America, Japan, and Australia) and *two-thirds world* (to refer to the rest of the world) as discussed by Gustavo Esteva and Madhu Prakash (1998). We do so for three reasons: to encourage critical thinking about how income and opportunity are distributed among regions of the globe, to indicate that most of the world's population lives outside the advanced economies, and to eschew judgments about people's quality of life.

Defining Corporate Social Responsibility

Corporate social responsibility (CSR) is an ambiguous and constantly evolving term that has various definitions and conceptions (Waddington, Chelladurai, & Skirstad, 2013). Numerous terms overlap with CSR, such as corporate sustainability, corporate sustainable development, corporate responsibility, and corporate citizenship. In its most narrow definition, CSR is a commitment to acting ethically and socially responsibly as a business or organization. In consumer sectors, CSR has been taken up by global **capitalism** as a way of legitimizing business interests as well as responding to the concerns of a broad coalition of consumers, governments, labor, and community activists. In this definition, CSR connotes four comprehensive ideas about how companies will behave (Hayhurst and Kidd, 2012):

1. that the company will abide by internationally accepted labor practices and ensure that its suppliers and sellers do the same;

2. that its production and business practices, from the initial extraction of raw materials through the manufacture, advertising, and distribution of products to the ultimate disposal of its used products, will be environmentally sustainable;

3. that it will be transparent and accountable; that is, it will provide regular reports on its business practices to its shareholders, employees, governments, and members of the public; and

4. that it will be supportive of human rights, or rights that one has because one is a human being. These rights aim to preserve and protect human dignity and ensure civil, economic, and social well-being.

Corporations who practice CSR see it as a benefit—whether it be that CSR makes them more competitive, allows for better recognition in society, or adds to the organization's legitimacy. CSR has been adopted in various ways by a number of organizations based on the idea that it positively benefits the company as well as society. It is also seen as a necessary business function by many scholars, one that responds to, as Carroll (1991, 1999) suggests, the "pyramid of CSR," encompassing economic, legal, ethical, and philanthropic aspects of society that businesses face. Note here that CSR, at least in this definition, is distinct from **philanthropy**—the act of donating money or goods resulting in no financial or material reward to the donor—to a religious, charitable, or educational organization or social

cause. Nevertheless, philanthropy is often closely linked to CSR, especially in the case of sport corporations and professional athletes, many of whom have established foundations for philanthropic purposes (Babiak, Heinze, Pil Lee, & Juravich, 2013). In Toronto, for example, the two major sport corporations, Maple Leaf Sport and Entertainment and the Toronto Blue Jays, have established foundations to channel fan contributions and private donations into community sport; both foundations were explicitly formed to strengthen brand recognition and legitimacy. CSR is also distinct from celebrity or cause-related marketing, the practice of sponsoring individual athletes, teams, or social campaigns to increase a firm's legitimacy, brand, or market share, although such marketing may blend with the support of human rights. For example, in 2007 Puma launched its Peace One Day football collection, linking the sale of a special line of gear and accessories to the United Nations International Day of Peace and the 2008 African Cup of Nations (Peace One Day, 2009). Keeping these distinctions in mind is important, as table 24.1 sets out. That being said, because philanthropy, cause-related marketing, and other forms of global corporate social engagement stem from the same or similar

Table 24.1 Taxonomy of Global Corporate Social Engagement Activities and Examples in Sport and International Development

Type of GCSE activity	Example
Corporate social responsibility (CSR)	Adidas partnered with the SOS Children's Villages and FIFA (International Federation of Association Football) campaign to raise funds for 20 villages across Africa for 2010 (SOS Children's Villages, 2017).
Professional sport league philanthropy	The NBA uses community outreach activities to enhance their public image and strengthen relationships with local communities in the two-thirds world (see Kwak and Cornwell, 2013).
Cause-related marketing	The NFL partnered with Breast Cancer Awareness (see Gaines, 2012).
Private foundation philanthropy	Nike Foundation funds activities for adolescent girls in the two-thirds world (see Calkin, 2015a).
Sport celebrity diplomacy	Right to Play's athlete ambassadors (see Cooper, 2007, for more about celebrity diplomacy in international development more broadly).
Consumer-based philanthropy	Right to Play joined forces with Roots Canada through a partnership that sees all items bought from the Canada Collection by Roots share a donated portion of the proceeds to Right to Play (see Roots, 2017).
Social entrepreneurship	Nike's Changemakers competition, a partnership with Ashoka, the largest social entrepreneurial NGO in the world (see Changemakers, 2007).
Corporate-NGO partnership	Tesco's partnership with the Homeless World Cup (see Homeless World Cup, 2016).
Market multilateralism	Nike's partnership with UNHCR (see Nike, 2007).

Data adapted from Hayhurst and Kidd (2012).

Learning Activity

Identify an example of CSR in sport that has not been mentioned in this text. To what extent does it conform to the definition that we have used?

impulses and pressures as CSR, we will analyze them as a broad grouping in this chapter.

Emergence of Corporate Social Responsibility

Corporate social responsibility has grown for a number of reasons. Although recent developments in the corporate world have seen an increasing number of firms and businesses becoming involved with practices and processes associated with social responsibility, the effort and the expectation that corporations act responsibly is not new per se. The trend is but a renewed focus on corporate ethics in response to the tremendous expansion of corporate activity and the corresponding reduction of the role of government during the recent ascendency of neo-liberal ideas of society, which argue for greater and less restricted international trade, deregulation of markets, and the privatization of previously publicly provided and democratically accountable services like education, health, and social services (Levermore & Moore, 2015). The expectations that corporations act responsibly have risen and declined in step with the growth of capitalism since at least the 18th century, when various entrepreneurs as well as civil society began to question the responsibilities of firms to the public (Babiak & Wolfe, 2013). Corporate philanthropy has a similar history, beginning when companies sought to give back to consumers and other parts of society. Such companies were seen as providing more than just standard business opportunities to the public; instead, they were viewed as a positive aspect of society through their philanthropic activities. The responses to unfair and unhealthy work practices, predatory business practices, and industrial pollution in the form of labor organizing, consumer boycotts, the creation of co-ops, and government legislation and scrutiny date from the 19th century and continue to this day. For example, in the face of growing public outcry

about forced labor practices during World War II, in 1998, more than half a century after the fact, car manufacturer Volkswagen compensated its workers from that time, and the program continues today (Schrempf-Stirling, Palazzo, & Phillips, 2016). In recent years, a number of companies have faced boycotts because of unethical or unfair practices. For example, in northern Canada demonstrators have protested the high cost of food that North West Company stores charge in remote communities; because of limited options, most families must buy their food from a retail chain owned and operated by North West Company (CBC, 2015). In 2014 boycotts were initiated against the world's largest online shopping retailer, Amazon, as a protest against the company's avoidance of corporate taxes. Because of the boycott, Amazon agreed to pay a fairer tax rate, but it still faces questions about its business practices, especially the stress on employees and accusations of suspicious firings and promotions (Heritage, 2015). From a historical perspective, CSR is the most recent response to a long and turbulent debate about the role of corporations in societies.

In 1948 the United Nations (UN) approved the **Universal Declaration of Human Rights**, a statement of the political, legal, economic, and social rights that every person in the world should enjoy. The Universal Declaration led to increased scrutiny by the public and civil society on firms operating in the two-thirds world in unhealthy, exploitative ways. The development of CSR in the last two decades follows the centuries-old dynamic of public criticism, labor organizing, consumer boycotts, and government and corporate response. An important instructional battleground in the 1970s was the Swiss-based corporation Nestlé. Health activists and journalists in Britain and the United States became concerned that the company's marketing of infant formula as a replacement for breast milk in the two-thirds world contributed unnecessarily to the malnutrition of children and impoverishment of families. They began a boycott, which quickly spread around the world. The issue was then taken up by the United States Senate, the United Nations Educational Scientific and Cultural Organization (UNESCO), and the World Health Organization (WHO). In 1981 the World Health Assembly (WHA) adopted an international code of conduct for the marketing of breast milk substitutes. The code bans the promotion of breast milk substitutes and sets out labeling requirements. In 1984 Nestlé agreed to implement the code, and the boycott was lifted, although debate continues about compliance. Nestlé Canada's CSR practices fall under its mandate of "creating shared value" (Nestlé Canada, 2017). The International Baby Food Action Network (2017) remains critical of Nestlé and the entire industry.

Corporate Social Responsibility in Sport

CSR among sporting goods companies emerged during the 1990s, in response to activism related to child labor and exploitative practices in the production of athletic shoes, uniforms, insignia gear, and equipment like footballs in the two-thirds world. As leading companies like Nike moved more production into the two-thirds world, it became evident that children and women were the primary laborers, receiving paltry wages in unsafe conditions in return for their work. In North America, a coalition of U.S. and Canadian university students, Students Against Sweatshops, brought these abuses and the moral contradictions involved to the attention of consumers and university buyers of branded apparel, through boycotts and sit-ins (Sage, 1999). At the University of Toronto, for example, a week-long sit-in in the president's office in the spring of 2000 persuaded the university to adopt a code of conduct for the production of all clothing and merchandise, including athletic uniforms, bearing its name. The university was the first Canadian university to do so. Today, at least 24 other Canadian universities, six major municipalities, and a growing number of school boards have such policies. U of T's code requires suppliers to agree to a set of fair labor conditions and accept independent monitoring (University of Toronto, 2001). Industry leaders like Nike and Adidas followed with their own undertakings.

Global companies, including sport organizations, have committed themselves to the realization of human rights and have created their own codes of conduct, complete with self-monitoring and reporting. Many corporate leaders and their supporters accept that capitalism should be socially responsible (Buhr & Grafström, 2006; Thorpe, 2013). Capitalism—defined as the economic system characterized by private property and wage labor, in which some people own the means of production, hire others to carry out the work, and sell the resulting goods and services to make a profit—has been the dominant economic system in much of the world for many years. But capitalism is constantly evolving in response to changing conditions and technology. In countries like the United States where neoliberal governments have watered down or eliminated state regulation of the economy and the environment, corporations had to show that self-regulation can work (Dashwood, 2014; Jenkins, 2001; Levi-Faur, 2005). Employees in the companies involved contributed to the articulation, elaboration, and monitoring of codes of conduct and other practices of CSR (Filatotchev & Stahl, 2015; van Tulder & Kulk, 2001). But in virtually every case, the impetus for them came from outside pressure and the fear that if they did not self-regulate, then fair trade campaigners might persuade governments to impose regulation (Okhmatovskiy & David, 2012; Pritchard, 1991).

Understanding Corporate Social Responsibility in Sport

In the next sections, we select two theoretical approaches used to explain the development of CSR in the area of international sport management and human rights. The first, managerial-based approaches, generally examines how CSR may be profitable for business and adhere to a neoliberalist ideology. The second approach uses **critical theory** to challenge those in power to consider how CSR shapes the lives of those who are marginalized and disadvantaged within society, and who are sometimes the supposed "targeted beneficiaries" of CSR initiatives.

Managerial Theory

Managerial theory, the dominant body of knowledge in sport management studies, has been used by many scholars within the field of CSR to display the uniqueness and beneficial aspects of CSR for firms and organizations. Many who adopt a managerial perspective or theoretical understanding also accept the legitimacy of neoliberal capitalism. They believe that the capitalist rise of businesses, including the free market, allows businesses to be actively involved in solving social problems. In the past,

CASE STUDY

Maquila Solidarity Network

The Maquila Solidarity Network (MSN) is a Toronto-based labor and women's rights organization that "supports the efforts of workers in global supply chains to win improved wages and working conditions and a better quality of life." MSN conducts research into conditions of employment, primarily in Central America and Mexico, evaluates the CSR undertakings of global companies, particularly in the apparel and sporting goods industries, and publishes annual reports on conditions and report cards on the major companies. For example, its 2006 report, Revealing Clothing Transparency Report, graded 30 global companies and retailers selling clothes in the Canadian market, including Nike, Adidas, H&M, Roots, La Senza, and Reitmans, on their labor practices and the transparency and accountability of their policies and programs. MSN has also contributed to and coordinated many campaigns to force change in both the two-thirds world (helping workers organize) and the one-third world (by pressuring large purchasers to adopt codes for suppliers). In Canada, it inspired and assisted the successful Students Against Sweatshop campaign to persuade the University of Toronto to impose a code of conduct on suppliers, and it coordinated the Clean Clothes and Fair Play at the Olympics campaigns to win the same from the Canadian Olympic Committee. It has created the Ethical Trading Action Group, a coalition of religious, labor, and nongovernmental organizations that has significantly broadened the campaigns to induce public institutions to adopt ethical purchasing policies and companies to disclose their factory locations in the interests of transparent monitoring. Its website provides a history of the anti-sweatshop movement, clear statements of what activists expect from companies practicing CSR,

and a compendium of relevant resources (Maquila Solidarity Network, 2017). Most recently, MSN has begun to enter into discussions directly with companies to bring about acceptable conditions of employment. As cofounder Bob Jeffcott wrote,

> Our focus has always been on supporting the efforts of the women and men who make our clothes to organize to improve their wages and working conditions, not on shutting down factories with bad conditions or giving shoppers ethical choices. From the beginning, the labor rights/anti-sweatshop movement has criticized retailers and brands whenever they cut and run from factories where worker rights violations had been reported, rather than staying to fix the problem. And while we often work with other organizations that describe themselves as corporate social responsibility (CSR) groups, we've always been more interested in and committed to finding new ways to make corporations more accountable rather than in helping them to better regulate themselves.

Organizations like MSN have been leading advocates of purchasing policies that require internationally accepted standards of production. The adoption of such policies by governments, universities, and major games organizing committees—an important achievement of the last 20 years—would simply not have occurred without them. They also provide an indispensable source of independent analysis of CSR for consumers, policy makers, researchers, and the corporations themselves, and advice and other resources to those directly affected, such as the workers and communities where the production of sporting goods takes place.

---

neoliberals believed that the only social responsibility of firms was to increase their profits within the confines of the law (Friedman, 1970; Waddington et al., 2013). In terms of CSR and sport management, however, neoliberals in contemporary society argue that CSR initiatives and programs positively benefit organizations in the long term. Thus, using management theory, many scholars emphasize how

adopting CSR strategies may lead to an enhanced public image, increased revenue and public recognition, and improved avenues to new and previously unreached audiences or consumers (Breitbarth, Walzel, Anagnostopoulos, & van Eekeren, 2015). For example, in 2007 Reebok (which is owned by Adidas) introduced its Global Corporate Citizenship platform, involving "a series of programs designed to support underserved communities and groups. They provide underprivileged youth with the tools they need to fulfill their potential and lead healthy, happy and active lives" (Adidas Group, 2007, p. 4). From a managerial perspective, this CSR platform should be evaluated primarily in terms of its effectiveness in enabling Reebok to penetrate new consumer markets and enhance its image.

Benefits to Companies

A great deal of CSR research focuses on producing practical findings and recommendations that corporations could use to strengthen their accountability to shareholders, enhance customer relations, and improve their bottom lines. Examples include shareholder studies, marketing research, feasibility studies, economic impact studies, and evaluation research (Frisby, 2005). In the context of marketing and sponsorship, Kwak and Cornwell (2013) discuss how aligning a brand with a meaningful cause is not only socially responsible but also potentially profitable. Specifically, they discuss various initiatives within the sporting context that are examples of cause-linked marketing (partnering with a non-profit organization or providing financial support to a specific cause), including partnerships between the NFL and American Cancer Society, MasterCard and Stand Up 2 Cancer MLB program, and Roger Federer and "The Match for Africa," a specific tennis match that Federer participated in to raise money for underprivileged children in Africa. Using these partnerships, Kwak and Cornwell identify potential benefits of CSR sponsorship and marketing practices engaged in by corporations and sport organizations, including the following:

- Increase public visibility
- Boost positive word-of-mouth between consumers and viewers
- Offset damaging publicity
- Improve brand and corporate image
- Enhance brand awareness and recognition
- Strengthen corporate citizenship
- Encourage repeat purchases
- Attract new market segments and geographic audiences
- Promote increased usage of products

Although the authors discuss these benefits, they also suggest that firms must tread carefully when considering the application of cause-related marketing or sponsorship as part of their CSR practices. In particular, they argue that, if done incorrectly (e.g., not providing enough information to consumers or incongruently aligning a cause to a business, such as Breast Cancer to Kentucky Fried Chicken), cause-related marketing may harm both the cause (e.g., raising money for cancer survivors) and the organization (e.g., the NFL), because consumers will believe that the partnership is profit oriented only. In addition, consumers have questioned some CSR initiatives as exploitative, because of the potential for firms to benefit from links to causes while not fully committing themselves to being involved with the program or the partners implementing the social initiative. Gaines (2012) explained how some critics questioned the NFL's launch of pink-themed merchandise for breast cancer awareness and emphasized that some fans may be discouraged from the cause because of the NFL's lack of transparency on such an initiative (i.e., the NFL did not publish or inform how much money goes to the campaign from the merchandise).

Walker, Heere, and Kim (2013) suggested that although CSR is a responsibility of modern-day firms and organizations, little is known about the tangible benefits of CSR. For example, the authors noted that limited information is known about how "targeted beneficiaries" are affected by the NBA Cares program that operates various social initiatives such as Basketball without Borders, Read to Achieve, and NBA Fit. In contrast, NBA Cares readily advertises more quantitative data in relation to its philanthropic activities, such as the $175 million it spends on charitable initiatives. In turn, Walker et al. (2013) argued that evaluations of CSR programs must examine the experiences of program beneficiaries as targets of CSR programs, while also critically considering the social impact of corporations and other partner organizations.

Because of questions of legitimacy such as ones the NFL and NBA faced, program evaluations and economic impact studies have become popular, and needed, in CSR studies to allow corporations to show or prove the societal and profitable impact that CSR has on its operations, consumers, and business.

In a study conducted by Ibrahim and Almarshed (2014), the researchers examined the effect that a CSR event had on consumers. Specifically, the event impact they measured was the Danone Nations Cup (DNC), an international football competition organized every year for children aged 10 to 12. The Groupe Danone is a French multinational food-product business based in Paris that operates globally. By conducting field surveys with consumers at the event, the researchers suggested that the event influenced individual perceptions of Groupe Danone in a number of ways, including increasing consumer commitment to the company, consumer intent to purchase Danone products, and an increased sense of recognition and trust with the company. The study's findings showed that the CSR event by Group Danone appears to benefit the corporation and better associates its brand with consumers and participants of the Danone Nations Cup.

Other research explores how sport managers may gain competitive advantage by viewing CSR as an opportunity-driven concept that can assist in accomplishing an enhanced strategic direction (Heinze, Soderstrom, & Zdroik, 2014). Still other research examines the ethical and discretionary components of CSR to understand how corporations can improve their reputations and build brand image outreach programs. Instructive examples can be drawn from professional sport; both teams and entire leagues use community outreach activities to enhance their public image and strengthen relationships with local communities (e.g., Hindley & Williamson, 2013). Kihl, Babiak, and Tainsky's (2014) assessment of Major Leagues Baseball teams' corporate community involvement initiatives sought to understand how CSR initiatives could be better implemented to improve relationships with local communities where the programs were run. Using evaluative program theory, the authors sought to understand perspectives from different community members and organizations. In doing so, they concluded that, based on interview responses, there were concerns of program implementation in four areas: (1) the partnership agreement, because of a lack of understanding between MLB teams and the community partner, resulting in misalignment of expectations; (2) the ecological context, because of inadequate social (limited number of parents and coach provision) and material (insuf-

ficient transportation for participants to attend programs) support; (3) protocol and implementation, influenced by the demand and need for increased human resources; and (4) a varied target population, resulting in different levels of team ability and experiences of dissatisfaction by participants. These issues illuminate how program evaluations are important not only for the implementation of CSR initiatives but also for the intended outcomes that stakeholders hope to see. Assessments such as this one can also provide information for primary and secondary stakeholders.

Primary and Secondary Stakeholders

CSR may also be explored using stakeholder theory to uncover how corporations seek to improve relations with communities, suppliers, consumers, investors, and the environment when implementing profit-driven activities (Misener, 2008). Such research is primarily concerned with identifying and analyzing how corporations are accountable to the various stakeholders who are affected by and involved in CSR interventions. For example, Walters and Tacon (2013) explored the issue of stakeholder engagement in CSR by examining how European football clubs engaged with various stakeholders, such as communities, employees, and environmental groups. Their study demonstrated that primary stakeholders (i.e., players, employees, and other groups central to the achievement of organizational goals, such as fans who watch the games) were often easy to connect with through fan engagement programs and employee-focused events and training. On the other hand, secondary stakeholders, such as community members, environmental organizations, and volunteers, were difficult to connect with. Although most of the football league clubs who engaged in CSR activities had community engagement initiatives, many executives interviewed stressed that connecting with local communities was challenging, leading to the suggestion that although certain views of football clubs paint them as "community institutions, clubs are not automatically embedded within their communities" (Walters & Tacon, p. 246). Besides struggling to connect with communities, few of the football clubs engaged in environmental activities, despite the growth of such initiatives in other sectors (Trendafilova, Babiak, & Heinze, 2013).

As outlined in table 24.1, other research has considered the socially responsible practices in mega sporting events (e.g., Dowling, Robinson, & Washington, 2013), the role of professional athletes as philanthropists (e.g., Babiak, Heinze, Lee, & Juravich, 2013), and the intersections among CSR, corporate citizenship, and sport management studies (e.g., Chelladurai, 2016). Smith and Westerbeek (2007) asserted that there is a distinct connection between sport and CSR, because sport builds community and fosters powerful connections between people, facilitating trust and strengthening ties between neighbors and nations. Babiak and Wolfe (2013) also suggest that sport is unique in regard to CSR, stating that the four features of passion, economics, transparency, and stakeholder management allow a unique connection of sport to CSR. It has also been suggested that sport corporate social responsibility has been recognized by the corporate world as "a powerful vehicle for the employment of CSR" (Bason & Anagnostopoulos, 2015). Therefore, various benefits of the unique attraction of sport for corporations seeking to be socially responsible remain popular.

Despite the benefits that it may bring, sport corporate social responsibility is not always an uncomplicated beneficial strategy for companies. At times it is controversial, messy, unpredictable, and therefore worthy of critical investigation. Although it may benefit some, it may not benefit all, and it may unwittingly set back the communities directly affected. One of the goals of this chapter is to encourage sport managers, especially those working in the areas of sport, CSR, and international development, to broaden their focus and ask how they can contribute to the enhancement of the entire society, not just their own corporations (Frisby,

Learning Activity

Think of an example of CSR not discussed in this chapter or consider the example that you discussed in the first learning activity in this chapter. Identify the primary recipients affected. How well has the CSR initiative you have studied addressed the needs of the intended recipients?

2005). Many standpoints outside managerial theory hold immense potential for critically investigating the intersections between sport, international development, human rights, and CSR. In the next section, we argue that critical theory is one of the most useful viewpoints in terms of uncovering the relationship between global capital and power, and for understanding domination and resistance in terms of CSR, development, and human rights.

Critical Theory

If those who use managerial perspectives tend to focus on how and whether corporations benefit from CSR, those who study it from a critical perspective tend to apply a more comprehensive lens and investigate the effects of CSR on entire societies, emphasizing a human-centered approach, one that aims to include the views of those who are ignored or exploited in managerial approaches (Sharp, 2006; Prieto-Carron, 2006; Levermore, 2013). Prieto-Carron (2006) refers to this as the "people case" of CSR, as opposed to the business case. Critical theory focuses on social relations, including the struggles over social power, representation, and ideology. It does not assume that either the corporation or the state acts in beneficial ways. Instead, it attempts to understand their roles and effects in our complex, dynamic, globalizing world. Critical thinking also involves reflecting on one's social position in the world (in terms of class, gender, ethnicity and race, sexuality, ability, and age) and holding up one's own beliefs to scrutiny, recognizing that the world contains significant inequality and that people from different backgrounds may experience a particular intervention quite differently. In the realm of sport management, a key consideration may also be to examine which voices are represented or unaccounted for in sporting practices, policies, and organizations. From this perspective, it is important to recognize the complexity of CSR as an intricate system that involves not only corporations, other stakeholders, and partnerships but also the recipients of programs and the societies in which they live. In particular, critical approaches focus on how CSR activities influence and affect those targeted by these programs.

For example, Benson (2017) critically examined the National Football League's (NFL) strategies for handling criticisms of concussions in football by investigating the multisided CSR campaign that the league engages in to reduce negative public relations. Through the league's CSR engagement, the NFL seeks to use philanthropic practices and injury reduction techniques such as technologically improved helmets and more biomechanically appropriate tackling methods to minimize risk of player concussions. Benson argues that through its initiatives, the league seeks to create its own discourse about concussions, one that normalizes the nature of football and its danger, depoliticizes the underlying reason of harmfulness (i.e., the roughness and inherent danger of football), and builds on simple, technical managerial solutions that strategically lead to an antipolitics of what is regarded as regular (i.e., the violent nature of the American pastime of football) in the United States. Through his critical analysis of the NFL and its concussion issues, Benson (2017) focuses on how such CSR initiatives may actually serve to create an alternative discourse about player safety to draw attention away from the concussion problem and the privileges of America's racial order. In this case, questions arise when adopting a critical lens to examine CSR: What is the long-term effect of concussions on the players in the NFL and other football leagues? How are the players, and the broader audience of the NFL, influenced by the CSR initiatives of the NFL? How are decisions made, not only in the NFL but also in the socially responsible practices of the league, from a bottom-up or top-down process? Who holds the power in this CSR initiative? Whose perspectives are being represented, and how are taken-for-granted beliefs about concussions and the racial order of America being produced, strengthened, or resisted through this CSR initiative? Here, using critical theory to understand the CSR activities of corporations allows us to uncover not only the norms embedded within acts that are claimed to be socially responsible but also the power, authority, and influence interwoven within such actions.

An important strand of critical theory is critical feminist theory, which assumes that social order and social life are highly gendered, that is, organized around gender, and that within contemporary societies, the interests of men with power tend to predominate. A key question from this standpoint pertains to "how gender relations privilege men over women, and some men over other men" (Coakley & Donnelly, 2004, p. 47). In contemporary one-third world and two-thirds world societies, researchers in

sport, health, and management have documented the upsurge in cause-related marketing campaigns that focus on girls. Hayhurst (2014) and Calkin (2015a, 2015b) are postcolonial feminist theorists who examined the recent focus on girls as "targets" of CSR initiatives, most especially the Nike funded Girl Effect campaign, which claims that girls are "agents of social change" and hold the answer to ending poverty for themselves, their families, their communities, and their countries (Nike, 2017). Hayhurst (2014) discussed how young women in many sport for development CSR initiatives, such as the Girl Effect, are framed as corporatized agents of change positioned to promote neoliberal discourses around gender equality, development, and sport in two-thirds countries. Put differently, Hayhurst (2011, 2014) highlighted how sport for development programs that target young women in the two-thirds world and are privately funded by corporations reproduce neoliberal forms of development.

Calkin (2015b) noted three themes that are shaped in the discourse of the online marketing videos used for the Girl Effect CSR project. The themes that Calkin (2015b) identified include (1) the "reflexive spectator," in which Westerners are persuaded to donate even though they have been fatigued by numerous attempts of charity; (2) a "breakdown of solidarity," which presents girlhood as a duality (i.e., a young woman can be either a can-do or an at-risk girl); and (3) a "marketing morality," which occurs when young women are marketed as tools of economic growth. Although campaigns such as the Girl Effect may generate financial support and awareness about the need to improve young women's lives and be recognized as important contributors to economic and social development, this campaign comprises a number of important complexities. From a critical and postcolonial feminist perspective, the Girl Effect promotes CSR and sport for development programming in ways that suggest that young women have unlimited choices and are able to foster individual self-growth regardless of the structural inequalities they (may) face. Here, the Girl Effect hones in on the promise of the individual young woman as a catalyst for development, rather than tackling the (global) structural inequalities and systemic structures that have historically marginalized young women in various areas of the world. That is, the Girl Effect campaign distracts attention away from the urgent necessity of addressing structural violence and inequalities that grossly oversimplify the process of social change, while enabling Nike to pose as a white knight and simultaneously conduct a profitable business. In the #MeToo moment, these issues seem evermore pressing. Indeed, SDP programs are increasingly targeting young women, and girl-focused SDP program curriculums often focus on teaching young women about sexual and reproductive health while also discussing how to avoid and navigate gender-based domestic and sexual violence in and through sport. But research has demonstrated, somewhat contradictorily, that when gender relations and culture are ignored in such programs, young women may in fact experience more sexual harassment and violence through their involvement (Hayhurst, 2014; Shehu, 2010), emphasizing the importance of understanding SDP from a critical perspective to highlight taken-for-granted assumptions of "development."

Taken together, Hayhurst's and Calkin's research demonstrates the gendered nature of CSR programs and the importance of using critical and postcolonial feminist lenses in thinking through the (neo) colonial landscape of global capital, particularly in relation to international development and sport. The research also reminds us to question whose interests are being served by such philanthropic endeavors.

CASE STUDY

CSR at Nike

Nike is one of the top 50 brands in the world. It sells products in more than 160 countries and employs over 800,000 workers worldwide in contracted factories (Nike Inc., 2017). Long before CSR became a popular term, the company and its foundation contributed significantly to the popularization of adult fitness, girls' and women's sport, and other progressive campaigns, and Nike has been an industry leader in the development and elaboration of CSR. Nevertheless, a history of anti-sweatshop activism has plagued the corporation for many years, creating an "image problem by setting the company's self-identity at odds with a growing public reputation for sweatshop practices" (Knight & Greenberg, 2002, p. 565). The central issue for activists has been the working conditions of Nike factories located in Asia, where the corporation produces most of its products. Activists want Nike to improve the conditions for these workers, most of whom are women, pay them a living wage, enable them to organize on their own behalf, recognize their rights, and treat them with respect (Sage, 1999). Although considerable evidence shows that Nike has cleaned up its act and improved the working conditions in its factories (e.g., Nisen, 2013), there is still concern that a gap remains between its socially responsible rebranding and the reality of its local labor practices (Knight & Greenberg, 2002). The combination of this history with Nike's presence in the UN Global Compact and ongoing criticism of its marketing to girls and women have maintained the pressure on the company to demonstrate socially responsible practices on the global stage. Nike has always been interested in penetrating untapped markets, particularly the women's sport market. Its ads use feminist rhetoric, suggesting to girls and women that Nike products will help them overcome their historic marginalization in sport (Cole & Hribar, 1995). These campaigns are problematic and reveal a history of sexist, racist, and classist tendencies that contextualize Nike's recent activities related to girls' empowerment. As an attempt to revamp their image as the solution to the oppression of girls in sport, and the marginalization of girls more generally, Nike launched the Nike Foundation in 2005 to help overcome poverty alleviation through girls' empowerment and foster innovative models of corporate philanthropy (Nike, 2005). The foundation actually started as an initiative in 1994 called the Nike PLAY (Participate in the Lives of American Youth) Foundation, focused on supporting community-based entities in the United States, Australia, Canada, and Europe with programs based on youth, sport, culture, and social services (Nike, 2005). Currently, the foundation invests explicitly in activities related to girls' empowerment and poverty relation, principally in countries in the two-thirds world that already have a Nike presence. Another key component of the foundation's work is facilitating partnerships with NGOs, UN agencies, and partners with experience in addressing "developing-country" poverty (Nike, 2005).

In keeping critical theory and its various strands in mind, we now turn to consider CSR activities in the two-thirds world as they intersect with sport and international development.

Corporate Social Responsibility, Sport, and International Development

At the writing of the previous version of this chapter, little research had investigated CSR in the two-thirds world (Newell & Frynas, 2007), and most studies on sport and CSR pertained to critiques of Nike's labor practices in Asia (e.g., Sage, 1999; Knight & Greenberg, 2002). Since then, other studies have examined the practices of sport corporations and their labor practices in the two-thirds world (e.g., Jamali, Lund-Thomsen, & Khara, 2017; Khan & Lund-Thomsen, 2011). Increasingly, corporations have recognized that consumers in the two-thirds world, or what some have referred to as the "bottom of the pyramid" (three billion low-income consumers outside mainstream markets at the bottom of the pyramid), can potentially be a market in themselves that drives new forms of business and contributes to their bottom line. For a company such as Nike, the bottom of the pyramid is an innovative form of CSR that drives new forms of business and contributes to their bottom line. Because of the growth of corporations operating in the two-thirds world, as well as the proliferation of CSR initiatives, an increased amount of research has been conducted on firms' social responsibility in countries other than the one-third world. Jamali and Karam (2016) highlight the increased activity of research being conducted on CSR in the two-thirds world by carrying out a meta-analysis of 285 studies focused on, in their words, "CSR in developing countries." Included in their meta-analysis are various nuances and interesting notes about CSR in the two-thirds world, including the following:

- CSR in the two-thirds world must consider a much wider range of institutional stakeholders, contextual conditions, and institutional pressures than those in the one-third world (e.g., governments, national policies, political conditions, economic conditions, and so on).

- Conducting CSR in the two-thirds world may serve to generate not only physical and financial capital of corporations but also human and social capital, especially in terms of contributing to a more cohesive society in some countries.

- Corporations must be cautious in the two-thirds world (and one-third world) when implementing CSR because of detrimental impacts, such as the harming of the environment through firm operations (e.g., factories within small communities) or confusion about accountability in regard to traditional public functions being served by private, corporate-led actors.

- Although corporations conducting CSR in the two-thirds world may lead to mechanisms for sustainable community development, such as additional employment, economic activity, and increased wages, businesses may also leave other stakeholders underserved, such as is the case in many one-third world CSR initiatives.

Some scholars accuse governments, UN agencies, and **NGOs** (nongovernmental organizations, such as Oxfam or Save the Children) of failing to "rid the planet of underdevelopment and poverty," and argue that the time has come for large corporations to step in by taking responsibility for promoting economic development and filling the governance gap (Hopkins, 2006, p. 2). But the question must be asked, Is development really only about economics? Development is a complex idea that embraces multiple definitions and understandings, particularly depending on the context in which it is used. Here, we briefly give the history of development to help explain how it connects to CSR and sport.

Following World War II, the "development era" was initiated in U.S. president Harry Truman's 1949 inaugural address, in which he proposed to launch a worldwide "program of development" (under the leadership of the United States) to enable impoverished countries to industrialize (Rapley, 2007). Truman's understanding of development was inherently modernist, equating economic growth with notions of progress and liberation (Roy, 2007). Put differently, his conception of development sought to advance a country characterized as backward and primitive, and industrialize nonindustrialized economies. Since then, the concept of development has been further elaborated and revised, mostly in response to shifting ideological and political power. In the 1970s it focused on "satisfying basic human needs." In the 1980s the brief rise of two-thirds world alliances added the ambition that development ensures a broad distribution of economic growth and the spread of liberal democracy. In its Declaration on the Right to Development (1986), the United Nations defined development as a "comprehensive economic, social, cultural and political process, which aims at the constant improvement of the well-being of the entire population and of all individuals on the basis of their active, free and meaningful participation and the fair distribution of benefits." But with the end of the Cold War and the fall of the Soviet Union, neoliberal, market-based solutions to poverty became dominant. The current campaign concentrates on the achievement of the **United Nations Sustainable Development Goals (SDGs)** by 2030. In 2016 world leaders committed to realizing the SDGs that built on the success of the Millennium Development Goals from 2000. The 17 goals that aim to fight poverty and climate change and support a framework for designing and implementing development programs in nations throughout the two-thirds world include the following (United Nations, 2017):

1. End poverty in all its forms everywhere
2. End hunger and achieve food security through sustainable agriculture
3. Ensure healthy lives and promote well-being
4. Ensure inclusive education and lifelong learning
5. Reduce gender inequalities
6. Improve access to water and sanitation
7. Provide access to affordable and clean energy
8. Ensure decent work and economic growth for all
9. Build resilient industry, innovation, and infrastructure
10. Reduce inequality
11. Build sustainable cities and communities
12. Ensure responsible consumption and production
13. Take action towards climate action
14. Conserve life below water in seas, lakes, and oceans
15. Sustainably manage forests and life on land
16. Ensure peace, justice, and strong institutions
17. Build strong partnerships to achieve the SDGs

The SDGs uphold human rights by aiming to preserve and protect human dignity.

Similarly, the SDP movement seeks to promote and protect human rights. SDP has both old and new characteristics. It is an expression of the old idea of "sport for good" (as opposed to "sport for sport's sake") that has motivated school, municipal, religious, political, and community-based organizations in the one-third world for more than a century. But it remains new in its focus on the two-thirds world and on indigenous communities (particularly those in the one-third world); in its attempt to bridge sport and other forms of intervention in health, education, foreign policy, and social development; and in its youth leadership (Hayhurst, 2009; Darnell, 2012; Schulenkorf, Sherry, & Rowe, 2016). The SDP movement has received a great deal of attention from academics, UN agencies, NGOs, and other stakeholders seeking to demonstrate the potential of sport to contribute to the SDGs and other pressing international development issues and to advance human rights. SDP positions sport as a tool to fight HIV and AIDS, build social cohesion, foster peace among conflicted groups, and address gender inequities (Kidd, 2008; Sherry, Schulenkorf, & Phillips, 2016). Table 24.2 outlines three approaches to understanding the relationship between sport and development. SDP and high-performance sport development may be distinguished in terms of their diverging agendas and histories (Houlihan & White, 2002), in which the aim of SDP is to contribute to development objectives mostly in partnerships with governments in the areas of health, education, and sport, and the goal of high-performance sport development is to prepare athletes to participate in sport at an elite level through organized training and major competitions (Kidd, 2008).

Table 24.2   Approaches to Understanding the Relationship Between Sport and Development

Concept	Definition	Example
Sport humanitarian assistance	Focuses on supporting humanitarian interventions in the two-thirds world (e.g., vaccinations, emergency food, and clothing to children in war).	Right to Play, in cooperation with UNICEF, contributes to smallpox and TB vaccinations in Afghanistan.
Sport for development and peace (SDP)	Uses sport to contribute to international development issues encompassed by UN MDGs (e.g., using sport as a tool to fight HIV and AIDS, build social cohesion, foster peace among conflicted groups, and address gender inequities).	Mathare Youth Sports Association (MYSA), an organization based in Kenya, uses the power of football to encourage youth to challenge gender stereotypes, contribute to environmental sustainability, and empower young people (Willis, 2000).
Sport development	Uses sport to develop and prepare athletes to participate in elite sporting competitions through organized training, and major competitions.	Olympic solidarity.

Data from Kidd (2008).

In terms of CSR, sport, and international development, the growing area of SDP has led to an increase in research studies on CSR in the two-thirds world. A recent example is a study conducted by Banda and Gultresa (2015), who examined the IGO Euroleague Basketball's One Team program, a CSR initiative operating within both the two-thirds world and one-third world through sport for development practices. The research focused on exploring the needs of stakeholders in both areas of the world and understanding various levels of the organizational structure before the implementation of the CSR initiative. In their findings, the authors suggest that taking certain steps to CSR before implementing CSR programs may be mutually beneficial to stakeholders as well as firms, most especially in the case of Euroleague Basketball's strategic business approach to CSR. They used four steps in the stages leading up to the CSR program:

1. New CSR awareness and primary stakeholder interaction at the corporate level, involving the establishment of a new governance structure based on active engagement of stakeholders in decision making
2. Active interaction between Euroleague Basketball's Community Trust and professional clubs to provide contextual needs for each

community and club that ensures profound impact on target groups
3. Stakeholder involvement at the grassroots level, basketball in the community, whereby a thorough needs analysis is conducted for each community to shape specific CSR focus areas
4. Joined-up CSR project delivery, in which all stakeholders are involved in CSR implementation and collaborative setting of objectives and tasks for the purposes of the project

Their study demonstrated that the needs and decisions of both primary and secondary stakeholders remain critical to the implementation and success of a given CSR initiative, especially one operating in the international development sector. They emphasize and explain that when Euroleague Basketball first engaged in CSR programming without gaining insight from organizations and individuals from the two-thirds world, as well as the one-third world, the impact and benefits of CSR were not fully realized. After conducting in-depth research and exploring how the CSR initiative could be better executed for all stakeholders, regardless of location, size of organization, or importance of voice, the preceding four steps allowed a much more comprehensive and favorable CSR program that not only addressed concerns of all those involved, both at the global and community level, but also influenced how important each stakeholder felt in the initiative. They suggest that adhering to these steps for most CSR initiatives, especially ones operating internationally using SDP, would be well advised to adopt such a process before implementing the program.

Another example of CSR, sport, and international development, is Levermore's (2013) exploration of the 2010 football World Cup in South Africa. Using a critical lens, he highlights how CSR through sport initiatives may heavily favor top-down, one-third world, competitive, masculinist traits. Levermore argues that despite being sponsored and supported by large corporations such as McDonald's and Coca-Cola, the World Cup was largely driven by asymmetrical power relations underlying the event. In particular, Levermore highlights concerns centered on the way in which the World Cup privileged elite football at the expense of grassroots soccer and offers specific examples of exclusion during this megaevent, such as the eviction of poor communities from tourist areas and stadia to offer a "positive" display of South African culture (Levermore, 2013). Additionally, after the World Cup ended, attacks on African migrants resumed, which led to questions of how the World Cup "unified" the nation of South Africa and accusations of the event being "fake nationhood" (Levermore, 2013). Although many CSR initiatives or events in the two-thirds world seek to benefit the communities, regions, and countries they become involved with, corporations must be careful when operating in the international development sector through SDP, especially because of taken-for-granted ideas of program implementa-tion that can lead to oversight about benefits to those who have limited voice in such initiatives (e.g., poor communities displaced by the World Cup).

United Nations Global Compact

Since its launch in July 2000, the **United Nations Global Compact**, which is focused on building the social legitimacy of business and markets, has grown to be the world's largest global corporate citizenship initiative. The 10 principles of the compact ask companies to support and respect human rights and ensure they do not commit human rights abuses; uphold labor rights, including the rights to freely formed trade unions, collective bargaining, and the abolition of child labor and discrimination; exercise environmental responsibility; and work against corruption. The compact has now grown to over 12,500 participants, including over 8,500 businesses in 100 countries worldwide (UNGC, 2017). Not surprisingly, the socially responsible behavior of companies reflects patterns of corporate interests (Himmelstein, 1997). Despite the tensions of CSR, its normative values continue to shape the behavior of transnational corporations such as Adidas and influence those corporate interests. Therefore, examining the relationships between the UN Global Compact, corporations, and SDP NGOs is useful for understanding how CSR norms permeate the landscape of sport for development. For example, Nike has been a member of the UN Global Compact since its official creation. By enlisting in the compact, Nike was legitimized by the UN by agreeing to follow nine principles drawn from the Universal Declaration of Human Rights, the International Labour Organization's (ILO) Fundamental Principles and Rights at Work, and the Rio Declaration on Environment and Development. These principles are meant to influence and direct Nike's behavior by building a shared meaning of good corporate practices as defined by the wider global community (Ruggie, 2004). Indeed, the UN Global Compact and the commitments it has engendered from global corporations constitute a progressive step forward for the corporate world. On the other hand, critics contend that the UNGC is merely an innovative way for corporations to enter into new spheres of influence and to penetrate new markets, particularly in the two-thirds world (Voegtlin & Pless, 2014). Others worry about compliance, suggesting that the

Learning Activity

Discuss to what extent the growth of the sport for development and peace sector has influenced how corporations, sport organizations, and researchers approach and think about CSR. Has the increase of SDP influenced positive CSR initiatives in the two-thirds world? How has the SDP field both positively and negatively influenced how corporations approach CSR? How have companies responded to the increasing need to fill government gaps in the two-thirds world?

Learning Activity

Visit the UN Global Compact's (UNGC) website and examine the UNGC's 10 principles. Under what theoretical framework (as discussed in the chapter) do these principles fall? What, in your perspective, are some positive and negative aspects of these principles?

compact enables companies to be branded as socially responsible entities while they may be acting in opposition to the principles of the compact behind closed doors. The compact is voluntary and cannot be legally enforced; therefore, the social and environmental aspects of businesses cannot be strictly regulated (Capdevila, 2007). Given these issues, is the UN Global Compact then just a "band-aid solution" to addressing the negative effects of the increasingly globalized world economy, as corporations continue to prioritize short-term profits and promotion over social and environmental considerations? What are the implications of the compact in terms of CSR? Does it present a hope for a new democratic world order, or does it simply circumvent the challenge to existing institutions? Further questions for research include sport CSR and the environment, community sport initiatives and social responsibility, and sport CSR and social change.

Summary

Most who enter the field of sport management do so because they love sport and want to encourage others to participate, play, and engage in sporting opportunities. But those who work in the field need to think critically about the current sporting landscape and understand how multiple actors such as NGOs, UN agencies, elite sport organizations, and, of course, corporations, influence sporting experiences. Undoubtedly, throughout the last 20 years, the global expansion of the sport industry has both extended opportunities to many people and raised difficult questions. In response, many transnational sport corporations have taken up CSR practices, policies, and programs. Everyone working in sport management today will be acutely shaped by this development and will have the opportunity to contribute to its improvement. The definition, forms, and problems of CSR in sport and development are constantly evolving, and the issues arising from its influence cannot be neglected. Sport managers need to think critically about how sport can contribute to the improvement of society, foster social change, and improve the lives of disadvantaged groups, particularly those in the two-thirds world. We are not suggesting here that sport will cure all the world's ills, but we hope that this chapter has encouraged students to think more about the possibilities of its reach.

? Review Questions

1. What were the origins of CSR?
2. The authors have suggested that philanthropy stems from CSR causes, but others suggest that it is not a form of CSR. What do you think and why? To what extent is CSR altruistic? To what extent is it not?
3. What were the origins of sport for development?
4. Do corporations necessarily need to be involved in sport for development?
5. How do organizations like the Maquila Solidarity Network contribute to sport CSR?

International Sport Management
A Way Forward

Alison Doherty, PhD
Western University, Canada

Tracy Taylor, PhD
University of Technology Sydney

As demonstrated in this book, sport happens within and across national, regional, and international boundaries. To manage sport effectively, sport managers need to understand, and learn from, how it is governed, marketed, delivered, and evaluated in and across different contexts. Many examples of both have been offered in this text, including an examination of sport in various nations and regions (chapters 3-11), within different organizational forms (chapters 12-16), and across different functional areas and contemporary issues facing sport (chapters 17-24). The purpose of this chapter is to build on those chapters and identify several directions for future research that can continue to advance understanding of international sport and its management through interrogating phenomenon, testing and reshaping theory, and extending knowledge in this burgeoning area. We do this by outlining some contemporary issues in sport that may be examined from an international perspective, given their presence across more than one nation, and by highlighting international matters that have had little scholarly consideration to date. We also dedicate a portion of the chapter to sharing some

insights on the international and cross-cultural research process—insight that comes from our own experiences working together, and with others, across a variety of nations, cultures, languages, and approaches.

International sport is a function of globalization, which in turn is characterized by economic, political, and social affairs associated with the movement, interaction, and integration of people, products, and services. Although economics may be a driving, and primary, force for international sport (Pfahl, 2012), there is increasing recognition of the political and sociocultural aspects that impact sport (Houlihan & Malcolm, 2016), and the interconnectedness and complexity that is introduced when operating across and between different nation states (Bale & Sang, 2003; Bradbury & O'Boyle, 2017). These influences have been seen through the historical development and evolution of sport as an industry, as described in chapter 2. International sport encapsulates many forms, including sport that is played in multiple countries (e.g., rugby, golf) or in which participants represent different countries (e.g., world championships); sport organizations that administer specific sports across the world (e.g., international sport federations); leagues or competitions that operate in several countries (e.g., International Cricket League); multisport events that have national representations (e.g., the Olympic and Paralympic Games); and sport products that have international reach (e.g., Tour de France, NBA). The increasing complexity associated with international sport both challenges and demands systematic research aimed at uncovering and discovering new knowledge about this field.

Systematic research is fundamental to knowledge generation that facilitates understanding of phenomena in a field. This new knowledge helps with the recognition, description, prediction, and ultimately management of incidents and events by highlighting evidence-based implications for practice. Research both tests proposed explanations about behavior (e.g., fan loyalty, willingness to pay for tickets, motivation to participate in sport activity, ethical decision making), and uncovers and generates new understandings about phenomena (e.g., emergent model of positive youth development through sport [Holt et al., 2017]; theory of suffering as a result of sport rule violations [Kihl, Richardson, & Campisi, 2008]; sport policy process model emanating from an examination of how sport policies are developed [Weed, 2005]). Research allows a field to go beyond description (what) to explanation (why and how) (Doherty, 2013): Why is sport a more effective political tool in some nations than others? How do international fans come to identify with a league in another nation? Why is the Olympic Games becoming so formulaic? How connected is the world through sport, and why (or why not)? How do sport organizations effectively navigate the international sport industry? How is the global labor migration most effectively managed? Further, research that adopts a critical lens helps to uncover both sides of the story by critiquing unfolding assumptions about phenomena (Frisby, 2005). The research agenda we present here should be considered in the context of systematic, theory-based research that adopts a critical lens to advance understanding of international sport and its management. The international sport research agenda presented in this chapter is indicative rather than exhaustive with regard to what may be examined, why, and how.

International Sport Management Research Agenda

We consider several topics and issues that highlight possible directions for future research in the realm of international sport management. We arrived at these topics by reflecting on issues in international sport that have received limited scholarly attention, and questions that have received national- or regional-specific empirical consideration yet are present across at least several countries or regions. For each topic, we provide a brief overview of the issue and current state of scholarly knowledge. We then propose several research questions that we believe can be addressed to advance theory-based, empirical understanding of these international sport management issues, and national or regional issues from an international perspective. The topics we address include: (1) global sport volunteering among different cultures and within and across nations, (2) national compliance with international sport policy and global conventions in different countries, (3) transmission of national culture in a global sport marketplace, and (4) global labor mobility in sport.

Global Sport Volunteering

Much has been written about the extent and nature of sport volunteering in a number of countries around the world in the service of sport events, national and regional federations, and community sport clubs. Some of that volunteering takes place at major international sport events, such as the Olympic and Paralympic Games and single-sport world championships or competitions. Volunteering at these major sport events often has an international component, because at least a portion of the volunteers travel from other countries to be involved (Fairley, Kellett, & Green, 2007). For the most part, however, sport volunteers are engaged locally, in their own communities or at least within their own regions or countries. Research, similarly, has focused on volunteering within a city, region, or country. An informal tally indicates that research about sport volunteers and volunteer management has been done in over two dozen countries. This work includes the examination of volunteerism associated with at least nine different Olympic Games. But as Taylor and Morgan (2017) note, sport volunteer research is largely limited to North American, Western European, and Antipodean nations, so theory and knowledge about sport volunteering thus largely reflects those nations and their (volunteer) culture. An opportunity has been lost, or at least has been missed, to gain a better understanding of sport volunteering, its cultural meaning, and its management by examining it as an international phenomenon that takes place around the world. For example, Meijs and Bridges Karr (2004) note that volunteer management models vary between countries, distinguished by a focus on the volunteer (i.e., the individual) versus the tasks that volunteers undertake. Both approaches reportedly have advantages and disadvantages, but the authors ask which approach is relevant in different contexts (Meijs & Bridges Karr, 2004). Relatedly, the European Union study on volunteering (European Union, 2010) notes that some of its member states have longstanding traditions in volunteering and well-developed voluntary sectors (e.g., Ireland, the Netherlands, and the United Kingdom), whereas in other countries the sector is still emerging (e.g., Bulgaria, Greece, Latvia, Lithuania, and Romania). The report concludes that the requirements of sport volunteers are becoming more demanding in terms of skills and qualifications and that collaboration between countries to gain a better understanding of sport volunteering is needed. We believe that an opportunity is available to examine, with a critical lens, the different national (and regional, cultural) contexts in which different volunteer management models are used (cf. Meijs & Bridges Karr, 2004), and any variations, to enhance understanding of the nature and management of sport volunteerism as an international phenomenon. This effort may lead to a refined (and potentially broader) model that accounts for additional and alternative forms of sport volunteering (e.g., shared positions, shorter terms, nontraditional roles), individual motivations, and outcomes to be involved, that highlights or suggests effective management practices.

A broader understanding of this international phenomenon may also help to better explain, predict, and manage the international nature of sport volunteering within or across a city, region, or country. With increasing emigration, many (mostly Western) nations are experiencing a dramatic shift in their ethnic, racial, and cultural makeup (Hainmuller & Hopkins, 2014). Immigrants have, to date, a lower rate of volunteering than nationals do (Lee & Pritzker, 2013; Sundeen, Garcia, & Raskoff, 2009), but this evidence may be biased by social surveys not capturing all the ways in which they engage in volunteering and why (Wilson, 2012). For example, research outside the sport realm indicates that members of minority and marginalized groups, such as recent immigrants, are less likely to volunteer through formal organizations and do not necessarily "fit the profile of the typical volunteer" (Wilson, 2012, p. 185). This finding should prompt consideration of a potentially different model of sport volunteering, in local communities and around the world, than has been captured to this point. Meijs and Bridges Karr (2004) note that cultural factors, including language and social norms, affect how people perceive volunteering and how they expect the organization to treat them. Thus, scholars are encouraged to explore the meaning and nature of volunteering among ethnically and culturally different sport volunteers (at home and across different nations) and within sport volunteer contexts characterized by diversity, so that what may perhaps be an international model of volunteering can be uncovered. Future research may consider the following questions:

◆ What aspects of sport volunteerism are unique to different nations? What aspects are common around the world?

◆ What individual factors (e.g., gender, age, income, race, immigrant status, education, work) and aspects of a person's life course shape sport volunteerism in and across different nations?

◆ Is there an international definition of sport volunteer activity?

◆ What are recent trends in sport volunteering around the world?

◆ How may a broader understanding of sport volunteering shape an alternate model of sport volunteerism and allow a revised profile of the typical sport volunteer?

National Compliance with International Sport Charters, Conventions, and Declarations

Another direction for international sport management research is the examination of how international sport policies and global conventions, intended to guide strategy and action for social change around sport-related issues that are (presumably) meaningful around the world, are actually being played out in different countries. Numerous international conventions, treaties, and charters either directly or indirectly have a significant alignment with sport. These include the *International Charter for Physical Education and Sport* (UNESCO, 1978), the *United Nations Convention Against Corruption* (United Nations Office on Drugs and Crime, 2003), the *International Convention Against Doping in Sport* (UNESCO, 2005), the *United Nations Convention on the Rights of Persons With Disabilities* (United Nations, 2008), which was the first legally binding international instrument to address the rights of persons with disabilities and sport, and the 1994 *Brighton Declaration on Women and Sport*, which provides the principles that should guide action intended to increase the involvement of women in sport at all levels and in all functions and roles. In addition, various transnational charters are acted on by member countries that voluntarily and democratically agree on the rule of law, such as the Council of Europe's (2001) *Code of Sports Ethics* and its recent work that aims to set an agenda for social inclusion through volunteering.

Scholars such as Adriaanse and Claringbould (2016) and Henry (2016) have begun to explore the implications of such charters and conventions for sport in different national contexts. For example, Adriaanse and Claringbould examined the *Brighton Declaration*, as well as legacy initiatives of the International Working Group on Women and Sport World Conferences, namely, the *Windhoek Call for Action* (1998), the *Montréal Toolkit* (2002), the *Kumamoto Commitment to Collaboration* (2006), and the *Sydney Scoreboard* (2010). They determined that the construction of gender of these legacies mainly centered on social practices associated with production, power, and symbolic relations. Although Adriaanse and Claringbould do not consider the further implications of these nuances for adherence to the goals set out in the aforementioned proposals in different nations, the initiatives may be expected to align better with some countries and cultures than others and have different mechanisms for implementation. For example, the status of women can vary significantly in different cultures, which has implications for the adoption of initiatives around rights and opportunities in a given country. As such, Adriaanse and Claringbould recommend that global conventions be supported by collaborative networks that can assist countries in their respective challenges to engage with, for example, gender equity policy and initiatives.

Henry (2016) noted that the European Union has significantly expanded into sport policy, with a view to economic regeneration, social integration, and international relations. The EU established the "specificity of sport" as a legal concept through the rulings of the European Court of Justice and through decisional practice of the European Commission (2016). The *White Paper on Sport* (European Union, 2007) notes that the specificity of sport requires an assessment of the compatibility of sporting rules with EU law on a case-by-case basis. But nation states in the EU, as elsewhere in the world, have their own constitutions and laws related to sport and these often take precedent. Early research on the implications of the EU *White Paper*, both within and across nations, has included the effect on sport regulation and governance (Garcia, 2009; Geeraert, Alm, & Groll, 2014; Hill, 2009), players' rights (Platts & Smith, 2009), and intergovernmental agency (Garcia & Weatherill, 2012). With the complexity of governing multiple nations (and their sport systems) by a given international policy, continued research may provide valuable insight into such considerations as the alignment between policy and member nation legislation and social dictums, barriers to implementation and compliance, and ultimate impact.

Universal declarations are intended to generate and maintain some consistency in standards across nations and regions, for the purpose of aligning them with values laid out by international bodies or organizations. Mechanisms may or may not be in place to account for political, economic, cultural, and social differences in the various regions, which can have implications for successful implementation. An example was the IOC's minimum target of 20 percent female board members of all boards of national Olympic committees by 2005. In 2000, only 6.1 percent of NOC boards were women, whereas 2013 data indicated female representation was approximately 18 percent. In 2015 the IOC reported reaching the target of 20 percent (although 10 NOCs had no women on their executive board) (IOC, 2017). Clearly, this particular international sport edict was not attained within the set period, although an increase has been reported in national or sport-specific gender and diversity quotas, targets, and initiatives (Adriaanse & Schofield, 2014). Whether setting targets or quotas actually works is the subject of an emerging body of research (Kotschwar & Moran, 2015; Leberman & Burton, 2017).

Research could examine global or regional charters, conventions, and regulations using a critical lens to consider the "internationalness" of the principles, guidelines, and intended course of action. Longitudinal tracking of implementation, compliant cases, and associated data could be used to examine the degree to which countries have implemented the international convention principles and to explore whether there are patterns of constraints to achieving the change required or the espoused outcomes. Questions for future research include the following:

◆ To what extent is a particular international sport convention effectively implemented by its target nations, and what are the apparent trends?

◆ What are common and unique constraints to compliance across different nations?

◆ What has been the effect of compliance (e.g., gender representation) on sport organizations over time?

◆ Have the goals or principles set out in these international-level declarations cascaded into national or local policy, and what does this reveal?

Transmission of National Culture Through Global Sport

A valuable exercise is to consider the implications of sport in a global marketplace for the transmission of culture with respect to the home nation. This trans-

mission may happen through hosting international events, national team participation in international events, and the global reach of national leagues. Pfahl (2012, p. 7) notes, "As sport is internationalized, it carries with it cultural elements from the hearts and souls of people in local communities to people around the world" through various media.

Governments may use sport to promote, or even change, national and international perceptions of their country's image brand by hosting sport megaevents such as the Olympic Games and FIFA World Cup (Grix, 2012). A growing body of research is examining the influence of such large-scale international sport events on the image of the event host as a tourism destination and on the image of the country overall (e.g., Dinnie, 2004; Grix, 2012; Kim, Kang, & Kim, 2014; Li & Kaplanidou, 2013; Preuss & Alfs, 2011). Benefits are purported to include increased tourist visitation and a stronger branding of the country and its products, all of which drive economic gains (Kim et al., 2014). Participation of national teams in international events is another occasion, and thus opportunity, to transmit a nation's culture. For example, much time, effort, and expense goes into designing opening ceremonies uniforms, which are intended to reflect the values of a given country at that point in time (Markovinovic, 2016).

Part of the image of a country is its culture—its values, expectations, and priorities—as reflected in its people, their behavior, and various symbols. The "Viking thunder-clap," introduced to the world by Iceland at the Euro 2016 football (soccer) championships and quickly taken up by other European teams and fans, as well as almost 70,000 fans of the NFL's Minnesota Vikings (Chibber, 2016), is an example of local culture going international. This interest has been accompanied by a flurry of media forums discussing the origins and meaning of the phenomenon. International sport consumers may also be intrigued by how increasingly global leagues, such as the NBA and NHL, handle issues of racism and various transgressions among players and fans. Fan misbehavior, and even violence, in the NHL and NFL for example (Babbs & Rich, 2016; Peters, 2015), may shape global consumers' perception of the respective league, the fans, and the society within which they exist.

Certainly, the strategic reach of national leagues into new marketplaces in other nations (see chapter 15) presents not only an opportunity to grow the leagues' respective brands (Kunkel, Funk, & Hill, 2013) but also a situation that allows the new marketplace to learn something about the home nation. This process may be conceptualized as an additional brand extension of a sport product. Just as international travel and tourism has implications for the transmission and reception of new and different cultures, the availability of sport globally, including the globalization of sport leagues, means that it may play an important role in culture transmission. This development has implications for leagues and other potentially key stakeholders, such as tourism promoters and governments, to play a role in signaling (Preuss & Alfs, 2011) a nation or region's culture to a much wider international marketplace, and certainly to be aware of the culture that is being transmitted. Given that less research to date has examined the role of national leagues in the transmission of culture globally, we focus on the following questions, as examples of directions for future research:

◆ What is the perceived culture (values and so on) associated with a national league, both at home and abroad?

◆ How does the perceived culture shape international consumers' perceptions of the home nation?

◆ How can leagues, tourism promoters, and governments leverage the culture associated with a national league to promote itself?

◆ Is cultural knowledge a motive for watching sport from other countries?

◆ What methods (e.g., signaling) can and do key stakeholders use to transmit culture?

Global Labor Mobility in Sport

With the internationalization of sport, including sport leagues, competitions, and businesses, there is an increasing transnational flow of people (athletes, coaches, administrators, and so on), services, information, technology, commodities, and capital (Houlihan & Malcolm, 2016) in which a sport may be an active (e.g., scouting, identifying, and developing talent from other nations), passive (i.e.,

letting the market or the individual determine these flows), or even resistant participant (e.g., restricting the number of foreign players allowed in any given club). Global labor mobility has been extensively studied and has produced a wealth of research in the international business, international human resource management, and careers literature. The increasingly common occurrence of transnational athlete migration (Maguire & Falcous, 2011; Ryba, Haapanen, Mosek, & Ng, 2012) requires greater understanding of transnational perspectives on sports labor migration.

Because of increases in imported talent from international leagues, attention has been given to trading in athletes, player transfer rules that restrict the movement of players between countries in European and North American sport leagues (Dietl, Fort, & Lang, 2013), and the multiple local and global, material and ideational power relations of cross-border athlete movements (Besnier, 2015). Changes to the nature of broadcasting and social media have intensified the commodification of professional athletes: Their brand value has increased, and their appeal has gone far beyond national borders into a global market (Sage, 2015). Systematic examination of the nuanced career paths and management of transnational athletes, coaches, and administrative personnel is warranted to gain better understanding of this aspect of international sport.

In many ways, sport is a unique employer because athletes are often inducted or induced into a career path at a relatively young age, and this might even include corresponding expatriation (e.g., Kenya and athletics; Bale & Sang, 2003). The athlete, or her or his family, might self-initiate a move to a different city, region, or country to prepare for international sporting success; or the athlete might be recruited and groomed by a professional sport team or club. Because athletes' experiences will vary significantly across different country contexts, understanding the social support mechanisms and culturally based implications associated with such movement is important (e.g., Egilsson & Dolles, 2017). Arbena (2003) suggests that the field can benefit from research that considers the push and pull factors that lead to international athlete movements such as contract restrictions, family ties, cultural barriers, and nationalism. Besnier (2015) cautions, however, that if only the "whole of region" migration patterns are considered, such as the flow of personnel from the two-thirds world to the one-third world for economic gain, the more individualized and cultural reasons for this migration may be overlooked. Although the early research on sport labor migration framed athlete movements around globalization and dependency theory (Bale, 1991; Bale & Maguire, 2003) and the way in which socioeconomic power relations shape the nature and directional flow of sport migrants (Maguire & Falcous, 2011), future research may examine the dynamics of inequality, exploitation, economic gain, and other power relations of organizations to improve understanding of the global circulation of professional athletes and the related management implications.

Transnational studies have started to capture the athlete voice (Agergaard, 2017; Engh & Agergaard, 2015), scrutinize the personal experiences of transitory athletes, consider employment decision making (Mutter, 2017), examine the influence of family values and cultural expectations (van der Meij & Darby, 2017), and document the social implications of moving to another country (Roderick, 2013). Sport organizations seeking to recruit and retain a nonlocal workforce could benefit from research and evidence-based practice focused on these human resource management issues across countries, leagues, and sports. By examining power relations between different countries' contexts and institutions, sport management scholars can better understand recruitment strategy implications and people management decision making with a human resource management framework. The question is, how can these phenomena be theorized in sport management?

Research into the impetus and mechanisms of sport labor migration and the transnationalism of sport migrant experiences is gaining momentum. The majority of research on these global movements, however, has been on either the two-thirds world to one-third world migration or the Europe and North America markets (Carter, 2016). There is a need to consider and understand the institutional complexities of how sport organizations in other countries respond to and manage both outgoing and incoming migrant athletes (Chepyator-Thomson & Ariyo, 2017). Furthermore, the experiences of sport expatriates outside professional sport and noncorporate communities (i.e., not multinationals) is another avenue of research that lends itself to further investigations (McNulty, Vance, & Fisher, 2017).

The "Olympic Caravan" (Horne, 2017) is another example of global labor migration in sport. As noted earlier, Olympic and Paralympic Games and other major sport events are often serviced by volunteers from far beyond the local host community, because people travel the world to be involved with high-profile mega sport events. These events are also staffed by paid employees who may come from around the world, having implications for their effective integration within the pulsating (Hanlon & Cuskelly, 2002) and multicultural environment that is a major games or festival. A growing line of inquiry about megaevent staff (e.g., Odio, Walker, & Kim, 2013) may also consider the global migration aspect of professional employees and their social links, and networks and communities developed and maintained across national and transnational boundaries.

Future research on global sport labor mobility may address the following questions:

- What are various career paths for transnational athletes, coaches, and professional experts? How do age, gender, family situation, culture, sport, country movement, and so on, influence decision-making processes, and what role do associated sport organizations play in this?

- Is there a transnational or expatriate career model, and how do international assignments affect career advancement and personal development? For example, does spending a large part of one's career abroad continuously, working for two to three years in various locations, result in different career paths or different attitudes? How might the notion of boundary-less careers be conceptualized?

- What are the cross-cultural differences in sport labor mobility, and can one build a taxonomy of transnational sport careers?

- What are the political, economic, and social dynamics of sports labor migration in different countries, and how do these influence the push and pull of personnel and their management?

Conducting International Sport Management Research

In this section we suggest several important considerations for undertaking research in international sport management, including addressing the topics highlighted earlier. We consider international comparative research and cross-cultural research, and the challenges of both. We provide several recommendations for overcoming their respective challenges and ensuring that the individual and professional benefits and value of this type of scholarship are realized.

International Comparative Research

Several of the directions for future research identified earlier may rely on comparative research. The purpose of comparative research is to achieve better understanding of a phenomenon by contrasting two or more cases that allow insight into differences (sometimes extreme), similarities, or both. International sport management is an ideal field for comparative research because it provides a frame for comparing different nations with regard to a similar phenomenon (e.g., sport volunteering) or examining the impact of a global phenomenon in different nations (e.g., policy compliance). Henry (2007) notes that the globalization of sport has, in fact, contributed to a decline in comparative analysis, in which an assumption of the "interconnectedness of political, economic and social systems . . . has led some to question the appropriateness of using the individual nation state as the default unit of analysis" (p. 4). He also attributes the lack of comparative research to an overreliance on the "Western-centred nature of much social analysis" (Henry, 2007, p. 5). He, and we, counter the claims that

> Globalization diminishes the role of the nation state to such an extent that an understanding of the roles and activities of nation state actors is no longer essential to explanations of [phenomena]... [and] "Western" ways of viewing the world are incompatible with non-Western perspectives such that comparisons become impossible. (Henry, 2007, p. 5)

Instead, we argue for the vital role of international comparative research for understanding both global sport and nation-based sport. In identifying, presenting, and assessing similarities and differences between selected cases or societies (Bergsgard, Houlihan, Mangset, Nodland, & Rommetvedt, 2007), we may gain a better understanding of how, for example, different cultural, political, economic, and social circumstances affect the phenomenon of interest in a given country or across countries. Both differences and similarities can be useful to testing, and reshaping, theory as well as identifying effective practices. Houlihan (2017) notes that, at least in sport policy, comparative research has tended to focus on developed countries and that smaller and poorer states are seriously underresearched. We concur and, again, agree with Henry (2007) that not only is a wider focus of research needed to extend the scope of understanding of sport management in small and developing countries, but a critical cross-cultural lens can enlighten understanding of non-Western sociocultural contexts of sport and in relation to the better known (or at least studied) Western ways of sport delivery.

Several conditions, however, are required for effective comparative research, the most notable being the need for information on at least two or more cases, and explaining rather than just describing similarities and differences (Henry, Al-Taqui, Amara, & Lee, 2007). The latter ensures that new knowledge in the field of international sport management goes beyond the what to the why and how (Doherty, 2013). Systematic, rigorous, and meaningful comparative analysis may be enhanced by purposeful sampling (Patton, 2015), with consideration of cases that are extreme in terms of their differences, such as a comparison of international sport convention compliance in highly developed Western nations and developing countries; cases that are intense in terms of rich examples of a phenomenon, such as a comparison of culture transmission through international sport in two nations that are robust (or rapidly growing) markets for a host nation league such as the NBA; and cases that are matched on some criteria that enables an examination of what works (or does not), such as a comparison of international sport organizations that are considered to have successfully navigated global talent migration in sport.

Cross-Cultural Research

Cross-cultural research may be a focus of international comparative analysis, and it has its own particular challenges. The focus is generally field-level comparison of human behavior associated with culture in various societies, from a qualitative, quantitative, or mixed-methods approach. But the act of studying different cultures may come with challenges of understanding and navigating different languages, values, expectations for research, and approaches to scholarship. From the literature we identify several considerations for effective and meaningful cross-cultural research that avoids or at least minimizes miscommunication, misinterpretation, and bias, highlighted in the sidebar Considerations for Cross-Cultural Research.

Liamputtong (2008) and Yaprak (2008) suggest several conditions for engaging in effective cross-cultural research that begins with cultural sensitivity. This obligation involves knowing the cultural context of the group being studied, including the social, familial, religious, historical, and political background. It also involves, of course, checking one's ethnocentricity about the superiority of one country or culture over another. Different cultures can have different cultural norms for behavior (e.g., regarding time and status). Navigating such differences requires patience and flexibility. Cross-cultural differences may also be found in language, which has implications for ensuring a clear conceptualization of the phenomena of interest across cultures. Researchers must acknowledge that instruments developed in a specific country (and culture, language) may not be appropriate for cross-cultural comparison. These considerations are fundamental for navigating cross-cultural work and likely require translation or reinterpretation of conceptual meanings of a phenomenon across different cultures, languages, and perspectives, so that new knowledge is based on data that is not biased by one culture, language, or perspective.

Cross-cultural research also involves ethical dimensions, including consideration of the power relationship between the researcher and the researched and who benefits from the outcomes or knowledge, to ensure research integrity and the value of reflexivity in a cross-cultural investigation (Miller Cleary, 2013). Collecting meaningful and reliable

Considerations for Cross-Cultural Research

◆ Cultural sensitivity
- Know the cultural context of the group being studied
    Social, familial, religious, historical, political background
- Be aware of one's own ethnocentricity about the superiority of one culture over another
- Consider different norms for behavior; requires patience and flexibility in the research process
- Be aware that a phenomenon and its subconcepts may have a different meaning in other cultures and languages
    Appropriateness of instruments developed in one culture or language in other contexts

◆ Ensure that data is not biased by one language or culture
- Clarify meaning of phenomenon and concepts in the other culture

- Check translation of instruments
- Acknowledge role, and potential bias or misunderstanding, of interpreter or translator
- Engage in open, reflexive, and critical analysis of data across cultures

◆ Consider power relationship between the researchers in different cultures and between the researcher and researched

◆ Be aware of nonverbal communication that may have additional, and even contradictory, messages

◆ Establish a research advisory committee comprising members of the cultural group being studied (or someone with extensive knowledge of the group)

(Liamputtong, 2008; Miller Cleary, 2013; Patton, 2015; Yaprak, 2008)

data from individuals in different cultures depends on the development of a trusting relationship and a good rapport established and maintained through the research cycle.

Patton (2015) focuses on differences in language as well as norms and values as key challenges in cross-cultural interviewing in particular. Both of us have experienced the language challenge when working with research colleagues whose first (or even second or third) language is not English like ours. Of course, interpreting data collected from participants who speak another language can be fraught with misunderstanding. Investigators need to acknowledge when their work involves an interpreter or translator because another party is engaged and another step is occurring in the research process (see also Liamputtong, 2008). With regard to differing norms and values, Patton (2015) notes that the significance attached to science in Western countries means that studying almost any topic is culturally acceptable. But this viewpoint is not the case globally. Some topics are taboo in other parts of the world (e.g., asking a subordinate about a superior, asking a person about his or her migrant work). Interview etiquette also varies by culture; it is acceptable in some contexts but unheard of in others for a woman to interview a man, or a man to interview a woman unchaperoned, and so on (Patton, 2015). Finally, Patton (2015) notes that in cross-cultural research, nonverbal communication such as body language and hand signals can be essential to consider as it may help interpret what research participants are sharing and provide additional information that complements, or even contradicts, what is being said.

Despite these challenges, and with attention to considerations to address them, thinking about sport management issues in a cross-cultural context can help identify new research directions and domains, and guide the development of a broader and more inclusive interpretation of management issues in sport. Cross-cultural research can also lead to advances in study design and methodology, as well as the building of cross-cultural research competence through the establishment of multinational research networks and cross-cultural research collaborations. The latter is aided by technological advancements in communication, such as the use of digital files and archives, WeChat, WhatsApp, Google Docs, cloud storage, and international data repositories and alliances, which enable cross-cultural and multinational research to be conducted more easily.

Summary

With the growth of international sport comes a parallel need to engage in systematic research that builds knowledge about its development, impact, and effective management, within and across nations, regions, and communities. In this chapter, we provide an overview of the dimensions of international sport management research and note how sport spans geographical boundaries and can be examined from a cross-national, cross-cultural, and international or transnational perspective. We highlight examples that are only indicative, not exhaustive, of directions for future research. We do this by identifying sport phenomena that are happening at, or have been exclusively examined from, a regional or national level but may benefit from a wider scope of (international) attention (i.e., sport volunteerism). We also note international sport management phenomena that have been the focus of little if any research to date (i.e., transmission of national culture, transnational labor migration, international policy compliance). But these topics are only a sampling of issues that may be considered across the breadth of (international) sport management. Our intent is to prompt the reader to contemplate what aspects of sport offered in many different nations or offered across nations may be examined further to increase understanding of sport as an international phenomenon.

Comparative and cross-cultural research is foundational to this exercise, and these forms of scholarship can enhance understanding of knowledge and theories of sport management that are universal rather than limited to specific geographies. The development of approaches, methodologies, and instruments to study sport-related phenomena in organizations across culture and location allows researchers to draw comparisons of and between countries and identify culture-specific factors. Ensuring that data collection instruments and protocols are comparable, that measurement is equivalent, and that both linguistic meaning and psychometric properties are maintained across populations are challenges of cross-cultural and cross-national research. Although these aspects may increase the complexity of international sport management research, the potential benefits to theory, knowledge, and practice surely inspire scholars committed to and passionate about this field.

References

Chapter 1

Appadurai, A. (1990). Disjuncture and difference in the global cultural economy. *Theory, Culture, & Society*, 7(2/3), 295-310.

Baghdadi, G. (2009, 17 July). *Non-aligned nations vow to keep up "self-determination."* Retrieved July 25, 2009, from www.cbsnews.com/blogs/2009/07/17/world/worldwatch/entry5177137.shtml

Bairner, A. (2001). *Sport, nationalism, and globalization.* Albany: State University of New York Press.

Baxter, K. (2010, 14 June). World Cup: FIFA to fans—buzz off. *Los Angeles Times* (Internet edition). Retrieved June 25, 2010, from http://latimesblogs.latimes.com/sports_blog/2010/06/world-cup-fifa-to-fans-buzz-off.html

Baxter, L., & Montgomery, B. (1996). *Relating: Dialogues & dialectics.* New York, NY: Guilford Press.

Bode, M. (2014). Game on: America's sports leagues in emerging markets. *Harvard Political Review*. Retrieved from http://harvardpolitics.com/united-states/game-americas-sports-leagues-emerging-markets/

Bourhis, J., Adams, C., Titsworth, S., & Harter, L. (2004). *Selected material from human communication.* New York, NY: McGraw-Hill Custom.

British Esports Association. (2017). Esports: The world of competitive gaming—an overview. Retrieved from *www.britishesports.org/assets/WhatisesportsPDFOCT17V2pdf1.pdf*

Coakley, J. (2003). *Sport in society.* New York, NY: McGraw-Hill.

Coakley, J., & Donnelly, P. (1999). *Inside sports.* London, United Kingdom: Routledge.

Delaware North. (2015). The future of sports. Retrieved from http://futureof.org/wp-content/uploads/The-Future-of-Sports-2015-Report.pdf

Eschenfelder, M., & Li, M. (2006). *Economics of sport* (2nd ed.). Morgantown, WV: Fitness Information Technology.

Friedman, J. (1990). Being in the world: Globalization and localization. *Theory, Culture & Society*, 7, 311-328.

Giulianotti, R., & Robertson, R. (2009). *Globalization and football.* London, United Kingdom: Sage.

Giulianotti, R., Bonney, N., & Hepworth, M. (1994). *Football, violence and social identify.* London, United Kingdom: Routledge.

Hanvey, R. (1976). *An attainable global perspective.* Denver, CO: Center for Teaching International Relations.

Harris, P., & Moran, R. (1991). *Managing cultural differences* (3rd ed.). Houston, TX: Gulf.

Hersey, P. (1984). *The situational leader.* Escondido, CA: Center for Leadership Studies.

Horne, J. (2006). *Sport in consumer culture.* New York, NY: Palgrave.

Katz, D., & Kahn, R. (1978). *The social psychology of organizations* (2nd ed.). New York, NY: Wiley.

Keys, B. (2006). *Globalizing sport: National rivalry and international community in the 1930s.* Cambridge, MA: Harvard University Press.

Khanna, T., & Palepu, K. (2010). How to define emerging markets. *Forbes*. Retrieved from www.forbes.com/2010/05/27/winning-in-emerging-markets-opinions-book-excerpts-khanna-palepu.html#4df9d75060c4

Leonard, T. (2008, 21 July). West Ham fans brawl with Columbus Crew as football hooliganism hits the US. *Telegraph*. Retrieved July 14, 2009, from http://telegraph.co.uk

Maffesoli, M. (1996). *The time of the tribes.* Thousand Oaks, CA: Sage.

Magnússon, G. (2001). The internationalization of sports: The case of Iceland. *International Review for the Sociology of Sport*, 36, 59-69.

Maguire, J., Poulton, E., & Possamai, C. (1999). Weltkrieg III? Media coverage of England versus Germany in Euro 96. *Journal of Sport & Social Issues*, 23(4), 439-454.

Matchett, S. (2005). *The chariot makers: Assembling the perfect Formula 1 car.* London, United Kingdom: Orion Books.

McCormack, G. (2002). Things more important than football? Japan, Korea and the 2002 World Cup. In J. Horne and W. Mazenrieter (Eds.), *Japan, Korea and the 2002 World Cup* (pp. 29-42). London, United Kingdom: Routledge.

Mead, G. (1934). *Mind, self, & society from standpoint of a social behaviorist (volume 1).* Chicago, IL: University of Chicago Press.

Naisbitt, J. (1994). *Global paradox.* New York, NY: Avon Books.

Nielson. (2017). Commercial trends in sports 2017. *2017 Nielsen sports report*. Retrieved from www.nielsen.com/content/dam/nielsenglobal/ru/docs/Nielsen_Commercial%20Trends%20in%20Sports%202017.pdf

Newzoo. (2018). 2018 Global esports market report. Retrieved from https://asociacionempresarialesports.

es/wp-content/uploads/newzoo_2018_global_esports_market_report_excerpt.pdf

Olympic Day spreads Olympic values worldwide. (2010, 11 June). Retrieved June 22, 2010, from www.olympic.org/en/content/Olympism-in-Action/At-grassroot-level/Olympic_Day_spreads_Olympic_values_worldwide

Performance Communications. (n.d.). The future of the sports fan. Retrieved from www.fotball.no/globalassets/dommer/the-future-sports-fan_spilleregler_english.pdf

Perry, N. (2005). Close encounters of another kind: Nationalism, media representations and advertising in New Zealand rugby. In S. Jackson and D. Andrews (Eds.), *Sport, culture, and advertising: Identities, commodities and the politics of representation* (pp. 154-171). New York, NY: Routledge.

Pfahl, M. (2002). Buddhism and systems thinking: A conceptual framework for management actions in Thailand. *Journal of Global Business Review, 1*(1), 46-55.

Pfahl, M., & Bates, B. (2008). This is not a race, this is a farce: Formula One and the Indianapolis Motor Speedway tire crisis. *Public Relations Review, 34*(2), 135-144.

Plamintr, S. (1994). *Getting to know Buddhism.* Bangkok, Thailand: Buddhadhamma Foundation.

PWC. (2011). Changing the game: Outlook for the global sports market to 2015. Retrieved from www.pwc.com/sportsoutlook

Senge, P. (1994). *The fifth discipline: The art and practice of the learning organization.* New York, NY: Doubleday Business.

Socolow, B. (2016). Emerging sports—A decathlon of legal and business issues. New York, NY: Portfolio Media.

Wakeford, N. (2003). The embedding of local culture in global communication: Independent Internet cafés in London. *New Media & Society, 5*(3), 379-399.

Withers, T. (2009, 24 May). *Cavs sign ownership deal with China group.* Retrieved July 11, 2009, from http://sports.yahoo.com

Chapter 2

Adidas Group. (2016). *How we create value: Adidas Group annual report 2015.* Retrieved September 19, 2017, from www.adidas-group.com/media/filer_public/e9/73/e973acf3-f889-43e5-b3c0-bc870d53b964/2015_gb_en.pdf

Andreff, W., & Szymanski, S. (2006). *Handbook on the economics of sport.* Cheltenham, United Kingdom: Edward Elgar.

Armijo, L.E. (2007). The BRICs countries (Brazil, Russia, India, and China) as analytical category: Mirage or insight? *Asian Perspective,* 7-42.

Baker, R., Danylchuk, K., Gillentine, A., Johnson, P., Pitts, B.G., & Zhang, J.J. (2016). Internationalized sport management education: Bridging the gaps. In B.G. Pitts, &

J.J. Zhang (Eds.), *Global sport management: Contemporary issues and inquiries* (pp. 18-37). London, United Kingdom: Routledge.

Baker, T.A., Liu, X., Brison, N., & Pifer, N.D. (2017). Air Qiaodan: An examination of transliteration and trademark squatting in China based on Jordan vs Qiaodan sports. *International Journal of Sports Marketing and Sponsorship, 18*(1).

Banjeree, S., & Linstead, S. (2001). Globalization, multiculturalism and other fictions: Colonialism for the new millennium. *Organization, 8*(4), 683-722.

Barney, R.K. (1988). Physical education and sport in the United States. In E.F. Zeigler (Ed.), *History of physical education and sport* (pp. 173-219). Champaign, IL: Stipes.

BBC. (2016, May 14). *FIFA ends Indonesia's suspension from football after almost a year.* Retrieved August 26, 2017, from www.bbc.com/sport/football/36292992

Blinebury, F. (2016). Rockets embrace status as "China's Team." *NBA.* Retrieved April 9, 2017, from www.nba.com/article/2016/10/09/houston-rockets-chinas-team

Butler, B.N., & Dzikus, L. (2015). Sport labour migration: Understanding leisure activities of American professional basketball players abroad. *Leisure Studies, 34*(1), 67-81.

Coakley, J. (2017). *Sports in society: Issues and controversies* (12th ed.). New York, NY: McGraw-Hill.

Conn, D. (2016, October 18). Manchester City earns £20.5m profit on income of £392m in 2015-16 season. Retrieved August 26, 2017, from www.theguardian.com/football/2016/oct/18/manchester-city-record-income-2015-16-season

Cui, J. (2015, June). American influence on Chinese basketball. *Insight: The voice of the American Chamber of Commerce in Shanghai.* Retrieved May 5, 2017, from http://insight.amcham-shanghai.org/american-influence-on-chinese-basketball/

Darby, P., Akindes, G., & Kirwin, M. (2007). Football academies and the migration of African football labor to Europe. *Journal of Sport and Social Issues, 31*(2), 143-161.

Duerden, J. (2015). Chinese league draws big stars and top coaches. Retrieved August 27, 2017, from www.nytimes.com/2015/09/05/sports/soccer/chinese-league-draws-big-stars-and-top-coaches.html?mcubz=3

Dyreson, M. (2003). Globalizing the nation-making process: Modern sport in world history. *International Journal of the History of Sport, 20*(1), 91-106.

Eitzen, D.S. (2012). *Sport in contemporary society: An anthology* (9th ed.). Boulder, CO: Paradigm.

Feigen, J. (2016). NBA's presence in China grows on foundation built by Yao Ming, Rockets. *Houston Chronicle.* Retrieved April 9, 2017, from www.houstonchronicle.com/sports/rockets/article/NBA-s-presence-in-China-grows-on-foundation-built-9957515.php

FIFA. (2017). History of football—The origins. Retrieved May 5, 2017, from www.fifa.com/about-fifa/who-we-are/the-game/index.html

Fisher, L. (2017). Where are they now? A complete list of NHLers playing overseas. Retrieved September 19, 2017, from https://larry-fisher.com/2014/05/02/where-are-they-now-a-complete-list-of-nhlers-playing-overseas

García, B. (2004). Urban regeneration, arts programming and major events: Glasgow 1990, Sydney 2000 and Barcelona 2004. *International Journal of Cultural Policy, 10*(1), 103-118.

Gems, G.R., Borish, L.J., & Pfister, G. (2017). *Sports in American history: From colonization to globalization* (2nd ed.). Champaign, IL: Human Kinetics.

Glassford, R.G., & Redmond, G. (1988). Physical education and sport in modern times. In E.F. Zeigler (Ed.), *History of physical education and sport* (pp. 103-171). Champaign, IL: Stipes.

Green, B.C., & Chalip, L. (1998). Sport tourism as the celebration of subculture. *Annals of Tourism Research, 25*(2), 275-291.

Hallmann, K., Kaplanidou, K., & Breuer, C. (2010). Event image perceptions among active and passive sports tourists at marathon races. *International Journal of Sports Marketing and Sponsorship, 12*(1), 32-47.

Han, C.M. (1989). Country image: Halo or summary construct? *Journal of Marketing Research, 26*(2), 222-229.

Harris, N. (2013). New research: Foreign players at record levels across European football *Sporting Intelligence*. Retrieved May 9, 2017, from www.sportingintelligence.com/2013/01/21/new-research-foreign-players-at-record-levels-across-european-football-210102

Heaphy, L.A. (2003). *The Negro leagues 1869-1960*. Jefferson, NC: McFarland.

Henry, G. (2015). Blank makes it official: New MLS team is Atlanta United FC. Associated Press. Retrieved April 7, 2017, from www.espn.com/espn/wire?id=13218578&section=soccer

Hoang, H., & Rascher, D. (1999). The NBA, exit discrimination, and career earnings. *Industrial Relations, 38*(1), 69-91.

Howell, M.L., & Howell, R. (1988). Physical activities and sport in early societies. In E.F. Zeigler (Ed.), *History of physical education and sport* (pp. 1-56). Champaign, IL: Stipes.

Huang, H., Mao, L.L., Wang, J., & Zhang, J.J. (2015). Assessing the relationships between image congruence, tourist satisfaction and intention to revisit in marathon tourism: The Shanghai International Marathon. *International Journal of Sports Marketing and Sponsorship, 16*(4), 46-66.

International University Sports Federation. (2017). FISU history. Retrieved September 23, 2017, from www.fisu.net/fisu/history

Jain, S.C. (2006). *Emerging economies and the transformation of international business: Brazil, Russia, India and China (BRICs)*. Northamption, MA: Edward Elgar.

Kobrin, S.J. (2015). Is a global nonmarket strategy possible? Economic integration in a multipolar world order. *Journal of World Business, 50*(2), 262-272.

License Global. (2017, April 1). The top 150 global licensors. Retrieved August 26, 2017, from www.licensemag.com/license-global/top-150-global-licensors-3

Ling, Z. (2008). Basketball. In F. Hong, D. Mackay, & K. Christensen (Eds.), *China gold, China's quest for global power and Olympic glory* (pp. 37-40). Great Barrington, MA: Berkshire.

Lipsey, R.A. (2006). *The sporting goods industry: History, practices and products*. Jefferson, NC: McFarland.

Lipshez, K. (2017). College beat: Falcigno's eyes smiling as she continues education, basketball career in Ireland. *Record-Journal*. Retrieved September 17, 2017, from www.myrecordjournal.com/home/10804814-154/college-beat-falcignos-eyes-smiling-as-she-continues-education-basketball.html

Love, A., & Kim, S. (2011). Sport labor migration and collegiate sport in the United States: A typology of migrant athletes. *Journal of Issues in Intercollegiate Athletics, 4*(9), 90-104.

Maguire, J. (1996). Blade runners: Canadian migrants, ice hockey, and the global sports process. *Journal of Sport and Social Issues, 20*(3), 335-360.

Maguire, J. (2004). Sports and globalization. In J. Coakley & E. Dunning (Eds.), *Handbook of sports studies* (pp. 356-369). London, United Kingdom: Sage.

Maguire, J. (2008). "Real politic" or "ethically based": Sport, globalization, migration and nation-state policies. *Sport in Society, 11*(4), 443-458.

Maguire, J., Jarvie, G., Mansfield, L., & Bradley, J. (2002). *Sport worlds: A sociological perspective*. Champaign, IL: Human Kinetics.

Nadvi, K., Lund-Thomsen, P., Xue, H., & Khara, N. (2011). Playing against China: Global value chains and labour standards in the international sports goods industry. *Global Networks, 11*(3), 334-354.

NAFSA. (2017). Trends in U.S. study abroad. NAFSA. Retrieved September 21, 2017, from www.nafsa.org/Policy_and_Advocacy/Policy_Resources/Policy_Trends_and_Data/Trends_in_U_S__Study_Abroad

Naismith, J. (1941). *Basketball: Its origin and development*. New York, NY: Associates.

NBA. (2012). NBA continues to grow internationally. Retrieved April 8, 2017, from www.nba.com/2012/news/10/26/nba-international-growth.ap

NBA. (2016). NBA rosters feature record 113 international players from 41 countries and territories. Retrieved May 10, 2017, from http://pr.nba.com/nba-rosters-international-players-2016-17

NCAA. (2000). Sport sponsorship, participation and demographics search. Retrieved May 8, 2017, from http://web1.ncaa.org/rgdSearch/exec/saSearch

NCAA. (2016). Sport sponsorship, participation and demographics search. Retrieved May 8, 2017, from http://web1.ncaa.org/rgdSearch/exec/saSearch

NCAA. (2017). International student-athletes. Retrieved September 21, 2017, from www.ncaa.org/student-athletes/future/international-student-athletes

OECD. (2017). Education Database: Enrollment of international students by origin, OECD Education Statistics (database).

O'Rourke, P. (2016). Boca's Carlos Tevez offered record Shanghai Shenhua wage—sources. Retrieved May 13, 2017, from www.espnfc.com/story/3023887/boca-juniors-carlos-tevez-offered-record-shanghai-shenhua-wage-sources

Oates, T., & Polumbaum, J. (2004). Agile big man: The flexible marketing of Yao Ming. *Pacific Affairs, 77*(2), 187-210.

Pac12. (2016a). Pac-12 All-Stars end trip to Australia with new friendships, insights. Retrieved May 13, 2017, from http://pac-12.com/article/2016/07/15/pac-12-all-stars-end-trip-australia-new-friendships-insights

Pac12. (2016b). Pac-12 extends agreement with Alibaba Group to support basketball game in China. Retrieved May 11, 2017, from http://pac-12.com/article/2016/11/10/pac-12-extends-agreement-alibaba-group-support-basketball-game-china

Pedace, R. (2008). Earnings, performance, and nationality discrimination in a highly competitive labor market as an analysis of the English professional soccer league. *Journal of Sports Economics, 9*(2), 115-140.

Poli, R., Ravenel, L., & Besson, R. (2017). World expatriate footballers. Retrieved May 10, 2017, from www.football-observatory.com/IMG/sites/mr/mr25/en

Pope, S.W. (1997). *Patriotic games: Sporting traditions in the American imagination, 1876-1926.* New York, NY: Oxford University Press.

Pope, S.W. (2010). The World War I American military sporting experience. In D.K. Wiggins (Ed.), *Sport in America: From colonial leisure to celebrity figures and globalization* (Vol. II, pp. 199-219). Champaign, IL: Human Kinetics.

Preuss, H., & Alfs, C. (2011). Signaling through the 2008 Beijing Olympics—using mega sport events to change the perception and image of the host. *European Sport Management Quarterly, 11*(1), 55-71.

Price, S. (2017). Why Chinese clubs are breaking transfer records—and why players are wise to go. Retrieved May 12, 2017, from www.theguardian.com/football/these-football-times/2017/jan/05/china-chinese-super-league-oscar-carlos-tevez

Richard, S., & Jones, I. (2008). The great suburban Everest: An "insiders" perspective on experiences at the 2007 Flora London Marathon. *Journal of Sport & Tourism, 13*(1), 61-77.

Ridinger, L.L., & Pastore, D.L. (2000). International student-athlete adjustment to college: A preliminary analysis. *NACADA Journal, 20*(1), 33-41.

Rowe, D. (2003). Sport and the repudiation of the globe. *International Review for the Sociology of Sport, 38*(3) 281-294.

Sage, G., & Eitzen, D.S. (2013). *Sociology of North American sport* (9th ed.). New York, NY: Oxford University Press.

Schwartz, E., Jamieson, N.I., & Pitts, B.G. (2015). The role of demography and migration in shaping the future of leisure, recreation, and sport. *International Journal of Sport Management, 16*(4), 620-644.

Seymore, H. (1990). *Baseball: The people's game.* New York, NY: Oxford University Press.

Soper, S. (2015). NCAA basketball is coming to China, with help from Alibaba. Retrieved May 11, 2017, from www.bloomberg.com/news/articles/2015-05-13/ncaa-basketball-is-coming-to-china-with-help-from-alibaba

Sport Changes Life. (2017). About sport changes life. Retrieved September 21, 2017, from www.sandiegouniontribune.com/sdut-ny-startup-helps-us-student-athletes-play-abroad-2013oct20-story.html

STAC. (2015). *Canadian sepak takraw history.* Retrieved August 26, 2017, from http://takrawcanada.com/?q=node/6#block-block-3

Swanson, R.A., & Spears, B. (1995). *History of sport and physical education in the United States* (4th ed.). Dubuque, IA: Wm. C. Brown & Benchmark.

Tainsky, S., & Winfree, J.A. (2010). Discrimination and demand: The effect of international players on attendance in Major League Baseball. *Social Science Quarterly, 91*(1), 117-128.

Telegraph. (2016). Carlos Tevez signs £615,000-a-week deal with Shanghai Shenhua. Retrieved May 13, 2017, from www.telegraph.co.uk/football/2016/12/29/carlos-tevez-signs-shanghai-shenhua-latest-big-money-move-chinese

The history of soccer. (n.d.). Retrieved May 10, 2017, from www.athleticscholarships.net/history-of-soccer-football.htm

Thompson, C. (2013). NY startup helps U.S. student-athletes play abroad. Retrieved October 20, 2013, from www.sandiegouniontribune.com/sdut-ny-startup-helps-us-student-athletes-play-abroad-2013oct20-story.html

Thornburg, C. (2016). Opening Day rosters feature 238 international players. Retrieved May 10, 2017, from http://m.mlb.com/news/article/170477992/mlb-rosters-feature-238-international-players

Van Tulder, R., & Kolk, A. (2001). Multinationality and corporate ethics: Codes of conduct in the sporting goods industry. *Journal of International Business Studies, 32*(2), 267-283.

Woods, R.B. (2016). *Social issues in sport* (3rd ed.). Champaign, IL: Human Kinetics.

Zhang, J.J., Chen, K.K., & Kim, J.J. (2014) Leadership on a global scale. In J.F. Borland, G.M. Kane, & L.J. Burton (Eds.), *Sport leadership in the 21st century* (pp. 327-346). Burlington, MA: Jones & Bartlett.

Zhang, J.J., Huang, R.H., & Wang, J.J. (2017). Introduction. In J.J. Zhang, R.H. Huang, & J. Nauright (Eds.), *Development of international sport industry* (pp. 5-27). Beijing, China: Social Science.

Zhang, J.J., Pitts, B.G., & Kim, E. (2017). Introduction: Sport marketing in a globalized marketplace. In J.J. Zhang & B.G. Pitts (Eds.), *Contemporary sport marketing: Global perspectives* (pp. 3-22). London, United Kingdom: Routledge.

Chapter 3

Buist, E. A., & Mason, D. S. (2010). Newspaper framing and stadium subsidization. *American Behavioral Scientist, 53*(10), 1492-1510.

Canadian Collegiate Athletic Association. (2017). *CCAA overview.* Retrieved on May 24, 2017, from http://ccaa.ca/information/inside/overview

Canadian Heritage. (2002). *The Canadian sport policy.* Ottawa, Canada: Minister of Public Works and Government Services.

Canadian Heritage. (2012a). *Canadian sport policy summary sheet.* Retrieved on May 24, 2017, from http://sirc.ca/sites/default/files/content/docs/pdf/csp_sheet_en.pdf

Canadian Heritage. (2012b). *Sport participation 2010. Research paper.* Retrieved on June 6, 2017, from http://publications.gc.ca/site/eng/9.698943/publication.html

CBS News. (2018). *Super Bowl LII: Ratings for football's biggest game lowest since 2009.* Retrieved on October 4, 2018, from www.cbsnews.com/news/super-bowl-lii-tv-ratings/

Church, A. G. (2008). *Pressure groups and Canadian sport policy: A neo-pluralist examination of policy development.* PhD. Dissertation. London: The University of Western Ontario.

Fort, R., & Quirk, J. (1995). Cross-subsidization, incentives, and outcomes in professional team sports leagues. *Journal of Economic literature, 33*(3), 1265-1299.

Green, B.C. (2005). Building sport programs to optimize athlete recruitment, retention, and transition: Towards a normative theory of sport development. *Journal of Sport Management, 19,* 233-253.

Guttman, A. (1988). The Cold War and the Olympics. *International Journal, 43*(4), 554-568. DOI: 10.2307/40202563

Haring, B. (2017). *ESPN Tennis Triumph: US Open Women's Championship Ratings 36 Percent Higher.* Retrieved on October 4, 2017, from http://deadline.com/2017/09/espn-tennis-ratings-up-36-percent-for-us-womens-open-championship-triumph-us-open-womens-battle-36-percent-higher-1202166188/

Hill, J.B. (2007, April 14). Robinson affected American society. *MLB News.* Retrieved from http://m.mlb.com/news/article/1898206//

Houlihan, B. (1997). *Sport, policy and politics: A comparative analysis.* London, United Kingdom: Routledge.

Huma, R. & Staurowsky, E.J. (2012). The $6 billion heist: Robbing college athletes under the guide of amateurism. A report collaboratively produced by the National College Players Association and Drexel University Sport Management. Available online at http://assets.usw.org/ncpa/pdfs/6-Billion-Heist-Study_Full.pdf

Hums, M.A., & MacLean, J.C. (2017). *Governance and policy in sport organizations* (3rd ed.) New York, NY: Taylor and Francis.

Hylton, J.G. (1999). Why baseball's antitrust exemption still survives. *Marquette Sports Law Review, 9*(2), 391-402.

International Health, Racquet, and Sportsclub Association. (2017, May 31). *About the industry.* Retrieved from www.ihrsa.org/about-the-industry/

Johnson, E.L. (1979). *History of YMCA physical education.* Chicago, IL: Association Press.

Kennedy, S.S., & Rosentraub, M.S. (2000). Public-private partnerships, professional sports teams, and the protection of the public's interests. *American Review of Public Administration, 30*(4), 436-459.

Ligaya, A. (2013, February 1). *Why funding new sports stadiums can be a losing bet.* CBC News. Retrieved from http://www.cbc.ca/news/canada/why-funding-new-sports-stadiums-can-be-a-losing-bet-1.1378210 on July 5, 2018.

Macintosh, D., Bedecki, T., & Franks, C.E.S. (1987). *Sport and politics in Canada: Federal government involvement since 1961.* Montreal, Canada: McGill-Queen's University Press.

Macintosh, D., & Whitson, D. (1990). *The game planners: transforming Canada's sport system.* Montreal, Canada: McGill-Queen's University Press.

Metcalfe, A. (1987). *Canada learns to play: The emergence of organized sport, 1807-1914.* Toronto, Canada: McClelland and Stewart.

National Collegiate Athletic Association. (2010, November 8). *History.* Retrieved from https://web.archive.org/web/20110807060521/http://www.ncaa.org/wps/wcm/connect/public/ncaa/about+the+ncaa/who+we+are/about+the+ncaa+history

National Collegiate Athletic Association. (n.d.). *Divisional differences and the history of the multidivision classification.* Retrieved from http://www.ncaa.org/about/who-we-are/membership/divisional-differences-and-history-multidivision-classification

PFRA Research. (n.d.). *Camp and his followers: American football 1876-1889*. Retrieved from www.profootballre-searchers.org/articles/Camp_And_Followers.pdf

Physical Activity Council. (2017). *2017 Participation report.* Retrieved from www.physicalactivitycouncil.com/pdfs/current.pdf

Povich, E.S. (2016, July 13). Why should public money be used to build sports stadiums? *PBS Newshour.* Retrieved from http://www.pbs.org/newshour/rundown/public-money-used-build-sports-stadiums/

Rosenwald, M.S. (2016, May 17). Youth sports participation is up slightly, but many kids are still left behind. *Washington Post.* Retrieved from www.washingtonpost.com/news/local/wp/2016/05/17/youth-sports-participation-is-up-slightly-but-many-kids-are-still-left-behind/?utm_term=.0b2d3055b9d0

Sam, M.P. (2011). Building legitimacy at Sport Canada: Pitfalls of public value creation? *International Review of Administrative Sciences*, 77(4), 757-778.

Schaefer-Jacobs, D. (2012, August 2). *Civil War baseball.* Retrieved from http://americanhistory.si.edu/blog/2012/08/civil-war-baseball.html

Simeon, R., Robinson, I., & Wallner, J. (2014). The dynamics of Canadian federalism. In J. Bickerton & A.G. Gagnon (Eds.), *Canadian politics* (6th ed.) (pp. 156-178). Toronto, Canada: University of Toronto Press.

Southall, R.M., & Staurowsky, E.J. (2013). Cheering on the collegiate model: Creating, disseminating, and imbedding the NCAA's redefinition of amateurism. *Journal of Sport and Social Issues*, 37(4), 403-429.

Sparvero, E., Chalip, L., & Green, B.C. (2012). United States. In B. Houlihan & M. Green (Eds.), *Comparative elite sport development* (pp. 242–271). Kidlington/Oxford, United Kingdom: Elsevier Butterworth-Heinemann.

Springfield College. (2015, October 20). *The "birth of basketball."* Retrieved from http://springfieldcollegepride.com/information/birthplace_basketball

Thibault, L. (2017). Canada: An evolving sport system. In J. Scheerder, A. Willem, and E. Claes (Eds.), *Sport policy systems and sport federations: A cross-national perspective* (pp. 65-88). Palgrave-MacMillan, London, United Kingdom.

Toronto2015. (2015). *About the Pan Am Games.* Retrieved on October 4, 2018, from http://HYPERLINK "http://www.toronto2015.org/about-us/pan-am-games" www.toronto2015.org/about-us/pan-am-games

U.S. Department of Health and Human Services. (n.d.). *Our history.* Retrieved from www.hhs.gov/fitness/about-pcfsn/our-history/index.html

U Sports. (2017). *History of U Sports.* Retrieved May 24, 2017, from http://en.usports.ca/information/about_cis/cishistory

Vasilogambros, M. (2016, July 12). When athletes take political stands. *Atlantic.* Retrieved from www.the-atlantic.com/news/archive/2016/07/when-athletes-take-political-stands/490967/

Wang, C. (2016, April 5). How a health nut created the world's biggest fitness trend. *CNBC.* Retrieved from www.cnbc.com/2016/04/05/how-crossfit-rode-a-single-issue-to-world-fitness-domination.html

Chapter 4

Arbena, J.L. (2002). The later evolution of modern sport in Latin America: The North American influence. In J.A. Mangan & L.P. DaCosta (Eds.), *Sport in Latin American society* (pp. 43-58). London, United Kingdom: Frank Cass.

Arbena, J.L., & LaFrance, D.G. (2002). Introduction. In J.L. Arbena & D.G. LaFrance (Eds.), *Sport in Latin America and the Caribbean* (pp. xi-xxxi). Wilmington, DE: Scholarly Resources.

BDO. (2017). *10° valor das marcas dos clubes brasileiros. Finanças dos clubes.* Retrieved from www.bdo.com.br/pt-br/publicacoes/noticias-em-destaque/10%C2%BA-valor-das-marcas-dos-clubes-brasileiros

Bermejo Vera, J., Gamero Casado, E., & Palomar Olmedo, A. (2003). *Poderes públicos y deporte.* Sevilla, Spain: Consejería de Turismo y Deporte.

Berry, A. (2013, April 1). More than one quarter of players born outside US. *MLB.com.* Retrieved from www.mlb.com/news/more-than-one-quarter-of-mlb-players-born-outside-us/c-43619160

Bravo, G. (2013). Brazil. In I. O'Boyle & T. Bradbury (Eds.), *Sport governance: International case studies* (pp. 142-155). London, United Kingdom: Routledge.

Bravo, G., Shonk, D., Silva-Borquez, J., & González-Mesina, S. (2018). *Sport mega-events in emerging economies: The South American Games of Santiago 2014.* London, United Kingdom: Mega Event Planning. Palgrave Pivot.

Cabralis, S. (2016). Trinidad and Tobago Women's Premier Soccer League. In B.G. Pitts (Ed.), *Case studies in sport marketing* (pp. 125-130). Morgantown, WV: Fitness Information Technology.

Capretti, S. (2010). La cultura en juego. El deporte en la sociedad moderna y post-moderna. *Trabajo y Sociedad*, 16, 231-250.

CARICOM. (n. d.). Tourism: Overview. Retrieved from https://caricom.org/work-areas/overview/tourism/P80

Chalip, L. (2015). A challenge of why sport matters: Managing sport for society. In M. Bowers & M. Dixon (Eds.), *Sport management: An exploration of the field and its value* (pp. 1-14). Urbana, IL: Sagamore.

Cobley, A.G. (2010). The Caribbean. In S.W. Pope & John Nauright (Eds.), *Routledge companion to sports history* (pp. 375-390). London, United Kingdom: Routledge.

Corruption and sport: Building integrity and preventing abuses. (2009). *Transparency international.* Working paper 03/2009. Berlin, Germany. Retrieved from www.transparency.org/publications/publications/working_papers/wp_03_2009_sport_and_corruption_9_september_2009

Darko, N., & Mackintosh, C. (2015). Challenges and constraints in developing and implementing sports policy and provision in Antigua and Barbuda: Which way for now for a small island state? *International Journal of Sport Policy and Politics, 7*(3), 365-390.

Doig, A. (1995). Mixed signals? Public sector change and the proper conduct of public business. *Public Administration, 73*, 191-212.

Eakin, M.C. (2004). Does Latin America have a common history? *Vanderbilt e-Journal of Luso-Hispanic Studies, I*, 29-49.

ECLAC. (2015). *Statistical yearbook of Latin America and the Caribbean*. Santiago, Chile: Economic Commission for Latin America and the Caribbean.

Elsey, B. (2009). The independent republic of football: The politics of neighborhood clubs in Santiago, Chile, 1948-1960. *Journal of Social History, 42*(3), 605-630.

Geeraert, A. (2016). *The EU in international sports governance: A principal-agent perspective on EU control of FIFA and UEFA*. Houndmills, Basingstoke, United Kingdom: Palgrave Macmillan.

Graça, A., & Kasznar, I. (2002). *O esporte como industria: Solução para criação de riqueza e emprego*. Rio de Janeiro, Brazil: Confederação Brasileira de Voleibol.

Gregory, S. (2010, July 26). Struck out by béisbol. In the Dominican Republic, teens become prey to big-league dreams. *Time, 176*(4), 44-49.

Griggs, G. (2006). Calypso to collapso: The decline of the West Indies as a cricketing super power. *Journal of Sport and Social Issues, 30*(3), 306-314.

Grindle, M. (2010). *Constructing, deconstructing, and reconstructing career civil service systems in Latin America*. Faculty Research Working Paper Series. Harvard Kennedy School.

Houlihan, B., & Zheng, J. (2015). Small states: Sport and politics at the margin. *International Journal of Sport Policy and Politics, 7*(3): 329-344.

Hyde, M. (2017, September 6). IOC selective blindness continues but 2016 scandal looks all too familiar. *The Guardian*. Retrieved from www.theguardian.com/sport/blog/2017/sep/06/ioc-rio-2016-corruption-vote-buying

Keech, M. (2016). Sport policy as a tool for developing countries. In G. Bravo, R. López de D'Amico, and C. Parrish (Eds.), *Sport in Latin America: Policy, organization, management* (pp. 21-33). London, United Kingdom: Routledge.

Klein, A.M. (1991). *Sugarball: The American game, the Dominican dream*. New Haven, CT: Yale University Press.

Ksiazek, T. B., & Webster, J. G. (2008). Cultural proximity and audience behavior: The role of language in patterns of polarization and multicultural fluency. *Journal of Broadcasting and Electronic Media, 52*(3), 485-503.

Lagesse, D. (2016, April 3). Baseball is a field of dreams—and dashed hopes—for Dominicans. *NPR*. Retrieved from www.npr.org/sections/goatsandsoda/2016/04/03/472699693/baseball-is-a-field-of-dreams-and-dashed-hopes-for-dominicans

Latino Baseball. (2015, May 7). The Caribbean World Series. Retrieved from http://latinobaseball.com/the-caribbean-world-series/

López de D'Amico, R. (2012). Policy in Venezuela. *International Journal of Sport Policy and Politics, 4*(1), 139-151.

Mandle, J.R., & Mandle, J.D. (2002). The failure of Caribbean integration: Lessons from grassroots basketball. In J.L. Arbena & D.G. LaFrance (Eds.), *Sport in Latin America and the Caribbean* (pp. 163-174). Wilmington, DE: Scholarly Resources.

Masters, A. (2015). Corruption in sport: From the playing field to the field of policy. *Policy and Society, 34*(2), 111-123.

Miller, R. (2012): Great players, bad business. *Revista. Harvard Review for Latin America*. Retrieved from https://revista.drclas.harvard.edu/book/greater-players-bad-business

McCree, R. (2016). Sociology of sport: English-speaking Caribbean. In K. Young (Ed.), *Sociology of sport: A global subdiscipline in review* (pp. 343-359). Bingley, United Kingdom: Emerald.

Menin, R. (2013, December 17). A Industria do esporte. *InfoMoney*. Retrieved from www.infomoney.com.br/blogs/imoveis/blog-do-rubens-menin/post/3106092/industria-esporte

Montoute, A., & Abdenur, A.E. (2018). CARICOM and rising powers: India, China, and Brazil's South-South cooperation in the region. In P. Lewis, T. Gilbert-Roberts, & J. Byron (Eds.), *Pan-Caribbean Integration: Beyond CARICOM* (pp. 206-223). London, United Kingdom: Routledge.

Nef, J. (2007). Public administration and public sector reform in Latin America. In G. Peters & J. Pierre (Eds.), *Handbook of public administration* (pp. 323-335). Thousand Oaks, CA: Sage.

O'Boyle, I., & Bradbury, T. (2013). *Sport governance: International case studies*. London, United Kingdom: Routledge.

Perez, S., & Forero, J. (2015, May 25). The FIFA scandal: Arrests put Latin America in spotlight. *Wall Street Journal*. Retrieved from www.wsj.com/articles/fifa-scandal-puts-latin-america-in-spotlight-1432769540

Poli, R., Besson, R., & Ravenel, L. (2018, June). Football analytics. The CIES Football Observatory 2017/18 season. *CIES*. Retrieved from www.football-observatory.com

PWC. (2011). Changing the game. Outlook for the global sport market to 2015. Retrieved from www.pwc.com/gx/

en/industries/hospitality-leisure/publications/changing-the-game-outlook-for-the-global-sports-market-to-2015.html

Rampersad, A. (2011). The social and cultural consequences of Cricket World Cup 2007: Poor spectatorship in Trinidad and Tobago. In L. Jordan, B. Tyson, C. Hayle, and D. Truly (Eds.), *Sports event management: The Caribbean experience* (pp. 97-110). London, United Kingdom: Routledge.

Rocha, C.M. (2016). Public sector and sport development in Brazil. In G. Bravo, R. López de D'Amico, & C. Parrish (Eds.), *Sport in Latin America: Policy, organization, management* (pp. 77-88). London, United Kingdom: Routledge.

Soria, S., & Maldonado, A. (2016). The long and winding road of the football industry in Chile. In G. Bravo, R. López de D'Amico, & C. Parrish (Eds.), *Sport in Latin America: Policy, organization, management* (pp. 253-269). London, United Kingdom: Routledge.

Spagnuolo, D.L. (2003). Swinging for the fence: A call for institutional reform as Dominican boys risk their futures for a chance in Major League Baseball. *University of Pennsylvania Journal of International Economic Law, 24*(1), 263-287.

Toomer, R. (2015). Jamaica. *International Journal of Sport Policy and Politics, 7*(3), 457-471.

van Bottenburg, M. (2001). *Global games.* Urbana: University of Illinois Press.

Wiarda, H.J., & Kline, H.F. (2007). *Latin American politics and development* (6th ed.). Cambridge, MA: Westview Press.

Williamson, R.C. (1997). *Latin American societies in transition.* Westport, CT: Praeger.

Chapter 5

Andreff, W. (1999). Les finances du sport et l'éthique sportive. *Revue d'économie financière, 55*(5), 135-175. https://doi.org/10.3406/ecofi.1999.4939

Andreff, W., Bourg, J.F., Halba, B., & Nys, J.F. (1994). *Les enjeux économiques du sport en Europe : Financement et impact économique.* Strasbourg, France: Conseil de l'Europe.

Bergonzoni, A. (2016). Le poids économique du sport en 2013. La dépense sportive nationale croît plus vite que le PIB. *Stat-Info, 16*(03). Retrieved from http://sports.gouv.fr/IMG/pdf/le_poids_economique_du_sports_en_2013-2.pdf

Bodet, G. (2009), Sport participation and consumption and post-modern society: From Apollo to Dionysus? *Loisir et Société/Society and Leisure, 32*(2), 223-241.

Bosscher, V.D., Sotiriadou, P., & Bottenburg, M. van. (2013). Scrutinizing the sport pyramid metaphor: An examination of the relationship between elite success and mass participation in Flanders. *International Journal of Sport*

Policy and Politics, 5(3), 319-339. https://doi.org/10.1080/19406940.2013.806340

Chantelat, P. (2010). *Sport, économie et management.* Paris, France: Economica. Retrieved from www.economica.fr/livre-sport-economie-et-management-chantelat-pascal,fr,4,9782717856019.cfm

Council of European Union. (2017). *Resolution of the Council and of the Representatives of the Governments of the Member States, meeting within the Council, on the European Union Work Plan for Sport (1 July 2017-31 December 2020), Council Resolution (23 May 2017)* (resolution No. 9639/17 SPORT 41). Brussels, Belgium: General Secretariat of the Council. Retrieved from http://data.consilium.europa.eu/doc/document/ST-9639-2017-INIT/en/pdf

Department for Culture, Media and Sport. (2011). *Taking part: The national survey of culture, leisure and sport, 2010-2011; adult and child data* [computer file]. Colchester, Essex, United Kingdom: UK Data Archive [distributor], August 2011. SN: 6855.

Downward, P., & Rasciute, S. (2011). Does sport make you happy? An analysis of the well-being derived from sports participation. *International Review of Applied Economics, 25*(3), 331-348. https://doi.org/10.1080/02692171.2010.511168

European Commission. (2014), *Special Eurobarometer 412: Sport and physical activity,* Brussels, Belgium: European Commission.

Estadistica. (2015). Encuesta de habitos desportivos en Espana 2015. Subdirección General de Estadística y Estudios, Secretaría General Técnica Ministerio de Educación, Cultura y Deporte.

Groupe AMNYOS Consultants. (2008). *Study of public and private financing of sport in Europe.* Minister for Health, Youth, Sport and the Voluntary Sector. Retrieved from www.amnyos.com/documents/amnyos_sport_synthese_FR.pdf

Lamprecht, M., Fischer, A., & Stamm, H.P. (2014). *Sport Suisse 2014: Activité et consommation sportives de la population suisse.* Macolin, Switerland: Office fédéral du sport OFSPO.

Lefèvre, B., & Ohl, F. (2012). Consuming sports: distinction, univorism and omnivorism, *Sport in Society, 15,* 44-63.

Lefèvre B., & Thiéry, P. (dir.). (2010). *Les pratiques des activités physiques et sportives en France 2010.* MEOS/INSEP/CNDS.

Llopis-Goig, R., Lefèvre, B., & Routier, G. (2017). Un análisis comparativo de las prácticas físico-deportivas en España y Francia a partir de encuestas nacionales. *Revista Española de Educación Física y Deportes, 6*(16), 482490.

NACE classification. (2002). http://ec.europa.eu/eurostat/ramon/nomenclatures/index.cfm?TargetUrl=LST_NOM_DTL&StrNom=NACE_1_1&StrLanguageCode=

EN&IntPcKey=&StrLayoutCode=HIERARCHIC&CFID =1110191&CFTOKEN=3ca0f6dadb71d377-1F2DE4F0-F7BF-BCAE-31C18C386EA88F92&jsessionid=ee30bfd 4a9bb1c743436)

NACE classification. (2008). http://ec.europa.eu/eurostat/ ramon/nomenclatures/index.cfm?TargetUrl=LST_ NOM_DTL&StrNom=NACE_REV2&StrLanguageCo de=EN&IntPcKey=&StrLayoutCode=HIERARCHIC)

OECD. (2016) https://data.oecd.org/gdp/gross-domes-tic-product-gdp.htm#indicator-chart

Scheerder, J., & Vos, S. (2011). Social stratification in adults' sports participation from a time-trend perspec-tive: Results from a 40-year household study. *European Journal for Sport and Society*, 8(1-2), 31-44.

SportsEconAustria, Sport Industry Research Centre, Sta-tistical Service of the Republic of Cyprus, Meerwaarde Sport en Economie, Federation of the European Sporting Goods Industry, & Ministry of Sport and Tourism of the Republic of Poland. (2012). *Study on the contribution of sport to economic growth and employment in the EU.* European Commission, Directorate-General Education and Culture.

Sullivan, O., & Katz-Gerro, T. (2007). The omnivore thesis revisited: Voracious cultural consumers. *European Socio-logical Review*, 23(2), 123-137.

Chapter 6

Balyi, I. (2001) Sport System Building and Long-term Athlete Development in British Columbia. Canada: SportsMed BC. Retrieved from http://iceskatin-gresources.org/ SportsSystemDevelopment.pdf

BBC. (2004a). Sport 'improves boys' behaviour. Retrieved June 14, 2004, from http:// news.bbc.co.uk/2/hi/ uk_news/education/3804793.stm.

BBC. (2004b). Specialist schools now a majority. Retrieved January 29, 2004, from http:// news.bbc.co.uk/2/hi/ uk_news/education/3438825.stm.

Bompa, T. O. (1983). *Theory and methodology of training: The key to athletic performance.* Dubuque, IA: Kendall/Hunt.

Bompa, T. O., & Haff, G. G. (2009). *Periodization: Theory and methodology of training.* Champaign, IL: Human Kinetics.

Bundesliga. (2017). German soccer rules: 50+1 explained. Retrieved February 26, 2018, from www.bundes-liga.com/en/news/Bundesliga/german-soccer-rules-50-1-fifty-plus-one-explained-466583.jsp

CBC. (2016, November 3). Russia approves anti-doping law targeting coaches. Associated Press. Retrieved February 26, 2018, from www.cbc.ca/sports/olympics/russia-anti-doping-law-coaches-1.3834669

Cafebabel. (2008, June 3). Football in Poland is more cor-rupt than in Italy. Retrieved May 10, 2017, from www. cafebabel.co.uk/lifestyle/article/football-in-poland-is-more-corrupt-than-in-italy.html

Chien, P.M., Kelly, S.J., & Weeks, C.S. (2016). Sport scandal and sponsorship decisions: Team identification matters. *Journal of Sport Management*, 30(5), 490-505.

Cooper Institute for Aerobics Research. (2013). The Cooper Institute signs agreement with Hungarian School Sport Federation. Retrieved from http://cooperinstitute.org/ pub/news.cfm?id=146

DaCosta, L.P. & Miragaya, A. (Eds.) (2002). *World experi-ences and trends of sport for all.* Oxford, United Kingdom: Meyer & Meyer Sport.

Davies, G. (2008). Specialist sports colleges make the grade. *Telegraph.* Retrieved February 1, 2008, from http:// www.telegraph.co.uk/sport/2290634/Specialist-Sports-Collegesmake-the-grade.html.

Duerden, J. (2017, November 16). Russia's chance to get into 2018 Winter Olympics suffers another blow after WADA decision. Associated Press. Retrieved from https://globalnews.ca/news/3863861/russia-doping-2018-olympics-wada/

Gál, A. (2012, July). Society and sport in Central Europe, particularly in Hungary. Glasgow, United Kingdom: World Congress of Sociology of Sport, Glasgow Cale-donian University.

Giles, T. (2017, 16 December). Russian Duma adopts new law allowing removal of coaches who violate doping rules. Retrieved from www.insidethegames.biz/arti-cles/1059194/russian-duma-adopts-new-law-allowing-removal-of-coaches-who-violate-doping-rules

Girginov, V., & Bankov, P. (2002). Bulgaria: Sport for all from a way of life to a matter of choice. In, DaCosta, L. P. & Miragaya, A. (Eds.). *World experiences and trends of sport for all.* Oxford: Meyer & Meyer Sport.

Giulianelli, E., & Malyon, E. (2017, January 25). Wracked by corruption and mismanagement, Romanian football is in crisis as players start to walk away. *The Independent.* Retrieved from www.independent.co.uk/sport/football/ european/wracked-by-corruption-and-mismanage-ment-romanian-football-is-in-crisis-as-players-walk-away-from-the-a7543666.html

Igoshev, M.V., & Apletin, A.A. (2014, May). Current human resources situation in Russia and need to increase the role of physical culture and sport. International Con-gress "Nations' Health: Systems of Lifelong Physical Education as a Foundation of Public Health," Moscow, Russia.

Inchenko, I.V. (2014, May). Solving social problems through sport and physical culture services. International Con-gress "Nations' Health: Systems of Lifelong Physical Education as a Foundation of Public Health," Moscow, Russia.

Johnson, S. (2012). Russian Olympic Committee prom-ises huge financial rewards for winning Olympic gold. Retrieved from http://ca.sports.yahoo.com/olympics/ news?slug=ycn-10877957

Keating X.D., Smolianov, P., Liu, X., Castro-Piñero, J., Smith, J. (2018). Youth fitness testing practices: Global trends and new development. *Sport Journal*. Retrieved March 1, 2018, from http://thesportjournal.org/article/youth-fitness-testing-practices-global-trends-and-new-development/

Kihl, L.A., Skinner, J., & Engelberg, T. (2017). Corruption in sport: Understanding the complexity of corruption. *European Sport Management Quarterly, 17*(1), 1-5.

lenta.ru (2016, October 11). Putin called to reduce public funding of professional sport. Retrieved October 11, 2016, from https://m.lenta.ru/news/2016/10/11/putin-sportbudget/

Matveev, L. P. (1964). *Problema periodizatsii sportivnoj trenirovki (Periodization of sport training)*. Moscow: Physical Culture and Sport.

Matveev, L. P. (2008). Teoriya i metodika fizicheskoj kul'tury (Theory and methodology of physical culture). Moscow: Physical Culture and Sport-SportAcademPress.

Platonov, V. N. (1988). *L'entrainement sportif: Theorie et methode. (Sport training: Theory and method)* Paris: Ed. EPS.

Platonov, V. N. (2005). *Sistema podgotovki sportsmenov v Olimpijskom sporte (System of preparation of athletes in Olympic sport)*. Moscow: Soviet Sport

Pochinkin, A.V. (2006). *Formation and development of professional commercial sport in Russia*. Moscow,: Soviet Sport.

Riordan, J. (1980). *Sport in Soviet society: Development of sport and physical education in Russia and the USSR*. Cambridge, United Kingdom: Cambridge University Press.

Ruizjan, R.R. (January 10, 2017). National antidoping groups, citing doping, want Russian athletes barred. *New York Times*. Retrieved January 10, 2017, from www.nytimes.com/2017/01/10/sports/olympics/national-antidoping-groups-citing-doping-want-russian-athletes-barred.html?action=click&contentCollection=Sports&module=RelatedCoverage&region=Marginalia&pgtype=article

RT. (2010). Gazprom to spend $130 mln on Russian Olympians. Retrieved from http://rt.com/sport/gazprom-russian-olympic-sponsorship/

Salzman, B. (2015, January 26). A bleak future for Eastern European soccer. Retrieved January 26, 2015, from https://sites.duke.edu/wcwp/2015/01/26/a-bleak-future-for-eastern-european-soccer/

Schwartz, M. (2008). A major tuneup for a sports machine. *New York Times*. Retrieved July 29, 2008, from www.nytimes.com/2008/07/29/sports/olympics/29russia.html?th&emc=th

Shneidman, N. N. (1978). *The Soviet road to Olympus: Theory and practice of Soviet physical culture and sport*. Toronto, Canada: The Ontario Institute for Studies in Education.

Smirnova, L. (2018). Football supporters hit the pitch at the fan World Cup. *The Moscow Times*. Available at: https://themoscowtimes.com/articles/fan-world-cup-62036. Accessed 1st July 2018.

Smolianov, P., & Zakus, D.H. (2008). Exploring high performance management in Olympic sport with reference to practices in the former USSR and Russia. *International Journal of Sport Management, 9*, 206-232.

Sport Ministry. (2012, 2017). Ministry for Sport, Tourism and Youth Policy of the Russian Federation. Retrieved January 10, 2012, and May 1, 2017, from http://sport.minstm.gov.ru

Stasik, E. (2012, June 6). Polish soccer plagued by cronyism and corruption. Deutsche Welle. Retrieved May 10, 2017, from www.dw.com/en/polish-soccer-plagued-by-cronyism-and-corruption/a-15980132

Suciu, A., Balota, I., & Oana, O. (2002). Romania: Sport for all as a change of mentality and new lifestyle. In L.P. DaCosta & A. Miragaya (Eds.), *World experiences and trends of sport for all*. Oxford, United Kingdom: Meyer & Meyer Sport.

To, W.W.H., Smolianov, P., & Semotiuk, D.M. (2012). Comparative high performance sport models. In Sotiriadou, P., & De Bosscher, V. (Editors). Managing High Performance Sport. London and New York: Routledge.

USA Hockey (2018). 2009-2019 Annual report. Retrieved on October 4, 2018, from https://cdn3.sportngin.com/attachments/document/0039/8267/2010_USAH_Annual_Report_FINAL2.pdf

Vinogradov, I. (2016, June 16). Muscovites pass GTO tests. Evening Moscow. Retrieved from http://vm.ru/news/2016/06/15/normi-gotov-k-trudu-i-oborone-gorozhane-vipolnyayut-legko-323474.html

Way, R., Repp, C., & Brennan, T. (2010). Sport schools in Canada: The future is here. Canadian Sport Center Pacific. Retrieved May 10, 2017, from www.vancouver-sun.com/pdf/NationalPaper2.pdf

Wynhausen, E. (2007). Crossing the greatest of divides, *The Australian*. Retrieved December 1, 2007, from http://www.theaustralian.news.com.au/story/0,25197,22850153-2722,00. Htm

Chapter 7

Abdl-Galil Muhammad, S., & Abdallah, M. (2016). Time management of obstacles among swimming and table tennis coaches in Egyptian sports clubs. *Ovidius University Annals, Series Physical Education and Sport/Science, Movement and Health, 16*(1), 91-97.

AllAfrica.com. (2018). *Kenya: How KPL Spent Sh270 Million Revenue From Last Season*. Retrieved on August 3, 2018, from https://allafrica.com/stories/201708010315.html

Bobst, C. (2015) The gris-gris wrestlers of Senegal. Retrieved May 26, 2017, from https://maptia.com/christianbobst/stories/the-gris-gris-wrestlers-of-senegal.

Boshoff, G.B.E. (1997). Barefoot sport administrators: Laying the foundation for sports development in South Africa. *Journal of Sport Management, 11*(1), 69-80.

Brewer, R. M., & Pedersen, P. M. (2010). Franchises, value drivers and the application of valuation analysis to sports sponsorship. *Journal of Sponsorship*, 3(2), 181-193.

Chappel, R. (2005). Sport in Namibia. *International Review for the Sociology of Sport*, 40(2), 241-254.

Chepyator-Thomson, J.R. (2014). Public policy, physical education and sport in English-speaking Africa. *Physical Education and Sport Pedagogy*, 1(5), 512-521.

Darby, P., & Solberg, E. (2010). Differing trajectories: Football development and patterns of player migration in South Africa and Ghana. *Soccer and Society*, 11(1-2), 118-130.

Delgado, D.R.L. (2016). Opening ceremonies of international sports events: The other face of Chinese soft power. *International Journal of the History of Sport*, 33(5), 607-623.

Eksteen, E., Malan, D.G. J., & Lotriet, R. (2013). *African Journal for Physical, Health Education, Recreation & Dance*. 19(4), 928-936.

Federal Ministry of Youth and Sports Development. (2017). Federal Ministry of Youth and Sports Development organogram. Abuja, Nigeria.

FIFA.com. (2018). 2010 FIFA World Cup South Africa. Retrieved on August 4, 2018, from https://www.fifa.com/worldcup/news/study-reveals-tourism-impact-south-africa-1347377

Gedye, L. (2017, April 26). Building the business of rugby. Retrieved June 1, 2017, from www.fin24.com/Finweek/Featured/building-the-business-of-rugby-20170426

Giampiccoli, A., Lee, S.S., & Nauright, J. (2013). Destination South Africa: Comparing global sports mega-events and recurring localised sports events in South Africa for tourism and economic development. *Current Issues in Tourism*, 18(3), 229-248.

Grix, J., & Houlihan, B. (2014). Sports mega-events as part of a nation's soft power strategy: The cases of Germany (2006) and the UK (2012). *British Journal of Politics and International Relations*, 16(4), 572-596. doi:10.1111/1467-856X.12017.

Grundlingh, M. (2015). Showcasing the Springboks: The commercialization of South African Rugby heritage. *South African Review of Sociology*, 46(1), 106-128.

Heuler, H. (2006). Senegal's traditional wrestling evolves. Retrieved May 26, 2017, from www.washingtonpost.com/wp-dyn/content/article/2006/05/31/AR2006053101606_pf.html

Hamza, A., & Abdelmonem, M. (2018). The relationship between transformational leadership and employee empowerment in certain Egyptian sports federations. *Ovidius University Annals, Series Physical Education & Sport Science, Movement & Health*, 18(2), 119-124.

Hill, S., Kerr, R., & Kobayashi, K. (2016). Questioning the application of Policy Governance for small-scale sports clubs in New Zealand. *Managing Sport & Leisure*, 21(4), 203-217. DOI: 10.1080/23750472.2016.1252686

Horne, J., & Manzenreiter, W. (2006). An introduction to the sociology of sports mega-events. *Sociological Review*, 54, 1-24.

Houlihan, B. (2005). Public sector sport policy: Developing a framework for analysis. *International Review for the Sociology of Sport*, 40(2), 163-185.

Isabirye, D. (2017, June 29). Uganda She Cranes win 2017 Africa Netball Championship. *Kawowo Sports*. Retrieved from https://www.kawowo.com/2017/06/29/uganda-she-cranes-lift-the-2017-africa-netball-championship-trophy/

Kamweru, J. (2008, July 2). Safari Rally set to return to the world championships. Ezine articles. Retrieved from http://ezinearticles.com/?Safari-Rally-Set-to-Return-to-the-World-Championships&id=1293364

Kenyan Premier League Limited (2018). Retrieved on August 3, 2018, from https://www.kenyanpremier-league.com/

League Management Company. (2017). Proposal for community ownership of football clubs in Nigeria. Retrieved from www.npfl.ng>pdf>proposal_for_com. on June 16th 2017.

Ndee, H. (2010). Modern sport in independent Tanzania: Agents and agencies of cultural diffusion and the use of adapted sport in the process of modernization. *International Journal of the History of Sport*, 27(5), 937-959

Oonk, G. (2004). The changing culture of the Hindu Lohana community in East Africa. *Contemporary South Asia*, 13(1), 7-23.

Parker, M. (2013). South Africa the history of rugby. *New African*, (533), 102-105.

Pilger, J. (2010). Why sharks should not own sport. *New Statesman*, 139(4998), 21.

Rotberg, R., & Obadina, E. (2007, January). Chapter 4: NIGERIA: Modern politics of ethnic entitlement. *Ethnic Groups In Africa* [serial online] (pp. 56-77). Available from: Book Collection: Nonfiction, Ipswich, MA. Accessed April 15, 2017.

Saayman, M., Saayman, A., & du Plessis, C. (2005). Analysis of spending patterns of visitors of three World Cup cricket matches. *Journal of Sport Tourism*, 10(3), 211-221.

Seidman, A., & Anang, F. (1992). Towards a new vision of self-sustainable development in Africa. In A. Seidman and F. Anang (Eds.), *21st Century Africa: Towards a new vision of sustainable development* (pp. 1-21). Trenton, NJ: Africa World Press; Atlanta, GA: Africa Studies Association Press.

Stander, F.W., & van Zyl, L.E. (2016). See you at the match: Motivation for sport consumption and intrinsic psychological reward of premier football league spectators in South Africa. *SAJIP: South African Journal if Industrial Psychology*, 42(1), 1-13. doi:10.4102/sajip.v42i1.1312.

Steyn, E., Hollander, W., & Roux, C.J. (2014). Sport event management curricular outcomes in the South African higher education context. *African Journal for Physical, Health Education, Recreation and Dance, 20*(4.1), 1492-1504.

Yeboah, T.N., Adams, M., & Akotia, P. (2017). Records management and football. *African Journal of Library, Archives and Information Science, 27*(1), 29-39.

Versi, A., & Nevin, T. (2003). Bonanza for South Africa. *African Business, 284,* 20.

Vidacs, B. (2011). Banal nationalism, football, and discourse community in Africa. *Studies in Ethnicity and Nationalism 11*(1), 25-41.

Chapter 8

Al Jazeera. (2017, July 3). *Free running Gaza.* Retrieved from www.aljazeera.com/programmes/aljazeera-selects/2017/07/free-running-gaza-170703090104743.html

Amara, M. (2012). Football sub-culture and youth politics in Algeria, *Mediterranean Politics, 17*(1), 41-58.

Amara, M., & Theodoraki, E. (2010). Transnational network formation through sports related regional development projects in the Arabian Peninsula. *International Journal of Sport Policy, 2*(2), 135-158.

Chen, S., & Henry, I. (2012). Women in management and leadership in the Olympic movement in Muslim majority countries: An empirical evaluation of Huntington's clash of civilisations typology. *International Journal of the History of Sport, 29*(15), 2131-2144.

Fatès, Y. (1994). *Sport et Tiers-Monde.* Paris, France: Presses Universitaires de France.

Giulianotti, R., & Robertson, R. (2004). The globalization of football: A study in the glocalization of the "serious life." *British Journal of Sociology, 55*(4), 545-568.

Josoor Institute. (2017). Sports and event industries in MENA. In collaboration with Repucom (now Nielsen Sports).

Nassif, N., & Amara, M. (2015). Sport, policy and politics in Lebanon. *International Journal of Sport Policy and Politics, 7*(3), 443-455.

Reiche, D. (2011). War minus the shooting? The politics of sport in Lebanon as a unique case in comparative politics. *Third World Quarterly, 32*(2), 261-277.

Thorpe, H. (2014). The emergence of action sports in the Middle East: Imagining new mobilities with parkour in Gaza. In *Transnational Mobilities in Action Sport Cultures* (pp. 242-261). London, United Kingdom: Palgrave Macmillan UK.

Tuastad, D. (2014). From football riot to revolution. The political role of football in the Arab world. *Soccer and Society, 15*(3), 376-388.

von der Lippe, G. (2014). Football, masculinities and health on the Gaza Strip. *International Journal of the History of Sport, 31*(14), 1789-1806.

Chapter 9

AERU. (2015). *The economic value of sport and outdoor recreation to New Zealand: Updated data.* Christchurch, New Zealand: Lincoln University.

All Blacks. (2017). Retrieved September 11, 2017, from www.allblacks.com/Teams

Australian Bureau of Statistics. (2017). Retrieved September 7, 2017, from www.abs.gov.au/ausstats/abs@.nsf/Web+Pages/Population+Clock?opendocument

Australian Olympic Committee. (2017). Minutes and letter of agreement with the Australian Sports Commission. Sydney, Australia: Author. Retrieved March 1, 2017, from http://aoc-cdn.s3.amazonaws.com/corporate/live/files/dmfile/ASC-and-AOC-Basis-for-Partnership-Agreement-reduced.pdf

Australian Sports Commission. (2011). Strategic plan 2011-2012 to 2014-2015. Canberra, Australia: Author. Retrieved March 13, 2017, from www.ausport.gov.au/__data/assets/pdf_file/0004/472738/ASC_Strategic_Plan_2011-12_to_2014-2015.pdf

Boyd, M. (1996). New Zealand and the other Pacific Islands. In K. Sinclair (Ed.), *The Oxford illustrated history of New Zealand* (pp. 295-322). Melbourne, Australia: Oxford University Press.

Cashman, R. (1995). *Paradise of sport: The rise of organised sport in Australia.* Sydney, Australia: UNSW Press.

Chelladurai, P., Radzi W.M., & Daud, M.A. (2017). Organisational structure and theory of non-profit sport organisations (chapter 3). In T. Bradbury & I. O'Boyle (Eds.), *Understanding sport management: International perspectives* (pp. 27-43). London, United Kingdom: Routledge.

Collins, C., & Jackson, S. (2007). *Sport in Aotearoa/New Zealand society.* Victoria, Australia: Cengage Learning.

Commonwealth of Australia. (2011). *National sport and active recreation policy framework.* Canberra, Australia: Author. Retrieved March 1, 2017, from http://www.health.gov.au/internet/main/publishing.nsf/Content/3B6F37C705F4F8CFCA257C310021CD4B/$File/nsarpf.pdf

FIFA statutes. (2015). FIFA. Zurich, Switzerland: Author. Retrieved September 13, 2015, from www.fifa.com/mm/document/affederation/generic/02/58/14/48/2015fifastatutesen_neutral.pdf

High Performance Sport New Zealand. (2013). *Strategic plan 2013-2020.* Wellington, New Zealand: Author.

Hoye, Russell. (2005). Professional sport in Australia and New Zealand: An introduction to the special issue. *Sport Management Review, 8,* 89-93. 10.1016/S1441-3523(05)70034-6.

Khoo, C., Schulenkorf, N., & Adair, D. (2014). The benefits and limitations of using cricket as a sport for development tool in Samoa. *Cosmopolitan Civil Societies: An Interdisciplinary Journal, 6*(1), 76-102.

McMillan, P. (2011). *Sport organisations and other sports services in Australia*. Melbourne, Australia: IBIS World Industry Report.

Ministerial Taskforce on Sport, Fitness and Leisure. (2001). *Getting set for an active nation: Report of the Sport, Fitness and Leisure Ministerial Taskforce*. Wellington, New Zealand: Sport, Fitness and Leisure Ministerial Taskforce. Retrieved March 15, 2017, from www.srknowledge.org.nz/wp-content/uploads/2012/06/Sport-Fitness-and-Leisure-Ministerial-Taskforce-2001.pdf

Ministry of Health. (2017). *Activity levels in New Zealand*. Retrieved September 7, 2017, from www.health.govt.nz/your-health/healthy-living/food-and-physical-activity/physical-activity/activity-levels-new-zealand

New Zealand Football. (2016). *NZF key milestones 2016*. Auckland, New Zealand: Author.

New Zealand Olympic Committee. (2017a). *About the NZOC*. Retrieved March 15, 2017, from www.olympic.org.nz/about-the-nzoc/

New Zealand Olympic Committee. (2017b). *Statement of purpose*. Retrieved March 15, 2017, from www.olympic.org.nz/assets/Uploads/OC4462-A3-doublesided-folded-Strategic-Document-HR2.pdf

NZ Institute of Economic Research. (2000). *The government's role in sport, fitness and leisure. Report to the Ministerial Taskforce on Sport, Fitness and Leisure*. Retrieved March 5, 2017, from https://nzier.org.nz/static/media/filer_public/79/2a/792ad28c-e6ab-4338-9e66-a75d36ca28c8/governments_role_in_sport_fitness_and_leisure.pdf

Olympic results, gold medalists and official records. (2017). Retrieved March 13, 2017, from www.olympic.org/rio-2016/rugby/rugby-7-men

Owen, P.D., & Weatherston, C.R. (2002). Professionalization of New Zealand Rugby Union: Historical background, structural changes and competitive balance. *University of Otago Economics Discussion Papers No. 0214*, pp. 1-30. Dunedin, New Zealand: University of Otago.

Pacific Games Council Charter. (2010). Apia, Samoa: Author. Retrieved September 12, 2015, from www.oceaniafootball.com/ofc/Portals/0/Images/Articles/PGC%20Charter%202010.pdf

Paralympics New Zealand. (2017). *Vision & mission*. Retrieved March 15, 2017, from www.paralympics.org.nz/About/Vision-Mission

Sak, N., & Karymshakov, K. (2012). Relationship between tourism and economic growth: A panel Granger causality approach. *Asian Economic and Financial Review*, 2(5), 591.

SANZAAR. (2017). *About SANZAAR*. Retrieved March 15, 2017, from www.sanzarrugby.com/about-sanzar/

Sotiriadou, K. (2009). The Australian sport system and its stakeholders: Development of cooperative relationships. *Sport in Society*, 12(7), 842-860.

Sotiriadou, K., Quick, S., & Shilbury, D. (2006). Sport for "some": Elite versus mass participation. *International Journal of Sport Management*, 7(1), 50-66.

Sotiriadou, K., Shilbury, D., & Quick, S. (2008). The attraction, retention/transition, and nurturing process of sport development: Some Australian evidence. *Journal of Sport Management*, 22(3), 247-272.

Sotiriadou, P., & Brouwers, J. (2012). A critical analysis of the impact of the Beijing Olympic Games on Australia's sport policy direction. *International Journal of Sport Policy and Politics*, 4(3), 321-341.

Sotiriadou, P., & De Bosscher, V. (2017). Creating high performing non-profit sport organisations (Chapter 6). In T. Bradbury & I. O'Boyle (Eds.), *Understanding sport management: International perspectives* (pp. 75-94). London, United Kingdom: Routledge.

Sport and Recreation New Zealand. (2002). *Annual report*. Wellington, New Zealand: Author. Retrieved March 13, 2017, from www.clearinghouseforsport.gov.au/__data/assets/pdf_file/0004/559228/Sport_and_Recreation_New_Zealand_Annual_Report_2002.pdf

Sport New Zealand. (2012). *Sport and recreation in the lives of young New Zealanders*. Wellington, New Zealand: Sport New Zealand.

Sport New Zealand. (2015). *Sport NZ Group strategic plan 2015-2020*. Wellington, New Zealand: Author.

Sport New Zealand. (2015). *Statement of performance expectations 2015-2016*. Wellington, New Zealand: Author. Retrieved March 13, 2017, from www.sportnz.org.nz/assets/Uploads/attachments/About-us/2015-16-Sport-NZ-Group-SOPE.pdf

Sport New Zealand. (2017). Retrieved September 7, 2017, from www.sportnz.org.nz/news-and-events/media-releases-and-updates/articles/sport-and-recreation-sector-makes-a-significant-economic-contribution-to-new-zealand

Statistics NZ. (2017). Retrieved September 7, 2017, from www.stats.govt.nz/browse_for_stats/snapshots-of-nz/top-statistics.aspx

UTSNZ. (2017). *History of university & tertiary sport NZ*. Retrieved March 13, 2017, from www.utsnz.co.nz/history.html

Chapter 10

Abdul Wahid, Z.A. (Ed.). (1970). *Glimpses of Malaysian history*. Kuala Lumpur, Malaysia: Dewan Bahasa dan Pustaka.

Abraham, C. (1988). Inter-cultural management at the crossroads. *Malaysian Management Review*, 24(1), 58–65.

ASEAN. (2018). About ASEAN. Retrieved on September 16, 2018, from https://asean.org/asean/about-asean/

Brownfoot, J.N. (2003). "Healthy bodies, healthy minds"; sport and society in colonial Malaya. *International Journal of the History of Sport*, 19(2), 126–156.

Central Intelligence Agency. (2017). *The world factbook*. Retrieved from www.cia.gov/library/publications/resources/the-world-factbook/fields/2107.html

Chatterjee, Samir R., & Pearson, Cecil A.L. (2003). Ethical perceptions of Asian managers: Evidence of trends in six divergent national contexts. *Business Ethics: A European Review, 12*(2), 203–211.

Chelladurai, P., Shanmuganathan, D., Jothikaran, J., & Nageswaran, A.S. (2002). Sport in modern India: Policies, practices and problems. *International Journal of the History of Sport, 19*(2), 366–383.

Chelladurai, P., Nair, U., & Stephen, S. (2013). India. In K. Hallman & K. Petry (Eds.), *Comparative sport development: Systems, participation & public policy*. New York, New York: Springer Science + Business Media.

Cheng, E., & Jarvis, N. (2010). Residents' perception of the social-cultural impacts of the 2008 Formula 1 Singlet Grand Prix. *Event Management, 14*(2): 91-106

Chong, T. (2005). *Modernization trends in Southeast Asia*. Singapore: Institute of Southeast Asian Studies.

DeSensi, J.T., Kelley, D., Blanton, M.D., & Beitel, P.A. (1988). *Employer expectations of sports managers and evaluation of sports management programs in the United States*. Paper presented at the North American Society for Sport Management Conference, Urbana, IL.

Green, M. (2007). Olympic glory or grassroots development? Sport policy priorities in Australia, Canada and the United Kingdom, 1960-2006. *International Journal of the History of Sport, 24*(7), 921–953.

Hashim, M.Y. (1992). *The Malay Sultanate of Malacca*. Kuala Lumpur, Malaysia: Dewan Bahasa dan Pustaka.

Horton, P.A. (2002). Shackling the lion: Sport in independent Singapore. *International Journal of the History of Sport, 19*(2), 243–274.

International Monetary Fund. (2016). World economic outlook database. Retrieved from www.imf.org/external/pubs/ft/weo/2016/02/weodata/index.aspx

International Sepak Takraw Federation. (2016). LSTAF Law of the Game 2016. Retrieved on September 16, 2018, from http://sepaktakraw.org/index.php/law-of-the-game/

Lizandra, M. (1993). *Sports management curricula: Identification of minimum core content areas and courses to be included in each content area for undergraduate and graduate (master's) sports management programs*. Unpublished doctoral thesis, Temple University, Philadelphia, PA.

Mangan, J.A. (2003). Prologue: Asian sport: From the recent past. *International Journal of the History of Sport, 19*(2), 1–10.

Manzenreiter, W. (2007). The business of sports and the manufacturing of global sport inequality. *Business of Sports, 2*(6), 1–22.

Megat Daud, M.A.K. (2000). *The sports industry in Malaysia*. Paper presented at the 3rd ICHPER.SD Asia Congress, Kuala Lumpur, Malaysia.

Mendoza, G. (1992). *Management: The Asian way*. Petaling Jaya, Malaysia: Eddiplex.

Nalapat, A., & Parker, A. (2005). Sport, celebrity and popular culture: Sachin Tendulkar, cricket and Indian nationalism. *International Review for the Sociology of Sport, 40*(4), 433–446.

National sport policy. (1989). Kuala Lumpur, Malaysia: Ministry of Youth and Sport, Malaysia.

Nielsen, L. (2011). *Classifications of countries based on their level of development: How it is done and how it could be done*. International Monetary Fund Working Paper. Retrieved from https://www.imf.org/external/pubs/ft/wp/2011/wp1131.pdf

Parks, J.B., & Quarterman, J. (Eds.). (2003). *Contemporary sport management* (2nd ed.). Champaign, IL: Human Kinetics.

Radzi, W. (2000). *Challenges and future directions of sports management in Malaysia*. Paper presented at the Proceedings of the 3rd ICHPER.SD Asia Congress, Kuala Lumpur, Malaysia.

Roberts, K. (2005). *Land of new opportunity*. Sport Business.

Sepak takraw. (n.d.). In *Wikipedia*. Retrieved from https://en.wikipedia.org/wiki/Sepak_takraw

Sports investment, events and media to power growth in the Singapore sports industry. (2009). Retrieved from www.sportsingapore.gov.sg/newsroom/media-releases/2009/3/sports-investment-events-and-media-to-power-growth-in-the-singapore-sports-industry

Sriboon, N. (2007). Sport and recreation activities and economic crisis in Thailand. *Asian Sport Management Review, 1*(1), 2–7.

World Bank. (2018). International comparison program database. Retrieved from https://data.worldbank.org/indicator/NY.GDP.MKTP.PP.CD?year_high_desc=true

World Bank Group. (2016). *The World Bank Group A to Z 2016*. Washington, DC: World Bank. Retrieved from https://openknowledge.worldbank.org/handle/10986/22548

Chapter 11

Central Intelligence Agency. (2017). *The world factbook*. Retrieved from www.cia.gov/library/publications/the-world-factbook/

Chehabi, H.E. (2001). Sport diplomacy between the United States and Iran. *Diplomacy and Statecraft, 12*(1), 89-106.

Cheng, P. (2006). The development of Asian sport industry. Retrieved from http://140.122.100.146/acad/ebook/9301/ld41.doc

Chinese Olympic Committee. (2009). *Official web site of the Chinese Olympic Committee*. Retrieved July 30, 2009, from http://en.olympic.cn

Daxue Consulting. (2018). Bright perspectives of China's sporting goods industry: Kids, millennials and elder people are most promising customers [Blog post]. Retrieved from http://daxueconsulting.com/chinas-sporting-goods-industry/

Daly, A. & Kawaguchi, A. (2003). Professional sport in Australia and Japan: League rules and competitive balance. *Otemon Journal of Australian studies, 29*, 21-32.

Eschenfelder, M.J., & Li, M. (2006). *Economics of sport* (2nd ed.). Morgantown, WV: Fitness Information Technology.

Harada, M. (2010). Development of the sport industry: Japan's experience. Paper presented at the 2010 Annual Conference of the Asian Association for Sport Management, Kuala Lumpur, Malaysia.

Hong, F. (2003). Epilogue—into the future: Asian sport and globalization. In J.A. Mangan & F. Hong (eds.), *Sport in Asian society*. London, United Kingdom: Frank Cass.

Hu, L.K. (2006). *Culture coherence and regional economic cooperation in Northeast Asia*. Retrieved July 27, 2009, from http://faculty.washington.edu/karyiu/confer/beijing06/papers/hu_lk.pdf

IBISWorld. (2017). *Sports equipment manufacturing—China market research report*. Retrieved from www.ibisworld.com/industry-trends/international/china-market-research-reports/manufacturing/stationery-sporting-goods/sports-equipment-manufacturing.html

Jones, R. (1999). Sport in China. In J. Riordan & R. Jones (eds.), *Sport and physical education in China* (pp. 1-19). London, United Kingdom: Spon.

Kim, S.S. (2004). Northeast Asia in the local-regional-global nexus: Multiple challenges and contending explanations. In S.S. Kim (ed.), *The international relations of Northeast Asia*. Lanham, MD: Roman & Littlefield.

Klingelhöfer, C. (2017). *Expert tips: How sports brands ensure their brand rights for the Chinese market*. ISPO.com. Retrieved from www.ispo.com/en/markets/id_79711826/tips-ensuring-brand-rights-for-the-chinese-market.html

Korean Overseas Information Service. (2007). *Government policies*. Retrieved January 10, 2008, from www.korea.net/korea/kor_loca.asp?code=J010102

Liu, D.F. (2017, April 14). The sports industry: The next big thing in China? *China Policy Institute: Analysis: The online journal of the China Policy Institute*. Retrieved from https://cpianalysis.org/2017/04/14/the-sports-industry-the-next-big-thing-in-china/

Ministry of Culture, Sport and Tourism. (2006). *Physical education white book* (Korean). Seoul, South Korea: KyeMoon.

Ministry of Education, Culture, Sports, Science and Technology (MEXT). (1991). *Japanese government policies in education, science, and culture 1991*. Retrieved July 27, 2009, from www.mext.go.jp/b_menu/hakusho/html/hpae199201/hpae199201_2_005.html

Ministry of Education, Culture, Sports, Science and Technology (MEXT). (2000). *Basic plan for the promotion of sports* [Press release]. Retrieved July 27, 2009, from www.mext.go.jp/english/news/2000/09/000949.htm

Ministry of Education, Culture, Sports, Science and Technology (MEXT). (n.d.). Law and plan. www.mext.go.jp/en/policy/sports/lawandplan/index.htm

Ok, G. (2007). *Transformation of modern Korean sport: Imperialism, nationalism, globalization*. Elizabeth, NJ: Hollym International.

Seoul Olympic Sports Promotion Foundation. (2007a). *ChongHapEopMuHyunHwang* (Korean).

Seoul Olympic Sports Promotion Foundation. (2007b). *SOSFO vision*. Retrieved November 12, 2007, from http://sosfo.or.kr/english/sosfo/vision.asp Sohu.com. (2017). The sports population in China 434 million: How hot is its sports consumption market? Retrieved from http://sports.sohu.com/20170129/n479682493.shtml

State General Administration of Sport. (2011). 2011-2020 Olympic Glories Plan. Retrieved from www.sport.gov.cn/n16/n1077/n1467/n1918952/1919010.html

Statista. (2018). Share of sports fans in 2016, by country. Retrieved from www.statista.com/statistics/655880/share-of-sport-fans-by-country/

Stevenson, C. & Nixon, J. (1987). A conceptual scheme of the social functions of sport. In A. Yiannakis, T. McIntyre, M. Melnick, & D. Hart, (Eds.), *Sport sociology: Contemporary themes* (3rd ed.) (pp. 23-39), Dubuque, IA: Kendall/Hunt.

The Economist Corporate Network. (2016). *China gets its game on: The emerging power of China's sports and fitness industry*. Retrieved from https://www.corporatenetwork.com/media/1637/china-gets-its-game-on-201701.pdf

The State Council. (2014). Opinions on accelerating the development of sports industry and promoting sports consumption. Retrieved from www.gov.cn/zhengce/content/2014-10/20/content_9152.htm

The State Council. (2015). General administration of sport of China. Retrieved from http://english.gov.cn/state_council/2014/09/09/content_281474986284050.htm

The State Council. (2017). China issues national nutrition plan (2017-2030). Retrieved from http://english.gov.cn/policies/latest_releases/2017/07/13/content_281475725038850.htm

United Nations Environment Programme. (2004). *Environmental indicators: Northeast Asia*. Retrieved from http://rrcap.unep.org/pub/indicator/Vertical%20North%20East%20Asia.pdf

Web Japan. (2009). *Sports: Promoting health for people. Japan factsheet*. Retrieved July 28, 2009, from http://web-jpn.org/factsheet/pdf/12Sports.pdf

World Taekwondo Federation. (2007). *Introduction: About the World Taekwondo Federation*. Retrieved August 31, 2007, from www.wtf.org/site/about_wtf/intro.htm

Yao, X.Z. (2000). *An introduction to Confucianism.* Cambridge, United Kingdom: Cambridge University Press.

Chapter 12

2018 Olympic candidates confirmed. (2010, August). SportsPro, 24, 31.

Around the Rings. (2017). Argentina to host first gender equal games.

Retrieved from http://aroundtherings.com/site/A__59874/title__Argentina-to-Host-First-Gender-Equal-Games/292/Articles

Battistoni, P. (2010, August 22). No need to combine Olympic and Paralympic Games, chief insists. Retrieved on March 14, 2011, from www.olympics-now.com/2010/03/12/no-need-to-combine-olympic-and-paralympic-games-chief-insists

Bell, D. (2002). Are all Paralympic elite athletes? International Games Archive 1998-2002: 1-12.

Brazil's decade of sport. (2010, August). SportsPro, 24, 54-57.

Britain, I. (2010). The Paralympic Games explained, Routledge, London.

British Columbia Supreme Court (2009). Sagen v Vancouver Organizing Committee for the 2010 Olympic and Paralympic Winter Games, 2009 BCSC 942.

Burton, R. & O'Reilly, N. (2010a). UN role offers IOC change to place sport amid global priorities, SportBusiness Journal, 12(48): 21.

Burton, R. & O'Reilly, N. (2010b). Assessing Vancouver after the fact, accusations, shades of truth, SportBusiness Journal, 13(19), 21.

Business model. (2017, March 16). The business model for the Olympic Games is running out of puff. *The Economist.* Retrieved from www.economist.com/news/business/21718938-budapest-latest-city-withdraw-its-bid-host-them-business-model-olympic

Carr, S. (2007). Title IX: An opportunity to level the Olympic playing field, Journal of Sports and Entertainment Law, 19: 149.

Centre on Housing Rights and Evictions Report, Fair Play for Housing Rights. (2007).

Clark, J. (1992, August) Fifth Wheels. The XXV Olympiad is the XXVth to exclude disabled jocks, Village Voice, p. 4.

Clarke, M. (2017). U.S. men's hockey team will stand with women in World Championship boycott, per reports. Retrieved from www.sbnation.com/nhl/2017/3/26/15066902/united-states-mens-hockey-womens-hockey-world-championship-boycott-usa-hockey

China embraces (2009). Retreived on March 14, 2011, from http://news.xiuhuarnet.com/english/2009-02/26/content_10901530.htm

Christie, J. (1997, December 5). Disabled athletes get full status, Globe and Mail, A21.

Crary, D. (2010, February). Organizers strive to achieve inclusiveness, sustainability, Daily Hampshire Gazette, pp. D1-2.

Council on Foreign Relations. (2017). The economics of hosting the Olympic Games. Retrieved from www.cfr.org/backgrounder/economics-hosting-olympic-games

Geekwire. (2017). Competitive gaming will overtake mainstream sports. Retrieved from www.geekwire.com/2017/competitive-gaming-will-overtake-mainstream-sports-years-says-momentum-ceo/

Geiling, N. (2016, August 2). We were promised the greenest Olympics ever—we got an ecological disaster. Retrieved from https://thinkprogress.org/we-were-promised-the-greenest-olympics-ever-we-got-an-ecological-disaster-6fba72f30aad

Gillis, C. (2010). Chantal Petitclerc, Retrieved on March 14, 2011, from http://historywire.ca/en/atricle/20908

Goldman, T. (2010, July 10). Runner Semenya cleared after gender test. All think Considered, NPR Radio, Retrieved February 6, 2011 from http://www.npr.templates/story/story.php?storyId=128342113.

Hums, M. & MacLean, J. (2009). Governance and policy in sport organizations, Holcomb Hathaway, Scottsdale.

IOC. (2015). *Factsheet: Sochi 2014 facts & figures.* Retrieved from https://stillmed.olympic.org/Documents/Games_Sochi_2014/Sochi_2014_Facts_and_Figures.pdf

Kommenda, N. (2017). How evictions have laid bare Rio's Real Olympic legacy. *The Guardian.* Retrieved from www.theguardian.com/sport/ng-interactive/2016/aug/02/how-evictions-have-laid-bare-rios-real-olympic-legacy

Klingbeil, A. (2017, March 3). Author fears Calgary Olympic bid committee infected with Olympic fever. *Calgary Herald.* Retrieved from http://calgaryherald.com/news/local-news/author-fears-calgary-olympic-bid-committee-infected-with-olympic-fever

Legg, D. & Steadward, R. (2011) The Paralympic Games and 60 years of change (1948-2008): Unification and restructuring. In Disability in The Global Sport Arena: A Sporting Chance. Special edition of Sport in Society, ed. Jill M. Le Clair. London: Taylor & Francis.

Legg, D. Burchell, A., Jarvis, P., & Sainsbury, T. (2009). The Athletic Ability Debate: Have we reached a tipping point? *Palaestra, 25*(1): 19-25.

Legg, D., Fay, T., Hums, M., & Wolff, E. (2009). Examining the Inclusion of Wheelchair Exhibition Events within the Olympic Games: 1984-2004. *European Journal of Sport Management, 9*(3): 243-258.

Lombardo, J. (2010). FIBA event expect revenue jump. *SportBusiness Journal, 13*(17), 6.

London 2010 budget cut by new British government. (2010, July). SportsPro, 23, 27.

Longman, J. (2010, March 30). South African runner plans return. New York Times. Retrieved on February 6, 2010 from http://www.nytimes.com/2010/03/31/sports/31semenya.html

Maki, A. (2017). Women make their mark in the sports executive suites. *Globe and Mail*. Retrieved from www.theglobeandmail.com/sports/women-make-their-mark-in-sports-executive-suites/article35105298/

Mickle, T. (2010a). Recalling Olympic Leader's Legacy, *SportBusiness Journal, 13*(2): 7.

Mickle, T. (2010b). Rogge's Youth Games reaching the starting line, *SportBusiness Journal, 13*(15): 26.

NOC & Athletes. (n.d.). Retrieved on March 14, 2011, from www.games-encyclo.org/?id=11837&L=1

Olympic History. (n.d). Retrieved on March 11, 2011 from http://olympics-india server.com/Olympics-history.html

Olympic Women. (2008) Some early history about women and the Olympics. Retrieved on April 11, 2010, from www.olympicwomen.co.uk/Potted.htm

Olympic Movement. (2017a). IOC subsidies for participation in Olympic Games. Retrieved from www.olympic.org/olympic-solidarity-world-programmes

Olympic Movement. (2017b). The IOC announces the composition of its commissions. Retrieved from www.olympic.org/news/ioc-announces-composition-of-its-commissions-38-per-cent-of-members-now-women

Panja, T. (2017, February 23). Olympics in "crisis" as just two cities vie to host Summer Games. Retrieved from www.bloomberg.com/news/articles/2017-02-23/olympics-in-crisis-as-just-two-cities-vie-to-host-summer-games

Paralympic Movement. (2016). IOC and IPC agree principles for new agreement through to 2032. Retrieved from www.paralympic.org/news/ioc-and-ipc-agree-principles-new-agreement-through-2032

Paralympic Movement. (2017a). Highlights from the Rio 2016 Paralympic Games. Retrieved from www.paralympic.org/rio-2016

Paralympic Movement. (2017b). Breaking down barriers—Sochi 2014 Paralympic Winter Games. Retrieved from www.paralympic.org/sochi-2014

Paralympic Movement. (2017c). The IPC—who are we. Retrieved from www.paralympic.org/the-ipc/about-us

Paralympic Movement. (2017d). Sports. Retrieved from www.paralympic.org/sports/summer

Pfister, G. (2000). Women in the Olympic Games 1900-97, In B.L. Drinkwater (Ed.), Women in sport, The encyclopedia of sports medicine, London: Blackwell Science, an IOC Medical Committee Publication.

Preuss, H. (2004). The economics of staging the Olympics: A comparison of the Games 1972-2008, Edward Elger, Northampton, MA.

Preuss, H. (2008). The impact and evaluation of major sporting events. European Sport Management Quarterly, London.

Rosner, S. & Shopshire, K. (2011). The business of sports (2nd Ed). Pp. 453-476, Jones & Barlett Learning, Sudbury.

Steadward, R. (1995). Integration and sport in the Paralympic movement. *Sport Science Review, 5*(1): 26-41.

Sportsnet. (2017). Gary Bettmann reaffirms NHL won't participate in 2018 Olympics. Retrieved from www.sportsnet.ca/hockey/nhl/gary-bettman-re-affirms-nhl-wont-participate-2018-olympics/

TV by the Numbers. 2014. USA–Canada men's hockey semifinal highest -rated hockey game ever on NBCSN. Retrieved from http://tvbythenumbers.zap2it.com/network-press-releases/usa-canada-mens-hockey-semifinal-highest-rated-hockey-game-ever-on-nbcsn/

United Nations General Assembly. (2009). *Report of the Special Rapporteur on adequate housing as a component of the right to an adequate standard of living, and on the right to non-discrimination in this context.* Retrieved from www2.ohchr.org/english/bodies/hrcouncil/docs/10session/A.HRC.10.7.Add.3.pdf

United Nations (2006). The Mellennium Developmental Goals Report, 2006. Retrieved March 14, 2011, from http://mdgs.un.org/unsd/mdg/Resources/Static/Products/Progress2006/MDGReport2006.pdf

United Nations (2007). Convention on the Rights of Persons with Disabilities. Retrieved March 11, 2011 from http://www.un.org/disabilities/convention/conventionfull.html

Wamsley, K. (2008, February). Social science literature on sport and transitioning / transitional athletes. Retrieved April 11, 2010 from www.athleticscan.com

Wolbring, G. (2008). One World, One Olympic: Governing Human Ability, Ableism and Disablism in an Era of Bodily Enhancements. In A. Miah (Ed.), Human Futures: Art in the Age of Uncertainty (Liverpool: Liverpool University Press).

Women are missing. (2016). Women are missing in sport leadership positions and it's time that changed. Retrieved from https://theconversation.com/women-are-missing-in-sport-leadership-and-its-time-that-changed-69979?platform=hootsuite

Wong, J. (2010, December 3). Chantal Petitclerc, 2004. Retrieved March 14, 2011 from www.theglobeandmail.com/news/nationa/matino-builder/chantal-petitcler-2004/article723009

Chapter 13

Association of IOC Recognized International Sports Federations (ARISF). (2017). *About ARISF*. Retrieved February 9, 2017, from www.arisf.org/who-we-are.aspx

Association of Summer Olympic International Federations (ASOIF). (2017). *Members*. Retrieved February 9, 2017, from www.asoif.com/members

Chavez, C. (2016, August 3). Baseball & softball, karate, surfing, climbing and skateboarding added to 2020 Olympics. *Sport Illustrated*. Retrieved February 9, 2017, from www.si.com/olympics/2016/08/03/2020-olympics-new-sports-baseball-softball-surfing-skateboarding-karate

Chen, L. (2004). Membership incentives: Factors affecting individuals' decisions about participation in athletics-related professional associations. *Journal of Sport Management, 18*(2), 153-173.

Crouse, K. (2009, July 24). Swimming bans high-tech suits, ending an era. *New York Times*. Retrieved from www.nytimes.com

Fairley, S., & Lizandra, M. (2011). International sport. In L.P. Masteralexis, C.A. Barr, & M.A. Hums (Eds.), *Principles and practice of sport management* (4th ed., pp. 187-216). Gaithersburg, MD: Jones and Bartlett.

Fédération Internationale de Football Association (FIFA). (2016). *FIFA financial and governance report, 2016*. Retrieved February 15, 2017, from www.fifa.com/mm/document/affederation/administration/01/03/94/23/fifa_ar08_eng.pdf

Fédération Internationale de Football Association (FIFA). (2017). *About FIFA*. Retrieved February 15, 2017, from www.fifa.com/aboutfifa/federation/associations.html

Fédération Internationale de Natation (FINA). (2017a). *FINA organizational chart*. Retrieved February 20, 2017, from www.fina.org/project/index.phfp

Fédération Internationale de Natation (FINA). (2017b). *Press releases: PR58—FINA bureau meeting*. Retrieved February 20, 2017, from www.fina.org

Fermoso, J. (2008, June 6). High-tech swimsuits approved by Olympic committee promise to even the competition. *Wired*. Retrieved from www.wired.com/gadget-lab/2008/06/high-tech-swims

Hums, M., & MacLean, J. (2004). *Governance and policy in sport organizations* (pp. 257-294). Holcomb Hathaway.

International Association of Athletics Federations (IAAF). (2017). *IAAF national member federations*. Retrieved February 9, 2017, from www.iaaf.org/about-iaaf/structure/member-federations

International Basketball Federation (FIBA). (2017). *FIBA organization*. Retrieved February 19, 2017, from www.fiba.com

International Biathlon Union (IBU). (2017). *Competitions*. Retrieved February 10, 2017, fromwww.biathlonworld.com/

International Olympic Committee (IOC). (2016, August 3). *IOC approves five new sports for Olympic Games Tokyo 2020*. Retrieved February 10, 2017, from www.olympic.org/news/ioc-approves-five-new-sports-for-olympic-games-tokyo-2020

International Olympic Committee (IOC). (2017a). *International sports federations*. Retrieved from www.olympic.org/ioc-governance-international-sports-federations

International Olympic Committee (IOC). (2017b). *The International Olympic Committee*. Retrieved February 10, 2017, from www.olympic.org/ioc-governance-international-sports-federations

International Olympic Committee (IOC). (2017c). *The International Olympic Committee*. Retrieved February 19, 2017, from www.olympic.org/the-ioc

International Tennis Federation (ITF). (2017). *International Tennis Federation—The world governing body of tennis*. Retrieved February 19, 2017, from www.itftennis.com/home.aspx

International Table Tennis Federation (ITTF). (2017). *International Table Tennis Federation*. Retrieved February 19, 2017, from www.ittf.com

Olympic Charter. (2016a). *Chapter 3: The international federations (IFs)*. Retrieved February 9, 2017, from www.olympic.org/documents/olympic-charter

Olympic Charter. (2016b). *Chapter 5: The Olympic Games*. Retrieved February 10, 2017, from www.olympic.org/documents/olympic-charter

Roberts, B.S., Kamel, K.S., Herick, D.E., McLean, S.P., & Sharp, R.L. (2003). Effect of a FastSkin Suit on submaximal freestyle swimming. *Medicine and Science in Sports and Exercise, 35*(3), 519-524.

SportAccord. (2017a). *About SportAccord*. Retrieved February 19, 2017, from www.sportaccord.com

SportAccord. (2017b). *Mission*. Retrieved February 10, 2017, from www.sportaccord.com/members

Theodoraki, E. (2007). *Olympic event organization*. Burlington, MA: Elsevier Linacre.

USA Swimming Association (USSA). (2010, June 1). *Amendments to conform USA swimming open water swimsuit rules to FINA open water swimsuit rules*. Retrieved from www.usaswimming.org

World Archery Federation (WA). (2017). Retrieved February 19, 2017, from www.olympic.org/world-archery-federation

World Baseball Softball Confederation (WBSF). (2017). Retrieved February 19, 2017, from www.wbsc.org

Chapter 14

Andren-Sandberg, A. (2016). *The history of doping and antidoping, a systematic collection of published scientific literature (2000-2015)*. Karolinska Institutet at Karolinska University Hospital, Stockholm, Sweden.

AP. (2010, January 11). Former slugger Mark McGwire admits steroid use throughout 1990s. AP.com. Retrieved from www.nj.com/sports/index.ssf/2010/01/former_slugger_mark_mcgwire_ad.html/

Barry, M. (2012). Basic ethical theories. Retrieved from https://visualunit.files.wordpress.com/2012/06/basic_ethics_theories.pdf

BBC. (2014). It's not the winning. Retrieved from www.bbc.co.uk/ethics/sport/overview/introduction.shtml

Beller, J.M., & Stoll, S.K. (2013). Sportsmanship: An antiquated concept? *Journal of Physical Education, Recreation & Dance, 64*(6), 74-79.

Carroll, W., & Carroll, W.L. (2005). *The juice: The real story of baseball's drug problems*. Chicago, IL: Ivan R. Dee.

Clark, N. (2016). Get ready to watch the Opening Ceremony: Olympic oath. NBCOlympics.com Retrieved from www.nbcolympics.com/news/get-ready-watch-opening-ceremony-olympic-oath

ESPN. (2012, March 4). NFL: Saints defense had "bounty" fund. Retrieved from www.espn.com/nfl/story/_/id/7638603/new-orleans-saints-defense-had-bounty-program-nfl-says

Hanson, K.O., & Savage, M. (2012). *What role does ethics play in sports?* Santa Clara University Resources. Retrieved from www.scu.edu/ethics/focus-areas/more/resources/what-role-does-ethics-play-in-sports/

Hassett, K.A., & Veuger, S. (2012, July 15). The Saints ain't sinners. AEI.com. Retrieved from www.aei.org/publication/the-saints-aint-sinners/

Haynes, C., Thielk, A., & Montilla, E. (2011). The champ [recorded by hip-hop artist Nelly]. San Monica, CA: On Digital Download, Universal Music Group.

Howman, D. (2015, October). Challenges to the integrity of sport [Speech]. Australian and New Zealand Sports Law Association Annual Conference (ANZSLA), Melbourne, Australia. Retrieved from www.wada-ama.org/en/media/news/2015-10/speech-by-wada-director-general-david-howman-challenges-to-the-integrity-of-sport

Kretchmar, R.S. (1994). *Practical philosophy of sport*. Champaign, IL: Human Kinetics.

Macur, J. (2014). *Cycles of lies, the fall of Lance Armstrong*. New York, NY: Harper Collins.

McLaren R. (2016). The Independent Person Report – WADA Investigation of Sochi Allegations. Retrieved from https://www.wada-ama.org/sites/default/files/resources/files/20160718_ip_report_newfinal.pdf

Mehaffey, J. (2012, July 31). Johnson scandal still reverberates. *Chicago Tribune*. Retrieved from http://articles.chicagotribune.com

Miller, J. (Producer), & McKay, A. (Director). (2006). *Talladega nights: The ballad of Ricky Bobby* [Motion picture]. Culver City, CA: Columbia Pictures.

Moore, R. (2012) *The Dirtiest Race in History: Ben Johnson, Carl Lewis and the 1988 100m Final*, London, UK: Wisden Publications

PBS. (2016). *Secrets of the dead unearthing history, the state-sponsored doping program* [TV series]. Retrieved from www.pbs.org/wnet/secrets/the-state-sponsored-doping-program/52/

Potter, D. (2012, July). *Cheating is as old as the Olympics*. CNN.com. Retrieved from www.cnn.com/2012/07/29/opinion/potter-olympics-cheating/index.html

Rankin, J. (2012, November). Part 1: If you're not cheating. Running Competitor.com. Retrieved from http://running.competitor.com/2012/11/features/part-1-if-youre-not-cheating_61401

Sawyer, T.H., Bodey, K.J., & Judge, L.W. (2008) *Sport governance and policy development: An ethical approach to managing sport in the 21st century*. Champaign, IL: Sagamore

Shaven, N. (2016, August). The ancient history of cheating in the Olympics. Smithsonian.com. Retrieved from www.smithsonianmag.com/history/ancient-history-cheating-olympics-180960003/

Thomas, E. (Producer), & Nolan, C. (Director). (2008). *The dark knight* [Motion picture]. Burbank, CA: Warner Bros.

UKAD (2017). What We Do. Retrieved from https://ukad.org.uk/our-organisation/what-we-do/

USADA. (2012, October 10). Statement from USADA CEO Travis T. Tygart regarding the U.S. Postal Service pro cycling team doping conspiracy. U.S. Postal Service pro cycling team investigation statement. Retrieved from http://cyclinginvestigation.usada.org/

Volkwein, K.A. (1995). Ethics and top-level sport—a paradox? *International Review for the Sociology of Sport, 30*, 311–321.

WADA (2017). Who We Are. Retrieved from https://www.wada-ama.org/en/who-we-are

Chapter 15

Amara, M., Henry, I., Liang J., Uchiumi, K. (2005). The governance of professional soccer: Five case studies—Algeria, China, England, France and Japan. *European Journal of Sport Science, 5*(4), 189-206

Arthur, D. (2003). Corporate sponsorship of sport: Its impact on surfing and surf culture. In J. Skinner, K. Gilbert, & A. Edwards (Eds.), *Some like it hot: The beach as a cultural dimension* (pp. 154-168). Oxford, United Kingdom: Meyer & Meyer Sport.

Burton, R., & Cornilles, R.Y. (1998). Emerging theory in team sport sales: Selling tickets in a more competitive arena. *Sport Marketing Quarterly, 7,* 29-37

Daly, A., & Kawaguchi, A. (2003). Professional Sport in Australia and Japan: League rules and competitive balance. *Otemon Journal of Australian Studies, 29,* 21-32

Edwards, A., & Skinner, J. (2006). *Sport empire.* Oxford, United Kingdom: Meyer & Meyer Sport.

FIFA. (2017). *Associations.* Retrieved from https://www.fifa.com/associations/index.html

Fitzsimons, P. (1996). *The rugby war.* Sydney, Australia: Harper Collins.

Giulianotti , R. (1999). *Football: Sociology of the game.* Cambridge, United Kingdom: Polity Press.

Hoye, R., & Cuskelly, G. (2007). *Sport governance.* Oxford, United Kingdom: Elsevier.

IFAF. (2018). *Nations.* Retrieved from https://www.ifaf.org/

International Cricket Council. (n.d.). Retrieved from www.icc-cricket.com/

Law, A., Harvey, J. & Kemp, S. (2002). The global sport mass media oligopoly: The three usual suspects and more. *International Review for the Sociology of Sport, 37*(3-4), 279-302.

Lee, J. (2001, April 11). *Chairman of the board.* Retrieved January 6, 2007, from http://bulletin.ninemsn.com.au/bulletin/eddesk.nsf/6df5c28ed2c6c605ca256a1500059f03/fb66f9a95a7f08feca240007f310?OpenDocument/

Masters, R. (1997). *Insideout: Rugby league under scrutiny.* Sydney, Australia: Ironbark.

Meenaghan, T. (1991). Sponsorship—legitimising the medium. *European Journal of Advertising, 25*(11), 5-10.

Morgan, M. (2002). Optimizing the structure of elite competitions in professional sport: Lessons from rugby union. *Managing Leisure, 7,* 41-60.

Noll, R.G. (2003). The organization of sports leagues. *Oxford Review of Economic Policy, 19*(4), 530-551

Peng, Q., Skinner, J., & Houlihan, B. (2017, September). An Organisational Analysis on the Chinese Football Association Reform: Philosophical and Methodological Considerations. Paper Presented at the 25th European Sport Management Conference, Magglingen, Switzerland.

PGA Tour. (2018). Retrieved from https://www.pgatour.com

Oebbecke, M. (1998). Toward a framework of total quality management (TQM) in professional sport team organizations: Identification and validation of TQM constructs, and the development of an associated measurement instrument. *EDD Dissertation.* Temple University, Philadelphia, PA, Proquest Dissertations.

Tadeo, A. J. P., & Gómez, F. J. G. (2009). *Does playing several competitions influence a team's league performance? Evidence from Spanish professional football.* Documentos de Trabajo FUNCAS, (455).

Ross, S. (2003). Competition law as a constraint on monopolistic exploitation by sport leagues and clubs. *Oxford Review of Economic Policy, 19*(4), 569-584.

Sage, G. (1998). *Power and ideology in American sport.* Champaign, IL: Human Kinetics.

SANZAR. (2018). *Tournament Format.* Retrieved from https://sanzarrugby.com/superrugby/about-super-rugby/tournament-format/

Shaw, S., & Amis, J. (2001). Image and investment: Sponsorship of women's sports. *Journal of Sport Management, 15*(3), 221-248.

Skinner, J., Stewart, B., & Edwards, A. (2003). The postmodernisation of rugby union in Australia. *Journal of Football Studies, 6*(1), 51-69.

Smith, A.C.T., & Stewart, B. (2010). The special features of sport: A critical revisit. *Sport Management Review, 13,* 1-13.

Stewart, B., Nicholson, M., & Dickson, G. (2005). The Australian Football League's recent progress: A study in cartel conduct and monopoly power. *Sport Management Review, 8*(2), 95-118.

Swanson, S. (2015). Globalisation strategies of the NFL and NBA. Sport Industry Group. Retrieved September 18, 2017, from www.sportindustry.biz/cutting-edge-sport/blog/globalisation-strategies-nfl-and-nba

Szymanski, S. (2003). The assessment: The economics of sport. *Oxford Review of Economic Policy, 19*(4), 467-477.

Szymanski, S., & Kuypers, T. (1999). *Winners and losers.* London, United Kingdom: Penguin Books.

Tomlinson, A. (2005). The making of the global sports economy: ISL, Adidas and the rise of the corporate player in world sport. In M.L. Silk, D.L. Andrews, & C.L. Cole (Eds.), *Sport and corporate nationalisms* (pp. 35-65). Oxford, United Kingdom: Berg.

Zhang, J.J., Pease, D.G., & Smith, D.W. (1998). Relationship between broadcasting media and minor league hockey game attendance. *Journal of Sport Management, 12,* 103-122.

Chapter 16

2012 Winter Youth Olympics. (n.d.). In *Wikipedia.* Retrieved March 6, 2017, from https://en.wikipedia.org/wiki/2012_Winter_Youth_Olympics

AOC. (n.d.). AYOF 2013. Retrieved February 20, 2017, from http://corporate.olympics.com.au/games/ayof-2013

Asian Paralympic Committee. (n.d.). Asian Youth Para Games Retrieved February 20, 2017, from www.asianparalympic.org/asian-youth-para-games

AYG 2013. (2013). Nanjing 2nd Asian Youth Games 2013. Retrieved February 20, 2017, from www.singaporeathletics.org.sg/nanjing-2nd-asian-youth-games-2013

Bahamas 2017. (2017). Bahamas 2017 CYG Organizing Committee. Retrieved February 20, 2017, from www.

bahamas2017cyg.org/organizers/bcyg-2015-organising-committee/

CGF. (2014). The Commonwealth Youth Games: Samoa 2015. Retrieved August 22, 2017, from https://thecgf.com/games/samoa-2015

Chappelet, J.-L., & Kübler-Mabbott, B. (2008). *The International Olympic Committee and the Olympic system: The governance of world sport*. Oxon, United Kingdom: Routledge.

Digel, H. (2008). The risks of the Youth Olympic Games. *New Studies in Athletics, 23*(3), 53-58.

EOC. (2017). EYOF—Vision, mission and values. Retrieved February 20, 2017, from www.eyof.org/vision-mission-and-values/

EYOF. (n.d.). About EYOF. Retrieved February 20, 2017, from www.eyof.org/who-can-take-part/#

FIFA. (n.d.). About FIFA. Committees. Retrieved June 2, 2017, from www.fifa.com/about-fifa/committees/index.html

Girginov, V. (2012). Governance of the London 2012 Olympic Games legacy. *International Review for the Sociology of Sport, 47*(5), 543-558.

Hall, V. (2016, June 7). Ontario passes Rowan's Law, but it's just one step in protecting kids from concussions. *National Post*. Retrieved June 13, 2017, from http://news.nationalpost.com/sports/ontario-passes-rowans-law-but-its-just-one-step-in-protecting-kids-from-concussions

Hanstad, D. V., Parent, M. M., & Kristiansen, E. (2013). The Youth Olympic Games: The best of the Olympics or a poor copy? *European Sport Management Quarterly, 13*(3), 315–338.

Hanstad, D.V., Parent, M.M., & Houlihan, B. (Eds.). (2014). *The Youth Olympic Games*. London, United Kingdom: Routledge.

ICG. (2013). Statutes. Retrieved February 20, 2017, from http://international-childrens-games.org/icg/index.php/about-icg/statutes-of-icg

ICG. (2016). History of the Games. Retrieved January 30, 2017, from http://international-childrens-games.org/icg/index.php/the-games

ICG. (n.d.) Alkmaar 2015. Retrieved February 20, 2017, from http://international-childrens-games.org/icg/index.php/2015alkmaar

IOC. (2015). Factsheet. The YOG: Vision, birth, and principles. Retrieved February 22, 2017, from https://stillmed.olympic.org/media/Document%20Library/OlympicOrg/Factsheets-Reference-Documents/Games/YOG/Factsheet-The-YOG-Vision-Birth-and-Principles-December-2015.pdf

IOC. (2016, November). Factsheet: IOC debriefing Olympic Games Rio 2016. Update—November 2016. Retrieved June 13, 2017, from https://stillmed.olympic.org/media/Document%20Library/OlympicOrg/Factsheets-Reference-Documents/OGKM/OGKM-factsheet-IOC-Debriefing-Olympic-Games-Rio-2016.pdf#_ga=2.73146899.1465123984.1497298992-1264564570.1463506977

IOC. (2017). Olympic Games Knowledge Management (OGKM). Retrieved June 13, 2017, from www.olympic.org/factsheets-and-reference-documents/olympic-games-knowledge-management-ogkm

IPC. (n.d.) 2017 Youth Parapan American Games. Retrieved February 20, 2017, from www.paralympic.org/news/sports-programme-confirmed-2017-youth-parapan-american-games

Judge, L.W., Petersen, J., & Lydum, M. (2009). The best kept secret in sports: The 2010 Youth Olympic Games. *International Review for the Sociology of Sport, 44*(2-3), 173-191.

Judge, L.W., Kantzidou, E., Gilreath E., Bellar, D., Petersen, J.C., & Surber, K. (2014). The promotion of the Youth Olympic Games: A Greek perspective. *Journal of Research in Health, Physical Education, Recreation, Sport & Dance, 6*(1), 6-12.

Kristiansen, E. (2015). Competing for culture: Young Olympians' narratives from the first Winter Youth Olympic Games. *International Journal of Sport and Exercise Psychology, 13*(1), 29–42.

Kristiansen, E., Strittmatter, A.-M. & Skirstad, B. (2016): Stakeholders, Challenges and Issues at a Co-Hosted Youth Olympic Event: Lessons Learned from the European Youth Olympic Festival in 2015, *The International Journal of the History of Sport 33*(10), 1152-1168.

Kristiansen, E.. MacIntosh, E., Parent, M., & Houlihan, B. (2017). Competing at the Youth Olympic Games: A facilitator or barrier on the high performance sport development pathway? *European Sport Management Quarterly, 18*(1), 73-92.

Leopkey, B., & Parent, M.M. (2015). Stakeholder perspectives regarding the governance of legacy at the Olympic Games. *Annals of Leisure Research, 18*, 528-548.

Lesjø, J.H., Strittmatter, A.-M., & Hanstad, D.V. (2017). Patterns of influence: Relations with the IOC as seen by the organizers of the Youth Olympic Winter Games 2016. *International Journal of Sport Management and Marketing, 17*(4/5/6), 331-350.

Lillehammer 2016. (2016). *Report to the Norwegian Ministry of Culture June 30, 2016*. Lillehammer, Norway: Lillehammer Youth Olympic Games Organizing Committee.

Little League. (n.d.). World series history. Retrieved March 6, 2017, from www.littleleague.org/World_Series/world-serieshistory/WSTournamentResults/pastchampsSLBB.htm

Little League. (2017). About Little League. Retrieved June 7, 2017, from www.littleleague.org/Little_League_Big_Legacy/About_Little_League/Who_We_Are.htm

Little League World Series. (n.d.). In *Wikipedia*. Retrieved June 6, 2017, from https://en.wikipedia.org/wiki/Little_League_World_Series

Loland, S. (2014). The Youth Olympic Games and the Olympic ideal. In D.V. Hanstad, M.M. Parent, & B. Houlihan (Eds.), *The Youth Olympic Games* (pp. 19-33). London, United Kingdom: Routledge.

MacIntosh, E. (2017). Young athlete major event experiences: Brand co-creators and ambassadors. *Sport in Society, 20*, 438-453.

McDaid, D. (2016, February 12). Winter Youth Olympic Games. BBC Scotland. Retrieved February 20, 2017, from www.bbc.com/sport/winter-olympics/35558833

Naraine, M.L., Schenk, J., & Parent, M.M. (2016). Coordination in international and domestic sports events: Examining stakeholder network governance. *Journal of Sport Management, 30*(5), 521-537.

New Taipei City 2016. (2016a). Introduction of International Children's Games (ICG). Retrieved January 30, 2017, from www.icg-newtaipeicity2016.com/about.php

New Taipei City 2016. (2016b). Organization. Retrieved January 30, 2017, from www.icg-newtaipeicity2016.com/organization.php

Parent, M.M. (2008). Evolution and issue patterns for major-sport-event organizing committees and their stakeholders. *Journal of Sport Management, 22*(2), 135-164.

Parent, M.M. (2010). Decision making in major sport events over time: Parameters, drivers, and strategies. *Journal of Sport Management, 24*(3), 291-318.

Parent, M.M. (2013). Olympic Games stakeholder governance and management. In S. Frawley & D. Adair (Eds.), *Managing the Olympic Games* (pp. 15-32). London, United Kingdom: Palgrave Macmillan.

Parent, M. M., Kristiansen, E., Skille, E. Å. & Hanstad, D. V. (2015). The sustainability of the Youth Olympic Games: Stakeholder networks and institutional perspectives. *International Review for the Sociology of Sport, 50*(3), 326–348.

Parent, M.M. (2016a). The governance of the Olympic Games in Canada. *Sport in Society, 19*(6), 796-816. doi: 10.1080/17430437.2015.1108652

Parent, M.M. (2016b). Stakeholder perceptions on the democratic governance of major sports events. *Sport Management Review, 19*(4), 402-416. doi: http://dx.doi.org/10.1016/j.smr.2015.11.003

Parent, M.M., Kristiansen, E., & Houlihan, B. (2017). Governance and knowledge management and transfer: The case of the Lillehammer 2016 Winter Youth Olympic Games. *International Journal of Sport Management and Marketing, 17*(4/5/6), 308-330.

Parent, M.M., Kristiansen, E., & MacIntosh, E.W. (2014). Athletes' experiences at the Youth Olympic Games: Perceptions, stressors, and discourse paradox. *Event Management, 18*(3), 303-324.

Parent, M.M., MacIntosh, E., Kristiansen, E., & Naraine, M.L. (2016). Report on the young athletes' feedback regarding the Lillehammer 2016 Winter Youth Olympic Games. Ottawa, Canada: University of Ottawa.

Parry, J. (2012). The Youth Olympic Games—some ethical issues. *Sport, Ethics and Philosophy, 6*, 138-154.

Samoa 2015. (2015, December). Samoa 2015 Commonwealth Youth Games 5-15 September, APIA, Post Games Report. Retrieved January 30, 2017, from www.thecgf.com/cyg/Samoa-2015-CYG-Post-Games-Report.pdf

Sand, T.S., Strittmatter, A.-M. & Hanstad, D.V. (2017). 2016 Winter Youth Olympic Games: Planning for a volunteer legacy. *International Journal of Sport Management and Marketing, 17*(4/5/6) 242-260.

Séguin, B., Ferrand, A., & Chappelet, J.-L. (2014). Extending the Olympic brand into new territories. In D.V. Hanstad, M.M. Parent, & B. Houlihan (Eds.), *The Youth Olympic Games* (pp. 177-196). London, United Kingdom: Routledge.

Skille, E. & Houlihan, B. (2014). The contemporary context of elite youth sport: The role of national sport organisations in the UK and Norway. In D.V. Hanstad, M.M. Parent, & B. Houlihan (Eds.). *The Youth Olympic Games* (pp. 34-50). London, United Kingdom: Routledge.

Strittmatter, A.-M. (2016). Defining a problem to fit the solution: A neo-institutional explanation of legitimising the bid for the 2016 Lillehammer Winter Youth Olympic Games. *International Journal of Sport Policy and Politics, 8*(3), 421-437.

Strittmatter, A.-M. (2017a). A neo-institutionalist analysis of sport event leveraging strategies and tactics. *International Journal of Sport Management and Marketing, 17*(4/5/6), 261-282.

Strittmatter, A.-M. (2017b). *Legitimation processes of sport organizations—the case of Norwegian youth sport policy and the 2016 Lillehammer Winter Youth Olympic Games.* Doctoral dissertation. Oslo, Norway: Norwegian School of Sport Sciences.

Strittmatter, A.-M., & Skille, E.Å. (2017). Boosting youth sport? The implementation of Norwegian youth sport policy through the 2016 Lillehammer Winter Youth Olympic Games. *Sport in Society, 20*(1), 144-160.

Strittmatter, A.-M., Kilvinger, B., Bodemar, A., Skille, E.Å. & Kurscheidt, M. (2018). Dual governance structures in action sports: Institutionalization processes of professional snowboarding revisited. Sport in Society. DOI: 10.1080/17430437.2018.1440696

Theodoraki, E. (2001). A conceptual framework for the study of structural configurations of organising committees for the Olympic Games (OCOGs). *European Journal for Sport Management, 8*(Special issue), 106-124.

Theodoraki, E. (2007). *Olympic event organization.* London, United Kingdom: Butterworth-Heinemann.

Val Di Fassa 2019. (2018). Alpine Junior World Ski Championships. Retrieved May 19, 2019, from http://www.valdifassa2019.com/EN/junior-world-championships.php

Wong, D. (2011). The Youth Olympic Games: Past, present and future. *International Journal of the History of Sport, 28*(13), 1831-1851.

World Rugby Under 20 Championships. (n.d.). In *Wikipedia.* Retrieved June 6, 2017, https://en.wikipedia.org/wiki/World_Rugby_Under_20_Championship

Chapter 17

Ahmadi, A. (2018, January 3). Dallas Mavericks announce new official Chinese name. *RSS Mavs News.* Retrieved March 15, 2018, from www.mavs.com/dallas-mavericks-announce-new-official-chinese-name

Allen, D.G. (2006). Do organizational socialization tactics influence newcomer embeddedness and turnover? *Journal of Management, 32*(2), 237-256.

Blanchard, P. (n.d.). *Information and knowledge management at the IOC.* International Olympic Committee. Retrieved May 1, 2018, from www.lboro.ac.uk/microsites/ssehs/olympic-studies/cv_abs/Philippe%20Blanchard-%20IM%20and%20KM%20at%20IOC-Final.pdf

Blauvelt, H. (2003, October 9). Stephenson to play with seniors, says Asians hurt LPGA. *USA Today.* Retrieved May 15, 2018, from https://usatoday30.usatoday.com/sports/golf/champions/2003-10-09-stephenson-champions_x.htm

Boyes, B. (2016, August 19). Is the Olympic Games Knowledge Management (OGKM) program effective? Retrieved April 20, 2018, from https://realkm.com/2016/08/19/is-the-olympic-games-knowledge-management-ogkm-program-effective

Cable, D.M., & Parsons, C.K. (2001). Socialization tactics and person-organization fit. *Personnel Psychology, 54,* 1-23.

Carte, P., & Fox, C. (2004). *Bridging the culture gap: A practical guide to international business communication.* London, United Kingdom: Canning.

Chaney, L.H., & Martin, J.S. (2004). *Intercultural business communication* (3rd ed.). Old Tappan, NJ: Prentice Hall, Pearson Education.

Chun, S., Gentry, J.W., & McGinnis, L.P. (2004). Cultural differences in fan ritualization: A cross-cultural perspective of the ritualization of American and Japanese baseball fans. *Advances in Consumer Research, 31,* 503-508.

Dawson, L. (2008). Building the Bird's Nest. *Architectural Review, 223*(1337), 96-97.

Dunning, E. (1989). Multinational enterprises and the growth of services: Some conceptual and theoretical issues. *Services Industries Journal, 9,* 5-39.

Eng, K., & Shear, A. (2006). *Kokoyakyu: High school baseball* [Motion picture]. Projectile Arts.

Gregg, E.A. (2014). Interview with Brian Carroll, vice president for television and emerging media, LPGA. *International Journal of Sport Communication, 7*(1), 52-55.

Hardman, A., & Iorwerth, H. (2014). Player quotas in elite club football. *Sport, Ethics and Philosophy, 8*(2), 147-156.

Hofstede, G. (1980). *Culture's consequences: International differences in work-related values.* Beverly Hills, CA: Sage.

Hofstede, G. (1991). *Cultures and organizations. Software of the mind.* London, United Kingdom: McGraw-Hill.

Hofstede, G., & Bond, M.H. (1984). Hofstede's culture dimensions: An independent validation using Rokeach's value survey. *Journal of Cross-Cultural Psychology, 15,* 417-433.

Holt, R., & Ruta, D. (2015). *Routledge handbook of sport and legacy: Meeting the challenge of major sports events.* London, United Kingdom, and New York, NY: Routledge.

Jackson, S.J., Brandl-Bredenbeck, H.P., & John, A. (2005). Lost in translation: Cultural differences in the interpretation of commercial media violence. *International Journal of Sport Management and Marketing, 1*(1/2), 155-168.

Lockstone-Binney, L., Holmes, K., Shipway, R., & Smith, K.A. (2016). Evaluating the volunteering infrastructure legacy of the Olympic Games: Sydney 2000 and London 2012. *Final Report.*

Lombardo, J. (2010, May 24). After two years, NBA China on steady course. *Street & Smith's SportsBusiness Journal.* Retrieved August 20, 2010, from www.sportsbussiness-journal.com

MacIntosh, E., Couture, L, & Spence, K. (2015). Management challenges in delivering an international sport and development program. *Sport, Business, Management, an International Journal, 5*(3), 276-296.

MacIntosh, E., & Doherty, A. (2008). Inside the Canadian fitness industry: Development of a conceptual framework of organizational culture. *International Journal of Sport Management, 9*(3), 303-327.

MacIntosh, E., & Spence, K. (2012). An exploration of stakeholder values: In search of common ground within an international sport and development initiative. *Sport Management Review, 15,* 404-415.

Maguire, J., Jarvie, G., Mansfield, L., & Bradley, J. (2002). *Sports worlds. A sociological perspective.* Champaign, IL: Human Kinetics.

Martin, J. (1992). *Cultures in organizations: Three perspectives.* New York, NY: Oxford University Press.

Parent, M., & MacIntosh, E. (2013). Organizational culture evolution in temporary organizations: The case of the 2010 Olympic Winter Games. *Canadian Journal of Administrative Sciences, 30*(4), 223-237.

Rabotin, M. (2008, July). Deconstructing the successful global leader. *American Society for Training and Development*, pp. 54-59.

Samiee, S. (1999). The internationalization of services: Trends, obstacles and issues. *Journal of Services Marketing, 13*, 319-328.

Schein, E.H. (1985). *Organizational culture and leadership.* San Francisco, CA: Jossey Bass.

Schaub, C., & Schindhelm, M. (2008). *Bird's Nest: Herzog & de Meuron in China* [Motion picture]. Brooklyn, NY: Icarus Films.

Shenkar, O., Luo, Y., & Yeheskel, O. (2008). From "distance" to "friction": Substituting metaphors and redirecting intercultural research. *Academy of Management Review, 33*(4), 905-923.

Smith, D.C. (2008). Pulling the plug on culture shock: A seven step plan for managing travel anxiety. *Journal of Global Business Issues, 2*(1), 41-46.

Sofka, J. (2008, October 27). Any company's China strategy must account for obstacles. *Street & Smith's SportsBusiness Journal.* Retrieved August 20, 2010, from www.sportsbussinessjournal.com

Wilson, R. (2008, September 3). LPGA's English-only rule backfires, could lead to lost sponsors. Retrieved September 10, 2010, from http://golf.fanhouse.com/2008/09/03/lpgas-english-only-rule-backfires-could-lead-to-lost-sponsors

Xi, X., & Duncombe, R. (2016). Knowledge management and transfer in 2010 Vancouver Olympic Winter Games. *American Journal of Engineering and Technology Research, 16*(1), 78-85.

Zhou, L., Wang, J.J., Chen, X., Lei, C., Zhang, J.J., & Meng, X. (2017). The development of NBA in China: A glocalization perspective. *International Journal of Sports Marketing and Sponsorship, 18*(1), 81-94.

Chapter 18

Ahlert G., an der Heiden, I. (2015). *Die ökonomische Bedeutung des Sports. Themenreport.* Osnabrück, Germany.

Arsenal Holdings plc. (2007, May). *Statement of accounts and annual report 2006/2007.*

Asafu-Adjaye, J. (2005). Environmental economics for non-economists (2nd ed.). Singapore: World Scientific.

A.T. Kearney. (2014, November 4). Sports industry growing faster than the GDP. Retrieved April 17, 2017, from www.atkearney.com/news-media/news-releases/news-release/-/asset_publisher/00OIL7Jc67KL/content/id/5273085

Atkinson, G., Mourato, S., Szymanski, S., & Ozdemiroglu, E. (2008). Are we willing to pay enough to "back the bid"?: Valuing the intangible impacts of London's bid to host the 2012 Summer Olympic Games. *Urban Studies, 45*(2), 419-444.

Baxter, K. (2014, July 21). Manchester United uniform is pricey real estate as Chevrolet knows. *Los Angeles Times.* Retrieved April 17, 2017, from www.latimes.com/sports/soccer/la-sp-manchester-united-20140722-story.html

Bayoli, L., & Bekker, M. (2011). Causes of construction cost and price overruns: The 2010 FIFA World Cup stadia in South Africa. *Acta Structilia, 18*(1).

CCTV.com. (2014, July 2). Manaus travel: Impact of the World Cup on tourism in Amazon. Retrieved April 17, 2017, from http://english.cntv.cn/2014/07/02/VIDE1404231958717510.shtml

Cobb, S., & Weinberg, D. (1993). The importance of import substitution in regional economic impact analysis: Empirical estimates from two Cincinnati area events. *Economic Development Quarterly, 7*(3), 282-286.

Cornelissen, S., Bob, U., & Swart, K. (2011). Towards redefining the concept of legacy in relation to sport mega-events: Insights from the 2010 FIFA World Cup. *Development Southern Africa, 28*(3), 307-318

Department of Culture, Media and Sports. (2015). *2010 Sport satellite account for the UK. Statistical release.* London, United Kingdom.

European Commission, DG Education and Culture. (2011). *Sport satellite accounts—A European project: New results.* Brussels, Belgium.

Garcia-Navarro, L. (2015, May 11). Brazil's World Cup legacy includes $550 million stadium turned parking lot. Retrieved April 17, 2017, from www.npr.org/sections/parallels/2015/05/11/405955547/brazils-world-cup-legacy-includes-550m-stadium-turned-parking-lot

Heyne, M., Maennig, W., & Suessmuth, B. (2007). *Mega-sporting events as experience goods.* Hamburg Working Paper Series in Economic Policy, No. 5.

International Licensing Industry Merchants Association (LIMA). (2016), *Statistics and facts on sports drinks in the U.S.* Statista.com

Knott, B., Allen, D., & Swart, K. (2012). Stakeholder reflections of the tourism and nation-branding legacy of the 2010 FIFA World Cup for South Africa. *African Journal for Physical Health, Education, Recreation and Dance,* September (supplement 1), 115-125.

Mankiw, N. (2015). *Macroeconomics* (9th ed.). New York, NY: Freeman.

Manchester United Football Club. (2012). World's most popular FC. Retrieved April 17, 2017, from www.manutd.com/en/News-And-Features/Club-News/2012/May/manchester-united-global-following-confirmed-as-659million.aspx?pageNo=1

Manfred, T. (2015, May 13). Brazil's $3 billion World Cup stadiums are becoming white elephants a year later. *Business Insider.* Retrieved April 17, 2017, from www.businessinsider.com/brazil-world-cup-stadiums-one-year-later-2015-5

Nolan, R. (September 11, 2008). Protestors crash Berlin arena's opening party. *Spiegel Online International.*

Retrieved August 7, 2009, from www.spiegel.de/international/germany/0,1518,577656,00.html

Olmstead, L. (2015). Luxury active travel at Backroads: Expertly guided bikes, hikes, and more. *Forbes*. Retrieved April 17, 2017, from www.forbes.com/sites/larryolmsted/2015/07/31/luxury-active-travel-with-backroads-expertly-guided-bikes-hikes-more/2/#1f37b0e761e3

Ormiston, S. (2014, June 9). In Amazon's Manaus, Brazil's dreamiest World Cup adventure. *CBC news*. Retrieved April 17, 2017, from www.cbc.ca/news/world/in-amazon-s-manaus-brazil-s-dreamiest-world-cup-adventure-1.2669024?cmp=rss

Pareto, V. (1971). *Manual of political economy*. New York, NY: Kelley.

Preuss, H. (2004). Calculating of the regional impact of the Olympic Games. *European Sport Management Quarterly*, *4*(4), 234-253.

Preuss, H. (2005). The economic impact of visitors at major multi-sport events. *European Sport Management Quarterly*, *5*(3), 283-305.

Preuss, H. (2007). The conceptualisation and measurement of mega sport event legacies. *Journal of Sport & Tourism*, *12*(4), 207-228.

Preuss, H. (2014, February 10). Global spectatorship at FIFA Football World Cups. Presentation at Conference of the World Association of Sport Management, Madrid, Spain.

Preuss, H. (2015). A framework for identifying the legacies of a mega sport event. *Leisure Studies*, *34*(1). doi:10.1080/02614367.2014.994552

Preuss, H. (2016). IOC legacy framework. Presented at the conference for the Union of World Cities, Lausanne, Switzerland.

Solberg, H.A., & Preuss, H. (2007). Major sport events and long-term tourism impacts. *Journal of Sport Management*, *21*(2), 215-236.

Spilling, O.R. (1999). Long-term impacts of mega-events: The case of Lillehammer 1994. In C. Jeanrenaud (Ed.), *The economic impact of sport events* (pp. 135-166). Neuchâtel, Switzerland: Editions CIES.

Statistics Netherlands. (2015). *Sport in focus—The contribution of sport to the Dutch economy in 2006, 2008 and 2010 (Summary)*. The Hague, Netherlands.

TechinBrazil. (2015, March 26). Brazilian demographics per state. Retrieved April 17, 2017, from https://techinbrazil.com/brazilian-demographics-per-state

Varian, H. (2010). *Intermediate microeconomics* (8th ed.). New York, NY: Norton.

Chapter 19

Adams, S. (2015, December 1). MLB ratifies new NPB posting system, formally announces Shohei Ohtani will be posted today. Retrieved from www.mlbtraderumors.com/2017/12/mlb-ratifies-new-npb-posting-system-formally-announces-shohei-ohtani-will-be-posted-today.html

Alyce, A. (2015). Interviews: J-League clubs budget is between 30 and 50 million USD. Retrieved from www.ecofoot.fr/interview-iriondo-j-league

Aspen Institute Project Play. (2017). *State of play 2017: Trends and developments*. Retrieved March 7, 2018, from www.aspeninstitute.org/publications/state-of-play-2017-trends-and-developments

Association of Road Racing Statisticians. (2018). Life-time prize money. Retrieved March 6, 2018, from www.arrs.net/PM_Life.htm

Benedictus, L. (2016, August 20). Why are deadly extreme sports more popular than ever? *The Guardian*. Retrieved from www.theguardian.com/sport/2016/aug/20/why-are-deadly-extreme-sports-more-popular-than-ever

Bennett, G., Henson, R., & Zhang, J. (2002). Action sports sponsorship recognition. *Sport Marketing Quarterly*, *11*(3), 174-185.

Blackshaw, I.S. (2017). *International sports law: An introductory guide*. Berlin, Germany: Springer-Verlag.

Bogage, J. (2017, September 6). Youth sports study: Declining participation, rising costs and unqualified coaches. *Washington Post*. Retrieved on March 7, 2018, from www.washingtonpost.com/news/recruiting-insider/wp/2017/09/06/youth-sports-study-declining-participation-rising-costs-and-unqualified-coaches/?utm_term=.1d6c151212a8

Bose, M. (2012). *Game changer: How the English Premier League came to dominate the world*. London, United Kingdom: Marshall Cavendish International.

Boston Marathon 2017. (2018). 2017 prize structure. Retrieved on March 6, 2018, from www.bostonmarathonmediaguide.com/prize-structure

Brown, M.T., Rascher, D.A., Nagel, M.S., & McEvoy, C.D. (2017). *Financial management in the sport industry*. Scottsdale, AZ: Holcomb Hathaway.

Chelladurai, P. (2014). *Managing organizations for sport and physical activity: A systems perspective* (4th ed.). New York, NY: Holcomb Hathaway.

Circuit-booking.com. (2018). Circuit overview Asia. Retrieved from www.circuit-booking.com/en/circuits/asia

Dan, G.C. (2014, 18 February). S-League braced for hurdles in bid to continue improving attendances. *Today*.

DeCotta, I. (2008). *The Singapore Grand Prix: 50 Years in the making*. Singapore: MediaCorp.

Dilworth, K. (2015, February 11). Would you let your child quit a sport midseason? Retrieved from www.nays.org/blog/would-you-let-your-child-quit-a-sport-mid-season

Duerden, J. (2018, April 17). Interest in K-League on the wane as South Korea hope for World Cup success. Retrieved from www.espn.com/soccer/blog/football-asia/153/post/3459660/interest-in-k-league-on-the-wane-as-south-korea-hope-for-world-cup-success

Deloitte. (2018). Roar power: Annual review of football finance 2018. Retrieved from www2.deloitte.com/uk/en/pages/sports-business-group/articles/annual-review-of-football-finance.html

European Commission. (1998). The European model of sport: Consultation document of DG X. Brussels: European Commission.

Football Association of Singapore. (n.d.). *Annual report April 2016-March 2017*. Singapore.

Fort, R. (2000). European and North American sports differences (?). *Scottish Journal of Political Economy, 47*(4), 431-455.

Gaines, C. (2017, August 6). Neymar's move to PSG will cost the French soccer giant more than $500 million. *Business Insider*. Retrieved from www.businessinsider.com/how-much-neymar-salary-transfer-fee-psg-barca-2017-8

Gregory, S. (2017, August 24). How kids' sports became a $15 billion industry. *Time Magazine*. Retrieved on March 7, 2018, from http://time.com/4913687/how-kids-sports-became-15-billion-industry

Harris, N. (2013, 9 September). Revealed: Asia driving boom as Premier League foreign TV cash hits £2.23BN. Retrieved from www.sportingintelligence.com/2013/09/16/revealed-asia-driving-boom-as-premier-league-foreign-tv-cash-hits-2-23bn-160901

Henderson, J.C., Foo, K., Lim, H., & Yip, S. (2010). Sports events and tourism: The Singapore Formula One Grand Prix. *International Journal of Event and Festival Management, 1*(1), 60-73.

Humphreys, B.R., & Watanabe, N.M. (2012). Business and finance of international sport leagues. In M. Li, E. MacIntosh, & G. Bravo (Ed). *International sport management*. Champaign, IL: Human Kinetics.

International Health, Racquet, and Sportsclub Association (2018). Market size of the global health club industry from 2009 to 2016 (in billion U.S. dollars). Retrieved March 7, 2018, from www.statista.com/statistics/275035/global-market-size-of-the-health-club-industry

Kaiser, L.L. (2004). The flight from single-entity structured sport leagues. *DePaul Journal of Sports Law, 2*(1), 1.

Kawai, K., & Nichol, M. (2015). Labor in Nippon Professional Baseball and the future of player transfers to Major League Baseball. *Marquette Sports Law Review, 25*(2), 491-52

Kyodo. (2017, February 9). J. League reveals breakdown of prize money, funds. *Japan Times*. Retrieved from www.japantimes.co.jp/sports/2017/02/09/soccer/j-league/j-league-reveals-breakdown-prize-money-funds/#.Wyrk6qdKjIU

Lee, A. (2015, February 24). 7 charts that show the state of youth sports in the US and why it matters. Retrieved March 7, 2018, from www.aspeninstitute.org/blog-posts/7-charts-that-show-the-state-of-youth-sports-in-the-us-and-why-it-matters/

Lim, B. (2018, May 10). The NBA is looking at a handful of Asian countries to become big markets. Retrieved from www.cnbc.com/2018/05/10/the-nba-is-looking-at-a-handful-of-asian-countries-to-become-big-markets.html

Mason, D. (1999). What is the sports product and who buys it? The marketing of professional sports leagues. *European Journal of Marketing, 33*(3/4), 402-419.

Matuszewski, E. (2017). Here's why we should be bullish about golf in 2017. *Forbes*. Retrieved from www.forbes.com/sites/erikmatuszewski/2017/01/23/heres-why-we-should-be-bullish-about-golf-in-2017/#6fdb34775660

Meng, W.M. (2017, September 15). Formula One: Singapore Grand Prix signs 4-year extension to host night race. The Straits Times. Retrieved from https://www.straitstimes.com/sport/formula-one/formula-one-singapore-grand-prix-signs-four-year-extension-to-host-night-race

Mohan, M., & Leng, H.K. (2015). *Motivations of football fans in Singapore*. Paper presented at the 7th International Conference on Humanities and Social Sciences, Hat Yai, Thailand.

Nagel, M.S. (2011) Free agents. In L.E. Swayne & M. Dodds (Eds.). *Encyclopedia of sports management and marketing*. Thousand Oaks, CA. Sage.

National Golf Foundation. (2018). Golf industry report. Jupiter, FL.

National Physical Activity Plan Alliance. (2014). The 2014 United States report card on physical activity for children & youth. Retrieved on March 7, 2018, from www.physicalactivityplan.org/reportcard/NationalReportCard_longform_final%20for%20web.pdf

Noll, R. (2003). The organization of sports leagues. *Oxford Review of Economic Policy, 19*, 530-551.

O'Connor, T. (2017). Our 12th annual state of the industry report: Old faithful? Is the sports events market really as predictable & dependable as we think? *Sports Events Magazine*, March 2017.

Outdoor Foundation. (2017). Number of participants in surfing in the United States from 2006 to 2016 (in millions). Retrieved March 5, 2018, from www.statista.com/statistics/191328/participants-in-surfing-in-the-us-since-2006/

Page, S.J., Steele, W., & Connell, J. (2006). Analysing the promotion of adventure tourism: A case study of Scotland. *Journal of Sport & Tourism, 11*(1), 51-76.

Plunkett Research. (2018). Sports industry statistics and market size overview. Retrieved from www.plunkettresearch.com/statistics/Industry-Statistics-Sports-Industry-Statistic-and-Market-Size-Overview/

Puchan, H. (2004). Living "extreme": Adventure sports, media and commercialisation. *Journal of Communication Management, 9*(2), 171-178.

Remember Singapore. (2016, 26 November). Vroom vroom . . . Looking back at the old Singapore Grand

Prix. Retrieved from https://remembersingapore.org/2016/11/26/singapore-grand-prix-sixties-seventies/

Rockerbie, D.W., & Easton, S.T. (2017). Revenue sharing in professional sports leagues as a hedge for exchange rate risk. *International Journal of Sport Finance, 12*(4), 342-358.

Rosen, S., & Sanderson, A. (2001). Labour markets in professional sports. *Economic Journal, 111*(469), 47-68.

Runner's World. (2016, November 7). Marathons by total number of finishers worldwide in 2016. Retrieved March 5, 2018, from www.statista.com/statistics/280473/marathons-by-number-of-finshers-worldwide/

Sandler Research. (2016, October 14). Adventure tourism market growing at nearly 46% CAGR to 2020. Retrieved March 5, 2018, from www.prnewswire.com/news-releases/adventure-tourism-market-growing-at-nearly-46-cagr-to-2020-597059331.html

Selvam, S. (2015). Rationalizing sport spectatorship: Analysis of fan behaviour in S-League. In H.K. Leng & N.Y. Hsu (Eds.), *Emerging trends and innovation in sports marketing and management in Asia.* Hershey, PA: IGI Global.

Sheinin, D. (2018, March 3). No longer sports' dirty little secret, tanking is on full display and impossible to contain. *Washington Post.* Retrieved from www.washingtonpost.com/sports/no-longer-sports-dirty-little-secret-tanking-is-on-full-display-and-impossible-to-contain/2018/03/02/9b436f0a-1d96-11e8-b2d9-08e748f892c0_story.html?utm_term=.76eb727c24ec

Singapore GP. (2013). 2013 Formula1 Singtel Singapore Grand Prix. Retrieved from www.singaporegp.sg

Singapore GP (2017, September 15). Singapore to host the Formula 1 World Championship until 2021. Retrieved from www.singaporegp.sg/media/press-release/236

Sport Singapore. (n.d.). *National sports participation survey 2011.* Singapore.

Star Online. (2010, June 7). Ministry to encourage extreme sports in Malaysia. Retrieved March 5, 2018, from www.thestar.com.my/news/nation/2010/06/07/ministry-to-encourage-extreme-sports-in-malaysia/#HjVF1m03mjUfuapx.99

Stoddart, B. (1990). Wide world of golf: A research note on the interdependence of sport, culture, and economy. *Sociology of Sport Journal, 7,* 378-388.

Technavio Research. (2016, June 20). Nearly 1.74 million people in North America surf at least once a year, making it the largest region for the global bodyboard market until 020, reports Technavio. Retrieved March 5, 2018, from www.businesswire.com/news/home/20160620005500/en/1.74-Million-People-North-America-Surf-Year

The R&A. (2015). Golf around the world 2015. Retrieved from www.randa.org/~/media/Files/DownloadsAndPublications/Golf-Around-The-World-2015.ashx

Wade, A., & Fuehrer, D. (2014, October 29). Running's most lucrative road races, biggest earners: The races with the most prize money, and the runners with the greatest lifetime prize money earnings. *Runner's World.* Retrieved March 6, 2018, from www.runnersworld.com/run-the-numbers/runnings-most-lucrative-road-races-biggest-earners

Wahba, P. (2015). Why big business loves marathons. *Fortune.* Retrieved March 6, 2018, from http://fortune.com/2015/10/26/business-marathons/

Weinstein, A. (2017, July 13). Report: NFL teams shared $7.8 billion in revenue last year, up 10 percent. *Sporting News.* Retrieved from www.sportingnews.com/nfl/news/nfl-teams-shared-8-billion-2016-10-percent-increase/xq0olewhxo2d1a5mmrll4w4fz

Wood, J. (2017, September 19). Report: Nine NBA teams lost money in 2016-17 after revenue sharing. *Sports Illustrated.* Retrieved from www.si.com/nba/2017/09/19/revenue-sharing-losses-net-income-cavs-spurs-wizards

Woods, R.B. (2011). *Social issues in sport* (2nd ed.). Champaign, IL: Human Kinetics.

Zegers, C. (2017, March 24). Revenue sharing and North America's major pro sports leagues. Retrieved from www.thoughtco.com/revenue-sharing-and-north-americas-major-pro-sports-leagues-326039

Zimbalist, A.S. (2002). Competitive balance in sports leagues: An introduction. *Journal of Sports Economics, 3*(2), 111-121.

Chapter 20

Aaker, D.A. (1991) *Managing brand equity: Capitalizing on the value of a brand name.* New

Abeza, G., O'Reilly, N., Séguin, B., & Nzindukiyimana, O. (2017). The world's highest-paid athletes, product endorsement, and Twitter. *Sport, Business and Management: An International Journal, 7*(3), 332-355.

Abeza, G., Pegoraro, A., Naraine, M.L., Séguin, B., & O'Reilly, N. (2014). Activating a global sport sponsorship with social media: An analysis of TOP sponsors, Twitter, and the 2014 Olympic Games. *International Journal of Sport Management and Marketing, 15*(3-4), 184-213.

Anderson, D. (1979). Sport spectatorship: Appropriation of an identity or appraisal of self. *Review of Sport and Leisure, 4*(2), 115-127.

Andrew, D. P., Kim, S., O'Neal, N., Greenwell, T. C., & James, J. D. (2009). The Relationship Between Spectator Motivations and Media and Merchandise Consumption at a Professional Mixed Martial Arts Event. *Sport Marketing Quarterly, 18*(4), 199-209.

Armstrong, K. (2014). Sport marketing. In P.M. Pedersen & L. Thibault (Eds.), *Contemporary sport management* (5th ed.) (pp. 251-269). Champaign, IL: Human Kinetics.

Beech, J.G., & Chadwick, S. (2007). *The marketing of sport.* Harlow, United Kingdom: Pearson Education.

Boyle, R., & Haynes, R. (2000). *Sport, the media, and popular culture*. Harlow, United Kingdom: Pearson Education.

Copeland, R., Frisby, W., & McCarville, R. (1996). Understanding the sport sponsorship process from a corporate perspective. *Journal of Sport Management, 10*(1), 32-48. Retrieved from Academic Search Premier database.

Crompton, J. (2004). Conceptualization and alternate operationalizations of the measurement of sponsorship effectiveness in sport. *Leisure Studies, 23*(3), 267-281. doi: 10.1080/0261436042000183695

Crow, B.R., Byon, K.K., & Tsuji, Y. (2011). International sport marketing. In M. Li, E. Macintosh, & G. Brave (Eds.), *International sport management* (pp. 395-407). Champaign, IL: Human Kinetics.

Ferrand, A., Chappelet, J.L., & Séguin, B. (2012). *Olympic marketing*. New York, NY: Routledge

Foster, G., O'Reilly, N., & Dávila, A. (2016). *Sports business management: Decision making around the globe*. New York, NY: Routledge.

Funk, D.C., & James, J. (2001). The psychological continuum model: A conceptual framework for understanding an individual's psychological connection to sport. *Sport Management Review, 4*(2), 119-150.

Garland, R., Charbonneau, J., & Macpherson, T. (2008). Measuring sport sponsorship effectiveness: Links to existing behavior. *Innovative Marketing, 4*(1), 46-51.

Gladden, J.M., & Funk, D.C. (2002). Developing an understanding of brand associations in team sport: Empirical evidence from consumers of professional sport. *Journal of Sport Management, 16*, 54-81.

Gray, D., & McEvoy, C. (2005). Sport marketing strategies and tactics. In B. Parkhouse: *The management of sport: Its foundation and application*, 4th Edition, pp. 228-255.

Harris, L.C., & Ogbonna, E. (2008). The dynamics underlying service firm customer relationships: Insights from a study of English Premier League soccer fans. *Journal of Service Research, 10*, 382–399.

Humphreys, B.R., & Mondello, M. (2008). Determinants of franchise values in North American professional sports leagues: Evidence from a hedonic price model. *International Journal of Sport Finance, 3*(2), 98-105.

Hunt, K.A., Bristol, T., & Bashaw, R.E. (1999). A conceptual approach to classifying sports fans. *Journal of Services Marketing, 13*(6), 439-452.

Lee, C., Bang, H., & Lee, D. (2013). Regaining fans' trust after negative incidents: fit between responses and nature of incidents. *Sport Marketing Quarterly, 22*(4), 235-245.

Madrigal, R. (1995). Cognitive and affective determinants of fan satisfaction with sporting event attendance. *Journal of Leisure Research, 27*(3), 205-227.

Madrigal, R. (2001). Social identity effects in a belief-attitude-intentions hierarchy: Implications for corporate sponsorship. *Psychology & Marketing, 18*(2), 145-165.

Retrieved from Communication & Mass Media Complete database.

Mahony, D.F., Madrigal, R., & Howard, D.A. (2000). Using the psychological commitment to team (PCT) scale to segment sport consumers based on loyalty. *Sport Marketing Quarterly, 9*(1), 15.

Man United. (2008). United store opens in China. Retrieved from www.manutd.com/en/News-And-Features/Club-News/2008/Feb/United-store-opens-in-China.aspx

Mason, D. (1999). What is the sports product and who buys it? The marketing of professional sports leagues. *European Journal of Marketing, 33*(3/4), 402-419.

Masteralexis, L.P., Barr, C.A., & Hums, M.A. (Eds.). (2015). *Principles and practice of sport management*. Burlington, MA: Jones & Bartlett Learning.

McCarville, R., Flood, C., & Froats, T. (1998). The effectiveness of selected promotions on spectators' assessments of a nonprofit sporting event sponsor. *Journal of Sport Management, 12*(1), 51. Retrieved from Academic Search Premier database.

Meenaghan, T. (1998). Current developments and future directions in sponsorship. *International Journal of Advertising, 17*(1), 3-28.

Mullin, B.J., Hardy, S., & Sutton, W. (2014). *Sport marketing* (4th ed.), Champaign, IL: Human Kinetics.

NBA. (2017). Locations. Retrieved from http://careers.nba.com/locations/

Neale, L., & Funk, D. (2006). Investigating motivation, attitudinal loyalty and attendance behaviour with fans of Australian football. *International Journal of Sports Marketing and Sponsorship, 7*(4), 12-22.

O'Reilly, N., Pound, R., Burton, R., Séguin, B., Brunette, M. (2015). *Global sport marketing: Sponsorship, ambush marketing, and the Olympic Games*. Morgantown, WV: Fitness Information Technology.

O'Reilly, N., & Séguin, B. (2013). *Sport marketing: A Canadian perspective*. Toronto, Canada: Thomson Nelson.

Pitts, B. G., & Stotlar, D. K. (2007). *Fundamentals of sport marketing*. Morgantown, WV: Fitness Information Technology.

Pitts, B. G., & Stotlar, D. K. (2013). The sport business industry. *Fundamentals of sport marketing*. Morgantown, WV: Fitness Information Technology.

Ratten, V., & Ratten, H. (2011). International sport marketing: Practical and future research implications. *Journal of Business & Industrial Marketing, 26*(8), 614-620.

Schwarz, E.C., Hunter, J.D., & LaFleur, A. (2012). *Advanced theory and practice in sport marketing*. New York, NY: Routledge.

Sandler, D., & Shani, D. (1989). Olympic sponsorship versus ambush marketing. *Journal of Advertising Research, 20*(4), 11-18.

Shank, M.D., & Lyberger, M.R. (2014). *Sports marketing: A strategic perspective* (5th ed.). New York, NY: Routledge.

Sky sports. (2017). Premier League has highest percentage of foreign players—UEFA report. Retrieved from www.skysports.com/football/news/11661/10725849/premier-league-has-highest-percentage-of-foreign-players-8211-uefa-report

Smith, A.C., & Stewart, B. (2010). The special features of sport: A critical revisit. *Sport Management Review, 13*(1), 1-13.

Stavros, C., & Westberg, K. (2009). Using triangulation and multiple case studies to advance relationship marketing theory. *Qualitative Market Research: An International Journal, 12*(3), 307-320.

Stewart, B., & Smith, A. (1999). The special features of sport. *Annals of Leisure Research, 2*(1), 87-99.

Stewart, B., Smith, A.C., & Nicholson, M. (2003). Sport consumer typologies: A critical review. *Sport Marketing Quarterly, 12*(4), 206-216.

Tapp, A. (2004). The loyalty of football fans—We'll support you evermore? *Journal of Database Marketing & Customer Strategy Management, 11*(3), 203-215.

Taylor. J. (June 15, 2008). Should EC Law accommodate the unique characteristics of sport? Retrieved from http://sportsagentblog.com/2008/06/15/should-ec-law-accommodate-the-unique-characteristics-of-sport/

Wann, D.L. (1995). Preliminary validation of the sport fan motivation scale. *Journal of Sport & Social Issues, 19*(4), 377-396.

Wann, D.L., & Branscombe, N.R. (1990). Die-hard and fair-weather fans: Effects of identification on BIRGing and CORFing tendencies. *Journal of Sport & Social Issues, 14*(2), 103-117.

Wann, D.L., Grieve, F.G., Zapalac, R.K., & Pease, D.G. (2008). Motivational profiles of sport fans of different sports. *Sport Marketing Quarterly, 17*(1), 6-19.

Wann, D.L., Melnick, M.J., Russell, G.W., & Pease, D.G. (2001). *Sport fans: The psychology and social impact of spectators.* New York, NY: Routledge.

Waters, R.D., Burke, K.A., Jackson, Z.J., & Buning, J.D. (2011). Using stewardship to cultivate fandom online: Comparing how National Football League teams use their web sites and Facebook to engage their fans. *International Journal of Sport Communication, 4*, 163-177.

Westerbeek, H., & Smith, A. (2002). *Sport business in the global marketplace.* New York, NY: Springer.

Chapter 21

Brodie, R.J., Ilic, A., Juric, B., & Hollebeek, L. (2011). Customer engagement: Conceptual domain, fundamental propositions and implications for research. *Journal of Service Research, 14*, 1-20.

Brodie, R., Ilic, A., Juric, B., & Hollebeek, L. (2013). Consumer engagement in a virtual brand community: An exploratory analysis. *Journal of Business Research, 66*, 105–114.

Karg, A., & Lock, D. (2014). Using new media to engage consumers at the FIFA World Cup. In S. Frawley & D. Adair (Eds.), *Managing the football World Cup* (pp. 25-46). London, United Kingdom: Palgrave MacMillan.

Karg, A.J., & McDonald, H. (2011). Fantasy sport participation as a complement to traditional sport consumption. *Sport Management Review, 14*, 327-346

Kietzmann, J.H., Hermkens, K., McCarthy, I.P., & Silvestre, B.S. (2011). Social media? Get serious! Understanding the functional building blocks of social media. *Business Horizons, 54*, 241-251.

Legal Sports Report. (2016, June 14). Growth of fantasy sports participation flattens out, little growth for DFS. Retrieved April 10, 2017, from www.legalsportsreport.com/10464/2016-fantasy-sports-data/

Naraine, M.L., & Parent, M.M. (2016). "Birds of a feather": An institutional approach to Canadian national sport organizations' social-media use. *International Journal of Sport Communication, 9*, 140-162.

Naraine, M.L., & Parent, M.M. (2017). This is how we do it: A qualitative approach to national sport organizations' social-media implementation. *International Journal of Sport Communication, 10*, 196-217.

Time. (2015, August 25). Fantasy sports spending has real growth spurt. Retrieved April 10, 2017, from http://time.com/money/4010096/fantasy-sports-spending-daily-growth-money/

Vivek, S.D., Beatty, S.E., & Morgan, R.M. (2012). Consumer engagement: Exploring customer relationships beyond purchase. *Marketing Theory and Practice, 20*, 122-146.

Chapter 22

Australian Sports Commission. (1998). *Vista Downunder: Proceedings from the international conference on athletes with disabilities,* P. Mayne (ed.), November 1-7.

Brettapproved. (2015). *2015 Brettapproved report on the disabled traveler market.* Retrieved August 31, 2017, www.brettapproved.com/wp-content/uploads/2015/07/Brettapproved-Report-on-Disabled-Traveler-Market-%E2%80%93-2015.pdf

Bull, C., & Lovell, J. (2007). The impact of hosting major sporting events on local residents: An analysis of the views and perceptions of Canterbury residents in relation to the Tour de France 2007. *Journal of Sport and Tourism, 12*, 229-248.

Chalip, L. (2005). Marketing, media and place promotion. In J. Higham (Ed.), *Sport tourism destinations: Issues, opportunities and analysis* (pp. 162-175). Oxford, United Kingdom: Elsevier.

Chalip, L., & Costa, C. (2006). Building sport event tourism into the destination brand: Foundations for a general theory. In H. Gibson (Ed.), *Sport tourism concepts and theories* (pp. 86-105). London, United Kingdom: Routledge.

Crafton, A. (2017, July). McDonald's discuss FIFA sponsorship withdrawal take-away after rising ethical concerns. *MailOnline*. Retrieved May 22, 2017, from www.dailymail.co.uk/sport/sportsnews/article-4678314/McDonald-s-discuss-FIFA-sponsorship-withdrawal.html

Crompton, J.L. (2006). Economic impact studies: Instruments for political shenanigans? *Journal of Travel Research, 45*(1), 67-82.

Delpy Neirotti, L. (2003). An introduction to sport and adventure tourism. In S. Hudson (Ed.), *Sport and adventure tourism*. New York, NY: Howarth Press.

Dimeo, P., & Kay, J. Major sports events, image projection and the problems of "semi-periphery": A case study of the 1996 South Asia Cricket World Cup. *Third World Quarterly, 25*(7), 1263-1276.

ESP Properties. (2017). What sponsors want and where the dollars will go. Retrieved November 30, 2017, from www.sponsorship.com/IEG/files/7f/7fd3bb31-2c81-4fe9-8f5d-1c9d7cab1232.pdf

Francken, D., & van Raiij, M. (1981). Satisfaction with leisure time activities. *Journal of Leisure Research, 13*, 337-352.

Flyberg, B., Stewart, A., & Budzier, A. (2016). The Oxford Olympics Study 2016: Cost and cost overrun at the Games. Retrieved May 22, 2017, from https://arxiv.org/ftp/arxiv/papers/1607/1607.04484.pdf

Fredline, L., Jago, L., & Deery, M. (2003). The development of a generic scale to measure the social impacts of events. *Event Management, 8*(1), 23-37.

Getz, D. (2008). Serious sport event tourists. Presentation at the European Association for Sport Management Congress, September 13, 2008, Heidelberg, Germany.

Gibson, H. (1998). Sport tourism: A critical analysis of research. *Sport Management Review, 1*(1): 45-76.

Glover, T. (2013, July 7). ECB runs behind big hitter of the international game. *The National*. Retrieved May 22, 2017, from www.pressreader.com/uae/the-national-news-business/20130707/281608123024194

Green, B.C., & Jones, I. (2005). Serious leisure, social identity and sport tourism. *Sport in Society, 8*(2), 164-181.

Greig, M. & McQuaid, R. (2003). The economic impact of a sporting event: A regional approach. Paper presented at 43rd European Regional Science Association Congress, Finland, August 27-30, 2003.

Heitner, D. (2015, October 19). Sports industry to reach $73.5 billion by 2019. Retrieved May 22, 2017, from www.forbes.com/sites/darrenheitner/2015/10/19/sports-industry-to-reach-73-5-billion-by-2019/#6590c5fe1b4b

Higham, J.E.S. (Ed) 2005. *Sport tourism destinations: Issues, opportunities and analysis*. Oxford: Elsevier Butterworth-Heinemann.

Hinch, T., Jackson, E.L., Hudson, S., & Walker, G. (2006). Leisure constraint theory and sport tourism. In H. Gibson (Ed.), *Sport tourism concepts and theories* (pp. 10-31). London, United Kingdom: Routledge.

ICC. (2015). ICC Cricket World Cup gives economic boost to Australia and New Zealand. Retrieved May 22, 2017, from www.icc-cricket.com/news/181588

Jackson, E. (2005). *Constraints to leisure*. State College, PA: Venture.

Jackson, E., & Searle, M. (1985). Recreation non-participation and barriers to participation: Concepts and models. *Loisir et Societe, 8*, 693-707.

Johnson, A. (2012). Huge Olympic effect on value of homes in London's East End. Retrieved, June 24, 2017, from www.independent.co.uk/property/huge-olympic-effect-on-value-of-homes-in-londons-east-end-7966087.html

Kraus, R. (2001). *Recreation and leisure in modern society* (6th ed.). Sudbury, MA: Jones and Bartlett.

Lamont, M., Kennelly, M., & Moyle, B. (2014). Costs and perseverance of serious leisure careers. *Leisure Sciences, 36*(2): 144-160.

Li, S., & Jago, L. (2013). Evaluating economic impacts of sport tourism events. *Current Issues in Tourism, 16*(6): 591-611. Retrieved from www.tandfonline.com/doi/abs/10.1080/13683500.2012.736482

Lohmann, P., Knott, B., Swart, K., Zouain, D.M., De Laurentis, G., Virkki, K., & Martelotte, M.C. (2017). Residents' perceptions of the tangible and intangible impacts of the R2016 Olympic Games and the implications for host city mega-event stakeholders. Paper presented at European Association for Sport Management Conference, Bern, Switzerland, September 5-8, 2017.

Menarey, S. (2017, April 17). FIFA struggles to secure sponsors. *The National*. Retrieved, August 31, 2017, from www.thenational.ae/business/fifa-struggles-to-score-sponsors-1.80224

NASC. (2015). Report on the sports travel industry. Retrieved from www.sportscommissions.org/Portals/sportscommissions/Documents/About/STI_report_June_15_final.pdf

Osborn, C. (2017, August 4). Residents of a crisis-ridden Rio caution future Olympic hosts. *PRI's the World*. Retrieved September 5, 2017, from www.pri.org/stories/2017-08-04/residents-crisis-ridden-rio-caution-future-olympic-hosts

Plunkett Research Group. (n.d.). Sport industry statistic and market size overview. Retrieved August 31, 2017, from www.plunkettresearch.com/statistics/Industry-Statistics-Sports-Industry-Statistic-and-Market-Size-Overview/

Preuss, H. (2005). The economic impact of visitors at major multi-sport events. *European Sport Management Quarterly, 5*(3), 281-301.

Preuss, H. (2007). The conceptualisation and measurement of mega sport event legacies. *Journal of Sport and Tourism, 12*(3-4), 207–227.

Preuss, H., & Schutte, N. (2008). *Football tourists and their contribution to the economic impact—evidence from EURO 2008 in Austria/Switzerland*. Paper presented at the 2008 European Association for Sport Management Conference, Heidelberg, Germany.

Sandomir, R. (2008, June 18). How big is the "Tiger Effect"? Networks will soon learn. *New York Times*. Retrieved August 22, 2017, from www.nytimes.com

Scott, A.K.S., & Turco, D.M. (2007). VFRs as a segment of the sport event tourist market. *Journal of Sport and Tourism*, 12(1), 41-52.

Stebbins, R.A. (2007). *Serious leisure: A perspective for our time*. New Brunswick, NJ: Aldine/Transaction.

Tang, Q., & Turco, D.M. (2001). A profile of high-value event tourists. *Journal of Convention and Exhibition Management*, 3(2), 33-40.

Turco, D.M., Riley, R.W., & Swart, K. (2002). Sport tourism. Morgantown, WV: Fitness Information Technology.

UNWTO. (2016, September, 24). UNWTO International Conference on Tourism and Sports. Da Nang, Viet Nam. Retrieved May 22, 2017, from http://cf.cdn.unwto.org/sites/all/files/pdf/technical_note_8.pdf

UNWTO. (2017, January 17). Sustained growth in international tourism despite challenges. Retrieved May 22, 2017, from www2.unwto.org/press-release/2017-01-17/sustained-growth-international-tourism-despite-challenges

Weed, M., & Bull, C. (2009). *Sports tourism: Participants, policy and providers* (2nd ed.). Amsterdam, Netherlands: Butterworth-Heinemann.

Western Cape Government. (2016). Two Oceans Marathon event evaluation report. Unpublished report.

Wicker, P. (2017). The carbon footprint of active sport tourist: An empirical analysis of skiers and boarders. *Journal of Sport and Tourism*, 19(1), 1-21.

World Health Organization. (2011). *World report on disability*. Retrieved August 20, 2017, from www.who.int/disabilities/world_report/2011/report.pdf

Yu, Y., & Turco, D.M. (2000). Issues in tourism event economic impact studies: The case of the 1995 Kodak Albuquerque International Balloon Fiesta. *Current Issues in Tourism*, 3(2), 138-149.

Chapter 23

Alavy, K., Gaskell, A., Leach, S., & Szymanski, S. (2006). On the edge of your seat: Demand for football on television and the uncertainty of outcome hypothesis. International Association of Sports Economists Working Paper Series, Paper No. 06-31, pp. 3-42.

BBC. (2013, August 8). Four-year doping bans for athletes to be reintroduced by the IAAF. Retrieved from www.bbc.com/sport/athletics/23621134

BBC TV. (2012). London Olympics Closing Ceremony, speech by Lord Sebastian Coe, August 12.

Crittenden, V.L., Hanna, R.C., & Peterson, R.A. (2009). The cheating culture: A global societal phenomenon. *Business Horizons*, 52, 337-346

Czarnitzki, D., & Stadtmann, G. (2002). Uncertainty of outcome versus reputation: Empirical evidence for the First German Football Division. *Empirical Economics*, 27, 101-112.

Davis, J.H., & Ruhe, J.A. (2003). Perceptions of country corruption: Antecedents and outcomes, *Journal of Business Ethics*, 43(4), 275-288.

Day, J. (2006). OrganGrinder Blog: Sports sponsors and doping scandals. *The Guardian*. Retrieved from www.theguardian.com/media/organgrinder/2006/jul/31/sportssponsorsanddopingsca

Den Nieuwenboer, N.A., & Kaptein, M. (2008). Spiralling down into corruption: A dynamic analysis of the social identity processes that cause corruption in organisations to grow. *Journal of Business Ethics*, 83(2), 133-146.

Drake, M. (2007, March 25). Did a cricketer kill Woolmer? *Daily Express*. Retrieved from www.express.co.uk/news/uk/2710/Did-a-cricketer-kill-Woolmer

European Union. (2013). Principles of good governance in sport. Retrieved from http://ec.europa.eu/assets/eac/sport/library/policy_documents/xg-gg-201307-dlvrbl2-sept2013.pdf

Gorse, S. (2014). Corruption in international sport: Implications for sponsorship management. Unpublished doctoral thesis, Coventry University, United Kingdom.

Gorse, S., & Chadwick, S. (2010). Conceptualising corruption in sport: Implications for sponsorship programmes. *European Business Review*, July/August, 40-45

Hodgetts, R. (2016, January 14). Athletics: "Corruption embedded within IAAF"—anti-doping report. CNN. Retrieved from http://edition.cnn.com/2016/01/14/sport/athletics-corruption-embedded-within-iaaf--anti-doping-report/index.html

Hughes, R., & Coakley, J. (1991). Positive deviance among athletes: The implications of overconformity to the sport ethic. *Sociology of Sport Journal*, 8(4), 307-325.

Jennings, A. (2006). *Foul! The Secret World of FIFA: Bribes, Vote Rigging & Ticket Scandals*. London, UK: HarperSport

Kelso, P. (2012, 1 August). Badminton pairs expelled from London 2012 Olympics after "match-fixing" scandal. *Telegraph*. Retrieved from www.telegraph.co.uk/sport/olympics/badminton/9443922/Badminton-pairs-expelled-from-London-2012-Olympics-after-match-fixing-scandal.html

Major sponsor suspends Mohammed Amir and threatens to cut ties with Pakistan team over betting scandal. (2010). *Telegraph Australia*. Retrieved from www.dailytelegraph.com.au/sport/cricket/boomboom-youre-sacked-as-pakistan-sponsor-dumps-mohammad-amir-over-betting-scam/story-e6frey50-1225913105790

Mason, D.S. (1999). What is the sports product and who buys it? The marketing of professional sports leagues. *European Journal of Marketing*, 33(3/4), 402-418.

Maennig, W. (2005). Corruption in international sports and sport management: Forms, tendencies, extent and countermeasures. *European Sport Management Quarterly*, 5(2), 187-225.

Moore, R. (2012). *The dirtiest race in history: Ben Johnson, Carl Lewis and the 1988 100m final.* London, United Kingdom: Wisden.

Neale, W.C. (1964). The peculiar economics of professional sports. *Quarterly Journal of Economics, 78*(1), 1-14.

Park, H. (2003). Determinants of corruption: A cross-national analysis. *Multinational Business Review, 11*(2): 29-48.

Reuters. (2009, September 24). Spanish insurer cancels Renault sponsorship. Reuters Canada. Retrieved June 19, 2013, from www.reuters.com/article/us-motor-racing-prix-renault/spanish-insurer-cancels-renault-sponsorship-idUSTRE58N47R20090924

Reuters. (2013). Sponsors rewarded for keeping faith in road cycling. Eurosport Australia. Retrieved from http://au.eurosport.com/cycling/tour-de-france/2013/sponsors-rewarded-for-keeping-faith-in-road-racing_sto3817241/story.shtml

Rottenberg, S. (1956). The baseball player's labour market, *Journal of Political Economy, 64*, 242-258.

Schurr, P.H., Hedaa, L. & Geersbro, J. (2008). Interaction episodes as engines of relationship change. *Journal of Business Research, 61*, 877-884.

Schweitzer, M.E., Ordonez, L., & Douma, B. (2004). Goal setting as a motivator of unethical behaviour. *Academy of Management Journal, 47*(3), 422-432.

Smith, A.C.T. & Stewart, B. (2010). The special features of sport: A critical revisit, *Sport Management Review, 13*(2010): 1-13.

Szymanski, S. (2001). Income equality, competitive balance and the attractiveness of team sports: Some evidence and a natural experiment from English soccer. *Economic Journal, 111*, 69-84.

Tanzi, V. (1998). Corruption around the world: Causes, consequences, scope and cures. *IMF Staff Papers, 45*(4), 559-594.

USADA. (2012, October 10). Statement from USADA CEO Travis T. Tygart regarding the U.S. Postal Service pro cycling team doping conspiracy. USADA press release. Retrieved March 16, 2013, from http://cyclinginvestigation.usada.org/

Weir, K. (2012). Cycling sponsors face doping dilemma after Armstrong scandal. Reuters. Retrieved from http://uk.reuters.com/article/2012/10/20/uk-cycling-armstrong-sponsorship-idUKBRE89J0AD20121020

Westerbeek, H., & Smith, A. (2003). *Sport business in the global marketplace.* Basingstoke, United Kingdom: Palgrave MacMillan.

Chapter 24

Adidas Group. (2007). *Giving 110%: Our efforts to be a responsible business in 2007.* Retrieved April 25, 2017, from www.adidas-group.com/en/sustainability/_downloads/social_and_environmental_reports/2007_adidas-Group_printed_report.pdf

Babiak, K., Heinze, K., Pil Lee, S., & Juravich, M. (2013). A foundation for winning: Athletes, charity and social responsibility. In J.L.P. Salcines, K. Babiak, & G. Walters (Eds.), *Routledge handbook of sport and corporate social responsibility* (pp. 221-235). New York, NY: Routledge.

Babiak, K., & Wolfe, R. (2013). Perspectives on social responsibility in sport. In J.L.P. Salcines, K. Babiak, & G. Walters (Eds.), *Routledge handbook of sport and corporate social responsibility* (pp. 17-35). New York, NY: Routledge.

Banda, D., & Gultresa, I. (2015). Using global south sport-for-development experiences to inform global north CSR design and implementation: A case study of Euroleague Basketball's one team programme. *Corporate Governance, 15*(2), 196-213.

Bason, T., & Anagnostopoulos, C. (2015). Corporate social responsibility through sport: A longitudinal study of the FTSE100 companies. *Sport, Business and Management: An International Journal, 5*(3), 218-241.

Benson, P. (2017). Big football: Corporate social responsibility and the culture and color of injury in America's most popular sport. *Journal of Sport and Social Issues, 41*(4), 307-334.

Breitbarth, T., Walzel, S., Anagnostopoulos, C., & van Eekeren, F. (2015). Corporate social responsibility and governance in sport: "Oh, the things you can find, if you don't stay behind!" *Corporate Governance, 15*(2), 254-273.

Buhr, H., & Grafström, M. (2007). The making of meaning in the media: The case of corporate social responsibility in the financial times. In F. Hond, F.G.A. de Bakker, & P. Neergard (Eds.), *Managing corporate social responsibility in action: Talking, doing and measuring* (pp. 15-32). Farnham, United Kingdom: Ashgate.

Capdevila, G. (2007). Global compact with business "lacks teeth"—NGOs. Retrieved from http://ipsnews.net/news.asp?idnews=38453

Carroll, A.B. (1991). The pyramid of corporate social responsibility: Toward the moral management of organizational stakeholders. *Business Horizons, 34*(4), 39-48.

Carroll, A.B. (1999). Corporate social responsibility: Evolution of a definitional construct. *Business & Society, 38*(3), 268-295.

Calkin, S. (2015a). Globalizing "girl power": CSR and transnational business initiatives for gender equality. *Globalizations*, 1-15.

Calkin, S. (2015b). Post-feminist spectatorship and the girl effect: "Go ahead, really imagine her." *Third World Quarterly, 36*(4), 654-669.

CBC. (2015). North West company boycott challenges high prices in North. Retrieved from www.cbc.ca/news/canada/north/north-west-company-boycott-challenges-high-prices-in-north-1.2938410

Changemakers. (2007). Sport for a better world. Retrieved from www.changemakers.com/sport-better-world

Chelladurai, P. (2016). Corporate social responsibility and discretionary social initiatives in sport: A position paper. *Journal of Global Sport Management, 1*(1-2), 4-18.

Coakley, J.J., & Donnelly, P. (2004). *Sports in society: Issues & controversies.* Toronto, Canada: McGraw-Hill Ryerson.

Cole, C.L., & Hribar, A. (1995). Celebrity feminism: Nike style post-Fordism, transcendence, and consumer power. *Sociology of Sport Journal, 12*(4), 347-369.

Cooper, A.F. (2007). Beyond Hollywood and the boardroom-celebrity diplomacy. *Georgetown Journal of International Affairs, 8*(2), 125.

Darnell, S. (2012). *Sport for development and peace: A critical sociology.* New York, NY: Bloomsburg.

Dashwood, H.S. (2014). Sustainable development and industry self-regulation: Developments in the global mining sector. *Business & Society, 53*(4), 551-582.

Dowling, M., Robinson, L., & Washington, M. (2013). Taking advantage of the London 2012 Olympic Games: Corporate social responsibility through sport partnerships. *European Sport Management Quarterly, 13*(3), 269-292.

Esteva, G., & Prakash, M.S. (1998). Beyond development, what? *Development in Practice, 8*(3), 280-296.

Filatotchev, I., & Stahl, G.K. (2015) Towards transnational CSR: Corporate social responsibility approaches and governance solutions for multinational corporations. *Organizational Dynamics, 44,* 121-129.

Friedman, M. (1970). A theoretical framework for monetary analysis. *Journal of Political Economy, 78*(2), 193-238.

Frisby, W. (2005). The good, the bad, and the ugly: Critical sport management research. *Journal of Sport Management, 19*(1), 1-12.

Gaines, C. (2012). Is the NFL profiting off of breast cancer? *Business Insider.* Retrieved from www.businessinsider.com/why-is-the-nfl-profitting-off-of-breast-cancer-2012-10

Hayhurst, L. (2009, May). Manufacturing sport for development interventions? Exploring the discourses and dangers of global corporate social engagement (GCSE) programs. Paper presented at the Bodies of Knowledge Conference, Toronto, Canada.

Hayhurst, L.M. (2011). Corporatising sport, gender and development: Postcolonial IR feminisms, transnational private governance and global corporate social engagement. *Third World Quarterly, 32*(3), 531-549.

Hayhurst, L.M. (2014). The "girl effect" and martial arts: Social entrepreneurship and sport, gender and development in Uganda. *Gender, place & culture, 21*(3), 297-315.

Hayhurst, L., & Kidd, B. (2012). Corporate social responsibility, sport, and development. In M. Li, E. Macintosh, & G. Bravo (Eds.), *International sport management* (pp. 345-379). Champaign, IL: Human Kinetics.

Heinze, K.L., Soderstrom, S., & Zdroik, J. (2014). Toward strategic and authentic corporate social responsibility in professional sport: A case study of the Detroit Lions. *Journal of Sport Management, 28*(6), 672-686.

Heritage, S. (2015). Why I'm finally going to boycott Amazon. Retrieved from www.theguardian.com/technology/commentisfree/2015/aug/17/why-i-am-finally-going-to-boycott-amazon

Himmelstein, J.L. (1997). *Looking good and doing good: Corporate philanthropy and corporate power.* Bloomington, IN: Indiana University Press.

Hindley, D., & Williamson, D. (2013). Measuring and evaluating community sports projects: Notts county football in the community. In J.L.P. Salcines, K. Babiak, & G. Walters (Eds.), *Routledge handbook of sport and corporate social responsibility* (pp. 317-327). New York, NY: Routledge.

Homeless World Cup. (2016). Tesco on-side for Homeless World Cup. Retrieved from https://homelessworldcup.org/tesco-on-side-for-homeless-world-cup/

Hopkins, M. (2006). What is corporate social responsibility all about? *Journal of Public Affairs, 6*(3-4), 298-306.

Houlihan, B., & White, A. (2002). *The politics of sports development: Development of sport or development through sport?* London, United Kingdom: Routledge.

Ibrahim, H., & Almarshed, S.O. (2014). Sporting event as a corporate social responsibility strategy. *Procedia Economics and Finance, 11,* 3-14.

International Baby Food Action Network. (2017). The issue. Retrieved from http://ibfan.org/the-issue

Jamali, D., & Karam, C. (2016). Corporate social responsibility in developing countries as an emerging field of study. *International Journal of Management Reviews.* doi: http://dx.doi.org/10.1111/ijmr.12112.

Jamali, D., Lund-Thomsen, P., & Khara, N. (2017). CSR institutionalized myths in developing countries: An imminent threat of selective decoupling. *Business & Society, 56*(3), 454-486.

Jenkins, R. 2001. Corporate codes of conduct: Self regulation in a global economy. (Last updated April 2001.) United Nations Research Institute for Social Development (UNRISD). Retrieved from www.researchgate.net/profile/Rhys_Jenkins2/publication/37150822_Codes_of_Conduct_Self_Regulation_in_a_Global_Economy/links/5448d2f30cf2f14fb8144837.pdf

Khan, F.R., & Lund-Thomsen, P. (2011). CSR as imperialism: Towards a phenomenological approach to CSR in the developing world. *Journal of Change Management, 11*(1), 73-90.

Kidd, B. (2008). A new social movement: Sport for development and peace. *Sport in Society, 11,* 370-380.

Kihl, L., Babiak, K., & Tainsky, S. (2014). Evaluating the implementation of a professional sport team's corporate community involvement initiative. *Journal of Sport Management, 28*(3), 324-337.

Knight, G., & Greenberg, J. (2002). Promotionalism and subpolitics: Nike and its labor critics. *Management Communication Quarterly, 15*(4), 541-570.

Kwak, D.H., & Cornwell, T.B. (2013). Cause-related marketing/sponsorship in sport. In J.L.P. Salcines, K. Babiak, & G. Walters (Eds.), *Routledge handbook of sport and corporate social responsibility* (pp. 285-297). New York, NY: Routledge.

Levermore, R. (2013). Viewing CSR through sport from a critical perspective: Failing to address gross corporate misconduct? In J.L.P. Salcines, K. Babiak, & G. Walters (Eds.), *Routledge handbook of sport and corporate social responsibility* (pp. 52-61). New York, NY: Routledge.

Levermore, R., & Moore, N. (2015). The need to apply new theories to "sport CSR." *Corporate Governance, 15*(2), 249-253.

Levi-Faur, D. (2005). The global diffusion of regulatory capitalism. *Annals of the American Academy of Political and Social Science, 598*(1), 12-32.

Maquila Solidarity Network. (2017). About us. Retrieved from www.maquilasolidarity.org/en/aboutus

Misener, L. (2008). Mega-events and corporate social responsibility: A stakeholder perspective of compatibility. In *North American Society for Sport Management Conference (NASSM 2008)* (pp. 312-313).

Nestlé Canada. (2017). Creating shared value. Retrieved from www.corporate.nestle.ca/en/creatingsharedvalue/csv%20in%20canada/home

Newell, P., & Frynas, J.G. (2007). Beyond CSR? Business, poverty and social justice: An introduction. *Third World Quarterly, 28*(4), 669-681.

Nike. (2005). Nike news. Retrieved from http://news.nike.com/news/nike-foundation-steps-on-to-new-field

Nike. (2007). Nike news. Retrieved from http://news.nike.com/news/nike-celebrates-partnership-with-un-refugee-agency

Nike. (2017). The girl effect. Retrieved from http://about.nike.com/pages/girl-effect

Nike Inc. (2017). About Nike. Retrieved from http://about.nike.com/

Nisen, M. (2015). How Nike solved its sweatshop problem. *Business Insider.* Retrieved from www.businessinsider.com/how-nike-solved-its-sweatshop-problem-2013-5

Okhmatovskiy, I., & David, R.J. (2012). Setting your own standards: Internal corporate governance codes as a response to institutional pressure. *Organization Science, 23*(1), 155-176.

Peace One Day. (2009). U.S. Congressional resolution. Retrieved from www.peaceoneday.org/us-resolution

Prieto-Carron, M. (2006). Corporate social responsibility in Latin America: Chiquita, women banana workers and structural inequalities. *Journal of Corporate Citizenship, 21*, 85-94.

Prichard, D. (1991). The role of press councils in a system of media accountability: The case of Quebec. *Canadian Journal of Communication, 16*. Retrieved from www.cjc-online.ca/index.php/journal/article/view/583/489

Rapley, J. (2007). *Understanding development: Theory and practice in the third world.* Boulder, CO: Lynne Rienner.

Roots. (2017). Support Right to Play. Retrieved from www.roots.com/ca/en/Support_righttoplay.html

Roy, A. (2007). In her name: The gender order of global poverty management. In A.L Cazebas, E. Reese, & M. Waller (Eds.), *The wages of empire: Neoliberal policies, repression and women's poverty* (pp. 28-40). Boulder, CO: Paradigm.

Ruggie, J.G. (2004). Reconstituting the global public domain—issues, actors, and practices. *European Journal of International Relations, 10*(4), 499-531.

Sage, G.H. (1999). Justice do it! The Nike transnational advocacy network: Organization, collective actions, and outcomes. *Sociology of Sport Journal, 16*(3), 206-235.

Samsung C & T. (2016). Samsung C & T Corporation: CSR report 2016, Report from the Corporate Strategy Office Planning & Management Team. Gyeonggi-do, Korea: Samsung C & T.

Schrempf-Stirling, J., Palazzo, G., & Phillips, R.A. (2016). Historic corporate social responsibility. *Academy of Management Review, 41*(4), 700-719.

Schulenkorf, N., Sherry, E., & Rowe, K. (2016). Sport for development: An integrated literature review. *Journal of Sport Management, 30*(1), 22-39.

Sharp, J. (2006). Corporate social responsibility and development: An anthropological perspective. *Development Southern Africa, 23*(2), 213-222.

Shehu, J. (Ed.). (2010). *Gender, sport and development in Africa: Cross-cultural perspectives on patterns of representations and marginalization.* Dakar, Senegal: Council for the Development of Social Science Research in Africa.

Sherry, E., Schulenkorf, N., & Phillips, P. (Eds.). (2016). *Managing sport development: An international approach.* New York, NY: Routledge.

Smith, A., & Westerbeek, H. (2007). Sport as a vehicle for deploying corporate social responsibility. *Journal of Corporate Citizenship, 25*, 43-54.

SOS Children's Villages. (2017). FIFA for SOS children's villages—sport and social responsibility. Retrieved from www.soschildrensvillages.ca/fifa-sos-childrens-villages-sport-and-social-responsibility

Thorpe, D. (2013). Why CSR? The benefits of corporate social responsibility will move you to act. *Forbes*. Retrieved from www.forbes.com/sites/devinthorpe/2013/05/18/why-csr-the-benefits-of-corporate-social-responsibility-will-move-you-to-act/2/#3b540b6f6403

Trendafilova, S., Babiak, K., & Heinze, K. (2013). Corporate social responsibility and environmental sustainability: Why professional sport is greening the playing field. *Sport Management Review, 16*(3), 298-313.

United Nations. (2017). Sustainable development goals. Retrieved from https://sustainabledevelopment.un.org/?menu=1300

United Nations Global Compact. (2017). Who we are. Retrieved from https://www.unglobalcompact.org/what-is-gc

University of Toronto. (2001). University of Toronto code of conduct for licensees. Retrieved from http://trademarks.utoronto.ca/wp-content/uploads/2012/03/Code-of-Conduct.pdf

van Tulder, R., & Kolk, A. (2001). Multinationality and corporate ethics: Codes of conduct in the sporting goods industry. *Journal of International Business Studies, 32*(2), 267-283.

Voegtlin, C., & Pless, N.M. (2014). Global governance: CSR and the role of the UN Global Compact. *Journal of Business Ethics, 122*(2), 179-191.

Waddington, I., Chelladurai, P., & Skirstad, B. (2013). CSR in sport: Who benefits? In J.L.P. Salcines, K. Babiak, & G. Walters (Eds.), *Routledge handbook of sport and corporate social responsibility* (pp. 35-51). New York, NY: Routledge.

Walker, M., Heere, B., & Kim, C. (2013). The paradox of CSR measurement: Putting the "responsibility" back in CSR through program evaluation. In J.L.P. Salcines, K. Babiak, & G. Walters (Eds.), *Routledge handbook of sport and corporate social responsibility* (pp. 309-316). New York, NY: Routledge.

Walters, G., & Tacon, R. (2013). Stakeholder engagement in European football. In J.L.P. Salcines, K. Babiak, & G. Walters (Eds.), *Routledge handbook of sport and corporate social responsibility* (pp. 236-248). New York, NY: Routledge.

Willis, O. (2000). Sport and development: the significance of Mathare Youth Sports Association. *Canadian Journal of Development Studies/Revue canadienne d'études du développement, 21*(3), 825-849.

Chapter 25

Adriaanse, J.A., & Claringbould, I. (2016). Gender equality in sport leadership: From the Brighton Declaration to the Sydney Scoreboard. *International Review for the Sociology of Sport, 51*(5), 547-566.

Adriaanse, J., & Schofield, T. (2014). The impact of gender quotas on gender equality in sport governance. *Journal of Sport Management, 28*(5), 485-497.

Agergaard, S. (2017). Learning in landscapes of professional sports: transnational perspectives on talent development and migration into Danish women's handball around the time of the financial crisis, 2004-2012. *Sport in Society, 20*(10), 1457-1469.

Arbena, J. (2003). Dimensions of international talent migration in Latin American sports. In J. Bale & J. Maguire (Eds.), *The global sports arena: Athletic talent migration in an independent world* (pp. 99-111). London, United Kingdom: Frank Cass.

Babbs, K., & Rich, S. (2016, October 28). A quietly escalating issue for NFL: Fan violence and how to contain it. Retrieved September 16, 2017, from www.washingtonpost.com/sports/redskins/a-quietly-escalating-issue-for-nfl-fan-violence-and-how-to-contain-it/2016/10/28/4ec37964-9470-11e6-bb29-bf2701dbe0a3_story.html?utm_term=.49bf08d46156

Bale, J. (1991). *The brawn drain: Foreign student-athletes in American universities*. Urbana, IL: University of Illinois Press.

Bale, J., & Maguire, J. (Eds.) (2003). *The global sports arena: Athletic talent migration in an independent world*. London, United Kingdom: Frank Cass.

Bale, J., & Sang, J. (2003). Out of Africa: The "development" of Kenyan athletics, talent migration and the global sports system. In J. Bale & J. Maguire (Eds.), *The global sports arena: Athletic talent migration in an interdependent world* (pp. 206-25). London, United Kingdom: Frank Cass.

Bergsgard, N.A., Houlihan, B., Mangset, P., Nodland, S.I., & Rommetvedt, H. (2007). *Sport policy: A comparative analysis of stability and change*. Oxford, United Kingdom: Elsevier.

Besnier, N. (2015). Sports mobilities across borders: Postcolonial perspectives. *International Journal of the History of Sport, 32*(7), 849-861.

Bradbury, T., & O'Boyle, I. (Eds.). (2017). *Understanding sport management: International perspectives*. Milton Park, United Kingdom: Taylor & Francis.

Carter, T. (2016). Labor migration, international politics and the governance of Latin American sport. In G. Bravo, R. Lopez de D'Amcio, and C. Parrish (Eds.), *Sport in Latin America: Policy, organization, management* (pp. 135- 141). New York, NY: Routledge.

Chepyator-Thomson, J.R., & Ariyo, E.S. (2017). Out of eastern Africa: An examination of sport labour migration in the post-independence era. *International Journal of the History of Sport*, 33(15), 1-21.

Chibber, K. (2016, September 26). The odd origins of the primal, heart-stopping Viking war chant that is spreading from sport to sport. Retrieved September 16, 2017, from https://qz.com/790797/minnesota-vikings-the-odd-origins-of-the-heart-stopping-war-chant-that-comes-from-iceland-via-the-film-300/

Council of Europe. (2001). *Code of sports ethics.* Retrieved September 19, 2017, from www.coe.int/t/dg4/epas/resources/texts/code_en.pdf

Dietl, H., Fort R., & Lang, M. (2013) International sport league comparisons. In L. Robinson, P. Chelladurai, G. Bodet, & P. Downward (Eds.), *Routledge handbook of sport management* (pp. 388-404). Milton Park, United Kingdom: Routledge.

Dinnie, K. (2004). Place branding: Overview of emerging literature. *Place Branding, 1*, 106-110.

Doherty, A. (2013). Investing in sport management: The value of good theory. *Sport Management Review, 16*, 5-11.

Egilsson, B., & Dolles, H. (2017). "From Heroes to Zeroes"–self-initiated expatriation of talented young footballers. *Journal of Global Mobility: The Home of Expatriate Management Research, 5*(2) 174-193.

Engh, M.H., & Agergaard, S. (2015). Producing mobility through locality and visibility: Developing a transnational perspective on sports labor migration. *International Review for the Sociology of Sport, 50*(8), 974-992.

European Commission. (2016, June). *Mapping and analysis of the specificity of sport: A final report to the DG Education & Culture of the European Commission.* Brussels, Belgium: Directorate-General for Education and Culture Directorate C—Youth and Sport.

European Union. (2007). *White paper on sport.* Brussels, Belgium: Commission of the European Communities.

European Union. (2010). *Volunteering in the European Union.* Brussels, Belgium: Educational, Audiovisual & Culture Executive Agency (EAC-EA) Directorate General Education and Culture (DG EAC).

Fairley, S., Kellett, P., & Green, B.C. (2007). Volunteering abroad: Motives for travel to volunteer at the Athens Olympic Games. *Journal of Sport Management, 21*, 41-57.

Frisby, W. (2005). The good, the bad, and the ugly: Critical sport management research. *Journal of Sport Management, 19*, 1-12.

García, B. (2009). Sport governance after the White Paper: The demise of the European model? *International Journal of Sport Policy, 1*(3), 267-284.

Garcia, B., & Weatherill, S. (2012). Engaging with the EU in order to minimize its impact: Sport and the negotiation of the Treaty of Lisbon. *Journal of European Public Policy, 19*(2), 238-256.

Geeraert, A., Alm, J., & Groll, M. (2014). Good governance in international sport organizations: An analysis of the 35 Olympic sport governing bodies. *International Journal of Sport Policy and Politics, 6*(3), 281-306.

Grix, J. (2012). "Image" leveraging and sports mega-events: Germany and the 2006 FIFA World Cup. *Journal of Sport & Tourism, 17*, 289-312.

Hainmueller, J., & Hopkins, D.J. (2014). Public attitudes toward immigration. *Annual Review of Political Science, 17*, 225-249.

Hanlon, C., & Cuskelly, G. (2002). Pulsating major sport event organizations: A framework for inducting managerial personnel. *Event Management, 7*(4), 231-243.

Henry, I. (2007). Globalisation, governance and policy. In I. Henry and the Institute of Sport and Leisure Policy (Eds.), *Transnational and comparative research in sport* (pp. 3-21). London, United Kingdom: Routledge.

Henry, I. (2016) Sport, the role of the European Union. In B. Houlihan and D. Malcolm (Eds.), *Sport and society* (3rd ed.) (pp. 533- 552) London, United Kingdom: Sage.

Henry, I., Al-Taugi, M., Amara, M., & Lee, P-C. (2007). Methodologies in comparative and transnational sports policy research. In I. Henry and the Institute of Sport and Leisure Policy (Eds.), *Transnational and comparative research in sport* (pp. 22-35). London, United Kingdom: Routledge.

Hill, J. (2009). The European Commission's White Paper on Sport: A step backwards for specificity? *International Journal of Sport Policy, 1*(3), 253-266.

Holt, N.L., et al. (2017). A grounded theory of positive youth development through sport based on results from a qualitative meta-study. *International Review of Sport and Exercise Psychology, 10*, 1-49.

Horne, J. (2017). Sports mega-events—three sites of contemporary political contestation. *Sport in Society, 20*(3), 328-340.

Houlihan, B. (2017). Sport policy and politics. In R. Hoye & M. Parent (Eds.), *The sage handbook of sport management* (pp. 183-200). London, United Kingdom: Sage.

Houlihan, B., & Malcolm, D. (2016). *Sport and society: A student introduction* (3rd ed.). London, United Kingdom: Sage.

International Olympic Committee [IOC]. (2017). Statistics. Retrieved October 19, 2017, from www.olympic.org/women-in-sport/background/statistics

Kihl, L.A., Richardson, T., & Campisi, C. (2008). Toward a grounded theory of student-athlete suffering and dealing with academic corruption. *Journal of Sport Management, 22*, 273-302.

Kim, J., Kang, J.H., & Kim, Y.K. (2014). Impact of mega sport events on destination image and country image. *Sport Marketing Quarterly, 23*(3), 161-175.

Kotschwar, B., & Moran, T. (2015). *Pitching a level playing field: Women and leadership in sports* (No. PB15-22). Washington, DC: Peterson Institute for International Economics.

Kunkel, T., Funk, D., & Hill, B. (2013). Brand architecture, drivers of consumer involvement, and brand loyalty with professional sport leagues and teams. *Journal of Sport Management*, 27, 177-192.

Leberman, S., & Burton, L.J. (Eds.) (2017). *Women in sport leadership: Research and practice for change.* London, United Kingdom: Routledge.

Lee, S., & Pritzker, S. (2013). Immigrant youth and voluntary service: Who serves? *Journal of Immigrant & Refugee Studies*, 11, 91-211.

Li, X.R., & Kaplanidou, K.K. (2013). The impact of the 2008 Beijing Olympic Games on China's destination brand: A US-based examination. *Journal of Hospitality and Tourism Research*, 37, 237-261.

Liamputtong, P. (2008). Doing research in a cross-cultural context: Methodological and ethical challenges. In P. Liamputtong (Ed.), *Doing cross-cultural research: Ethical and methodological* (pp. 3-20). New York, NY: Springer.

Maguire, J., & Falcous, M. (Eds.). (2011). *Sport and migration: Borders, boundaries and crossings.* London, United Kingdom: Routledge.

Markovinovic, M. (2016, August). These designers were enlisted to create Olympic uniforms for the opening ceremony. Retrieved September 15, 2017, from www.huffingtonpost.ca/2016/08/04/olympic-uniform-designers_n_11339454.html

McNulty, Y., Vance, C.M., & Fisher, K. (2017). Beyond corporate expatriation-global mobility in the sports, religious, education and non-profit sectors. *Journal of Global Mobility: The Home of Expatriate Management Research*, 5(2), 110-122.

Meijs, L.C.P.M., & Bridges Karr, L. (2004). Managing volunteers in different settings: Membership and programme management. In R.A. Stebbins and M. Graham (Eds.), *Volunteering as leisure, leisure as volunteering: An international assessment* (pp. 177-193). Oxfordshire, United Kingdom: CABI.

Miller Cleary, L. (Ed.) (2013). *Doing cross-cultural research with integrity: Collected wisdom from researchers in social settings.* New York, NY: Palgrave Macmillan.

Mutter, J. (2017). The global mobility decisions of professional sailors' spouses. *Journal of Global Mobility: The Home of Expatriate Management Research*, 5(2) 203-219.

Odio, M., Walker, M., & Kim, M. (2013). Examining the stress and coping process of mega-event employees. *International Journal of Event and Festival Management*, 4, 140-155.

Patton, M.Q. (2015). *Qualitative research and evaluation methods* (4th ed.). Thousand Oaks, CA: Sage.

Peters, C. (2015, April 20). WATCH: Multiple cases of awful fan behavior mar Stanley Cup playoffs. Retrieved September 16, 2017, from www.cbssports.com/nhl/news/watch-multiple-cases-of-awful-fan-behavior-mar-stanley-cup-playoffs/

Pfahl, M.E. (2012). Key concepts and critical issues. In M. Li, E. MacIntosh, and G. Bravo (Eds.), *International sport management* (pp. 3-29). Champaign, IL: Human Kinetics.

Platts, C., & Smith, A. (2009). The education, rights and welfare of young people in professional football in England: Some implications of the White Paper on Sport. *International Journal of Sport Policy*, 1(3), 323-339.

Preuss, H., & Alfs, C. (2011). Signaling through the 2008 Beijing Olympics—using mega sport events to change the perception and image of the host. *European Sport Management Quarterly*, 11, 55-71.

Roderick, M. (2013). Domestic moves: An exploration of intra-national labor mobility in the working lives of professional footballers. *International Review for the Sociology of Sport*, 48(4), 387-404.

Ryba, T.V., Haapanen, S., Mosek, S., & Ng, K. (2012). Towards a conceptual understanding of acute cultural adaptation: A preliminary examination of ACA in female swimming. *Qualitative Research in Sport, Exercise and Health*, 4(1), 80-97.

Sage, G.H. (2015). *Globalizing sport: How organizations, corporations, media, and politics are changing sport.* Milton Park, United Kingdom: Routledge.

Sundeen, R.A., Garcia, C., & Raskoff, S.A. (2009). Ethnicity, acculturation, and volunteering to organizations. *Nonprofit and Voluntary Sector Quarterly*, 38, 929-955.

Taylor, T., & Morgan, A. (2017). Managing volunteers in grassroots sport. In T. Bradbury and I.O'Boyle (Eds.), *Understanding sport management: International perspectives* (pp. 130-144). Milton Park, United Kingdom: Taylor & Francis.

United Nations Educational Scientific and Cultural Organization (UNESCO). (1978). *International charter of physical education and sport.* Retrieved September 19, 2017, from www.unesco.org/education/pdf/SPORT_E.PDF

United Nations Educational Scientific and Cultural Organization (UNESCO). (2005). *International convention against doping in sport.* Retrieved September 19, 2017, from www.unesco.org/new/en/social-and-human-sciences/themes/anti-doping/international-convention-against-doping-in-sport/

United Nations Office on Drugs and Crime. (2003). *United Nations convention against corruption.* Retrieved Septem-

ber 19, 2017, from www.unodc.org/documents/brussels/
UN_Convention_Against_Corruption.pdf

United Nations. (2008). *United Nations convention on the
rights of persons with disabilities.* Retrieved September 19,
2017, from www.un.org/development/desa/disabilities/
convention-on-the-rights-of-persons-with-disabilities.
html

van der Meij, N., & Darby, P. (2017). Getting in the game
and getting on the move: Family, the intergenerational
contract and internal migration into football academies
in Ghana. *Sport in Society.* Advance online publication.
doi:10.1080/17430437.2017.1284807.

Weed, M.E. (2005). A grounded theory of the policy process
for sport and tourism. *Sport and Society, 8,* 356–377.

Wilson, J. (2012). Volunteerism research: A review essay.
Nonprofit and Voluntary Sector Quarterly, 41, 176-212.

Yaprak, A. (2008). Culture study in international marketing: A critical review and suggestions for future research.
International Marketing Review, 25, 215-229.

Index

Note: The italicized *f* and *t* following page numbers refer to figures and tables, respectively.

About the Editors

Eric W. MacIntosh, PhD, is an associate professor of sport management at the University of Ottawa in Canada. MacIntosh researches and teaches on various organizational behavior topics, covering concepts such as culture, leadership, satisfaction, and socialization. His principal research interests are the functioning of the organization and how a favorable culture can transmit positively internally and outwardly into the marketplace.

MacIntosh has consulted for and conducted research with many prominent national and international sport organizations, including the Commonwealth Games Federation, NHL, Right to Play, U Sports, and Youth Olympic Games. He is well published in leading peer-reviewed sport management journals and is a member of several prominent editorial boards.

Photo courtesy of the University of Ottawa.

Gonzalo A. Bravo, PhD, is an associate professor of sport management at West Virginia University in the United States. A native of Santiago, Chile, Bravo has a master's degree in sport administration from Penn State University and a doctorate in sport management from Ohio State University. Before joining academia, he worked as sport director in a large sport organization in Chile.

His research examines policy and governance aspects of sport as well as organizational behavior in sport. His work has been published in journals such as *International Journal of Sport Management and Marketing*, *Managing Sport and Leisure*, *International Journal of Sport Policy and Politics*, and the *Journal of Sport Management*. He is also the coeditor of *Sport in Latin America: Policy, Organization, Management* (Routledge, 2016) and the author of *Sport Mega Events in Emerging Economies* (Palgrave, 2018).

He is a founding member of the Latin American Association for Sport Management (ALGEDE) and the Latin American Association of Sociocultural Studies of Sport (ALESDE). In 2016, Bravo completed a sabbatical in Brazil, and from 2014 to 2017 he was a visiting scholar at the University of Pittsburgh's Center for Latin American Studies.

Photo courtesy of West Virginia University–CPASS

Ming Li, EdD, is a professor of sports administration and the chair of the department of sports administration in the College of Business at Ohio University in the United States. Li received his doctorate in sport administration from the University of Kansas. His research interests are in financial and economic aspects of sport as well as management of sport business in a global context.

Li is a former president of the North American Society for Sport Management (NASSM) and is currently serving as commissioner of the Commission on Sport Management Accreditation (COSMA). He is a member of the editorial board of *Journal of Sport Management* and *Sport Marketing Quarterly* and has coauthored two books in sport management. He is a guest professor at six institutions in China, including the Central University of Finance and Economics and Tianjin University of Sport.

Li served as an Olympic envoy for the 1996 Atlanta Olympic Games. He also served as a consultant for the 2010 Guangzhou Asian Games organizing committee.

Photo courtesy of Ming Li

Contributors

Gashaw Abeza, PhD
Towson University

Samuel M. Adodo, PhD
University of Benin, Nigeria

Mahfoud Amara, PhD
Qatar University

Emma Ariyo, MS
University of Georgia

Govindasamy Balasekaran, PhD
Nanyang Technological University, Singapore

Guillaume Bodet, PhD
University Lyon, University Claude Bernard Lyon

Clayton Bolton, EdD
Texas A&M University–Commerce

Trish Bradbury, PhD
Massey University, New Zealand

Li Chen, PhD
Delaware State University

Jepkorir Rose Chepyator-Thomson, PhD
University of Georgia

Alison Doherty, PhD
Western University, Canada

Ted Fay, PhD
State University of New York at Cortland

Lyndsay Hayhurst, PhD
York University, Canada

Kevin Heisey, PhD
American University in the Emirates

Megat A. Kamaluddin Megat Daud, PhD
University of Malaya, Kuala Lumpur

Adam J. Karg, PhD
Swinburne University

Shannon Kerwin, PhD
Brock University

Bruce Kidd, PhD
University of Toronto Scarborough, Canada

Euisoo Kim, MBA
University of Georgia

Kazuhiko Kimura, MS
Waseda University, Japan

Yong Jae Ko, PhD
University of Florida

Brice Lefèvre, PhD
University Lyon, University Claude Bernard Lyon

David Legg, PhD
Mount Royal University, Canada

Ho Keat Leng, PhD
Nanyang Tenchological University, Singapore

Mitchell McSweeney, MA
York University, Canada

Laura Misener, PhD
Western University, Canada

Jacqueline Mueller, MSc
Loughborough University London

Michael L. Naraine, PhD
Deakin University

Michael Odio, PhD
University of Cincinnati

Milena M. Parent, PhD
University of Ottawa

Charles Parrish, PhD
Western Carolina University

Demetrius W. Pearson, EdD
University of Houston

Michael Pfahl, PhD
Bangkok University

Holger Preuss, PhD
University Mainz, Germany

Tyreal Y. Qian, MS
University of Georgia

Wirdati M. Radzi, PhD
University of Malaya, Kuala Lumpur

Samantha Roberts, PhD
Texas A&M University–Commerce

Guillaume Routier, PhD
University Lyon, University Claude Bernard Lyon

Benoit Seguin, PhD
University of Ottawa

David J. Shonk, PhD
James Madison University

James Skinner, PhD
Loughborough University London

Peter Smolianov, PhD
Salem State University

Popi Sotiriadou, PhD
Griffith University, Australia

Anna-Maria Strittmatter, PhD
Norwegian School of Sport Sciences

Steve Swanson, PhD
Loughborough University London

Kamilla Swart, EdD
American University in the Emirates

Tracy Taylor, PhD
University of Technology Sydney

Douglas Michele Turco, PhD
Sport Business School Finland

Doyeon Won, PhD
Texas A&M University-Corpus Christi

Di Xie, PhD
Active Sport International Co., Ltd., China

Chia-Chen Yu, EdD
University of Wisconsin–La Crosse

James Zhang, PhD
University of Georgia